Advertising

Advertising

Tony Yeshin

SOUTH-WESTERN
CENGAGE Learning

Australia • Brazil • Japan • Korea • Mexico • Singapore • Spain • United Kingdom • United States

SOUTH-WESTERN
CENGAGE Learning

Advertising

Tony Yeshin

Publishing Director: John Yates

Commissioning Editor: Charlotte Loveridge

Production Editor: Helen Oakes

Manufacturing Manager: Helen Mason

Senior Production Controller: Maeve Healy

Marketing Manager: Vicky Fielding

Typesetter: J&L Composition Ltd

Cover design: Jackie Wrout

For product information and technology assistance,
contact **emea.info@cengage.com**.

For permission to use material from this text or product,
and for permission queries,
email **clsuk.permissions@cengage.com**.

The Author has asserted the right under the Copyright, Designs and Patents Act 1988 to be identified as Author of this Work.

British Library Cataloguing-in-Publication Data
A catalogue record for this book is available from the British Library.

ISBN: 978-1-84480-160-2

Cengage Learning EMEA
High Holborn House, 50-51 Bedford Row
London WC1R 4LR

Cengage Learning products are represented in Canada by Nelson Education Ltd.

For your lifelong learning solutions, visit
www.cengage.co.uk

Purchase e-books or e-chapters at:
http://estore.bized.co.uk

Printed by CTPS, China
3 4 5 6 7 8 9 10 – 11 10 09

Contents

List of figures, tables, and case studies

TABLES

CASE STUDIES

Acknowledgements

I would like to thank the many people who have helped in the construction of this book. Apart from my friends within the profession who are too many to mention, I would like to single out Janet Mayhew at the Institute of Practitioners in Advertising together with Matthew Coombs at the World Advertising Research Center for giving me permission to use the case studies, which are extracted from the IPA Effectiveness Awards and other published papers. Thanks to the many authors of the IPA and other case studies who are acknowledged alongside the individual extracts from their original papers. Also thanks to Lynne Robinson for her superb assistance in obtaining the images to illustrate the case studies.

I would also like to thank Marco Rimini at J Walter Thomson for permission to reproduce the agency briefing form. And to the people at Grolsch for granting permission to use one of their advertising images for use on the front cover of this text.

Finally, my very special thanks to Hamish Pringle, Director General of the IPA. Not only did he read the book in its proof form and make very valuable suggestions (many of which have been incorporated), but he also supplied a foreword.

I am grateful to you all.

Tony Yeshin
May 2005

Foreword

For the student, academic or practitioner interested in the advertising business there are still so many unanswered questions, and that's one of the things that makes this industry so challenging.

For example, will personal video recorders, which turn viewers into 'programmers', destroy traditional spot advertising, and if so, how will advertiser-funded broadcasters finance their businesses without it? And who will win the battle for scarce customer attention – the TV or the PC, or perhaps a hybrid technology?

Will brand and response advertising converge as a result of the rise of interactive digital platforms, and what sort of agencies will prosper in the era of permission for personal data and consent to communications from brands?

Is a 'viral' inside or outside the self-regulatory framework, and does it make a difference if it's uploaded by a user from a website as opposed to transmitted by an advertiser as an attachment to an e-mail?

Will the new customer-centric research enable far more sophisticated media planning and how will we measure the effectiveness of multi-channel integrated campaigns?

How long will it take before the City fully appreciates the role of marketing, and the agencies they employ, in the creation of 'intangible' brand assets that, on average, account for a third of all shareholder value?

All these questions and many more will need to be addressed by the next generation and who knows what the nature of the answers will be? But one thing we can be certain of is that a deep understanding of the way things are now, and how they got that way, will be an essential precursor to finding the solutions.

This book is a tour de force in its assembly of an astonishing array of content, an absorption of which would make for the lion's share of the due diligence required, and there are generous signposts to many other sources. All the answers may not be found within these pages, but all the vital clues certainly can be.

Hamish Pringle
Director General
Institute of Practitioners in Advertising

Preface

Having taught advertising and marketing communications over a number of years, I have long sought a text that combined practitioner experience with a solid academic underpinning. Moreover, whilst there are many extremely sound American texts, I wanted one with a more international scope that provided access to an understanding of the principles of advertising using European and other international examples.

My professional career was spent entirely within the fields of advertising and marketing communications, having worked at and run a number of agencies both large and small, and handled a wide variety of international clients with major brands. Since becoming an academic, I have learned to appreciate the importance of the work other academics and practitioners have done to further the understanding of the way in which advertising works, together with the insights they offer into other aspects of the advertising profession.

I have attempted to combine those two strands in order to produce the text I have so long sought. Whether I have achieved that is for you to judge. I hope this book will provide a solid basis for those both at undergraduate and postgraduate level to gain an appreciation of the roles and contribution of the advertising industry as well as an insight into the ways in which advertising in its variety of forms is developed and measured.

Additional material can be found on the accompanying website at www.cengage.co.uk/yeshin. This material includes additional case material and references, useful web links and PowerPoint slides.

For those of you who are planning to write a dissertation on some aspect of the advertising industry, this book should provide an effective starting-point, with many references to the important papers mentioned above. For the rest, my hope is that it provides you with additional knowledge about the profession and forms the starting-point for many careers within the advertising and related industries.

Tony Yeshin
September 2004

Glossary of terms

Above the line Any paid form of advertising (television, press, radio, cinema, posters) on which commission is paid by the media to the agency.

Account executive The person within the advertising agency responsible for the administration of a client's business.

Account planner The advertising function which seeks to develop an understanding of the consumers' relationship with the brand in order to brief creative development.

ACORN An acronym for A Classification of Residential Neighbourhoods which enables consumers to be classified on the basis of the area of residency.

Adoption process The mental and behavioural stages through which an individual passes before making a purchasing decision.

Advertising Any form of paid-for media used by the marketer to communicate with his target audience.

Advertising agency A company that develops and implements advertising activity.

Advertising appeal The particular approach, based on rational or emotional arguments, which seeks to develop a direct link between the product or service and the consumers' needs or wants.

Advertising campaign The development of a series of advertisements placed in one or more media in order to communicate a proposition to a designated target audience.

Advertising manager The person within a company or organisation who is responsible for the development and co-ordination of advertising activities.

Advertising objectives The specific tasks which advertising is designed to fulfil.

Advertising planning The establishment of a sequence of events relating to the intended activity, including strategies to identify the target audience, developing the advertising message, selecting the appropriate media and implementing the plan.

Advertising strategy A statement of the broad goals that the advertising is designed to achieve.

Advertorial A style of advertising which seeks to depict the message as editorial.

Advocacy advertising   Campaigns designed to disseminate ideas, often of public importance, in a way that promotes the interests of the advertiser.

Affordability method   The apportionment of a communications budget after deduction of the desired level of profit and all other costs.

AIDA   A model of personal selling subsequently used to explain the process of advertising.

Appropriation   The sum of money allocated to a campaign.

Art director   The person primarily responsible for the visual aspects of the advertising campaign.

Attention   The process of arousing the interest of an individual in some activity.

Attitude   Knowledge and feelings – both positive and negative – towards a subject.

Attributes   The physical or emotional qualities which a product or service possesses.

Audience   The number of individuals reached by an advertising medium.

Average frequency   The average number of times that the target audience has to be exposed to the advertising message during the period of the advertising campaign.

Awareness   The stimulation of knowledge about a person or object.

Banner advertising   Small graphics, usually at the top of a web page.

Beliefs   A conviction regarding the existence or characteristics of something.

Below the line   Marketing communications activities which are not subject to commission being paid to the advertising agency.

Benefit segmentation   A grouping of consumers based on the specific benefits they desire from a product.

Billings   The agency's revenue derived from direct advertising expenditure.

Black box model   A simple model of the communications process relating level of expenditure to sales effect.

Body copy   The text contained in an advertising message.

Brand   A name, term, design, symbol or any other feature that identifies one seller's goods or services from those of other sellers.

Brand equity   The assignment of a capital value to a brand. Sometimes used to describe the intangible benefits associated with the use of a brand.

Brand image   The total impression created in the consumer's mind by a brand and all its associations, functional and non-functional.

Brand loyalty   A measurement of the extent to which consumers are committed to a particular brand.

Brand manager   The person within the company responsible for the marketing of a specific brand.

Brand personality The character of a brand expressed as if it were a human being.

Brand stretch The ability of a brand to be extended to include products or categories beyond the original product.

Brand switchers Consumers who alternate purchases between different manufacturers products.

Branding The process of creating a unique identity for the product or service.

Broadcasting Media designed to reach the mass market.

Budget The amount of money allocated to a campaign.

Burst A pattern of media expenditure in which activity is concentrated into a comparatively short period.

Business to business (B2B) The promotion of its products or services by one company to another.

Campaign An all-embracing plan indicating the choice of media and other activities designed to support the brand within an identified timeframe.

Case rate method A method of budget calculation in which expenditure is calculated as a percentage of the sales value of a case of product.

Category management The responsibility for co-ordinating the activities of all the company's brands within a particular market sector.

Cause marketing The process of sponsoring a charitable activity designed to achieve a positive impact on the brand image.

Circulation The number of issues of a media title that are sold.

Classified advertising Usually typeset messages carried by print media often arranged by category of interest.

Clickthrough A measure of the effectiveness of web advertising based on a measurement of the number of surfers who click on the ad.

Clutter The surrounding messages that interfere with the comprehension of advertising.

Cognitive dissonance The discrepancy between the advertising message and what is expected by the viewer or reader of the advertising.

Cognitive response The interpretation of stimuli and the organisation of thoughts and ideas.

Commission The method of remunerating advertising agencies by means of a payment directly from the media – traditionally set at 15 per cent of the advertising expenditure.

Communication The process of dissemination of information to establish shared meaning between the sender and the receiver.

Comparative advertising The contrasting of one manufacturer's products or services with those of another either by naming the competitor or inferring its identity.

Complex problem solving Purchasing decisions in which the consumer will require additional information on which to base an evaluation of alternatives. Most often used where the capital outlay is great or the risk is high.

Comprehension The creation of an understanding about a product, service, object or person.

Concept testing A research procedure in which outline ideas are exposed to current and potential consumers to learn about their response.

Consumer behaviour The activities in which people engage in order to satisfy needs, wants and desires.

Contingency A sum of money held in reserve to respond to unforeseen circumstances.

Continuous advertising A media plan in which the budget is spread to enable the advertising campaign to be visible at all times, without interruption.

Co-operative advertising A programme in which the manufacturer pays an agreed percentage of the retailer's advertising costs in return for the featuring of the manufacturer's brand.

Copy testing The process of using market research to gain an understanding of consumer response towards an advertising proposition.

Copywriter The person responsible for writing the headline and text for the advertising.

Core values The central values associated with a product or service.

Corporate advertising Campaigns created to promote awareness and understanding of a company.

Corporate identity The programme of communication and change that a company undertakes in order to communicate its values.

Corporate image The way in which a company is perceived, based on its history, its beliefs and philosophy.

Corporate strategy The determination and definition of the long-term goals of an organisation.

Cost per thousand A calculation of the cost of exposing an advertising message to 1000 members of a designated target audience.

Coverage A calculation of the size of the audience that will be exposed to an advertising message using a particular media vehicle.

Creative brief The agency document that defines the key elements that direct the development of the advertising message.

Creative director The person responsible for managing the work of the creative department.

Creative strategy The identification of the specific goals which advertising is designed to fulfil.

Crisis management The establishment of procedures for anticipating and dealing with communications problems.

Culture The shared values, beliefs and behaviours of a society.

DAGMAR A model of the advertising process developed by Russell Colley. Incorporates a precise method for the selection and quantification of communications tasks.

Database A computer-based listing of the names, addresses and other details of current and potential customers, which can be used for purposes of direct marketing.

Database management The process of maintaining and refining accurate customer information.

Decision-making unit Those individuals who participate in the purchasing decision process, usually in the context of company purchases.

Decision stage That part of the process of consumer buying behaviour which results in an evaluative judgement about the alternatives.

Decoding The means by which the recipient of a message transforms and interprets it.

Demographics Groupings of individuals based on characteristics such as age, sex, race and income.

Diffusion The spread of a new idea throughout a group of individuals.

Direct mail The use of postal and other delivery techniques to communicate with a defined target audience.

Direct marketing An interactive system of marketing which uses one or more advertising media to effect a measurable response and/or transaction at any location.

Direct response A method whereby the advertiser provides the consumer with a means of communicating directly with the organisation.

Direct selling The process of achieving the sales of products or services without the use of intermediary sales channels, such as wholesalers and retailers.

Display advertising Press advertising using visual components to communicate a message relating to the brand.

Drip A pattern of media expenditure in which the budget is deployed at a comparatively low level over an extended period.

E-commerce The process of selling goods and services through the internet.

Emotional responses Those non-rational reactions to a proposition which are based on intangible benefits or associations which a product or service can induce.

Emotional strategy The identification of non-rational stimuli as the basis for an advertising campaign.

Encoding The process of putting information into a symbolic form of words, pictures or images.

Endorsement The recommendation of a product or service by someone other than the advertiser.

Ethics   The principles that guide an individual's or organisation's conduct in its relations with others, and the values it wishes to communicate.

Evaluation of alternatives   The consumer's consideration of the various options available to resolve an identified need or want.

Event sponsorship   The association of a company or brand name with a public activity.

Everyday low prices (EDLP)   A pricing policy adopted by some companies in which short-term promotional pricing is either reduced or eliminated and replaced by a consistent level of lower prices.

Exposure   The consequence of presenting an advertising campaign to target audiences.

External databases   Computer-based records compiled from external sources which can be used for the purposes of direct marketing.

Family life cycle   A sequence of stages through which the individual passes over time.

Feedback   The process of ensuring an understanding of the recipients comprehension of a message by the sender.

Flighting   A pattern of media scheduling in which periods of advertising are alternated with periods of inactivity.

Focus group   A qualitative group discussion structured to discuss specific issues.

Frequency   A calculation of the number of times a target audience is exposed to an advertising message during a given period.

Full service agencies   Those which offer a comprehensive creative, account handling, planning and media service to their clients.

Geo-demographic segmentation   A method of segmenting the market using a combination of psychographic and geographic data.

Geographic segmentation   The identification of market or audience segments solely based on geographic factors.

Generic branding   A policy by which products or services are sold using their category name.

Global branding   Where the manufacturer utilises the same name and design in all markets.

Global marketing   The adoption of a common marketing strategy and implementation plan for all countries in which a manufacturer markets his or her goods.

Gross margin   The calculation of net sales value minus the cost of goods over a defined period.

Guerrilla marketing   The use of unconventional approaches that associate the brand with a sponsored event without gaining official recognition from the organiser.

Halo effect   The creation of an aura or beneficial image that is transferred from one category to another.

Hard sell An advertising approach using a rational message and emphasising the arguments in favour of the brand.

Hierarchy of effects The identification of a sequence of stages to explain the working of advertising.

Image The creation of an identity for a product or service by its association with other values.

Impulse purchase Products or services bought without prior consideration, usually in response to some stimulus at the point of purchase.

Integration The process by which the tools of marketing communications are used in combination to reinforce each other.

Internal databases Computer-based records compiled from internal records such as sales registrations, warranty cards and other sources for the purpose of direct marketing.

International advertising Campaigns designed to promote the product or service in a number of different countries.

Just noticeable difference (JND) The amount by which a product or service needs to be changed to ensure that the change is observed by the consumer.

Learning The process of change to an individual's behaviour resulting from experience.

Lifestyle The way in which a person lives, identified by his or her activities, interests and opinions.

Lifetime value An evaluation of loyal customers whose value to the organisation is expressed in terms of the long-term value of their purchases.

List broker An organisation which provides mailing lists to companies.

Local brand One that is marketed in a specific country.

Logical appeals Advertising approaches based on the performance, features or attributes of a product or service.

Look-alikes Products which adopt the visual cues of another brand in order to facilitate the inclusion of the product within the category of choice.

Loyalists Consumers who exhibit a consistent purchasing preference for a particular brand.

Manufacturer branding The use of a manufacturers name or logo to identify the products or services produced by the company.

Market analysis Research that assists in the identification of markets for a product or service and which details information relating to consumer behaviour, competitive activity and similar factors.

Market research The gathering and assessment of data and other information.

Market segmentation The means by which the characteristics of homogeneous groups of consumers can be determined.

Market structure The ways in which a market for any product or service can be defined or segmented.

Marketing The management process responsible for identifying, anticipating and satisfying consumers, profitably.

Marketing communications The process by which a marketer develops and presents stimuli to a defined target audience with the purpose of eliciting a desired set of responses.

Marketing communications mix The combination of the various communications activities to create a sustained campaign of activity to support the brand.

Marketing concept The process by which the marketer responds to the needs and wants of the consumer.

Marketing mix The combination of the elements of the marketing programme, including product, price, place and promotion.

Marketing objectives The determination of specific and measurable goals to be achieved by the marketing programme.

Marketing plan The formal document containing the information designed to guide the development and implementation of the marketing strategy.

Marketing strategy Specific plans of action for the achievement of designated marketing objectives.

Mass marketing An approach in which the advertiser attempts to appeal to the entire market using a single marketing mix.

Mature market The stage at which a market for a product or service ceases to expand.

Media The vehicles of communication by which a message is transmitted to its audience.

Media mix The combination of two or more different media to be used to fulfil a media plan.

Media plan The document embodying the specific media objectives, strategy and tactics designed to support a brand.

Media planning The process of determining the means by which an advertising message will be communicated to a defined audience.

Media schedule A graphic representation of the dates, times and media sources in which advertising is to be placed.

Merge and purge The process of eliminating the duplication of names and addresses contained within two or more mailing lists.

Motive An aroused need that directs behaviour towards a specific goal.

Multi branding A strategy adopted by some manufacturers in which the parent name is subservient to those of the individual brands which they produce.

Multinational advertising The process of developing advertising campaigns to run in several different countries based on the identification of common values and needs.

Multinational agencies Those which operate a network in many different countries and offer clients a common approach to the resolution of advertising requirements.

Narrow-casting The fragmentation of media audiences resulting from the increase in the number of media channels.

Needs The gap between a consumer's current state and the desired state.

Noise The external stimulus factors in the environment which surround the communications message and inhibit its effective transmission.

Non-verbal communications The process of ensuring the transmission of a message without the use of words or language.

Objective and task method The nature of the task is determined and the cost of achieving the specific objectives is calculated and a budget allocated accordingly.

Objectives The specific goals to be achieved during the timescale of a plan.

Opinion leader An individual who reinforces an advertising message and to whom others look for guidance.

Outcomes The results and consequences of any activity.

Percentage of sales method A budgeting procedure by which the expenditure is calculated as a finite percentage of the sales value.

Perception The process by which an individual receives, organises and interprets information.

Perceptual mapping A technique of market research in which the key attributes of a product or service are identified and competing products rated according to their ability to satisfy the desired ratings.

Permission marketing The process whereby an individual agrees to receive communications from a company.

Personal selling The process by which a salesperson communicates with one or more prospective purchasers for the purpose of making sales.

PEST+C An acronym standing for the political, economic, social, technological and consumer factors used in the analysis of a marketing environment. Sometimes written as PESTI+C, the 'I' standing for international.

Planning The process of anticipating the future, establishing goals and objectives.

Point of purchase Promotional items designed to attract the attention of the consumer in those placed where the products are purchased, sometimes referred to as point of sale.

Positioning Identifying the place in the market or the mind of the consumer which the company or product wishes to occupy.

Post-purchase dissatisfaction A response to a purchasing decision in which the consumer feels that the product or service has failed to deliver the expected performance on some dimension.

Post-purchase satisfaction A response to a purchasing decision in which the consumer's direct experience of the product or service matches or exceeds its expected performance.

Problem identification The recognition of an unfulfilled want or need.

Problem solving The process by which the consumer resolves an identified need.

Product differentiation The process of creating a point of difference between the product and its competitors by identifying physical or emotional dimensions of the brand.

Product life cycle A management technique in which a product is depicted as passing through a series of progressive stages.

Product placement The inclusion or mention of products or services in films, television programmes or elsewhere, usually in exchange for a fee.

Promotion That element of the marketing mix which includes all forms of marketing communications.

Promotion management The process of determining and co-ordinating the elements of the promotional mix.

Promotional mix The use in any combination of advertising, sales promotion, public relations, direct marketing and personal selling to achieve specific objectives.

Psychographics The understanding of the psychological profiling of prospective consumers.

Public relations (PR) All forms of planned communications between any organisation and its publics with the purpose of establishing mutual understanding.

Publicity Any communication concerning a company, product or service which is not paid for or sponsored.

Pull strategy A promotional strategy in which the manufacturer or supplier promotes a product or service to the end consumer with the aim of stimulating demand.

Pulsing A media scheduling approach in which short heavy bursts of advertising are followed by extended periods of low level expenditure.

Push strategy A promotional strategy in which the manufacturer or supplier promotes a product or service through a series of marketing intermediaries with the aim of pushing the product through the channels of distribution.

Qualitative research Techniques used amongst relatively small groups in order to identify and evaluate subjective opinions.

Quantitative research   The collection of data from samples of the target population to enable quantification and analysis.

Rate card cost   The published costs of advertising in a specific media outlet.

Rating point   A measurement of a media audience – usually television – in which the size of the audience is calculated and expressed as a percentage. One rating point is equivalent to one per cent of the total viewing potential.

Rational decisions   Decisions based on the qualitative assessment of the performance of a product or service and relate to specific features, attributes and benefits.

Reach   The percentage of a total audience which will be exposed to a message during a defined period of time.

Readership   The calculation of the number of individuals who read a single copy of a media title.

Receiver   The target audience for whom a communications message is intended.

Reference groups   Those groups within society with which the consumer identifies and would wish to belong.

Relationship marketing   The process of getting closer to the customer by means of customer service and quality delivery.

Remuneration   The income received in return for the provision of services.

Response rate   The percentage of the target audience who respond to a direct-response campaign.

Road blocking   A media approach in which the same advertisement appears simultaneously on several different channels.

Routine problem solving   Situations in which the consumer possesses sufficient prior knowledge to take a purchasing decision without seeking additional information.

Sales promotion   The use of short-term, often tactical, techniques to achieve short-term sales objectives.

Sales quota   A quantitative expression of a target to be achieved by a salesperson or team during a given period of time.

Sampling   The process of encouraging the consumer to try a specified product or service.

Secondary research   The use of information that has previously been compiled and published.

Segmentation   The process of dividing a market into smaller groupings based on an understanding of consumer needs and wants.

Selective attention   The process by which receivers only notice some of the messages to which they are exposed.

Selective distortion   The process by which receivers modify or change received information to fit in with existing attitudes and beliefs.

Self-regulation   The process by which manufacturers agree to abide by codes of practice without the force of law.

Semiotics   The study of the nature of meaning.

Sender   The person or organisation transmitting a communications message.

Share of voice   A calculation of the share of category media expenditure.

Slogan   An advertising copyline that is closely associated with the brand.

SMS   Text message sent on a mobile phone.

Social class   An open grouping of people with similar social ranking.

Social marketing   Marketing campaigns that recognise the general 'good of society'.

Soft sell   Advertising that uses an emotional message to create a response.

Source   The sender of a message.

Source credibility   The extent to which the consumer believes in the trust-worthiness of the source of the message.

Sponsorship   The connection of a company or product with a public event in which the manufacturer contributes towards part or all of the costs in return for the benefit of association.

Storyboard   A pictorial representation of how a commercial will develop.

Strategy   The determination of the means by which longer-term goals and targets will be achieved.

SWOT   An acronym standing for strengths, weaknesses, opportunities and threats used in the analysis of a company or brand's competitive position.

Subliminal advertising   A message communicated below the normal levels of comprehension such that the viewer is unaware of having received it.

Symbolic representation   Words, pictures or images used to convey a message.

Tactics   Specific actions designed to implement strategies.

Target audience   The identification of a group of potential consumers who have specific characteristics in common.

Target marketing   The selection of specific markets segments at which to aim marketing or marketing communications.

Telemarketing   A form of personal selling in which the communications process is conducted via the telephone.

Test market   An area or region selected as being representative of the market as a whole used to test elements of the campaign either individually or in combination.

Tracking study   A market research technique which analyses consumer response and buying behaviour over an extended period of time.

Trade allowances   Sums of money negotiated by manufacturers with distribution channels in return for the carrying out of certain functions or activities.

Unique selling proposition (USP)   An advertising approach developed by Rosser Reeves which is designed to make the product the focus of the advertising message by identifying a unique aspect, attribute or benefit.

Viral marketing   A form of advertising in which an advertising message is sent by e-mail to selected recipients who, in return, pass that message onto others.

Want conception   The process of activating latent needs or wants.

Want development   The identification of new uses for an existing product.

Want focus   The identification of a consumer need or want in order to establish a relevance with the product or service being promoted.

Want satisfaction   The provision of reassurance to the consumer to confirm the purchasing decision.

Wearout   A measure of the loss of advertising effectiveness over time.

Word of mouth   Information about products and services conveyed from one individual to another.

Zapping   The use of a remote control device to change channels during commercials.

Zipping   The avoidance of television commercials that have been pre-recorded on video tape.

1 The advertising context

Learning outcomes

By the end of this chapter you should have a clear understanding of:

- the nature of advertising
- the historical development of advertising
- the environment in which advertising exists
- the classification of advertising
- the functions and roles of advertising
- the benefits and limitations of advertising
- the social and ethical issues related to advertising
- the legal and regulatory framework which controls advertising.

The nature of advertising

A recent study conducted on behalf of the Advertising Association indicated that consumers consider anything a brand does in terms of communication to be advertising (Ford-Hutchinson and Rothwell 2002). This is an extremely wide definition and does not satisfy academic rigour, although it is entirely consistent with the views of one of the greatest advertising luminaries, David Ogilvy (1983), who made the same suggestion in his book.

In more precise terms advertising is paid-for, non-personal communication from an identified organisation, body or individual designed to communicate information and to influence consumer behaviour.

Advertising is one of a variety of marketing communications tools that companies can use to achieve their defined objectives. Historically, advertising has always played the lead role in terms of communications activity, although that position is being eroded dramatically as the other tools of marketing communications gain more widespread use. This is particularly evident in the United States (Jones 1995) where the amount of money spend on promotional activity is now significantly greater than that spent on advertising.

Whilst a similar trend is observable in the UK and elsewhere, it is significantly less marked. Not only does advertising continue to play a greater role in overall terms, it continues to dominate strategic thinking regarding the application of marketing communications in many areas of marketing.

At just over £3.9 billion, the quarterly adspend in the UK reached its highest ever level in 2003. Outdoor and radio continue to be the strongest growing sectors.

Expenditure on outdoor media grew by 38 per cent between 2001 and 2003. Both national and regional newspapers have produced growth rates that are higher than at any time since 2001. Meanwhile TV advertising has grown by only 1.6 per cent (WARC 2004).

The breakdown of UK advertising expenditure can be seen more clearly in Table 1.1 which compares 2001 and 2002.

Table 1.1 Advertising expenditure by media, 2001 and 2002

	2001 (£m)	2002 (£m)
Television	3031	3091
National press	2504	2600
Regional press	2931	2990
Consumer magazines	775	798
Radio	512	532
Cinema	141	151
Outdoor	772	817
Online	180	240/250
TOTAL	10 845	11 224

SOURCE: Advertising Association 2003

The historical development of advertising

The reality is that advertising is not a new phenomenon. In one form or another, advertising has been with us for centuries. Advertising as we know it can be dated back at least some 300 years. Newspapers of the early eighteenth century carried whole pages of text-based advertisements, very similar to the lineage advertising with which we are familiar today.

The post-war period in the West witnessed a considerable boom in consumer affluence and with it an increased desire for material possessions. However, advertising remained somewhat constrained. Firstly, there were limits on the breadth of the media. The most powerful advertising medium, television, although available, was only installed in the homes of the few. Even then, in the UK, commercial television did not commence until 1955. So advertising was limited to printed media.

Secondly, people were dismissive of advertising, regarding it as possessing no redeeming qualities. In the eyes of many it contributed nothing to society as a whole. Instead, it was seen as 'stirring the dormant, unconscious desires of civil society' (Boutlis 2000).

It was not until the relaxation of the 'moral code' in the 1960s that consumerism became a vocal movement. The growth in affluence, particularly amongst the young, opened up the opportunity for the exploitation of new markets. Increasingly, academics including Levitt (1960) and Kotler and Levy (1969) sought to define a new approach to marketing in which the consumer became the focus of all business activities.

Advertising, in turn, became a primary means of achieving marketing goals. It moved from the simple task of conveying information about products to integrating image dimensions to enhance its appeal to consumers. The evolution of marketing is seen most vividly in the way that advertising has developed to respond to changes in the level of consumer sophistication. There has been a progression from the 1950s' hard- and straight-selling approach to the conspiratorial debunking references to the brand and the commercial world in much current advertising, certainly in the West.

Mary Goodyear (2000) indicates that there is an increasing use of exaggeration, symbolism, metaphor, conventions borrowed from other advertising, and pastiches of television and cinema styles – all crediting the consumer with increased commercial knowledge and understanding. Moreover, advertising increasingly appeals to the emotions rather than the intellect.

The thinking of Rosser Reeves and the Unique Selling Proposition – which sought to find specific product features to exploit within the advertising message – gave way to the desire for creativity espoused by American agencies including Doyle, Dane, Bernbach and Papert, Koenig, Lois and in the UK by Collett, Dickenson, Pearce and Boase, Massimi, Pollitt.

It was Stanley Pollitt of the latter agency who, along with Stephen King at J. Walter Thompson, vocalised the need to delve more deeply into the minds of the consumer to identify their needs and wants more precisely. And with it, the need for a new agency function – that of the planner – whose skills would be used to hone the creative brief and provide the guidance for the development of effective advertising.

Today's advertising embodies a higher level of creativity than in the past. Recognising fundamental changes in society, advertising desires to appeal to a consumer who is more aware about its role, to invite the consumer to participate more fully and transfer the qualities of the advertising to the brand that it supports. The proliferation of advertising in a plethora of media demands real differentiation to cut through the clutter and reach the desired target audience in a way that will enhance the appeal of the brand.

The challenge facing advertising today is that, according to a study by Kroeber-Riel (1990, cited in Appelbaum and Halliburton 1993) in Germany, as much as 90 per cent of the information provided to the consumer is ignored. They argue that advertising will need to capture the consumer's attention and deliver the message in an original way that will enable the consumer to remember and identify with both the message and the brand.

The environment in which advertising exists

The relationship between advertising and marketing

Marketing is the process by which companies satisfy consumer needs through the provision of products and services. It is most aptly described using the definition provided by the Chartered Institute of Marketing: 'The management process responsible for identifying, anticipating and satisfying consumer needs, profitably'.

Marketing uses a variety of tools, known collectively as the four Ps. These are the product, the place, the price and promotion. The latter consists of a series of communication techniques which includes advertising, sales promotion, direct marketing and public relations. The specific task of advertising is to deliver persuasive messages to a target audience that may comprise actual and potential users of the product or service.

The fundamental aim of marketing is to create and maintain offerings of products and services that satisfy the needs of consumers. Consumers communicate their needs, wants and desire through various forms of market research. Marketers communicate information about their products through forms of marketing communications, including advertising. The goals of advertising are to stimulate interest in the brand, create positive brand values, demonstrate how a product can satisfy consumers' wants, differentiate between their brands and those of their competitors and persuade consumers to respond in particular ways – to try a new product, to make a purchase, visit a particular retail outlet, etc.

Advertising and the economy

Although it is widely criticised, it can be argued that advertising, particularly within a capitalist society, provides the means for encouraging competition. By making information about competing products and services widely available, it ensures that no single product can, ordinarily, dominate a market.

In support of advertising, Bullimore (1995) argues that 'without advertising, we would not have brands, or innovation, consumer choice, value for money, or our diverse media'.

The advertising context

Undeniably, the context for advertising changes continuously. On the one hand, as several commentators have indicated, advertising is perhaps more ubiquitous than ever before. Advertising is present in almost every aspect of daily life. On the other, there are increasing pressures for regulation to control what are seen as the more damaging aspects of advertising campaigns. For some, advertising represents a major catalyst for change, not all of it positive and, perhaps because it is an easy target, advertising is often blamed for all of the 'evils within society'. Public debates held at the House of Commons have recently reflected on the role of advertising in the context of 'binge drinking', obesity and other social problems (Debating Society 2003). Various countries have indicated that more extensive controls on advertising may be necessary to counter its perceived impact on social behaviour.

On a more precise micro level, several factors have impacted on the advertising environment over the past decade. Kiely describes the various force as follows (cited in Eagle et al. 1999):

- The mass media have fragmented and a proliferation of entertainment options has weakened television's dominance as an advertising medium.
- The mass market have fragmented and there are more selective markets and an increase in niche marketing which have replaced traditional broad market groups.
- The impact of economic recession is still being felt, with advertising spending significantly reduced and a resultant move to alternative techniques that generate 'instant' sales responses, such as sales promotion, and those that are more easily measured, e.g. direct marketing.
- Retail chains have increased their power over manufacturers, including influencing how advertising and promotional resources are allocated.

Similarly, Mole (1999) identifies a series of important trends and changes within the competitive environment:

- Competition is becoming increasingly multidimensional. Where once supermarkets competed for a share of the grocery market, they are now involved in hardware, pharmacy, financial services, petrol and the internet.
- Companies are competing for a share of the customer relationship. By providing a broader range of services, they increase their overall relationship with the

customer. Companies who fail in this will increasingly be sidelined into niche areas.

- Markets are transforming – the old definitions of what constitutes a market break down as consumers are able to satisfy their needs outside the traditional market boundaries.

- Branding is going beyond awareness and imagery into the core capabilities of the organisation and the establishment of new relationships with the customer.

The classification of advertising

It would be wrong to consider advertising as a single entity. There are, clearly, several different types of advertising and it is important to understand the role and purpose of each within the context of a specific advertising campaign. Advertising can be classified in four key ways, as shown in Figure 1.1.

Figure 1.1 **The classification of advertising**

- By target audience
- By purpose
- By medium
- By geographic region

By target audience

One simple way of discriminating between types of advertising is to examine the target audience at which the advertising message is aimed. Here we can distinguish between advertising aimed at the consumer and that which is aimed at some other audience. Much of what we see on a day-to-day basis consists predominantly of advertising targeted specifically at different consumer groups. For example, all of the major supermarket chains aim their campaigns at shoppers who, they hope, can be persuaded to use their outlets in preference to those of their competitors for their regular purchases. Kellogg's and their main competitor, Cereal Partners, mount different campaigns to promote the sales of each of their breakfast cereals.

Against this form of advertising, however, can be contrasted that aimed at the 'trade' audience. The same products may well be involved, but the underlying nature (and, of course, the content) of the advertising will be different. Brands will use trade advertising to communicate the advantages of their brand to particular retailers, to encourage them to stock and display their products alongside competitive products, including the retailer's own. A considerable amount of advertising is designed to communicate between businesses, either in the instances like those above or where the target audience is the end user of, say, the raw materials which the company processes. This category would also include advertising by 'professional' companies, such as solicitors and accountants, promoting their services to potential users. Yet another target audience will be the financial community. Such advertising will, for the most part, appear in the broadsheet newspapers and specialist magazines (although it is by no means restricted to these). Here the purpose will be to communicate some aspect of the company's performance, such as its financial results.

By purpose

An alternative way of describing advertising is in terms of its specific purpose. Most advertising takes the form of commercial activity designed to promote the particular products or services offered by the company. Whilst brands receive the majority of the expenditure on advertising, there are instances where a company seeks to develop an image for itself beyond that of the brands it manufactures. Corporate advertising is attracting increasing attention with the recognition that many consumers wish to identify the values of the company from which it buys products and services. Similar campaigns may be mounted by industry groups, designed to promote a category of products.

There are few current examples of generic advertising. The 1970s saw a number of generic campaigns exhorting consumers to drink tea, eat eggs, use seat belts, etc. Recently, however, the carpet industry mounted a campaign to encourage the return to their form of floor covering – the industry having lost considerable volumes to the adoption of wood floors.

During the BSE crisis, the Meat and Livestock Commission, representing the farming community, mounted a campaign to encourage people to eat more meat – against the adverse publicity of the BSE scare. In the same way, although for different reasons, the video industry has developed advertising to encourage video rental in general rather than promoting any particular film title or even the outlets from which the videos can be obtained. However, Ehrenberg and Barnard (1997) argue that there is little evidence that such campaigns actually work.

Against this is the considerable amount of non-commercial advertising undertaken by governmental bodies and charitable organisations. These latter are often designed to affect people's attitudes and opinions rather than to sell anything specific.

By media

The third method of classifying advertising is in terms of the media used. Although we will examine media and their suitability in greater depth in Chapter 11, it is important to recognise that not only does each medium provide different opportunities to the advertiser, they also represent different means of communicating information about the product or service which is being promoted. In most markets, advertisers have access to:

- television
- radio
- newspapers
- magazines
- poster and other outdoor media
- cinema
- the 'new' media.

By geographic Region

A final way of classifying advertising is in terms of the geographic area that it is intended to cover. In most countries, there are a variety of local media (press, posters, etc.) which enable the advertiser to restrict the geographic coverage to a very narrow area. This might encompass a village, town or city, perhaps the area in which the particular product or service is available.

At the next level, various media offer regional facilities to extend coverage to a wider area. These will include local radio, cinema and even regional television. Once again, the selection might be dictated by the availability of the product or service or, alternatively, a desire on the part of the manufacturer to take advantage of some particular regionality, to upweight the level of expenditure placed behind the brand or to run some form of test operation prior to extending the coverage of the campaign.

Much advertising, particularly that for major brands, runs on a national basis. Here, the advertiser can access all of the media available to promote the brand, often utilising several media channels in combination to create a campaign with wide coverage of the desired target audience.

Equally, advertising is sometimes run on an international basis. Increasingly, as we will see later in this book, companies seek the opportunity to standardise their campaigns across several countries. Major brands which have an international presence will sometimes use the same advertising campaign across many countries to achieve economies of scale in the production of the advertising as well as the management time and energy which goes into the planning of the campaign.

Advertising can also be considered in terms of the role that it fulfils in terms of the marketing context.

Further classifications

Pioneer advertising

Pioneer advertising serves to inform consumers about the existence of a new product category. The purpose of this is to stimulate primary demand for a product which is previously unknown in the marketplace, rather than identifying the particular attributes of a specific brand. However, many new products are specifically introduced by manufacturers with a strong branding presence, in the hope that they will continue to 'own' the category even when joined by other, similar products. The portable tape player continues to be known as the 'Walkman' even though it is manufactured by several other companies other than the originator, Sony.

Competitive advertising

This seeks to persuade consumers of the particular benefits and advantages which derive from a particular brand. The intention is to increase selective demand by providing information regarding the product attributes and benefits which may not be available from competitive products, or even where the attributes are shared, to create the impression that they are the 'property' of the advertised brand. Intel, the manufacturers of computer chips, has used this approach to successfully brand a component within another manufacturer's product with such success that it is almost impossible to sell a computer without 'Intel inside' in the mainstream market. This campaign has undoubtedly contributed to the growth of Intel, which is ranked by Interbrand (2004) as the fifth most valuable brand in the world.

Comparative advertising

This relates to specific campaigns that directly compare one product's attributes with those of its competitors. It is important to recognise that, in the UK at least, such advertising is a relatively new phenomenon. Under the provisions of the Trade Marks Act, 1938, the trade mark of a brand was protected from infringement and could only be used with the express permission of the owners of the mark – hardly likely to be given to a competitor for use in such advertising. Under the Trade Marks Act introduced in October 1994, however, the restrictions on comparative advertising have been lifted. The result has been the appearance of a number of new campaigns making direct and overt comparisons between brands. Many campaigns now directly name competitors and make overt comparisons between the various products, services offered or prices charged, in order to develop a competitive advantage. Hardly a day passes without the technique being employed by companies within the mobile telephone sector, for example. Similarly, the technique is a common feature of financial advertising in which, for example, a bank compares its lending rates with those of its competitors.

At the time of writing, the Alliance & Leicester were mounting a campaign to assert their advantages over financial services companies. The advertising specifically identifies the rate charged to borrowers which is compared to the rates of other leading named financial institutions.

Subliminal advertising

Subliminal advertising is the embedding of material in print, audio or video messages so faintly that they are not consciously perceived.

According to Rogers and Smith (1993), although a great deal has been written about this topic, little evidence exists to support the notion that it has any effect. Indeed, most academic researchers on the subject have reported no practical or predictable effect in an advertising setting. Despite these findings, many articles and books are published which promote the notion that subliminal advertising is used and is effective.

The functions and roles of advertising

The particular roles that advertising can play are many and varied, although they fall within three broad areas, as shown in Figure 1.2.

Figure 1.2 **The key roles of advertising**

- to inform
- to persuade
- to sell.

The informational function

In certain instances, advertising simply seeks to provide the public with specific pieces of information. In many cases, this has a neutral content, such as public announcements or some forms of governmental advertising. In other instances, manufacturers may use advertising to inform previous consumers of some deficiency in their product. This is apparent in the case of product recalls, where the manufacturer uses advertising to communicate the particular problem to the widest possible audience in order to ensure a speedy dissemination of information and an equally rapid response on the part of the owners of such products.

In the case of a manufacturer introducing a new product, there is a need to inform potential consumers about the new product. This may take the form of a simple announcement, or may provide detail about the product, its functions and some form of comparison or claim about the product in the context of alternative product offerings.

In order to extend the appeal of an existing product, manufacturers may attempt to use advertising to suggest new uses for a product. In many instances, responses to consumer research will identify different ways in which the consumer uses the product, and these may assist in the identification of new opportunities. A manufacturer may wish to inform the market of a price change or some other aspect of the product proposition. Recently, for example, Immac have focused advertising on the new name 'Deet' for their brand. The national daily newspapers frequently mount promotions wherein the price is reduced to encourage greater levels of trial. This has particularly been the case following the introduction of tabloid versions of the quality national daily newspapers. *The Times*, for example, distributed vouchers to the readers of the broadsheet version to encourage them to sample the new format.

Sometimes, it will be necessary to provide some form of explanation of how a product works. When Dyson introduced their revolutionary new vacuum cleaner, it needed to explain to potential purchasers the operating differences between its product and those of its competitors – the Dyson cleaner does not use a bag and claims to filter out more dust than rival manufacturers products. Currently, the company is advertising the fact that, unlike competitive vacuum cleaners, the Dyson does not use suction. Services companies may need to provide information concerning the range of available services to the consumer. This is seen clearly in the context of banking services, where a company may offer the ability to maintain a current account with a cheque book, credit card facilities, domestic and foreign services, such as the ability to withdraw funds whilst on holiday abroad, together with deposit accounts, investment programmes, and so on. The list of services may be quite extensive.

If the manufacturer identifies a dissonance between the product performance and consumer perceptions, it may be necessary to use advertising to correct false impressions. Similarly, when a product deficiency has been identified, it may be necessary to reduce consumer fears. Following the withdrawal of the Perrier brand, the brand owners used advertising extensively to inform customers of the steps that they had taken to remedy the problem and to reassure them that the new product was safe and reliable. In contrast, most manufacturers do little more than use advertising to recall the defective product and fail to respond to consumer fears which might result from the identification of a problem.

As we will see, it is not only brands that are important. An increasingly important element of reassurance derives from the image of the company which produces the product. Advertising can assist in the process of building a company image.

The persuasive function

Either because of changes to the product formulation or because of a previous miscommunication, manufacturers may wish to change customer's perceptions of product attributes or benefits. Following the reformulation of many products within the soap powder market, and the removal of the bleaching agent, it was important to provide a new basis for product comparisons. Advertising stressed the products' powers to ensure colour fastness and de-emphasised their ability to get clothes whiter.

Much 'cause' advertising attempts to persuade consumers to alter their attitudes towards a particular issue. Political parties use this form of advertising, especially during the run up to an election, to persuade the audience that their policies are the most appropriate and to motivate them to vote for a particular party. Similarly, charities often attempt to focus attention on a specific concern. For several years, the RSPCA has campaigned to improve conditions for animals and has used a variety of advertising approaches to alter public opinions. Government departments sometimes use this form of advertising to bring about a change in attitudes towards issues of general concern. Over many years, for example, the Department of Transport has used advertising messages to influence attitudes towards drink driving or child road safety.

In some market sectors, advertising may be used as a precursor to other activities. It may, for example, attempt to provide specific information to the target audience in order to persuade potential customers to take a sales call.

The selling function

Most advertising seeks to promote the sale of particular goods or services. To achieve this objective, the advertising provides the potential or existing customer base with information about the product or service. In the majority of instances, such advertising seeks to reinforce existing attitudes by explaining how the product is appropriate to the potential users' existing needs or lifestyle.

Some advertising, particularly that of a promotional nature, will attempt to persuade the customer to make a purchase now, rather than delay it until some later time. The advertising will convey a sense of urgency, often by placing some form of time constraint on the offer being made. This is particularly the case with 'sale' advertising. Potential customers are notified of the sale dates and reminded that they can only obtain the particular 'bargains' at that time. Similarly, retailers will make 'time-limited' offers which impose restrictions as to when customers can take advantage of the offer price.

A key role of advertising is to bring about the building of brand preferences and to encourage brand switching. This is the form most advertising campaigns take, where the advertiser stresses aspects of brand superiority and will sometimes make direct comparisons with competitive products. Often, it will not be sufficient merely to inform the consumer of the existence of the brand. It will be important to direct them to those outlets that stock the product and to remind them where to buy it. Many campaigns feature a list of stockists, and this serves two purposes. On the one hand, it provides the consumer with the necessary information to enable them to locate the product. On the other, it provides an incentive to the featured outlets to continue to stock the brand.

Some products have a distinctly seasonal appeal. Advertising may be used to remind consumers that the product may be needed in the future and to ensure that the brand is kept in mind during the off season. Finally, even dominant brands have to ensure the maintenance of 'front of mind' awareness. The consumer has a comparatively short memory and, even with familiar brands, needs to be reminded of the benefits and advantages they provide.

Many organisations, both commercial and those in the not-for-profit sector, use advertising to achieve their goals. It is important to recognise that the users of advertising can control the specific nature of the message and, to a large degree, the composition of the audience to whom that message is addressed.

The role of advertising has traditionally been seen as an aid to sales. This it does in four main ways by:

1 creating awareness
2 providing essential information
3 helping to build a relevant brand image
4 acting as a regular reminded to try, buy or use the brand.

However, as Fletcher (1993) points out, advertising needs to be targeted precisely and to arouse the interest of potential consumers in order to achieve effectiveness. As he notes:

- People are exposed to a large number of advertisements in their lives. They respond to a very small minority of them.
- Selective perception focuses people's attention on those advertisements which interest them.
- Many advertisements evoke little interest because they relate to goods and services which people do not buy.
- Most marketing companies seek to increase sales of their brands. For a brand to show a significant increase in sales it is necessary for only a minority of people to buy it instead of or as well as their usual brand.
- The task of advertising is to discover who these minorities are and to say 'exactly the right things to them'.
- Such minorities are not difficult to identify because experience suggests that they will be very similar to the existing buyers of the brand.

The purpose of advertising is to modify the way individuals relate to the product or service being advertised. Depending on the advertising strategy, it is anticipated that consequent changes in brand awareness or predisposition will change behaviour. The purpose of testing advertising or other communication is to predict these effects.

The benefits and limitations of advertising

Benefits

Advertising can create images of products that serve to differentiate them in the marketplace. Since, as we have already seen, the increasing convergence of technology has resulted in a situation in which many products cannot be differentiated in physical terms, manufacturers must utilise other methods to create some distinction for their products or services. In many product categories, consumers are unable to discriminate between competing brands in blind tasting, yet they express preferences for particular brands. The basis of their selection, in many instances, is the positive associations of the brand in terms of the image or appeal of the product derived from the style and content of the advertising supporting that brand.

Advertising can assist in the creation and maintenance of brand equity. Today's brands have a real financial value which is significantly greater than the investment required to produce them. De Chernatony and McDonald (1992) report the addition of some £127 million to the balance sheet of Reckitt & Colman following their acquisition of Airwick Industries. This sum was attributed solely to the intangible benefits of 'goodwill, heritage and loyalty conveyed by the newly acquired brand names'.

Advertising can create a unique personality for a brand. It is undeniably true that it is the brand personality that is the key to sparking consumer desire. Advertising creates specific impressions of a brand which are left beyond the actual message being communicated. There are many examples of this, including Levis, Tango, John Smith's Bitter and Nike. All of these demonstrate the important part played by the personality created through advertising as a major contributor to the consumer's propensity to purchase the brand.

Advertising can be used to reduce overall selling costs. Imagine a sales force attempting to communicate with millions of potential consumers of a product category without access to conventional media!

Feldwick (1997) summates the contribution of advertising in the following way:

> Advertising has the ability to work as a catalyst, providing images that transform perceptions to the brand both among its consumers, and those who are responsible for delivering the brand to those consumers. So, apart from its direct effects, it may have equally powerful indirect effects. As a result, other marketing activities may become more productive. But, more than this, all those involved with the brand – the staff who deal with customers, the R&D people, the marketing group, the other agencies who work on the brand – will share a clear and inspiring vision of how this brand is different.

Winston Fletcher in his book *Advertising, Advertising* (1999) argues the benefits provided by advertising:

- It provides stimulating information.
- It facilitates choice and helps the consumer overcome the 'information mountain'.
- It increases the user's satisfaction in using the product.
- It fosters competition and, thereby, reduces prices.
- It subsidies the media.
- It creates demand, which creates sales, which creates employment.
- It creates brands which provide the consumer with an assurance of quality, thereby justifying their price premium.
- It often makes a contribution to societal well-being – encouraging charitable donations, more careful driving, etc.

Limitations

Against these advantages, it is important to recognise the limitations inherent in advertising: it is not a universal panacea. Whilst it can introduce consumers to a new product concept and may encourage them to try it, if the product fails to live up to the expectations, even the most powerful advertising campaign will seldom overcome consumer rejection of an ineffectual product or service.

Advertising is inherently an expensive means of communicating with a desired target audience, at least in capital terms. With some exceptions, advertising media costs are extremely high and involve varying degrees of wastage. Even the best-planned media schedule will reach consumers who have little or no interest in the product category.

As a vehicle for communication, advertising essentially represents a one-way medium. Increasingly marketers are recognising that there is a need to establish a two-way dialogue with the potential consumer. Unless some form of feedback mechanism is built in to the execution, such dialogue is inhibited. Advertising tends to be somewhat impersonal. Whilst it is effective in communicating simultaneously to large numbers of people, the specific needs and wants of the individual cannot be recognised and responded to.

It is important to remember that the other tools of marketing communications offer alternative means of communication with both existing and potential consumers. Each of these tools has distinctive advantages which advertising may not be able to match.

Advertising and society

Advertising needs to respond to social pressures. The content of advertising changed through the 1960s from the presentation of pseudo-scientific support for a brand proposition to the presentation of 'real' people with 'real' emotions.

There needs to be a fundamental truth in the advertising for a brand. Advertising will not work if the product fails to live up to the expectations created by the advertising.

Kotler (1972) in a paper in the *Harvard Business Review* was amongst the first to recognise that what consumers desire may not necessarily be good for them and that the long-term consequence may well be that both consumers and society may suffer. He proposed that marketing adopt a more societally responsible approach in order to achieve a more satisfactory outcome.

Social responsibility in marketing covers a diverse range of issues such as consumerism, environmentalism, regulation, political and social marketing.

Criticisms of advertising

One of the most common complaints about advertising is 'if they spend less on commercials, maybe I could buy the product for a lot less'. Scipione (1997) conducted a study into public perceptions of advertising expenditures and found that consumers have no idea of how much companies really spend. Indeed, for the most part they tend to overestimate the levels of expenditure. Despite this, their perceptions are important since, if they believe that the company is spending too much, it may impact upon their purchase decisions related to the advertised brand.

Shimp (1997) identified several areas where critics contend that advertising has a negative effect on society. They are as follows:

- Advertising is untruthful and deceptive, manipulative, offensive and in bad taste.
- It creates and perpetuates stereotypes.
- It encourages people to buy things that they don't really need.
- It plays upon fears and insecurities.

In her book, *No Logo*, Naomi Klein (2000) makes several assertions that corporate expansion and marketing have detrimentally affected consumers' lives:

- **No space**: She claims that marketing communications now dominate much of our physical environment (via advertising, product placement, sponsorship, etc.). Moreover, she suggests that corporations are even starting to dictate the content of magazines, newspapers and television channels. The consequence, she asserts, is that it undermines our freedom of thought and expression.
- **No choice**: The dominance of very few corporate players means that we face a restricted choice of goods and services.
- **No jobs**: As companies become more successful, they reduce the size of their workforces and employees face redundancy and exploitation.

Pollay and Gallagher (1990) have tabulated many of the consequences of commercialisation, which is the direct result of much advertising. We show their results in Figure 1.3.

Figure 1.3 Possible cultural consequences of commercialisation

Advertising typically is:

Promoting goods and objects
- as satisfying all needs
- as all that is important
- as good for everyone

Intense advocacy
- insisting, exhorting
- half-truths, incomplete information

Appealing to individuals

Easily understood, using:
- social stereotypes
- strong symbols

Idealising 'the good life'

When advertising appeals to:
- mass markets
- sexuality
- fears
- status
- youth
- newness

So it seems to foster:

Materialism
- psychological belief in consumption as the source of all satisfaction
- political properties favouring private over public goods
- spiritual displacement of religion

Submission and seduction
- compulsive consumption, indulgence disregarding consequences
- cynicism, distrust, dishonesty

Selfishness and greed
- sacrificing community, charity, co-operation, compassion

Simplistic symbols
- racism, sexism, etc.
- religious and political iconoclasm

Creates dissatisfaction
- loss of self-esteem, self-respect
- frustrations, powerlessness
- criminality, revolution

It also promotes:
- conformity
- pornography
- chronic anxieties
- envy, social competitiveness
- disrespect of family elders
- disrespect of tradition

The consumer and advertising

According to Li et al. (2002) public perceptions of advertising have been studied for decades, and findings show that consumers' attitudes towards advertising as an institution are usually more favourable than unfavourable. Many consumers recognise not only the negative societal effects of advertising, but also the positive economic impact of the advertising industry. However, individual advertisements differ from advertising as an institution of society, and research indicates that the content and tactics of certain ads 'offend' or 'irritate' consumers.

In a study by Mittal (1994) approximately one-third of the respondents acknowledged advertisements to be a good source of marketplace information. Some found them entertaining and a good source of social-image information.

Many felt that advertising had good economic benefits, i.e. raising standards of living. However, on the negative side, Mittal found that a sizeable proportion indicted advertising for furthering materialism, overselling sex and promoting unwholesome values. Nearly everyone believed that advertising increased the cost of goods.

Consumers tend to think virtually every form of commercial promotional activity, from concert sponsorship to telemarketing, is a form of advertising (Schultz 1995). Industry practitioners and academics, however, tend to distinguish certain forms of promotion as 'not advertising' (Rust and Oliver 1994). Certain activities might better be classified, they suggest, as sales promotion, promotional products, direct marketing or public relations. But even these professionals might find it challenging to pigeonhole some activities, such as word of mouth and product placement in movies. It is often stated that consumers are exposed to something like 3500 advertisements each day (e.g. Godin 1999 and White 2002, both cited in Richards and Curran 2002), but that number varies by what we classify as advertising.

Abernethy and Franke (1996) argue that the evidence on consumer attitudes toward advertising shows that consumers prefer advertising that helps in decision making. Providing information that differentiates a brand from its competitors tends to increase commercial recall, comprehension and persuasion. They cite a 1995 study by Ducoffe that found information in advertising to be the single factor most strongly correlated with overall advertising value. Their review of audiences' perceptions of commercials revealed the informative/effective factor to be the best predictor of ad likeability and brand attitudes. Their summary is that advertising information is an important influence on consumers' responses to both the ad and the brand.

The Advertising Standards Authority Report (Ford-Hutchinson and Rothwell 2002) similarly identified a series of consumer attitudes towards advertising and confirmed many of the previous studies:

- Advertising is everything with a name on it. As noted earlier, from the consumer perspective, the term 'advertising' encompasses every piece of brand, product or service communication. It obviously includes the key media of advertising but also other aspects of 'selling' such as direct mail, door drops, the internet, branded clothing, sponsorship, branded text messages and even telephone sales.
- Life without advertising would be dull. Advertising is part of the environment. For some, mainly older respondents, there is, perhaps, too much advertising, but the majority embrace it as part of life. They indicate that without it there would be less information, entertainment and street colour, and less to talk about.
- Advertising is an indicator of business health.
- Advertising has got better. It is felt to be cleverer, more reflective of real life, more entertaining and more tuned to different targets.
- Consumers are concerned about 'untruthful truthful advertising', advertising that does not lie, but is economical with the truth. It mainly concerns the advertising of financial products that highlights substantial benefits but is vague about risk or downsides. It is epitomised by advertising for accident claims companies, consolidation of debts and loan offers.

- Overall, the regulatory bodies were felt by the public to 'be doing a good job'. However, in the area of 'untruthful, truthful advertising' it was felt that 'they' should be more active, invasive and controlling in order to protect consumers.

Arnold (2001) argues that consumers are becoming ever more sophisticated and there is a need on the part of advertisers to respond to this new sophistication. One indication is the growth of interactive advertising, by which consumers can access additional information to supplement the content of a particular advertising execution during the commercial break. Advertising literacy is a relatively recent phenomenon. Remember that in the UK TV ads only started in 1955.

Schultz and Barnes (1995) consider the ways in which consumers process information on products and services.

> They simply take in all the information they need in various ways, over time and from varying sources. They have a constantly changing dynamic approach to the brand. Through a plethora of brand contacts, each brand develops its own history with each customer.

Gordon and Langmaid (1999) quoted respondents as experiencing a feeling of being 'mesmerised' in front of the television, and being mesmerised is not a cognitive state. They proposed that respondents to ads were processing them at a low involvement level, and stored the information and conclusions in some passive memory store from which it was not readily retrievable.

Yet consumers apparently welcome advertising. Gordon and Ryan (1982) indicate that advertising is thought to brighten the environment, add interest to boring journeys and offer relief from the tensions and frustrations of everyday travelling.

However, many consumers are sceptical towards advertising claims. Hardesty et al. (2002) carried out research in order to investigate the ability of consumers' scepticism toward advertising to moderate the effects of advertised price claims that employ external reference prices (i.e. invoice prices) to frame offers as attractive. The use of external reference prices is common in the marketplace, and the potential for consumer deception is well documented. Scepticism toward advertising is the general tendency of disbelief of advertising claims and represents a basic marketplace belief that varies across persons and is related to its level of general persuasion.

Social and ethical issues

Inevitably, advertising attracts considerable attention in the public debate concerning ethics and morality. The very public nature of advertising draws both commentary and criticism. There are some who argue that the very nature of advertising itself is unethical. They suggest that advertising persuades people to consume products and services or to adopt patterns of behaviour which are unethical. Moreover, they argue that advertising raises the cost of products generally, is often untruthful and tends to target vulnerable groups within society, such as the old, the young or the impressionable.

Bush and Bush (1994) argue that ethical and moral issues resulting in controversy will always surround advertising because of the nature of the creative process. Creative advertisers take risks and chart new frontiers. However, by breaking new ground, they challenge components of the narrative paradigm and create controversy. Because ethics is such a pluralistic, complex and situational phenomenon, it is important for advertisers to establish boundaries or latitudes of ethicality for their creative campaigns. Once these boundaries are established, advertisers can anticipate the controversy that may be generated by their advertising.

Advertising has become a fundamental aspect of society with Leiss et al. (1986) suggesting that we accord what it says a place of special prominence in our lives – being one of the great vehicles of social communication.

Marketers are generally more likely to be faced with ethical issues than managers in other functions because of the nature of their role. They have to deal with multiple parties, often external to the company, who may have conflicting interests. Marketing transactions often involve more than one community which creates the potential for conflicting ethical norms. One of the dilemmas in the area of marketing ethics rests in the difficulty of determining which stakeholder interests should take priority and who should make the final decision if conflict exists between those interests.

Whilst it is true that managers concerned with ethical and environmental issues are beginning to appear within corporate structures, they are commonly attached to any one of the traditional departments rather than having individual departmental responsibility. The differences in individual attitudes, professional roles and hierarchical position are all likely to influence the way in which corporate morality is perceived and understood (Cone 1999).

Advertising practitioners and academicians are becoming more aware of and concerned about the ethicality of advertisements (Reidenbach and Robin 1988) and advertising/marketing in general. In fact, in the past decade participation in workshops, training seminars, and academic research on ethical dilemmas in marketing has increased (Zinkhan, Bisesi and Saxton 1989).

Definitions

In 1973 William Frankena (cited in Zinkhan 1994) defined ethics as a set of moral principles directed at enhancing societal well-being. He sub-divided this into two moral principles: benificence – which concerns doing good; and justice – which is the practice of being fair. Bush and Bush (1994) defined ethics as 'just or right standards of behaviour between parties in a situation, based on individual moral philosophies'.

A major difficulty in determining ethical standards is the fact that attitudes and values evolve over time. Inherently, therefore, the standards which apply themselves change. Ethics is an area that requires each individual to take a stand. In the end, each individual must not only decide what is right and what is wrong but must also be able to justify these personal decisions to critics.

Zinkhan (1994) acknowledges that when making these difficult moral choices there are many places to turn for guidance including personal conscience, company policy, industry standards, governmental law or regulation, and organised religion.

Understanding the ethics of advertising

One approach for understanding advertising ethics is to identify those advertising practices which have potentially harmful effects for society as a whole or a particular segment. Zinkhan (1994) suggests that actions which involve harmful effects present a difficult set of moral choices and options.

Robin and Reidenback (1998) take a much broader view of ethics in marketing communications and point out the degree to which the basic functions are seen to be ethical or unethical. They suggest that advertising, in particular, must be measured within an understanding of our history, the times in which they are applied, their context, the expectations of society, the requirements of capitalism and our best understanding of human behaviour.

According to Carrigan and Attalla (2001) the study of marketing ethics has evolved in response to what they term as the 'smugness' of marketers. They argue that, 'theoretically, in the exchange process marketers made a reasonable profit, consumers got the product they desired and everyone was happy'. This somewhat simplistic notion has been increasingly challenged. First by writers such as Vance Packard and Ralph Nader who championed the corner of the consumer, and more recently by far more organised consumer activists such as Greenpeace, Friends of the Earth, the Consumers' Association and others.

Pollay and Gallagher (1990) conducted a review of social science commentaries on advertising which drew together a wide range of material into a general framework. This synthesis suggested that advertising was seen by social scientists as a powerful and intrusive means of communication and persuasion whose effects could be to reinforce materialism, cynicism, irrationality, selfishness and a number of other undesirable outcomes.

Ethical criticism

Many researchers claim that consumers now have limited tolerance with advertisers, claiming them to be more cynical. Murphy (2000) believes that 'the arrival of the conscience driven consumer' is one of the most interesting sociological forces today.

Advertising has been charged with a number of ethical breaches, most of which focus on its apparent lack of societal responsibility. Pollay (1986) suggests that advertising has profound consequences due to its pervasiveness, stereotypical portrayals, manipulative and persuasive nature, preoccupation with materialism and consumption, frequent use of sex appeals and lack of information. Other criticisms include advertising's targeting practices to potentially vulnerable groups such as children, minorities and the disadvantaged, the overly dramatic and increasingly graphic use of fear appeals, and unethical or irresponsible handling of potentially harmful or offensive products.

Several of these points of contention can be structured into more general categories, such as:

targeting minorities, the disadvantaged, children, teens and the elderly; message strategies: the use of fear appeals, sex appeals, negative appeals or attacks, and offensive humour; product or brand issues: advertising for controversial, unusual, or embarrassing products or services; and broad societal issues: advertising's effects on values, religion, cultural literacy, or materialism.

(Treise and Weigold 1994; Boddewyn 1991)

Shimp (1997), however, claims that 'advertising reflects the rest of society and any indictment of advertising probably applies to society at large'.

| **Establishing ethical guidelines** | One approach for understanding advertising ethics is to identify advertising practices (e.g. subliminal advertising, advertising to children) which have potentially harmful effects for society (or potentially harmful effects for some segment of society). Actions which involve harmful effects certainly present a difficult set of moral choices and options. |

Many within the field of marketing seek to establish ethical guidelines and practice and disseminate these throughout the industry. This is reflected in the increasing number of papers published in academic journals on the issues involved. Similarly, many major multinational companies have published codes of conduct to demonstrate their commitment to better business behaviour, as have professional marketing bodies. Advertising ethics has been an important subject area, for example, in the *Journal of Advertising*. During the first 20 years of its publication, there were 159 articles published on topics related to advertising ethics.

Increasingly it is recognised that advertisers should apply these principles to avoid offending members of the public. Hyman and Tansey (1990) stressed the importance of advertisers identifying and distinguishing ethical issues and boundaries in preparation of potentially negative consequences. The International Chamber of Commerce, for example, states that: 'advertising should be decent, prepared with a due sense of social responsibility and not be such as to impair public confidence in advertising'. This is similar to the principles established by the Advertising Standards Authority which states that 'advertising should be legal, decent and honest'.

David Ogilvy, writing in *Ogilvy on Advertising* (1993), argues that the public and the media should be made to share greater responsibility for not permitting (such unethical) advertising to appear in the first place.

| **The consequences of unethical behaviour** | Unethical conduct often has negative consequences. These range from adverse publicity to diminished corporate reputation, to lower employee morale, to customer boycotts and even legal sanctions. |

Some countries have already banned specific categories of product from advertising. Others have more limited controls. This area has been drawn into sharp focus with the worldwide concern over obesity, for example, with much debate centring on the morality of advertisers promoting the sale of products which encourage people to eat poor diets. To this must be added the wider range of products – alcohol and tobacco, for example – which are acknowledged to cause health problems, and the advertising of products targeted to children.

In every instance, there is the potential risk that, if the advertising industry fails to self-regulate effectively, governmental controls will be introduced to curb what is perceived as unethical behaviour.

A further consequence is the impact of consumer activism. Whilst it is evident that consumer activism is on the increase, it is difficult to determine whether the consumer is overtly concerned with the ethical behaviour of the companies from whom they buy products and services.

Various authors have demonstrated that boycotts and other campaigns against unethical behaviour have resulted in the loss of considerable sums of money to the companies involved. According to Klein (2000), Shell were estimated to have lost more than 20 per cent of sales during the Brent Spar boycott. Similarly, the Nestlé boycott is said to have cost the firm some $40 million.

However, despite the widespread publicity surrounding the 'unethical' behaviour of many international and multinational organisations, many consumers continue to buy their products and their profitability continues to increase.

TV advertising and children

There are several reasons why advertising and its influence on children's behaviour takes up public and political discussion to such a pronounced extent. Berger (1999) presents a summary of the main arguments:

- Advertising is universally present and it is salient; everyone is affected by it and can evade it only to a very limited extent. The numerous stimuli and their intensity automatically result in emotional reactions of sympathy or antipathy: the subject-matter of the mass media determines both the relevant political and private discussion.
- An advertisement can be looked upon as a brief but exaggerated and highly emotionally charged burst of information, usually directed at a specific group. Everybody is exposed to advertising, yet most people are not in the targeted segment of the population for much of the advertising they see. There is no one who has not at some time been enraged about a certain advertisement or commercial spot – all forms of aversion to advertising stem from this feeling.
- Advertising is always perceived to be equivalent to the effect that it has – in the sense of influencing behaviour. The demand for bans on advertising is based on the assumption that there are direct links between advertising and the effect it has on behaviour. The central argument of all political discussion is that advertising aims at influencing and 'leading astray'.
- The diversity as well as the increase in child and juvenile misbehaviour (aggressiveness, crime, school failure), is often blamed on the nature of advertising.

A recent paper by Bandyopadhyay et al. (2001) identifies a series of ethical issues which surround the relationship between children and advertising:

- Are children consumers?
- Is the selling intent of advertising understood by children?
- Are advertisers unfair to children?
- Are television commercials distinguishable from television programmes?
- Are children affected negatively by commercials?

In it, they set out the specific concerns, together with the views of those who would prefer to see the maintenance of the status quo. See Table 1.2.

Table 1.2 Ethical issues around children and advertising

Concern	Response of advertising proponents
Children should be viewed as consumers' offspring: passive and naïve.	Children need products for growth as an individual – both socially and personally.
A parent–child conflict may result in disharmony within the family.	Children receive pocket money and should be allowed to spend it on products they desire.
Children are unable to understand the selling intent of a commercial.	Children are sophisticated and aware of the advertising world. They know that somebody is putting together an advertisement with the intention of getting them to buy the product. Various studies have demonstrated that children as young as 4 can demonstrate an awareness of the intent of commercials.
Children are being exploited before they are cognitively aware and fail to distinguish commercials from programmes.	Commercials and programmes are perceptually different and children understand the differences in content.
Information provided in commercials is insufficient and inadequate.	Advertising serves as an information source for children and enables them to learn to function in the marketplace.
Advertising directed at children creates materialism, stifles creativity, creates conflict between parents and children and hinders the development of moral and ethical values.	Commercials extol the virtues of consuming and promote a way of life. They provide information about products from which an evaluation can be made.
Children become expert at pressuring parents with constant requests and threats to buy advertised products.	Much of this pattern of behaviour is learned in the playground and 'pester power' exists even in those countries where advertising to children is banned.

SOURCE: Bandyopadhyay et al. 2001

European governments display a diversity of responses to the issue of advertising and children. Sweden has the most stringent controls, banning advertising to children under 12. The issue has caused much debate with the EU although, thus far, individual countries remain free to determine their own policies towards advertising and children. The Australian government is currently considering a total ban on the advertising of food and snacks to children.

Social marketing

Social marketing faces special ethical problems that are linked to the ultimate ends it promotes. Brenkert (2002) argues that these ends cannot be assumed to be justified in the same manner in which the ends of commercial marketing are justified.

He suggests that in contrast to commercial marketing, which is focused on market exchanges, social marketing is focused on welfare exchanges.

However, social marketing's analysis of social problems gives rise to another group of ethical challenges. Brenkert suggests that it may unwittingly substitute a marketing rationale for relevant moral rationales called for by the social problems it addresses. In addition, because of their partition of social problems and market segmentation, social marketers may not be able to focus on the background and structural features that underlie the social problems they attack. Accordingly, although social marketing has been offered as 'a new and better' solution to these problems, it may be able to offer only temporary solutions that do not significantly affect the underlying problems.

Social marketers seek to bring about social change through marketing techniques, This raises ethical questions about the effects of social marketing on self-determination and democracy.

Social marketing has clear relations to commercial marketing. Still, social marketing is distinct from commercial marketing in that social marketing focuses on resolving social problems, whereas commercial marketing focuses on producing various goods or services for a profit.

Public service advertising

A paper by Baggozzi and Moore (1994) discusses the development and effect of public service advertisements. The authors suggest that these may be divided into two types:

- Those aimed at the individual to protect or help themselves (where fear is often used) such as the recent campaign designed to encourage householders to install smoke detectors.
- Those which use an indirect appeal and are aimed at people to give time and money to help others in danger.

They argue that in the latter context emotional advertising elicits a far greater response than those which present a rational argument. It is argued that the emotional ads, by stimulating empathy directly through the viewers' perceptions of the activity depicted, engender negative emotions and stimulate the desire to help. Their study indicated that the greater the magnitude of the negative emotions (i.e. anger, sadness, fear and tension) the stronger the empathic response and hence the desire to help.

This is very much the approach taken by National Children's Homes (NCH) in their recent campaign. However, stimulating too much emotion may also cause a negative reaction. A similar campaign for Barnado's (which previously had won an effectiveness award) was widely condemned for the graphic nature of the content in subsequent executions.

Green advertising

Over the past 20 years, public support for environmental protection has fluctuated somewhat. Despite this, the green movement is unarguably one of the more important social movements in recent history. Many national polls indicate that public concern for the environment remains consistently high, although in many instances government statistics demonstrate that comparatively few consumers take direct action to adopt a more environmentally friendly approach.

An increasing number of marketers are targeting the green segment of the population. Recycled paper and plastic goods and environmentally friendly detergents, amongst others, are examples of products positioned on the basis of environmental appeal. A number of major brands, including Ben & Jerry's ice cream and Green & Black's chocolate, have launched products with an ethical or green positioning. Several companies have adopted the Soil Association logo and the Fair Trade Marks, which are increasingly sought out by consumers.

According to research conducted by OMD for *Marketing* magazine, over half of all consumers have now purchased a Fair Trade product which guarantees a premium to farmers in the developing world. The products purchased by these consumers include:

Coffee	65%
Chocolate/cocoa	42%
Tea	34%
Fresh fruit	28%
Snacks	16%
Fruit juice	14%

Banerjee and Gulas (1995) indicate that green advertising is on the rise as more and more manufacturers are informing their consumers about positive environmental aspects of their products and services.

Advertising is defined as green if it meets one or more of the following criteria:

1 Explicitly or implicitly addresses the relationship between a product/service and the bio-physical environment.
2 Promotes a green lifestyle with or without highlighting a product/service.
3 Presents a corporate image of environmental responsibility.

The legal and regulatory framework

Advertising is designed to persuade people either to do or not to do something specific. A consequence, therefore, is that advertising does not adopt a neutral stance. There are those who are concerned about the content of advertising. By its very nature, advertising attempts to present products and services in the best possible light. However, by failing to communicate the negative aspects of those products, some believe that it fails to tell the whole truth.

Advertising is, increasingly, expected to entertain. It follows from this that advertising relies more heavily on images and emotional content to attract the consumer's attention and interest, some of which may offend some members of the community.

Throughout most societies, there are specific regulations that govern the use of advertising. These range from controls over specific product categories which may or may not be advertised, the timing of specific advertising which might be considered offensive to certain age groups, and so on.

Harker and Harker (2000) state that the regulation of marketing activity, particularly the advertising component, is necessary to protect those who cannot protect themselves from undesirable behaviour or conduct. The system of regulation adopted provides authority to control the exchange process. In many countries, advertisers opt for a system of self-regulation for a variety of reasons, not the least being to stave off unwanted government intervention that would itself be difficult to administer, given the dynamic nature of advertising.

A key foundation of most self-regulation systems is the code of conduct, which acts as a set of guidelines to which the advertising industry must adhere and a framework for advertising regulators to test the value of a complaint. Codes of conduct that provide extensive coverage of prevailing community issues and are concisely written using precise language will be of greater use in the determination process than those that do not.

Self-regulation is well developed in only some 20–40 countries, but a number have strengthened their voluntary codes and guidelines regarding sex and decency in advertising – notably, Canada, Ireland, New Zealand, Sweden (where an Ethical Council has recently been created) and the United Kingdom.

Advertising regulators attempt to deal with this issue of acceptable advertising by considering prevailing community standards, ensuring that complaints boards include representatives from throughout the community (Boddewyn 1988) and participate in code creation and revision. There is also a call to publicise their adjudications widely (Wiggs 1992). These measures mean that acceptability is defined by default as advertising that did not clearly fall foul of legal or self-regulatory standards. This approach is pragmatic since advertising regulators must make decisions, but it needs also to be recognised that, as with other control systems, these decisions are subjective.

Ads that are indecent, sexist, sexy, exhibit violence to women or treat them as mere objects present a constant and even growing problem in many countries. Both the law and voluntary guidelines find it difficult to handle such ads because of the wide range of attitudes towards sex and decency in advertising, and the fact that these attitudes change. Three recent adjudications by the Advertising Standards Authority indicate specific concerns. Ads by the lingerie manufacturer Agent Provocateur were banned as being degrading to women. Similarly, ads for Nokia's N-Gage mobile gaming device were banned for encouraging 'sexual violence towards women'. The final example is the decision by the ASA to vet all campaigns featuring the logo 'FCUK'. It ruled that clothing retailer French Connection has persistently produced advertising designed to offend the public. As a result, all future ads will have to be submitted for approval by the Committee of Advertising Practice.

Advertising bodies and practitioners are improving their responses to this situation which threatens their autonomy but promises to increase their effectiveness. However, these responses also generate unwelcome implications and consequences for advertising's role and freedom. Some commentators suggest that government regulation of advertising curtails the rights of advertisers to communicate with their publics and of people to receive information about products. This is a complex issue pitching those who distrust advertising and conceive of practically no limits to what can be prohibited or restricted by law against those who promote 'freedom of commercial speech' as essential to the functioning of the market system.

Most self-regulatory codes are concerned with 'decency'. This can be defined as conformity to recognised standards of propriety, good taste and modesty. In advertising, such standards typically cover:

- controversial behaviours (e.g. drinking, gambling and contraception);
- the promotion of 'unmentionable' or 'offensive' goods and services such as undergarments, feminine-hygiene products, funerals, toilet paper, contraceptives and massages;
- the communication of messages about cigarettes, alcoholic beverages, pornographic materials, violence-ridden films and comic books as well as other items whose consumption is considered undesirable by some groups or the government;
- the use of tasteless images, vulgar language and offensive appeals.

Soft advertising issues, including sex and decency, are difficult to control – short of outright bans and government censorship, which are not uncommon. There are still 'Ministries of Information' in various countries (for example, in Malaysia, Singapore and Saudi Arabia) that must be consulted beforehand and can suspend offending publications, while the advertising of various products and services (contraceptives, casinos, cigarettes, etc.) is prohibited in many Western countries.

Advertising regulations

In the UK, the new Office of Communications (OFCOM), has taken over the functions of five existing regulators: the Independent Television Commission (ITC), the Broadcasting Standards Commission (BSC), the Radio Authority, the Radio Communications Agency and the Office of Telecommunications (OFTEL). It now acts as the new regulator for the UK's broadcasting industries, which include television, radio, telecommunications and wireless communications services. One of the many responsibilities of OFCOM is to monitor advertising content, through the established ITC Code of Advertising Standards and Practice.

The Advertising Standards Authority is the independent body set up by the advertising industry to police the rules for non-broadcast advertisements, sales promotions and direct marketing that are laid down in the Committee of Advertising Practice (CAP) Code. Members of CAP include agency representatives, service suppliers and media owners, all of whom enforce the code on advertisers.

Since November 2004, Ofcom has contracted out some aspects of advertising regulation to the ASA and has created a new body – the BASA – to regulate broadcast advertising. What is interesting about the new arrangements is that these two bodies now overlap, having the same chairman – Sir Gordon Borrie – and share several council members to ensure consistency in the rulings relating to all forms of media activity.

The guidelines of the code state that advertisements should not be misleading or offensive to the public and, in particular, should be:

- legal, decent, honest and truthful
- prepared with a sense of responsibility to consumers and to society
- in line with the principles of fair competition generally accepted in business.

These statements are embodied in a series of rules:

- Legal: Marketers have the primary responsibility to ensure that their marketing communications are legal.
- Decent: Advertising must avoid serious or widespread offence.

- Honest: Marketers should not exploit the credulity, lack of knowledge or inexperience of consumers.
- Truthful: No marketing communications should mislead, or be likely to mislead by inaccuracy, ambiguity, exaggeration, omission or otherwise.

For comparison, advertising content in Australia is regulated through the Trade Practices Act and the Australian Broadcasting Authority Act. Until 1996, the guidelines for self-regulation were established by the Media Council of Australia. Since that date, a more comprehensive code has been established by the International Chamber of Commerce. Considerable concern has been expressed that the new codes are somewhat less comprehensive than those they replaced, and that they embody no real enforcement mechanisms. Whilst the majority of advertisers have withdrawn or modified their advertising when required to do so under the terms of the code of practice, in reality, there is no method of enforcement if they refuse to do so (Kerr and Moran 2002).

Advertising clearance

The advertising clearance process has three major stages:

1 a screening review;
2 potential requests for changes in the advertisement submission due to taste, audience fit, or for the advertiser to substantiate the truthfulness of claims;
3 rejection or acceptance of the submission.

Not every advertisement goes through all three stages. One station might accept any advertisement as long as advance payment is made. A second station might review advertisements for problem areas but not review all submissions. A third station may carefully review every advertisement and reject many advertising submissions (Abernethy 2001).

Case study

IPA Effectiveness Awards 2002 GOLD AWARD

Agency: Fallon

Authors: Laurence Green and Felicity Morgan

'It's A Skoda. Honest.'

Introduction

British consumers know nothing of Skoda's genuinely splendid engineering heritage, having first become acquainted with the brand during the dog days of communist rule in Czechoslovakia and Skoda's unhealthy monopoly on car production. The Skoda joke, a uniquely British phenomenon, was the unfortunate outcome. As the jokes peaked in the late 1980s, change was afoot. Czechoslovakia's 'Velvet Revolution' prompted a partnership with Volkswagen and which resulted in the production of the Felicia, a car impressive enough to win seven consecutive *What Car?* 'Budget Car of The Year' awards. Though ridiculed as a brand, Skoda's UK sales grew through the mid-1990s and extraordinary levels of loyalty were achieved.

No one could argue that the Skoda brand was ill-defined or its franchise particularly open to competitive incursion. But nor could it be argued that Skoda was making genuine inroads against the broader consumer base; rejection figures for the brand remained stubbornly fixed at around 60 per cent over the period. And as the brand's future product reality became more obvious, it was apparent that Skoda's image deficiencies would soon become a critical commercial limitation. Higher-quality, more expensively priced cars would be rolling off the production line (as VW moved to a shared platform production strategy), Skodas that would have

to compete for different consumers and against a new competitive set.

The first demonstration of the product transformation led by Volkswagen was the launch of the Octavia in 1998. Launch reviews were invariably flattering. The Octavia's £10 million launch advertising budget remains Skoda's largest ever. However, the launch was a failure. Only 2569 Octavias were sold in 1998 (that's an advertising cost per car in the region of £4000). By the year end, Octavia accounted for only 12 per cent of Skoda sales, so that the Felicia remained overwhelmingly the Skoda car most often seen on the road.

The 'new' Skoda

It was clear a new approach would be needed if Skoda's next launch wasn't also to fail. Although the Fabia was once again rumoured to be a 'great product' it was clear that product alone wouldn't be enough to drive people to reappraise the Skoda brand. And indeed that we had to win reappraisal of the Skoda brand for any product to achieve its potential.

We concluded that the stigma attached to Skoda had become a shared cultural phenomenon. To target only those who might consider buying one was to ignore the vast mass of their friends, neighbours, colleagues and even children who were likely to ridicule that decision.

To summarise our two key strategic building blocks:

1 A new role for advertising: use the Fabia to confront the biggest barrier to buying a Skoda – the irrational prejudice against the brand.
2 A new target audience: create a general shift in attitudes so that potential buyers feel confident they can choose Skoda without being laughed at.

As a result, our media plan was contrary, rejecting the narrowcast and the new in favour of an old-fashioned broadcast plan: *Coronation Street*, posters and all. PR played a critical role at launch; since press coverage was part of the problem, it had to be part of the solution. PR was charged with convincing opinion-formers that Skoda had changed (with car and campaign as evidence) and more generally to create an impression of success for the advertising to work against.

The creative idea

The creative response to our brief was summarised in the line 'It's a Skoda. Honest.' Skoda would make advertising featuring people who still thought their cars were poor. But by gently ridiculing these people, the consumer would conclude that he/she 'wasn't one of them'. The creative work didn't so much reposition the brand as reposition the consumer's attitude to the brand.

The Fabia launch/Skoda relaunch campaign broke in March 2000 and key TV spend since has comprised the following: Fabia executions launched March 2000; Octavia executions launched January 2001 as shown in the table below:

After only one burst of advertising, key image measures had responded rapidly as shown in the table below:

	Pre(%)	Post(%)	Change
Skodas are better than they used to be	54	79	+25
Skoda make cars you can't take seriously	47	32	−15
I'd be proud to have one on my drive	20	33	+13

There was also dramatic impact on consideration. The number of prospects who would not consider Skoda dropped from 60 per cent to 42 per cent, a rejection figure now lower than the equivalent figures for Fiat and Citroen for the first time ever.

The Fabia relaunch was the start of an amazing two-year period for Skoda. The advertising and PR campaigns spearheaded a dramatically rethought marketing programme that included innovative media thinking, new 'brand-led' direct marketing, point-of-sale (POS) material and website. Collectively, these efforts have had a striking business impact.

Since the Fabia launch, volume growth has easily outstripped the market, winning record share for the brand, shown in the table below.

	Skoda volume (%)	Market growth (%)	Skoda market share growth (%)
1999	5	−2	1.0
2000	35	1	1.3
2001	23	11	1.5

In years 2000 and 2001, then, Skoda's business accelerated. Comparing actual sales to projected sales, we see an incremental revenue uplift of £185 million and profit uplift of £18.5 million, an uplift that already pays back on a total marketing spend of £15.4 million over the period. Factoring in predicted repeat sales and profit from those incremental customers, this profit uplift amounts over the long run to £37 million.

We have a dramatic sales uplift that we can logically ascribe to the Skoda brand's repositioning in communications. We believe that we can demonstrate a short-term return on advertising investment. (A return on investment achieved despite the brand's history and a category share of voice of less than 2 per cent.).

SOURCE: This case study is adapted from the paper presented at the IPA Effectiveness Awards. The full version is available at www.warc.com and is reproduced by kind permission of the Institute of Practitioners in Advertising and the World Advertising Research Center.

Questions

1 Describe the different ways in which advertising is classified.
2 Identify the various functions of advertising.
3 Argue the benefits of advertising.
4 Identify the limitations of advertising.
5 Discuss the various criticisms that are levelled at advertising.
6 Why is it important to consider the social and ethical impacts of advertising?
7 What are the different approaches towards the regulation of advertising?

2 The theoretical background to advertising: how advertising works

Learning outcomes

This chapter explains:

- the nature of the communications process
- the models of advertising
- the criticisms of advertising models
- how theory relates to practice
- the issues around advertising awareness and effectiveness.

The communications process

Before we can begin to examine the models that relate to the development of advertising, we must first understand how communication itself takes place. We can begin by examining a simple model that identifies the fundamental elements of communication. See Figure 2.1.

Whilst this model is oversimplistic, it depicts the three basic elements of communication. The first is the source of the message which, in this context, is the advertiser. Second, there is the message itself, designed to deliver specific information to the third part of the equation, namely the receiver. Whilst the basic elements are present, the model fails to communicate the depth of the process since it ignores other important factors which come into play.

A somewhat better understanding of the communications process is provided by a more detailed model shown in Figure 2.2. This model introduces a number of new elements that serve to demonstrate the complex nature of communications.

When we send any form of advertising message, we need to encode it into some form of symbolic representation. Most advertising consists of words, colours, shapes, pictures and possibly music, each of which is designed to convey some form of impression to the reader or viewer. All of these elements are intended to be understood by the receiver of the message and, together, they combine to deliver a

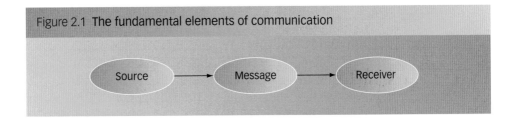

Figure 2.1 The fundamental elements of communication

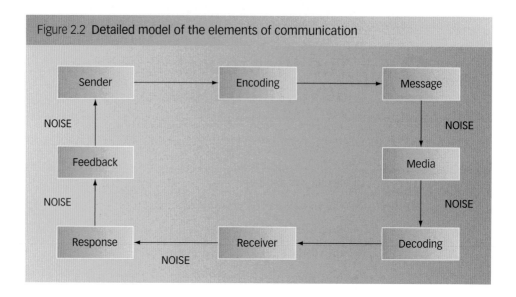

Figure 2.2 Detailed model of the elements of communication

desired impression of the product or service to the consumer. The message will need to be placed into some form of medium or carrier that the sender believes will be seen or heard by the receiver. This might be television, a newspaper, radio or any other medium available to the sender.

It is important to recognise that the message is only one of the many which the intended receiver will be required to deal with. It is estimated that the average person is exposed to around 1300 commercial messages in a normal day (White 1998). The inevitable consequence is that the advertiser's message becomes confused with the others. This is what we refer to as 'noise' – the general clutter of information within which the advertising message is placed and through which it must penetrate in order to achieve effective impact on the desired audience.

The consequence is that the intended message may well be incompletely communicated or confused by this surrounding 'noise'. Moreover, whatever message is received will be impacted by the recipient's preconceptions related to the sender or the message or both. If the receiver regards the company as reliable and trustworthy then the message will be interpreted in that context. However, the opposite might also be true, particularly if the receiver has previously had some negative experience with the same company or product.

A further complication is that the decoding process is reliant upon the receiver understanding the signs and symbols used by the advertiser. For the most part, we grow up with an understanding of the 'language' used by advertisers. We are mostly familiar with the 'shorthand' and symbols that are used to convey particular meaning. However, this is not true of all cultures, particularly those in which advertising is not the norm, or where the chosen signs and symbols may deliver alternative meanings. We will examine this issue more fully in the context of International Advertising in Chapter 13.

However, Stern (1994) argues that the standard communication model proposed by information theorists (sender, message, addressee – in which the message is decoded on the basis of a code shared by both the virtual poles of the chain) does not describe the actual functioning of communication.

The existence of various codes and subcodes, the variety of sociocultural circumstances in which a message is omitted (where the codes of the addressee can be different from those of the sender) and the rate of initiative displayed by the addressee in making presuppositions and abductions – all result in making a message (in so far as it is received and transformed into the content of an expression) an empty form to which various possible senses can be attributed. Moveover what one calls 'message' is usually a text, that is, a network of different messages depending on different codes and working at different levels of signification.

The particular response which the receiver makes will itself be dependent on a variety of factors. Some advertising simply conveys information to the consumer; other forms are intended to elicit some form of invitation to purchase or to take some other specific type of response. Clearly, the response of the receiver to the message will be of considerable importance to the sender. Accordingly, the sender will often build in some form of feedback mechanism in order to understand the nature of the response which, in turn, can be used to refine the message if it fails to deliver the desired response.

In Chapter 6 we will consider the wide variety of other factors which influence the consumer's perception of the advertising message.

Understanding the advertising process: the models of advertising

It is clear that advertising is but one of the elements of marketing communications. Although, as we saw in Chapter 1, it is capable of fulfilling a number of different roles, the specific function must reflect the objectives contained within the marketing plan. In the development of any advertising campaign, the starting-point for the planner must be to determine the specific objectives. A key determinant of the nature of the advertising campaign will be the available budget, since this will affect the type of media that can be afforded.

Since before the beginning of the last century, many of the models designed to explain how advertising works have been based on identifying and describing the sequence of events which the consumer 'goes through' following exposure to advertising. Each of these models attempts to describe the ways in which advertising is supposed to impact on the viewer and the hierarchy of effects that result. Despite frequent and repeated criticisms of many of these models, they continue to remain at the forefront of much current advertising research.

Certainly, the earliest model used in most of the literature is that of AIDA, variously attributed to St. Elmo Lewis (1898) and Strong (1925). It was Lewis's contention that salespeople needed to pursue a sequence of actions in order to achieve success. It was somewhat later that the model and its sequence of events were applied to advertising. In the ensuing decades a great many similar models were described in the literature, sometimes changing the words used or adding or deleting stages (Barry and Howard 1990; McDonald 1992).

The AIDA model proposed a simple hierarchical structure to identify the stages of the communications process (see Figure 2.3). Originally proposed at the turn of the century to explain the process of personal selling, it was rapidly adopted as a model to explain the process of communications in advertising.

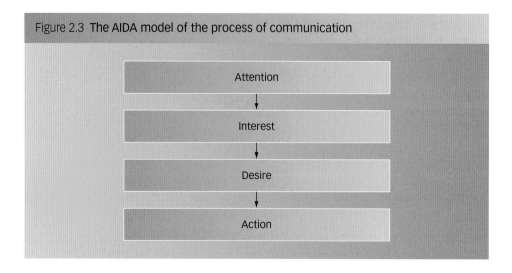

Figure 2.3 **The AIDA model of the process of communication**

The basic tenet was that, in order to have effect, the first task of any campaign was to gain the attention of the viewer or reader. From the outset, it was recognised that a fundamental aim of communication was to cut through the surrounding clutter and arrest the attention of the potential purchaser. Moreover, it suggested that the process of communication required the audience to pass through a series of sequential steps, and that each step was a logical consequence of what had gone before. The principle of sequential activity or learning is used commonly in many marketing models, and is often referred to as a hierarchy of effects. The attention phase is key to the process, since whatever follows will be of little value if the attention of the audience has not been achieved.

The second stage is the stimulation of an interest in the proposition. In most cases, it would be reasonable to assume that if the first requirement – attention – had been met, the second would follow on almost automatically. Indeed, if the communications message has been properly constructed, this will be true. However, in some instances, particularly where an irrelevant attention-getting device has been employed, the potential consumer does not pass fully to the second stage.

The third stage is to create a desire for the product or service being promoted. Often, this will take the form of a 'problem–solution' execution in which advertisers seeks to position their product as the answer to a problem which they have previously identified. Soap powder advertisements often follow this sequence of events, although many other examples can be found from contemporary marketing activity. Personal care, hair care, and do it yourself products are other areas where this approach is currently employed.

The fourth and final stage of the AIDA model is the stimulation of some form of response on the part of the audience – the action stage. Most advertisements have a specific call to action, and many are linked with promotional offers designed to induce a purchase of the product or some other desired end result.

This sequential pattern – or something like it put in different words – is treated as common sense: it only says that people need to be aware of a brand before they can be interested in it, and that they need to desire it before they can take action and buy it. This imputes two roles to advertising: (1) an informational role – making them aware of the product – and (2) a persuasive role – making people desire it before they have bought it.

In its informational role, it might seem that when there are no deeper benefits to guide a consumer's brand choice, he/she will be influenced by the last advertisement seen or by the general weight of past advertising. This assumption has led to the use of awareness and recall measures in pre-testing and monitoring advertisements. But there is little direct evidence that advertising for established brands works like this. The evidence that does exist is either negative or at best shows effects which are not dramatically large and which still require confirmation.

In its persuasive role, advertising is thought to create a desire or conviction to buy, or at least to add value to the brand as far as the consumer is concerned. For this reason advertisements take on persuasive methods like creating a brand image, highlighting a unique selling point (USP) or informing consumers that they need a special product to meet a special need (for example, a special shampoo for oily hair). But again, there is no empirical evidence that advertising generally succeeds in this aim, when there are no real differences to sell.

Many other hierarchical models have been developed to identify and explain the process of advertising communication. Two of these models are worthy of specific consideration. The first was developed by Robert Lavidge and Gary Steiner (1961) and offers a number of points of difference against the AIDA model.

Their model can be depicted as shown in Figure 2.4.

A major premise of this model is that the receiver of the advertising message must pass through a series of distinct stages in a defined sequence in order to ensure a

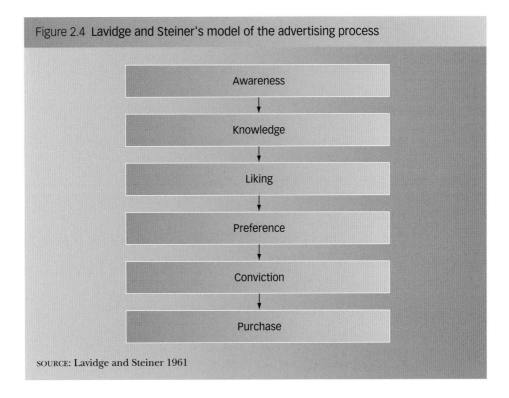

Figure 2.4 Lavidge and Steiner's model of the advertising process

Awareness

↓

Knowledge

↓

Liking

↓

Preference

↓

Conviction

↓

Purchase

SOURCE: Lavidge and Steiner 1961

purchase of the product or service that is being advertised. The implication is that, if any of the stages are missed out, the desired outcome will not be achieved. The starting point, and one which is held in common with many of the other models, is that the consumer must be stimulated to become aware of the product or service being advertised. Given the previous commentary on the general clutter of communication – both of a general and of an advertising nature – it is clear that the message must be capable of breaking through to gain the receiver's attention.

Following this, he or she needs to be provided with specific information about the product which improves their knowledge and understanding of the brand. This may relate to the attributes, features or benefits of the product or service or, as we will see later, may relate to some emotional facet of the brand proposition. This state of knowledge must then be developed into a liking for the product or service. At the very minimum, the task is to ensure that the consumer includes the product alongside other known brands within the product category.

The next stage is that of creating a preference. The task of advertising must be to offer some point of distinction to create a separation in the mind of the consumer between the product being advertised and others within the category, always providing this point of difference can be established. Implicit in this statement is the assumption that there is a correspondence between this point of difference and the consumer's needs and desires. The penultimate stage of conviction is the result of the consumer forming a specific purchase intention towards the advertised product or service. Lavidge and Steiner suggest that, only when all of these stages have been concluded will the consumer convert intention into action and purchase the brand.

In the early 1960s, Russell Colley proposed a new approach to advertising planning entitled **d**efining **a**dvertising **g**oals for **m**easured **a**dvertising **r**esults often referred to by the acronym DAGMAR. Unlike some previous models, the DAGMAR approach proposed a precise method for the selection and quantification of communications tasks which, in turn, could be used as the basis for measuring performance. Like his predecessors (and many others subsequently), Colley also used a hierarchy of effects model to describe the advertising process, seen in Figure 2.5.

Since the elements of the Colley model broadly follow those of earlier models, it is not proposed to describe the individual stages. However, Colley's main contribution to the advertising process rests in his identification of a procedure to ensure that the goals established for advertising were precisely formulated and capable of being monitored.

An imperative of the approach was to ensure that the objectives established were capable of unbiased measurement. This is not simply a question of, for example, quantifying levels of awareness, or of trial, but rather of defining precise levels to be achieved for specific aspects of comprehension of the message. At the same time, Colley suggested that precise timescales be determined for the achievement of the objectives set. In order to enable such measurements, it was suggested that a series of benchmarks should be identified. Apart from the obvious benefit of providing the base against which subsequent achievements could be measured, the benchmarking process has a far more important role in the process of strategy determination. It provides a major contribution to the overall planning process by indicating areas in which marketing communications activity might be appropriate.

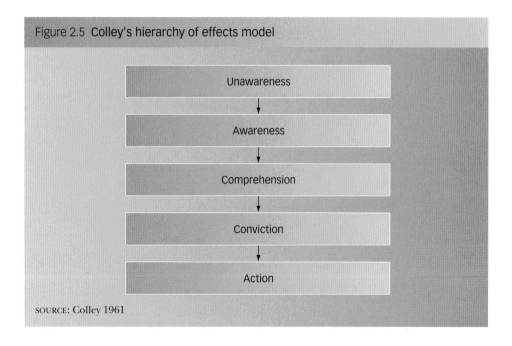

Figure 2.5 **Colley's hierarchy of effects model**

Unawareness

↓

Awareness

↓

Comprehension

↓

Conviction

↓

Action

SOURCE: Colley 1961

Importantly, the proponents of the DAGMAR approach argue that benchmarking is an essential prerequisite of the planning process.

Targeting is a further dimension of DAGMAR whereby a detailed understanding would first be developed regarding the target audience(s). Again, it is argued that, without such knowledge, the impact of the message is likely to be weakened. By understanding exactly who (age, sex, class, usership patterns, lifestyle factors, etc.) represents the best prospect for the proposition, not only can they be targeted more effectively by careful media selection but, similarly, the message can be made to appeal directly to them, rather than potential users as a whole.

Needless to say, Colley recommended the adoption of a written approach to the procedure. He argued that this was partially to impose a discipline on the process – the need to express thoughts clearly and precisely in written form demands far more care and attention to the meaning given than the verbal expression of an idea – and partially to ensure that all participants to the process are both aware of and committed to the task.

Although the DAGMAR model continues to be widely used, it is often criticised for implying that consumers are essentially *passive* in the marketing communications process. Whatever the criticisms made of it, however, it is the essential nature of his process of defining objectives which has ensured the enduring appeal of the DAGMAR process.

Although considerable progress has been achieved in the measurement of results, with new techniques being developed, it has to be recognised that some aspects of the marketing communications process remain unclear. Frequent attempts are made, for example, to determine the precise way in which advertising works. In a book by Colin McDonald (1992) some 150 pages are devoted to an examination of current theories and, although the author makes some valid recommendations, there is no definitive answer to the question of how advertising works. Indeed, since its publication, several new theories have been propounded, which add to the debate, but fail to resolve it. Similarly, in 1999 Vakratsas and Ambler reviewed more than 250 journal articles and books to establish what is known and should be known about how advertising affects the consumer – how it works.

Various alternative models have been suggested. One, which appears in many academic works, is that developed by the advertising agency, Foote, Cone and Belding (1979). They proposed that advertising can be distinguished on two key dimensions – thinking versus feeling and low-involvement versus high-involvement products. This results in a four-quadrant diagram, depicted in Figure 2.6.

The first consideration is whether the product is selected primarily in terms of its functional benefits or whether the purchase is based on emotional factors. In reality, of course, many purchases involve aspects of both of these, although there may be a dominance of one rather than the other. For example, whilst the purchase of a car might be thought to be based exclusively of the functional dimensions – seating capacity, fuel economy, safety, etc. in reality, many such decisions are based as much on the emotional values of the car – what it looks like, impressions of the marque, other people's reaction to the ownership of the brand, and so on.

The second dimension relates to whether the purchasing decision is one of low or high involvement. Low-involvement purchases are those which, by definition, do not take much consideration on the part of the consumer. For the most part, they consist of frequently purchased products, with which the consumer has considerable familiarity. As such, the purchase decision can be made quickly without any deliberation. By contrast, high-involvement purchase are those which are less frequently made, where the cost is often high and which involve a variety of risks.

Rossiter et al. (1991) proposed a new model for the planning of advertising. Although derived from the FCB grid, it contained other dimensions to overcome, what they perceived as the shortcomings of the FCB model. Within their grid, they argue that brand awareness is a necessary precursor to the creation of brand attitude. They argue that brand attitude without prior brand awareness is an insufficient advertising communication objective. Hence, it is first necessary to determine

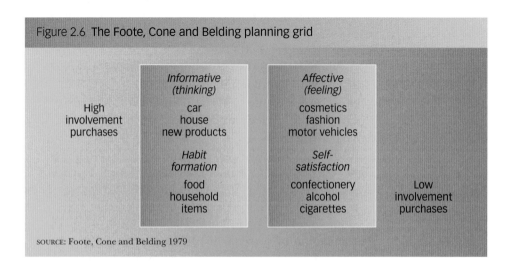

Figure 2.6 **The Foote, Cone and Belding planning grid**

	Informative (thinking)	Affective (feeling)	
High involvement purchases	car house new products	cosmetics fashion motor vehicles	
	Habit formation	Self-satisfaction	
	food household items	confectionery alcohol cigarettes	Low involvement purchases

SOURCE: Foote, Cone and Belding 1979

whether the potential consumer has heard about the product or service before identifying their feelings. See Figure 2.7.

They also expanded the think–feel dimensions of the FCB grid to cover the other motivations that people may have when buying products. These include three 'transformational' motives and five 'informational' motives.

A particular model of advertising response, which summarises the key facets of the process, is that used by George and Michael Belch in their 1993 book on advertising and promotion. Their model is shown in Figure 2.8.

This model proposes that the consumer is influenced in the construction of his or her opinions of a brand by a series of interacting factors. Following exposure to the advertising message, three important areas exert an influence on the consumers' attitudes. The first are a series of thoughts that relate specifically to the message contained in the advertisement. The advertiser may seek to make reference to particular facets of the brand, its performance, its attributes or some other dimension that will enhance perceptions of the product. To these are added source-oriented thoughts that relate to the environment in which the advertising is seen. Some media will enhance the credibility of the message whilst others will have the

Figure 2.7 The Rossiter–Percy planning grid

		Low involvement (lower risk)	High involvement (higher risk)
Transformational motives	Sensory gratification		
	Intellectual stimulation		
	Social approval		
Informational motives	Problem removal		
	Problem avoidance		
	Incomplete satisfaction		
	Mixed approach avoidance		
	Normal depletion		

SOURCE: Rossiter et al. 1991

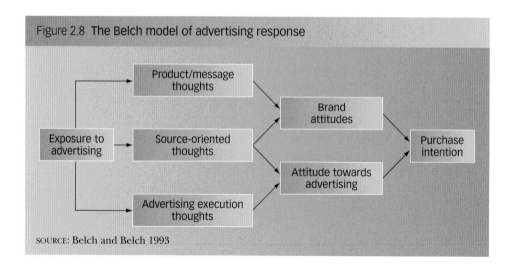

Figure 2.8 **The Belch model of advertising response**

SOURCE: Belch and Belch 1993

opposite influence. Finally, there are a series of issues that relate to the advertising execution itself.

It has long been recognised that consumers are as much influenced by the nature and content of the advertising itself as the message it seeks to convey. Several studies, including that conducted by the advertising agency Lowe, Howard-Spink (1995), suggest that the content of advertising may actually cause viewers to 'turn off'. Their work claims to identify a third of the population who actively avoid advertising.

The combination of these three factors establishes a series of attitudes in the minds of the consumer, both towards the brand and to the advertising itself which, in turn, have a decisive impact on their purchase intention.

An alternative model to explain the process of advertising communication is that of 'heightened appreciation' (Yeshin 1993). The model, depicted in Figure 2.9, suggests that the responsibility of the planner is to identify the specific dimension of the brand which has significance to the consumer in order to focus attention on it. By stressing a particular aspect or attribute of the brand in advertising, the consumer becomes more aware of that attribute in a use situation, resulting in an enhanced image for the brand.

A more recent model is one proposed by Professor Andrew Ehrenberg (1997). Essentially, Ehrenberg rejects earlier models based on the principles of persuasion. He argues that the notions of persuasion and conversion before the action of purchase takes place are not supported by empirical evidence. In their place, he proposes a new model based on four dimensions shown in Figure 2.10.

The 'awareness' stage reflects the fact that the consumer has, first, to become aware of and interested in a new brand. This, he suggests, can be achieved in a number of different ways – through advertising, retail displays, promotions, media mentions, direct marketing, word of mouth, and so on. For an existing brand, the consumer will already have some familiarity and the various tools of marketing communications will be required to persuade the consumer to take a closer look, especially where an existing brand is re-packaged or re-formulated. Curiosity may

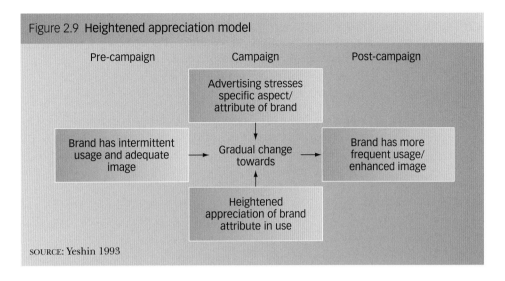

Figure 2.9 Heightened appreciation model

Pre-campaign   Campaign   Post-campaign

Advertising stresses specific aspect/ attribute of brand

Brand has intermittent usage and adequate image → Gradual change towards → Brand has more frequent usage/ enhanced image

Heightened appreciation of brand attribute in use

SOURCE: Yeshin 1993

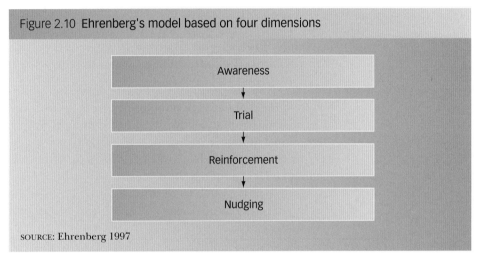

Figure 2.10 Ehrenberg's model based on four dimensions

Awareness
↓
Trial
↓
Reinforcement
↓
Nudging

SOURCE: Ehrenberg 1997

inspire 'trial' and an exploratory purchase may, therefore, be made. Such trial purchases are he argues, prompted by advertising, word of mouth and retail availability, and so on.

The third stage of the model – 'reinforcement' – is a further area where advertising and marketing communications can play an important part. Advertising, for example, can maintain awareness of the newly purchased brand and, in some instances, provide brand reassurance. It is here that positive beliefs about the brand may develop, with the brand entering the consumer's brand repertoire.

The final stage of 'nudging' is where consumers, both those who have already tried the product and those who have yet to try, can be persuaded to buy it or purchase it again. The stage is designed to reinforce a steady habit on the part of the consumer. Although 'reminder' advertising will often be used by established brands to fulfil this role, in some instances, more concerted efforts will be required. It is here that relaunches and similar devices may be employed to draw specific attention to the brand and encourage potential consumers to think about it afresh.

Three main steps can account for the known facts of brand choice behaviour:

1 gaining awareness of a hand;
2 making a first or trial purchase; and
3 being reinforced into developing and keeping a repeat buying habit.

Some initial awareness of a brand usually has to come first, although occasionally one may find out a brand's name only after buying it. Awareness operates at different levels of attention and interest and can be created in many different ways, of which advertising is clearly one. Awareness may build up into the idea of looking for more information about the brand, asking someone about it, and so on.

A trial purchase, if it comes, will be the next step. This does not require any major degree of conviction that the brand is particularly good or special. Buyers of Brand A do not usually feel very differently about A from how buyers of Brand B feel about B. If that is how one feels afterwards, there is therefore no reason why a consumer should feel strongly about a different brand *before* he has tried it. All that is needed is the idea that one might try it. A trial purchase can arise for a variety of reasons: a cut price offer, an out-of-stock situation of the usual brand, seeing an advertisement or display, boredom, and so on (Ehrenberg 2000).

Like many other authors, Hall (1998) suggests that, rather than one model of how advertising works, there are four major models:

- The sales response model: Advertising seeks short-term changes in consumer behaviour. It stimulates direct interest in and, hence, sales of a brand, but does little in terms of brand building. In this context, advertising tends to adopt a promotional approach, featuring a special price or other offer.
- The persuasion model: The role of advertising is to persuade consumers about the functional superiority of the brand.
- The involvement model: Here, advertising seeks to encourage consumers to buy into the brand values because it stands for something that the consumer wants to be associated with.
- The salience model: Advertising seeks to get consumers interested in the brand because it stands out, is radically different and is self-assured.

Criticisms of advertising models

Various authors have been extremely critical of the models put forward to explain the process of advertising. Terry Prue writing in *Admap* (1998) says of the various early models of advertising (AIDA, AIETA, DAGMAR) 'They all assume a passive consumer whose brand knowledge, attitudes and consideration to buy are influenced by advertising'. It could be argued that they are less models than descriptions of the key aspects of good and effective advertising. This view is similar to that expressed by Brierley (1995) 'there is no evidence to suggest that people behave in this rational, linear way'.

All of the hierarchy models presume that those exposed to advertising (and other forms of marketing communications) respond to those messages in an ordered and sequential manner. Most contain common elements that relate to thinking (cognitive effects), feeling (affect) and doing (conative). Certainly, the model that is most often used to illustrate the hierarchy of effects is that developed by Lavidge and Steiner (1961). Like others both before them and since, the authors proposed that consumers were moved through a sequence of events that started with their lack of product awareness and concluded with their purchase of the advertised product.

Similarly, Weilbacher (2001) identifies a series of fundamental weaknesses in the hierarchy of effects models:

- The only form of marketing communications that the models are concerned with is advertising. Whilst advertising alone may, in some situations, result in increased sales, in the vast majority of marketing scenarios, sales are the result of a combination of marketing factors.
- These models are overly simplistic in their portrayal of human behaviour and response. Advertising is considered as a discrete stimulus that causes the consumer to follow an inflexible path resulting in the ultimate response of brand selection or purchase.
- Such models are based on the now discredited theories of 'behaviourist formulation'.
- Hierarchy models make the assumption that all advertising works in the same way.

Others, including Ambler and Varatsas (1999), argue that persuasive hierarchy models are flawed on two counts:

- Such models assume that the brain works through a series of stages, as if it were a computer.
- They ignore the consumer's experience of previous product usage.

Hierarchy of advertising effects models have been around in the literature of advertising for more than 100 years. Yet, as Vakratsas and Ambler (1999) stated 'the concept of hierarchy on which they are based cannot be empirically supported'.

In another paper, White (1999) states 'these [the first of the so-called hierarchy of effects models] continue to dominate much thinking about what advertising does, although they are clearly a gross, misleading and mistaken over-simplification.'

Most models see the consumer as a passive individual whose brand knowledge, attitudes and consideration to buy are influenced by advertising. These include:

- STARCH: See, read, remember, act upon
- DAGMAR: Awareness, comprehension, conviction, action
- AIDA: Attention, interest, desire, action
- AIETA: Awareness, interest, evaluation, trial, adoption

In their review and critique of the advertising hierarchy, Barry and Howard (1990) considered five alternative order hierarchies of effect. In addition to the traditional cognition-affect-conation model, they investigate the following additional five models:

- cognition–conation–affect
- affect–conation–cognition
- conation–affect–cognition
- conation–cognition–affect
- affect–cognition–conation

Barry and Howard (1990) dismiss the conation-affect-cognition and the conation-cognition-affect models because of the little likelihood that advertising first affects behaviour without any prior cognition and/or affect, no matter how little. The researchers present the criticisms of the remaining four model sequences and state: 'On a theoretical (or empirical) level it appears that there are no clear grounds to dismiss any of the four [remaining] models noted above. On a practical level, the value of the debate is unclear.'

In spite of the criticisms of Weilbacher (2001) and others, including this author, the hierarchy of effects remains important to both the practitioner and academic communities. It makes sense to suggest that before people consume most goods and services, they have some information about these goods and services and form some attitude, no matter how weak that attitude or how quickly the attitude was formed. And it makes intuitive sense to say that all prior experiences impact how the information is processed and how the attitude(s) is (are) formed.

Benefits of advertising models

Although these models are widely challenged, they nonetheless offer a series of potential benefits:

- they allow us to predict behaviour
- they provide us with information as to which advertising strategy is appropriate to particular circumstances
- they identify a series of important concepts which need to be addressed in the development of advertising.

Barry and Howard (1990) argue that, in addition to its simplicity, intuitiveness, and logic, the hierarchy of effects model provides a number of important benefits:

- It helps us to predict behaviour, no matter how imperfect those predictions are.
- It provides information on where advertising strategies should focus (cognition, affect, conation) based on audience or segment experiences.
- It provides us with a good planning, training and conceptual tool.

John Little in his overview of modelling in 1994 has contrasted the two kinds of models – decision models and descriptive models – as follows:

Decision models are for solving problems. They should include the variables and phenomena that are vital for the problem at hand, i.e., controllable activities like price, promotions, and advertising, but leave out those that are not ('artful incompleteness').

Descriptive models seek to uncover marketing phenomena and to represent them. This is the classical task of science. Descriptive models without marketing decision variables go back to the work of Ehrenberg (1959, 1988) and others.

Ehrenberg et al. (2001) state:

Decision models are so called because they contain marketing-mix variables that a manager could, in principle, control or change. We doubt, however, whether decision problems can be resolved by any such simple one-off 'if-this-then-that' formula. Our difficulties concern (1) the decision variables themselves, (2) the model's ability to predict the effects, and (3) the implied causal links with sales.

The decision variables. The variables in a decision model seldom seem very specific. Lower spending on 'promotion' (as in the above formulation) could for example work in the following way (and more).

- Some retailers reducing your shelf space, or some deciding to de-list you altogether.
- The salespeople becoming de-motivated (or conversely trying harder, so as to still earn their commission).
- Fewer consumers buying (or the same number buying less, or fewer being retained, or fewer converted).

Many other such 'explanatory' variables are typically not even included in the above model. Yet more comprehensive econometric models have seldom if ever been claimed to work out the problem of overfitting. It seems a case of damned if you do (put more variables in) and damned if you don't (leave them out).

The alternative is descriptive models. These seldom contain push-button-if-this-then-hopefully-that decision inputs. Instead, good descriptive models just describe regular observed patterns. Such models can then provide grounded benchmarks and insights for evaluating marketing action. But that will occur as separate subsequent steps.

How advertising works: from theory to practice

Whilst the debate continues, one thing we can safely say is that there is no consensus on how advertising works! However, the learning over several decades has given us a somewhat greater grasp both of the process and the means by which advertising effectiveness can be achieved.

Duckworth (1995) reflects that the issue of 'how advertising works' has become something of a holy grail for advertising analysts. The absence of any definitive consensus reflects the problematic nature of the question. He concludes that any meaningful discussion of how advertising works needs to consider advertising in relation to the brand whose symbolic meaning it seeks to modify or reinforce.

There are two broad perspectives on how advertising works.

On the one hand, there are a number of authors who argue that, in order to work effectively, advertising has to impact on people's attitudes towards the brand in order to create the desired behaviour. By differentiating brands from their competitors, the role of advertising is to give them added value and secure consumer commitment towards the brand. This is the 'strongly persuasive' view of advertising.

The opposing view is that the role of advertising is to provide publicity for the brand. This publicity helps to maintain the brand within the consumers' 'portfolio' of brands from which the select on a given purchase occasion.

Foremost amongst the latter group are Barnard and Ehrenberg (1998) who, along with others, suggest that many advertisements do not embody overtly differentiating messages or values and, those that do, still do not have a significant impact on the way people think or feel about the brand. They argue that it is the process of trying the brand which brings about a change in attitudes. Equally, they argue that the attitudes held by customers to a brand are, in fact, somewhat similar to those held about a competitive brand by its customers.

When an advertisement shows up in a consumer's immediate environment, it may or may not be perceived consciously. If it is attended to at all, it will be in the context of whatever the consumer already has retained about the advertised brand and the product category in which it competes. What the consumer already knows about the brand will depend on what he or she has processed and remembered from previous advertising for it, as well as other sponsored marketing communications for it, past experience with the brand (either personal or second-hand as reported by family members, friends, acquaintances, strangers, or impersonal outside evaluators like consumer reports) and any other past information about the brand from other non-advertising marketing communications as well as information from other media sources not controlled by the marketer. In addition to whatever the consumer remembers about the brand from such past exposures, his or her perception of an advertisement will also depend on several personal habits and attitudes that are part of his general reaction to advertisements.

Advertising, specifically, and sponsored marketing communications, generally, must somehow upset whatever the consumer now perceives about the brand and transform that perception into some sort of feeling that the brand is among those that are totally acceptable within the product category. Advertising, specifically, and sponsored marketing communications, generally, must be thought of as devices to increase brand acceptability. Only by making a brand seem more acceptable is it likely ever to join the brands that are already perceived as acceptable or continue its current membership within that group.

Advertising and sponsored marketing communications must be created in the context of whatever consumers now know and think about the brand. Advertising and marketing communications must be used to modify the existing perception of the brand, making it always more compatible with everything that the consumer expects and wishes to find in brands in the product category within which it competes (Weilbacher 2003).

Jones (1998) illustrates the working of advertising as shown in Figure 2.11.

He also describes the process of persuasion within advertising as shown in Figure 2.12.

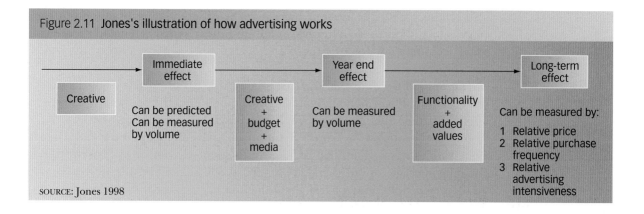

Figure 2.11 Jones's illustration of how advertising works

SOURCE: Jones 1998

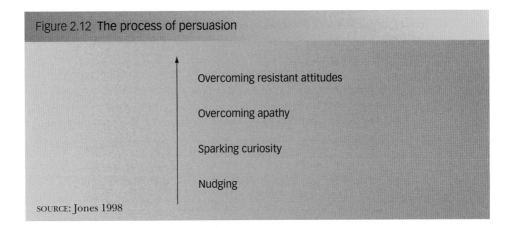

Figure 2.12 **The process of persuasion**

Overcoming resistant attitudes

Overcoming apathy

Sparking curiosity

Nudging

SOURCE: Jones 1998

Similarly, Prue (1998) proposes a new 'alphabetical' model based on four elements:

- Appreciation: For any ad to be effective it must first be appreciated by its target audience. It must be considered to have sufficient value for it not to be screened out and ignored at any deeper conscious level.
- Branding: Advertising must be sufficiently well branded in such a way that the advertising is inextricably linked to the brand. Unfortunately, much advertising fails to achieve this.
- Communication: The advertising should communicate something that is strategically relevant to the brand.
- Desired effect on the brand: None of the previous steps is of any value in isolation unless the target group is affected by the advertising.

In effect this is less of a model than a description of the elements which make up solid advertising.

Heath (2002) summarises the process of creating effective advertising as having a number of key elements as follows:

- Because brands match each other's performance so swiftly, there is an expectation among consumers that most reputable brands will perform similarly. This deters them from trying to make purchase decisions using rational performance factors, and encourages them to use alternative criteria – word-of-mouth recommendation, instinct and intuition.
- Intuitive decisions are strongly influenced by emotional 'markers'. For example, most of us believe that German engineering is the best, and this is why German cars, washing machines and power tools can command a premium over others. Ads that influence such emotional markers are especially powerful.
- In general, consumers do not expect to learn anything of importance about brands from advertising and are therefore not pre-disposed to pay much attention to it. The result is that any message that requires active evaluation or reinterpretation to be understood is likely to be poorly registered.
- Brand information is not so much actively 'sought after' as passively 'acquired'. Passively 'acquiring' information relies greatly on an automatic learning process

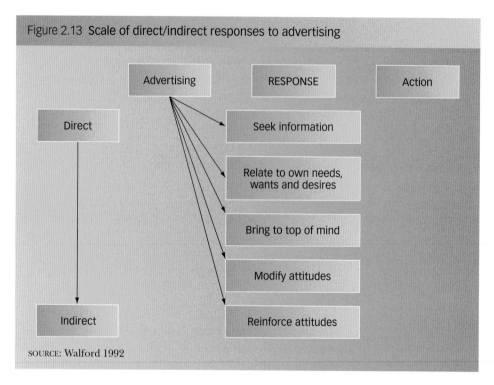

Figure 2.13 Scale of direct/indirect responses to advertising

SOURCE: Walford 1992

known as implicit learning. This cannot analyse or reinterpret anything: it simply stores what is perceived, plus any simple conceptual meanings attached to these perceptions.

- Because implicit learning is automatic, you use it every time you see or hear an ad. This means that each occasion on which an ad is processed at high involvement (and its content is learned actively) will be outnumbered two, five, ten, even fifty times by the occasions on which it is processed at low involvement (and its content learned implicitly).

Certainly, it is generally accepted that advertising can work in several different ways, and can have both direct and indirect influences. Walford (1992) depicts these graphically, as shown in Figure 2.13.

Advertising awareness and effectiveness

There is considerable interest, not surprisingly, in the extent to which advertising has an appreciable impact on short-term sales. Many academic studies suggest that the direct short-term sales effect of advertising is quite low. Jones (1995) goes somewhat further. He reports on the findings of a study wherein 70 per cent of advertising campaigns were effective in the current week, but only 46 per cent sustained that success over the course of a year. However, other studies suggest that such advertising has a beneficial effect on other important variables, most notably brand equity.

Juchems (1996) argues that advertising awareness, in itself, is not the advertising effect but merely the precondition for advertising effectiveness.

If awareness of the advertising campaign is low, then the campaign is unlikely to be very effective. If awareness is average to above average then, Juchems suggests, advertising has cleared the first hurdle. Successful communication of the intended advertising content does not necessarily mean that the brand in question will actually be bought or become more attractive to the potential consumer. In order to achieve a positive response, it is essential that the advertising is relevant to the consumer.

However, this perspective is contradicted by Blackston (2000). He points to a mechanism called 'pre-attentive processing' in which attitudes and behaviours can be shown to have been influenced by stimuli such as advertising that the person concerned has no conscious recall of having seen.

It is widely accepted that the content of advertising has to undergo processing by the brain in order for it to have any effect. The more the content is processed, the more likely it is to bring about some changes in attitudes or behaviour. He argues that it is possible to be very attentive to advertising, but process it at a very low level; equally, one can be inattentive to the advertising – at least consciously – yet thoroughly process it.

He emphasises that although a high level of active processing is a necessary condition, it is not sufficient by itself to ensure effective advertising. It matters crucially what is processed and the nature of the meaning that results. The more it is processed, the more the advertising is potentially able to do whatever it is designed to do. A high level of processing reflects the ability of the advertising to make the effects of its specific messages more meaningful and long-lived.

The criteria for the determination of advertising effectiveness must be derived from the specific objectives – recall, improved image, heightened purchase consideration, etc. – that have been set for the advertising.

Blackston suggests that there are four advertising effects that are of significance:

- Intrusiveness/stand-out qualities of the advertising: Only advertising that is consciously and attentively recalled can have this effect and, whilst it is not essential to have this effect, it is conceded that it is better to be intrusive than not.
- Creative quality of the advertising: The consumer responds to advertising with a level of appreciation – including likeability – and uses a number of descriptors such as 'lively', 'imaginative', and 'worth watching again'.
- Effect on the brand: This is the main measure of effectiveness since it measures the ability of the advertising to enhance perceptions of the brand in line with its objectives.
- Call to action (persuasiveness): This is, clearly, of major importance for advertising designed to stimulate purchasing in the short term.

Whilst sales are important as a measure of advertising effectiveness, they do not tell the whole story. Often we tacitly assume that advertising hasn't worked because we can't point to an immediate increase in sales. We need to recognise that advertising has other roles such as maintaining sales, reducing consumer willingness to switch to competitive brands, etc.

Campbell and Dove (1998) found that adspend was not correlated with total market sales, i.e., whatever the total market expenditure, total sales will be much the same. However, if you take out private (also known as own) label from that equation, total advertised sales do correlate. In other words, total advertising may well pay for advertised brands. Stephan Buck writing in a monograph published by the World Advertising Research Council (2001) – *Advertising and the Long-term*

Success of Premium Brands – demonstrated a similar outcome. He argued that the continued success of premium brands was largely a consequence of almost constant advertising within the sector. Where brands withdrew advertising support in favour of alternative promotional tools, private label products increased their share of the overall sector.

Other research conducted by Boulding et al. (1994) demonstrated clearly that

> when firms increase their unique communications activities, this leads to a future increase in brand differentiation. Conversely, when firms increase their non-unique communications activities, this leads to a future decrease in brand differentiation.

They conclude that their study shows two types of effects that communication can have when it alters the brand's positioning:

- it can affect the desirability of the brand relative to other competitive offerings;
- it can affect the salience of price and, thus, the brand's price sensitivity.

They argue, further, that advertising activities are often undervalued relative to promotional activities, given a long-run view.

Weak versus strong theories of advertising

An enduring debate within the advertising industry relates to the appropriateness of two alternative strands of theory.

In an interesting analysis of the 1998 IPA Advertising Effectiveness awards, Ambler (2000) reveals that the traditional persuasion theory (based on AIDA) remains, after 100 years, the most frequently used practitioner model to explain how advertising works. He indicates that when asked to identify how they thought their advertising had worked, the persuasive hierarchy was indicated by 17 out of 48 respondents. The weak theory of advertising was endorsed by only three respondents. In a similar manner, Meyers-Levy and Prashant (1999) writing in the *Journal of Marketing* effectively argue that the persuasive hierarchy is the only model worthy of serious consideration.

But, is this true? Does advertising only work through persuasion? There are many proponents of the 'weak' theory of advertising – Ehrenberg, White, etc.

One of the earliest expositions of the weak theory of advertising was that of Ehrenberg (1974) which stated that advertising worked through a sequence of awareness, trial and reinforcement (ATR). Ehrenberg argues that product preferences are formed after initial trial, with the role of advertising being to reinforce existing habits. It also serves to provide a framework for the product experience and assists in the defence of the brand's consumer franchise.

Ambler (2000) argues that our understanding of how advertising works is not simply a choice between the 'weak' and 'strong' theories of advertising. Rather each can explain particular situations and, moreover, it is unlikely that any single theory of advertising can always be right.

He suggests that all 'persuasion' theories possess a series of defining characteristics:

- There is a sequence of stages, although the nature of the elements may be different.

- Advertising is received by consumers in a manner which is processed.
- Advertising seeks to change the consumer's knowledge and attitudes in such a way that behaviour will also change.
- Persuasion theories address only part of the topic. They consider how advertising is processed, but do not explain how the processed ads impact upon consumer choices, i.e. behaviour.

The theory of low involvement asserts that repetition of exposure has an effect which is not readily apparent until a behavioural trigger comes along. Even then, the immediate effect is only a subtle restructuring of what was there all along – i.e., a shift in salience.

Franzen (1999) describes low-involvement processing as follows: 'we are constantly scanning our surroundings, unconsciously and automatically, to determine whether there is something deserving of our focused attention'.

Krugman (2000) suggests that advertising researchers have argued about the relative merits of using recognition or recall as measures of advertising effect. Because the criterion of recognition is much more easily achieved than that of recall, it has been criticised as being less sensitive. Underlying this 'technical' controversy, however, is the fact that the use of recognition justifies modest advertising expenditures, while the use of recall justifies far larger expenditures. I would reposition the recognition versus recall problem with this proposed addition to the theory of involvement – i.e., the nature of effective impact of communication or advertising on low-involvement topics, objects or products consists of the building or strengthening of picture-image memory potential. Such potential is properly measured by recognition, not by recall. The use of recall obscures or hides already existing impact. The use of recall may be justified by advertisers who don't mind paying for a strategy that may include some 'overkill'. However, the use of recall obscures non-commercial cultural effects of the medium, especially television.

In contrast to the above, the proper measure of high-involvement impact is indeed recall, along with clear verbalising and correct perception of the stimulus. In this connection it is interesting that our tradition of research in public opinion has been heavily invested in reporting public reaction to the news, initially newspaper news. The news is very factual stuff, left-brain stuff. The continuous and very prominent reporting of public reaction to news probably overrepresents the extent of that reaction, while the cultural impact of 'right-brain' television, though presumed to be enormous, is difficult to demonstrate.

- First, generally, most advertising is familiar and somewhat in the expected pattern or style for commercial products and brands. Here, the inference is that it only takes a very quick look, in most cases, to effectively get the message.
- Second, and more specifically, recall and attitude effects are not necessary for advertising to do its job of aiding in-store purchasing. I had proposed a theory of low involvement with advertising which suggested that faint impressions could build up into an in-store-triggered purchase with very little trace of the advertising effect prior to that purchase. And this may include very little evidence of advertising perception prior to the purchase. Krugman concludes that quick and/or faint perceptions of product advertising, even unremembered, do their

job in most cases and that the 'actual' exposures are closer to the media-scheduled exposures than we give the media credit for.

Salience

An important dimension of advertising effectiveness is that known as 'salience'. As Romaniuk and Sharp (2002) indicate:

> salience in our terms refers to the presence and richness of memory traces that result in the brand coming to mind in relevant choice situations. It is not an attitudinal concept, being about a relevant brand's 'share of mind'.

But it is much more than mere awareness of the brand in its product category (however this is measured). Thus with awareness has to come familiarity and, almost inevitably, a belief that the brand is reputable or acceptable (like some other such brands). They argue that such broad salience is vital for a brand to become and remain in one's 'consideration set' as a brand that one might or does buy.

Successful publicity for Brand X affects the 'salience' of the brand, especially if the product or service is one that is broadly relevant to the recipient (including friends and neighbours).

Most advertisements do not seem to feature or imply strong selling propositions but 'mere talking-points' (visual or verbal), i.e. creative and impactful ways of referring to the brand to help bring it before the public again. These may be:

1 Proclaiming the brand.
2 Presenting the brand as the product.
3 Providing information.
4 Establishing distinctiveness.
5 Appealing to emotions. Some advertisements command attention through family values, gorgeous scenery, sex, humour, cute children, animals, music, being ethical or some other warm experience.
6 Proffering a reason. Quite a few advertisements (a decided minority?) do present a reason (other than just announcing a price cut) for choosing that brand (e.g. has four airbags). 'Carlsberg – Probably the Best Lager in the World.'
7 Hard sell. Some advertisements do overtly try to coax people to buy here and now:

> 'While Stock Lasts!'
> or
> 'BUY X NOW!'

Salience concerns the 'size' of the brand in one's mind i.e. all the memory structures that can allow the brand to come forward for the wide range of recall cues that can occur in purchase occasions. With this 'share of mind' come feelings of being familiar and feelings of assurance ('Yes, I've heard of it. It should be all right.'). That is our broad designation of 'salience': awareness and memory traces, plus familiarity plus assurance.

Salience is not exclusive. An individual usually has a consideration set of several competitive brands that he or she may choose to buy over a series of purchases (and others not). Opting for one or another salient substitute on any specific purchase occasion need then be for no special reason. But the choice can also vary with the context – availability, a desire for variety, a mood, advertising or retail display, an offer or a whim of the moment (e.g., the parents-in-law are visiting).

For a brand to be in a consumer's consideration set or to be actually chosen, the brand does not have to be seen as 'best,' but only as 'good enough.'

For any individual buyer some brands are more salient than others, and, in a repertoire, some are bought more often. This will be a consequence of the many 'reinforcers,' often small, which can act upon a buyer over time (Foxall and Goldsmith 1994), e.g. aspects of distribution, product features, advertising, etc. Even for highly competitive brands that match each other's advantages, individual features differ in various 'minor' ways. For example, the bottle-tops, place on a retailer's shelf, the specific ingredients in particular mueslis and/or their degrees of sweetness, or the style of door handles on a car.

Such minor differences are seldom individually advertised. They are often not even consciously noticed by the consumer, or evaluated, at least not until after the brand has already been fairly extensively tried. The consumer 'acts first and thinks later' (Swindells 2000). Therefore, minor differences rarely influence a consumer's initial choice of brand.

Such minor brand differences can, however, lead to lasting longer-term brand preferences and subsequently foster extended use ('I like that muesli'). They can influence why one brand slowly becomes much bigger than its otherwise very similar competitors. Advertising can help in this even by merely publicising the brand name. This can remind consumers of their own personal reasons for considering that brand (Ehrenberg et al. 2002).

Ambler (1998), however, argues that the word is being as a 'catch-all' which includes all of the ways in which a brand is notable or stands out for consumers; they would:

- be aware of the brand
- have it in their wider consideration set
- have it in their actual purchase repertoire (for frequently bought products)
- express an intention to buy it again
- be willing to pay its price
- feel brand assurance
- express positive attitudinal beliefs and liking
- choose it as 'the brand I would buy if my usual brand were unavailable'.

It cannot be denied that advertising affects memory. Whether it switches motivation on (expressed as the strong theory of advertising) or stops it switching off (the weak theory) the outcome on memory is the same.

Ambler argues that the sum of brand memories, that is, everything we have thought or felt about the brand is brand equity.

Case study

IPA Effectiveness Awards 2002

Agency: J Walter Thompson

Authors: Sameer Modha and Donald Kerr

Shell Optimax: reintroducing branding to a commodity market

Introduction

By the end of the 1990s, petrol had become like milk, bread or eggs – a commodity. Generally you tried to buy it cheap, but if you were running low you would nip into the nearest place to top up and pay whatever price you had to. There was no point in paying more because they were all the same.

The commoditisation of petrol seemed inevitable, and the oil companies powerless to resist because their freedom to innovate had been curtailed. How could they succeed in pushing back the tide of supermarket own-label goods where so many others had failed? Their strategies themselves admitted defeat. BP went green and Esso decided to join 'em rather than beat 'em, with its PriceWatch approach.

There are 1100 Shell service stations in the UK, taking many thousands of tanker deliveries per year. That is a huge logistical operation, where you have to try and do things as cheaply as possible. Pricing Optimax was tricky – charge too much and it wouldn't pay its way, charge too little and the pricing would actually undermine the brand Shell was trying to create. It turned out that at around 4–5p per litre more than unleaded, Optimax, if it was positioned as a fuel that gave extra performance and engine protection, could expect to get perhaps 10 per cent of Shell petrol sales.

Targets

Optimax therefore had to meet the following targets by the end of 2001:

- 10 per cent of Shell petrol sales
- a higher unit margin 3p per litre above regular unleaded
- 1 per cent increase in Shell petrol sales.

The task

So what was the role of marketing, in the narrow sense, within all of this? There were two audiences to talk to. First, a tightly defined consumer target of upmarket motor enthusiasts, but second there were the retailers themselves – the people on the forecourts.

The six key claims that Shell wanted to make about Optimax were that it:

- is a completely new unleaded petrol
- is the UK's best performance petrol
- is exclusive to Shell
- gives you the power to respond, just when you need it
- protects your engine like no other petrol
- was created by the Shell scientists who fuel the Ferrari F1 cars.

Radio advertising was a natural choice for reaching motorists on the road, using morning and evening 'drivetime' spots to reach drivers just as they were thinking of filling up. Radio advertising focused on London, Central and Granada regions, and was supported by a dedicated promotion in each area, using a mechanic, specifically designed to reinforce the performance benefits of the fuel. The ads were run on Capital Radio, BRMB and Key 103.

Endorsement was an important decision criterion for consumers, so significant spend was directed at motoring magazines such as *Top Gear* and *F1 Magazine*, using both advertising and advertorials to expand the technical aspects of the product, and ensure readers would see Optimax within an environment they valued and trusted.

The advertising

In the same way that the market had been commoditised, petrol communications had become formulaic and predictable. If Optimax was to ask consumers to stop thinking about fuel as a commodity, the advertising had to break the conventions of the market.

The launch television commercial, created by JWT for use globally by Shell, avoided all the clichés of the category by replacing the real world with that of the undersea environment, using fish getting around their world as a metaphor for cars getting around town. The unique benefits of Optimax gave the 'hero fish' an edge, allowing him to dart out of difficulties and demonstrate, without fear of accusations of recklessness, the benefits of the new fuel to the motorist.

The results

Optimax has been Shell's most successful marketing initiative in the UK for many years. Not only has it already beaten its financial targets but it has also had a profound impact on how customers and staff perceive Shell. The results of the launch can be considered from three perspectives; financial, staff and customer.

- Financial: The target of 1 per cent increase in sales in the business case has been considerably surpassed with 4 per cent 'new to Shell' sales. Unit margins have also exceeded target. All this means that Optimax broke even after just eight months and had already generated over £5 million gross profit for Shell.
- Shell staff: Retailer focus groups following the launch have shown that the launch of Optimax has had a major impact on staff morale and enthusiasm. Optimax is Shell's most popular initiative for many years among forecourt sales staff.
- Customers: Consumer research following the advertising campaign has shown that not only are Optimax users extremely loyal to the product itself but they are also far more loyal to Shell than standard unleaded users. Many of these core users were previously only occasional Shell users, which explains why we have had such good incremental sales.

Shell now makes an average £2.40 per fill of Optimax compared to an average of only £1.50 from unleaded users, which is naturally delivering significant growth in customer value to Shell.

SOURCE: This case study is adapted from the paper presented at the IPA Effectiveness Awards. The full version is available at www.warc.com and is reproduced by kind permission of the Institute of Practitioners in Advertising and the World Advertising Research Center.

Questions:

1 Describe the communications process. Why do we need to use the 'more complex' model described in this text?
2 Why is it important to understand the 'process of advertising'?
3 What was Russell Colley's contribution to the debate surrounding the creation of advertising?
4 Why are most models of advertising criticised, particularly by those in the profession?
5 How do the models contribute to our understanding of how advertising might work, and what are their benefits?

3 The importance of integrated marketing communications (IMC)

Learning outcomes

This chapter will help you understand:

- the background to IMC

- the current debate around IMC

- the impact of external factors

- forces driving the growth of IMC

- the benefits of IMC

- the process of achieving integration

- organisational approaches to IMC

The background to IMC

It must be remembered that advertising does not exist in isolation from the other tools of marketing communications. Whilst for many, advertising still remains the lead tool of the marketing communications mix (although even that position is being challenged by some, as alternative forms of communication become more important) there are few campaigns in which advertising is used on its own. More frequently, campaigns consist of a number of elements such as public relations, sales promotion and direct marketing used alongside advertising.

A significant debate over recent years has been the significance of ensuring the integration of these tools of marketing communications. A paper by Caywood et al. (1991) commenced a process of academic and professional discussion that continues today.

The study conducted by Schultz and Kitchen published in 1997 indicated that even then 75 per cent of all agencies in the USA devoted 25 per cent of their client time to IMC programmes. Interestingly, the smaller the size of the agency (and presumably, their client base) the greater the percentage of time devoted to achieving IMC.

Whilst the numbers of interviews was relatively small, it revealed that 59 per cent of small agencies devoted 50 per cent or more of their time to integrated marketing communications programmes. This compares with 45 per cent amongst medium-sized agencies and 36 per cent amongst large agencies.

In contrast to the opinions of Schultz and Kitchen (1997) Duncan and Everett (1993) suggest that IMC is not a new issue in that smaller communications agencies have been doing co-ordinated planning for their clients for years. Furthermore, on the client side, small marketing departments have also had a quasi-integrated approach by the mere fact that all of them knew what was going on because all of them were involved with major communications programmes.

Integrated marketing communications is significant for consumers, although they may be unaware of the concept. They recognise integration and see it logically as making it easier for them to build an overall brand picture. In essence, links between the media are seen as:

- providing short cuts to understanding what a brand stands for
- adding depth and 'amplifying' a particular message or set of brand values
- demonstrating professionalism on the part of the brand owner.

The blurring of the edges of marketing communications

Recent years have seen significant changes in the way that marketing communications campaigns have been developed and implemented. In the 1960s and 1970s, the primary source for the development of all forms of marketing communications activity was the advertising agency. At that time, separate departments within the agency provided their clients with advice in all of the appropriate areas.

Since then, two strands of change have taken place. Firstly, the wider appreciation of the techniques themselves and the need for specialist personnel to develop them have resulted in the creation of specialist companies which deal with specific areas of marketing communications. The consequence has been a progressive fragmentation of provisions within the area. Initially, there was an emergence of specialists in each of the major fields of marketing communications, in areas such as sales promotion, public relations, direct marketing and so on.

Today, that specialism has been taken even further. Specialist companies that deal with e-marketing, product placement, the organisation of trade and consumer events, sponsorship activities and so on now abound. Individual companies can now provide clients with inputs in such areas as the design and production of point-of-sale materials, the creation of trade and consumer incentives, pack design and guerilla marketing techniques, amongst many others. Even in the mainstream areas, agencies have become specialised in terms of youth or grey marketing, FMCG or retail marketing communications, dealing with pharmaceutical products or with travel and tourism. And the specialisms continue.

Secondly, and in contrast to this, there has been an increasing tendency for this wide variety of specialists to provide inputs which encompass a range of executional devices. Today, several different companies will have the ability and expertise to develop campaigns utilising a wide range of marketing communications formats. Moreover, few marketing communications campaigns utilise a single component or element. Rather marketers will tend to employ several different devices that, previously, were the domain of dedicated and specialist companies.

The consequence has been a distinct blurring of the divisions between previous specialist practitioner areas, as Cook (1994) notes:

> Discipline overlap is blurring long standing distinctions. It's becoming increasingly difficult to categorise work as sales promotion or direct marketing. Most direct marketing offers contain some form of sales promotion or vice versa. And with the growth of direct response press and TV advertising, direct marketing is moving closer to conventional advertising.

The strategic challenges facing organisations

Marketing, and for that matter, marketing communications, are being readdressed by major corporations to determine the values which they derive from the adoption of their principles. Indeed, the very nature of these principles is being challenged and re-evaluated to determine their relevance to the challenges being faced by companies at the start of the new millennium.

Nilson (1992) suggested that marketing had 'lost its way'. Despite employing high-quality management, organisations have in many instances seemed unable to face the challenges which they face in the broader environment. Growth has come more from acquisition than brand development. The consequence of chasing niche markets has been the continued and growing failure of new products to attract substantial and profitable audiences. The continued growth of private label products in a wide variety of market sectors evidences the fact that retailers are often more successful in their identification and satisfaction of consumer needs. New and innovative competitors have stolen share from the large multinational FMCG companies, despite their comparatively smaller scale, which should have precluded entry into the market.

The essential requirement of the 'new marketing' approach is the development of a close customer focus throughout the organisation which, in turn, demands an understanding of customers as individuals in order to appreciate their perceptions, expectations, needs and wants. The increasing availability of tools to enable the marketer to achieve this deeper understanding of the consumer, similarly demands the re-evaluation of the ways in which the tools employed to communicate with those consumers are used.

Strategic marketing communications

Schultz et al. (1992) argue that marketing communications often presents the only differentiating feature that can be offered to potential consumers. By recognising the fact that everything a company does consists, in some form, of communication between itself and its customers, it becomes aware of the increasingly important role of marketing communications as a strategic tool.

Just as the premise of the 'new marketing' places the consumer at the centre of all activity, so too, marketing communications must be considered from the essential perspective of understanding consumer behaviour. This implies a consideration of more than just the content of the message itself. Close attention needs to be paid to the context of the message (the vehicle used to communicate with the target audience), as well as the timing and tone of the message. The underlying imperative is the need for an identification of clear, concise and measurable communications objectives that will enable the selection of the appropriate communications tools to achieve the tasks set.

By developing an understanding of the identity of the consumer, and their particular needs and wants, we can determine the nature of the behaviour which the communications programme will need to reinforce or change. And, in turn, the specific nature of the message that will affect that behaviour, and the means by which we can reach them.

The strategic role that marketing communications can play is increasingly evidenced by the impact of specific campaigns. These not only affect the way in which consumers think about the particular products and services which are offered to them, but the very way in which they consider the categories in which those products and services exist.

The forces driving the integration of marketing communications

A major contemporary issue in the field of marketing communications is the drive towards integrated activity. There are a number of reasons for this fundamental change of thinking which need to be examined.

The marketing methods businesses used in the 1980s, such as the constant focus on new products, generic competitive strategies, promotional pricing tactics, and so on, are no longer working and have lost their value as competitive weapons. Today's marketing environment has been described as an age of 'hyper-competition' in which there exists a vast array of products and services, both new and variations on existing themes. A casual look in the supermarket will confirm this view. Take, for example, the 'cook-in-sauce' sector. The variety available to the consumer is little short of mind-blowing, whole fitments devoted to ethnic and other varieties, and with each product replicated by several different brands.

Many of the fastest-growing markets are rapidly becoming saturated with large numbers of competitors. And each competitor has similar technology. The consequence is that, as Schultz et al. (1995) put it, sustainable competitive advantage has been eroded. In many categories new products and services are copied in days or weeks rather than years. And, significantly, anything a company can do, someone else can do cheaper.

Consumers are searching for more than a single element in any transaction. Instead, they seek to buy into the array of relevant experiences which surround the brand. Successful marketing in the 1990s required total consumer orientation. It must be quality-driven and focused on communication with the individual, creating long-term relationships with the aim of customer satisfaction, not just volume and share.

Many writers on the subject, most notably Schultz (1999), argue that IMC is the natural evolution of mass-market media advertising towards targeted direct marketing. Schultz sees IMC as a logical and natural progression within the field of marketing communications. As he describes is 'it appears to be the natural evolution of traditional mass-media advertising, which has been changed, adjusted and refined as a result of new technology'. This author concurs with those who believe that IMC is significantly more than 'merely a management fashion' as attested by Cornellisen et al. (2000). Many companies strive to achieve total integration of their marketing communications efforts, recognising the undeniable benefits which derive from the practice, not least of which is the ability to deliver consistency in their messages to their target audiences.

Integration, however, is not a new phenomenon, as the following quote from J. Walter Thompson in 1899 illustrates:

> We make it our business as advertising agents to advise on the best methods of advertising, in whatever form . . . as the best combination of work, such as we give, is the cheapest, as it brings the best results.

Proctor and Kitchen (2002) argue that the brand is the hub of all marketing communications and depict this as the 'wheel of integration' as shown in Figure 3.1.

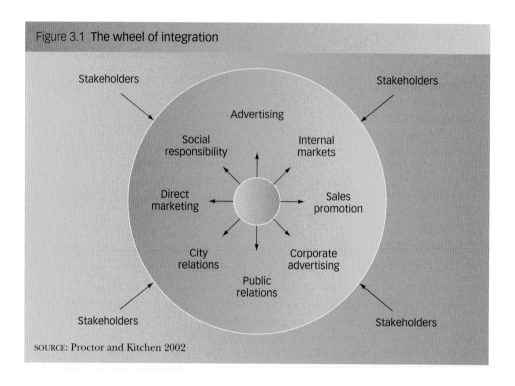

Figure 3.1 The wheel of integration

SOURCE: Proctor and Kitchen 2002

The current debate around IMC

Much debate surrounds the very nature of integrated marketing communications, with the consequence that several alternative definitions have been proposed. Cornellisen et al. (2000) argue that one of the problems with the interpretation of IMC is the lack of a consensus decision as to what the phrase actually means in practice. They point to the fact that various writers have argued about the move away from the traditional distinction between 'above-the-line' and 'below-the-line' to 'through-the-line' and 'zero-based' communications. What they fail to recognise is that the practitioners within the field operate as brands and seek to provide a distinctive offering to their clients. Hence the adoption of a variety of nomenclatures for the practice of IMC.

They argue that the theoretical concept of IMC is ambiguous and 'provides the basis for researchers to adopt whichever interpretation of the term best fits their research agendas at any given time'.

There appears to be a discordancy between academic thinking and practice in the marketplace. Schultz and Kitchen (1997) argue that most marketing communications activities in the past have focused on breaking down concepts and activities into even more finite specialisms. Few marketing communications approaches have involved integration or holistic thinking. Whilst it is acknowledged that the pace of change towards the adoption of an holistic approach has been relatively slow, none the less, many practitioners and clients have moved progressively towards a focus on IMC.

Schultz in Jones (1999) defines IMC as 'a planning approach that attempts to co-ordinate, consolidate and bring together all the communications messages, programmes and vehicles that affect customers or prospects for a manufacturer or service organisation's brands'.

Jeans (1998) provides greater clarity by proposing that 'IMC is the implementation of all marketing communications in such a way that each project, as well as meeting its specific project objects, also

- conforms with the brand platform
- is synergistic with all other projects related to the brand
- actively reinforces the agreed brand values in any dialogue with the market
- and is measured by its short- and long-term effects on consumer behaviour.'

Shimp (1996) suggests 'that the marketer who succeeds in the new environment will be the one who co-ordinates the communications mix so tightly that you can look from medium to medium and instantly see that the brand is speaking with "one voice"'. The one voice definition refers to an organisational effort to unify brand and image advertising, direct response, consumer sales promotions and public relations into a 'single positioning concept'.

Brannan (1995) argues that 'Our communications are fully integrated when we identify a single, core message which leads to one great creative idea which is implemented across everything we do'.

However, perhaps the clearest definition of integrated marketing communications is that of the American Association of Advertising Agencies (1993):

> A concept of marketing communications planning that recognises the added value of a comprehensive plan that evaluates the strategic roles of a variety of communications disciplines and combines them to provide clarity, consistency and maximum communications impact through the seamless integration of discrete messages.

The important dimension of this definition is the recognition of the need for a *comprehensive* plan that considers the strategic aspects of each of the tools of marketing communications in an holistic manner, rather than the development of them as separate elements. This approach represents a substantial shift in the underlying planning process, since it aims to ensure cohesion and the delivery of a single minded message to the target audience.

Paul Smith writing in *Admap* (1996) states:

> Integrated marketing communications is a simple concept. It brings together all forms of communication into a seamless solution. At its most basic level, IMC integrates all promotional tools so that they work together in harmony.

Key to the issue is the fact that the consumer does not see advertising, public relations, sales promotion and other marketing communications techniques as separate and divisible components. As the receivers of a variety of messages from an equally wide range of sources they build up an image of a company, its brands and its services – both favourable and unfavourable. As far as they are concerned, the source of the message is unimportant. What they will be concerned with is the content of the message.

> A surge of interest by marketers in integrated communications strategies, where promotional messages are co-ordinated among advertising, public relations and

sales promotion efforts, brings with it the implicit acknowledgement that consumers assimilate data about popular culture from many sources.

(Solomon and Englis 1994)

Equally, according to Lannon (1994):

> Consumers receive impressions of brands from a whole range of sources – first hand experience, impressions of where it can be bought, of people who use it or people who do not, from its role in cultural mores or rituals, from movies, literature, television, editorial, news, fashion, from its connections with events and activities and finally from paid advertising media.

A parallel consideration is the fact that the communicator desires to achieve a sense of cohesion in the messages which the company communicates. If, for example, advertising is saying one thing about a brand and sales promotion something different, a sense of dissonance may be created with the consumer left in some confusion as to what the brand is really trying to say.

There is little doubt that marketing communications funds spent on a single communications message will achieve a far greater impact than when a series of different or contradictory messages are being sent out by the brand. And, with the pressure on funds, marketers desire to ensure that they are presenting a clear and precise picture of their products and services to the end consumer.

Few companies are specifically concerned with issues of whether to spend their money on advertising, sales promotion, public relations or elsewhere. They are concerned with ensuring that they develop a cohesive marketing communications programme that most effectively communicates their proposition to the end consumer. The particular route of communication is far less important than the impact of the message. And, in budgetary terms, companies need to consider where their expenditure will best achieve their defined objectives. The previous notions of separate and distinct advertising, sales promotion, public relations and other budgets fails to appreciate that the considerations of the overall marketing communications budget needs to be addressed as a matter of priority.

But at the heart of the debate is the recognition that the consumer must be the focus of all marketing communications activity. If we consider the Chartered Institute of Marketing's definition of marketing, we can see that the primary need is the anticipation and satisfaction of consumer wants and needs. It is the development of an understanding of the consumer and his or her wants and needs that will ensure that marketing communications works effectively to achieve the objectives defined for it. This represents a fundamental change of focus. A shift from the functional activity of creating marketing communications campaigns to an attitudinal focus in which the consumer's needs are at the heart of all marketing communications planning. And, with it, a change from a focus from the product itself to the ultimate satisfaction of the end consumer. Of course, there are functional implications.

Above all else, there is an increasing recognition that companies need to identify what position their product or service occupies in the minds of the consumer relative to that of other products or services. Only when they have gained that knowledge can they begin the process of planning marketing communications to either alter or enhance that position.

As choice becomes an ever greater factor for consumers, both in the products they use and the way they learn about those products, it is increasingly clear that no marketer can rely on advertising alone to deliver its message. Integration permits us to focus the power of all messages. It holds the greatest, most exciting promise for the future.

(George Schweitzer, Senior Vice President,
Marketing and Communications, CBE's Broadcast Group)

In general, some consistent themes may be drawn from prominent IMC definitions identified in the literature, including:

- a sound knowledge of the organisation's stakeholders, acquired through two-way interaction with these parties;
- the selection of communication tools which promote the achievement of communications objectives, are reasonable in regard to the organisation's resources and favourable to the intended recipient;
- the strategic co-ordination of various communication tools in a manner consistent with the organisation's brand positioning and which maximises their synergistic effect so as to build strong brands and stakeholder relationships;
- the use of appropriate, timely and data-driven evaluation and planning to determine the effectiveness of this process;
- strong inter-functional and inter-organisational relationships with those responsible for implementing marketing communications campaigns;
- impact on customer relationships, brand equity and sales.

IMC is recognised increasingly for the strategic role it can play in managing the 'intangible side of business', through assisting in building relationships with customers and other stakeholders and in creating positive perceptions, attitudes and behaviours towards brands (Reid 2003).

One of the difficulties with many definitions of integrated marketing communications is the narrow ambit which they suggest. For the most part, authors concentrate on the primary tools of marketing communications, rather than the broader aspects which impact on their target audiences. Since, to reiterate the notion of David Ogilvy, that everything that a company does, communicates, then the notion of IMC should realistically embrace every dimension of company activity.

Some authors do stretch the definitions somewhat. Much contemporary thinking can be depicted as in Figure 3.2.

However, for IMC to become the significant factor that it should be, it must go further. It must embrace the reputational facets of the company's behaviour. We are increasingly witnessing concerns voiced by the consumer about the reputation of the company with whom they do business. Whether or not they buy the brands of that company will depend as much on how they regard the organisation as the efficacy of the products and services it provides. Whilst what is depicted above might be considered as a 'short-term' perspective of IMC, a longer-term view would encompass a number of other significant variables which mould the way that consumers and others view the organisation. These new dimensions can be depicted graphically, as in Figure 3.3.

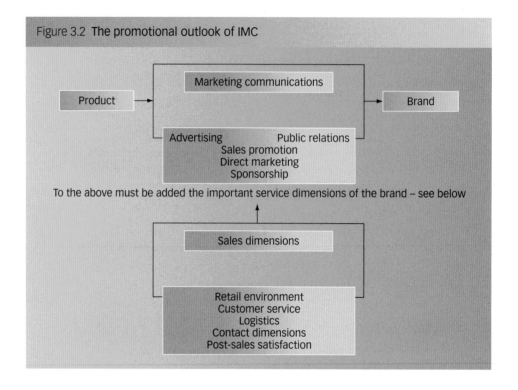

Figure 3.2 The promotional outlook of IMC

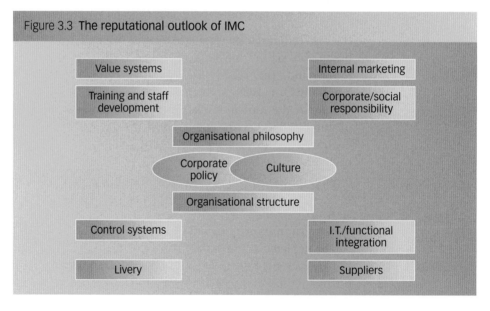

Figure 3.3 The reputational outlook of IMC

This notion is reinforced by the writing of Picton and Hartley (1998) who assert 'Integration should not just involve the marketing communications activities, but all the messages delivered by the company.'

Dimensions of IMC

These can be summarised as follows:

- Need for internal communications to ensure consistency of activities.
- Clearly identified marketing communications objectives which are consistent with other organisational objectives.
- Cohesive and planned approach encompassing all dimensions of marcom (marketing communications) activity in a synergistic manner.
- Range of target audiences.
- Management of all forms of contact which may form the basis of marketing communications activity.
- Effective management and integration of all promotional activities and people involved.
- Incorporates all product/brand and corporate marketing communications efforts.
- Range of promotional tools, including personal and non-personal communications.
- Range of messages derived from a single consistent strategy. This does not imply a single, standardised message. The IMC effort should ensure that all messages are determined in such a way as to work to each other's mutual benefit and minimise incongruity.
- Range of media including any vehicle capable of transmitting marketing communications messages (Picton and Hatley 1998).

The search for integration should not be taken to infer creative uniformity. Creative treatments need to be mutually consistent, but it is perfectly acceptable to implement a range of different messages targeted at different audiences. The essential is to avoid confusion and inconsistency.

The impact of external factors on marketing communications

Information overload

External and environmental factors have forced marketers to undertake a fundamental rethink both of marketing strategies and the positioning of products and this, in turn, must impact on the process of marketing communications.

The consumer is continuously bombarded with vast quantities of information. According to Dan O'Donoghue (1997), whereas the average consumer was subjected to about 300 commercial messages a day in 1995, today that figure has risen to around 3000. Whether the information is orchestrated by the marketer or the media in general is less relevant than the fact that there is simply too much information for the average consumer to process effectively. The inevitable consequence is that much of the material is simply screened out and discarded. The result is that the consumer may make purchasing decisions based on limited knowledge, or even on a misunderstanding of the real facts. The individual is far less concerned with the average advertising message, which makes the task of ensuring appropriate communications with the target audience an even more daunting prospect.

An important dimension of the screening process is what I have described elsewhere as the 'submarine mentality'. In essence, since none of us can absorb all of the information around us, we establish personal defence mechanisms to screen out unwanted or irrelevant information. The analogy would be that of a submarine which goes underwater and, hence, avoids the surface bombardment. At periodic intervals, the submarine lifts its periscope to examine particular aspects of the world around it. And when it has finished gathering the new information, it descends again – oblivious to any changes which might be taking place.

As consumers, our awareness of specific advertising messages is treated in a similar way. Some form of trigger mechanism is usually required to encourage us to pay attention to the variety of marketing communications messages. Usually, this is an internal recognition of an unfulfilled need which heightens the levels of awareness of pertinent advertising and other information. The principle can be commonly observed. If, for example, you have recently purchased a new car, your awareness of the marque will be enhanced and you will immediately become aware of similar vehicles all around you.

However, in the process of attempting to find better and more effective ways of communicating, we have also gained a greater appreciation of the nature of marketing communications itself. Much work has been done in the area of model construction and theoretical examination which has helped us to enhance areas of implementation.

The discerning consumer

Recent decades have seen the progressive improvement in levels of education which, in turn, has made consumers both more demanding concerning the information they receive and more discerning in their acceptance of it. Marketing communications propositions developed in the 1950s and 1960s would be treated with disdain by today's more aware consumers. Specious technical claims and pseudo scientific jargon which were at the heart of many product claims are no longer given quite the same credence.

This change is reflected in the comment of Judy Lannon (1996): 'Consumers have changed from being deferential and generalised to personal and selective'. She argues that we need to re-examine the way in which consumers use sources of commercial information. A particular issue to be addressed is, as she describes it, the 'credibility dimension' which involves not only the underlying credibility of the message, but the credibility of the sponsor delivering the message.

A contradiction

The inability to store and process new information, coupled with the demand for a greater focus in marketing communications messages, has resulted in the consumer relying more on perceptual values than on factual information. All consumers build up a set of 'values' which they associate with a company or a brand. Some of these values will be based on personal experience or the experience of others. Many of them will be based, however, on a set of 'short-handed conclusions' based on overheard opinions, the evaluation of third-party organisations, even the misinterpretation of information. These two factors combine to create a new dynamic for marketing communications.

However these thought processes are developed, and however the information is received, is less important than the fact that for the individual their views represent the truth. A product which is perceived to be inferior (even though there is factual evidence to contradict this view) is unlikely to be chosen in a normal competitive environment. The imperative, therefore, is to understand the process of perceptual encoding and relate it to the task of marketing communications. A simple example will suffice.

Most consumers are responsive to a 'bargain' proposition. And certain assumptions are made particularly in relation to well-known and familiar brands. If a potential consumer sees a product on sale in a market environment, there is some expectation that the price will be lower than, say, in the normal retail environment. If the brand name is well established, then it is likely that they will be able to draw from it the confidence and reassurance which will be necessary to the making of a purchase decision. Indeed, there is considerable evidence that these perceptual factors, influenced by the environment, will for some consumers induce them to make a purchase even though they might have been able to purchase the same product at a lower price elsewhere.

Many retailers have recognised this situation and have adopted a positioning relative to their competitors of low price. By marking down the prices of a narrow range of products, they encourage the consumer to believe that all products are similarly discounted. The result is that the consumer will decide to make all of his or her purchases at that outlet based on the perceptions derived from a limited comparison of those brands upon which the retailer has focused marketing communications activity. Since few consumers are in a position to make objective comparisons across a wide range of comparable outlets, these perceptions are accepted and become the reality.

The situation is compounded by the fact that price is only one consideration in a purchase decision. Most people have an ideal view of a price and quality combination. Needless to say, such a view is highly personal and subjective, but it becomes the basis of making subsequent purchase decisions for that individual. Thus reputation, both for retailers and brands, will be an important consideration in the purchase selection.

Changes in family composition

Long gone are the notions of the family comprising two adults and 2.4 children. In all countries, the notion of family itself has different meanings. Some communities perceive the family as a small integrated unit, others adopt a model of the extended family with the elder children having responsibility for ageing members of the family – either parents or grandparents. The increasing levels of divorce and the growing acceptance, by some, that marriage is not a norm to which they wish to comply, has resulted in growing numbers of single parent families. In all these situations, their needs and expectations will be substantially different from each other, and effective marketing communications needs to recognise and respond to these underlying changes in society.

The ageing population

In many countries, improved standards of living and better health care have resulted in two parallel changes. On the one hand, in order to sustain living standards, people are deferring having children or are having fewer of them. On the other, life expectancy is improving as medical care is enhanced. These forces have resulted in a progressively ageing population in most developed markets. And with it, a change in the values, needs and wants which consumers exhibit about products and services.

The green imperative

Increasing numbers of consumers are concerned with the environmental impact of the products and services they consume. The abandonment of CFCs, the reduction in the volume of packaging waste, the consumption of scarce and irreplaceable resources and similar factors have all impacted on the consumer's perceptions of desirable products and services.

No longer is the single focus of their attention the efficacy or otherwise of the products they might buy. They require reassurance that not only do the products perform in the way that they expect, but they also contribute to a better environment.

The changing face of media and the growth of narrow casting

The advent of an increased number of media channels – land-based, cable and satellite television, an increasing number of radio networks, and a mammoth explosion in the number of 'specialist' magazine titles – have resulted in a fundamental shift in terms of media planning. Where once the advertiser had to recognise that the use of a chosen media might, whilst providing excellent coverage of the desired target audience, carry with it a substantial wastage factor, the situation has now changed somewhat. Consumer groups can be targeted with a far higher level of precision. A specific message can be developed to appeal to a sub-group of users accessed by the nature of the television programmes they watch or the magazines they read. And, the increasing use of direct marketing techniques has resulted in the possibility of one-to-one marketing – where the proposition can be tailored specifically to respond to the individual needs of the single consumer. 'Mass media advertising dominated marketing communications for decades, however, the nineties have seen companies place a greater emphasis on alternative communications mediums' (Lannon 1996).

Most people are aware of the increasing fragmentation of media channels. However, perhaps more importantly, there is a wide variety of new channels of communication which can be used by brand owners to communicate with potential consumers and others – postcards, mobile internet, till receipts, fuel pumps, hoardings around sports grounds, product placement, to name but a few. Research must be capable of monitoring the impact and ability of all of these communications channels to influence the 'viewer'.

Franz (2000) argues that the proliferation of new media adds complexity to the media landscape, since these new media channels rarely replace old media. Rather, they tend to complement each other. What is significant is the way that media are used. Consumers tend to be more selective in their use of media, both because of time and money. The consequence is that media selection tends to be more specific than ever before.

Non-verbal communications

We have already seen that the emergence of new media has enabled a more precise focus on target groups of consumers. But it has also demanded a new approach to the execution of marketing communications propositions, particularly on television.

Increasingly, satellite channels are unrestricted in their availability. The same programmes can be watched simultaneously in France and Finland, Germany and Greece. And, if that is true of the programming, it is equally true of the advertising contained within. Whilst programmers have the opportunity to overcome language and other barriers to communication within their formats, the same is not so readily true for the advertiser.

The response has been a growth in the recognition that visual communication has a vital role to play in the overall process. Increasing numbers of television commercials are being made with a pan European or global audience in mind. The emphasis is less on the words being used than the impact of the visual treatments employed.

At the time of writing, a constant visual treatment is being utilised by Gillette to support their Series range of products across diverse markets. Here, the voiceover is modified to verbalise the proposition in each marketplace. In fact, the company has adopted an integrated approach for their six-year-old campaign embracing everything the company does. 'It is a much more single minded strategic platform for the brand', according to Bruce Cleverly, General Manager for Gillette Northern Europe. 'It is the strategic premise of the entire Gillette grooming business.'

Other companies have gone considerably further. The verbal component of the proposition has been minimised with the storyline being developed entirely, or almost so, in visual form. Television commercials for Dunlop, Levis and Perrier are examples of this approach.

Speed of information access

Not only has the growth of information technology meant that information can be processed more rapidly, it has also meant that access to that information can be made far more speedily than at any time in the past. This has significant import for the marketer.

Census information which was previously tabulated by hand, or on comparatively slow computers – and which was substantially out of date by the time it was made available – is now available within a relatively short period of time. Marketers can determine with far greater precision than at any time in the past, the likely audience for their propositions, and can more readily segment markets into groups of users, rather than communicating with them as an aggregation.

At the same time, of course, this improved level of communication has a direct impact on the consumer. An increased level of media coverage of consumer-related issues means that any problem with a product or service is almost bound to receive media exposure. News stories about product withdrawals, and the focus on product deficiencies within programmes like *Watchdog*, all ensure that large groups of consumers become aware of these issues within days or even hours of the occurrence.

The growth of global marketing

The changes brought about, substantially by mass communications, have, to some degree, encouraged the movement towards global marketing. With the recognition that national and cultural differences are growing ever fewer, major manufacturers have seized upon the opportunity to 'standardise' their marketing across different markets.

It is now possible to purchase an ostensibly similar product with the same name, same identity and similar product ingredients in many different markets. From the ubiquitous Coca-Cola, now available in almost every different country, to products like the Mars Bar, manufacturers are seizing the opportunity to ensure a parity of branding throughout all of the markets they serve, and to extend the territories in which they operate. The latter company has unified its branding of the Marathon Bar to Snickers and Opal Fruits to Starburst to achieve international parity. Similarly, Unilever recently consolidated the various names of Jif and Vif into Cif for the same reason.

There are few markets (although the product contents may well be different) which would not recognise the Nescafé coffee label or what it stands for. The big M means McDonalds in any language, and Gillette run the same copy platform for its series range of male shaving preparations in many different countries.

The forces driving the growth of IMC

Various studies have focused on the factors which are encouraging the adoption of integrated marketing communications programmes (Yeshin 1996; Duncan and Everett 1993; Schultz and Kitchen 1997; Grein and Ducoffe 1998; Kitchen and Schultz 1999).

A further dimension of the study by Kitchen and Schultz (1999) was an identification by respondents of the forces driving the move towards IMC, as follows:

- call for synergy among promotional tools
- rapid growth and development of database marketing
- recognition that agency's future success depends on helping clients develop IMC programmes
- emergence of a variety of compensation methods
- rapid growth of IMC importance
- fragmentation of media markets
- shift in marketplace power from manufacturers to retailers
- escalating price competition
- traditional advertising too expensive and not cost effective.

Duncan and Everett (1993) identify several factors underlying the pressure to integrate marketing communications:

- agency mergers and acquisitions
- increasing sophistication of clients and retailers
- increasing cost of traditional advertising media
- increased global competition
- increasing pressure on organisations' bottom lines
- decreasing effectiveness of traditional media
- decreasing cost of database usage
- trends such as zapping, zipping, media fragmentation and loss of message credibility.

The key factors behind the drive to IMC are briefly discussed below.

Value for money The recession of recent years and increasing global competition have brought about substantial changes in the way that client companies are managed. On the one hand, there has been the impact of shrinking marketing departments, in which fewer people are allocated to the management of the products and services which the company produces. On the other, the pressure on margins has encouraged clients to become tougher negotiators. Companies are keen to gain the maximum value for money and the maximum impact from all relevant disciplines.

Increasing pressure on organisations' bottom lines The inevitable consequence of the variety of economic pressures has resulted in a close focus on company profitability. As all forms of cost increase, so companies seek to make compensatory savings throughout all of their activities.

Increasing client sophistication This is particularly true of areas such as an understanding of retailers, customers and consumers. There has been an increasing confidence in the use of other marketing communication disciplines, especially sales promotion, and the greater ability to take the lead in terms of their strategic direction.

Disillusionment with advertising This has resulted in clients turning to other disciplines in the search to improve customer relationships and more sales.

Disillusionment with agencies Advertising agencies, in particular, which were often the primary source of strategic input for the clients with whom they worked, have lost significant ground in this respect. Specialist consultancies and others are now being retained by client companies to advise them of the strategic directions they should be taking, with the agency role becoming progressively smaller in many instances.

Fragmentation of media channels As we have seen earlier, the changing face of the media scene is demanding the re-evaluation of the contribution that the variety of media channels can make to the delivery of the message. With new ways of communicating with the target audiences, new approaches are necessary to achieve maximum impact from marketing communications budgets.

Traditional advertising too expensive and not cost effective There is an increased recognition that, for many companies, the use of traditional forms of advertising no longer provides the means of achieving cost-effective reach of their target audiences. As media costs escalate, many companies are turning to other forms of marketing communications to achieve their objectives.

Rapid growth and development of database marketing The increasing availability of sophisticated database techniques has enabled manufacturers and service providers alike with a more precise means of targeting consumers. The move away from traditional mass marketing towards closely focused communications techniques is a reflection of the increasing cost of traditional advertising techniques.

Power shift towards retailers In most consumer markets, comparatively small numbers of retailers have come to dominate their respective categories. In the grocery field, for example, the major supermarket chains – Tesco, Asda, Sainsbury's, and Safeway (now part of Morrisons) – account for a substantial part of the retail business. Together, these four companies account for over 50 per cent of retail sales. Inevitably, this has resulted in their taking the initiative in terms of the marketing to consumers. To a large degree, even major manufacturers have to bow to the demands of the retailers or face the prospect of their products being de-listed from their shelves.

Escalating price competition As brands increasingly converge in what they offer to consumers, companies are striving to overcome the debilitating impact of the downward price spiral. The recognition that marketing communications is often the only differentiating factor between competing brands has led to an increased focus on how the tools can be used to achieve brand distinction.

Environmental factors Consumers are becoming increasingly concerned with the way in which products impact on the general environment. In turn, companies have been forced to adopt a more environmentally friendly approach or risk consumers rejecting their products in favour of those which they consider to be more responsive to these broader concerns.

Emergence of a variety of compensation methods Where once agencies were bound by a compensation based on commission (a fixed percentage of the monies spent on advertising), today's marketing communications companies are rewarded in many different ways. The most important impact of this change has been to free them (and the perception of their income) as being tied to recommendations to increase their clients' spend.

Agency mergers and acquisitions Responding to the needs of the marketplace and, in particular, to pressures from their clients, agencies are increasing merging to form larger groups. Partly, this has been driven by the need to provide client services across a variety of territories. However, a further dimension has been the desire to provide a comprehensive service to clients across the variety of areas encompassed by marketing communications. The large agency groups exist as holding companies controlling operational companies in all of the relevant communications fields.

Increased global competition The drive towards globalisation has increased the necessity to achieve synergy between all forms of marketing communications. Where once a brand might be sold in a single country, today's mega-brands are available across the globe. Significant savings can be achieved through the implementation of a constant communications campaign across all of the territories in which the product is sold.

The impact on marketing communications

We have already seen that marketing communications needs to focus on the end user rather than on the nature of the product or service provided. But, it is suggested, marketing communications needs to respond more rapidly to these underlying changes in the social and environmental framework.

In their important work on IMC, Schultz, Tannenbaum and Lauterborn (1992) propose that it is time to abandon the principles of the 4 Ps for the four Cs.

'Forget **P**roduct. Study **C**onsumer wants and needs. You can no longer sell whatever you make. You can only sell something that someone specifically wants to buy.

Forget **P**rice. Understand the consumer's **C**ost to satisfy that want or need.

Forget **P**lace. Think **C**onvenience to buy.

Forget **P**romotions. The word in the 90's is **C**ommunications.'

If marketing communications is to be effective, it is vitally important that we move from a situation of specialisation – in which marketers are experts in one area of marketing communications – to people who are trained in all marketing communications disciplines.

At the same time, as we have already seen, the process of change requires us to look at focused marketing approaches rather than adopt the litany of the 1960s – that of mass marketing. With the recognition that all consumers are different and, hence have different needs and wants – even of the same product or service – there is the need to ensure that we are able to communicate with them as individuals rather than as a homogenous unit. The aim increasingly is to communicate with ever smaller segments of the global market and, in an ideal world, to reach a position where we can communicate with them individually. This desire manifests itself in the increasing drive towards direct marketing techniques, the most rapidly growing sector of the marketing communications industry.

There needs to be a clear statement of the desired outcomes of marketing activity as a whole. This requires a totally new approach since most people working within marketing have been brought up in a disintegrated environment. Objectives need to be longer term and expressed more strategically than would be the case for the short-term objectives of mores individual marketing tactics.

Schultz (1999) argues that as the tools of marketing communications are progressively diffused into a variety of specialisms, there has been a natural inclination for those individual specialists to focus entirely within their own area – often to the detriment of the brand or communication programme. The consequence has been a natural drift towards less integrated, less co-ordinated, less concentrated marketing communications activities.

The task of IMC is to strategically co-ordinate the various elements of the promotional mix in order to achieve synergies and to ensure that the message reaches and registers with the target audience.

Novak and Phelps (1994) have suggested that there are several important dimensions to the process of integration:

- the creation of a single theme and image
- the integration of both product image and relevant aspects of consumer behaviour in promotional management (as opposed to a focus on one or the other of these two)
- the co-ordinated management of promotion mix disciplines.

Similarly, Low (2000) identified four components that contribute to the co-ordination of marketing communications activities:

1 planning and executing different communications tools as one integrated project
2 assigning responsibility for the overall communications effort to a single manager
3 ensuring that the various elements of the communications programme have a common strategic objective
4 focusing on a common communications message.

Relationship marketing

A development of the marketing communications process as it moves through the early 2000s is the area known as 'relationship marketing'. With the ability to reach consumers on a highly segmented or even one-to-one basis, so too has come the recognition that the process itself can become two way. Hitherto, marketing communications primarily concerned itself with the process of communicating *to* the end consumer. By encouraging the process of feedback, we can now communicate *with* the consumer.

Increasingly, companies such as Nestlé and Heinz have announced moves into club formats which enable the establishment of a direct relationship between the manufacturer and the consumer. Many loyalty programmes, such as the Frequent Flyer and Frequent Stayer programmes now run by most international airlines and hotel groups, have a similar objective of establishing a relationship with the consumer, to their mutual benefit. The increasing use of customer loyalty programmes within the major retail chains is further evidence of the desire to establish direct contact with the customer base – for long-term advantage. The encouragement of a 'feedback' loop is a facet of marketing communications which is destined to grow apace over the next few years and, as companies perceive the benefits of encouraging a positive relationship with their customers, their consumers, their suppliers and others, so we will witness the growth of developed two-way marketing communications programmes.

It has to be recognised that contemporary marketing is more complex than at any other time in the past. No longer is it sufficient to rely on the traditional marketing mix variables to achieve differentiation between manufacturers. Areas such as product design and development, pricing policies and distribution in themselves are no longer capable of delivering the long-term differentiation required. With an increasing level of convergent technologies, product innovation may be going on in parallel between rival manufacturers even without their knowing what the other is doing. And, even where this is not the case, any new feature can rapidly be copied by the competition. Where once, a new feature, ingredient or other product attribute would enable a manufacturer to achieve a unique stance for an extended period, today this is no longer the case. One has only to look at the area of the rapid innovation within the soap powder and detergent markets to see just how speedily rival manufacturers catch up with each other.

With the concentration of distribution into relatively few hands, the opportunities for achieving solus distribution of brands is minimised. Indeed, the retailers themselves represent an increasing threat to the manufacturers' brands as their packaging moves ever closer to that of the manufacturers' own.

Pricing, once a major area of differentiation, similarly provides less scope. The pressure on margins brought about by the increasingly competitive nature of retailers' own products, has restricted the scope to use price to differentiate effectively. Clearly, this is particularly true of fast-moving consumer goods, where price dissimilarity can only operate over a very narrow range. Other products, such as perfumes and toiletries, and luxury goods ranging from hi-fis to cars, still have more flexibility in the area of price.

We are left, therefore, with only one of the four marketing mix variables which can be utilised to achieve effective brand discrimination – marketing communications. Schultz, Tannenbaum and Lauterborn (1992) argue that the area of marketing communications will, increasingly, be the only opportunity of achieving sustainable competitive advantage.

If all other things are equal – or at least more or less so – then it is what people think, feel and believe about a product and its competitors which will be important. Since products in many areas will achieve parity or comparability in purely functional terms, it will be the perceptual differences which consumers will use to discriminate between rival brands. Only through the used of sustained and integrated marketing communications campaigns, will manufacturers be able to achieve the differentiation they require.

To appreciate the impact of this statement, it is worth looking at a market which replicates many of the features described above. In the bottled water market, several brands coexist, each with unique positionings in the minds of the consumer. Yet, in repeated blind tastings, few consumers can identify any functional characteristics which could be used as the basis for brand discrimination.

> The increasing need to manage relationship building has brought forth a variety of 'new generation' marketing approaches – customer focused, market-driven, outside-in, one-to-one marketing, data-driven marketing, relationship marketing, integrated marketing and integrated marketing communications.
>
> (Duncan and Moriarty 1998)

The benefits of IMC

Undeniably, the process of integration affords a great number of benefits to the companies which adopt it. Linton and Morley (1995) suggest 10 potential benefits of IMC:

- creative integrity
- consistent messages
- unbiased marketing recommendations
- better use of media
- greater marketing precision
- operational efficiency
- cost savings
- high-calibre consistent service
- easier working relations.

Similarly, the Kitchen and Schultz study (1999) identified a series of benefits which could be derived from IMC programmes. These included:

- increased impact
- creative ideas more effective when IMC used
- greater communications consistency
- increases importance of one brand personality
- helps eliminate misconceptions
- provides greater client control over communication budget
- provides clients with greater professional expertise
- enables greater client control over marketing communications
- helps eliminate miscommunications that result from using several agencies
- enables greater control over budgets

- provides client with greater professional expertise
- necessitates fewer meetings
- enables client consolidation of responsibilities
- agencies can provide faster solutions
- provides method of effective measurement
- reduces cost of marcom programmes
- greater agency accountability.

The key benefits are discussed below.

Consistency of message delivery: By approaching the planning process in an holistic manner, companies can ensure that all components of the communications programme deliver the same message to the target audience. Importantly, this demands the adoption of an overall strategy for the brand, rather than developing individual strategies for the separate tools of marketing communications. The avoidance of potential confusion in the minds of consumers is a paramount consideration in the development of effective communications programmes.

Corporate cohesion: For the company, IMC can be used as a strategic tool in communicating its corporate image and product/service benefits. This has important consequences both on an internal and an external level. As consumers increasingly gravitate towards companies with whom they feel comfortable, it becomes important to ensure that the overall image projected by the organisation is favourably received. This demands, in turn, the development of a cohesive communications programme within the organisation – to ensure that all people working for the company fully understand the organisation's goals and ambitions – and externally – to present the company in the most favourable light.

Client relationships: for the agency, it provides the opportunity to play a significantly more important role in the development of the communications programme, and to become a more effective partner in the relationship. By participating in the totality of the communications requirements, rather than having responsibility for one or more components, the agency can adopt a more strategic stance. This, in turn, yields significant power and provides important advantages over competitors.

Interaction: IMC ensures better communication between agencies and creates a stronger bond between them and the client company. By providing a more open flow of information it enables the participants in the communication programme to concentrate on the key areas of strategic development, rather than pursue individual and separate agendas.

Motivation: IMC offers the opportunity to motivate agencies. The combined thinking of a team is better than the sum of the parts (and unleashes everyone's creative potential).

Participation: Everyone owns the final plan, having worked together on the brainstorming and implementation, avoiding any internal politics. Potentially, this can overcome the divisive nature of individual departments 'fighting their own corner'.

Measurability: Perhaps the most important benefit is the delivery of better measurability of response and accountability for the communications programme.

The process of achieving integration

The task of developing and implementing marketing communications campaigns is becoming increasingly divergent. No longer it is the task of one pair of hands. As the specialist functions develop further, the marketer must seek and co-ordinate the input from a number of different sources. Many organisations will retain an advertising agency, a public relations consultancy, a sales promotion company and perhaps even a media specialist. Ensuring that all of these contributors work to the same set of objectives and deliver a cohesive message to the consumer is a task which is an increasingly challenging one.

The key requirement is the establishment of a feedback mechanism between all elements of the strategic development process and, importantly, the consideration of all of the tools of marketing communications designed to fulfil the promotional objectives established for the campaign. It is the adoption of an holistic approach to campaign development which is at the heart of integration, a fundamental shift from the practice of developing each of the elements on a piecemeal basis.

'Integrated marketing communications offers strategic and creative integrity across all media' (Linton and Morley 1995). This ensures that the company maintains a constant theme and style of communication which can be followed across all applications. In turn, this provides for a strong and unified visual identity in all areas of communication.

This does not imply that all material should have the same copy and visual execution, but all items used must serve to tell the same story and to reinforce the overall message to the consumer. This enables each element of a campaign to reinforce the others and to achieve the maximum level of impact on the target audience. The best platforms for integrated campaigns are ideas that can be spread across the whole marketing communications mix, e.g. American Express 'Membership has its privileges' and Gillette's 'The best a man can get' will work in any discipline.

Andrex has, for many years, used the image of a Labrador puppy in its advertising to symbolise softness. More recently, however, the device has been extended into other promotional areas. Its 'Puppy tales' campaign offered a series of books about the adventures of a puppy, which was featured on-pack and in television advertising. The promotion gained editorial coverage both for the promotion itself and by way of reviews of the author, Gerald Durrell. All of these devices reinforced the brand message.

Some companies go further. They produce a visual identity manual to which all items produced on behalf of the company must comply. This establishes a series of specific requirements which may cover the typefaces used, the positioning of the logo and other important visual elements which provides a high level of commonality in all materials produced. Often this is associated with a redesign of the corporate image. When the author was working with the Prudential Corporation, Woolf Olins were engaged to redesign the company look and, as part of the package, created a corporate ID manual which covered all of the above areas, and to which all agencies were required to comply.

An essential part of IMC is the process of ensuring that the message conveyed is consistent. Whereas this is achievable in the context of a single agency which produces all of the materials required by its client, in the vast majority of case, companies will employ several different agencies, often independent of each other. Indeed, some of the material will be produced by the company in-house. In this instance, someone must take overall responsibility for ensuring the consistency of the various items to ensure that there is an overall coherence in what is produced. This means that the person or department must consider not only the obvious items such as advertising, point of sale and direct mail pieces, but everything else which is prepared to support the brand. This may include product leaflets and other literature, presentations and audio visual material, sales training items, exhibition stands and so on.

A key area within the requirement of IMC is the need for recommendations which are without structural bias. Historically (and still to a large degree) it was inevitable that agencies promoted their own particular corners. Advertising agencies would often present advertising solutions, promotions companies would offer sales promotion responses, and so on.

The move towards IMC has been hastened by the desire for agencies to become more accountable for their recommendations. Inherently, agencies have to be confident, as far as it is possible to be so, that the recommendations they make are those most likely to achieve the outcome desired by the client company.

To many writers on the topic, the central part of the IMC process is the maintenance of an effective database. Not only does this provide the opportunity to gain a greater understanding of existing customers, from an examination of their profiles (and using those profiles to identify similar target groups) it is possible to achieve a greater degree of precision in all subsequent communications activity.

At the conceptual level, integration is about capturing a single thought which expresses what we wish the brand to stand for and of ensuring that this thought is expressed, whatever the medium. At the process level, it is about ensuring that the development and implementation of communications lives up to that brand thought, and drives forward the relationship between the brand and the consumer.

As John Farrell, then Chief Executive of DMB&B (now incorporated into Leo Burnett) said: 'Unless there is close involvement of senior client personnel who truly have a full communications perspective, it's simply unfair on the agencies involved to expect them to drive the integration process from the outside.' Clients do not need specialist implementation functions within their businesses, rather at a conceptual stage there has to be a structure and attitude which actively encourages the agency to recommend the most appropriate media solution to solve the particular problem.

Integration is not just about execution. It is about the single brand thought that expresses the essence of the brand personality and then interpreting that thought for the appropriate audience without changing or denigrating it. Integration extends to the point where the client and agency work together as a single team. The total team across all communications requirements is fully integrated with the customer and brand requirements and that is what drives the focus of the team.

Winston Fletcher (1998) seeks to make the distinction between good and bad integration. He argues that badly done integrated marketing campaigns squeeze different communications media into strait-jackets which minimise their individuality. 'To force all types of communications to use the same message, instead of allowing them to deploy their own strengths and complement each other, is direly inefficient.'

The position is summarised by the approaches adopted by two different companies. After Bisto's annual marketing communications plan has been developed, it is presented at a meeting with all of the Bisto agencies represented. Paula Ross, a group product manager as RHM says:

> this creates a more open flow of information with all of the agencies focusing on the key objectives, not just their ideas. It motivates all that take part and everybody has ownership in the brand plan. And, most important, the combined thinking of the team is better than the parts.

Similarly, Tetley implements the IMC process by holding quarterly meetings when marketing staff meet with its advertising agency, PR consultancy and sales promotion consultancy.

Van Raaij (1998) summarises the differences between classic forms of marketing communications with the IMC approach as shown in Figure 3.4.

Figure 3.4 Classic marketing communications and integrated communications: a comparison

Classic communications	Integrated communications
Aimed at acquisition	Aimed at retention and relationship management
Mass communications	Selective communications
Monologue	Dialogue
Information is sent	Information is requested
Information provision	Information self-service
Sender takes initiative	Receiver takes initiative
Persuasive 'hold-up'	Provides information
Effect through repetition	Effect through relevance
Offensive	Defensive
Hard sell	Soft sell
Salience of brand	Confidence in brand
Transaction oriented	Relationship oriented
Attitude change	Satisfaction
Modern, linear, massive	Post-modern, cyclical, fragmented

SOURCE: Van Raaij 1998

Increasingly, attempts are being made by companies to co-ordinate some, if not all, of the marketing functions to benefit from the resultant synergy. In this regard, many companies adopt a 'consistency' approach to ensure that the brand messages created by different marketing activities do not conflict with the agreed strategic positioning of the brand. In some instances, much more complete integration is achieved by ensuring that a similar device is used across all marketing activities – for example, Coca-Cola advertise their sponsorship of various events, especially football, and also use them as the basis of sales promotion activities.

Very few companies have really developed a comprehensive approach towards integration where the overall responsibility for all communication functions is lodged in a single location, either internally or externally.

A survey by Duncan and Everett (1993) found that, at that time, there was a relatively low familiarity with the concept of IMC. However, once the concept was defined, most regarded it as a valuable concept.

They identified that a significant number of companies were co-ordinating the functions of marketing communications both internally and externally. An increasing number of clients stated that they were likely to hire agencies with an understanding of IMC and believed that IMC would grow within their organisations.

The way in which companies are organised into different departments which reflect the various functions of marketing communications is a key cause of disintegrated communications where different messages are communicated to consumers about the same brand. In the worst case scenario, the messages delivered by marketing communications may actually contradict each other (Alanko 2000).

Some writers suggest that the most efficient means of achieving integration is to appoint a single agency which is responsible for all aspects of the campaign, contracting out certain areas. The reality, except for a relatively small number of companies, is that such an approach is generally not possible. The need for specialist services in the wide variety of areas which make up the tools of marketing communications, requires staff who are skilled in those specialisms.

Research by Gronstedt and Thorson (1996) suggests that integrated approaches are necessary because most work related to communications cuts across different knowledge and skills domains, whilst Schultz et al. (1992) argue that IMC results in the creation of communications programmes that are both tonally and visually coherent.

The question of how to organise external communications disciplines has been a continuing source of debate within the arena of marketing communications (Cornellisen et al. 2001). The conundrum is whether organisation should be of a functional nature, that is, with the various departments merged together to create a single entity which can deal with all communications requirements or whether, as suggested by Gronstedt (1996) it is more about integrating the processes of marketing communications. Schultz et al. (1992) argue that the different mind-sets of professionals operating within the various disciplines inhibit the level of cross-functional operation and the ways in which the disciplines can contribute to the achievement of the desired objectives.

Gronstedt and Thorson (1996) suggest five possible models for an integrated organisational structure:

1 **The consortium** One agency performs the role of main contractor to a consortium of specialist agencies. The main agency helps its client to develop a strategy and decides which persuasive tools to use. It typically executes traditional advertising but subcontracts other tools. The account team at the main agency co-ordinates the specialist agencies to ensure that messages and timing are integrated.

2 **Consortium with a dominant agency** Agencies that have the capacity to plan an integrated campaign and execute traditional advertising as well as some other communications tools. The main agency has various combinations of in-house services and outside suppliers.

3 **Corporation with autonomous units** All the specialists are brought in-house as separate and autonomous units. The specialist units are separate profit centres, sometimes with separate names and in separate buildings.

4 **The matrix organisation** Agencies not only have specialists in-house but they are integrated in a matrix structure. The matrix design combines functional division and cross-functional taskforce teams. The matrix structure requires that professionals work across functions whilst maintaining the functional division.

5 **The integrated organisation** All disciplines are incorporated into the advertising agency structure rather than forming separate units for each persuasive tool. The agency is no longer structured by functional departments but by accounts. Each person works for a particular client not for a direct marketing or sales promotion department. Each account group comprises personnel who are capable of handling all communications disciplines.

Duncan and Everett (1993) suggest four agency client relationships which could foster integration:

1 The client and its agencies collectively establish strategies, then each communications function is executed by a different agency.

2 The client and its agency establish the strategies, then the 'integrated' agency is responsible for the executions of all or most of the communications functions.

3 The client determines overall strategies and assigns individual functions to individual agencies, but requires that all of these suppliers stay in touch with each other.

4 The client alone determines overall strategies, then each communications function is executed by a different agency.

Grein and Gould (1996) identify five factors which, they suggest, impact on the organisational dimensions and affect its effective implementation:

1 inter-office co-ordination
2 co-ordination of promotional disciplines across country offices
3 the degree of centralisation
4 the frequency of inter-office communication
5 the use of information technology.

Jeans (1998) argues that the most likely route to achieving IMC is in team-building, rather than any hierarchical or matrix method of control. Since the necessary practitioner skills are unlikely to be embodied in any single individual, a team of people will be essential to provide the necessary inputs.

A study by McArthur and Griffin published in 1997 demonstrated the extent to which marketing organisations perceived integration to have been fulfilled. Almost half of the companies surveyed indicated that all marketing communications activities of their companies were co-ordinated either by a single person or as a result of some reporting relationship. A further quarter co-ordinated the majority of their marketing communications programmes. Interestingly, and confirming the results of other studies, the areas of business which indicated the highest level of co-ordination of activities were retail and business to business.

The study identified a series of 'inconsistencies' in the sourcing of activities across the different business types. Their study revealed, for example, that consumer marketers tended to use external suppliers for creative input more extensively than others. The business-to-business sector relied more heavily on their advertising agencies for all communications activities. Retailer marketers were significantly more prone to source activities in-house.

There are sound historical reasons for these differences in practice sometimes, but not always, related to the level of marketing communications expenditures within specific categories. Within the consumer sector, budgets tend to be large and activities more extensive. Inevitably, companies involved with these programmes seek high levels of expertise within the respective fields and source suppliers who, in the main, have a demonstrable track record of being able to deal with the market sector. Elsewhere, where budgets are somewhat lower, companies tend to rely more heavily on a single supplier to achieve economies across the range of activities which they implement. The retail sector, by contrast, inevitably demands a greater speed of response and, hence, is more prone to produce material in-house where those with the specialist skills can be located.

Nor should it be presumed that IMC is the exclusive province of FMCG and branded manufacturers. Alanko (2000) argues that 'integration in B2B goes beyond co-ordinating media and other communications channels and their messages. It "enters the heart of the enterprise and its core processes, customer acquisition, retention and development"'.

He makes the point that, as with other forms of business, integration within the B2B sector occupies a strategic role and must involve senior management.

Interesting differences in the global acceptance and implementation of IMC are seen in various recent works.

A survey conducted by Griffin and McArthur (1997) sought to identify the extent to which IMC was practised within companies. Respondents were shown a series of seven marketing communications functions (including creative, media, sales promotion, etc.) and asked to indicate the nature of co-ordination between them and the extent of that co-ordination.

The results were as shown in Table 3.1.

A study conducted by Kitchen and Schultz (1999) indicated the extent to which the premise of IMC had been adopted in a number of countries, as shown in Table 3.2.

A further aspect of their research was the amount of client budgets devoted to IMC activities as shown in Table 3.3.

Table 3.1 Extent of marketing communications co-ordination within companies

	Business focus				
	All (%)	Consumer (%)	B2B (%)	Service (%)	Retail (%)
Companies where all activities co-ordinated	46.2	46.2	62.5	34.5	50.0
by a single person	24.0	30.8	31.3	17.2	15.0
through a reporting relationship	22.1	15.4	31.3	17.2	35.0
Companies where 5–6 activities co-ordinated	28.7	33.3	18.8	20.7	35.0
by a single person	7.7	5.1	6.3	3.4	20.0
through a reporting relationship	21.0	28.2	12.5	17.2	15.0
Companies where 3–4 activities co-ordinated	18.3	12.8	12.5	31.0	15.0
by a single person	12.5	7.7	12.5	27.6	—
through a reporting relationship	5.8	5.1	—	3.4	15.0

SOURCE: Griffin and McArthur 1997

Table 3.2 Amount of time devoted to IMC programmes for clients, by country

Amount of time (%)	USA (%)	UK (%)	New Zealand (%)	Australia (%)	India (%)
75% or more	25	11	21	5	—
50%–74%	25	32	11	—	—
25%–49%	25	25	25	26	23
10%–24%	15	30	37	37	46
10% or less	10	11	5	32	31

SOURCE: Kitchen and Schultz 1999

Table 3.3 Client budget devoted to IMC, by country

Country	% of budget
USA	52
UK	42
New Zealand	40
Australia	22
India	15

SOURCE: Kitchen and Schultz 1999

The study showed significant differences between the five countries surveyed. In response to a question about the amount of time devoted to IMC programmes for client firms, for those indicating more than 50 per cent of their time, the percentages were 50 per cent for the US, 43 per cent for the UK, 32 per cent for NZ, 5 per cent for Australia and 0 per cent for India. From the expenditure perspective, respondents were asked to identify the percentage of their overall budgets devoted to IMC activities, with similar results: US 52 per cent, UK 42 per cent, NZ 40 per cent, Australia 22 per cent and India 15 per cent.

According to Kitchen and Schultz (1999)

> whilst IMC is recognised as offering significant value and importance to clients and agencies alike, the fact that no clear proposal, method or acceptable disposition of measurement and evaluation has been offered and/or found widespread acceptance weakens conceptual application in a global sense.

Pickton and Hartley (1998) summarise the different dimensions of integration:

- Promotional mix integration: Synergy between the individual promotional elements.
- Promotional mix with marketing mix integration: Synergy between the elements of the marketing mix with those of the marketing communications mix, since each element of the marketing mix has a communications value of its own.
- Creative integration: Themes, concepts and messages across all marcom activities.
- Intra-organisation integration: All relevant internal departments, individuals and activities within the organisation.
- Inter-organisation integration: All external organisations involved in marketing communications on behalf of the organisation.
- Information and database systems: Databases are rapidly becoming the primary management tool that drives the organisation's business strategy.
- Integration of communication targeted towards internal and external audiences: A variety of audiences need to be considered within the context of IMC, both internal and external. They will represent a variety of potentially disparate groups.
- Integration of corporate and brand/product communications: Corporate communications is often considered as a separate entity and, often, has different people who have the responsibility as 'corporate guardians'. Organisations must recognise the strategic and tactical impact of corporate identity on their other marketing communications activities.
- Geographical integration: Integration cross both national and international boundaries.

The barriers to integration

Despite the undeniable advantages afforded by integration, an examination of the market situation suggests that relatively few companies have yet reached the stage of fully integrating their communications campaigns.

Various studies (Mitchell 1996; Yeshin 1996; Schultz and Kitchen 1997; Kitchen and Schultz 1999) have described the progressive adoption of the philosophy of IMC across many major and sophisticated client companies. None the less, many barriers continue to exist.

These studies indicate that, whilst much has been written on the topic, the subject remains largely misunderstood by many of those responsible for its implementation. This is clearly seen by the diversity of 'definitions' provided for IMC by the respondents.

'Co-ordinating all of the tools of promotion to ensure a consistent message.'

'Rolling out a single creative theme across all executions.'

'Using a single agency to deliver all requirements.'

Clearly there is considerable confusion as to the nature of IMC, with some respondents regarding it as a process; others perceiving it as a facility for 'one-stop' shopping, whilst for others it was a means whereby cohesion might be achieved between creative executions and strategies, even if provided by a multiplicity of suppliers.

Several factors can be identified as presenting barriers to the integration process, both of an internal and an external nature.

Internally, the lack of management understanding of the benefits of IMC, the short-term outlook adopted towards much of the planning process, the inherent nature of the 'political' battles between departments battling for supremacy and the fear of departmental budget reductions, with the consequence of staff reductions, together with the turnover of staff and the fear of losing expertise in specialist areas, were all identified as contributing to the general lack of adoption of IMC within companies. Externally, issues such as agency egos, the agency's fears of losing control, the lack of expertise in the individual areas of communications, the concern over reductions in the scale of the communications budget and the problems of the system of remuneration were further restrictions of the progress of integration.

Structurally, few companies are in a position to ensure integration. Often various functions compete with each other for the responsibility of briefing and implementation of the tools of marketing communications. These include the brand manager, the marketing manager, the marketing director, in a few instances, a communications director, together with a variety of 'specialist' heads of departments covering public relations, sales promotion and so on. Often these individuals represent 'vested' interests and are protective of their own sectors to the preclusion of an integrated approach. Most importantly, few companies have truly recognised the issue of responsibility for the custodianship of the brand and the negative implications of divisive communications messages. '. . . In practice, the situation is even worse. Company structures perpetuate this division, giving each "speciality" a different owner, based on technical skills required to execute, rather than conceptual skills required to plan' (Lannon 1994).

Undeniably, there are significant problems for the client in terms of commissioning and managing several different agencies, especially in the context of the reduction in the size of marketing departments. The temptation of the integrated one-stop concept is for many too great to resist. The attraction of using several different agencies is the possibility of selecting the best people in each field.

Moreover, there is a general lack of experienced people within the field of marketing communications who exhibit expertise in the variety of fields which make up the total communications process. The need for individuals with a 'broad perspective' and an understanding of the contribution which each of the marketing communications disciplines can provide is underlined by a study by Cleland (1995).

The study by Kitchen and Schultz (1999) identified a number of barriers, real or perceived, to achieving IMC:

- requires staff to be more generalist
- integrated agencies do not have talent across all marcom areas
- IMC means staff have to develop new skills
- IMC give a few individuals too much control
- client staff lack expertise to undertake IMC programmes
- client centralisation difficulties
- client organisational structures constrain IMC.

Lannon (1994) asserts that most company communications policies are rooted in an outmoded past, when competition was less intense and the retailer wasn't anything like the powerful force it is today.

- The discontinuities of the 1980s and into the 1990s have fractured and fragmented not only the conventional media scene, but also the corporate structures and cultures of a more stable past.
- Differing agendas of clients and agencies have eroded productive and trusting relationships between clients and their agencies.

Perhaps the most significant barrier to integration is the approach to communications budgeting. In most cases budgets are substantially determined on a 'historic' basis – considering what has been spent in the past – rather than against an evaluation of specific objectives. Often, individual departments are required to argue for budget tenure, or an increase if the situation demands it. In the majority of cases, budgets are considered on a line-by-line basis, rather than holistically.

Despite this, some market sectors are more advanced than others in the adoption of an integrated approach. Two, in particular, stand out as having made significant progress in the integration of their campaigns – the financial sector and retailers. In each case there has been a more widespread recognition of the benefits of integration. Campaigns by many of the commercial banks together with high street retailers such as Safeway underpin the advantages of integration. Certainly, most companies agree that the process of integration will increase apace, as much because of the need to deal with substantial communications budgets in a more positive manner, as from the drive towards global considerations where the desire for a common communications policy and the obvious financial benefits are of major importance.

The consumer and integrated marketing communication

At the heart of the debate is the undeniable need to ensure the clear and effective communication of brand messages to consumers and others. The process demands a change of focus from share and volume to a detailed understanding of the extent to which the manufacturer can satisfy the needs and wants of consumers. The essential focus has to be on customers, relationships, retention levels and satisfaction.

Several authors have suggested that IMC, as well as benefiting the manufacturers of products and services, also works for the consumer. David Iddiols (2000) suggests that IMC works on three levels for the consumer.

1 It provides short-cuts to understanding what a brand stands for.
2 It adds depth and amplification to a particular message or set of brand values.
3 It demonstrates professionalism on the part of the brand owner.

Iddiols identifies three potential mechanics for providing integration across activities:

1 The use of some form of mneumonic device, such as the red telephone used by Direct Line, or the tea folk by Tetley.
2 A consistent proposition reinforced across all communications activities, such as Tesco's 'Every little helps'.
3 Conveying a consistent set of brand values, as in the examples of Coca-Cola, Guinness or Levis.

Further, he identifies three ways in which integration represents a coherent approach as far as consumers are concerned:

1 Values-driven – Guinness, Coca-Cola, Halifax, Levis.
   Conveying a consistent set of values is the strongest approach.
2 Proposition driven – BT, Royal Mail.
   Consistently delivering a proposition is important when establishing or shifting a brand's identity. This is apparent, for example, with the Tesco line 'Every little helps' or L'Oréal's 'You're worth it'.
3 Mnemonic driven – Direct Line, Scottish Widows, Walker's Crisps; Orange.
   Employing a mnemonic device: the red phone for Direct Line and the orange colour for Orange mobile phones enabled both brands to establish an identity and gain a place in the public's consciousness.

A key contributor to the achievement of effective and integrated marketing communications is the appropriate use of market research – to gain greater insight and understanding of consumer behaviour, as well as to achieve an understanding of the contributions of the individual tools of marketing communications.

The difficulty, as many writers acknowledge, is changing the focus of market research from a disintegrated mode into a holistic practice. Archer and Hubbard (1996) suggest that the vast bulk of market research carried out continues to reflect the outdated theories and structures of disintegrated marketing communications. They argue that a more holistic approach needs to be adopted to measure the aggregate outcomes of all marketing activity whilst, at the same time, monitoring the specific actions which contribute to that outcome.

The clear advantages of a more holistic approach to research are that it is more comprehensive, embracing all activities and both short- and long-term objectives; it provides the used with greater flexibility; and it is more realistic in that it measures the end result of all activities on the target audience.

International dimensions of IMC

Recent works reflect the increasing growth and impact of global marketing communications. Grein and Gould (1996) have suggested that the concept of IMC should be broadened and renamed global integrated marketing communications. Since increasingly manufacturers seek to implement communications campaigns across national boundaries, IMC requires integration beyond that of disciplines to encompass global management of campaigns. The management of international brands demands that strategic marketing decisions are integrated and co-ordinated across all relevant global markets.

They offer a new definition to incorporate the international dimension:

> A system of active promotional management which strategically co-ordinates global communications in all of its component parts both horizontally in terms of countries and organisations and vertically in terms of promotion disciplines.

A study conducted by Grein and Ducoffe (1998) revealed the extent to which advertising agencies in particular are becoming global enterprises, reflecting the needs of their, increasingly global, clients. They indicated that clients wish to use more standardised campaigns, which are easier and cheaper to administer, have proven track records in some countries and result in a unified brand image and position around the world. For many companies, these benefits were considered sufficient to outweigh the less than perfect outcomes in some operating countries.

A direct consequence, confirmed by the study is a reduction in the extent of local creativity on international accounts. Once campaigns have been developed, usually in one country, they are implemented with relatively few variations on a world-wide basis.

However, as indicated by the work of Grein and Gould (1996), the level of inter-office communications made the task of effective integration difficult to achieve.

IMC – a summary

Using the analogy of Kitchen and Schultz (1999) who considered the state and acceptance of IMC against the product life cycle, it can be reasonably concluded that IMC is a marketing concept which is still emerging. As such, it might be positioned somewhere between its introduction and growth stage.

A point of issue is the difference between academic understanding of the concept and its role in the context of the practitioner. Kitchen argues that IMC, from the academic standpoint, is just over 10 years old, pointing to the work of Caywood et al. (1991) as the starting point for academic study.

In practice, the notion of IMC – albeit not the words – has been around for a considerably longer period. The author of this text was responsible for the establishment of a marketing communications agency, The Above and Below Group, in 1972, whose existence was founded on the provision of integrated communications activities to its clients.

However, several important dimensions of the practice of integrated marketing communications can be recognised:

- IMC is an increasingly importance facet of the practice of marketing communications.
- An increasing number of client companies and their agencies strive to achieve deeper and better integration of their marketing communications activities.
- It reflects both an underlying conceptual as well as a practical change in the way in which marketing communications programmes are developed and implemented.

- The desire to achieve global presence for their brands drives companies towards the achievement of consistent imagery for their brands, and coherent messages in their communications programmes.
- In contrast to the views of Cornellisen and Lock (2000), IMC is not a management fad.
- A continued inhibition to the development of IMC remains the internal structure of client companies and the defence of departmental independence.
- IMC will require the emergence of a new breed of communicators who can command a generalistic overview of all of the tools of marketing communications from a brand management perspective.
- Whilst it remains true that some brands can still achieve effective communications despite disintegration, 'all of the evidence points to the fact that it will take longer and runs the risk of confusing the very people you wish to sell to along the way' (Iddiols 2000).

The way forward is summarised in the paper prepared by the American Productivity and Quality Centre Study in 1998. The study identifies a series of key best practice issues which focus on the achievement of excellence in terms of brand development and communication. Those companies which most exemplified best practice:

- concentrate on a few key brands and provide streamlined and sophisticated brand support
- provide the leadership and support of senior management in developing and sustaining successful brands
- provide the consumer and customer-led informational infrastructure to achieve an all-round view of the brand network
- define their brands in terms of core values, promise and personality that provide guidance, meaning and focus for all brand-related activities
- view communication as an opportunity to project a unified image, not just of individual brands, but also of the company itself
- have started to move towards the financial measurement of brands and related communications activities.

Kitchen and Schultz (2000) argue for the imperative of integrated market communications and suggest that it will become the essence of competitive advantage:

- because of the four goals of business – to increase, accelerate, stabilise cash flows and build shareholder value;
- because firms with strong brand relationship have significant competitive advantages, including getting a higher 'share of wallet' and obtaining price premiums, both of which result in increased revenues;
- because of the long-term effects of building brand equity and shareholder value;
- because of their contribution to business goals.

Similarly, Reid (2003) argues that IMC is 'not only about doing better marketing communications, but having a broader link to establishing a basis for competitive advantage'.

Case study

IPA Effectiveness Awards 2002 SILVER AWARD

Agency: Leo Burnett

Authors: Gurdeep Puri and Janey Bullivant

Kellogg's Real Fruit Winders

Background

Kellogg's has been making cereals for over 100 years. By the 1990s, the search was on to find new growth opportunities beyond the breakfast table. There appeared to be an opportunity with kids. Kids' purchasing power was on the increase and kids' need for snacks seemed set to grow as meal occasions fragmented. Kellogg's had built a successful adult snack business while, with kids, it had done little more than give them their favourite cereals in another form. For Kellogg's the kid snack opportunity lay in leveraging its strength as a 'kid enjoyed/mum endorsed' brand that would provide a point of difference in the market.

Kellogg's struck upon a market that was dynamic in the States but non-existent in the UK – fruit roll-ups worth $400m. The 'fruit' sector would allow Kellogg's to exploit its nutritional heritage in a new area.

The challenge

The challenge was to successfully launch Real Fruit Winders as the first non-cereal product from Kellogg's, creating a platform for future growth in fruit snacks. Real Fruit Winders represent a significant departure from the tried and tested for Kellogg's. This was a new

proposition in a new sector. In business terms, Kellogg's was aiming for a value of £25m by the end of year two, against £15.9m for cereal and milk bars.

Campaign development

The search was on for groundbreaking ideas, not 30-second launch ads. We needed something that would fire the imagination of kids in an intensely crowded marketplace. Our key strategic breakthrough was to redefine the business we're in – entertainment not just taste satisfaction. We would only target kids in communications. We would position Real Fruit Winders as a genuinely cool snack that every 10-year-old in the playground wanted.

Target insight

In their struggle to make sense of the world and to assert themselves, kids have a deep desire for control. One of the things in their universe that satisfies this desire is interactivity. It was the common theme of the things kids were most into: Gameboy, CD-ROMS, the internet, email, SMS messaging. Interactivity put them in charge, allowed them to make the decisions and express themselves freely. By contrast, there was little true interactivity in the snack market. It was often just an add-on such as a website with some games rather than the glue which held the brand together.

Our big idea

This gave us our big idea – to take on some of these interactive properties and position Real Fruit Winders as an edible toy.

The creative brief

The creative brief for the launch campaign read as follows:

- Role for advertising: Put Real Fruit Winders into the hands and minds of kids.
- Target audience: 10–12-year-old kids (broader audience 6–12 years).
- Proposition: Interactive fruity fun that goes on and on.
- Tone of voice: Street smart and groundbreaker.

Our brief was for an integrated and inescapable campaign that explored where kids were hanging out and what they were doing.

The creative solution

The invention of a 'language' gave our idea its edge. The Chewchat gang would converse in Chewchat, an iconic symbol language, initially composed of 22 symbols. Chewchat would also be used to spread the word about the brand virally and to take kids' involvement with it to another level. Collectable stampers connected the language back to the food. These would allow kids to stamp their favourite messages into the food and chat with their mates in a new and exciting way.

Media strategy

Phase one: underground – pre-launch. The aim of phase one was to seed the Chewchat language among opinion leaders. A PR programme was created to direct them to www.chewchat.com and this included distributing chewchat.com stickers at concerts, in magazines and in cinemas. Chewchat clothing was created for key kids' celebrities and a giant Chewchat symbol appeared at Victoria station. On the website, kids could use the 'Chatterbox' to download symbols and email them to friends. This activity was all unbranded.

Phase two: kids' discovery – launch. The objective of phase two was to put kids 'in the know' about Chewchat, the gang and the product. Again, activity focused on reaching playground leaders who could be relied upon to spread the word, ensuring a trickledown effect on awareness and sales. A total of 300 000 branded chewchat.com stickers were inserted into kids' magazines. Terrified fruit and members of the Chewchat gang began to appear on the website.

Phase three: mass awareness and trial. Phase three aimed to get the Real Fruit Winders message across to a broader audience of kids and mums and build critical mass for the brand. TV broke at the beginning of June, with two ads. Prior to this, a series of fruit 'wind up' stunts occurred around the country. These included

blocking roads with giant strawberries and blackcurrant rain showering a stately home. On April Fool's Day, it was revealed that this was a hoax from Kellogg's in the *News of the World*.

The launch of Real Fruit Winders has been a resounding success. By the end of December 2001, it achieved the following:

- Real Fruit Winders has a market value of £21.5m RSP (retail selling price). (This is based on Kellogg's ex-factory volume.) This compares favourably with a figure of £14.4m for cereal and milk bars in its first year. It is already close to its second-year objective of £25m.
- It has outsold several key kids' brands in grocery. It has achieved penetration of 32 per cent in households with children. This is almost double the launch target of 17 per cent. It has attained strong repeat rates – 51 per cent first repeat and 65 per cent second repeat among households with children, against targets of 46 per cent and 65 per cent.
- It has built Kellogg's equity outside of cereal for the first time and created a platform for future growth in fruit snacks.

Real Fruit Winders achieved a remarkable 59 per cent prompted awareness among kids with only PR and web activity. This rose to 77 per cent after the first TV burst and peaked at 93 per cent in October. Not only did the TV create awareness, it was very efficient at doing so. It achieved an awareness index score of 30, versus the norm of 11 for kids' ads.

The strong status of Real Fruit Winders among kids has also increased the salience of the parent brand. For the first time, kids are happy to eat a Kellogg's product in the playground in front of their mates.

Econometric modelling has shown that the campaign accounted for 22 per cent total Real Fruit Winder sales. In fact, the actual contribution is higher than this, as the model does not include the effect of online advertising or the viral impact of PR. Even without these other media effects, the campaign has paid for itself and generated incremental revenue. TV advertising, the combined effect of TV and web and the combined effect of PR and web account for 13.9m roll sales, equivalent to £3.1m value sales.

The integrated multimedia campaign of PR, ambient media, web and TV was used to create a very different brand experience – one that went far beyond simple enjoyment of the product and gave kids the means to interact with Real Fruit Winders on a number of different levels on their own terms.

SOURCE: This case study is adapted from the paper presented at the IPA Effectiveness Awards. The full version is available at www.warc.com and is reproduced by kind permission of the Institute of Practitioners in Advertising and the World Advertising Research Center.

Questions

1 Identify the factors that are encouraging the move towards integrated marketing communications.
2 Discuss the benefits of IMC.
3 What are the forces that restrain companies from fully implementing an integrated approach, and how can these be overcome?
4 How does IMC impact upon the consumer?
5 Why is IMC especially important in the context of international advertising?

4 The importance of branding and the advertising contribution

Learning outcomes

This chapter should give you a solid grounding in:

- the role of the brand
- the advantages of branding
- the dimensions of branding
- brand valuation and brand equity
- the elements of branding strategy
- the roles of advertising
- the challenges facing brands.

The role of the brand

In many ways, an understanding of brands underpins much of what we attempt to achieve within the field of advertising since, of course, the brand is at the centre of all such activity. Ultimately, the key responsibility of brand managers is to sustain and develop the product or service for which they are responsible in such a way that it can respond positively to all eventualities. Stewardship of the brand is key since the profitability of these brands will determine the eventual survival of the companies which own them.

Branding itself is a comparatively recent process evolving from the essential need for manufacturers to distinguish their products and services from the commodity sectors within which they operate. There is considerable debate as to when the process of branding began. It has been suggested by Griffiths (1992) that Sunlight Soap was one of the first true brands. William Lever recognised that consumers were dissatisfied with the characteristics of unbranded soap products then available. They were inconsistent in quality, smelt unpleasant, offered no consistency in weight and had no packaging. Products were produced by a crude process of mixing tallow and the remnants of raw alkali in cauldrons into large bars which were to be sliced into lengths by the grocer. The Sunlight brand remedied these defects. In February 1884, Lever registered the brand name and in 1885 created a formula comprising a mix of coconut and cottonseed oil, resin and tallow. The formula remained unchanged for many years. By the 1890s the company was producing nearly 40 000 tons of soap. The process followed by Lever encapsulates some of the roles of branding.

As Adam Lury (1998) puts it:

The practice of branding, although over 2,000 years old, is primarily a 20th century phenomenon. Indeed, it is one of the most important phenomena of the century. It ranks with the decline of imperialism, the growth of feminism and the arrival of the atomic age.

Major brands represent significant commercial value to their owners. Table 4.1, representing the 20 largest UK brands, reveals that even the 11th is worth over £100 million.

The importance of brands (and their sustenance) is exemplified by the fact that many of the brands that occupy positions of leadership today were introduced as long as 100 or more years ago. Coca-Cola, Hovis and Heinz were all first launched in the late nineteenth century, whilst Cadbury's Dairy Milk is a product of the early 1900s. Only 9 of the top 50 UK brands have been launched since 1975.

The significance of developing a strong brand is underpinned by a study conducted by Buzzell and Gale (1987) which indicated that strong brands achieve significantly more profit than their weaker counterparts. Their research of some 2600

Table 4.1 Top 20 UK brands, 2003

Brand	Sales to June 2003 (£m)	% change 2002/03	Manufacturer
1 Walkers crisps	240–245	3.6	Walkers
2 Persil	210–215	2.7	Lever Fabergé
3 Diet Coke	195–200	20.3	Coca-Cola
4 Hovis bread	190–195	11.9	British Bakeries
5 Coke	185–190	0.3	Coca-Cola
6 Kingsmill bread	190–185	10.6	Allied Bakeries
7 Warburtons bread	160–165	10.9	Warburtons
8 Ariel	150–155	9.2	Procter & Gamble
9 Nescafé	135–140	−4.9	Nestlé
10 Pampers	110–115	6.1	Procter & Gamble
11 Muller	100–105	−0.8	Müller
12 PG Tips	95–100	−7.6	Unilever Bestfoods
13 Bold	90–95	3.7	Procter & Gamble
14 Heinz soup	90–95	9.3	Heinz
15 Colgate toothpaste	90–95	2.2	Colgate Palmolive
16 Kit Kat	90–95	−7.3	Nestlé
17 Comfort	85–90	7.3	Procter & Gamble
18 Cadbury Dairy Milk	85–90	20.9	Cadbury Trebor Bassett
19 Tetley tea	80–85	0.2	Tetley GB
20 Silver Spoon white sugar	80–85	4.6	White Spoon

SOURCE: *Marketing* 2003 (based on A.C. Nielsen figures)

business revealed that products with a market share of 40 per cent are capable of generating a return on investment three times greater than those with a share of 10 per cent. Moreover, according to the *Financial Times* (1997): 'Companies which base their businesses on brands have outperformed the stockmarket in the past 15 years.'

According to Brandt and Johnson (1997), the strongest brands are those that have developed unique, meaningful differences that set them apart in the mind of the consumer. These discriminators can be functional or emotional, or a combination of the two. Biel (1991), however, recognises that the functional/physical differences between brands have diminished significantly and it is, therefore, the emotional differences that operate as the real discriminators. 'The key to remember is that brand success and brand equity live in the heart and mind of individual consumers.'

Branding definitions

A brand is defined as a name, term, design, symbol or any other feature that identifies one seller's good or service as distinct from those of other sellers. A brand name may identify one item, a family of items or all items of that seller. Bennett (1998) and de Chernatony and McDonald (1992) argue that:

> A successful brand is an identifiable product, service, person or place, augmented in such a way that the buyer or user perceives relevant unique added values which match their needs most closely. Furthermore, its success results from being able to sustain these added values in the face of competition.

Clifton and Maughan (2000) define brands as 'a mixture of tangible and intangible attributes, symbolised in a trade mark, which if properly managed, creates influence and generates value.'

We will see in the next section how the process of branding creates a unique identity for a product or service in the mind of the consumer and, with it, a level of distinctiveness that sets it apart from all of its competitors. Reassurance derives from the fact that the consumer can readily identify the maker of the product and consider the company reputation and, importantly in the context of marketing communications activity, it provides the sense of focus for the promotion of the brand.

The advantages of branding

Branding offers important advantages to the manufacturer and consumer alike. By branding a product, the manufacturer can obtain legal protection for its composition and other features in order to avoid the problems of being copied by competitors. It creates a unique identity in the marketplace which assists in the process of attracting consumers who, over time, will establish patterns of loyalty to the product and, in turn, will enable the company to enhance its profitability. In many instances, branding enables manufacturers to charge a premium price for their products by associating a desirable image with it for which consumers may be encouraged to pay a higher price. It helps manufacturers to plan their inventories more efficiently and to ensure the rapid processing of orders. Finally, it helps in the process of segmenting markets by providing distinctive product offerings designed to satisfy the needs of smaller groups of consumers.

A critical element of the debate is an understanding of the fact that, for the most part, consumers are unable to differentiate between competing products. Sampson (1993) states that 'most markets have a convergence of brands. They look alike, taste the same and have the same formulation. Brand choice is no longer about the rational product attributes. It is, and increasingly will be, all about brand personality.' In most instances the core product offered by a manufacturer may be indistinguishable from that of his competitors. Indeed, given the nature of technology, the specific product advantages which one manufacturer has over his competitors will often be readily and rapidly duplicated by them.

In countless 'blind taste' tests, consumers are unable to identify the identity of the brands and, often, select as 'the best' a product that they decry once the brand names are revealed. The perennial example of Coca-Cola vs Pepsi (de Chernatony and McDonald 1992) serves to illustrate. In a direct comparison of the brands with the identities concealed, the preferences expressed were:

prefer Pepsi	51%
prefer Coke	44%
equal/can't say	5%

Once the brand identities were revealed, the following preferences were expressed:

prefer Pepsi	23%
prefer Coke	65%
equal/can't say	12%

During the 1980s, the Stella Artois 'Reassuringly expensive' campaign captured the spirit of the times and resulted in the brand becoming number one in the premium lager market. As Duckworth (1996) explains: 'Interestingly, the brand comes last in blind taste tests! Add the brand name and it becomes first choice – a clear demonstration of the power of brand potency overcoming the limitations of product reality.'

The consumer also benefits. Branding provides the potential buyer with a reassurance of quality. Consumers can reasonably expect that a branded product will, other things being equal, offer a consistency over time. They enhance the process of shopping since the consumer can rapidly identify products and services with which they are familiar. Finally, they enable consumers to identify new products in which they might be interested.

Advertising exists to communicate information about and promote brands. Brand owners, it might be concluded, are therefore promoting their own interests. Brands provide economic value for money, functionality in developing the requisite quality of products to solve consumer problems and psychological satisfaction. Thus, according to Ambler (1997), functional benefits are intrinsic to the brand and its component products, psychological benefits are in the minds of the consumer, and economic benefits relate to the exchange transaction. Brands are diverse, offering different benefits in different ways to different consumers at different times.

Economic benefits:

- Brands promote competition (consumers gain from brands competing strongly for their patronage).
- Brands improve consumer value (whether branding brings higher or lower prices, it still ensures value for money).
- Brands insure consumer risks (brands provide 'insurance' satisfaction to consumers in that they can rely on the brand's consistency and quality assurance standards).

- Brands provide consumers with choice (competition implies a variety from which consumers can make their individual selections to match their needs most closely).

Functional benefits:

- Brands require, and thus create, horizontal differentiation. Branding offers assortments of added values – both in terms of services and psychologically.
- Brands require, and thus create, vertical differentiation (consumers want goods of the best quality they can afford and they would like choices of different levels of quality to suit different needs and situations).
- Brands provide reliability and thus reassurance (the brand/consumer relationship provides reassurance that the manufacturer will look after the consumer's best interest since it is also in the interest of any manufacturer who intends to build the brand over the longer term).
- Branded products are fit for the use for which they are advertised (consumers do not buy brands for the sake of buying but to solve a problem or to meet a need).
- Manufacturer brands are more widely available.
- Brands subsidise consumer usage of media and sporting, arts and other events through advertising and sponsorship.

Psychological benefits:

- Brands simplify consumer problem solving and information processing.
- Brands help consumers feel good about their purchases.
- Brands have social benefits for consumers.

Similarly, Davis (2002) identifies a series of benefits of successful branding:

- Strong brands command higher price points and higher margins.
- Brand loyalty drives repeat business.
- Strong brands lend immediate credibility to new product introductions.
- Strong brands embody a clear, valued and sustainable point of difference.
- Strong brands offer internal focus and clarity within an organisation.
- Customers are more likely to be forgiving if a company makes a mistake when the customers have a consistently positive experience with the brand.
- Brand strength is a lever for attracting the best employees and keeping satisfied employees.

Brand building

King (1991), the co-founder of the concept of planning, argues:

> Most people in marketing would agree that success will depend on developing skills in brand building. That is, using all the company's particular assets to create unique entities that certain customers really want; entities which have a lasting personality, based on a special combination of physical, functional and psychological values; and which have a competitive advantage in at least one area of marketing.

Peter Doyle (1997), writing in *Excellence in Advertising*, suggests that to succeed, a brand must have sustainable, differential advantage. He argues that 'differential advantage' is the reason that consumers prefer the brand to those provided by competitors. 'Sustainable' is the provision of an advantage that is not easily copied by competitors. He further asserts that brands only become assets to the company if they possess both of these attributes. Brands which are negative (Lada, Hoover) achieve their profits as a result of property or distribution arrangements rather than as a result of differential advantage. Importantly, brands depreciate if they do not receive constant investment. However strong a brand may be, unless it continues to receive investment in the form of quality enhancement, service dimensions and brand image, then the brand will, inevitably, decline.

Successful brands are those which create a distinctive image or personality. By associating particular attributes with a brand, the product is differentiated in the minds of the consumers. Attributes may be real and tangible, such as product performance, value for money, or other aspects of quality, or emotional and intangible, providing status or being associated with trendiness.

A slightly different perspective is offered by Southgate (1994) who identifies branding as initially being purely a defensive device – to make it harder for the competition to steal one's products. In fact, branding is both defensive and aggressive. A strong brand will actively communicate with potential customers on a variety of levels providing them with all manner of reasons to buy a product or service.

Brandt and Johnson (1997) have suggested a set of guidelines for the building of successful brands and managing the brand within the technology sector, which they present as the six Cs:

1 customer focus, from the start of planning;
2 champions of the brand, companies really need to be leaders in their field;
3 capability, in terms of the organisation and the resources available;
4 common practices and policies;
5 consciousness of brand issues guiding everyday activities;
6 consistency of messages, processes, methods and experiences with the brand.

The same authors have provided a series of guidelines for brand building in the IT sector (Brandt and Johnson 1997). They argue that the marketing strategy must:

- develop a mission statement for the brand which is agreed throughout the company;
- outline and implement processes for assessing the market to keep up with competition, market trends and demand;
- develop a brand image that is unique, recognisable, controllable and won't date;
- develop an internet site that will allow e-business transactions;
- strive to develop plans and processes to position the company as a leader within its field;
- endeavour to keep all processes, messages and experiences with the brand constant.

Differentiation is the first step in creating a brand (Agres and Dubitsky 1996). Differentiation can take many forms – from the clear-cut, physical or functional to the emotional and 'distinguishing but irrelevant differentiators such as the colour of the packaging or 'stripes in toothpaste' (Barnard et al. 1998). The overriding objective is to gain competitive advantage by building sustained customer loyalty towards products or services, meeting the demands of closely defined markets precisely.

Developing and managing a brand's image is a fundamental part of a firm's marketing programme (Roth 1992). Many practitioners have long advocated the use of a clearly defined brand image as a major basis for achieving market success. A well-communicated brand image enables consumers to identify the needs satisfied by the brand (Park and MacInnis 1986) and thereby differentiate the brand from its competitors (Reynolds et al. 1984). In fact, developing a brand image strategy has been prescribed as the first and most vital step in positioning a brand in the marketplace (Park and MacInnis 1986). As a long-term strategy, a consistent and effective brand image helps build and sustain brand equity. Moreover, brand images can provide a foundation for extending existing brands.

Selame (1997) argues that a brand builds itself on three important dimensions:

- Trust: Consumers have faith in a particular product or service because they believe they are able to rely on the brand.
- Perception: Consumer choice lies with specific brands because of the perceived value of the product or service that is communicated.
- Promise: The brand name provides reassurance to the consumer and represents an expected level of quality.

Agres and Dubitsky (1996) suggest that the building of successful brands occurs through a succession of consumer perceptions:

- Differentiation: The perceived distinctiveness of the brand. This is particularly important for new brands that seek success since established brands can rely on past perceptions.
- Relevance: The personal appropriateness of the brand. High differentiation with low relevance puts the onus on the marketer to know how the brand is relevant to consumers' lives. Mature brands in the early stages of decline may have high relevance but low differentiation.
- Esteem: How highly customers regard the brand.
- Knowledge: Understanding what the brand stands for. It is the end result of the communications process.

Louro and Cunha (2001) establish four brand management paradigms, which reflect the differential degree of consumer and firm orientation in defining brand meaning and value. They identify two dimensions that differentiate the brand management paradigms, namely, the brand centrality dimension and the customer centrality dimension. The brand centrality dimension revolves around tactical orientation, where brands are conceptualised and managed as tactical instruments, together with brand orientation in which the processes of the organisations revolve around the creation, development and protection of the brand identity. The customer centrality dimension provides two approaches – unilateral and multilateral. The former approach concentrates on the organisation's internal capabilities in creating value to the brand. The latter approach is based on a dialogue between the customer and the organisation.

Chris Cleaver (2000) sets out some basic principles in order to guide brand development. In his view, great brands:

- have breadth, depth, power, substance, personality, rational justification, emotional appeal and are memorable;
- have a declared point of view on the world;
- have a well-understood value set and philosophy;
- have clear propositions;
- enable choice;
- exert influence on their markets – even to the point that they can establish the category elements such as packaging shape, colour etc., which enable choice;
- have a strong vision of their own future;
- allow for premium pricing;
- are a valuable intangible asset;
- enrich the experience of using the product in an intangible way.

The dimensions of branding

The dimensions of a brand are depicted in Figure 4.1.

At the centre of the branding task is the core product. This may or may not be different from the products of competitive manufacturers. Indeed, increasingly, it is unlikely that there will be any significant difference at a level which the consumer can discriminate. What makes it different are the perceptual and tangible values which are associated with the core product and are depicted above. Any or each of these important dimensions can be used by a company to distinguish its product or service from those of its competitors.

As King (cited in Haigh 1996) states

A product is something that is made in a factory; a brand is something that is bought by a consumer. A product can be copied by a competitor; a brand is unique. A product can be quickly outdated; a successful brand, properly managed, can be timeless.

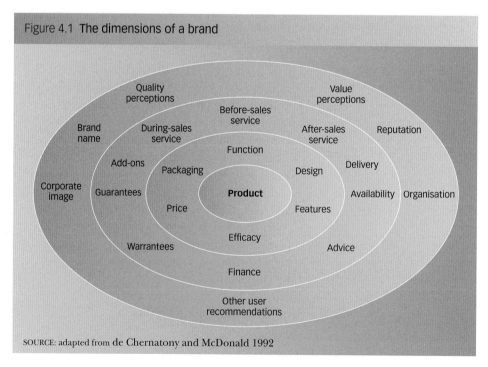

Figure 4.1 **The dimensions of a brand**

SOURCE: adapted from de Chernatony and McDonald 1992

To the consumer a product is something that satisfies needs or provides a solution to a particular problem. It is important to recognise that these needs are just as likely to be emotional as they are to be functional and economic. The capacity of a product to fulfil the consumer's needs and desires are what, over time, builds its value.

It must be remembered, of course, that not all of the listed dimensions apply to all products and services. In some instances, the tangible aspects of the proposition will be more important; in others, differentiation may be achieved as a result of the quality of the services – before, during and after-sales, guarantees, etc. – which are provided; in yet other instances, it will be the brand image and identity which will assume the greatest level of importance.

McEnally and de Chernatony (1999) identify six stages of branding:

- Stage 1 Unbranded goods: Producers at this stage where producers make little or no effort to distinguish their brand from those of competitors, the result being that the consumer is unable to differentiate between products from different manufacturers.
- Stage 2 Brand as reference: This stage develops from competition in the marketplace when producers find it necessary to differentiate themselves from their competitors, achieved primarily through the identification of physical product attributes. The consumer begins to use brand names as a device to aid decision making.
- Stage 3 Brand as a personality: With many products being essentially similar, physical attributes are no longer sufficient to enable the differentiation of brands. Producers move on to a process of differentiation through giving their brands personalities. In turn, this enables the consumer to develop a more personal relationship with the brand.
- Stage 4 Brand as icon: The brand is now 'owned' by the consumer. The customer now has an extensive knowledge of the brand and this information is used to create their self-identity.
- Stage 5 Brand as a company: This is where the company and the brand are as one. The brand must be viewed in the same fashion by all stakeholders.
- Stage 6 Brand as policy: At this stage, the brand is established through an alignment with the company policy. The company establishes an identity against such dimensions as fair trade, animal testing, human rights, the protection of the environment, etc. Consumers who purchase the brand equally support the causes the company is promoting. Again, by making this commitment, consumers may be said to own the brand. A pioneering example of this is Anita Roddick's Bodyshop, one of the first successful 'ethical' brands.

The brand name

Branding and packaging are the overt and tangible aspects of a product, and serve to distinguish a manufacturer's product from that of his or her competitors'. In the crowded retail environment, it is these aspects of the product which assist the brand in standing out from the crowd.

Most brand names are made up of letters and numbers, and in some instances, may also include an additional graphic design that is unique to that product. In most instances, manufacturers will register these logo designs to ensure legal

protection of their mark, and to avoid the risks of 'passing off'. Bass beer, with its red triangle logo, became the first registered trade mark in the UK.

The source of brand names is interesting:

- BMW derives from Bayerische Motorenwerke.
- Aktien Gesellschaft für Anilinfabrikation becomes AGFA.
- The first two letters from Durability and Reliability and one from Excellence spell out DUREX.
- Joel Cheek named his instant coffee after the first hotel that agreed to try the product – Maxwell House.
- Adi Dassler created Adidas from his own name.
- The founder of IKEA, Ingvar Kampryd, combined his initials with those of his home town and the farm where he was born.
- Nivea is taken from the Latin for snow white – *nivis*.
- Hovis derives from *hominis vis* (the strength of man).

Other names derive from 'functional' aspects of the product. The detergent, Daz, gets its name from a derivation of the product benefit – 'dazzle'.

It is important to remember that in most cases a brand name will only be protected within the specific category of trading and, thus, other manufacturers will, potentially, be free to use the same name in another category. In the 1960s Granada, which had registered the name in the context of television production, TV rental and associated areas, attempted to preclude its use by Ford in the automotive industry. The legal case decided in favour of Ford and they were able to retain the use of the name for a range of cars.

There are many examples of brand names that have lost their ability to be unique to a particular brand owner and, instead, have become category descriptors. These include:

Cellophane
Thermos
Sellotape
Linoleum
Corn Flakes.

Oakenfull and Gelb (1996) have summarised the most common causes of what they term 'genericism':

- A company develops a unique product but does not develop a generic description beyond the brand name. The company may lose its trade mark rights if it doesn't create a generic name for others to use when they begin to sell competing versions.
- Consumers use the company's brand name to identify a certain type of product because the brand name is shorter and easier to use than the product's category.
- A particular brand achieves such a high share of market that the brand becomes the category.

Brand image

If, for one moment, we strip away the brand marks of Levis, Kellogg's, Cadbury's, Mercedes, and Johnson & Johnson, to name but a few, we are left with commodity products shorn of all of the brand values normally are associated with those names. All the investment made by those companies over many years into the creation of image values through the use of marketing communications is lost. It is the function of marketing communications to establish a series of defined images and values in the minds of consumers that are instantly recalled on exposure to the brand name. Consumers buy brands. Thus, the loyalty that the brand identity can create in the marketplace is fundamental to the ability of a company to offset competitive activities

The brand values are equally important to the company in terms of its longer-term extension of activities. Many brand names have positive values associated with them which extend beyond the particular product with which the name is identified. These intangible values can be used by the company to extend its portfolio into other areas. Within the soap and detergent markets, two brands stand out as examples of the positive values of branding. Fairy and Persil have both been used as brands which have taken their owners into extended categories by the association of related new products with the positive values built up around those names.

However, the brand image is made up, as we have seen, of a combination of function and emotional value. Sampson (1993) states:

> It is not sufficient to measure the rational attributes of a brand alone. That gives only a partial picture. The emotional attributes must also be measured to obtain the complete picture. And it is the emotional benefits that usually account for brand choice, to a larger degree than rational ones.

Similarly, Patterson (1999) says 'Brand image has a number of inherent characteristics or dimensions which include, among others, brand personality and user image'.

According to Belen del Rio et al. (2001) brand image can be defined as perceptions about a brand as reflected by the cluster of associations that consumers connect to the brand name in memory, whilst Ambler (1997) suggests that 'Brands offer a guarantee to their user that it is reliable, carries out its functions efficiently and meets consumer expectations associated with the brand name'.

The brand personality

One of the key issues in contemporary marketing communications is that of the brand personality, described by the advertising agency, J. Walter Thompson (n.d.) as 'The total impression created in the consumer's mind by a brand and all its associations, functional and non-functional'.

Since, as we have seen, few consumers can differentiate between products on purely functional grounds, other dimensions become important to their task of product selection. Over time, brands – substantially as a result of the investment made through marketing communications – develop a 'personality' of their own. They are seen by consumers to be 'young' or 'old', 'fashionable and trendy' or 'boring and out of date'. Inevitably this is a major reflection of the contribution made by the tools of advertising and promotion which serve to invest brands with a particular image.

As Sampson (1993) states 'Consumers should feel that by buying a particular brand they are buying into their desired way of life or derived personality, that the brand is a symbol of external gratification.'

An important distinction is that the difference between brand image and identity is that identity is sent whilst image is received/perceived (Meenaghan 1995).

De Chernatony and McDonald's (1998) illustration of the relationship between brand identity and image is shown in Figure 4.2.

Cowley (1999) suggests that brand personality as one aspect of brand image. He comments that many practitioners fail to separate the concepts as they are so closely related. Patterson (1999) has developed a model to depict the elements of the brand image, as shown in Figure 4.3.

Figure 4.3 suggests that brand image is a composite term that encompasses brand personality as something that derives from the process of interpretation of the various images that are perceived by the consumer.

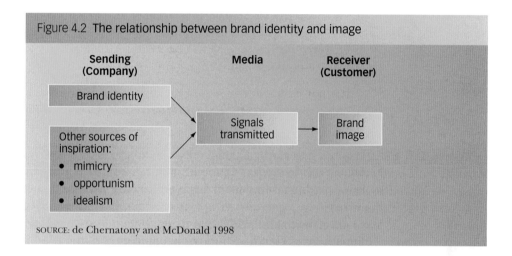

Figure 4.2 The relationship between brand identity and image

SOURCE: de Chernatony and McDonald 1998

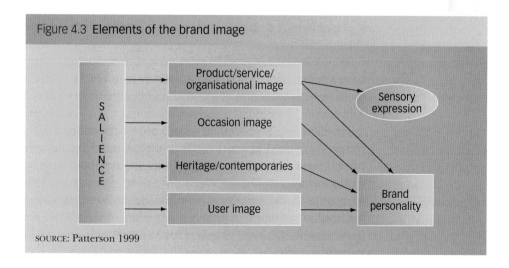

Figure 4.3 Elements of the brand image

SOURCE: Patterson 1999

As Upshaw (1995) puts it:

> Brand personalities are, almost by definition, more emotion than logic driven because they reflect the feelings people have about brands, and the way those brands transmit feelings back to them . . . The personality must be just as strategic in the sense that it must appear to be a natural continuation of what the positioning represents, only from a tonal, emotional, more human perspective.

Siracuse (1998) identifies the importance of the brand personality and suggests that the brand should be treated as a 'live organism that evolves and adapts depending on the environment and the audience, whilst still maintaining his or her identity'. This confirms that brand personalities are not fixed but, with the appropriate use of the tools of marketing, can be changed over time.

Jennifer Aaker (1997) defines brand personality as 'the set of human characteristics associated with the brand'. She argues that the symbolic use of brands is possible because consumers often imbue brands with human personality traits. Various authors including Fournier (1995) and Plummer (1985) have suggested different dimensions of brand personality, including dimensionalising brands as celebrities or the relationship between the brands and oneself.

Jennifer Aaker (1997) defines five brand personality dimensions which might be perceived by consumers:

- sincerity
- excitement
- competence
- sophistication
- ruggedness.

Brand personality can significantly affect brand equity. Keller (2000) states that, in strong brands, equity is not only tied to the actual quality of the product or service but to various other intangible factors including user imagery, usage imagery and brand personality. It is suggested that it is these qualitative dimensions which create brand value.

Brand protection

If the positive values associated with a brand are sufficiently strong, it will enable the owner to overcome major problems with product quality. Both in the UK and elsewhere, major brands have suffered from such things as contaminants which have required the company to withdraw temporarily from the market. Early in 1990, some bottles of Perrier were found to contain benzene. Despite its dominant presence, and the obvious implications of its decision, the company determined to remove all stocks of its products from the shelves of supermarkets and other outlets. Advertising and public relations were used to inform the public of the action the company had taken and, following exhaustive research to eliminate the problem, the brand was relaunched. The fact that Perrier was able to regain much of its market share is a testament both to the strength of the brand name and to the positive approach taken by the company in dealing with the issue.

In the United States, Tylenol suffered similar problems when a dangerous chemical was introduced into a few containers on retailers' shelves. A similar response in dealing with the problem enabled the brand to return to the market with many of the values associated with the name intact.

The issue of contamination is one which, unfortunately (in terms of what it says about society), marketers need to address. In the recent past, several products have been removed from supermarket shelves following the disclosure of tampering with the product contents, sometimes with disastrous consequences for the purchaser. The issue of brand protection is an important one, in both a domestic and an international context, and we will return to the topic throughout this chapter.

Other uses of the brand

Brand names and identities may be used in a variety of other ways. Once a brand has built up a high level of recognition amongst consumers, it may be sold or leased to other manufacturers to provide them with an immediate entrée into another sector of the market.

Mars demonstrated the power of their brands with their move into the ice cream market. Despite the fact that the company had no prior representation within the sector, the values associated with the names of Mars, Bounty and others gave an immediate identity to the ice cream products that bore these logos. This issue will be considered in more detail in the section on 'Brand extensions and brand stretch'.

Brand valuation

Although the value of branding has been long understood, it was brought into sharp focus with the valuation of the brand name of Guinness on the balance sheet during the Distillers takeover battle.

The practice has been followed by others ensuring that the valuation of brands is given close consideration, since the value placed upon them may exceed the value of the tangible assets of a company. The brand has increasingly come to represent an important financial asset to the company that owns it. Rupert Murdoch, for example, capitalised the value of some of his newspaper titles. In 1985, Reckitt & Colman capitalised Airwick, followed two years later by GrandMet who capitalised Pillsbury following its acquisition. In 1988 the real debate commenced when Rank Hovis McDougall identified more than 50 existing brands on its balance sheet with a combined value of £678 million. Thus, the goodwill represented by these brands was worth almost 60 per cent of the total value of the company. In 1996, Grand Metropolitans' brands were estimated to be worth £2.8 billion – 70 per cent of total shareholder funds. Similarly, companies, including Cadbury Schweppes, United Biscuits, Pernod Ricard and others, used this device to inflate the size of their balance sheets, in part, as a device to avoid takeover or to make the process more expensive.

In *The Economist* of 14 November 1996, the value of the physical components of McDonald's – which Interbrand named as the world's leading brand of that year, overtaking Coca-Cola for the first time – were calculated as being worth $17 billion. At that time, the value of the company on the New York Stock Exchange stood at $33 billion. The difference of $16 billion can be attributed to the brand value.

Tom Blackett (1996) reports on the impact this has had. Whereas in 1981 net tangible assets represented some 82 per cent of the amount bid for a company, by 1987 this had fallen to just 30 per cent. Solid evidence that companies were no longer being sought for their tangible assets but rather their intangible assets – their brands.

In 1988, Phillip Morris the American food and tobacco company bought Kraft for $12.9 billion, approximately four times the worth of the company's tangible assets. In the same year, Nestlé bought Rowntree for $4.5 billion – more than five times Rowntree's book value. In 1997, the then head of Procter & Gamble, Paul Polman stated that: 'the difference between the value of P&G's assets as measured by accountants – $12bn – and its market value of $55bn is mostly accounted for by the value of its brands'.

However, outside of the UK, regulations have made the process of the valuation of intangible assetts somewhat less attractive. In both Germany and Italy, such intangibles cannot be included within the balance sheet. In the USA, they are treated as 'goodwill' and must be amortised over a period of not greater than 40 years.

Philip Barnard (1993) of the Research International Group identified the monetary value of strong brands using PIMS data. His results are shown in Table 4.2.

Table 4.2 Monetary value of strong brands	
Rank	**Return on investment (%)**
Market leaders	
Dominator	34
Marginal leader	26
Competitors	
No. 2	21
No. 3	16
Followers	12
SOURCE: PIMS Data	

In the USA, a study examined the yearly stock returns against the yearly brand equity changes of 34 American companies between 1989 and 1992. They compared the return on investment of these companies and found that the yearly stock return correlated positively against the return on investment (ROI). The more established companies with higher brand equity achieved a yearly stock return of approx. 30 per cent whilst those with lower brand equity experienced a stock return of approx. -10 per cent.

Feldwick (1998) depicts the components of brand value as shown in Figure 4.4.

A number of companies including The Henley Centre, Interbrand and the accountants, Arthur Andersen, have developed methodologies for valuing brands. Their intent is to isolate and quantify the contribution that the brand is making and to use that as the basis for valuation, either as an earnings multiplier or a discounted cash flow.

Brand valuation techniques have been developed, according to Birkin (1995b) for a number of purposes:

- to help in merger and acquisition negotiations
- to establish royalties for brand licensing

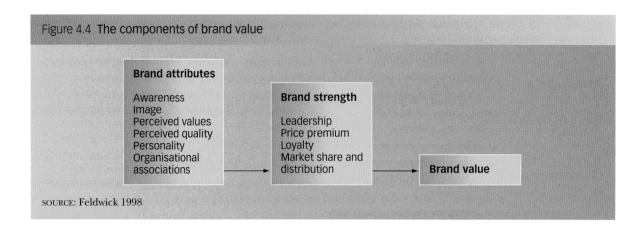

Figure 4.4 **The components of brand value**

SOURCE: Feldwick 1998

- to develop systems for the internal licensing of brands within a group of companies
- to support bank lending decisions
- to quantify damages in trade mark disputes
- to develop brand strategies to allocate marketing resources between brands
- to establish brand measurement systems.

Birkin suggests that the process of brand valuation extends beyond the mere need to determine the current value of the brand. It is designed to answer a number of wider questions such as:

- What factors most contribute to or inhibit brand value?
- What factors are likely to increase or reduce brand value in the short term?
- What effect will the existing brand strategy have on brand cash in the short and long term?
- What can be done to maximise the value of individual brands and the overall brand portfolio?
- What effect will planned brand extensions have on brand value?
- What effect will competitor strategies have on brand value?
- Are existing procedures sufficient to monitor and understand brand value?

According to Alexander Biel (1990), strong brands have recognised properties contributing to asset value: trade leverage, extendibility, endurance and high prices and margins for their owners; time-saving qualities, dependability, and intrinsic as well as functional benefits for their consumers. Analysis of a large sample of US and European businesses shows a clear relationship between relative advertising expenditure relative to sales and three key indicators – market share, perceived quality and return on investment.

The same author indicates that the profitability of companies selling branded products grew at twice the rate of the commodity dominated firms over a five-year period from 1988 to 1993 (Biel 1997).

Despite this ongoing debate, comparatively few companies use a brand valuation approach. A survey, conducted by a specialist business research agency Business Marketing Services (cited in High 1994) on behalf of Public Dialogue, amongst 120 senior marketing decision makers identified that only 23 per cent of the sample used brand valuations as a measure of marketing performance, and only 12 per cent included brand valuations in their balance sheets. Despite this, some 67 per cent of respondents believed that brand valuations would become more important over the next few years.

Brand equity

There are two contrasting views of brand equity. On the one hand there is the financial perspective, as described above. Here, the brand is viewed as an asset that can be used to deliver incremental cash flows. Thus, brands with greater brand equity can be expected to result in greater market shares, opportunities for premium pricing, reduced promotional costs, and increased trade leverage. The alternative is the marketing view of brand equity. In essence this views the situation from the perspective of the consumer. Those brands that have achieved substantial equity are those which can sustain a platform of premium quality, differentiated clear imagery and a uniqueness of proposition.

Brand equity needs to be defined with some degree of precision. One of the difficulties is that the term 'brand equity' is used in a variety of different ways and, therefore, means different things to different people. Feldwick (1997) identified three alternative uses of the term:

1 The brand's value or valuation, either at sale or on the balance sheet. Since this will vary as a result of changes in market conditions it can only be a one-off measure.
2 The brand strength, which is a measure of the relative value of consumer demand for the brand.
3 Brand description, meaning a collection of brand image data and attributes.

He argues that 'brands need to be managed with a view to their long-term market position, respecting their contract and relationship with the consumer'.

Several definitions serve to illustrate the difficulties:

- O'Shaughnessy (1995), for example, defines brand equity as 'the set of assets such as name awareness, loyal customers, perceived quality and other associations that are linked to a brand'.
- Mark Uncles (1995) suggests that Interbrand's checklist of characteristics is a good starting-point – market leadership, market growth, advertising and promotional support, internationality, technological stability, brand trend and brand protection. The company has developed a specific approach to brand valuation which consists of both objective and subjective evaluations of the brand performance, and currently is one of the most widely used devices for assessments of a brand's strengths and weaknesses.
- Aaker (1996a) defines brand equity as a set of assets (or liabilities) linked to a brand's name and symbol that adds to (or subtracts from) the value provided by a product or service to a firm and/or that firm's customers.
- Farr (1996) argues that the ideas, associations and images that people have of a brand determine the demand side of the brand equity equation. They define the brand's worth to the consumer. If a brand's standing in strong enough in the consumers' minds to warrant them paying the price asked for it, then the brand will have converted its brand equity into sales equity.

- Brand equity is defined by Cooper (1998) as 'the description and assessment of the appeal of a brand to all the target audience who interact with it'.

However, it is recognised that there is a series of important components of brand equity:

- **Perceived quality** is a measure of brand equity which, in research, has been show to correlate closely to sales performance, price sensitivity and company value.
- **Salience** indicates the proportion of people who have sufficient knowledge of a brand to rate its equity.
- **Association** of a brand with positive images is vital to brand success.
- **Customer satisfaction** is self-explanatory.
- **Customer loyalty** is an indicator of market success and of the strength of a brand.
- **Likelihood to purchase** on next occasion is also key.
- **Willingness to recommend** reflects the level of regard for a brand.
- **Price premium potential** is the extent to which a brand is able to command a premium over the price of other products in its category.

David Aaker (1996b) sets out a series of measures designed to identify the value of brand equity which he describes as the 'brand equity ten'.

> Loyalty measures:
>   Price premium
>   Satisfaction/loyalty
> Perceived quality/leadership measures:
>   Perceived quality
>   Leadership
> Associations/differentiation measures:
>   Perceived value
>   Brand personality
>   Organisational associations
> Awareness measures:
>   Brand awareness
> Market behaviour measures:
>   Market share
>   Price and distribution indices.

These brand functions are important in the context of determining the value that the brand possesses for the company which manufactures or provides them. A positive brand image offers the company significant competitive advantages:

- The brand can command higher margins and/or volume, more inelastic consumer response to price increases, increased marketing communication effectiveness and greater trade co-operation.
- Brand loyalty means less vulnerability to competitive marketing actions and to marketing crises (e.g., Coca-Cola).
- Possible licensing opportunities, that is, the ability to introduce new products as brand extensions.

In a paper published in 1997, Alan Cooper and Paul Simmons have added an important new dimension to the consideration of brand equity. They suggest that brand equity consists of three elements:

- Brand description: This means the image and associations that a brand has. This includes its distinctiveness, its quality and the esteem in which it is held.
- Brand strength: This is the prominence and relative dominance of that brand, which is based on levels of awareness, penetration, loyalty and personal involvement on the part of consumers.
- Brand future: This is the additional new dimension proposed by Cooper and Simmons (1997). This not only reflects the brand's ability to thrive despite future changes in legislation, technology, retail structure and consumer patterns, but it also indicates its growth potential.

Strong brand equity can be a powerful defence against competitive incursions and new product launches. It provides the brand owner with a springboard for brand extension, not just brand growth. There are various methods designed to measure brand equity, although there is no common standard. David Aaker, for example, believes that the important dimensions are loyalty, perceived quality, market leadership, associations, awareness, differentiation and market behaviour; Interbrand base their assessment on an analysis of the brand together with financial and market analysis; Millward Brown monitor presence, relevance to consumer needs, product performance, competitive advantage and bonding.

If a company cannot keep firm control over the integrity of the brand equity, they may alienate the already cynical consumer with a stream of brand extensions and relaunches with no real selling point (Birkin 1995a).

Schuring and Veerman (1998) argue that high levels of brand equity are a direct result of the possession of a strong brand name. It brings with it a number of significant competitive advantages:

1 Reductions in marketing costs are more likely to occur, due to the level of consumer brand awareness and the loyalty which already exists.
2 The brand has a greater degree of trade leverage when bargaining with distributors since customers have expectations of where to find the brand.
3 The brand has the power to charge a higher price because customers have a higher perceived quality of their product.
4 Companies are able to launch brand extensions more easily based on pre-established credibility.

The elements of branding strategy

We can discriminate between a series of very different branding strategies adopted by companies.

MANUFACTURER BRANDING
   MULTI-PRODUCT BRANDING
   MULTI- BRANDING
   COMBINATION BRANDING
MIXED BRANDING
PRIVATE BRANDING
GENERIC BRANDING

Manufacturer branding

A key decision to be taken by all manufacturers is the branding policy towards the products which they introduce to the market.

In some instances, the manufacturer will choose to adopt a **multi-product branding** strategy. Here, the manufacturer uses the strength of the parent name to communicate a series of common values which 'endorse' all of the products which bear that name. Undeniably, there has been a gradual shift from product branding to umbrella branding – 3M, Heinz – or dual branding – Nestlé and Kit Kat – or co-branding arrangements with complementary businesses IBM Personal Computers and Intel chips, Diet Coke and NutraSweet. Coca-Cola often uses its name to endorse other products than its primary brand. However, it is not always consistent in its approach. When the company attempted to introduce its bottled water product into the UK market, it used the brand name 'Dasani' without any reference to the parent company. However, in other markets, its water brands carry the Coca-Cola endorsement. In Turkey its water brand is 'Turkuaz' with the Coca-Cola logo clearly evident on the label. Similarly, in India, their brand is 'Kinley' which is underpinned with the statement 'A product of the Coca-Cola Company'.

Sony and JVC, for example, have both established strong reputations within various sectors of the consumer electronics market. Whether the consumer is intending to purchase a television, a CD player or a video recorder, the endorsement and reputation of the parent company singles out the appropriate product as being worthy of consideration. The name of Kellogg's is synonymous with breakfast cereals and Colgate with dental care. Similarly, the standing of the Automobile Association lends credibility to its offering of car and other insurance facilities.

Usually, although not always, manufacturers restrict such activity to directly related markets, since it can be reasonably expected that the products all have common values and attributes. If, for example, the consumer perceives the names of Black & Decker or Bosch as being those of manufacturers of quality power tools, those names can reasonably be expected to carry a similar weight within the broader do-it-yourself markets. Both of those companies have moved into gardening tools, for example.

In many instances, manufacturers maintain several brand names which are used to endorse separate market categories, but the names are kept distinct from each other to avoid the creation of confusion in the minds of the consumer. For example, Gillette maintains its name for the personal care market, but uses the Braun brand for the related electrical appliances market, embracing dry shaving, electric hairdryers, toothbrushes and so on. The company is now part of Procter & Gamble.

Manufacturers who choose to keep the parent name subservient to the end user adopt a strategy called **multi-branding**. For example, the name of Procter & Gamble is little known by consumers, although the brands they produce are all major players in their respective markets. P&G is the manufacturer of a variety of brands including, amongst many others, Ariel and Daz in the detergents market, Olay, Vicks, Pampers and Pantene.

In some instances, the benefit of a multi-branding approach is that it enables the parent manufacturer to have competing products within the same sector of the market. This principle can be seen from the example of Procter & Gamble, as well as Kraft, Jacobs and Suchard (itself a subsidiary of Philip Morris), which maintains several brands of coffee including Maxwell House, Kenco, Mellow Birds, Jacobs and

Gevalia, which variously compete with each other in different sectors of the market. This same principle is adopted in the retail environment where, for example, Dixons has the same parent as Currys, as does The Link, and PC World. Each chain presents a different image and identity to the potential consumer allowing for more appropriate targeting of differing consumer needs.

An important dimension of multi-branding which deserves mention, is the use of third-party endorsement. Increasingly, manufacturers are recognising the importance of names which may be only distantly related to the product category as underpins to the product message. When P&G acquired the name of Olay, it was used to establish major credibility in the cosmetics sector. By the same token, the addition of names such as Chanel and other couture houses has added a believable dimension to products which might otherwise be indistinguishable from their competitors.

In certain instances, typified by the approach of Nestlé, a **combination branding** approach is taken, whereby the parent name is used to endorse some products – directly or indirectly – but where others are left to stand alone. In the instant coffee market, for example, the brand name for their main product is a derivation of that of the parent company, Nescafé; Gold Blend, their premium quality product, is endorsed with the Nescafé logo; in the cereals, confectionery and other markets, the Nestlé symbol is used alongside that of brand names such as Cheerios and Kit Kat; whilst in the bottled water market, the name of Perrier is left to stand alone.

Mixed branding

Several manufacturers adopt a mixed branding approach to distinguish between products which they manufacture under their own brand names and identities and those which are supplied to retailers and packaged with their retail identities.

Although several manufacturers refuse to supply product to private label – including Kellogg's – and indeed have used advertising to communicate that fact; others such as Allied Bakeries, United Biscuits, Dalgety and Britvic, to name just a few, simultaneously sell products under their own brand names to compete on-shelf with retail competitors which they have supplied.

Private branding

Within the retail sector, operators are being increasingly concerned with issues relating to branding. For many years they were content to use their operating name on the products which were manufactured on their behalf and sold by them. Consumers derived their perceptions from the support activity which surrounded the store identity. Retailers, such as Sainsbury's, Safeway and others, developed distinctive positionings within the marketplace in relation to quality, value for money and other dimensions, and the products which bore their logos reflected those values.

In recent years, however, the retailers have seen the need to elevate their own (private label) products to brand status. Sainsbury's introduced Novon – a range of washing powder and liquid products – and Gio – a competitor in the soft drinks market – with their own distinct identities. More recently, Tesco have announced a brand called 'Unbelievable' to compete with Unilever's 'I can't believe it's not butter'. Safeway maintains a comprehensive range of products with distinctive packaging and identities to compete with manufacturer's brands. We will consider other aspects of 'look-alike' brands later in this chapter.

Generic branding

In some instances, manufacturers or retailers have been content to sell their products under generic or 'no brand' identities. Often this stance is taken to emphasise dimensions such as value for money. The notion of the 'white pack' originated in France to provide consumers with a range of 'no frills' products at considerable discounts against conventional brands. The approach has been met with mixed success, although there is little doubt that many of those consumers who purchased the products packaged in this way expressed satisfaction and rated them highly in terms of value for money.

Onkvisit and Shaw (1989) provide an overview of the possible branding scenarios as shown in Table 4.3.

Table 4.3 Overview of possible branding scenarios

	Advantages	Disadvantages
No brand	Lower production cost Lower marketing cost Lower legal cost Flexible quality and quantity control	Severe price competition Lack of market identity
Branding	Better identification and awareness Better chance for product differentiation Possible brand loyalty Possible premium pricing	Higher production costs Higher marketing costs Higher legal costs
Private brand	Better margins for dealers Possibility for larger market share No promotional problems	Severe price competition Lack of market identity
Manufacturer's brand	Better price due to more price Brand inelasticity Retention of brand loyalty Better bargaining power Better control of distribution	Difficulties for small manufacturers with unknown brand or identity Brand promotion required
Single brand (in one market)	Marketing efficiency More focused marketing permitted Brand confusion eliminated Advantage for product with good reputation	Market homogeneity assumed Existing brand image damaged when trading up or down Limited shelf space
Multiple brands (in one market)	Market segmented for varying needs Competitive spirit created Negative connotation of existing brand avoided More retail shelf space gained Existing brand image not damaged Possible halo effect	Higher marketing costs Higher inventory costs Loss of economies of scale
Local brands	Meaningful names Local identification Avoidance of taxation on international brand Diffused image Quick market penetration as a result of acquiring local brand Variations of quality and quantity across markets allowed	Higher marketing costs Higher inventory costs Loss of economies of scale

	Advantages	**Disadvantages**
World-wide brands	Maximum marketing efficiency Reduction of advertising costs Elimination of brand confusion Advantage of culture-free product Advantage of prestigious product Easy identification and recognition for international travellers Uniform world-wide image	Market homogeneity assumed Problems with grey and black market Possibility of negative associations Quality and quantity consistency required Local opposition and resentment Legal complications

SOURCE: Onkvisit and Shaw 1989

Brands and consumer perceptions

Brands continue to maintain a considerable price premium, despite expressions to the contrary. It was anticipated that pressure on disposable income during the recession would force consumers progressively towards cheaper products.

A study published in 1997 (Buck and Passingham 1997) reinforces previous findings that manufacturers' brands continued to attract significant market share despite their higher prices. From an analysis of the AGB Superpanel data, involving over 10 000 respondents, the study found that consumers were continuing to pay a significant premium for branded products, as Table 4.4 shows.

Despite a significant increase in the power and competitive position of the main supermarket chains, the leading premium brands in most packaged grocery categories have proved remarkably successful in maintaining both their position and sales (Buck 2000).

Using Taylor Nelson Sofres data from the AGB Superpanel, Buck demonstrates that recent years have seen both an increase in the strength of the major supermarkets, and a corresponding increase in the share held by supermarket brands. In 1975, the top four supermarket groups held 22 per cent of the packaged groceries market. By 2000, the figure for the top four approached 70 per cent. Similarly,

Table 4.4 Price comparison of brand types, groceries

	Average prices in Tesco stores		
Category	**Premium brand**	**Tesco own-label**	**Tesco value label**
Instant coffee	185p	139p	57p
Baked beans	33p	23p	10p
Cola	65p	30p	13p
Washing up liquid	136p	82p	20p
Muesli	202p	156p	132p
Yoghurt	184p	161p	95p
Average index	100	69	35

SOURCE: AGB Superpanel

supermarket (private label) sales have shown a similar pattern. Their sales more than doubled to around 40 per cent of the market in the late 1990s. There remain very few packaged grocery categories into which private label has not made deep inroads.

It would be reasonable to conclude that the era of the premium brand is at an end. However, using the same data source, Buck analysed sales in 26 leading grocery categories. Of these, 19 of the brand leaders in 1975 remained leaders in 1999. Half of these had succeeded in increasing their market share despite the growth of private label across all of these categories.

The subsequent analysis of the data, using a comparison between levels of advertising expenditure and brand share, led Buck to conclude that there was a direct correlation between them.

> The general conclusion here is that there is a significant positive relationship between relative advertising/sales ratios and brand growth, and that there is also evidence of a causal link, since the high ratios preceded growth in market share.

Both studies support the belief that, although many consumers suggest that there is little to choose between branded and private label products, the perceptual values continue to be vitally important. The consequence is that major brands continue to hold significant shares of their market sectors.

A parallel study by Campbell and Dove (1998) came to a similar conclusion. They demonstrated that 'wherever the advertising trend is down . . . sales of own label outstrips the growth of brands; and that increased levels of advertising are depressing own-label sales'.

We have already seen that consumer perceptions are influenced by a variety of internal and external factors. However, we have also seen that advertising and other marketing communications plays an important role in influencing those perceptions and the creation of images which go far beyond the normal functional factors which may affect the choice of a brand. There are, of course, some areas where these added values may indeed be real and tangible. Virgin Airlines have stressed several key dimensions of their service delivery in their business class advertising – additional seating room, provision of in air 'lounge facilities', choice of movies, car pick-up at destination, and so on. In most cases, however, especially with low-involvement products – which include the vast majority of fast-moving consumer goods – it is the combination of the physical attributes of a brand together with the values created by marketing communications, which are important to the creation of perceptual values.

According to Blackston (1995) we can distinguish between the objective and subjective meanings of the brand:

- **The objective brand** consists of the set of associations, images and personality characteristics around which there is, more or less, a consensus. They represent the common or 'public' meaning of the brand in that people who know about the brand, more or less, share the same perceptions. Nike, for example, means personal achievement, going for it, not accepting limitations; Apple means mould-breaking, being anti-establishment.

- **The subjective brand** represents what the brand thinks of me. In addition to knowing whether I like the brand, respect the brand, trust the brand it encompasses how the brand feels about me: does it like me? Does it respect me? Does it think it is smarter than me? Does it condescend to me?

In an article in *Campaign* magazine Max Burt (1994), then at Abbott Mead Vickers BBDO, argued that it is the brand personality which is the key to sparking consumer desire. We need to consider the impressions of the brand that are left, beyond the actual message being communicated. He cites, amongst others, Tango, John Smith's, Courage Best and Fosters as examples where the personality created by advertising is a major contributor to the consumer's propensity to purchase the brand. In many instances, the consumer may be more concerned with the intangible benefits delivered by the brand than the physical performance of the product itself. The reputation and lifestyle factors involved in, say, owning a Rolex watch or wearing a Pierre Cardin suit, have little to do with direct performance comparisons with other watch brands or other clothing manufacturers (Burt 1994).

A study conducted in the United States throws light on the nature of brand leadership. The study asked a large sample of people to identify the brand leader in a number of product categories. In most instances, the consumer's view of the brand leader coincided with the facts, but in some they didn't. What consumers were talking about is 'leader brands', in terms not so much of size but of leadership characteristics. Similar conclusions derive from a study conducted by DMB&B (Ford-Hutchinson 1996). In a comprehensive survey conducted in some 16 different countries, consumers were asked to identify which brand or company was the leader in one of 56 different markets.

In categories as diverse as cereals, instant coffee, tea bags, toothpaste and lager, the majority of consumers were able to clearly identify a 'leader'. In some markets, the dominant brand was clearly identified, elsewhere, the position, even for the most significant brand is less clear-cut, as Table 4.5 shows.

Table 4.5 Consumer-identified brand leaders

Examples of strength of overall leadership in different categories

1st leader	%	2nd leader	%
Kodak	78	Fuji	6
AA	58	RAC	17
Heinz	51	Batchelors	13
Whiskas	44	Kit-e-Kat	25
Nescafé	42	Kenco	12
Tetley	40	PG Tips	22
Michelin	28	Dunlop	17
IBM	24	Apple	12
Carlsberg	19	Heineken	17

SOURCE: DMB&B Data 1992/95

Qualitative work associated with this study indicates that most consumers prefer to purchase a product which they consider to be the brand leader, even if they do not always do so.

Hankinson and Cowking (1995) illustrate the way in which a brand attempts to build a relationship with their target consumer, as shown in Figure 4.5.

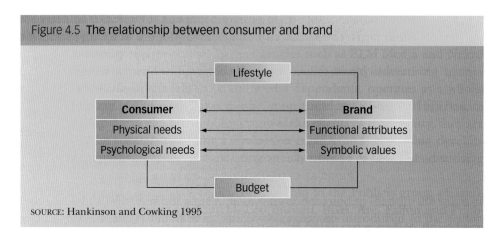

Figure 4.5 The relationship between consumer and brand

SOURCE: Hankinson and Cowking 1995

The relationship revolves around the ability of the brand to satisfy the consumer's physical and psychological needs by offering the right mix of functional attributes and symbolic values. This is reinforced by Uncles (1995) who argues that more and more emphasis is being given to the creation of brands with powerful symbolic features and personalities.

De Chernatony and Dall'Olmo Riley (1998) suggest that the brand purchased does not have to reflect the personality of the consumer, rather the personality that they wish to project. 'It is a powerful aspect of branding since there is evidence showing that when consumers choose between competing brands they do so according to the brands' personality and the personality they wish to project.' Moreover, 'Buyers often use brands as non-verbal clues to communicate with their peer groups'.

An important dimension of consumer perception is trust in the brand, which can only be built over time. A study published in the Reader's Digest in 2004, based on a sample of 10 000, asked consumers to identify which brands they most trusted and identified these brands in a wide variety of markets. The survey confirms that consumers' faith in brands remains solid and provides the benchmark by which they choose products. Some examples given in Table 4.6 illustrate this point.

Identifying and building brand values

The process of identifying and building brand values is interactive with that of marketing communications. As we have already seen, the environment of the message which is communicated to the potential consumer is equally important as the nature of the message itself.

Tony O'Reilly, Chairman and CEO of Heinz commenting on brand values in the BBC programme 'Branded' (O'Reilly 1996) said:

> the process of creating a popular brand is a long slow process and trying to take brand share away from a dominant brand is a very long and expensive process. In modern retailing, not to be attempted . . . that's why brands are so valuable.

Table 4.6 Consumers' most trusted brands

Category	Company	Share of vote (%)	I use the brand (%)
Airline	British Airways	41	69
Bank	Lloyds TSB	17	87
Breakfast cereal	Kellogg's	59	94
Car	Ford	18	71
Coffee	Nescafé	54	89
Credit card	Barclaycard	18	85
Food retailer	Tesco	33	96
Hair care	Head and Shoulders	12	96
Household cleaner	Cif	23	93
Internet company	AOL	16	75
Margarine	Flora	27	93
Mobile phone	Nokia	57	85
PC	Dell	27	45
Petfood	Pedigree Chum	22	53
Skincare	Olay	18	83
Soap powder	Persil	35	93
Soft drink	Coca-Cola	22	93
Tea	PG Tips	24	88
Toothpaste	Colgate	50	92

SOURCE: *Reader's Digest* 2004

What values and expectations consumers have of a brand must be clearly identified before work on advertising can commence. The whole issue of positioning is one of great significance, but it starts with the consumer, rather than ending with them. The key to a proper understanding of the brand in the context of consumer expectations is market research. However, it is not possible to simply ask consumers what they think about a brand, or at least, not if the purpose it to identify the underlying characteristics which make up a brand image. In response to a question 'what do you think *xxx* product is like', answers are likely to be physical and tangible; for example, it tastes good, it lasts a long time, and so on.

One approach to the problem is to use a series of projective techniques, which enable the respondent to use a series of other stimuli in order to make some form of meaningful response. The simplest technique is to ask consumers (and potential consumers) to identify the sorts of people that they think use the product. This will allow us to access the important dimension of user image. If consumers identify brand users as being substantially different from themselves, it is apparent that there is some form of dissonance between them and the offering. Where consumers identify more closely with the product being investigated, they will tend to describe users as 'people like me'. Identifying such dissonance may be a key dimension in rectifying an image problem, especially if the 'real' product delivery is felt to be appropriate to users who perceive themselves in a different light. An example will illustrate the point:

In the UK, users of cruises tend to be identified by non-users as being older (perhaps retired), fairly sedentary (what is there to do on board a ship), wealthy (cruising is expensive), and so on. However, if exposed to the product many non-users tend to find it attractive and rapidly become converts. Accordingly, companies like Royal Caribbean and P&O have sought to associate other values with their proposition to make it more appropriate to a younger audience.

An alternative research approach is to ask respondents to imagine what sort of personality the product would have if it were human. Some interesting results emerge which are directly applicable to the identification of brand personality. A product might be seen as young or old, male or female, passive or aggressive, wealthy or impoverished. All of these, and many other dimensions, will provide important clues as to how the individual perceives a product or service. Other techniques involve getting the consumers, often in a group discussion format, to use visual elements – providing them with illustrations taken from newspapers and magazines – and inviting them to prepare a collage of their impressions of a product or service. The key factor is that we identify what it is that makes a product 'behave' in the way that it does, in order that we can then determine whether the image is close to the one desired, or whether we will have to take action to change it.

An important way of depicting brand positionings is with the use of a perceptual map. Using the techniques outlined above, it is possible to build up a typology for all of the brands which compete in a market category. By identifying the key considerations in the minds of the consumer (to isolate the important dimensions of a desired brand) and placing them on a matrix we can illustrate the relative positions of the competing brands within a market. The resultant 'map' relates all brands to each other, and allows for exploration of their relationship to an idealised position to occupy. Sometimes, it will be necessary to build up multiple maps, where the market is segmented and where the desired values of each segment differ from those of the others.

Simon Clemmow (1997) has developed a framework to assist in identifying the status of the brand. The model, shown in Figure 4.6, stresses the importance of considering both the market and consumer context in which the brand is seen.

The task of enhancing brand equity is a long-term consideration and, importantly, should be a primary responsibility of the chief executive of the company. In many cases, the management and development of the brand has traditionally fallen to the marketing director who apportions the annual marketing budget. Often, this is a reflection of a short-term orientation designed to achieve immediate sales goals. Moreover, the tenure of the marketing director may, of itself, militate against taking a longer-term perspective. A survey conducted by Data Management Services in 1996 indicated that some 53 per cent of top marketing personnel in the leading 3,000 advertisers has changed their job within an 18-month period. In contrast, the average tenure of CEOs in leading PLCs is 8 years, whilst the average length of service with the company is 25 years. Clearly, it is the CEO who is best placed to take on the custodianship of the brand and its equity.

A strong brand is salient – it pops into the mind automatically when one thinks of the product class. It stands out sharply in the mind of the consumer. Various stud-

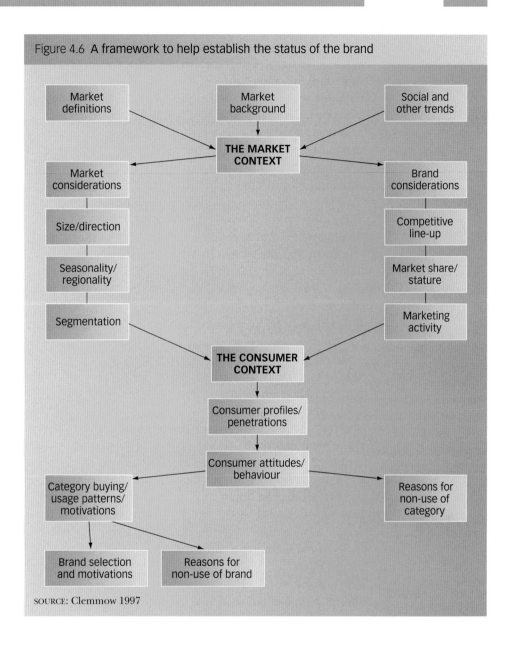

Figure 4.6 A framework to help establish the status of the brand

SOURCE: Clemmow 1997

ies have shown that strong brands are distinguished from their weaker counterparts in that they have shape and substance, form and content. Visual images and words or phrases linked to them frequently come to mind when people think of strong brands, for example, 'Nike – just do it' and the 'tick'; 'Coca-Cola is the real thing'. Similarly, a strong brand is held in high regard. Just because a brand is well known does not qualify it as a strong brand unless it is well thought of.

Altering brand imagery

It is important to understand that brand images are not fixed. They can be amended or changed completely by the appropriate use of marketing communications tools. Lucozade was historically a product associated with recovery from illness; today, marketing communications has transformed it into a product that is seen by its young audience as a trendy and refreshing beverage. Tango has been converted from a brand that was, at best, a conventional carbonated soft drink into something uniquely associated with 'orangeness' and an 'icon' brand to its target consumers. Hellmann's have transformed salad dressing from an old fashioned to a modern and desirable accompaniment to food.

In the 1980s, the Levis brand had become associated with a corporation rather than an aspiration. The ads were highly product-oriented and featured middle-aged men engaged in middle-aged pursuits. They were perceived as being 'uncool' and communicated none of the values that the desired target market desired. The 'Laundrette' and subsequent commercials created by BBH changed all of that. Today, the brand is cool, carries 'street cred' and is aspirational. It is now the dominant brand with a significant share of the overall jeans market.

Cooper and Simmons (1997) have suggested that there is a new dimension in marketing based on the altering of values. They identify a series of companies as 'entrepreneurial revolutionaries'. These are companies and brands which set out to take risks in order to take control of a market by changing the equilibrium of values that, hitherto, have been regarded as important. They create fresh motivations in the consumer agenda based on the premise that consumers have, or can be changed. Their objective is to change the 'rules of the game'. By the actions they take, they are able to reposition the current sector leaders and undermine their brand equities. Such brands would include Virgin, First Direct, Daewoo, Microsoft and PlayStation. They contrast the performance of First Direct with other banks; First Direct has not only had a dramatic impact within the consumer banking sector but has also altered the choice criteria by which consumers assess competitive offerings. Successful growing brands take share from competitors but do not alter their fundamental perceptions. It is the former which fulfils their definition of 'revolutionaries'.

One of the most important contemporary transformations of a brand is that carried out on Skoda, where advertising has altered perceptions from a car which few people would consider to one which is now seen as good value for money and which many would be happy to own and drive.

Brand extensions and brand stretch

The area of brand extension – also referred to as 'brand stretch' – has been the subject of considerable debate in recent years. In essence, the process is one of transference in which the name of an existing successful brand is attached to additional products. The process provides the company with a series of potential benefits:

1 The existing awareness of the brand name tends to encourage consumer confidence in a new brand.
2 The same impact may be apparent within the retail environment, providing the opportunity to secure rapid distribution for a new product.
3 It may offer economies of scale in marketing communications, since several related brands can be grouped under a single umbrella campaign.

Brand elasticity is a concept that is undeniably gaining in importance. According to David Howard (1997), there are two key reasons for this phenomenon. First, the existence of brand elasticity is beginning to upset accepted areas of influence in terms of the demarcation of the particular market sectors in which a brand can operate. Second, the potential for brand extensions and new brand opportunities has focused corporate minds on the company brand as a new type of financial asset. Brand elasticity is a measure of the ability of the individual brand to establish itself in new areas. To achieve this, the brand has to be able to exploit its values and reputation so as to create market confidence in a product or service new to the brand.

The issue of brand stretch is an increasingly important one (Ford-Hutchinson 1998). As more and more manufacturers are seeking to maximise their return on investment and their return on their assets, so brand stretching into new markets is seen as a possible route. We have seen supermarkets move into banking and insurance, confectionery brands into ice cream and Virgin into everything from records to airlines to financial services.

Doyle (1997) identifies three areas in which brand extension may be considered:

1 if the brands appeal to the same target market segment and have the same differential advantage,
2 if the differential advantage is the same, but the target market is different,
3 if a company has different differential advantages, it may find synergy of the brands appeal to the same target market.

It has been argued that it is tempting to think that a basis for measuring brand stretch is to determine how close a potential new product is to the established core competencies. Over time, elasticity would be generated by the accumulation of brand extensions, each one related to the previous one. However, this notion of 'proximity' does little to explain the failure on the part of the financial sector, especially the banks, to develop into other financial services. Moreover, it does equally little to explain the success of brands that cover a divergent range of sectors. Virgin appears to have developed brand credibility across a range of apparently unrelated products and services. Similarly, retailers have encompassed not only a wide variety of product offerings, but are increasingly moving into other areas such as credit cards, holidays, insurance, petrol and banking services.

However, it is argued by many, amongst others Trout and Rivkin (1996), that brand extensions represent a dangerous trap for unwary companies. The existing awareness of the brand name may create an unrealistic confidence in the new product, with the result that the research process is either compressed or ignored. And, of course, if the new product fails, it may have a detrimental impact on the reputation of the original brand.

It is interesting to compare the Levi Strauss extension into Levis tailored classic suits which failed because the brand held the wrong connotations. It is vitally important to consider what the brand means in consumer terms. When Levis introduced a range of men's suits in the mid-1980s it failed to recognise that the new range was inconsistent with its original position of young, defiant, anti-establishment and individualist. The brand extension failed. Despite this failure, Levis have more recently achieved success with Dockers – possibly because of its disassociation from the Levis name.

The publishing group, Emap, is to extend its FHM men's magazine brand into the fashion and boardgame markets with a number of new products. The magazine has signed a merchandising deal with the watchmaker Zeon to produce a range of FHM collection branded watches. The products will be promoted via the magazine and on the FHM website. Distribution deals have been signed with Debenhams and H. Samuel. Emap has also signed a deal with boardgame manufacturer Upstarts to produce three FHM-branded drink-themed games. FHM already has a number of brand extensions including a credit card, together with books, calendars and posters.

In the same way, The Easy Group, fronted by Stelios Haji-Ioannou, is moving into the men's grooming market with the lauch of a range of products called Easy4Men. The company which already owns EasyJet, Easycar and EasyInternet Café brands is emulating the Virgin model of expanding the brand into consumer products.

Many other companies are considering the potential value of brand extensions. P&G's leading skincare brand Oil of Olay has moved successfully into the cosmetics market with its make-up range being priced to match mid-market brands such as Boots No.7 and Revlon. Other examples of include Virgin Cola, Persil dishwashing liquid and Sony mobile phones.

Research conducted by Bates Dorland identified a series of products which are associated with cigarettes in the minds of consumers. Amongst these was coffee. As a result, a concept was developed for Benson & Hedges to launch B&H Bistros which sell B&H quality blend coffee. The concept is on test in Malaysia, where a ban on cigarette advertising is already in place. After two years, the decline in the B&H share of the cigarette market has been arrested and the advertising for the B&H Bistro is amongst the most frequently recalled TV ads. Elsewhere, other tobacco companies have developed similar propositions. Tabacalera, the Spanish tobacco group has licensed the brand name of its leading cigarette – Ducados – to enable a chain of Ducados cafes to be developed. The same company launched a record label – Duca2 – whose media activities have been censured by the Spanish regulatory authorities as constituting an illegal promotion of the Ducados cigarette brand.

Several cigarette brands have diversified into branded clothing. Marlboro and Camel are two brands which have been so extended. In the UK the Camel clothing and boots range has created a turnover of some £14 million, and £363 million worldwide. Similarly, the Marlboro Classics clothing range is now the second-largest mail order brand in the USA, whilst over 1000 Marlboro Classic retail outlets have been opened throughout Europe and Asia. Other brand extensions include John Player Whisky in Japan, Stuyvesant travel agency in Germany, and Kent travel agency in Malyasia.

Virgin has broken all of the rules of branding. Instead of asking the question: 'What business are we in?' Virgin has pursued a policy of which business can the brand go for. Will Whitehorn, Corporate Affairs Director for the Virgin Group, supports the diversity of Virgin branding: 'The UK's definition of a brand has remained far too narrow, too closely associated with a product rather than a set of corporate values.' The Virgin brand does not represent a faceless company. It embodies the positive aspirational associations and charisma derived from Richard Branson, according to Phillippe Mihailovic (1995). He argues that the order of brand extensions made by Virgin has been significant to its overall success. Importantly, the brand symbolised music first, then entertainment megastores, then an airline, publishing business, a radio station and so on. The consumer accepted each of these extensions and, far from diluting its core properties or weakening its existing associations, the Virgin brand appears to be adding core properties with each new launch. The brand conveys fun, excitement, quality, value for money, innovation and more. Virgin is no longer considered a market specific brand – Virgin has become the *people's* brand.

Mihailovic suggests that a house brand can stretch across various product markets and categories, although some house brands have less limitations than others. Coca-Cola, for example, has the problem of a house brand name derived from a specific product such that other products carrying the name would be unlikely to benefit from it. Neither Fanta nor Sprite was launched as a Coca-Cola brand extension as a result of the corporate decision not to jeopardise the core brand. Most house brands have a much broader positioning – Revlon, Sony, Yves Saint Laurent, etc. Colin Macrae (1995) argues that the Japanese have shown the business world that perceived quality is highest when the brand carries a corporate guarantee.

However, brand extensions are no panacea. The *Journal of Consumer Marketing* reported that Nielsen conducted a large-scale study of 115 new products launched in the UK and USA. Share was measured two years after launch. Brand extensions performed significantly less well overall than those product launches with new brand names. In general, the most positive brand extensions have occurred when there is a high brand concept consistency together with high product feature similarity.

Doyle (1989) defines brand extensions as 'the use of a brand name successfully established for one segment or channel to enter another one in the same broad market'. Kotler et al. (2001) uses the following definition: 'a brand extension strategy is any effort to extend a successful brand name to launch new or modified products or lines'.

Line extensions are described by Reddy et al. (1994) as extensions which involve the use of an established name for a new offering in the same product category. Examples are Ariel Colour, Diet Coke and Mercedes S Class. The distinction between brand and line extensions is substantially dependent on the definition of the category in which the company currently operates. It is important therefore to consider the category definition carefully.

Tauber (1988) reviews a sample of 276 brand extensions to evaluate the different ways of extending brands and concluded that there are seven types of brand extensions.

1 Same product in a different form, e.g. Mars bars extended into Mars Ice Cream.
2 Distinctive taste, ingredient or component which is used to create a new item in a new category, e.g. Kraft extended the distinctive taste of Philadelphia into Philadelphia cream cheese salad dressing.
3 Companion product, e.g. Sony batteries in a Sony TV remote control.
4 Same customer franchise, e.g. the AA extended its offering into books, insurance policies, etc.
5 Expertise – where a brand extends its original brand into areas which exploit its special knowledge or experience, e.g. Canon extending its expertise in optics into photocopiers.
6 Unique benefit, attribute or feature owned by the brand, e.g. Dyson.
7 Designer image or status – using status or expertise in one area to underpin offerings in another, e.g. Saab make aircraft as well as cars.

According to Tauber (1988): 'with the huge costs and risks involved in launching new brands, many of which fail, extending an existing brand is seen by many as a more cost effective and lower risk method of launching new products'.

However, there is limited evidence to suggest that brand extensions have a higher rate of success than new brands. One study, in a single firm, found that of products launched six years earlier, 30 per cent of the new brands survived compared with 50 per cent of brand extensions. Brand extensions carry the risk of diluting what the brand name means to consumers, especially in the case of extensions that are inconsistent with the brand image or fail to meet consumer expectations in other ways (Roedder et al. 1998). Farquar et al. (1992) suggest that any extension away from the product category may risk diluting the strength of the parent brand in its original product category. For example, when Cadbury extended into mainstream products such as mashed potato, dried milk, soup and beverages its association with chocolate and confectionery was weakened.

A company can successfully leverage a brands' existing equity in new categories. Rangaswamy et al. 1993 showed that highly valued brands (i.e. those with high brand equity) tend to extend more readily. Whilst good brand extensions can have a positive effect on the core brand, poor brand extensions can dilute a brand.

Hart and Murphy (1998) suggest some basic brand extension guidelines:

- The key to determining the direct that brand extension should take is to identify product categories where the functional values of the parent brand are just as important to the consumer as they are in the original category.
- Consumer research is then required to determine the extent to which consumers will find the existing brands' participation in the target categories plausible and persuasive.
- Brand extension should only be undertaken when the parent brand is healthy, stable and, ideally, growing. Not when it is already on the decline.
- Brand extension should only be contemplated when serves to reinforce the existing vision, mission and values. The extension initiative should in no way change the positioning of the parent brand. If it is likely to do this, then the company should consider some form of new brand or sub-brand.

Aaker and Keller (1990) and Sunde and Brodie (1993) concluded that the consumer's acceptance of a brand extension increases if:

1 the parent brand is perceived as being of high quality;
2 there is a perception of 'fit' between the new product category and the brand;
3 the category is seen as 'difficult to make', i.e. some expertise is needed.

The issue of fit has also been explored by Park et al. (1991) whose research supported the notion that, in evaluating brand extensions, consumers consider the perceived degree of fit between the extension and the brand. Thus, fit relates to product feature similarity (attributes, usage occasions, etc.) and brand concept consistency (i.e. unique abstract meanings). The most positive evaluations of brand extensions are given to those that have a high degree of fit on both dimensions.

McWilliam (1993) suggests that the difficult of determining fit is one of identifying which conceptual dimension of the brand is appropriate to base the extension on. The study found that despite large amounts of consumer research, these key dimensions may not be discovered until after the launch and subsequent failure of the extension.

In contrast, however, Broniarczyk and Alba (1994) found that brand-specific associations that are relevant to a new category can be leveraged even if the new category is quite different from the original. Thus, opportunities to exploit a brand's value are not limited to similar extension categories.

Kapferer (1992) argues that 'The greatest handicap to the brand is its vertical extension by which brands try to cover every level of quality and status.'

There are a series of benefits and advantages that derive from brand extensions:

- instant recognition of new brand;
- significantly cheaper to associate new product with a known and trusted brand name than to develop a totally new one;
- enables company to enter a product category more easily;
- desirable aspects of brand image transferred to new brand;
- considerable cost savings, especially in media, since audience are already familiar with the brand and its values;
- opportunity to secure rapid distribution since retailers are aware of brand features;
- potentially increases the brand's customer base and binds them more closely to the brand;
- provides an opportunity to change the brand image in a positive way by associating new attributes to the brand name.

Effects of brand extensions

Positive
1. Creates awareness: existing familiarity with brand aids entry.
2. Brand and quality associations: the credibility of the extension will be judged by consumers on the strength of the original product.
3. Encourages trial purchase: a reassuring/recognised name.
4. Strengthens the brand.
5. Adds interest to the core brand (Mars dark and light bars, limited edition mint Kit Kat).
6. Updates the image/extends the appeal to a wider audience.
7. Gives greater presence in the market (Nestlé in instant coffee market).

Negative
1. Neutral effect: the product simply falls in line with what is expected of the brand.
2. Negative associations.
3. Name confusion.

Kapferer (1992) illustrates the ability of brands to extend, as shown in Figure 4.7.

Brand extension is a common strategy to launch products into new markets within all types of industry. Often, when a company wishes to move into a related market it may use the premise of extending the parent brand name. Estimates of the extent of this practice vary considerably. Morrin (1999) adapts Ourusoff (1997) and suggests that as many as eight out of ten new products are introduced as an extension of the parent brand. Jevons and Gabbott (2000) estimates that over 95 per cent of all new products introduced in the USA every year are brand extensions.

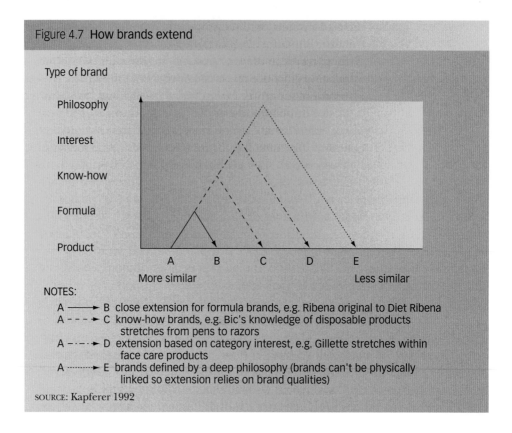

Figure 4.7 How brands extend

Type of brand

Philosophy

Interest

Know-how

Formula

Product

A   B   C   D   E

More similar   Less similar

NOTES:

A ——————► B close extension for formula brands, e.g. Ribena original to Diet Ribena

A - - - - ► C know-how brands, e.g. Bic's knowledge of disposable products
                    stretches from pens to razors

A -·—·—·► D extension based on category interest, e.g. Gillette stretches within
                    face care products

A ··········► E brands defined by a deep philosophy (brands can't be physically
                    linked so extension relies on brand qualities)

SOURCE: Kapferer 1992

However, not all brand extensions are guaranteed to be successful. Brands that stretch too far may result in failure and possibly dilute the image of the parent brand. The linkage between the parent product and the new product class is the central issue.

Research has suggested that the consumer's attitude toward the brand extension is a key factor in the determination of success. Their perception of 'fit' between the original and the extended product in relation to the product features and brand associations will be a key dimension of acceptance. Research by Aaker and Keller (1990) and Park et al. (1991) amongst others suggests that brands with abstract attitudes have a greater extendibility across different product classes that those which are associated with functional or concrete attitudes.

The roles of advertising in branding and building brand values

David Ogilvy (1983) states, 'every advertisement should be thought of as a contribution to the brand image. It follows that your advertising should project the same image, year after year.' In the context of current thinking, the analogy should be taken to include more than just advertising. It is vitally important that all communications messages on behalf of the brand communicate a singular and consistent image. We have seen that the consumer may be unaware of the source of the message, in specific terms. Often, he or she will be unable to determine whether the impressions were created by advertising, public relations, packaging or any other dimension of the brand activity. Nor, for that matter, does it really matter, providing that the impression the consumer receives is a favourable and positive one.

John Bartle (1997) argues that advertising has a unique ability to communicate the totality, the crucial combination of the rational and emotional ways in which the consumer can benefit from a product. Moreover, he argues that advertising can add emotional values in a way and a scale that no other tool within the marcom mix can. John Hegarty (2001), his partner in the advertising agency BBH, says 'We need to be concerned about where the company thinks the brand ought to be. The intention of advertising is to realise brand ambition. Great advertising has a vision for its products. Advertising focuses that vision.'

Heath (1998) argues that:

> advertising fits in in two ways. It can help set up brands by introducing them to the public; but more often it is used to enhance the appeal and increase the value of the brand. It is self evident that advertising must do this: if it did not, no-one would spend vast sums of money on doing so.

Advertising is one important source (although not the only one) of brand image and personality. Consumers interpret the actions, language, location and dress of a brand and, thereby, interpret the brand's intentions. The task is to dramatise the pluses in the brand. However, continuity is vitally important: communications that constantly change direction are far less effective. As Meeneghan (1995) states 'Advertising provides the most important source of brand imagery because it positions the brand against consumer expectations and attaches values to it that are attractive to the target audience'.

Kim (1990) states that the role of advertising in the process of creating brand identity is significant. It exploits product features that deliver meaningful benefits to consumers and are generally central to the brand image creation by demonstrating the product's ability to satisfy the buyer's needs.

Other authors confirm this view. 'Advertising's role, therefore, is to make consumers, whatever the current state of attitudes toward, information about, or images of a brand, more informed about the brand and more generally favourable to it' (Weilbacher 2001) whilst Walker and Dubitsky (1994) suggest 'positive attitudes towards an advertisement lead to favourable attitudes toward the advertiser or the advertised brand'. Similarly, Meeneghan (1995) asserts that:

> Advertising has a central role to play in developing brand image, whether at the corporate, retail or product levels. It informs consumers of the functional capabilities of the brand whilst simultaneously imbuing the brand with symbolic values and meanings relevant to the consumer.

Advertising is capable of contributing to the growth of brands but, to do this, the creative idea within the campaign must have a sharp enough cutting edge to generate sales in an increasingly competitive marketplace. But it does demand that the marketer examine all aspects of the communications message to ensure that the elements are consistent with each other, and that the consumer does not receive contradictory impressions of the brand.

Biel's study on branding (1990) provided a number of important conclusions:

1 Advertising makes a measurable direct contribution to perceived quality and share of market which, in turn, lead to profitability.

2 Advertising appears to have carry-over sales effects that extends beyond the period in which the advertising is actually running.

3 Businesses emphasising advertising over other forms of marketing communications enjoy a higher return on invested capital.

4 There is a significant relationship between market share and advertising spending. Money invested in advertising not only drives profits, but also builds strong brands.

However, Doyle (1997) argues that brands are rarely created by advertising and that advertising is not the basis for brands. He suggests that advertising's job is merely to communicate and position brands.

Brand relationships

According to Max Blackston (1993), the concept of brand relations has substantially been applied to the development of advertising. It has proved invaluable in identifying the 'problem' advertising is required to address and in providing specific direction for the attitude the brand should adopt in the advertising. The importance is not only to understand what the consumer thinks of the brand, but also what the consumer feels the brand thinks of them, i.e. are they an appropriate person to own or to use the brand. However, as he points out, advertising is but one of the ways in which a brand communicates with its consumers via attitudes and behaviours. Consequently, brand relationships have a broad relevance for all areas of marketing communications.

This has been the greatest spur to the development of 'relationship' marketing. with its objective of marketing to consumers 'one at a time'. Similarly, brands' attitudes and behaviours, expressed through packaging, sales promotion, and public relations, should all be consistent with their relationships. Tango, for example, have developed a positive relationship with their customers. Substantial numbers of their target audience – teenagers – have answered the invitations in advertising to call special Tango lines. According to Tango, over 2.5 million called the Apple Tango helpline and the Orange Tango Genetics 'demand' line.

The challenges facing brands

The real brand challenges facing today's firms can be grouped into four. First the collapse of boundaries between markets, industries and technologies. More and more markets are now becoming global with international sourcing and competition. The erosion of boundaries between industries means that, for example, Barclays Bank faces competition not just from other high street bank brands but more dangerously from Tesco, Virgin and Microsoft. Businesses too are ceasing to be technologically specific. Cars, for example, are increasingly about electronics rather than mechanical engineering. Such changes mean that the knowledge base managers now require is much broader and the brand competition their firms face is much greater.

The second challenge is the erosion of customer loyalty. Customers' expectations of value from all industries are rising. In particular, customers want individually tailored, rather than mass-market, solutions. Excess production capacity in most industries means that profit margins are shifting from supplying products to service and software solutions. Third, is the sheer speed of change. Novelty and fashion are becoming the norm in all markets. IT and the new media are creating new means to market making traditional distribution channels obsolete. Unless brands adapt to these real changes they soon lose their saliency to today's customers. The final challenge is the changing role of marketing in the firm (Doyle 1998).

The weakening of brands

Recent years have seen a progressive weakening of the position of brands in the marketplace which, in turn, has given rise to the overall debate as to whether the 'era of brands' is drawing to a close. Undeniably, brand owners face increasing pressures from a variety of fronts. These pressures include:

- a broader choice of products, each of which can satisfy differing consumer requirements;
- the lessening of product differentiation, as technology enables rival manufacturers to achieve the same, or very similar, product performance;
- the increasing sophistication of consumers, which results in a greater degree of scepticism surrounding manufacturers' claims.

Scott Davis (1994) identifies several reasons for the erosion of brand strengths:

1. private label intrusion
2. price discount back breaking
3. image devaluation
4. new entrant encroachment
5. investment-level withdrawal.

Where once the supermarket shelves were stocked with a wide variety of brands, and offered extensive choice to the consumer, the progressive erosion of retail margins has resulted in a concentration on a comparatively few brands. In many cases, the consumer is offered the choice between the brand leader, the second brand and a private label alternative. Inevitably the consequence, particularly for smaller brands, has been their removal from the shelves of the major retailers. Whilst in some sectors the impact of price pressures is squeezing out even well-established brands.

The changes in retailing

Recent years have seen fundamental changes in the retail scene. Most significant amongst these has been the growing power of the major retailers. The progressive number of mergers and takeovers has resulted in a comparatively small number of substantial retailers dominating their market sectors. In turn, this consolidation of retailing is shifting the centre of power away from brand owners. The level of concentrated buying power has given the advantage to many large operators in mass-market retailing – Boots, Toys'R'Us, Tesco, Asda (now part of Walmart). And, as a consequence, manufacturers must submit to the demands of these powerful retailers or risk the consequence of being de-listed from their shelves. At the same time, these leading retailers have consolidated their hold on key consumer markets by becoming more efficient.

Using all of the tools of marketing communications, retailers have created their own brand personalities that automatically invest their own label products with the same image. Their brand power is combined with heavyweight activity of both advertising and in-store support.

The growth of private label

There are four key reasons why retailers are motivated to develop own label sales:

1 to increase margin
2 to build store loyalty
3 to mask price comparisons
4 to generate greater supply chain efficiency.

De Chernatony and McDonald (1998) have identified the following characteristics in markets where own label products are particularly strong:

1 excess manufacturing capacity
2 products perceived by consumers as commodities
3 low levels of manufacturer's investment
4 production process employs low technology
5 brand advertising is not that significant.

However, in some respects, events have overtaken these conclusions:

1 Private label brands are no longer dependent on major manufacturers to supply their products. New manufacturing facilities have been specifically built to produce own label products. Cott, the supplier of Virgin Cola, together with many supermarket brands is a prime example of this development.
2 In an increasing number of sectors, whilst the products are not perceived as commodities, there has been a failure on the part of the major manufacturers to differentiate their products sufficiently to prevent a switch to private label.
3 The growth of the international own label market allows the manufacturers to achieve considerable economies of scale.
4 As technology becomes cheaper and more accessible, manufacturers of private label can invest in higher technology production facilities.
5 Many brands with high levels of advertising investment have been subjected to considerable private label attack, both in generic form and from look-alikes. It would appear that the scale of the advertising spend is no longer seen as a deterrent to private label attack – examples are Coca-Cola and Procter & Gamble.
6 There has been a fundamental shift in consumer attitudes towards private label products.

The consequence of manufacturer failure

Three major manufacturer-led factors have contributed to the weakening of brand positions.

Firstly, many manufacturers have increasingly sought to compete on price, both with each other and with retailers' own products. This has served to erode the distinctive characteristics which, historically, set brands apart from their private label equivalents. The overuse of price-based promotional techniques has resulted in a focus on price as a purchase discriminator.

Secondly, partly to fund promotional activity and partly to improve overall short-term profitability, some manufacturers have withdrawn other forms of marketing communications support. It is clear that if manufacturers fail to reinforce brand images, particularly with advertising, consumers will rapidly forget the underlying reasons why they chose the brands in the first place. The only factor which remains is the comparative price of the products on the shelves. In this circumstance, the private label products will always win!

As Kotler and Armstrong (1996) explain:

> The barrage of coupons and price specials has trained a generation of consumers to buy on price. Product proliferation and the seemingly endless stream of brand extensions and line extensions have blurred brand identity. As store brands improve in quality and as consumers gain confidence in their store chains, store brands are posing a strong challenge to manufacturers' brands.

The third factor has been the move by manufacturers into the supply of private label products. Today, 5 of the world's top 12 food and drinks producers now produce own-label products for retailers. Companies include Phillip Morris, Nestlé, Campbell's Soup, Heinz and Sara Lee.

Both Unilever and Procter & Gamble avoid producing products for private label whilst Kellogg's have used the fact in their advertising. Heinz, however, which previously adopted the same stance, now produces products for retailers, although it claims that the 'B brands' are sufficiently differentiated from their brand leader to avoid confusion. Their approach is to sell these products on the open market rather than link with individual retail chains.

A study conducted by *Marketing* magazine (*Marketing* 1997) reveals the extent to which major brands are now involved with the supply of products for private label sale. The article identified several manufacturers who also produce own-label products:

cereals – Weetabix, Cereal Partners (Nestlé)
biscuits – McVitie's, Burton's
crisps – KP, Golden Wonder
chilled – Dairy Crest, St Ivel
bread – British Bakeries, Allied Bakeries
hot beverages – Premier Beverages, Kraft Jacob Suchard.

This serves to confuse the issue relating to copycat brands. Asda used the fact that their Wheat Bisks product bore a striking resemblance to the Weetabix brand to defend their position in the claimed confusion between their Puffin brand and the McVitie's Penguin brand. However, the reason that Weetabix had not complained was due to the fact that they manufactured the product for Asda.

Many consumers are now aware that major brand manufacturers also make retailers' own-label products. Given the increasing tendency for retailers to adopt the visual cues associated with major brand packaging identities, many consumers believe that the product is the same as the manufacturers' own.

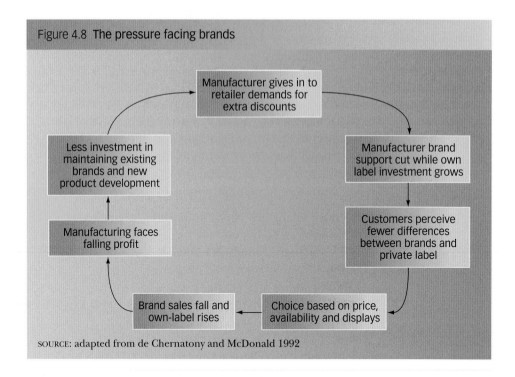

Figure 4.8 The pressure facing brands

SOURCE: adapted from de Chernatony and McDonald 1992

Brand look-alikes   The role played by packaging in communicating brand values is receiving considerable attention in the context of brand look-alikes. The increased number of retail
products which take on the visual appearance of the brand leader is causing great
concern for the manufacturers of branded products.

Increasingly, own brands are now being introduced into sectors with very strong
brands and, moreover, in very similar packaging: same size, same type and shape of
container and very similar graphics. The main reason for the growth of own label
and, increasingly, look-alikes, is the fact that supermarkets have become brands in
their own right, with added values which appeal to their customers. They have
achieved this using classic marketing techniques, including marketing communications. Retailers are now amongst the biggest advertisers.

A survey conducted for *Marketing* by NOP in March 1997 indicated that 41 per
cent of shoppers believe that manufacturers make a supermarket's own label product if its pack design is similar to the branded version. Significantly, nearly one in
five shoppers, 17 per cent, have mistakenly bought own label brands because they
confused their design with premium brand labels.

Recent years have seen a progressive quality improvement for private label products – a far cry from the days when their success was dependent entirely on their
price position – and, with it, the packaging brief. Today's private label products look
as good as their branded counterparts. However, at the same time there has been a
tendency to 'borrow' the packaging cues.

In 1994 Sainsbury's launched its Classic Cola with packaging strikingly similar to
that of the brand leader Coca-Cola. Tesco launched a low-fat spread called 'Unbelievable' corresponding to Unilever's 'I can't believe it's not butter'; Asda launched
'Puffin' against 'Penguin', and there are many other examples.

The response from the brands has been understandable, typified by the statement of Sir Michael Perry, former Chairman of Unilever:

> We understand that there are traditional packaging cues for certain product groups, such as a blue container for bleach. But look-alikes which set out to mislead are a parasitic form of competition, feeding on the investment in research, innovation and marketing expense of others.

As we have seen, in many instances, particularly in a crowded retail environment, the consumer devotes little time to brand selection. The decision to purchase is made on the basis of a series of visual clues as to the identity of the brand. Until comparatively recently, such clues as the pack shape, its colour, the style of the typeface and similar visual hints were a ready guide to the brand identity of the product purchased. Today, however, the situation is far less clear. Consumers could be forgiven for mistaking the identity of a product, given the number of packs that have been specifically designed to emulate the appearance of another. Retailers have, similarly, recognised the importance of packaging design and the contribution that it can make, not only to their profits but, importantly, to their overall images.

It is important to recognise that the issue of look-alikes is not limited to the FMCG sector, although most of the media attention has been devoted to that area. In fact, many other product categories as facing the same problem, sometimes as the hands of retailers, in other instances from rival manufacturers. Rolex look-alikes, for example, are produced by Seiko.

The designs of personal computers are similar because there are only a few mass-produced components available; in the case of many small cars, the designs converge because the leading companies all use similar design techniques and submit their designs to the same wind tunnel assessments; whilst in the field of telephony, the services are substantially interchangeable with each other and represent no discernible differences. Similarly, rival service providers may utilise the same creative devices to communicate their propositions to potential consumers. For example, Insurance Direct offer a similar service to Direct Line whilst Lloyds Bank Insurance Direct use a house/telephone device similar to Direct Line's car/telephone.

A quite separate problem, though no less worrying for the original manufacturers, is the dramatically increased numbers of fraudulent product copies. Many major brands face the problems of exact copies of the branded packaging and bearing the same name, for example, pirate CDs and perfumes sold in many retail outlets.

The brand response

The central issue for manufacturers is to create a brand with a sustainable differential advantage and provide it with a distinctive personality which customers can relate to. The concern is no longer brand versus own label, but brand versus brand. Manufacturers must constantly improve their brands to stay ahead of the competition. In this context, the role of marketing communications is to communicate the added value of the brand versus any other, including retailer own label and look-alikes.

A response to the weakening position of brands could be found in the following process. Companies must recognise the increasing importance of brands to their future survival. According to Chris Macrae (1991) whilst many brands have moved into the boardroom – as a result of the growing acceptance of the role of corporate branding, the role of the brand manager has either been downgraded or converted into a general management position. Often, the management of brands is devolved to promotions managers and service delivery managers. For brands to regain the initiative, there has to be a recognition of the important role of management of the branding process.

Manufacturers must ensure the continued investment in current brands and new product development. The withdrawal of brand support can only contribute to their further demise. At the same time, there is a need for improvements in both consumer and retailer communications programmes. This would encourage an increased recognition of the brand values resulting in the securing of a wider distribution base. The success of retailers is, ironically, dependent upon having strong brands. Ultimately, they can only improve their profitability – even in the context of their private label products – if they have the major manufacturers' brands alongside them. The change of direction indicated by Sainsbury's – from a concentration on private label, to an increased depiction of branded goods in their advertising – is a reflection of the fact that ultimately many consumers wish to purchase brands, even from their own preferred retailer.

The investment in research to identify the added values which are required by consumers is an important element within the process. And, there is a requirement for a continual investment in the new product development process. A similar investment will be required in terms of the communications programmes designed to associate the product benefits and justify the premium prices charged.

The move to get closer to the customer applies equally to the trade, inspiring increased co-operation between manufacturers and major retailers. The growth of category management is an important aspect of this co-operation. The retailer is less concerned with selling more of an individual brand than with maximising the overall profitability of the sector. By working together on ensuring greater efficiency in space planning and other joint initiatives in the areas of promotion and merchandising, manufacturers and retailers can co-operate to ensure increased sales and profits from each square foot of shelf space. For the manufacturer, this co-operation can bring about preferred supplier status and ensure that brand and private label strategies are implemented in a more harmonious manner.

White (2000) argues that since consumers are becoming more individualistic, choosy and demanding, brands will have to adapt if they are to develop or maintain significant franchises. He suggests that brands will have to become more multifaceted in order to appeal effectively to a more diverse set of consumer needs and attitudes.

His notion of a 'chameleon' brand which is capable of adapting to different target audience needs reflects a fundamental truth that brands are not what we make them, but what the consumer decides to make them.

Service brands

Although much of the chapter has referred to branding in the context of consumer goods, in reality much of the economy is devoted to service companies. According to Bateson (1995) the contribution of the service sector is significantly greater than that of manufacturing. Moreover, more people are employed within the services sector than in production. Dibb and Simkin (1993) suggest that some two-thirds of the British workforce is employed within service companies.

Most authors accept the premise that services possess four unique features:

- intangibility
- inseparability of production and consumption
- heterogeneity
- perishability.

De Chernatony and Riley (1997) identify several different service branding strategies. Amongst these, there is considerable empirical evidence to support the notion that the size and reputation of the firm is often used by the consumer as an indication of the quality of the service provision. In the absence of the normal branding devices, service providers must take alternative routes to ensuring that there are tangible clues as to the identity of the provider. In the financial sector, for example, it is commonplace to create a visual device that can be used to identify the service brand. Direct Line Insurance has, for many years, used a mnemonic of a red telephone; Lloyd's Bank has used the Black Horse.

In many instances, the tangible evidence of service quality is provided by the staff of the company who interface directly with the consumer. Considerable efforts must, therefore, be devoted to providing adequate training to ensure that the appropriate standards are maintained. Some companies go somewhat further. Avis staff are easily identified by their red uniforms, as are the staff of such diverse organisations as WH Smith, PC World and Eddie Stobart.

As noted earlier, a key role is played by the ability of the consumer to identify the company providing the service. To this end, several corporate campaigns have been specifically designed to establish the identity of the company in the mind of the consumer. However, this is potentially limiting in the sense that if different services are associated with the same company, consumers may have difficulty in differentiating between them. To avoid this, some organisations maintain the identities of several different brands to ensure clear separation for the consumers. First Direct has been given a distinctive identity which separates it from the Hong Kong SB (HSBC).

Although it is reasonable to assume that many of the dimensions of services branding are similar to those for FMCG products, in fact, few service providers go sufficiently far to develop clear and distinctive brand identities. Importantly, comparatively few of them associate clear emotional values with their branding devices to achieve differentiation. De Chernatony and Riley (1997) suggest that 'Service organisations, in particular, financial services, have not given sufficient attention to developing their brands as effective shorthand devices to simplify the complexity consumers perceive when choosing between competing services brands.'

In the field of retail, these factors are extremely important. Substantially, competitors in the same area of retail provision offer a very similar range of products to their customers. Their point of difference depends on the extent to which they are able to create a clear identity based on both physical and emotional differences between themselves and their competitors. Tesco and Asda have all done supremely well in providing consumers with discriminatory identities which enable them to occupy distinctive positions in the marketplace.

This should not be taken to imply, however, that advertising, like all of the other aspects of marketing communications, should not be subject to frequent review. Even long-running advertising campaigns may reach a point where the message needs to change. The advertising strategy should be re-examined and the executions monitored to ensure that the approach continues to be appropriate.

Case study

IPA Effectiveness Awards 2002 SILVER AWARD

Agency: BMP DDB

Authors: Andrew Deykin and Vicki Holgate

Hovis

Background

In the spring of 2001, British Bakeries was about to celebrate Hovis's 115th birthday. Hovis sales were rising. This was made all the more impressive by the fact that the bread was in decline (−4 per cent p.a.). Hovis's market share had almost doubled in the previous two years. However, under the surface, all was not well. British Bakeries was selling more and more bread, but it was making less and less money out of it. The average price that people were paying for Hovis fell by 10 per cent in real terms as a result of the EDLP (everyday low pricing) policy adopted by most of the major retailers.

Business strategy

Hovis's business objective was to increase profits significantly by the end of 2001. The aim was to increase volume and price together by increasing the underlying demand for the brand. Such a shift would allow Hovis to come off EDLP and put up its price (thereby improving margins) while increasing volume at the same time. Unfortunately Hovis's brand equity was declining. It is hard to increase the underlying demand for a brand when its value in consumers' minds is declining.

Spontaneous brand awareness of Hovis was in long-term decline. Conversely, spontaneous awareness of Kingsmill (Hovis's closest competitor) was on the rise, to the point that it had even overtaken Hovis for a brief spell in 2000. Hovis was seen as old fashioned and was becoming increasingly distant from bread buyers. Another contributor to Hovis's declining brand equity was that Hovis simply had not had enough advertising support in recent years, either in real or relative terms. Advertising funds had been be redirected to fund the EDLP activity, and Hovis had fallen victim to the vicious circle of EDLP.

The solution

In order to improve the underlying demand for the Hovis brand and break out of this vicious circle it was decided that Hovis would be relaunched on 11 June 2001 with a £4.2 million advertising investment. This was double the spend of the previous year and was anticipated to give Hovis at least an equal share of voice with Kingsmill. The relaunch would coincide with the planned price rises.

Holistic communications

The philosophy behind the relaunch communication plan was that it should include every opportunity people had to interact with the Hovis brand. It would therefore, comprise radical new packaging, new advertising, an updated website and significant PR.

The communications were going to have to build Hovis's brand equity. But more than that, if they were to increase the underlying demand for the brand, they were going to have to build brand equity in a way that was motivating.

Looking at all the qualities of the Hovis brand, one stood out as both differentiating and also very motivating for mums – goodness. 'Goodness' has always been at the heart of the Hovis brand. From its very inception, back in 1886, Richard 'Stoney' Smith found a way to retain the wheatgerm (the goodness) in the flour, thereby producing a loaf that was more nutritious. Unfortunately, the link between Hovis and brown bread was so strong that it threatened to jeopardise any attempt at communication about white bread, however full of goodness it was.

We realised that whatever we did in communication terms, it was going to have to be very noticeable and very different to get people to think again about Hovis.

The communications campaign – The creative brief put 'goodness' in a context that was relevant to today's hassled mums.

What do we want people to believe? If I buy Hovis for my family, then, whatever else might happen, at least I know I've given them a damn good start.

Proposition – Hovis is one good thing you can do for your family every day.

Target audience – Hassled mums who want to do the best for their family. Anything they can rely on for a spot of 'goodness' is appreciated.

Tone of voice – Honest, of the people. We just had to make sure that the ads looked totally different from anything that had gone before for Hovis, and they did. The advertising features a cartoon family who suffer all the problems and battles of real families – squabbling kids, rude words and so on. The endline for the campaign is 'Get something good inside'. A realistic and modern way to talk about 'goodness'. This line is featured throughout all the communication and has even been incorporated into the Hovis logo.

The media schedule – The advertising was bought against the core white bread market – housewives with children.

The packaging – It was decided that the packaging should change as radically as every other element of the communication mix. The 'goodness' message is communicated by photographs of good, honest, everyday food.

The website – Along with every other channel of communication, the site was redesigned to fit in with the new Hovis style. The site became 'Harry's site' and contained information on the new packs, the Hovis family and the new advertising.

The PR helped introduce people to the new pack designs through fly posters featuring baked beans and the Hovis logo.

Price rises – Hovis came off EDLP as planned and the price was increased dramatically over the first six months of the campaign. For example, the average price of a Hovis Great White loaf rose from 49p to 57p.

The combination of increases in volume at the same time as increases in price meant that the business objective of increasing profits significantly by the end of 2001 was soundly achieved. Hovis increased its share of white bread dramatically, becoming No.1 in white bread and therefore No. 1 in every area of the bread market.

Hovis's brand image improved on all the key dimensions communicated by the advertising and the packag-

ing. People loved the ads and genuinely felt they could relate to the characters and situations. We have evidence that both the advertising and packaging clearly communicated the core messages that helped to build brand equity.

Both Hovis's volume and value grew massively. Hovis is now No.1 in all areas of the market. The relaunch, in its entirety, has transformed the profitability of Hovis. Profits increased by over 32 per cent. The advertising paid for itself more than one and a half times over. Every £1 spent on advertising generates £1.67 of extra profit. This equates to a return on investment of 67 per cent.

SOURCE: This case study is adapted from the paper presented at the IPA Effectiveness Awards. The full version is available at www.warc.com and is reproduced by kind permission of the Institute of Practitioners in Advertising and the World Advertising Research Center.

Questions

1 Identify the important dimensions of branding (using the de Chernatony diagram) and consider the contribution that each of these makes to the differentiation of the brand.
2 What are the benefits of creating a strong brand?
3 Why do some companies concentrate on promoting a single brand name whilst others develop a portfolio of brands?
4 Consider any recent brand name change that has occurred. How did the manufacturer transfer the values of the original brand name to the new one?
5 Why is brand extension considered to be an important aspect of brand management? What are the dangers inherent in brand extension?
6 What contribution does advertising make to successful branding?
7 Consider the challenges facing brands and how these might be addressed.

5 Agency structures and the client/agency relationship

Learning outcomes

By the end of this chapter you should be familiar with:

- the UK agency scene
- advertising agency structures and personnel
- the debate relating to agency remuneration
- the agency/client relationship
- the criteria for agency selection.

Advertising agencies play a varied role in terms of the contribution they make to their respective clients' businesses. Indeed, this is the focus of much of the debate that is currently raging within the marketing communications industry. In some instances, this is a reflection of the structuring of the specific agency or consultancy which the company uses – its range and breadth of skills, and the relationship which exists between the organisations. In others, it depends to a substantial degree on the role that the client company perceives the agency or consultancy to be capable of fulfilling.

The UK agency scene

The top ten UK advertising agencies are truly global, with representation through wholly owned subsidiaries or partner agencies in most of the major marketing regions of the world. Their growth has been the result of acquisition and the organic development of new business. Often, reflecting the move to provide a greater range of services to their clients, agencies have formed substantial groups comprising not only the functions of advertising but also major subsidiaries operating in the fields of media specialisation, sales promotion, direct marketing, public relations and other areas.

The top ten UK agencies are shown in Table 5.1.

The structure of agencies will have a marked impact on the range of skills and services that they can offer their clients. It has to be said, however, that there is no single prescription for agency structuring. A key factor will be the scale of the agency. The larger it is, the greater the range of specialist skills it can afford to employ. By the same token, smaller agencies necessarily tend to employ personnel who are more 'generalist'. A further factor will be the underlying nature of the agency itself which, in turn, will largely determine the nature of the people it will need to employ to provide the services its clients expect and demand. As might be expected, the specialist skills of, say, an international advertising agency will demand

Table 5.1 The top 10 UK agencies

Rank 2003	Rank 2002	Agency	Billings Y/end Dec. 2003 (£m)	Billings Y/end Dec. 2002 (£m)	Year on year % change
1	1	Abbott Mead Vickers BBDO	349.96	341.17	2.57
2	2	McCann Erickson	302.56	298.50	1.35
3	7	J. Walter Thompson	268.18	244.87	16.86
4	6	Publicis	279.77	250.34	11.75
5	4	Ogilvy & Mather	253.24	273.36	−7.36
6	15	Euro RSCG	237.53	221.11	7.42
7	11	TBWA	236.98	172.17	37.64
8	5	M&C Saatchi	232.78	251.45	−7.42
9	3	Lowe	219.45	274.89	−20.17
10	8	Saatchi & Saatchi	212.58	234.30	−9.27

SOURCE: *Campaign* 2004

a different pattern of recruitment from, say, one which operates exclusively within a single country, or deals with a particular type of client. If the agency specialises in a particular type of advertising, for example, retail, medical or high-tech accounts, then it will need to employ the skills of people who have a particular understanding or aptitude for that field of activity.

From the outset, agencies tended to be generalist in their approach, that is, they attracted a wide variety of clients whose accounts demanded different inputs. However, as competition between advertising agencies intensified, so they began to concentrate their efforts into particular fields. To some degree, this was self-fulfilling. If an agency already had a portfolio of fast-moving consumer goods, for example, then it would tend to attract clients from similar fields.

They would be more able to demonstrate their expertise and achievements for existing clients and thus attract more similar accounts to their agency. By the same token, however, the effective fulfilment of clients' briefs often requires very specialist knowledge. A copywriter who has the skill to develop impactful consumer campaigns is unlikely to possess a knowledge and understanding of more technical areas. Accordingly, such clients will tend to be attracted to agencies that can provide the appropriate inputs.

Recent years have seen an increasing degree of specialisation within the field of advertising, although there will inevitably continue to be some degree of overlap between the different agency provisions. Much will depend on the overall nature of the clients' business. If the account is predominantly recruitment based, that is, the advertising is designed to recruit staff to their clients' companies then, not unreasonably, the client will tend to be attracted to an agency which can demonstrate expertise in that area. However, such clients may often have a requirement for other forms of advertising. Whether they use their specialist recruitment agency to develop such advertising will depend, to some degree, on the scale of their budget. If the advertising spend, in this case, for non-recruitment advertising is small, the client may prefer to remain with a single agency which, over time, will develop a substantial understanding both about the nature of the client's business and the specific advertising requirements.

The result has been the development of a very complicated advertising scene. Some agencies will operate within comparatively narrow fields, such as those indicated above, together with others such as financial specialisms, retail, pharmaceutical, business-to-business advertising, direct response, charity, tourism and so on. Such agencies will continue to develop their expertise within these areas which, in turn, serves to attract a number of clients operating within related areas.

If the budget is substantial, however, the client may divide the account between two or more agencies, to achieve a better match between the skills offered and the specific advertising requirements. This is particularly the case with global companies with substantial portfolios of brands. Companies such as Procter & Gamble, Unilever, Nestlé and others will retain the services of several major international agencies and will assign them the responsibility of handling several brands from that portfolio.

Reflecting the increasing move towards integrated marketing communications, most advertising agencies are subsidiaries of groups, usually operating on an international basis, which also incorporate specialists in the fields of public relations, sales promotion, direct marketing, sponsorship and other related areas of marketing communications.

The advertising agency: structure and personnel

Even within a specialist field such as advertising, the individual practitioners will have their own views of how to best structure themselves to meet the needs of their clients. In particular, agencies have an individual personality, and this will be reflected in the way that they set themselves up to deal with their clients' requirements. However, there are some common threads that run through most of them, as can be seen from Figure 5.1.

The agency management team

Providing the overall guidance and strategic direction of the agency will be a senior management team. They will come from a variety of different backgrounds and will offer a broad base of experience to the team. Commonly, the management team will comprise most or all of the heads of the various departments shown above, together with a financial director. They will fulfil a variety of different functions. On one level they will provide the essential cohesion which the agency requires. They will be responsible for establishing the central policies that will provide the basis upon which the agency operates with its client base. On another, they will provide the essential point of contact at the senior management level of the client company. This function is particularly important since, in other respects, the senior client management may not have regular contact with the agency and need to be apprised both of issues relating to their own businesses and other factors which will govern the working relationship between the companies. They will also be responsible for obtaining new business, either from existing clients or from companies that are new to the agency. And, in the case of the larger agencies, they may have a specialist team responsible for identifying and converting new clients.

The core functions of the advertising agency will be provided by a team representing the four major departments, each of which must work closely with each of

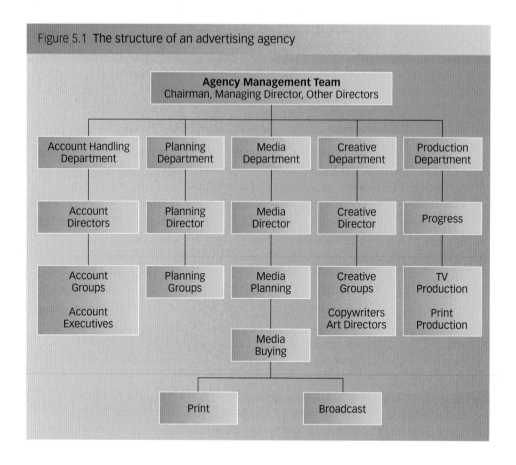

Figure 5.1 **The structure of an advertising agency**

the others to ensure the successful development of effective advertising and communications campaigns.

Account management

The account management team will vary considerably dependent upon the nature of the business for which they are responsible. Most agencies will have one individual who maintains the overall management responsibility for the account management function within the agency. The head of account management will have a key responsibility in maintaining the ongoing relationships with the clients and will hold frequent meetings with the senior client management team. He or she will be responsible for ensuring that the clients' needs are reflected in the performance of the agency, the recruitment and guidance of the account management team, and for setting the 'style' of the agency in relation to its account handling role.

Each account of the agency will be lead by an account director who may be a member of the main board of the agency. That individual will have the key responsibility of guiding the relationship with the client or clients (in many instances, the account director will be responsible for leading more than one piece of business) and providing the focus for the day-to-day handling of the business. In a simplistic sense, they are the clients' representatives within the agency and will be responsible for the guidance of the work that is produced by the agency.

Beneath the account director in structural terms will be a number of account handlers – various referred to as account executives, account managers and so on.

They will provide the day-to-day liaison with the client company and will be responsible for ensuring that the essential work required by the client is fulfilled both on time and within budget. Most importantly, they represent the channel through which the dialogue between the client and agency is conducted. They convey information between the two parties, providing the necessary interpretation to 'translate' client language into agency speak and vice versa. They have a co-ordinating responsibility in terms of bring together members of the agency team whose inputs will be required to satisfy the client's requirements at the various stages in the development of an advertising or communications campaign. They also have the responsibility for presenting the resultant work of the agency back to the members of the client team.

Agencies vary considerably in terms of their account handling structures but, in essence, their objective will be to mirror the client's own internal structure and provide appropriate contact points between the organisations at all relevant levels.

Planning	The role of planning is a comparatively new function within the advertising agency, but one that has evolved dramatically to change the nature and function of the agency response to its clients' communications needs. The reason that planning has become intrinsic to contemporary advertising development is that advertising is not a linear process. Account planners need to offer strategic solutions that lead to creative solutions.

Two individuals, above all others, can lay claim to having created this important agency function: Stanley Pollitt, who later went on to found an agency called Boase, Massimi, Pollitt (now part of DDB, the 14th-largest agency in the UK, with UK billings of £176 million in 2003) and Stephen King at J. Walter Thompson (in 2003, the 3rd-largest agency with UK billings of £286 million). So, how did they change the nature of advertising? Most significantly, they made the first real attempt to integrate the process of understanding the consumer with the function of creating advertising messages (*Campaign* 2004).

As King (1989) put it 'Marketing companies today are increasingly changing their viewpoints. They recognise that rapid response in the marketplace needs to be matched with a clear strategic vision. The need for well planned brand building is very pressing.'

Several factors have contributed to the emergence and growth of the account planning function, not only within this country, but within most major advertising agencies throughout the world. In part, it represented a response within the agency to the changing needs of their client companies. The increased understanding of the marketing function necessitated a closer focus on the consumer. Hitherto, dialogue with the consumer audience was provided by the research department of the agency, although its contribution was relatively minor and comparatively late in the advertising development process. Most often, research was used to test advertising rather than integrated into its development. The result was the creation of friction with the creative department who saw their ideas condemned by what they saw as inadequate research techniques.

The research departments themselves realised that their contribution to the development process was under-utilised. Their responsibilities were, largely, limited to providing an overview of the marketplace – often using the internal resource of a desk research or library facility – and evaluating the results of creative development. A major part of their function was that of copy testing – using prompts such as commercial scripts or storyboards to evaluate the consumers' response to an advertising message. Since the research department was considered a backroom function, it was rarely represented at the key meetings, both internally with the people responsible for creating the advertising, or with clients to provide an advocacy role of the material that the agency was presenting. At the same time, agency management began to appreciate the cost of misdirected creativity. Without adequate guidance, the creative department might waste enormous amounts of time – a precious resource – on the development of advertising that was irrelevant to the true needs of the consumer or, at best, misunderstood.

The development of account planning changed all that. Account planners have an important strategic responsibility within the agency. They are required to provide a far deeper understanding of both the consumers and the brands that they purchase. Often, it is their responsibility to guide the strategic direction of the advertising, isolating the positioning which the product or service should adopt to most closely correspond with the identified needs of the consumer. They are fully integrated with the creative process and work closely with the creative teams at all stages of the advertising development, not merely in terms of its final evaluation. They have a key voice in the agency–client dialogue. Unlike their research predecessors, they are represented at all key meetings and contribute to the development of the broader issues of strategic development being addressed by the client company. They occupy senior management roles within the majority of agencies and address similar issues on behalf of the agency itself. Ultimately, however, it is their ability to identify the critical consumer insight to the client and agency team alike that makes their contribution so important.

An important aspect of the planning role seems to be to impose some creative control on the advertising development process. According to Hackley (2003) the planner is there to ground the development of advertising in consumer insight so that the client's marketing objectives remain at the centre of the agency's thinking.

Stephanie Kugelman (1998), Vice Chairman and Managing Director of Young & Rubicam, NY, states

> Clients expect more strategic thinking from their agencies because competitors and consumers are changing so rapidly. The bar has been raised for all of us in terms of the understanding we have to have about the brand and the consumer, the level of understanding we have to bring to the client, and the level of insight that has to inspire or provoke the advertising for the product.

Stanley Pollitt (2000), one of the founders of the concept of planning, established a number of key principles:

- The planner is an 'expert in research'.
- The planner uses and understands quantitative research and market data together with qualitative data.
- The planner personally conducts a good deal of qualitative research and develops, at first-hand, an in-depth understanding of the target audiences.
- The planner is continuously involved in the campaign, in strategic thinking, in

developing the creative execution and in assessing the results of the campaign in the market.

- The planner forms part of a threesome with the account manager and creative who, together, share the responsibility for the creative advertising.

Similarly, Lisa Fortini-Campbell (1992) in her book *Hitting the Sweet Spot* defines five key functions of the account planner:

1 Discovering and defining the advertising task

   The account planner is the person who has the responsibility for organising information regarding the consumer and the marketplace. They use a variety of inputs including both existing client and agency data as well as specific primary research which they initiate.

2 Preparing the creative brief

   The account planner is the person within the agency who prepares the creative brief which will both inform and inspire the creative process. We will discuss the creative brief itself in Chapter 10, but suffice it to say at this stage that this document provides the focus on the key issues – most importantly, the critical consumer insight – which will guide the creative development process.

3 Creative development

   The account planner is integral to all stages of creative development, from the initial thoughts and rough ideas, to the final work that is presented to the client. They represent the custodian of the brand values and, critically, interpret these in the context of their understanding of the needs and wants of the consumer. In many instances, they may well go back to the consumer at a number of inter-mediate stages to ensure that their reaction to the advertising proposition is an appropriate one. This will provide additional guidance to the creative team to enable them to hone the proposition to its most effective level.

4 Presenting the advertising to the client

   Advertising may 'sell' itself to the client, but usually needs some interpretation to demonstrate how the advertising works with the consumer. It is the planner's function in this area to identify how the advertising campaign will work in the marketplace and to pinpoint the broader implications of the advertising approach in terms of the objectives – both short- and long-term – which have been established for it. They provide the essential rationalisation and justifica-tion for the advertising approach, often utilising information about the advertis-ing from research conversations with consumers. Their role is to provide an objective evaluation of the consumer response to the agency proposals.

5 Tracking the advertising's performance

   After the implementation of the advertising campaign, the planner continues to monitor consumer reaction to it. This process will provide important feedback to the agency and client teams, not only about the impact of the campaign itself, but also information that will guide the subsequent development of the campaign.

Account planning is aimed at generating strategic insights during three key phases of the campaign process: strategy generation, creative development and campaign evaluation. Account planners function as a liaison both between the account exec-utive and the creative department, and between the creative department and the consumer. The structure of planning across agencies varies somewhat. In some agencies the planning function leans more toward account management, whereas at others planners are considered members of creative departments (Kover and Goldberg 1995).

As Jones (1998) describes:

> A planner is essentially the account teams' primary contact with the outside world; the person who, through personal background, knowledge of all pertinent information, and overall experience, is able to bring a strong consumer focus to all advertising decisions.

Similarly, Newman (1994) states

> For the creative teams, the key benefit of the account planner is usable research. Not numbers, not arbitrary pre-post switching scores, not a quantitative research report put on their desks, but a person who explains and communicates, who seeks them out to bring them useful insights. A person who can argue conceptually about an idea and how it will work in the marketplace.

John Bartle (1985) is unequivocal about the role of planning. 'You cannot produce effective advertising without planning it.' He suggests that account planning is now very much part of the agency establishment. However, he points out that, of itself, it does not guarantee great advertising. It has no divine right of status or power. Its future depends upon planners being good enough and upon the function being deployed within the appropriate agency structure at the right level.

Similarly, Hall (1997) argues 'planners have to come up with unique insights and new angles that will help creatives capture the consumers' imagination. This is where the planner can create a real difference in the advertising process, providing a unique and invaluable input that leaves his or her validity beyond question.'

Butterfield (1985) argues that 'the planner has direct responsibilities and points of contact with the client's own personnel. He is no longer merely a discontinuous technical research advisor, he is a fundamental part of "business partnership" that exists between client and agency'.

The creative department

The creative department represents the public face of the agency. It is their responsibility to create the advertising messages that are ultimately seen by the target public or publics. The larger agencies employ a considerable number of people within their creative departments who not only possess the specific skills of art direction and copywriting, but additionally may also have built up extensive specialist experience within particular market sectors. Sometimes, if an agency has a number of different clients in a particular area, for example, retailing or pharmaceuticals, it may employ specific creative staff who will have demonstrated a clear understanding of those respective markets.

In most agencies, the creative department is headed up by a creative director, who has built up a wide range of experience. Not only is the creative director responsible for the final evaluation of the work produced by the members of the department, he or she is also responsible for the smooth running of the creative function within the agency. Often, the position will be held by someone who has established a strong reputation within the industry, since that reputation will contribute to the desired image of the agency in the minds of its clients and prospective clients.

It is most common for creatives to work as a team, usually comprising two people, one with art direction skills, the other with those of copywriting. Their role is to interpret the creative brief and translate that into an effective advertising message. In many cases, these teams work so closely that their individual contribution to the final work is indistinguishable. Either or both will contribute equally to the determination of the final idea – the copywriter contributing to the visual component as much as the art director suggesting the copy approach. Indeed, so close do these relationships become that they will often change jobs together and join a new agency as an established team. Here again, reputations become progressively important. Teams that have consistently produced effective advertising campaigns may well be a major reasons why clients are attracted to the agency at which they work.

The creative process is often augmented by a number of other functions within the agency. Since it is not an essential requirement that an art director can draw, he may need to call upon the services of a specialist visualiser who can translate his ideas into a form which others can readily recognise. Similarly, some agencies employ typographers whose responsibility is to ensure the appropriate use of typefaces that can contribute to the overall communication of the advertising message. Increasingly, however, this manual task is being replaced by people with computer skills and with experience of a wide variety of software packages which can be used to assist the process.

The media department

The media department fulfils the essential role of ensuring that the messages created by the agency are communicated in the appropriate media at the right time and at a realistic cost. The issue is complicated by virtue of the fact that there may well be multiple media solutions and the media department must use its skills and experience to ensure that the media selected contribute to the effectiveness of the communications process.

The media department usually consists of several people, each possessing discrete specialist skills. Central to this is a research and planning function. There is a vast array of data available to the media planner that will assist in the determination of the appropriate media for the task in hand. It is the planner's responsibility to interpret the available information and identify the route most relevant to the needs of the campaign. We will see later that, although cost effectiveness is an important consideration, it may be overridden in certain circumstances by the need to ensure that the media environment is the most appropriate for the effective communication of the specific message to the identified target audience.

Most media departments will also employ specialist buyers whose responsibility it is to implement the agreed media solution. Through the establishment of close relationships with their own designated area of the media – television, radio, press, posters, etc. – they are the people who ultimately conduct the negotiations designed to purchase time or space at the most cost-effective level. The fragmentation of the media has increased the number of specialisations within the department. In the larger agencies, for example, there will often be a number of media specialists who deal exclusively with the regional or local media, usually reflecting the specific needs of their client base.

The media function is an important one within the agency environment, but is an area which has been complicated by the comparatively recent trend towards the separation of this function from the rest of the agency with the creation of media independents and dependents. The former exist solely to provide their clients with the essential functions of a media department, the latter similarly fulfil these functions but operate as a wholly owned subsidiary of an advertising agency or other communications group. Specialist media agencies such as BLM Media and Naked Communications operate completely independently of any advertising agency grouping. MediaCom, the largest of the media dependants, operates as a wholly owned subsidiary of The Grey Advertising Group (now part of WPP). However, as well as fulfilling the media function for many of the clients of that agency, they are also retained by a number of companies whose creative and advertising development is the responsibility of an advertising agency outside of the that advertising agency.

ZenithOptimedia occupies a similar relationship to the Publicis group of agencies (which includes Saatchi & Saatchi, Leo Burnett, BBH, Arc, Fallon and Publicis). In fact, the Publicis group is the largest of the holding companies. Apart from owning several major international advertising agencies, it is also the owner of Starcom, Media Vision and Zed Media. Again, their media specialists plan and buy the media requirements for several of the clients of the agencies within the group but, additionally, work directly or indirectly for a number of clients who have no relationship with the agency.

It has to be recognised that scale has become an important facet of negotiating effectively with the media sellers. The larger the media agency, the greater the potential discounts that it can achieve on behalf of its clients. And, by removing the restriction of working for an individual agency and its clients, a media independent or dependent can, effectively, aggregate the business of several agencies or client companies. The latter facet has become increasingly important, with a number of large companies centralising their media planning and buying function within a single media specialist. The existence of these specialist agencies has meant that, in some instances, agencies maintain only a 'skeleton' media staff with the main task of media fulfilment being contracted out.

Production

The production department has the critical responsibility of ensuring that creative ideas are correctly translated into the final form appropriate to their appearance in the designated media. One function within the production department, which has a special role, is that of the progress or traffic manager. This individual (and there may well be several within the larger agencies) has the specific responsibility for ensuring that the various stages of the creative development are completed at an appropriate time to ensure that the advertising appears in the correct media on the due date. In many cases the development of the conceptual advertising campaign, which was presented to the client by the agency team and subsequently approved for appearance into the form in which it is required by the media, is a lengthy and complicated one. Individual elements will need to be brought together within an agreed timeframe. For example, specific photography may be required using selected models. Whilst the creative team will have the responsibility for choosing both the photographer and the artists required, it will be the task of the progress manager to ensure that each stage of the production process is completed within an agreed timeframe to meet the copy deadline. In this respect, it is vitally important that the progress manager works equally closely with the media department to identify such timetable requirements. The same principle applies equally to the production of television advertising.

It is important to note that most of the final components of any advertising campaign are sourced outside of the agency. It will be essential for any campaign to utilise the skills of outside photographers, television commercial production teams and so on. This is an important consideration since it will have a great bearing on the charges that the client will be called upon to pay during the development of the advertising campaign.

Other services to agency team

Information department

No agency can function effectively without a constant flow of relevant information. Every day, articles will be published which will have a bearing on the way in which the agency understands its client businesses. In the larger agencies, an internal function would be a library or management information service that would cull relevant journals and other periodicals in order to build an effective database of information from which agency staff could draw. In other instances, the department might be given the task of sourcing information pertinent to a new project from appropriate sources – industry associations, governmental bodies, etc.

In smaller agencies, this function would be fulfilled by some external resource. Several companies exist which can provide this input on an hourly, daily or other basis, obviating the need for the agency to tie up its resources in a function that might only be drawn upon at irregular intervals.

Personnel

Like any other business function, an advertising agency must be capable of dealing with a wide variety of personnel issues: recruitment, remuneration, dismissal and so on. An internal personnel or human resources department provides these functions, although in some instances, the responsibility may be fulfilled by a senior member of the management team assisted by other dedicated members of staff.

Finance

As organisations grow, the financial provisions of their operation have to be considered as a separate entity. Clearly, there is a close interrelationship between the financial function and that of personnel management, and often these departments are combined. However, whichever structure is employed, the agency must be capable of managing its cash flow, ensuring the prompt payment of its invoices and its discharging of its debts to other organisations that it uses from time to time.

Regional agencies

Although a large number of clients work closely with their main agencies, often centred on London or another major city, there are also a substantial number of regional agencies which have developed to provide a more local service to their clients. Some of these exist as subsidiaries of the major international agencies. Indeed, the largest regional agency in 2003 with media billings of slightly over £47 million was Cheetham Bell JWT which is part of the J. Walter Thompson group (itself part of WPP).

Others, such as PWLC with 2003 billings of £40.6 million and the Publicity Bureau (£33.8 million), operate independently.

An excellent source of information about all agencies is the special *Campaign* report, referred to previously which produces an annual survey of the Top 300 agencies and their billings during February each year.

The changing role of marketing communications

One important issue that must be considered is the nature of the fundamental changes which all forms of marketing communications agencies are being called upon to address.

We have already seen the underlying move towards integrated marketing communications. Perhaps more than any other single issue, this is resulting in significant changes to the nature of the agencies and the services that they seek to provide. This has manifested itself in a number of different ways. In some instances, agency groupings have been formed which provide their clients with access to a wide range of specific skills not usually associated with the world of advertising. If we look for example at several of the major international agency networks, many of them have established formal links with other companies within the field of marketing communications. In some cases, we are seeing the establishment of single integrated agency structures which seek to provide the totality of marketing communications input under a single 'roof' – effectively providing 'one-stop' shopping to their clients.

Ironically, of course, this has often been the nature of the service provision of several of the regionally based 'advertising' agencies. The inherent nature of their relationships and, perhaps, the size of the companies with which they deal has resulted in them being regarded as the major source of input, and certainly the 'guardians' of the communications process on behalf of their clients. At the same time, we are also witnessing moves in the opposite direction. Rather than providing the 'full service' of the larger advertising agencies, many companies have established themselves within comparatively specialised fields.

A la carte

In some instances, responding to the needs of their client base, some agencies provide an á la carte service in which client companies are invited to access only those services that they require. Often, a client will require a specific range of inputs from an agency corresponding to their position in the marketplace. This may be in the form of advice in the strategic area, involvement in the new product development process, the development of creative materials and so on. In most cases, the agency is remunerated in the form of a fee related to the volume of the work. Most importantly, the client has access to those inputs which it requires at a particular moment of time, but with the knowledge that, as its business or demands grow, so the agency can continue to service the expanding requirements of the business.

Media specialists

This has been the important growth sector of recent decades, and has significantly elevated the contribution of media to the communications mix. In response to the demands of their clients, most of the major agencies have separated the media function and can now provide a dedicated service distinct from its other functions.

There may be several different reasons for a company to use a single media source for its media planning requirements. Clearly, there are significant benefits to be derived from placing the totality of their media planning and buying requirements into a single media company. The economies of scale which can be obtained from negotiating the entirety of its spend will often represent significant savings to the client company. It can ensure the consistency of approach, despite using several different agencies to provide the creative and planning inputs.

Some companies retain an independent media specialist to evaluate the performance of their advertising agencies or media buying agencies, who retain the direct responsibility for the planning and buying of the media on their area of the clients' business.

Creative boutiques

In the same way that media has become a specialist function, so too the area of creative development has, in some areas, been separated from the rest of the advertising agency role. In some cases, creatives who have developed a strong relationship with the company have established themselves as independent operators who continue to provide the input in this area. In others, the client gains access to a pool of talented individuals who can be used either to supplement the creative work of their agency or to enable them to draw on these skills without the need to appoint a full-time agency.

This may be particularly useful when the company is developing new products, when it will require creative input, perhaps in the form of product concepts or positioning statements, but will not require them to be developed into advertising campaigns.

Specialised agencies

The specialist nature of some specific business areas has resulted in the development of agencies with parallel skills. Often, because of the particular nature of a market, the company will need to gain access to a number of individuals who have developed an understanding of the special requirements. This may result from the specialist nature of, for example, the regulatory requirements or the technical nature of the business area. In recent years, specialist agencies in the fields of high technology, medical and pharmaceutical products, and financial services have all emerged to provide specialist inputs to their clients. Apart from the obvious differences in terms of their knowledge base, there is a further difference that distinguishes these agencies from their mainstream counterparts.

The convention has long been established that the major agencies do not handle competing clients. Some companies insist that their agencies do not handle any business in those market areas in which they operate, even though the particular agency may not handle that aspect of the clients' business directly. This is becoming an increasingly difficult stance as major agencies could find themselves precluded from large areas of business potential. The involvement of major conglomerates in a wide variety of business areas might prevent an agency from handling major areas in which they would otherwise wish to become involved.

In the specialist agencies, no such restrictions exist. Client companies accept that, in order to gain access to the specialist skills, they must sacrifice the non-competition rules.

The agency/client relationship

All agency/client relationships are different, often reflecting the culture of the companies involved. Some companies attempt to establish enduring relationships with their advertising partners which, in many cases, are sustained for many years. J. Walter Thompson has handled the Kellogg's account since the 1930s. WCRS published a monograph celebrating 15 years of advertising for BMW (the paper won the Grand Prix in the IPA Advertising Effectiveness Awards in 1994), and still handle that account; Levis was the first account awarded to Bogle Bartle Hegarty and remains with that agency today.

Yet others tend to change on a more frequent basis, perhaps reflecting their insecurity with the area of advertising expertise or because they perceive that change will enhance other aspects of their overall business performance. Periodically, companies feel the need to check out what is available to them. In some cases this is the direct result of some deficiency – real or perceived – in the performance and contribution of their agency. At other times, the agency review may be a reflection of management changes within the client company, and the resultant desire to reflect those changes by selecting an agency with a similar personality. Yet again, some reviews are built in to the process. Some organisations specifically adopt a time-limited relationship with their agency – say, three to five years – at which time a review of the current agency scene is implemented irrespective of the performance of the incumbent.

Many senior managers maintain a 'watching brief' to be alert to changes in the marketing communications scene. The spate of mergers and takeovers during recent years has, inevitably, resulted in some conflicts of interest, with clients having to remove their business to another agency at relatively short notice. By maintaining an awareness of agency performances, clients can at least identify potential contenders for their business should they decide to move.

Clients do not usually have only one goal, one set of values and one homogeneous set of management experiences and backgrounds. Instead, client organisations are typically made up of individuals co-operating (or competing) in pursuit of unique sub-goals. For example, an account manager may interact with a variety of individuals in a client organisation, who may be distinguished by their different needs, responsibilities, attitudes and decision-making power when it comes to advertising. Thus, the potential exists for misevaluation by managers who are not involved in the creation of advertising, but who are involved in the selection, retention and termination of the relationship with an agency. Thus, the need to target communications to key managers and other personnel within the client firm is more critical in the advertising process than it might be with more tangible products.

The agency/client relationship is a dynamic decision-making process in which the participants identify, evaluate, and choose appropriate communication strategies and alternatives. Moreover, it is a dynamic evaluation process, in which agency and client learn about each other's strengths and weaknesses, preferences, and prejudices.

Beltramini and Pitta (1991) identify a number of benefits of effective relationship management between agency personnel and the various client-buying centre role players across advertising tasks. First, two-way flows of communication should enhance the quality of advertising. A knowledge of the client's marketing, public relations and consumer service departments is valuable for grounding any promotion initiative in reality. The potential of missing a great advertising idea, or of creating an inaccurate and poorly perceived message, should be reduced if agency personnel remain open to input from personnel working in the client firm which can be indirectly (as well as directly) influential in the advertising process.

Second, communicating with a larger variety of role players within the client firm should enhance acceptance of the agency and its advertising. It is reasonable to assume that as problems arise, a more 'personified' agency in contact with all the parties in the advertising decision and its subsequent evaluation should be more favourably evaluated than one which is not such an active communicator. There are no guarantees that merely talking to indirect influencers will eliminate major problems. However, agencies which maintain working relationships with their clients should find it somewhat easier to move through client approval cycles during newer tasks, and also find it easier to maintain a co-operative air when engaged in straight, routine tasks.

Third, the relationship management process conveys a potentially valuable insight into the true nature of the client firm. Knowing the real decision makers and their most important influencers can sharpen account managers' actions, and make them more effective in the long run. For example, investing in an understanding of the client network pays dividends in the early identification of informal decision influencers and insulated deciders, as well as gatekeepers of relevant information.

Fourth, the actions of the agency in responding to concerns of the client buying centre can lead to an overall positive evaluation of the agency and a reluctance to change agencies. Effective relationships require time to nurture, and no client is interested in having to brief a new agency unnecessarily. Over time, advertising tasks may vary from new and exciting to those of lesser interest. However, a genuine interest in servicing a client underscores an agency's commitment to maintaining a working and productive relationship.

Kulkarni et al. (2003) recognise that advertising agency changes are serious decisions for client firms because of the risks involved. Advertising agencies provide intangible services that may substantially affect sales, profits and market share. Yet these effects cannot be accurately predicted. Which agency will produce great ads and which will not? Manufacturing firms may routinely change suppliers of components, parts or materials because the product purchased can be exactly specified and tested ahead of time for compliance to specifications. This is simply not possible with advertising agencies.

Another risk for clients considering an agency change involves the possible communication effect from the change itself. Agency firings – particularly those involving well-known consumer products or firms – are public events, often covered in the business press. How will investors react to the news of the firing? Will they see it as good news or will they sell the stock? Overall, agency firings pose important managerial issues for agencies and their clients.

In many instances, the firing of an ad agency is preceded by a loss in the client's market share in the period immediately prior to when the agency is fired. This suggests that the agency is being held responsible for the share loss, although it may well be a means of avoiding the underlying issues that are truly responsible for the brand share.

In a paper by Mitchell and Sanders (1995) an attempt was made to explain why some clients choose to remain loyal to their advertising agencies over an extended period, whilst others move on a more frequent basis. A significant proportion of the sample felt that organisational and business environmental factors were the most important determinants of loyalty.

It suggests that termination is a process rather than a single decision, but that the formal break also appears to relate to highly specific incidents. Moreover, the study indicates that prolonged relationships are important because failure results in both significant cost and operational difficulties. The process of switching agencies, it argues, together with the development of positive new relationships, can take up to two years.

There are a wide variety of reasons why a client/agency relationship breaks down. A survey conducted for *Campaign* magazine (*Campaign* 2004b) identified several causes for the account move:

'It has lost its enthusiasm for your product/service'	85%
'It is not devoting enough time/resources to my account'	87%
'It lacks integrated communications skills'	32%
'It lacks the technology to service my account'	15%
'It is working on a conflicting account'	61%
'There is a personality clash'	44%
'You change agency regularly as a matter of course'.	2%

Many of these findings are reinforced in a paper by Jones (2001). He asserts that reasons commonly given by clients for changing agencies include:

- 'I want to be involved in the advertising process, rather than simply being a purchaser'
- 'I want my agencies to get on with each other' (see decision by Amanda McKenzie of BT (*Campaign* 2004b))
- 'I want my agency to be proactive'
- 'I want my agency to have a view on other communication disciplines'
- 'I want value for money'
- 'I want quality thinking'
- 'I want consistency'
- 'I want a bespoke solution'.

Agency philosophy

In the agency context, creative 'philosophy' is the policy, style or guiding principle that specifies the general nature of the advertising on the basis of an underlying assumption of how the advertising will work (Lannon 1986). Many agency philosophies relate more to strong CEOs and visionary public relations efforts than to any guiding principles based on communication. In the advertising business, ideas of how advertising works form the foundation for the complex development of an agency's creative philosophy.

Agency philosophies differ substantially and these have an important bearing on the client relationship. The inherent nature of the agency stance, its reputation in areas of creativity, account planning and handling, the style of its involvement with its clients' businesses, and other factors serve to distinguish any one agency from its competitors. Not surprisingly, agencies tend, in the main, to attract clients with similar personalities to their own.

Agency philosophies play an important role in the agency/client relationship, since they define the distinct style or approach used by the agency. Indeed, many commentators agree that accounts can be won or lost because of the nature of the agency philosophy.

Often, the philosophy of the agency reflects the viewpoint of the owner or manager and the ability of the agency to translate that into effective advertising campaigns. Research in the USA by Collins and Porras (1997) demonstrated that the adoption of a clear agency philosophy, almost irrespective of its nature, was what distinguished the top agencies from the also-rans. In effect, agencies attempt to create 'brand identities' for themselves in order to distinguish their offering from that of their competitors.

It is important to note that clients adopt similar philosophical approaches to the ways in which they wish their business to be handled. Not surprisingly, there is a close match between the overall agency approach or philosophy and that sought by their clients.

Advertising practitioners and researchers agree that accounts may be won or lost by the nature of the agency philosophy and dominant philosophies may differ cross-culturally. Effective philosophies can be so useful that they survive indefinitely (Patti and Frazer 1984). There has been such an interaction between advertisers and agencies over the years that advertiser creative strategies have shaped the overriding creative philosophies adopted by agencies. The earliest agency philosophies were developed in the inter-war years by prominent advertisers, such as Procter & Gamble (P&G), and then adopted by various agencies.

The process of forming an agency philosophy is complex, with considerable interactions among a variety of variables, such as the owner's or manager's viewpoint, the client's approach to communication, communication theory and the ability of the agency to translate the desired philosophy into a meaningful campaign procedure.

There are two predominant forms of agency philosophy, rational and emotional, as well as combinations thereof. Well-known examples of these philosophies are 'argument', 'problem–solution', 'pre-emptive', the 'USP' and 'positioning'.

Emotional philosophies, in contrast, tend to reflect the more impulsive, irrational and sensual models of buyer behaviour. They postulate that buyers are less rational in their purchase decisions and so moods, colours and feelings about products may be just as important as functional information (Ogilvy 1983). Well-known, primarily emotional philosophies include brand image and identity, resonance and anomaly. It is likely that the two philosophies will overlap, but for some, there may be a difference between the strategy and the tactics.

Since the Second World War, one of the most influential rational advertising philosophies has been Rosser Reeves' (1961) 'unique selling proposition' (USP). Reeves, of the advertising agency Ted Bates, stated that 'each advertisement must say to each reader: buy this product and you will get this specific benefit'. The USP school argues that advertisers must offer strong, unique and relevant benefits to be successful.

As West and Ford (2001) point out:

Advertising risk can relate to several specific decisions, such as media choice and timing, but the central risk taken in any campaign is the creative work. Creative risk is inherent in the advertising process because the success or failure of any advertisement is impossible to predict given the clutter of the environment. Most clients tend to accept evolutionary creative work more easily than they do the challenging because it is easier to relate to unoriginal advertising.

The debate relating to agency remuneration

An important dimension of the relationship will, inevitably, be a reflection of what the company is charged for the work that the agency produces and, with this, an agreement as to the ownership of this material. There is a variety of different bases for agency remuneration, and it is important that whichever method is used, agreement should be reached at the outset.

Duncan and Lace (1998) identify the underlying reasons for the changes in approach towards agency remuneration. The last 10 to 15 years have seen major fractures appearing in the agency remuneration landscape. The first of these was the de-coupling of media planning and buying from the core agency offering, manifested in the emergence of the media independents during the 1980s. Not only did they take their expertise with them, they also took some 3 per cent of the commission, which left clients asking themselves what it was they were really getting for their 12 per cent.

Then there was the recession, which saw the UK taken by surprise by the speed and ferocity of the economy's downturn, scrabbling to find the quickest way to cut costs. So-called 'soft' items like marketing and advertising were the first to go. With them went the advertising industry's once staunch loyalty to the commission system.

Third, the traditional agency has found itself slugging it out with a new competitive set – management/marketing consultancies on the one hand and a myriad of low-cost production services on the other. Finally, the emergence of globalisation and integration has added a new dimension to the shape and scale of deals.

Today, remuneration methods are more diverse than ever: there is no simple standard. Clients and agencies need to be more creative in devising a remuneration system to suit their needs. Better value and greater mutual respect might emerge if both parties were to work harder to arrive at more focused, leveraged remuneration deals.

However, before examining the various remuneration systems, it is important to make a distinction in terms of the work that an agency is involved in. It is important to make a separation between above- and below-the-line activities. In simple terms, above-the-line expenditure relates to media expenditure – that is, the cost of advertising on television, in the press and magazines, on radio and outdoor, and cinema. It is these areas from which the agency receives its commission payments. Below-the-line expenditure covers all other areas of marketing communications, whether on sales promotion, public relations or elsewhere.

1 **Commission:** The traditional commission system continues as the most common basis for calculating agency income. For many decades, the principle has been established that agencies receive the bulk of their income *not* from their clients, but from media proprietors. Indeed, this gives rise to the use of the word

'agency'. They were the agents of the media companies. Historically, agencies have received 15 per cent of the monies spent in the media as a direct discount from the television contractors, radio stations, media titles, and other sectors. You may, sometimes, see the figure of 17.65 per cent used. This is the amount required to uplift the net media expenditure to yield 15 per cent commission.

The important thing to remember is that this commission is already built in to the media rates. If, for example, a poster campaign is quoted as costing £100 000, it will already contain an agency commission of £15 000. When you are preparing budgets, remember not to double cost this element. Some students show the gross cost of media *plus* an agency charge of 15 per cent. This is wrong!

It is also important to remember that this commission payment covers only the cost of the internal charges (staff salaries and other overheads, predominantly). The charges incurred by the agency for the production of items or the commissioning of any work on behalf of the client will be passed on, usually uplifted by a similar rate of 15 per cent.

2 **Negotiated commission:** For several years, pressure has been applied on agencies to adjust the commission rate to more accurately reflect the volumes of work involved in handling a clients' business. Client companies, especially the larger ones, have long recognised that their account represents a highly desirable income source for an agency. Moreover, there will, usually, be several agencies well equipped to handle the business, whatever its nature. In these situations, they can well afford to apply pressure to competing agencies to reduce the overall costs of their advertising activities.

Today, many agencies are prepared to negotiate a level of commission lower than 15 per cent. Sometimes, this will be a straight reduction on the entirety of the business, say to 12 per cent or 10 per cent. In other instances, it will be based on a sliding scale. In these cases, the first £million of billings might be charged at the full rate of 15 per cent, the second £million at, say, 12 per cent, and so on down to an agreed level. In part, this is a reflection that agencies, like other businesses, achieve economies of scale and that, as income rises, the associated costs rise at a slower rate.

It is also important to recognise that the calculation of commission can go the other way. In the case of a highly labour-intensive account, with a relatively low level of expenditure, the agency may require a higher level of commission to compensate it for the level of work involved. Some agencies, especially the larger ones, may operate on a minimum level of billings that they are prepared to service. This is a direct reflection of the fact that large agencies carry substantial overheads that have to be recouped from the activities of their clients, either in the form of billings or fees. Often, however, a company with comparatively small billings may wish to retain a large agency to have access to the skills and knowledge base that the agency possesses. The company may feel that the level of input, particularly of a strategic nature, may only be obtained by working with a large domestic or international agency. If a client wishes to retain one of these large agencies then it may be called upon to remunerate the agency by way of a supplementary fee.

However, whatever method of commission calculation is agreed, it is vitally important that it is formally agreed, in writing, at the outset of the relationship.

Seldom is there more ill feeling than when either party feels aggrieved, either that it is being overcharged or that it is being underpaid for the level of work required.

3 **Fee:** The majority of agency/client relationships are based on a level of fee being calculated and agreed at the outset. Here, some assessment of the level of work involved in handling the business is agreed and a fee reflecting this is determined. It is argued that, by removing the commission element, agencies are no longer predisposed to recommending increased levels of media expenditure on the basis of their own increased income needs. By the same token, since the agency receives no more (or less) for its large recommendations than its smaller ones, the client can feel more comfortable that these are based on a proper consideration of the strategic issues. Clients want advice that is neutral of how much is spent.

Fees provide for the agency's costs and profit, enabling even cash flow and budgeted expenditure. Fees also help to ensure that the agency's recommendations for the choice of communications are not biased towards commissionable above-the-line media. The principal drawback is that they provide little incentive or reward – there is no link between the value created and the remuneration paid.

In some instances a retainer fee is offered by the client to its agency where, for example, the company wishes to secure the input of an agency although, because of limited media expenditure, it recognises that the agency would not receive adequate compensation for its services. However, for the fee method to work smoothly, periodic reviews must be included within the contractual arrangements to ensure that both parties remain comfortable with the level of fee charged.

4 **Time-based:** In a few instances, the remuneration of agencies is based on similar principles to that of other professional bodies. Since, often, a great deal of time is involved in, say, the development of creative concepts, or media campaigns which for some reason do not run, an agreement is based on the time required to develop the work. The system is based on the maintenance of accurate time-sheets by all those personnel involved with the client's business, and the salary and associated costs raised by an agreed factor to deliver an appropriate level of profit.

5 **Cost-based:** An alternative approach is to apply the same principles as above to the costs of developing the associated work for a client. Again, an agreed percentage uplift is applied to all costs to ensure that the agency receives a profit for its efforts.

6 **Performance-based:** In a very few instances, the agency is rewarded on the basis of the results it achieves for its clients. Specific targets are established and agreed, and the agency is compensated for either achieving or exceeding the targets set. By the same token, the agency reimburses the client if it fails to reach the agreed levels of performance. Although this method of remuneration may spread more widely in those areas, such as media, where the buying performance of the agency can be directly measured, comparatively few full service advertising agencies are prepared to accept such a basis of compensation. Clearly, advertising is only one component of the overall mix and, if other areas of the

company fail to reach their goals, this will impact negatively on the agency income without their being able to control the level and nature of the activity.

The Incorporated Society of British Advertisers (ISBA 2000) defines payment by results as: 'an enhancement in the advertising agency remuneration agreement based on the achievement of mutually agreed targets or criteria for higher advertising satisfaction, providing an equitable return to the agency'.

Surguy (2001) suggests that performance-related payments resolve a number of difficulties:

- With the increasing need to justify advertising expenditures, relating the advertising budget to actual results provides real ammunition to the debate.
- It helps the agency to have the same objectives as the client and moves the relationship closer to that of a partnership.
- The agency is encouraged to develop more powerful creative solutions which operate on lower budgets and which use non-traditional media.
- The agency is encouraged to concentrate on improving efficiency and process.

Carter and Rainey (1998) have argued that it would be beneficial for agencies to be remunerated on the basis of brand equity performance – although, as yet, no satisfactory definition of 'brand equity' is available.

It is argued that this measure would help to determine the precise contribution which the advertising could be expected to make and, moreover, would encourage a high degree of mutual involvement between client and agency throughout the advertising development process.

However, it is recognised that agencies cannot be fully responsible for brand equity performance since it is affected by a variety of factors outside of the control of the agency – not least of which is the independent development of media strategies.

A survey conducted by Duncan and Lace (1998) demonstrated the decline of the traditional 15 per cent commission payment to agencies in the UK. Already, by that time, only one-third of all advertisers paid by commission with only 4 per cent continuing to pay the full 15 per cent.

The principal methods of remuneration at that time were:

Labour-based fees	43%
Fixed commission	24%
Fixed fees	12%
Commission + fees	11%
Variable commission	10%

They identified that fees accounted for 55 per cent of agency/client agreements, with these being more prevalent amongst those with 'younger' relationships and those with lower budgets.

Further, they found that one in five advertisers included an element of payment by results in their agency agreements. This was most common on accounts with higher annual budgets and at larger advertising agencies. It is interesting to note that, however, that some 80 per cent of clients who had included an element of payment by results in their agreements reported no change in the level of agency performance.

The remuneration of production is a widely reported source of friction between agencies and their clients. Clients are often concerned that agencies offer little or no added value for the additional payments made beyond the costs of production. The study indicated that around half of clients paid additional commission on production charges, whereas two-thirds of those advertisers paying a fee paid for production at cost.

The main issue for agencies has been a concern with the return on the investment they make on their clients' behalf. They invest a considerable amount of time and energy in the development of campaigns which may never appear. The consequence is that all of the agency's work – background analysis, strategy development, and the identification of the creative solution – may never be paid for.

The result has been a greater preparedness to negotiate a fee-based arrangement with their clients. In the worst situation, this provides a guarantee that the agency will be paid for its work.

An alternative source, Eagle et al. (1999), provides similar information for other countries, as summarised in Table 5.2.

Table 5.2 Remuneration methods, New Zealand and USA		
	New Zealand (%)	**USA (%)**
Full commission	12.5	5.3
Reduced commission	37.5	–
Fee	–	5.3
Project basis	12.5	–
Mix of commission/fee	37.5	89.5

According to Lace (2000), payment by results is now present in around 34 per cent of current UK agency/client agreements. Increasingly, it is estimated that nearly two-thirds of advertisers now pay for production at net cost (i.e. without mark-up). Historically, production mark-ups have been a significant source of agency income, but equally, have been a major source of dispute between some agencies and their clients.

According to a study by ISBA (2000) and the Advertising Research Foundation, the proportion of companies incorporating some form of performance-related pay into agency agreements had risen to 35 per cent in 2000 from 21 per cent in 1997.

Production costs

The issue of production costs remains a thorny problem, and is often the source of unsettling established relationships.

As noted above, whether the agency receives commission, a fee or income based on time or costs, clients must expect to pay the costs of production for the materials required to implement a campaign. Whether this is in the form of a television commercial, or a direct mail piece is, in itself, immaterial. The principle is that, rarely, do agencies maintain in-house production facilities.

At the time when an agency have agreed finished concepts for implementation, these will be passed on to some outside company for final production. This may involve, for example, the production of film and video, the casting of artists for a commercial or press advertisement, the photographers' charges, typesetting, any print items and so on. A proper approach is to agree cost estimates at an early stage in the process, so that the client company has a complete understanding of the likely costs involved in the costs of communications materials. Some, like a television commercial, may be extremely high. Inevitably, the more complicated the materials, the higher the relative costs. A complicated mail piece will cost considerably more than a simple letter.

If both parties know the 'ball park' costs of production early in the process of creative development, subsequent difficulties can, substantially, be avoided. There is no point continuing with the development of a complicated brochure involving expensive location photography, if the need is for a simple communications item! Some latitude must be built in to cost estimates. Almost inevitably, some changes will take place during the production phase and these must be paid for. But, at minimum, the likely cost parameters will be clearly understood by both parties, and the shock of receiving a production bill of £400 000 when the client was expecting to pay, say £250 000, will be largely overcome.

Ownership of creative material

An issue which surfaces at regular intervals is that of the ownership of the creative work produced by agencies. So long as the relationship between an agency and its client is sustained, this is not an important consideration. However, when a client moves on, for whatever reason, attention must be given to the transfer of the copyright in the advertising and related materials. Often, this problem is resolved by an examination of the contract between the two parties. In most instances, certainly in terms of the relationships between the larger companies, the agreement between them provides for the transfer of copyright either upon the payment of a supplementary fee or in consideration for a percentage of subsequent billings during the period in which the creative work continues to be used.

The agreement is important for two reasons. It protects the agencies and recognises that a major contribution is their ability to produce effective creative work. On the other, it provides for the client to continue to use the material whilst the new agency is 'bedded in'. Even after a company appoints a new agency to handle its business, the process of developing new materials may take several months. By continuing to have access to the work produced by the previous agency, the client can continue to support his or her business during the period in which the new work is being developed, researched and implemented.

The criteria for agency selection

The starting-point in any agency selection process must be the definition of the services that the client requires them to provide. Different agencies fulfil different specialist roles, and it is important to isolate which services will be required. The range is certainly broad enough to provide the flexibility to meet any circumstances.

1 Full service agencies offering directly or indirectly (often through subsidiary companies) a comprehensive range of marketing communications inputs.

2 Broad-based specialist consultancies in the fields of media planning and buying, sales promotion, public relations and direct marketing.
3 Narrow-based consultancies offering, for example, creative services (copywriting and art direction), planning, new product development and so on.

It is important to identify the particular services that will be required in order to isolate the nature of the organisation or organisations to be employed. If the needs of the organisation are, predominantly, in the area of sales promotion or public relations, for example, there is little point attempting to secure the services of an international advertising agency. Not only are the main skills likely to be under-utilised, the senior management are extremely unlikely to become involved with the management of your business. Having identified the services, the next step is to identify the qualitative and quantitative criteria that will be used to evaluate performance.

Do you require the agency, for example, to be skilled in areas such as market research? Is planning a key requirement? What type of creative skills do you require? And so on.

Should the agency have prior experience of your market sector? What size should the agency be? Do you wish to be a major player, or are you content to be a 'small fish in a big pond'? Should the agency be part of an international network or are you content with a domestic agency?

You can then begin the process of identifying a shortlist of agencies that can fulfil your brief. In this respect, it is important to consider a wide variety of inputs to help you in the selection process. Certainly, it is important to examine recent issues of the trade press that will help you identify which agencies are 'hot' and which are not. It may provide you with examples of work that they have produced for other clients – so that you can consider aspects such as creative performance. There are a number of specific publications that will also help you identify the current clients and other aspects of the agencies you might be considering. Amongst these are the *Campaign* publication – *Portfolio*, the BRAD *Advertiser and Agency List*, the *Blue Book* and similar titles. You might consider consulting the Advertising Agency Register (AAR) which maintains current portfolios of agencies in the respective fields and can help guide you towards a shortlist by offering advice based on their experience of agency structures and 'personalities'.

There is little doubt that rumours of an 'account change' are particularly unsettling to the working relationship with the incumbent agency. As far as possible you should avoid publicising any impending review until as late as possible.

It is important that you visit a number of agencies to get to know the personalities involved – relationships with agencies are dependent on people factors. These meetings will provide them with the opportunity to set out their credentials and, hopefully, to identify the personnel who would be working on your business, should they be appointed. At this stage, try to discriminate between the 'A' team of senior management who will be responsible for new business presentations and who (unless your account is of major significance) will be unlikely to work on your business, and the day-to-day team. It is the latter with whom you will have to develop a working relationship.

Some companies issue a preliminary questionnaire to agencies they are considering, which contains a number of specific questions to assist the process of 'shortlisting'. This may be used to ensure that the criteria you have established are met by the possible contenders and that other important areas, including agency remuneration, are covered before the shortlist is finalised. Similarly, there are a number of specialist selection companies who will undertake the preliminary stages on your behalf. The benefit of using such consultants rests in their experience gained from an involvement in the process over many years – unlike your own which is likely to be somewhat limited – and the fact that the identity of the company seeking to appoint may be protected for somewhat longer.

Whatever approach you adopt, the next stage is the creation of a shortlist and the issuing of a specific brief. The brief to the agency is used to enable them to demonstrate a specific response to your requirements. As such it needs to provide the contenders with as much information as can be provided – bearing in mind that the more vague you are at this stage, the less able they will be to provide a full response to your requirements. As far as possible, you must be prepared to allow the agencies to access the same information as you would require for the development of your marketing communications plan. Security can be maintained by inserting a confidentiality clause into the briefing document. Allow sufficient time for the agencies to absorb and analyse the information provided, and to carry out their own research, if necessary, when considering the date for the 'pitch'. If there is insufficient time between the briefing and the presentation, the response will inevitably be somewhat shallow.

Finally, establish some form of objective assessment against which to measure the agency presentations. Define the formal criteria so that all involved in the process can participate in the decision on the same basis. Whether the presentations will be assessed on the basis of strategic recommendations or on the basis of preliminary creative work is a somewhat subjective decision. Equally it is important that, as far as possible, the key people at the company end should be involved in the selection process. It is they, rather than the senior management, who will need to establish good working relationships on an on-going basis. The importance of these interpersonal relationships cannot be stressed enough.

The same *Campaign* survey referred to previously (*Campaign* 1994) and conducted amongst 117 marketing directors identified several important factors which were sought from an agency during a pitch.

'Quality of thinking'	94%
'Good chemistry between both parties'	90%
'Evidence the agency understands and can enhance your brand'	85%
'A powerful creative idea'	68%
'Strategy that offers value for money'	73%
'An agency culture that fits your own'	64%
'Presence of senior agency staff who will stay on your account'	81%
'Evidence of sound business/management skills'.	75%

Once the agency selection has been made, it is important to ensure that there is a smooth and efficient handover between them and the previous incumbent, so that there is no interruption to the flow of work on your business. Contacts need to be formalised and the winning agency announced.

The *Campaign* survey identified seven important dimensions that were sought from a new advertising agency:

'It has previous experience working in your market sector'	46%
'It offers a fully integrated service, including below the line'	35%
'It offers international resources'	16%
'It offers a remuneration system based on fees not commission'	41%
'It is fundamentally committed to creative excellence'	74%
'It has embraced new technology and uses it'	38%
'It is able to advise you on the information superhighway'.	22%

In some instances, as we have already seen, the reasons behind an agency change have more to do with the breakdowns in personal relationships and the perceptions of the agency service, rather than with the quality of the creative work produced by the agency. In other instances, the cause of the move will be an international realignment of the agencies on the client roster. There will be occasions when the client will wish to continue to use the creative material that has been previously produced, despite a change in the agency appointed to handle the business. Most agencies have made provision for this in their contracts. Usually, the client will be required to pay a compensatory fee which will ensure that the rights to the creative output are transferred to the company on the cessation of the agency contract.

In November 1995, the ISBA (Incorporated Society of British Advertisers) and the IPA (Institute of Practitioners in Advertising) issued a guide to best practice in the management of the pitching process. It embodies a 10-point pitch guide covering many of the key points made above. It makes the strong recommendation that the pitch list should be limited to three agencies, or four if the incumbent is included, and that all agencies participating should be informed of the number on the list. It also makes the suggestion that client companies should make an overt financial contribution to the costs of the presentation as a sign of commitment. Although it recognises that such payments are unlikely to cover the costs of the agency's involvement in the presentation process – often the costs run into many thousands of pounds – nonetheless, it does serve to demonstrate the seriousness of the intent towards the agencies involved.

According to Beard and Kim (2001) many marketers turn to independent consultants to help manage the search for a new advertising agency. In the USA, some estimates indicate that the majority of large account reviews involve the use of external consultants. However, as the authors point out, no empirical research has been conducted to evaluate the practice.

Undeniably, the task of appointing a new advertising agency is both important and complex. The consequence is that it becomes very time consuming which some suggest is very poor use of senior management time. However, it remains true that the greater the level of care and effort which is invested in selecting the right agency, the greater the likelihood that the subsequent relationship will be long lasting.

However, there are criticisms of the consultancy process. It has been suggested that they may introduce a level of bias into the process by only recommending particular agencies (with which they are familiar) or certain types of agencies. Moreover, consultancies which develop close relationships with client companies may well encourage those clients to place their accounts for review, since the process will ensure that they earn large fees for their involvement.

Their study, which was limited to the USA, determined that 52 per cent of account reviews were managed by consultants. Further, it indicated very limited bias on the part of the consultants.

Most review consultants are former executives of large corporate advertising departments or major advertising agencies. The use of review consultants has become prevalent, in much the same way the use of consultants has grown in all areas of sales, marketing and management. Estimates of the extent to which consultants are managing reviews range from 50 per cent to 70 per cent.

Consultants in many areas are used for a variety of reasons that appear to fall into three categories:

1 resources
2 specialisation and expertise
3 objectivity.

The trade literature on the topic suggests that these reasons likely hold true for the use of review consultants, although it has also been suggested that some advertisers use them primarily to handle agency compensation negotiations.

As Beard (2002) indicates:

The basic question driving this study is the following: Does the use of review consultants lead to more successful client–ad agency relationships? Initially, and based on the similarities between users and nonusers of review consultants, the answer to this question is no. The results clearly indicate that relationships beginning with a consultant-managed review are neither more nor less successful, based on the advertiser's perception of five key relational factors. Thus, the claim that review consultants are 'matchmakers' who produce superior client–ad agency relationships is somewhat overstated.

Case study

APG Creative Planning Awards

Agency: DMB&B

Author: Charlie Snow

The Reading and Literacy Campaign

Background

In a 1997 report on literacy skills among OECD nations, the UK came third from bottom, with 23 per cent of adults having literacy skills at the lowest level. The UK was outperformed by the USA and New Zealand; we had almost twice as many people in the lowest level as Germany. Only Poland and Ireland did worse. It was facts like these that supported the government's comment on the 'unacceptable' literacy levels in this country.

In the White Paper, 'Education in Schools', the government set out its plans for tackling the problem from the bottom up, focusing on young children. Again, the statistics indicated room for improvement: only 63 per cent of 11-year-olds were achieving the expected standards in English, and performances varied considerably among primary schools – 15 per cent in the worst, 100 per cent in the best.

Targets

An ambitious target was set: 80 per cent of 11-year-olds to reach the expected standard in literacy for their age by 2002. A number of initiatives were set up from September 1998 to help meet the objective: the National Year of Reading was launched, the daily Literacy Hour was introduced into all primary schools and commercial partners were invited to help get more books into schools.

The brief

The main elements of the advertising brief were as follows:

- The desired outcome was that more and more parents (guardians, carers) would give more help with reading to their children of pre-school and primary school age.
- The central theme should be the benefits of literacy.
- Beware antagonising or alienating teachers.

The brief indicated that parents from lower socio-economic classes (C2DE) were the most in need of encouragement. They were the people we talked to in qualitative research, and from them four key learnings emerged that proved pivotal to the communications strategy.

Learning One: Reading Matters. Every parent agreed unequivocally that they wanted the best for their child(ren). They all recognised that being able to read was a necessary skill for their child to progress through life.

Learning Two: Lack of Confidence, Especially From Dad. Whilst the willingness to help might be there, the means was not. Many lacked confidence, having had bad experiences from childhood. This lack of confidence manifested itself in a certain nervousness of teaching children the wrong methods. And it was the dads that felt the most uncomfortable with reading, even suggesting it was women's work, justifying this view by praising their partner's greater ability to act out stories and their higher levels of patience.

Learning Three: Haven't Got the Time. The main barrier to providing more help was lack of time. Dad was working longer hours, Mum was working more herself, leisure time was being squeezed. So the government telling parents that they should spend 20 minutes a day reading to the children was all very well, but ran the risk of showing a lack of understanding of the realities of family life, and worse still could wind people up.

Learning Four: The Dreaded Book at Bedtime. The immediate association with children's reading was the book at bedtime; an occasion which in theory was joyous and intimate, but in practice was when everyone was tired, and was often cut short. For many, the occasion had turned into a chore.

The advertising task

These learnings led us to a specific advertising task: rather than tell them what they already knew, we needed to give parents the means and therefore the confidence to help with reading, especially the dads – our core target.

But we were faced with two big problems: parents felt a tremendous time pressure, and the book at bedtime had become a chore. These were real issues that we couldn't just gloss over. So we started to think about what sort of reading there was that didn't put time pressures on people and wasn't a chore.

The answer

We were getting blocked by the 'book at bedtime'. Reading didn't have to just be books at bedtime, it was anything at any time: it was cereal packets at breakfast, road signs from the car, Ceefax on television and so on. These were natural reading opportunities that occurred spontaneously in everyday life. They were far removed from the recommended 20-minute reading period or the daunting book at bedtime.

What we could do in the advertising was to validate these alternative reading moments and encourage parents to exploit them. We could open their minds to the fact that reading can be more than the book at bedtime: it's road signs, recipes, computer screens, football programmes, instructions for toys . . . it's all valid, fun and easy. And it was stuff that dads could get involved with. We had a strategy to meet the task and sidestep the barriers of time and the book at bedtime chore.

The creative brief

Our advertising proposition was: 'There are lots of opportunities to read to or with your children in everyday life, beyond the book at bedtime.' To make the advertising work harder, and to push the desired change in behaviour, a direct response element became central to the brief. There needed to be a call to action to seek out a leaflet which extended our idea by offering parents more practical advice on how they could help and showing a number of further occasions that they could take advantage of.

The creative work

The skill of the creative team has been in structuring and crafting the wealth of examples that planning provided into clear and memorable advertising. Their solution reflects real people in real situations. A sense of naturalism and intimacy is heightened by casting parents with their own children.

The spine of the commercial is the familiar book at bedtime moment; this is offset by alternative reading moments, all of which can be a simple shared pleasure between parent and child. The effect is made more dramatic by the use of a famous nursery rhyme whose familiar, traditional refrain is broken by the vernacular from the everyday occasions.

The result is an entertaining and involving campaign that recognises the value of reading both books and other material, summarised in the line: 'A little reading goes a long way'. Having been drawn in, the viewer is then directed to phone for a leaflet filled with yet more practical advice.

Contribution to media

To increase the impact and effect and to enhance the creative work, the television occasion we recommended was 'mutual viewing' – Mum, Dad and the children enjoying programmes as a family. The schedule focused on early evening and weekend, and featured programmes such as *Coronation Street*, *Champions League Football* and *Stars in Their Eyes*. TV was supplemented by other 'mutual viewing' media: a half-term Disney cinema package was bought, as was a children's home video deal. The commercials also featured on a number of Premier League football clubs' jumbotrons before kick-off and at half time.

The results

The fact that the campaign has proved to be a huge success endorses the power of the work. Over a million leaflets have been sent out as a result of the advertising. Far from antagonising teachers, we have gained their full support – they have become a valuable distribution network.

The figures show that we have not only reached but motivated the C2DE dads: with advertising awareness among our core target at 57 per cent, and agreement with the statement – 'It made me feel I could really help my children' – at 79 per cent. This positive change in attitude seems to have converted into a positive change in behaviour. In follow-up telephone interviews with parents that responded to the advertising, 37 per cent claimed to have used the tips in the leaflet, with another 56 per cent saying they intended to use them.

Planning identified the key task for advertising: to provide parents with the means and therefore the confidence to help with reading, especially dads. It also identified two key barriers: time pressure, and the book at bedtime chore. Planning offered a clear solution to meet the task and side step the barriers: the validation of a range of everyday reading opportunities beyond the book at bedtime – opportunities that were easy to take, fun to do, and involved dads.

SOURCE: This case study is adapted from the paper presented at the APG Creative Planning Awards. The full version is available at www.warc.com and is reproduced by kind permission of the World Advertising Research Center.

Questions

1 Consider the different roles of agency personnel. What is their contribution to the overall task of the development of effective advertising?
2 Identify the different types of advertising agency and consider their role in respect of handling aspects of the clients' business.
3 Is there a conflict between the increasing specialisation of some agencies and their ability to make overall strategic recommendations to their clients?
4 Examine the different methods of agency remuneration. Why has there been a progressive move away from the traditional commission system?
5 Why do some clients seek to develop long-term relationships with their agencies whilst others move frequently? Identify the reasons why some clients change agency on a regular basis.
6 How would you go about seeking to appoint a new advertising agency to handle your business?

6 Analysing the advertising audience

Learning outcomes

This chapter aims to develop your understanding of:

- consumer behaviour in the context of advertising development
- influences on consumers' purchasing decisions
- underlying changes in the nature of the consumer and their impact on purchasing
- brand loyalty
- consumer understanding of advertising
- organisational buying behaviour.

At the outset of the planning process it is imperative to ensure that the planner has a deep understanding of the nature of the audience for advertising. Gaining an understanding of the ways in which people set about making their purchase decisions is an essential part of determining effective communications strategies. In simple terms, potential customers can be divided into two broad groups. For most products and services, the largest group is represented by the consumer market, comprising large numbers of both individuals and households who purchase products and services for their own use. For others, their potential purchasers are made up of companies, both those who operate for profit together with non-profit organisations who buy goods and services for their own use.

This chapter will explore each of those aspects.

Understanding consumer behaviour

The topic of consumer behaviour is an extensive one. It has been defined by Solomon (1996) as: 'The study of the processes involved when individuals or groups select, purchase, use or dispose of products, services, ideas or experiences to satisfy needs and desires'.

A considerable body of work exists in the attempt to understand the important dynamics of consumer behaviour. Early theoretical studies tended to concentrate on the economic variables to explain the differences that existed amongst consumers.

However, these provided only a limited understanding of the process since they ignored the important psychological factors. George Katona (1963) introduced a new approach known as behavioural economics, which sought to add these dimensions to the economic factors. However, the turning point for a proper appreciation of the complex nature of consumer behaviour was provided by Francesco Nicosia

(1966) who was amongst the first to recognise the important role of marketing communications in determining the nature of consumer purchases.

Two further studies provide the basis for our contemporary understanding of the process of consumer behaviour. The Engel, Kollat and Blackwell (1968) model first introduced the concept that the consumer passes through a series of separate stages during the decision-making process. A year later, John Howard and Jagdish Sheth (1969) developed their important model (known generally as the Howard-Sheth model) which introduced the notion that there are different levels of decision making dependent on the nature of the purchase being undertaken.

The decision-making process

The decision-making process consists, theoretically, of a number of separate and distinct stages. In practice, it is not necessary that all of the stages are followed in each purchasing decision, nor are the stages necessarily followed in the order shown below. However, the model in Figure 6.1 provides a useful basis from which to examine the separate dimensions of decision making and to explore the potential impact of marketing communications upon them.

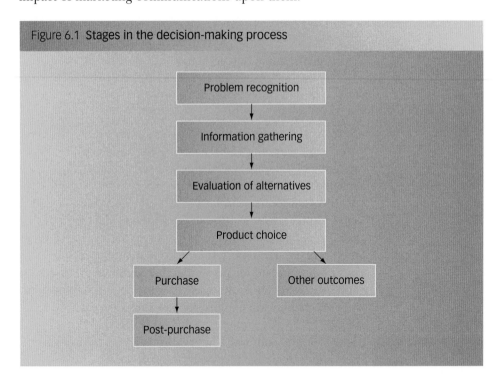

Figure 6.1 **Stages in the decision-making process**

Problem recognition

At the outset, the consumer experiences a need or problem situation which, in simple terms, is the appreciation of some difference between his or her existing state and the desired state. This might be the experiencing of thirst or hunger, or some more complicated problem such as dissatisfaction with, say, a domestic sound system.

Information gathering

Whereas the solution to the first problem is fairly straightforward – obtain a drink – in the second case, the individual will rarely possess sufficient knowledge on which to base a purchasing decision. It is likely, therefore, that he or she will set about obtaining relevant information from a variety of sources. These might include specialist publications, for example, *What Hi Fi*, and *Which Magazine*, together with the opinions of friends, relatives and others who might recently have gone through a similar process. Equally, he or she might visit a series of specialist outlets to gather leaflets, literature and the opinions of the dealers who stock the range of relevant products.

Evaluation Once sufficient information has been gathered the potential purchaser can consider the various alternatives on offer, and make an evaluation based on both objective and subjective criteria. An important consideration might be the amount of money available for the purchase, or the looks and styling of the different products. Familiarity with the various manufacturers' names might be a further basis of evaluation, similarly, the reputation of the retailer and so on. It is in this context that branding becomes a vital component, since the reputation of the brand may well be uppermost in terms of which product to purchase.

Purchase Once the evaluation stage has been completed, the individual may decide to make the purchase. However, it is important to recognise that in some situations the decision may be deferred. Perhaps the available models fail to meet the criteria applied, or the individual does not possess sufficient money at that time to enable the desired purchase to be made.

Post-purchase Even when the purchase has been made, the process depicted by the model does not cease. The purchaser will often seek justification for the purchase – which can be obtained from a number of sources. Advertising may serve to congratulate the purchaser on the wisdom of his or her choice; the comments of friends and others may similarly reinforce the purchase decision. However, in some instances, the consumer will fail to be satisfied with the product. Some consumers will complain directly to the outlet from which it was purchased, others will complain to the manufacturer, yet more will simply tell their acquaintances that the product failed to live up to expectations.

This notion of post-purchase dissatisfaction is important in the communications context since, if it is sufficiently widespread, it may undermine all of the efforts and investment that the organisation places into advertising.

Advertising is often used to provide consumers with decision rules and the necessary evaluative criteria to use when making purchase decisions. For example, advertising might emphasise a brand's performance on a particular dimension in order to establish that attribute as being important to consumers.

Brand decisions tend, for the most part, to be made intuitively rather than rationally and most brand communication is processed at very low attention levels. Heath (2001) challenges the view established in the models of consumer information processing that there is great benefit to be gained from collecting brand information necessary to make a rational decision. He argues instead that most brand decisions are made using instinct and intuition.

Similarly, Leith and Riley (1998) argue that it is imperative to understand the emotional and subconscious triggers leading to a product choice. However, it is necessary to understand that these 'need states' are a result of the situations individuals find themselves in at a particular point of time, and that these will change at different points in time.

This is reflected in a comment by Tyrrell (1994): 'there are often more differences between the same individual on two different occasions than there are between two different individuals on the same occasion.'

Swindells (2000) argues that for any consumer, the world is made up of a myriad of vague ideas, images, thoughts and feelings. They come together in a loose network of meanings which shape consumer behaviour. The consumer is bombarded with information which has practical implications for their actions.

The nature of problem solving

In the purchasing process we can distinguish between three types of purchase:

- **Routine problem solving:** Routine problem solving is most often associated with frequent or regular purchases. Such purchases are those in which the consumer already possesses sufficient information upon which to base the purchase decision. Choices between competing brands are often made routinely with minimal effort on the part of the consumer. Everyday purchases such as the purchase of a can of drink, a bar of chocolate or even a tube of toothpaste, generally, fulfil these criteria. Except for new products which may be introduced to the sector, the consumer is very familiar with the products which are available and, most importantly, the brands. The simple recognition of the packaging of a familiar brand within the retail environment may be the only cue that the consumer requires to make the purchasing decision.

- **Limited problem solving:** In those situations where a decision is required, such as a consideration of a new product or brand, some thought will be given to the nature of the purchase decision. In practical terms, this may simply consist of a comparison being made between a familiar brand and the new one on the basis of the ingredients, price or some other dimension. For the most part, the consumer follows a series of simple decision rules rather than become involved in a rigorous evaluation of the various alternatives. Here again, the brand name may be important since one which is familiar provides the confidence and reassurance necessary to make the purchase. And, as with routine purchase, the level of risk involved in the purchasing decision is low, hence the consumer is less concerned if the decision made subsequently proves to be the wrong one. For example, if the consumer purchases an unfamiliar bar of chocolate, perhaps one which is new to the market, but which bears a familiar brand name, the consequences of making a wrong decision is of little importance. If, on tasting the product, the consumer finds that it is not to his or her liking, they simply resolve not to purchase the product again.

- **Extended problem solving:** Purchasing decisions which are complex or involve the expenditure of considerable sums of money are, by their very nature more extended. Since there is a level or risk associated with the decision, the consumer may well follow several or all of the stages outlined in the decision-making process, described earlier.

Siamack Salari, head of behavioural research at J. Walter Thompson, has developed a model of the decision-making process within the shopping environment. It follows four stages. First, the consumer looks for a reference point, usually the benchmark brand. Then they compare other brands against the benchmark. The third stage is making a final selection, followed by making a final check, as described by Salari (1997):

> It is a model and not everybody goes by it – people sometimes jump stages. We have timed how long people spend in stores. In some product categories, they find the reference point in two seconds, in others it is longer. Where that happens, there is confusion and it is an indication that the brand mix is not helping people get into selection.

Increased complexity and choice

It has to be remembered, however, that the consumer is confronted by an increasing range of choices in terms of every single product purchase. A glance at any fitment in a supermarket illustrates the wide variety available to the consumer. The frequent introduction of new products and variants of existing ones, makes the process of choosing an appropriate product slightly more difficult. The recent growth of the coffee vendors (Costa, Starbucks, etc.) is further illustration. These outlets offer as many as seven different types of coffee (espresso, cappucino, latte, etc), five different toppings (cinnamon, vanilla, etc.), four variations on milk from skimmed to extra cream, four sugar alternatives, three different cup sizes, three variations on strength together with eight different syrups. This provides over 6000 different combinations and it is estimated that it would take over 17 years to try all of them!

Despite this, most purchases, particularly those of everyday items, are made very speedily. This can be seen readily by observing consumers making their purchase decisions in, say, a supermarket.

Faced with so much choice, what strategies do consumer adopt? The options are illustrated in Figure 6.2.

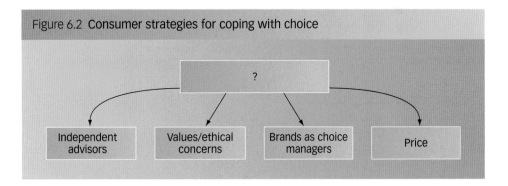

Figure 6.2 Consumer strategies for coping with choice

When making purchasing decisions, there are five types of value that the purchaser can derive from the brand:

1 Functional value: The specific benefits that the consumer perceives derive from the brand.
2 Social value: The value a brand can provide to link the purchaser with other users of the brand on a social level – particularly associated with high quality, luxury brands.

3 Emotional value: The emotional satisfaction which the consumer derives from ownership of the brand.

4 Knowledge value: The satisfaction of curiosity which the purchaser derives from trying a new brand.

5 Conditional value: The perceived utility of the brand within a particular situation.

Factors influencing buying behaviour

There are a wide variety of factors that influence the purchasing behaviour of consumers. These are summarised in Figure 6.3.

Consumers do not live in isolation from the environment that surrounds them. All the factors in Figure 6.3 may play a part in influencing the decisions taken on a daily basis. Such things as psychological influences; needs and motives; attitudes and lifestyle; personality and self-concept; culture; social status; reference groups; word-of-mouth communication; household and situational influences will often have a direct bearing on the nature of the decision taken.

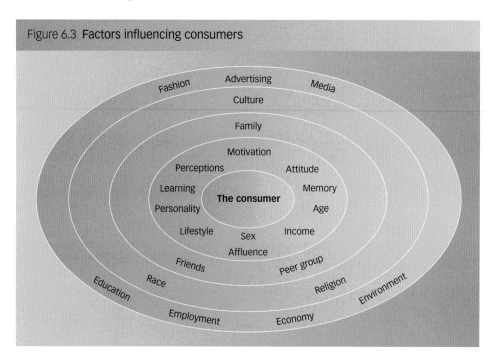

Figure 6.3 **Factors influencing consumers**

- **Age:** The age of the consumer will have a distinct bearing on the sort of products and services that he/she purchases. Products which are of interest to a younger audience will have little or no appeal to one which is older, and vice versa. Indeed, products which are aimed at a specific age group may alienate people of a different age. Significantly, the spread of population is undergoing major changes with the consequence that, in most Western countries, there are an increasing number of older consumers and a corresponding decline in the number of younger consumers. This will have important consequences for society in general but also in terms of the marketing of products and services.

  There is already widespread recognition that many older consumers have far greater disposable income and, hence, an increased number of products are being targeted towards them.

These changes can be seen from Table 6.1 showing population projections.

Table 6.1 **The ageing population in the UK**

	Population projections in millions			
Age	**2001**	**2011**	**2021**	**2031**
0–15	12 003	11 045	11 093	11 172
15–29	10 578	11 372	10 784	10 308
30–44	13 913	12 713	12 511	12 915
45–59	11 282	12 763	13 461	12 006
60–74	7 780	9 314	10 653	21 280
75+	4 452	4 940	5 602	6 985
TOTAL	59 987	61 956	64 105	65 568

SOURCE: UK census data and National Statistics

- **Sex:** Similarly, the sex of the individual may dictate both what he or she purchases as well as the purchase location. For the most part, it would be expected that the purchasing decisions of females in terms of clothing, cosmetics and magazines would be different from those made by males.
- **Income:** It is not only the absolute level of income that is important, but also the amount that is disposable after other commitments have been taken into account. For example, someone who owns a house will have to pay the mortgage out of their income, similarly with a loan to purchase a car. These, and other 'fixed' expenditures, such as food and clothing, will have to be taken into account before the consumer can make purchases of more 'indulgent' items. In turn, the amount that can be spent on such purchases will be dependent on how much is left.
- **Affluence:** There is no doubt that, over time, particularly in Western nations, individuals have become progressively more affluent. What were once considered as 'luxury' items, are now considered part of the ordinary. For example, in 1987 the number of meals eaten out stood at 3.5 million. In 2003 the figure was almost 5 million. Similarly, the number of holidays taken abroad has increased from 16.5 million in 1987 to around 36.5 million in 2003. Some other examples indicate the increased levels of affluence, as shown in Table 6.2.
- **Personality:** Personality can be defined as an individual's unique psychological composition that influences the way that the individual reacts to the environment. However, there is considerable debate as to whether personality traits are, in fact, consistent across time. None the less, in conjunction with other factors, personality may influence the nature of the products and services purchased by the individual.

  Some individuals are more active than others, yet others more inquisitive. A further distinction may be made in terms of the introvert versus extrovert dimension. This may, for example influence the nature of the clothes individuals wear, the type of entertainment they seek and so on.
- **Lifestyle:** This influences how people spend their time, the sort of activities in which they like to become involved and their general interests within their immediate surroundings. Again, it is an important behaviour dimension which

Table 6.2 Indicators of affluence, UK, 1987–2001

	1987 (%)	1997 (%)	2001 (%)
Home ownership:			
Owner-occupied, owned outright	24	26	27
Owner occupied, with mortgage	37	41	41
Car ownership:			
1 car	45	48	40
2 cars	16	29	35
Washing machine	87	92	93
Microwave oven	36	75	85
Central heating	73	88	91
Colour television	91	98	99

SOURCE: General Household Survey, National Statistics Office 2003

affects the way that people dress, their choice of hobbies and even the ways in which they decorate their houses or flats.

- **Learning:** This can be defined as those experiences that have an effect on personal behaviour. However, it has important implications in the context of advertising. People learn to understand the symbolic meanings conveyed within advertising campaigns. The significance is that it is often possible to communicate complex messages without using full descriptions. For example, the depiction of a kitchen in an advertisement might convey a particular lifestyle or create aspirational values to the reader.

- **Memory:** In many purchase decisions, consumers do not make a deliberate attempt to search their memory for previously encoded information. In these situations, implicit (versus explicit) memory retrieval may be dominant; therefore, there is a need for marketers to understand the effects of implicit memory. Consistent with this, low retrieval motivation seems to underlie findings that retail store consumers spend just five seconds on some brand choices (Shapiro and Shanker 2001).

- **Perceptions:** These relate to the way in which we derive meanings from the external environment and apply them to our own world. Importantly, perception relates to the way in which we 'translate' stimuli. Since all consumer activities such as shopping, purchasing and the way in which we use products require interaction with the outside world, the topic of perception is vitally important in the context of advertising.

  Perception is also the process by which stimuli such as sight, sound, colour, touch, taste and others are selected, organised and interpreted. External stimuli or sensory inputs represent a major part of the marketing communications process. Advertising, in particular, makes great use of these stimuli to communicate a message about a brand or service. The use of music in commercials is designed to evoke a series of memories or to create positive associations between the brand and the consumer, as shown in Figure 6.4.

Figure 6.4 **The perceptual process**

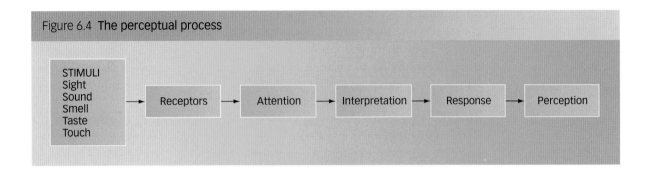

- Sight: The visual components of marketing communications are especially important. The shape, size and particularly the colour of an item of packaging conveys specific meaning to the consumer regarding the identity of the brand. Given the speed with which the selection of products from crowded supermarket shelves takes place, these visual cues are vitally important to the ability to convey specific brand information. So important, in fact, that recently British law has been altered to enable companies to protect the specific colours they use to identify their products and services. First amongst those to register for protection were BP (the specific colour green used on their forecourts) and Kodak (the shade of yellow used on packaging and other materials).
- Sound: The use of music in television commercials has already been mentioned. Often, the sound track selected is used to create associations with a particular product or service. Since the launch of 'Launderette' featuring Nick Kamen and accompanied by Marvin Gaye's 'I heard it through the grapevine' activity for the Levis brand has been synonymous with music. First Choice feature a track by Katrina and the Waves in their advertising and reinforce the proposition by playing the same music on their flights. The process has been taken to the extreme point of identification by Intel who use an audio link in the same way as a logo is used by other companies. Intel insists that every computer advertiser uses the mnemonic to identify the presence of the Intel chip inside the computer.
- Smell: The use of fragrance, especially within the retail environment, is designed to induce specific perceptions in the minds of shoppers. The smell of fresh bread or freshly roasted ground coffee is likely to create positive images regarding the outlet and induce sales, not only of the specific product categories but of others where the positive association of fresh produce induces a favourable response.
- Taste: Many product categories are differentiated on the basis of taste, either real or perceived. Indeed, the process of taste differentiation is used by several companies, the most notable of which is Pepsi, to identity the difference between the brand and its competitors.
- Touch: The feel of a product, or the benefits associated with the use of a particular brand, offer another dimension of differentiation. Lenor, Unilever's washing product, has long used the benefit of softness to create a positive association with the brand.

- **Motivation:** This relates to the way in which a person behaves in particular circumstances and deals with the issues of why the particular action is taken. A great deal of research in the context of advertising development is undertaken to understand why people behave in the way that they do and, in certain circumstances, to identify ways in which their behaviour can be changed for the benefit of the advertiser.
- **Attitude:** This relates to way in which we think about specific elements in the world in which we exist. Importantly, these attitudes also affect the ways in which we act in particular circumstances. They determine our likes and dislikes and, as with motivations, are important to understand from a planning perspective. By understanding the attitudes that people hold we can either seek to reinforce them – if they are positive – or to change them if they are negative.

As much as we are influenced by the dimensions briefly described above, we are also affected by the people who surround us and the beliefs and attitudes that they hold.

- **Family:** since attitudes and behavioural patterns are, as we have seen, learned experiences, one of the most important sources of such learning is the family to which we belong. Many of the belief patterns that we display derive directly from our previous family experiences. Patterns of behaviour are learned from a very early age and are directly influenced by family members. This extends beyond such dimensions as attitudes towards others, or to politics, but also includes our attitudes towards products and services.

  This is illustrated by a survey conducted by Decision Market Source Centre Inc. and reported by McNeal (1999) which found that of those interviewed in a sample of 40 000 college students, 62 per cent still buy the same brand they grew up on.
- **Friends and peer groups:** As with family, friends have a direct influence on our patterns of behaviour. To a very large extent we seek to emulate our immediate friends in terms of the way in which we dress, often the very foods we eat and so on. Most people seek to be accepted by the people around them and, hence, try to behave in a manner which will be endorsed by them. Much research has been conducted to determine the influence of peer groups. It has been found that even young children seek to copy the patterns of behaviour of their peers, to the extent that they favour the same brands of clothing, footwear and other products.
- **Culture, race and religion:** These are important dimensions of consumer behaviour, both in a domestic and an international context. Culture can be defined as those beliefs that an individual acquires as a member of society. It includes a wide variety of beliefs affecting morals, customs and knowledge. It serves to establish a variety of conventions which affect the way people think and act. The difficulty, particularly in terms of the development of international advertising, is that cultural beliefs are often different and, as we will examine in Chapter 13, cause potential difficulties in the development of advertising campaigns which are to be implemented across a number of geographic regions.

  Race and religion can be considered as distinct aspects of culture and which, similarly, impose specific patterns of behaviour. These might include, for example, foods which are proscribed and therefore cannot be eaten, patterns of dress, as well as personal values.

- **Education:** Levels of education are similarly important in determining individual behavioural patterns. It may, for example, impact on the extent to which the individual challenges information received from advertising. The higher the level of education, the greater the likelihood that the individual will be more demanding of products and services and will require more information, rather than accepting at face value the nature of an advertising message.

  An important aspect in this regard will be the level of literacy. Whilst in most societies, literacy is at a high level, there will remain some percentage of the population who are, for example, unable to read. In that context, press advertising will need to more graphic than descriptive.

  Similarly, educational achievement will also have an impact on the nature and level of employment which, in turn, will affect the level of income.

Perceptual selection

Today's consumer is bombarded with information. Information is available at every moment in the day – from news and weather broadcasts, to roadside posters, point-of-sale material in shop windows and, of course, advertising messages. The fact is that there is simply too much information available to be processed simply. The consumer adopts a defence mechanism to limit the amount of information they absorb, known as perceptual selection. In effect, they subconsciously choose to accept or ignore information available to them.

The brain is highly selective. The conscious brain allows in only the perceptions that reinforce its belief system. As Burdick (1997) puts it 'it [the brain] does not believe what it sees – it sees only what it believes'. He argues that it is the visual element of advertising that is more important – because it has direct access to the subconscious.

Attention

A consequence of perception selection is the fact that many consumers either actively ignore advertising messages or find that their attention is directed elsewhere during an advertising break. It is for this reason that the creation of advertising uses specific devices to attract the consumer's attention at the beginning of a television or radio commercial, for example.

The changing nature of the consumer

Recent years have seen fundamental changes in consumer aspirations, substantially the impact of 50 years of consumerism. As we have already seen, what was once perceived as luxury is today seen as an everyday requirement of household life.

In contemporary society, there is less deference, less guidance and more complexity.

- Although we still trust many professionals and institutions, we are less bound by their pronouncements.
- Gender roles are breaking down – there are fewer stereotypes.
- Peer pressure remains but this is less predictable.
- Scientific evidence appears to be contradictory.
- So, we worry about a wider range of issues.

The standard classification of consumers increasingly ceases to have real value. Values and lifestyles are far more significant variables than age or sex, for example. Judy Lannon (1991) writes: 'Such has been the enthusiasm for psychographic segmentations that perhaps the most predictive segmentation of all, lifestage, either is overlooked or somehow lost in the analysis.' Lifestage provides a means to transcend cultural differences and can be used to segment consumers across national boundaries.

In the same way, Gordon and Valentine (2000) argue that consumers are regarded too rigidly in the context of marketing. They argue that the concept of the 'target consumer' is outmoded. It implies not only rigidity, but also the idea of ownership and control of the target by the brand. They recognise that consumers are not fixed points in space and time. They are continuously evolving and changing, and have multiple identities. And, from an advertising perspective, it is vitally important to understand the nature of these changes in order that campaigns can respond to changing needs.

At a recent conference on changes in consumer behaviour Paul Flatters (2003) of The Future Foundation depicted these societal changes in a graphic form (Figure 6.5).

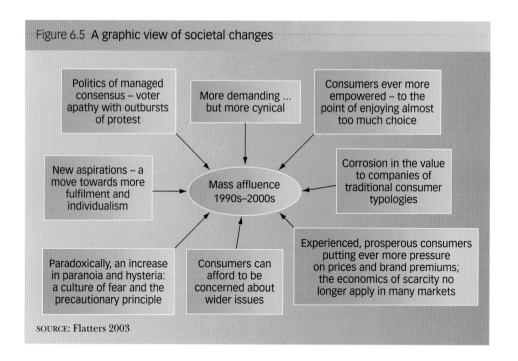

Figure 6.5 A graphic view of societal changes

Politics of managed consensus – voter apathy with outbursts of protest

More demanding ... but more cynical

Consumers ever more empowered – to the point of enjoying almost too much choice

New aspirations – a move towards more fulfilment and individualism

Mass affluence 1990s–2000s

Corrosion in the value to companies of traditional consumer typologies

Paradoxically, an increase in paranoia and hysteria: a culture of fear and the precautionary principle

Consumers can afford to be concerned about wider issues

Experienced, prosperous consumers putting ever more pressure on prices and brand premiums; the economics of scarcity no longer apply in many markets

SOURCE: Flatters 2003

Maslow's hierarchy of needs

As we have already seen, consumers experience needs. Essentially, these are the gap between their current condition and their ideal state. In 1954, the psychologist Abraham Maslow argued that these needs are organised in sequential levels which represent a series of priorities. These can be depicted graphically, as in Figure 6.6.

At the lowest level, there are a series of physiological needs that must be satisfied – hunger, thirst, sleep, shelter, etc. These needs are essential for the survival of the

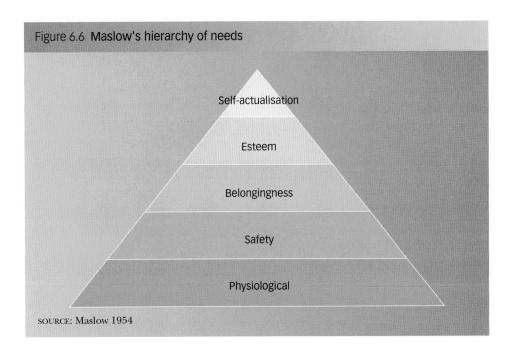

Figure 6.6 Maslow's hierarchy of needs

Self-actualisation

Esteem

Belongingness

Safety

Physiological

SOURCE: Maslow 1954

individual and must be met before the higher levels can be considered. At the next level, there are a series of needs that relate to a safe and secure life. Once these lower-level needs have been satisfied, the individual will move towards products and services which demonstrate their belonging to a particular group within society. These will include those items which are consumed by the identified peer group, in order that the individual can demonstrate membership of that group.

What Maslow describes as the esteem needs are those items that enable an individual to evaluate him or herself positively. They are often outward manifestations of success within society which enable the individual too convey his status to others. Expensive items such as branded watches, luxury cars and designer clothes all serve to convey this impression.

Finally, he identifies a level of self-actualisation. At this level, the individual will already have achieved much in life and will seek to fulfil personal needs, perhaps of enhancing knowledge, increasing overseas travel or other aspects of personal fulfilment. This will often, for example, include such things as devoting time to charitable activities, in order that the individual can 'give back' something of his or her success to society as a whole.

A brand itself does not consist of any value. However, it can be associated with values that meet the needs of the consumer. These brand values can be formed into a hierarchy, after Maslow, as in Figure 6.7.

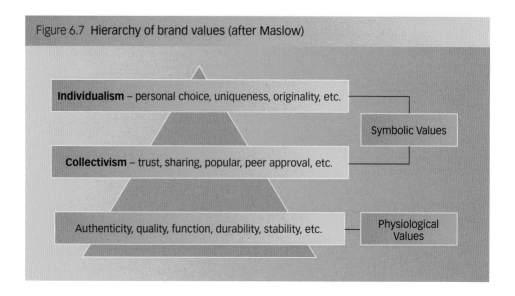

Figure 6.7 Hierarchy of brand values (after Maslow)

Individualism – personal choice, uniqueness, originality, etc.

Symbolic Values

Collectivism – trust, sharing, popular, peer approval, etc.

Authenticity, quality, function, durability, stability, etc.

Physiological Values

Self-image and symbolic consumption

Central to contemporary thinking is the recognition that the consumer does not make consumption choices solely from the nature of a product's functions but also from their symbolic meanings (Belk 1988). He argues that one of the key ways of expressing and defining group membership is through 'shared consumption symbols'.

Consumers are what they own, since their possessions are viewed as major parts of their extended selves. The symbolic meaning of the consumers' possessions may portray essences of his/her individuality or reflect his/her desirable connections with others.

Brands have, increasingly become the manifestation of the individual. As Sir Michael Perry (former Chairman of Unilever) (cited in Lury 1998) describes it 'in the modern world, brands are a key part of how individuals define themselves and their relationships with one another . . . More and more we are simply consumers. We are what we wear, what we eat, what we drive.'

We have seen that products provide a series of symbolic meanings that are largely determined by the advertising message that supports the brand. The functions of these symbolic meanings of products operate in two directions: outward in constructing the social world, social-symbolism; and inward in constructing our self-identity, self-symbolism (Elliott 1997). As consumption plays a central role in supplying meanings and values for the creation and maintenance of the consumer's personal and social world, so advertising is recognised as one of the major sources of these symbolic meanings. These cultural meanings are transferred to brands and it is brands that are often used as symbolic devices for the construction and maintenance of identity.

Advertising is recognised as one of the most potent sources of symbolic meanings (see for example Lannon and Cooper 1983). Within society, advertising is viewed as a guideline to map out all aspects of the consumer's existence. On the other hand, all aspects of the consumer's existence are also guidelines to map out advertising creativity. The relationship between advertising and the consumer is a two-way process: advertising not only helps in creating, modifying and transforming cultural meanings for the consumer, but also represents cultural meanings taken from the consumer's world view and invested into the advertised product. This relationship results in a flow of symbolic meanings derived from culture and transferred into the semiotic world of advertising, then interpreted and used by consumers to construct internally their self-concept and externally their social world. 'Finally as part of the external construction of an individual's life world the meaning returns back to its original starting point, the mass of flowing meanings that represents culture.' Thus, advertising is both a means to transfer or create meanings into culture and a cultural product itself.

As Lannon and Cooper (1983) state: 'Advertising not only helps in creating, modifying and transforming cultural meanings for the consumer, it also represents cultural meanings taken from the consumers' view of the world and invested into the advertised product.'

It is widely recognised that consumers can identify themselves with specific brands and develop feelings of affinity towards them. Various authors have suggested that the consumer can enhance their self-image through the images of the brands they buy or use. The consequence of this work is that the greater the level of consistency between a brand image and the consumer's self-image, the better the consumer's evaluation of the brand and the greater the intention to buy it.

Sirgy (1982) argues that consumers would approach products that possess images that serve to enhance their self-esteem and avoid those that don't.

Similarly, authors (including Long and Schiffman 2000) have indicated that brands fulfil a social identification function. In this respect, they allow the consumer either to identify with or dissociate from a particular social group. Consumers will positively value those brands that enjoy a good reputation among the groups to which they belong, or aspire to form part of.

Vigneron and Johnson (1999) propose that brands provide a status function. Brands enable the user to express feelings of admiration and prestige. The authors suggest that this function is based on five characteristics:

1 They represent a symbol of the individual's power and social status.
2 They represent a reflection of social approval.
3 They benefit from the exclusivity or limitation of the offer to a small number of people (gold/platinum credit card).
4 They offer a contribution to emotional experiences.
5 They are evidence of technical superiority.

De Chernatony and McDonald (1998) depict the self-image concept and its relationship to brand choice as shown in Figure 6.8.

The significance of this from an advertising perspective is that consumers often buy products which are consistent with their own self-image or the image they seek to portray. Most of the research conducted in this field has suggested that the greater the degree of match between the human characteristics that consistently describe an individual's self or desired self and those that describe a brand, the greater the likely preference for the brand.

Brands seek to become involved with their audiences' lifestyles – Evian sponsored 'chill out areas' in clubs, Rizla created the Rizla Rolling Roadshow, First Direct projected a message on the side of a building by London's Westway so that

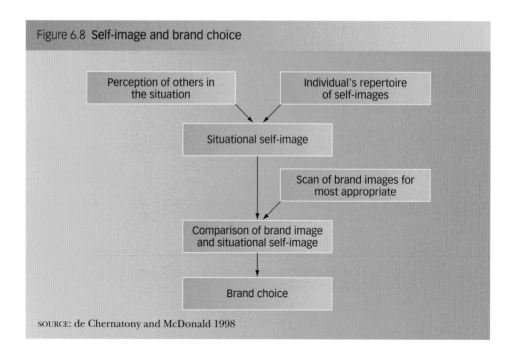

Figure 6.8 Self-image and brand choice

SOURCE: de Chernatony and McDonald 1998

clubbers, returning home in the early hours, would be greeted with the message 'We're awake too'. Similarly, Adidas have created 'urban culture programmes' to identify their brand with the attitudes of target consumers.

Brands can be used by the consumer as resources for the symbolic construction of the self. The symbolic consumption of brands can help establish and communicate some of the fundamental cultural categories such as social status, gender and age, and such cultural values as family, tradition and authenticity. Elliott and Wattasuwan (1998) comment that 'symbolic consumption does one of four things: portray individualism, reflect the desire to belong, categorise oneself in society, or carry out the process of self completion'. They go on to state that 'many products possess symbolic features and consumption of goods may depend more on their social meaning that their functional utility'.

The results of a study conducted by Jamal and Goode (2001) confirm previous findings that there is a strong relationship between self-image and brand preference. Consumers prefer brands that have images compatible with their perceptions of self. Moreover, the study confirms that consumers tend to prefer a brand based on its symbolic properties rather than its functional qualities.

Alreck and Settle (1999) describe this process as 'model emulation' as a way of belonging, i.e. copying others so as not to seem out of place, particularly in unfamiliar surroundings.

In his paper, Graeff (1996) found that the degree of similarity between brand image and self-image will have greater effects on the attitudes on consumers. Equally, consumers who exhibit a low degree of congruence between self-image and the brand's image are less persuaded by advertisements that encourage them to consider their self-image when evaluating the brand.

When there is low congruence between self-image and brand image, marketers can either attempt to change the brand image or de-emphasise the image of the brand in their advertisements and stress functional aspects of the brand.

Heath (2000) argues that successful advertising campaigns work by building up simple but potent associations and linking them to brands. These associations, by triggering different 'markers' in the brain influence brand choices at an intuitive level.

He illustrates his argument with a number of advertising campaigns for brands which establish these markers in the minds of consumers, summarised in Table 6.3.

Table 6.3 Product associations and benefits

Brand	Association	Benefit
Marmite	Unique salty taste	'Divisively unusual'
Toilet Duck	Curly bottle neck	Better for getting under rim
Dyson	Transparent	Better, more obvious cleaning
Body Shop	No animal testing	Stance against unnecessary cruelty
PG Tips	Pyramid bags	Stronger, more naturally brewed tea

SOURCE: Heath 2000

Although advertisers aim to create particular meanings for their brands in advertising, meanings interpreted by the consumer may be varied and diverse. There is growing recognition that the consumer is an active and participating audience. Moreover, work by Dube et al. (1996) demonstrated that there is a significant level of mismatch between the attitudes held by consumers and those reflected in the advertising aimed at them. In a sense, this contradicts the belief that attitudes should be matched. They concluded that the mismatch strategy may well be more persuasive on the grounds that it increases liking for the brand: 'If advertisements succeed in making consumers consider products from perspectives that they have not thought of before, it may help develop a richer, more elaborate network of associations.'

Consumers and brand loyalty

It has been consistently demonstrated that consumers buy and prefer brands (Buck 2001).

Having said that, however, consumers display differing levels of loyalty towards brands. Whilst some are absolutely loyal, buying the same brand on all occasions, others tend to be less so. The levels of brand loyalty can be depicted as shown in Figure 6.9.

The most important sector of consumers to any brand will be those who are absolutely loyal. Although these may only represent a comparatively small percentage of all purchasers (estimated at between 10 and 20 per cent depending on the brand), they are vitally important from the perspective of volume. Bearing in mind the 'Pareto' principle, these consumers may account for as much as 60–70 per cent of all products sold.

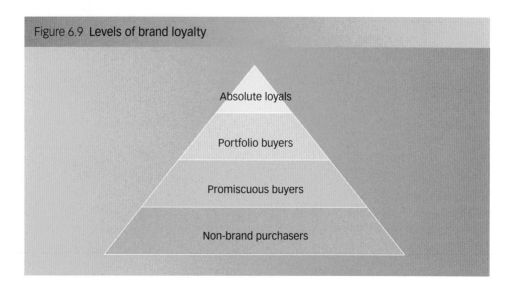

Figure 6.9 Levels of brand loyalty

Absolute loyals

Portfolio buyers

Promiscuous buyers

Non-brand purchasers

Many consumers are loyal to a comparatively few brands that represent their personal portfolios of preference. These consumers will be portfolio buyers. In effect, they have determined (possibly as a result of prior experience) that several alternative brands meet their personal criteria. They may well exhibit a specific preference towards one of them but where, for example, their preferred brand is out of stock or alternatively where a comparable brand is on special offer, they will choose to buy an alternative and be content with it. Often on any purchasing occasion, they will select the brand which they perceive as offering the best value for money. This may, for example, be a function of price or it may be some form of promotional offer which increases the perceived value. These consumers may also be referred to as brand switchers.

The third group of consumers can best be described as promiscuous buyers. In effect, they will purchase any product available based, usually, on price. They provide no loyalty and only make a repeat purchase of the same brand if it offers the best price.

Finally, there are a group of consumers who actively reject brands. For some this is an emotional decision based on the premise that brands are more expensive and offer no better value. For others, it is simply a question of price. Here the supermarkets' own label products reign supreme because they are invariably cheaper than manufacturers' products.

Understanding the motivations of these consumers will be part of the advertising planning process, since advertising will be required to perform a different role for each of these groups.

Whilst many advertisers target the loyal users and portfolio buyers, Anschuetz (2002) argues that in suggesting that a brand target a small group of profitable households, marketers want to ignore the large number of low-volume households, believing that increasing the small number of high-volume households is the route to growth. But dismissing the greater number of light- and moderate-buying households that are critical to brand growth as 'less valuable' is similar to dismissing a high-volume, low-margin brand as less valuable to a company's bottom line than a high-margin brand that sells very little. Although these consumers generate less profit per unit, the total number of units sold compensates for the lower margins contributing to the tremendous revenue and profit success of high-volume mass-marketed products. It is the combination of margin and quantity sold that produces a profitable bottom line, not margin alone.

Similarly, while generating less revenue or profit per household, the much larger number of lighter and moderate brand users makes them an important source of brand growth and, certainly, marketing communications attention.

So, in determining which consumers are most valuable to a brand, it is important that marketers consider the net impact on the bottom line, not just the revenue generated per household. A brand needs to focus on generating the greatest revenue and profits within its budget. That will mean generating purchase interest in the brand among light-, moderate- and heavy-buying households – even non-buyers. A brand needs to focus on increasing its profits from category consumers, not just on increasing the percent of its buyers that are the most profitable per household.

Barnard and Ehrenberg (1997) argue that many consumers are 'split loyals'. Each of these consumers chooses from his or her repertoire of brands with, mostly, steady purchase propensities, that is, only occasional shifts and departures from habit. Advertising to these multi-brand users, they argue, does not have to be strongly persuasive.

A paper by Baldinger and Rubinson (1996) suggests that loyal users can, in fact, be sub-divided into further groupings:

- 'real loyals', who are loyal in both attitude and behaviour;
- 'vulnerables', whose buying may be loyal, but whose attitudes are less strong;
- 'prime prospects', who actively favour a competitive brand in their attitudes.

They argue that there are specific links between attitude and behaviour, and it is the latter which can be used to predict the longer term performance of a brand. If attitudinal loyalty erodes over time the brand will continue to decline since, even loyal users, are likely to be wooed by other competitive brands.

A subsequent paper by Ilsley and Baldinger (1998) identifies three types of brand loyalty:

1 Behavioural loyalty: Are customers buying the brand?
2 Attitudinal loyalty: Are they buying it for the right reasons?
3 Category loyalty: Are there enough loyal buyers in the category?

In their analysis of brand purchasing patterns, they found that the average brand consists mostly of low loyal purchasers (74 per cent). Only 14 per cent were moderate loyals and 12 per cent high loyals to the brand.

We have already seen that there are a number of different types of buyer behaviour. Understanding the process of buying behaviour will have important implications for determining advertising strategy. Product categories exhibit differing levels of involvement for the consumer. Clearly, a frequently bought impulse item – such as ice cream or confectionery – requires little thought on the part of the consumer. In response to the felt need, the consumer will simply purchase a product which satisfies that need. Sufficient information will already be stored in the consumer's memory to facilitate the choice between different brands and to enable the purchase to be made with only a low-level consideration of the alternatives. At the other end of the spectrum, major purchasing decisions which involve significant sums of money or items which are only infrequently purchased – such as a new car or a holiday – will create a high level of involvement in the purchasing decision.

The involvement level of different product categories can be regarded as a continuum – from low level to high level – and understanding where a product is located on the scale will be important in deciding the nature of the advertising message. Advertising which is designed to support frequently purchased fast-moving consumer goods or services will, often, serve only to reinforce and underpin existing values. Advertising for expensive consumer durables will, in many instances, provide a great deal of information to provide a framework for an understanding of the products' features and benefits.

A further consideration will be the extent to which the decision is based on rational or subjective factors.

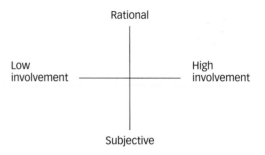

Rational decisions are those which are based on a careful consideration of the functional values of a product or service, and in which the perceived performance will be the primary criterion for choice. *Subjective* decisions are those which are based on such factors as taste or image. An important consideration, in both areas, is the role of the brand. Some brand names project an image of quality and performance – which will impact on the consumer's purchasing decision process. By the same token, other brand names are synonymous with style and fashion.

It is possible to create a simple matrix to depict these factors, and on which any product or service can be plotted. Identifying the position on this scale (using objective measures such as market research) will be important to the development of an effective advertising strategy.

It will also be important to understand the nature of the consumers of the brand. Clearly, at the introductory phase, all consumers will be trialists, some of whom may subsequently become loyal purchasers of the brand. At this stage, as we have seen, advertising will need to provide specific reasons to purchase.

New category users are non-users of the product category. Some will have a positive attitude towards the category, some will be unaware and have no attitude towards it, yet others will be negative. Needless to say, those who are positively disposed towards the category will be easier targets for an advertising message than those who are unaware or certainly those who are negative towards it. In reality, most consumers exhibit a varying degree of loyalty towards individual brands – as can be seen from the diagram. None the less, many established brands retain a small percentage of users who will, under most normal circumstances, be unwilling to switch from their preferred brand to some alternative, even when incentives are offered to them (this is exemplified by the Daz Challenge).

Research by Ehrenberg (1972) suggests that for buyers of the average supermarket product, some 15 per cent will switch brand within a single week of purchase, 70 per cent will switch over a period of six months, and 90 per cent by the end of a year. If we examine these figures from a different perspective, it suggests that the average brand enjoys only a 10 per cent of hardcore loyalists, although these will invariably be responsible for a significantly larger percentage of the brand's unit sales.

Advertising will have a differential impact on each of these groups and in some instances, the advertiser may develop specific campaigns to respond to the differing needs of each of these groups of consumers.

Consumer understanding of advertising

It has been recognised that it is critical that advertising reflects a deep understanding of consumer needs in order to reach and influence them effectively. Equally, it is vitally important that the advertising message is carefully constructed to appeal to the target audience, both in terms of its content and its composition.

Hirschman and Thompson (1997) suggest that consumers who use an aspiring and inspiring strategy interpret media images by as worthwhile goals and motivating examples. The relationship is one of emulation, in which the images provide motivation for the investment of personal time, effort and self-sacrifice to attain a certain body type or lifestyle. The existence of celebrity icons who at least appear to have certain looks, meet standards of success or defy the ageing process affirms that such goals are humanly attainable and that the consumer's efforts will ultimately provide personal reward.

Rather than accepting media images as representations of reality or authentic possibilities, consumers sometimes focus on their exaggerated, artificial and fantasy-like nature.

Much research has been carried out to measure the effectiveness of advertising on brand image, attitudes and attention towards the brand. Olney, Holbrook and Batra (1991) have carried out extensive research indicating that the brand and emotions portrayed affect empathy, attitudes towards the advertising, self/brand images and feelings and responses.

Gordon and Ryan (1982) define four types of consumer in terms of their appreciation of advertising:

- **The sophisticated critic:** Many people have grown up surrounded by television and other media and have acquired knowledge about advertising through increasingly frequent popular coverage in the media – TV programmes, newspaper and magazine articles, etc. Such consumers believe they know enough about advertising to evaluate them in terms of their effectiveness.
- **The uninhibited appreciator:** Typified by the view that 'the ads are often better than the programmes', they rate advertising highly. They enjoy advertising both for the information it provides as well as a form of entertainment.

- **The careful deliberator:** Enjoys some advertising, particularly where they feel that the intentions of the advertiser are straightforward and easily understood.
- **Suspicious rejectors:** These people tend to react negatively to all advertising.

Carphone Warehouse makes its recognition of individual needs crystal clear in its philosophy of objective advice. Go airlines train staff to watch for special problems and nip them in the bud by making eye contact at check-in, for instance, or telling customers in long queues that he or she recognises they're waiting. Southwest Airlines, the US low-cost airline, attributes its success to the key requirement of each member of staff – a sense of humour and the zanier the better.

And, as Valentine and Gordon (2000) point out 'On a larger scale, a whole range of specific policies demonstrate that Tesco sees the world from the individual customer's standpoint.'

Peter Fisk, the former CEO of the Chartered Institute of Marketing, argues that consumer insight is the best source of competitive advantage. He cites the following examples to demonstrate that where organisations understand the needs of their consumers, they establish a commanding position in the marketplace (Debating Society 2003):

Amazon
Pret a Manger
Apple iPod
Tesco
easyJet

Juchems (1996) states that 'Advertising must make the product seem more appealing to the consumer, superior to other products, more valuable, better tasting, more effective.'

Whilst Lannon (1996) argues that, despite its low credibility in terms of reputation/evaluation (compared with editorial), nothing can convey images, beliefs, feelings and impressions more powerfully than advertising. However, she points out that when companies face some form of crisis and the reputation of the organisation is at stake, third party editorial is seen to be the more powerful medium.

Successful advertising is bounded by two important constraints. Firstly, individuals must be exposed to it and pay some attention. Secondly, they must interpret it in the way that the advertiser intended. Several dimensions affect perception, summarised by Aaker in 1982.

Selection	**Organisation**	**Interpretation**
Selective attention	Closure	Irrelevant cues
Selective exposure	Grouping	First impressions
Perceptual defence	Figure and ground	Physical appearance
Perceptual blocking		Halo effect
		Stereotypes

Organisational buying behaviour

In this section, we are dealing with the buying decisions taken by organisations, as opposed to individuals, as in the consumer market. In many respects, there is a considerable overlap between the two. Indeed, an increasing number of writers in the area are applying directly, or with only slight modifications, the models developed for consumer behaviour to the organisational context. Although there are significant differences between the purchasing patterns of consumers and businesses, there is also an important similarity (Yeshin 1993).

The differences

Consumer
Uses own money
Large number of buyers
Individual (or family) decision
Often short timescales

Business
Uses company money
Small numbers of buyers
Group buying decision
Extend buying timescales

The similarity
All buying decisions are taken by people

The buying centre

A major difference between consumer and organisational buying behaviour may be expressed in terms of the people who make the buying decision and the nature of that decision. In the majority of instances, the organisational buyer is not the end user of the product, since the purchase is a part of the overall manufacturing process. He may be buying ingredients, raw materials or manufacturing plant, all of which will be used in different ways to produce the products for which the company is responsible.

In many cases, the responsibility for buying involves a number of different individuals who, together, comprise the decision-making unit (DMU). Frederick Webster and Yoram Wind in their paper on organisational buying behaviour identify several different roles undertaken within the DMU.

- Initiators: These are the people within a company who first identify the particular need for a product or service.
- Influencers: These are members of the organisation who can, directly or indirectly, affect a purchasing decision.
- Decision makers: Those who have the ultimate responsibility for deciding which supplier will be the source of the products or services required.
- Gatekeepers: These people control the flow of information within the company, and it is their responsibility to maintain information for the DMU.
- Purchasers: They are the individual(s) who actually make the purchase.
- Users: They will use the product or service purchased.

Whether all of these functions are maintained separately within an organisation will, to a large degree, depend both on its size and its operating culture. However, it is common for at least some of these functions to be maintained independently of the others. This, in turn, represents a level of complication in the communications process. It requires that the supplier will need to contact several different individuals in order to achieve a positive buying decision.

The organisational purchasing process

Although differently described, the nature of the organisational buying process has close parallels with purchases on the part of the consumer. In the same way that we distinguished between three types of buying decision amongst consumers, so too there are three types of organisational decision.

In many instances, the company will simply renew or repeat an order for products or services that have been purchased previously. Sometimes referred to as the 'straight rebuy' it reflects commonly purchased items that have been bought previously. Since substantial knowledge already exists concerning the quality of the items and of their supplier, the purchase is substantially similar to that of the 'routine' purchases made by consumers. The 'modified rebuy' is one in which the company purchases similar items as before, although against a somewhat different specification. In this instance, some information may be sought about the nature and facilities offered by alternative suppliers, although the purchase decision involves only limited problem solving. The final type of organisational purchase is that known as the 'new buy'. As with the extended problem solving scenario on the part of the consumer, this purchase may well involve a more complex analysis since the need for relevant information will be at a higher level. Potential suppliers will often need to be evaluated and the specifications of the purchase will need to be researched and prepared to meet the company requirements.

Derived demand

A further factor which needs to be considered in the context of organisational buying is that known as derived demand. The need for the products or services from a particular supplier will often be directly dependent on external considerations. If demand for the company's products increases, this will automatically increase its demand for raw materials. The converse is equally true. In the former context, it is difficult for a supplier to persuade the company to increase the level of purchases since the obvious consequence will be the stockpiling of supplies rather than immediate consumption.

In order to understand both consumer and business markets a series of questions must be answered:

1   Who is important in the buying decision?
2   How do they buy?
3   When do they buy?
4   Where do they buy?
5   What influences their choice decision?
6   How are choice criteria determined?

This information is an essential prerequisite to the planning of advertising and marketing communications strategies. The nature of the answers will have a substantial influence of the framing of the communication programme, its timing and targeting.

Case study

IPA Effectiveness Awards

Agency: McCann-Erickson Sydney

Authors: Carolyn Pigot, Alexander Flakelar

Fruitopia

Introduction

The Coca-Cola Company has long been recognised as the world's leading beverage marketer. Since the flagship brand Coca-Cola launched the company, the natural extension of the business was in the area of carbonated soft drinks. Around the world The Coca-Cola Company markets such brands as Sprite and Fanta and their diet variants. However, as consumers' lifestyles, preferences and tastes change, The Coca-Cola Company has recognised the need to diversify its offering to include beverages outside of the traditional realm of carbonates.

This market trend is borne out by figures from the US: growth in the carbonated soft drinks category in 2001 was 0.6 per cent, following 2000's figure of 0.2 per cent (source: *Beverage Digest*). This modest increase is happening at a time where non-carbonated and 'health and wellbeing' beverages such as bottled waters and energy drinks are in some cases experiencing double-digit growth. In Australia, while the carbonates portfolio has had continual growth, the challenge remained to diversify into the full range of non-alcoholic ready to drink beverages including bottled water, energy drinks and fruit juice.

Marketing background

Analysis of the competitive environment revealed that consumers had recognised the health benefiting qualities of juice but were frankly bored by the extrinsic offerings that they offered. The market had failed to sufficiently motivate consumers and there was a need for a healthy dose of brand imagery, injecting some life and fun into a dull environment.

The 100 per cent juice market in Australia is highly fragmented with no dominant national brand. There are seven major manufacturers and more than 35 brands active in the market, however, the brands tend to have strong regional skews. Spring Valley is the overall market leader with 25 per cent share, driven by heritage and hence strong brand recognition in the route market – an established brand in the larger states of New South Wales and Victoria. All other brands have a similar share, although Fruitopia has made very strong inroads since launch, currently growing at 35.3 per cent.

Consumer insight

Whilst the need for healthy beverages is acknowledged by almost everybody, communications in the category have tended to focus on a very tired formula that focuses largely on natural, high-quality product features. Missing has been the sense of dynamism that characterises the typical 100 per cent juice consumer. Younger, more affluent people leading busy lifestyles typically consume fruit juices – especially 100 per cent fruit juices.

Fruitopia has made its mark by providing consumers with colour, movement and verve, rewarding the consumer not just with a wholesome product, but enjoyable, 'consumable' advertising.

Target market

Demographics: People aged 18–29 years.

Psychographics (key insights of targets mindset): 'the free at heart'.

- Busy young people, always keen to follow their heart and not their head.
- These people have stopped worrying and started living.
- They know they buy their juice for boring health reasons (traditional, wholesome) and don't feel good about brands that just reinforce that – they're looking for emotional nutrition and fun!

Fruitopia provides a natural boost to make them feel physically good about themselves whilst the emotional dimension gives permission to have fun with the brand.

Research results

Limited qualitative research has been done into the two commercials produced, but it was clear that consumers responded very well to a brand that dared to have fun with 100 per cent juice. The research was of course conducted after this strategy was implemented, but underlines the sound thinking done up front:

'It's young and fresh. It's not like that Daily Juice ad which is just so old fashioned whereas this is young and funky.'

'. . . it's a good way of showing real juice without being boring.'

'Because you see them juicing you think pure juice – but this is funky juice.'

Core creative idea

The 'workers' in the Fruitopia Factory have the time of their lives producing Fruitopia 100 per cent juice.

Communications objectives

- Establish 25 per cent brand awareness.
- Communicate the 'natural optimism' and 'positive energy' of the brand through the way we deploy the media vehicles.
- Implement an exciting sampling programme that has synergy with the 'feel' of our above the line activity to drive trial of Fruitopia during launch phase.

Media strategy

Primary vehicles selected to deliver communication objectives were television and sampling.

Television – to establish awareness and amplify the proposition

TV promotion – driving awareness and amplifying the proposition:

- To leverage the TV component an activation was negotiated during the launch phase nationally on the 7 Network.
- The activation was a national competition with viewers being encouraged to call and enter to win a major prize for two to the La Tomitina Festival in Valencia, Spain.
- The competition spot displayed a 1900 number on the screen. The viewers were asked to leave their name and number to go in the draw to win.
- The competition line received 4820 entries.

Sampling – driving trial and amplifying the proposition:

A fundamental component of the success of new product launches is trial, and then re-trial. It was therefore crucial to get our product into the hands lives of our consumers. Sampling was conducted across five metro markets to capture the target in their working environment. Importantly, sampling activity was conducted on Monday mornings at 9 o'clock – the least energetic part of the week!

Results

Fruitopia was launched in September and advertising flighted until the end of January 2002. During this period Fruitopia's volume increased by 35.3 per cent whilst the total category experienced a negative growth of 0.6 per cent.

Sales figures to the end of January 2002 indicated that Fruitopia held a 7.1 per cent share of the total 100 per cent juice, under 600ml category. The corresponding 12 months to January 2001 saw Pacific Orchard hold 5.5 per cent of the market. This represents a 1.6 per cent increase in market share from only 11 weeks of media activity.

Brand awareness target was 25 per cent. The campaign achieved 53 per cent above expectations in the first six tracking periods.

SOURCE: This case study is adapted from the paper presented at the Effectiveness Awards. The full version is available at www.warc.com and is reproduced by kind permission of the World Advertising Research Center.

Questions:

1 Why is consumer behaviour an important factor to consider in the development of an advertising campaign?
2 What are the stages of the decision-making process and how can these be influenced by advertising?
3 What is the difference between rational decisions and emotional decisions, and why is it important to identify which is appropriate in a given buying situation?
4 Identify the many influences on consumer behaviour and consider their impact on the nature of consumer purchases.
5 Why is it important to identify the changing nature of the consumer as early as possible? How are these changes likely to impact on the development of advertising?
6 What are the differences between consumer buying behaviour and that of an organisation? In each case identify the target audiences for advertising campaigns.

The roles of segmentation, targeting and positioning

Learning outcomes

This chapter will offer you an insight into:

- how market segmentation works
- the process of targeting
- the nature of positioning
- the ways in which brand positioning can be achieved
- the difficulties of changing brand positioning
- the contribution of advertising.

Certainly, the vast majority of products and services, particularly those with large marketing communications budgets, appeal to consumers. However, it would be naïve in the extreme to assume that these products have an appeal to all consumers. Even the most popular products and services fail to appeal to all consumers. Take, for example, the ubiquitous Coca-Cola. Whilst, undeniably, one of the world's largest brands, even within its own sector, not all consumers drink the product. Some prefer Pepsi, others Virgin Cola or one of the myriad private label competitors. Some consumers reject cola beverages entirely, preferring instead other carbonated soft drinks or water, yet others consume hot beverages such as tea or coffee and so on. The range of drinks which can satisfy the basic need to quench a thirst is almost endless. It follows that for products to succeed, they must identify the critical consumer dimensions which will ensure that their product or service achieves appeal to some or other segment of the overall population.

How market segmentation works

Consumers can be differentiated against a wide range of variables both demographic and psychographic, which are largely self-explanatory but which were described in more detail in Chapter 6.

Demographic variables

Age
Sex
Race
Religion
Income
Occupation
Social class
Education
Geographic location
Family life cycle
Lifestage

Whilst these dimensions provide us with information about the consumer, it is important to remember that they often lack the ability to discriminate sufficiently. Simply because two consumers are of a similar age and gender, for example, does not indicate that their tastes and preferences for the products they desire will be similar.

Psychographic variables

Identifying the underlying psychological characteristics provides a much richer texture from which to develop an understanding of the important consumer variables. Psychographics is the understanding of the psychological basis of opinions and attitudes. Often, the term is used interchangeably with that of 'lifestyle' and, whilst there is some overlap, it is possible to distinguish between the two. The former term relates to the types of opinions which people hold, whereas lifestyle more appropriately describes the way that people live, and considers their personal values and actions in a social context.

Several factors can be considered in order to provide an understanding of the way people act in the way that they do – and, importantly, this can help us determine the reasons for the purchase of the products and services that they buy.

- Attitudes: It is clear that the attitudes people hold will impact on products and services.
- Motivation: Here we are considering the reasons which lie behind the particular purchase decision.
- Desired benefits: This involves segmenting the market on the basis of the benefits which purchasers seek from the product in question.

Lifestyle

Lifestyle covers a variety of important factors such as activities, interests and opinions (AIO) and is based on a paper presented by Dr Joseph Plummer in 1974. The important lifestyle dimensions can be seen from Table 7.1.

Lifestyle data that are assumed to reflect market behaviour are widely used by advertisers to identify and target market segments. The data generated by any one of a number of lifestyle-oriented clustering models are then used as input to creative and strategic decisions. As a result, the lifestyle categories that emerge from data-driven lifestyle segmentation schemes become more than convenient descriptive tools for marketers. Through their widespread use in marketing and advertising they become instantiations of 'social types' for consumers and advertisers alike. The strategic depiction of carefully selected social types is fundamental to many advertising campaigns.

Table 7.1 Key lifestyle factors		
Activities	**Interests**	**Opinions**
Work	Family	Themselves
Hobbies	Home	Social issues
Social events	Job	Politics
Vacation	Community	Business
Entertainment	Recreation	Economics
Club membership	Fashion	Education
Community	Mood	Products
Shopping	Media	Future
Sports	Achievements	Culture

SOURCE: Plummer 1974

Clearly, effective lifestyle advertising must relate marketer-generated lifestyle categories to desirable (and meaningful) social types for their target markets, and must do so in a manner that will be accepted as accurate by the audience (Englis and Solomon 1995).

One of the best-known applications of this principle is VALS2 – a values and lifestyles model developed by SRI International (Mitchell 1983). The model groups individuals into three broad categories based on their 'self-orientation' and considers their motivations against the characteristics of 'principles' – those who hold strong personal beliefs about what is or is not appropriate in given circumstances; 'status' – those who are influenced by the approval of others within their social environment; or 'action' – individuals who are motivated by activity, variety and risk. These categories can be further examined on the basis of the financial resources which the individuals possess. The VALS typology adds two further categories: 'strugglers' – whose financial situation is so restricted that their psychological characteristics are unimportant – and 'actualisers' – individuals who possess such sufficient financial resources that they can display all of the psychological orientations. All these types are shown in Figure 7.1.

Roberts (1999) argues that psychographics can help in the following ways:

- Creative teams are offered more precise, scientific guidance on target audience beliefs and attitudes to inspire their thinking.
- Market analysis is given an extra tool with which to evaluate and measure market potential and penetration.
- Planning is able to evaluate media channels in terms of their balance of viewer, listener or reader psychological types.

He states:

it is precisely because psychographics can achieve this aim [of identifying people who probably be interest in a product category] that makes it so interesting to brand managers and advertisers. So much above the line is concentrating on the brand experience, not on product attributes, and that requires advertising cre-

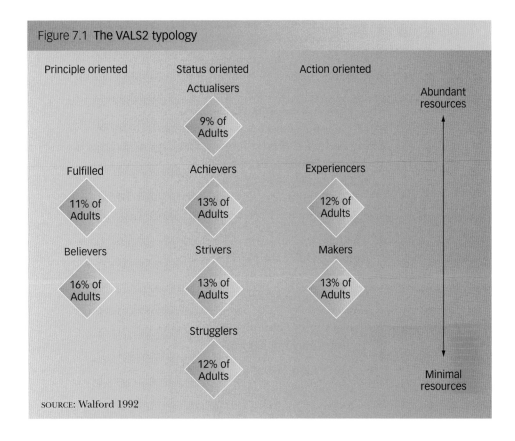

Figure 7.1 The VALS2 typology

SOURCE: Walford 1992

ative to 'get inside the head' of the existing and potential audiences. Effective nationwide psychographic codes enable this to be done so much m ore precisely than has previously.

However, the limitations of current lifestyle segmentations schemes have been well documented (e.g. Holt 2002). Different ethnically or minority-based interpretive communities, brand communities (Muniz and O'Guinn 2001), subcultures of consumption, and lifestyles provide a theoretical base for developing innovative socio-cultural segmentation methods that sensitively discriminate among consumers' similarities and differences, as is relevant to a product (Kates and Goh 2003).

The changing consumer

Recent years have witnessed fundamental changes in the values and lifestyles of consumers as the view of the world around us changes dramatically. A few facts will illustrate.

- We have seen the progressive shift of the woman out of the home and into the domestic economy.
- Family roles are changing. In many instances, women are the main family income earners, whilst some men remain at home and fulfil the traditional parent role.
- Job security, the underpinning of society for many decades, is breaking down. Comparatively short tenure is much more the norm and people are being hired on relatively short-term contracts.

- Expectations of the annual salary increase or bonus is rapidly diminishing and, even where it exists, it is constrained by economic circumstances.
- Continuing threats on personal safety are omnipresent.
- Public respect for the 'institutions of life' is diminishing.
- Personal values are changing. Things that were once the preserve of the 'middle classes' are now available to all.
- The office environment is losing its role. Already significant numbers of workers conduct their businesses from home rather than from within a structured organisation.
- Companies are no longer local or even national. In many cases, people are employed by organisations whose head offices are thousands of miles away.
- Environmental considerations apply to all aspects of daily life.

The data available form the Social Trends and General Household survey available from the Office for National Statistics provide us with an interesting picture of both contemporary and future society. The overall picture indicates that population growth will be comparatively slow. Currently, the figure stands at 59 million, with the projection for 2031 being only 61 million. Despite this, there are fundamental changes in the underlying composition of society – all of which have an important bearing on marketing futures.

- **Age:** The number of people over retirement age will increase progressively. The consequence of past fluctuations in fertility rates together with increasing longevity will result in an ageing population. Similarly, the number of children under 16 is projected to fall. The numbers of those of working age will continue to increase to around 2011 and then decline. These facts have important consequences for the consideration of both savings and pensions. There are some 18 million people in Britain aged over 50 and have a higher life expectancy than ever before (74 for men and 80 for women, compared to 45 and 49 in 1901). Whereas total consumer spending in the UK in 1991 was £335.5 billion, people over 40 spend £148.5 billion of this.

  The changing roles and perceptions of differing age groups is clearly seen from a recent article which appeared in *The Times* (1997) under the heading of 'Grandpa, what do you get up to all day?'. What made the article so interesting was the fact that in many instances, the grandparents depicted in the article were role models or icons for the youth generation. They included Linford Christie – a grandfather at 37 – Mick Jagger and Nanette Newman.

  As Myserson (2003) states: 'The very term "grey market" wraps a shroud around a market sector that should be vibrant; it also sends the wrong signal to creatives about a group of consumers as colourfully diverse and distinctive as everyone else.' Most marketers would take the trouble to analyse and understand any new national market they were entering. But marketers have been surprisingly slow to engage with the complex dynamics of an ageing population.

- **Households:** The number of households has increased dramatically from 18 million in 1971 to 24 million currently. This number is projected to rise by another 4.4 million in England alone by 2016. Inevitably, this will have a significant impact on the demand for mortgages and other household services. In 1971, single-person households represented around 18 per cent of the total. By 2016 they will represent 36 per cent.

- **The single consumer:** We can examine the reasons for the recent explosion in the proportion of singles within the population. There is a variety of characteristics that have converged to account for so many singles in most Western countries. First, young people are postponing marriage. Instead of marrying young, more women are enrolled in college or pursuing professional careers than ever before. Increasingly, concerns of economic success are causing young people to postpone marriage. Further, changing social values make it no longer necessary to be married in order to have children or to cohabitate.

  Second, there is a small increase in the proportion of individuals in society who have chosen to remain single on a permanent basis. They may be put off by the fragility of the institution of marriage or they may simply lack adequate partners for marriage. Whatever the reason, this group of 'never married' continues to increase.

  Third, the number of divorces continues to rise (although the actual divorce rate has begun to decrease). Although five out of six divorced men and three out of four divorced women will eventually remarry, the time that they spend between marriages has been growing. Thus, although they may be temporarily between marriages, there are more divorced singles than ever before.

  The consequence is that the new single consumer is one who engages in active lifestyles. They maintain high levels of activity and seek new challenges, accomplishments and experiences. This seeking behaviour leads them to search for new avenues of fulfilment. They seek convenience and variety and are willing to innovate into new and untried products in order to obtain this fulfilment. This seeking behaviour allows them to expose themselves to new relationships and product opportunities in their quest. This is especially true for those who are single by choice.

  In addition, singles may engage in compensating behaviours to make up for a lack of intimacy in their lives. They desire more intimate identification with an individual and compensate for this lack of identification by forming large networks of friends. Part of this behaviour is their tendency to identify more closely with brand names, possibly allowing the lifestyle depicted by the brand to be a reflection of their own. By choosing a certain set of brands they may be assuring themselves of their lifestyle. These singles may desire to fill some emotional gaps in their life. Affective messages and television shows may appeal to singles, as is indicated by their tendencies to watch a lot of television and display impulsive purchase behaviours. This is especially true for those who are single through circumstance rather than by choice (Donthu and Gilliland 2002).

Hofmeyr and Rice (1999) identified three kinds of consumer, each with a very different mindset related to marketing communications:

1 Committed brand users who are less likely to be in the market for competitive brand messages. The psychological involvement these consumers have with their brands makes them relatively resistant to competitive communications.

2 Uncommitted but involved users who are most likely to be the big users of

advertising. Whilst they are not unhappy with their current brand, they remain interested in information about other brands. They are susceptible to advertising, particularly if a brand communicates a perceptible product advantage and/or an emotional dimension which is relevant to them.

3 Uncommitted and uninvolved users who are less likely to be big consumers of advertising. They do not hold strong impressions of any brand and, whilst they are willing trialists, they remain promiscuous.

Targeting

The task of targeting is an essential part of the process of developing effective marketing communications campaigns. As with other words common in marketing and marketing communications, 'targeting' can be used in different contexts. There are two important dimensions to this task which affect various aspects of campaign development.

The targeting of markets

What is a market?

The words 'market' and 'category' tend to be used interchangeably.

A sector is a group of products, each of which is an acceptable substitute for each of the others. The consumer chooses between these products. The brown and white bread sectors; the regular and diet drinks market; the canned and ambient desserts sectors, and so on.

Within the sector any shopper is unlikely to choose equally between each of the brands. For any sector there is likely to be some degree of brand loyalty and preference. Most consumers satisfy their needs with a small number of brands. The objective of advertising is to add value to the brand in such a way that it becomes preferred by a significant number of consumers.

Ambler et al. (1998) make an important distinction between old and new markets which, in turn, has a significance for the development of advertising. A 'new' market is one in which advertising is about products which are not known (or are little known) to the shopper, because the type of product is new. An 'old' market is one where most of the products are broadly familiar to them. A 'new' market is where a substantial proportion of the sales are to first-time buyers whereas in an 'old' market very few sales are made to trialists.

However, it must not be assumed that 'old' markets are necessarily stable. Even a mature market is capable of innovation and growth. This may be the result of some change in the nature of the product offering, the packaging or the contribution made by advertising which serves to reposition the brand and its uses in the consumer's mind. Technological markets are vivid examples of this vibrant change. Who today uses a typewriter, for example?

When used in the broader context of marketing, the task of targeting implies the appropriate evaluation and identification of one or more market segments in which it is desired to operate. This is a fundamental strategic decision that will help define the subsequent development of both marketing and marketing communications programmes.

There are four distinct strategic approaches, any one of which may be appropriate to the task in hand:

- **Undifferentiated marketing:** This is sometimes referred to as mass marketing – in which the company offers the product to the entire marketplace. The company will ignore the differences that may exist between separate market segments an offer a single product designed to appeal to all consumers.

- **Differentiated marketing**: This is when the company develops different combinations of the marketing mix, each of which is designed to appeal individually to the separate identified segments of the market.
- **Concentrated or targeted marketing:** In this case the company identifies one or more target segments and develops different marketing mixes for each of them. In effect, rather than trying to obtain a share of the overall market, the company identifies one or market segments where its reputation or experience enables it to provide a closer match between what it provides and the segment requirements.
- **Custom marketing:** This is when in which the company develops campaigns to respond to the needs of individual consumers. Most commonly applied through the techniques of direct marketing, this is the ultimate in differentiation.

The targeting of consumers

The same word, 'targeting', is used somewhat differently in the context of marketing communications although, inevitably, there is some degree of overlap. Here we are concerned with the aspect of achieving coverage of a defined target audience through the use of appropriate media. We have already seen that we can apply many different consumer characteristics, either singly or in combination, to define the nature of one or more target audiences. This information will be used both in the development of the communications message and, particularly, in terms of the selection of the media vehicles which will be used to convey that message to the desired audience.

Bond and Morris (2002) highlight the fact that the segmentation process is something familiar within society: 'As young children, we naturally group things together . . . the concept of splitting people into groups is essential to our lives'. It is therefore not surprising that marketers regard segmentation as a natural process. Such segmentations are often used to identify unique groups of consumers for whom different types of product or marketing communications are appealing.

The process of targeting consumers has become significantly more sophisticated in recent years. Commonly, devices such as geodemographics have been used to classify people by where they live. Using this data to classify neighbourhoods is simple to effect and comparatively easy to use. Companies can access a variety of systems, such as ACORN; PiN; MOSAIC and DEFINE, all of which apply segmentation characteristics to regional neighbourhoods. To these has been added the establishment and growth of lifestyle databases, such as NDL, CMT and ICD. The retailing sector provided the initial impetus for the growth of the sector, although the subsequent growth of the financial services sector has continued to fuel that growth and enable the sophisticated application of direct marketing techniques.

Geodemographic systems, such as ACORN and Superprofiles, offer a well-established segmentation approach. More recently, with increasing penetration of lifestyle data, new segmentation products such as CACI's Lifestyles UK enable segmentation down to the household level, thus providing better discrimination. Marketing databases, with the addition of customer transaction data, enhance this even further.

Positioning

Positioning is a core concept within the framework of marketing. It is a strategic issue which informs, identifies and creates the relationships between the organisation and the markets it serves.

Its role was given focus with the publication of the Trout and Ries book *Positioning: The Battle for Your Mind* (1986). Since then, the concept of positioning has undergone much debate in an attempt to secure an accurate description of its contribution to marketing and communications strategy.

Hibbert (1995) defines positioning as the act of designing the organisation's image and value offering so that the organisation's customers understand and appreciate what the organisation stands for in relation to its competitors.

Marketers try to create images for their brands in order that they are positioned to fit a distinct market segment occupied by no other brand. They strive to create a brand image that is similar to the self-image of the target consumers. A brand is a belief. At its most powerful, it evokes passion – people are proud to work for the company; people are proud to be seen using a product that possesses a particular brand name. There is both internal and external faith in a particular set of values.

According to Marsden (2002) positioning may be simply defined in terms of how a brand is positioned in the mind of the consumer with respect to the values with which it is differentially associated or which it owns. For example, the association of Volvo with safety may describe a positioning in the minds of many consumers that has the capacity to render Volvo more or less attractive.

The commercial utility of positioning lies in how the imbuing of trade marks with unique, true and compelling values can influence purchasing decisions and impact upon sales.

The positioning of the brand is a vital component of the determination of the advertising strategy. It is, as we have seen, necessary to identify the role that it plays in the minds of its current and potential customers. It is important to develop a solid brand benefit positioning. This requires an identification of the consumer's needs and wants and a matching of what the product has or does in the form of a brand benefit positioning, and depends on the effective use of market research. Positioning involves the creation of an image for the product or service in order that consumers can clearly understand what the company provides relative to its competitors and, importantly, differentiates it from them.

The rationale for targeting a given segment is to achieve the benefits of association. Successful association facilitates the entry of the brand into the consumer's evoked set, as well as to place the brand in close proximity to the market leader.

At an individual level an advertising message results in a judgement about the brand's category membership. So, for example, if a brand advertisement makes a comparison between itself and the brand leader, the latter brand may serve to ensure that the consumer perceives the advertised brand as part of the market category. This is particularly important in the context of a new brand about which the consumer holds no opinions and which, therefore, possesses no perceptual values.

Robin Woods, head of the US company, Segmentation Marketing, suggests that there are five specific requirements of a distinctive brand benefit position (Woods 1993):

1 The position must be based on primary consumer needs used to select one brand from another.
2 It is important to convey why the brand meets those needs better than the brand with which it competes.
3 No other brand can be substituted with the same consumer message or proposition.
4 No other product class can be substituted and still leave consumers with the same message.
5 The message must be precisely and specifically communicated to consumers.

It has been argued that positioning can be sub-divided into two components:

- What the product does: functional positioning
- What the product means: emotional positioning.

The relationship between the functional and emotional components will change somewhat over time. Inevitably, at the beginning of the product's life, the need will be to convey information about the product and relate it to the consumer's need – felt or unfelt. However, as time goes by the consumer's need for information about the product becomes less and less. The consumer is not only aware of the product and its competitors, but knows all about the ways in which the product can satisfy his or her needs (or at least thinks he or she does). In order for the advertising to continue to capture the imagination of the consumer, it must provide a far more emotional connection to the brand or adopt a different approach to engage the consumer's interest.

Some years ago, the author was involved with the advertising for a brand called Vick's Vapour Rub, prior to its acquisition by Procter & Gamble. The brand was mature in that most households kept a jar of the product in their bathroom cabinets. However, usage was not as high as it might have been. The task therefore was to regenerate interest in the brand. The problem faced by the creatives was the fact that users felt that they new everything they needed to know about the product. Accordingly, a television campaign was developed which provided 'new' information about the brand without revealing the brand identity until the very end of the commercial. The result was that consumers derived new attitudes towards the brand and usage levels increased.

There are a variety of positioning characteristics which can be adopted by an organisation, but the single-minded requirement is to identify a long-term proposition which positions the brand in the minds of consumers. For many years, Mars was the confectionery bar which 'helps you work, rest and play', while Gillette remains 'the best a man can get'.

Upshaw (1995) identifies several different types of positioning prompts:

- Feature-driven prompts: The use of specific features of the product to differentiate the brand. Dyson has done precisely this by focusing attention on its 'bagless' vacuum cleaner.
- Problem–solution prompts: The product is seen to be the 'unique' solution to a particular problem. This is an approach which is commonly used in the household detergents and cleansers market.
- Target-driven positioning: Uses the nature of the consumer to identify a place in the market. In essence, the message is that 'people like you use this brand'. Many

finance companies use this style of advertising, depicting 'consumers' who choose to use the particular organisation.

- Competitive-driven positioning: The product adopts an overt stance relative to an identified competitor. This is the approach taken by Avis vs Hertz.
- Emotional or psychological positioning: Perfume brands commonly attach emotional values to their brands.
- Benefit-driven positioning: That used by Virgin Airlines.
- Aspirational positioning: Successful people use this brand. Rolex is an example of this stance.
- Value positioning: Adopted by McDonald's Value Meals and Asda, for example.

The concept of category membership is important due to its relation to creating and communicating a brand's position within the field of competing alternatives (Adams and Van Auken 1995).

Brand positioning

Brand positioning starts with establishing a frame of reference, which signals to consumers the goal they can expect to achieve by using a brand. Choosing the proper frame is important because it dictates the types of associations that will function as points of parity and points of difference. In some cases, the frame of reference is other brands in the same category. Coca-Cola is a soft drink. It competes with Pepsi cola and retailer's cola. But in certain instances, the frame of reference might be brands in quite disparate categories. Coke, Gatorade and Snapple belong to the soft drink, sport drink and iced tea categories, respectively, but they potentially share the frame of reference that consists of all thirst-quenching drinks.

Some further examples will serve to illustrate the nature of brand positioning.

- The positioning of Häagen-Dazs ice cream targets a young, hedonistically oriented audience. In turn, the audience's response and perceptions underpin the brand's status – and so reflect its positioning and subsequent appeal. The creative strategy was to associate the dimensions of sexiness, fun and indulgence with the pleasure of eating Häagen-Dazs ice cream (Holbrook and Hirchman 1991).
- Coca-Cola's creative strategy is designed to ensure that the brand is always portrayed as the classic and original cola. Their advertising messages continue to reflect this brand positioning – 'Always Coca-Cola', 'You can't beat the real thing', 'Eat football, sleep football, drink Coca-Cola'.
- Subaru cars enhanced the brand status by making an overt comparison with an established brand in the field, Volvo, and even challenging its position: 'Volvo has built a reputation for surviving accidents. Subaru has built a reputation for avoiding them. Subaru Legacy – we built our reputation by building a better car.'

Bhat and Reddy (1998) confirm that positioning a brand through a clear and consistent image-building campaign remains a cornerstone of brand marketing practice.

Many academic papers have been written on the distinction between the utilitarian and emotional benefits of brands. In the latter context, consumers use either personal or subjective criteria such as taste, pride, desire for adventure and desire for expressing themselves in their consumption decisions.

Table 7.2 illustrates the differences between symbolic and functional positioning.

Table 7.2 Symbolic and functional brands, by product category		
Product category	**Symbolic brand**	**Functional brand**
Watches	Rolex, Breitling	Casio, Timex
Sports shoes	Nike, Adidas	Dunlop
Ice cream	Häagen-Dazs	Wall's

The findings of Bhat and Reddy (1998), however, appear to contradict those of Park et al. (1986). The latter had suggested that the functional and emotional requirements consumers have of a brand are entirely distinct and recommended that, in determining the best positioning for a brand, the managers decide which of those ends of the spectrum they wish to appeal to. Moreover, they argued, managers should not attempt to appeal to both since this would result in consumer confusion.

Although their research is somewhat limited in terms of the categories and brands tested, Bhat and Reddy found that it is entirely possible for some brands to possess both functional and emotional appeals to its target audience.

The issue of how brands and advertising messages realise several potential meanings has significant implications for advertising theory and practice. Traditionally, positioning has been viewed as a relatively stable set of consumer perceptions (or meanings) of a brand in relation to competitive alternatives. However, in contemporary social conditions, advertising and brands come to signify many other meanings than their intended positionings. Furthermore, segmenting a market into non-overlapping groups of consumers becomes a difficult task in a commercial environment in which consumers are increasingly aware of the advertisers' intentions, shift categories over time, and even straddle different segments depending on the consumption context.

Various authors have identified different positioning dimensions that may be adopted by brands.

1 A brand may be distinguished as a result of particular product characteristics or benefits. For many years, Jacob's Club biscuits were differentiated from competitive products with the statement: 'If you like a lot of chocolate on your biscuit, join our club'. The proposition served to associate more chocolate with the brand, inferring a superiority over competitors' products.

2 The brand positioning may reflect a positive price/quality relationship in the minds of prospective consumers. The John Lewis Partnership has become inextricably linked with the proposition 'Never knowingly undersold', whilst the Asda price check underpins their claimed price superiority.

3 Some brands are differentiated by the nature of the product user. By associating the brand with particular consumer groups, the brand seeks to fulfil a unique role relative to its competitors. Recently, Audi used this approach to differentiate its customer from the 'flash, yuppie driver' who would not be content with the understated nature of the car.

4 A similar process can be achieved by associating the product with a particular use or application.

5 In some cases, brands are differentiated by their position as a cultural symbol. They represent certain important dimensions of behaviour or self-expression, e.g. Levis or FCUK.

6 Finally, brands may adopt a particular position relative to an identified competitor. Avis have long been seen as the main challenger to the brand leader (Hertz), although in some markets this is far from being a reflection of their true position in the marketplace.

Changing brand positioning

It is important to remember that brand positionings are not fixed. It is an expensive process, but the position a brand occupies in the mind of the consumer can be changed over time. Brands such as Lucozade and Skoda are illustrations of the way in which consumer perceptions can be positively challenged by advertising campaigns to achieve fundamental changes that are positive towards the brand.

Many brands are not where they wish to be in the consumers' minds. Identifying the desired positioning will determine both the content and nature of their communication. In the case of Boddingtons, the objective was to heighten appreciation of the product and its characteristics. The creative approach was to condition drinkers to appreciate the large creamy head and to associate this with good quality. The various executions used for the brand used a variety of humorous metaphors to underpin the endline – 'The cream of Manchester' (Baker 1995).

Kates and Goh (2003) suggest that sometimes, working with cultural conditions to achieve brand morphing must go beyond changing slogans and pattern standardisation (i.e. using a unifying theme for the brand image but customising it to local meanings). This is particularly important in the international context. There may be certain local cultural meanings that are so deeply entrenched that simply customising an idea to a foreign market is not sufficient.

However, developing a competitive brand positioning is not an easy task. As Keller et al. (2002) state, many brands falter sooner than they should. They establish five potential pitfalls to the process of effective brand positioning.

1 Companies sometimes try to build brand awareness before establishing a clear brand position. You have to know who you are before you can convince anyone of it. Many dot-coms know this pitfall well. A number of them spent heavily on expensive television advertising without first being clear about what they were selling.

2 Companies often promote attributes that consumers don't care about. The classic example: For years, companies that sold analgesics claimed their brands were longer-lasting than others. Eventually, they noticed that consumers wanted faster relief more than sustained relief.

3 Companies sometimes invest too heavily in points of difference that can easily be copied. Positioning needs to keep competitors out, not draw them in. A brand that claims to be the cheapest or the most fashionable is likely to be overtaken by a competitor who can lower their price further or demonstrate greater 'trendiness'.

4 Certain companies become so intent on responding to competition that they walk away from their established positions.

5 Companies may think they can reposition a brand, but this is nearly always difficult and sometimes impossible. Although Pepsi cola's fresh, youthful appeal has been a key branding difference in its battle against Coca-Cola, the brand has strayed from this focus several times in the past two decades, perhaps contributing to some of its market share woes. Every attempt to reposition the brand has been followed by a retreat to the former successful positioning.

They confirm that brand positioning and repositioning is tough. They argue that once a brand has developed a successful positioning, it will be necessary to find a modern way to convey the position. Moreover, companies should think hard before they alter it.

Differentiation

Most profitable strategies are built on differentiation: offering customers something they value that competitors don't have. But most companies, in seeking to differentiate themselves, focus their energy only on their products or services. In fact, a company has the opportunity to differentiate itself at every point where it comes in contact with its customers – from the moment customers realise that they need a product or service to the time when they no longer want it and decide to dispose of it.

Barnathan et al. (2001) argue that:

a good brand can be decisive in differentiating products and services from an ever-larger array of competitors. A great brand is a promise, a compact with a customer about quality, reliability, innovation and even community. And while the concept of a brand is intangible, brand equity is far from it.

Macmillan and McGrath (1997) pose a series of questions that a company should address to identify points of differentiation against their competitors:

- How do people become aware of their need for your product or service?
  Are consumers aware that you can satisfy their need? Are they aware that they even have a need that can be satisfied? Your company can create a powerful source of differentiation if it can make consumers aware of a need in a way that is unique and subtle.
- How do consumers find your offering?
  Opportunities for differentiating on the basis of the search process include making your product available when others are not (24-hour telephone order lines), offering your product in places where competitors do not offer theirs (the mini Tesco outlets on petrol station sites) and making your product ubiquitous (Coca-Cola). Making the search process less complicated, more convenient, less expensive and more habitual are all ways in which companies can differentiate themselves. And when competitors can't or won't do the same – at least, not right away – you have the potential for a strategic advantage.
- How do consumers make their final selections?
  After a consumer has narrowed down the possibilities, he or she must make a choice. Can you make the selection process more comfortable, less irritating or more convenient?

- How do customers order and purchase your product or service?
  This question is particularly important for relatively low-cost, high-volume items. Can a company differentiate itself by making the process of ordering and purchasing more convenient?
- How is your product or service delivered?
  Delivery affords many opportunities for differentiation, especially if the product is an impulse purchase or if the customer needs it immediately.
- What happens when your product or service is delivered?
  How is your product installed? How is your product or service paid for? Many companies unwittingly cause their customers major difficulties with their payment policies. How is your product stored? How is your product moved around?
- What is the customer really using your product for?
  Finding better ways for customers to use a product or service is a powerful differentiator.
- What do customers need help with when they use your product?
  Can you provide an after-sales advice line which can be accessed by product users when they experience difficulties?
- What about returns or exchanges?
- How is your product repaired or serviced?
  Increasingly, companies provide service contracts at the time of purchase to overcome these difficulties.
- What happens when your product is disposed of or no longer used?
  In a world in which it is becoming increasingly economical simply to replace many products as they age rather than spend the money to fix them, what do customers do with the obsolete goods? In some countries, it is now mandatory for the manufacturer to provide recycling facilities when the product becomes obsolete.

A recent phenomenon has been the placing of emphasis on the brand in relation to the consumer, rather than on the product. As Woodward (1999) suggests: 'a complete role reversal in the role of brands has happened: instead of signifying something about a product, the brand signified things about the consumer'.

The role of advertising

For a new brand, advertising has a key role in placing the brand on the consumer's mental map. Success in creating awareness is a major step towards gaining sales success for a new brand. Consumers are unlikely to buy a brand they know nothing about – except in the lowest risk categories.

For established brands, the aim of advertising is to increase brand presence. The most successful brands have managed to take some aspect of their product performance and make it a perceived advantage. Alternatively, they have developed a distinctive brand personality and positioning which gives the brand a perceived consumer advantage in the marketplace. As a result, they continue to be able to command a premium price which, in today's market, may not be justified on the basis of physical product attributes alone.

Several authors comment on the positive contribution that advertising can make in the context of brand positioning. Meeneghan (1995) states: 'Brand image is reliant on both the informational and transformational abilities of advertising.' He goes on to state that 'advertising represents a most potent source of brand identity'.

It functions to present and thereby position the brand attributes against consumer expectations and to imbue the brand with values symbolically attractive to the target market.

Similarly, Cobb-Walgren and Ruble (1995) suggest that advertising is the primary mechanism for creating psychological differentiation among brands and for enhancing brand equity.

De Chernatony and McDonald (1998) argue that the 'use of vibrant advertising creates an identity for the brand and the resultant image perceived by consumers will either enhance or diminish their perception of the products or service'. Ehrenberg and Barnard (1997) reinforce the notion that advertising is often the only variable factor that enables a brand to distinguish itself from its competitors, whilst Anschuetz (1997) suggests that 'advertising is one of the few elements of the marketing mix that can build a groundswell of popularity of a brand through its use of broadly appealing, entertaining imagery and interesting information'.

The extent to which advertising is immediately motivating is dependent on a number of key factors:

- the extent to which there is new content in the advertising;
- the relevance of the message;
- enjoyment of the message;
- the effectiveness with which the message is integrated into the brand.

Micro-marketing

However, there are alternative viewpoints. Some authors, including Preston (2000), argue that manufacturers should aim for broader rather than narrow segments of a particular market.

While traditional media advertisements are designed to appeal to a particular audience, each of us is constantly adrift in a veritable sea of advertising that has not been designed for us, whether due to the nature of the message or the goods or services being advertised. They act as a constant reminder of consumption of one kind or another. They represent a mass.

Micro-marketers take a dim view of this aspect of advertising, citing it as wasteful in comparison to highly targeted communications wherein the individual or family unit becomes the focus of marketing activity. They do not stop to consider the cumulative effect of creative advertising on primary demand. Nor do they realise that internet advertising is essentially sales promotion elevated by the utilisation of computer technology and that retail point-of-sale promotions are merely targeted price promotion.

All manners of consuming behaviour are encoded with positive imagery, to the extent that all manners of consumption are positively associated with abstract relationships. The cumulative advertising effect is the provision of a vast repertoire of potential demand from which we are able to select for socially or personally useful reasons. The overwhelming message from advertising en masse is that consuming is imperative, simply because of the positive associations that are provided within the messages.

Case study

IPA Effectiveness Awards 2003

Agency: Ten Alps MTD and Mediacom Scotland

Authors: Vince Meiklejohn and Keith W. Crane

Bahlsen UK

Background

Bahlsen is a long-established (since 1889) German family-owned company, which manufactures high-quality continental biscuits, cakes, snacks and Christmas specialities. It has an annual turnover in excess of £1 billion, trades in at least 68 countries and has 15 manufacturing plants. Bahlsen has consistently invested in its number one product, Choco Leibniz. Once tried, consumers are loyal and Bahlsen has the second highest loyalty (second only to Chocolate Wholewheat). Penetration is therefore key.

Prior to the 2002 advertising campaign, prompted brand awareness of 18 per cent was regarded as low and, actually, advertising so far has made the lead product – Choco Leibniz – better known than the Bahlsen brand, which has limited the 'halo effect' on other products. For 2002, increased investment was made available for a strategy that accelerates the company mission.

Brand objectives

At the brand level, Bahlsen wished to generate a 38 per cent increase in sales on their four core products – Choco Leibniz, First Class, Messino and Pick Up. In addition, there were specific targets for increased distribution for each product, for improving the numeric rate (packs per store per week), overall household penetration and increasing Bahlsen users who buy two or more brands.

Advertising objectives

The role for advertising was dictated by Bahlsen's business strategy and objectives in the UK market, as follows:

- increase penetration of people buying two or more Bahlsen products;
- drive additional trial by 400 000 households;
- build awareness of Bahlsen = Continental by 40 per cent.

In addition, at a qualitative level, Bahlsen want to establish a 'continental repertoire' in consumers' minds, and to establish and build the idea and a personality for the 'Bahlsen family' through its product range. Lastly, but importantly, they wish to be seen as leaders in personal indulgence biscuits, particularly the 'special treats' sub-sector.

Advertising strategy

Some significant changes were made in strategy for 2002, compared with 2001 and before:

- Timing: normal market seasonality is April/May and September/October, but in addition the 'shoulder' periods of March, June and November were to be considered.
- Target audience: a major change was made here to change from the narrow ABC1 adult 'Indulgents' audience to the 'everyday treat/special treat' biscuit eaters, which in media terms was targeted as 'All Housewives'.
- Media: spearhead the campaign with TV (the indisputable proven medium) in an undeveloped region(s)

for Bahlsen and support with consistent presence in secondary media in the strongest markets for Choco Leibniz.

- Creative: use creativity, which is adaptable to work in all media, including small press spaces and provides high frequency against the target audience. In addition, the client wished to spend more of the budget delivering the message, rather than creating it.

Creative work

Three 20-second commercials were produced for Choco Leibniz, each promoting their own product benefits but also focusing on the creation of the Bahlsen 'family' concept. A key component of the commercials was the continuing the use of the 'More Chocolate than a Biscuit' endline. We wanted to establish a clear link between the individual products, and Bahlsen and quality continental ingredients.

A series of trade advertisements were produced for both independent and multiple grocery trade press, as a strong visible support to the effort to increase major multiple distribution.

Results

Sales effects: AC Neilsen Scantrack shows very significant increases in average weekly sales, compared with the 12-week average before the campaign. Whilst there was little effect on non-advertised Bahlsen products in the advertised area during the campaign, a significant lagged effect was experienced during the nine-week post-advertising period.

There was a similar significant effect and pattern on rate of sale during and post advertising, compared with the 12-week average prior to the campaign.

The advertised areas again show significant positive increases – 26.6 per cent during the campaign period and 144.9 per cent in the following nine weeks for advertised products and 54.6 per cent for non-advertised products, in the advertised areas.

Advertising tracking effects: A tracking study was carried out in the advertised areas in the spring of 2002, both pre and post the Bahlsen TV campaign. Spontaneous awareness of Bahlsen, as a brand of special continental biscuits, went up by 66 per cent (albeit from a low base) from 3 per cent pre- to 5 per cent post-campaign. Prompted brand awareness of biscuit brands showed

Bahlsen increasing by 90 per cent from 11 per cent to 21 per cent, with negative effects on awareness of individual product lines.

Sales effects: Consistent patterns have emerged, when comparing advertised regions with the rest of the UK, and there is a step change year-on-year comparing advertised and non advertised product lines. Sales are 67 per cent stronger (3 × rest of the UK); there is a 60 per cent increase in rate of sale (43 per cent better than rest of the UK); year-on-year growth: sales up 144 per cent year on year in the advertised areas (60 per cent better than rest of UK). Rate of sale has doubled year on year in the advertised areas.

There has been a measurable 'halo' effect on non-advertised lines within the advertised regions, directly attributable to advertising the Bahlsen brand name, before the specific product lines. Sales were 107 per cent stronger (nearly twice the rest of the UK) with a 98 per cent increase in rate of sale (82 per cent better than the rest of the UK) during the advertising period and the nine weeks after. Year-on-year sales were up 54 per cent, more than double the rest of the UK.

In addition, significant increases in brand and advertising awareness have been achieved for the Bahlsen brand, confirming success of the campaign in achieving the objective.

SOURCE: This case study is adapted from the paper presented at the IPA Effectiveness Awards. The full version is available at www.warc.com and is reproduced by kind permission of the Institute of Practitioners in Advertising and the World Advertising Research Center.

Questions

1 What are the methods applied to segment markets? Why are the psychographic variables considered to be more appropriate than demographic variables?

2 In what ways do changes in the nature of the consumer affect segmentation?

3 What are the strategic approaches to the targeting of markets?

4 What is positioning in the context of advertising and why is it important to consider the nature of brand positioning?

5 What is the difference between functional positioning and symbolic positioning?

6 How do brands change their positioning in the minds of consumers? Identify the difficulties involved in this process.

7 What elements might be used to differentiate one brand from another?

8 The contribution of market research

Learning outcomes

This chapter will familiarise you with:

- the market research process

- the stages of market research and the sources of information

- how market research helps advertisers to understand the market

- the contribution of market research to the strategic development of advertising

- the importance of evaluating advertising effectiveness.

The market research process

The market research process provides the means by which the various tasks of identifying consumer needs and wants, identifying an appropriate advertising strategy and evaluating campaign effectiveness can be achieved. The tools of market research are at the heart of planning effective marketing communications strategy. In a dynamic marketplace, the gathering and assessment of information is a vital precursor to the determination of strategy. Clearly, much information will already have been gathered to form the basis of marketing planning, and this will have equal relevance to the marketing communications process. Importantly, however, there is a number of specific aspects of market research that will have a more direct bearing on the planning of advertising.

We collect information in order that we can understand what is going on. We interview customers, record their views, analyse and map them. From this we can construct an understanding of the dynamics of the market, and we can classify brands into hierarchies, from new to established, from biggest to smallest. The key questions to which research may provide answers are:

- Is there a response to the advertising, and what is its magnitude?
- Which customers respond?
- What are the time dynamics of the response?

The Market Research Society defines research as:

> The collection and analysis of data from a sample of individuals or organisations relating to their characteristics, behaviour, attitudes or possessions. It includes all forms of marketing and social research such as consumer and industrial surveys, psychological investigations, observations and panel studies.

It involves a disciplined approach towards the collection of data and their interpretation in order to gain an understanding of the marketplace in which consumers exist. Its key role is to assist in the planning and evaluative processes and to help eliminate risk from the task of decision making.

The process of market research is relatively straightforward and consists of a series of separate stages of data collection, organisation and interpretation. The fundamental objectives of the process are twofold.

Firstly, there is the need to reduce or eliminate uncertainty in the various steps of the planning process. Although there will be a number of factors which are outside the direct control of the company, it is vitally important that the company is aware of those factors which may impact on the development and implementation of the strategic and marketing communications plan. By the same token, the company will need to be aware of fundamental movements in such areas as competitive activity, consumer purchasing patterns, attitudes and so on.

Secondly, there is the need to monitor the performance of the developed plan. Unfortunately, marketing is not an exact science. The more rapid the feedback of response to the plan, the more likely it is that the company can make the necessary changes to ensure its effectiveness. And, of course, the information gained will make a substantial contribution to the long-term strategic planning process.

There is a number of important areas of information which are required and on which the advertising campaign will be based. The planner will require detailed information as to the nature and behavioural patterns of the consumer to whom the message is to be addressed. Who are they; where are they; how, when and where they buy the product; how they use the product; what specific attitudes they hold, and so on. It is important to build up a finite picture of the target consumer in order that the message can be properly constructed and focused.

The underpinning of any successful advertising campaign will be the use of market research. As markets become increasingly complex, it is beyond the scope of advertising planners, or even the most highly paid creatives, to base their work entirely on some form of intuition.

As Goodyear (1994) argues:

> The success of advertising in the future seems likely to depend on the advertiser's knowledge of the social and temporal context in which his advertisements are being consumed. For example, are consumers likely to be channel surfing, the target group's attitudes toward advertising per se, and their familiarity with its conventions.

Moreover, with the costs of making a mistake increasing alarmingly, few advertising professionals would fail to seek guidance from the marketplace.

The stages of market research and the sources of information used

The market research process consists of a series of interlinked stages, as illustrated in Figure 8.1. It is important to remember that, although the stages are linked, work can be conducted in several areas concurrently, and in many instances not all of the stages will be required.

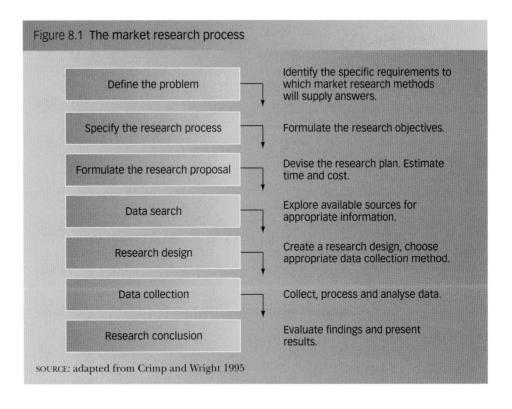

Figure 8.1 The market research process

Define the problem	Identify the specific requirements to which market research methods will supply answers.
Specify the research process	Formulate the research objectives.
Formulate the research proposal	Devise the research plan. Estimate time and cost.
Data search	Explore available sources for appropriate information.
Research design	Create a research design, choose appropriate data collection method.
Data collection	Collect, process and analyse data.
Research conclusion	Evaluate findings and present results.

SOURCE: adapted from Crimp and Wright 1995

Market planning

It is to be assumed that, in the development of the marketing strategy, considerable amounts of information will already have been gathered. Both from internal sources and published data (secondary research) and from the commissioning of specific research programmes (primary research), a picture will have been built up of the general environment in which the brand competes, the nature of the competition, growth rates and potential, as well as information regarding the consumer. It is this latter area which has most bearing on marketing communications. The value of desk research should not be underestimated. Much valuable information can be derived from available and published data, with the advantage that it will be significantly cheaper than commissioning dedicated research studies. Moreover, since in many cases much of the important work of interpretation will have been carried out by others, the information will be easier to assimilate.

There are many important sources of information that should be examined at this stage. They are discussed in the next three sections.

Internal information

This includes the frequent and currently available information sourced from inside the organisation, such as production information, inventory records, sales statistics, field sales reports, customer guarantees and other feedback, together with any previous research that has been conducted. The latter will provide an important base of benchmarking, which can be referred back to at several stages in the subsequent work.

**External
sources**

The company will be able to access considerable amounts of information from published sources. Important amongst these are the wide range of publications available from the Central Statistical Office (CSO). Although the list of publications is extensive, certain titles should be referred to on a regular basis.

These include the *Annual Abstract of Statistics*, the *Monthly* and *Quarterly Digests of Statistics, Social Trends* – which is an invaluable source of information for uncovering the underlying trends amongst the population – and special surveys, such as the *National Food Survey*; the *Family Expenditure Survey* and the *General Household Survey*. A comprehensive guide to government data is the *Guide to Official Statistics* which is published by HMSO.

A second but equally important source of market information is provided by a number of titles including The Economist Intelligence Unit's *Retail Business* and research by Mintel and Euromonitor. All of these and similar publications provide frequent 'overviews' of specific markets which aggregate much of the information available and present it in a comprehensive form.

Thirdly, there are a number of published surveys available that will provide valuable information on different aspects of brand and consumer behaviour. These include the AGB *Home Audits* and *Consumer Panels*; *Nielsen*; *BARB* – which provides television viewing data; the *JICNARS* readership survey; and the *Target Group Index* (*TGI*) which relates the purchasing of products to media habits. The fourth important source is the plethora of trade and specialist publications which, similarly, provide important information on issues relating to their own market areas.

An excellent source of general information and statistics relating to markets, consumers and brands are the pocket handbooks published by WARC. The *Marketing Pocket Book*, for example, provides a general overview of the marketplace with information on the economy, the consumer, retail and distribution, media, etc. There is also a limited section providing international data. However, much more detailed information and statistics are available from the more specialist pocket-books, for example, the European market, the Americas and the Asia Pacific region.

With the increasing availability of information on the internet, often provided by companies and industry groups, these too, can represent an important source of knowledge which can be incorporated into the planning process.

It should be noted that this is but a small selection of the wide variety of published sources. For a more comprehensive listing, the reader is recommended to consult a specialist text in the field such as Crimp and Wright's *The Marketing Research Process* (4th edition, 1995), Crouch and Housden's *Marketing Research for Managers* (2nd edition, 1996). These examples relate to the UK market, but comparable sources from government and other agencies are available in most countries, and represent an important contribution to the planning process in the international context.

In most countries there are syndicated advertising measurement services which already have large databases of previous studies. These are used to establish performance norms against which the brand's advertising can be measured.

It will be vital for the development of advertising to understand the nature of the competitive environment. Who are the competitors and what are their offerings? How are their products or services positioned to the consumer, and what images – either positive or negative – do they possess? What advertising approaches do they use, and so on.

In many instances, this information can be derived from the syndicated reports mentioned previously, although it should be noted that these may be somewhat dated. It may, therefore, be necessary to conduct a specific study to obtain the necessary data.

How market research helps advertisers to understand the market

A key area of understanding will be derived from usage and attitude (U&A) studies, since these provide a consumer perspective of the brand and the market in which it exists. Whilst it is difficult to be prescriptive in this area – as with other forms of market research – there will generally be a number of specific areas which will need to be covered.

- **Awareness:** U&A studies can indicate levels of awareness for own and competitors' products, as well as providing an indication of advertising awareness.
- **Usage:** There are a number if dimensions of usage which will be important to understand.

   On a general level, information will be required on the levels of loyalty and the propensity to trial other products on the part of the consumer. Since few consumers remain exclusively loyal to any one product – rather, they tend to build up a portfolio or repertoire of brands which they are prepared to consider as viable alternatives – it is important to understand the make-up of the portfolio. On a more specific level, information will be needed on patterns of usage, in terms of frequency of purchase, source of purchase, how the product is used, on what occasions the product is used, and so on.

- **Attitudes:** As the name suggests, a U&A study is the primary source of attitudinal information. And since marketing communications is concerned, in part, with the creation or reinforcement of attitudes, the study will provide important clues as to what potential consumers think about the brands available, their relative positionings and offerings

- **Needs:** Although the product purchased may be identical, the consumer needs that they fulfil may be very different. The U&A study will provide guidance as to the extent to which existing brands fulfil consumer needs and expectations and will also help in the identification of potential gaps in the market. It goes without saying that it will be necessary to collect the information across a wide sample in order to enable a statistical analysis in terms of the demographic breakdown of the existing or potential market which it is desired to penetrate.

Usage and attitude studies will often be supplemented with other forms of **qualitative** research.

For the most part, qualitative research is conducted either with small groups of individuals, or on a one-to-one basis. The specific purpose of such research is of an exploratory or investigative nature, although no attempt is made to draw definitive conclusions from the information gained. Its most important contribution is the ability to provide depth and texture to consumer information, which would not be available from quantitative studies. In some cases, the two forms of study are used in tandem. Qualitative studies are capable of making a valuable contribution to the strategic planning process because they are more flexible than the standardised form of research based on interviewing against a predetermined questionnaire. There are a number of specific areas where a qualitative approach will be favoured over a quantified one. A qualitative approach can be used:

- To identify potential problem areas more fully, and in greater depth.
- To enable the formulation of hypotheses which can be the subject of further research study.
- To explore patterns of consumer behaviour, beliefs, attitudes and opinions; as a precursor to a quantitative study, where it is important to pilot questionnaires for comprehension. This is especially true within the field of advertising, where it is possible to explore concepts prior to the further development. To establish the comprehension of communications campaigns both prior to and after they have been exposed to a mass audience, perhaps to assist in the identification of deficiencies in the communications process.

According to a study conducted by Brown and Stayman (1992) attitudes towards advertising, the message and the brand, are constantly changing, hence the need for obtaining attitudinal information that is as contemporary as possible. Advertising is having to face the uncertainty of functioning within a largely competitive environment. In today's competitive climate, customers are having to process three times as much information as was the case 50 years ago, and this is an important issue in the context of the way in which potential customers process advertising information. Franzen (1994) suggests that customers are:

- increasingly selective in what receives their attention;
- paying increasingly less attention to communications;
- processing communication at shallow, more superficial level;
- starting to 'consume' more pictures at the expense of words.

Qualitative research is a methodology which uniquely allows for the exploration of 'sensitive' or 'embarrassing' issues, since questions can be set in an oblique form for subsequent interpretation. Often, a one-to-one approach will enable access to consumer information that would not be available in a group context.

Although not an ideal situation, there are instances, resulting from the constraints of time or cost, where qualitative data is the only basis on which subsequent decisions are taken. This is particularly true, for example, in the development of advertising concepts. It is clear that, on these occasions, there is a greater need for caution and care in interpretation than where a quantified study is used. Often decisions will be based on the comments of a relatively small number of respondents. The importance, however, is not the number of respondents but the commonality of the directions of their responses. If a series of group discussions, say, are similarly negative in their views of an advertising proposition then, in most cases, it is reasonable to consider dropping the particular approach in favour of some alternatives that are more positively received.

The main contribution of such studies is in terms of the group dynamics that the techniques allow for. Unlike conventional questionnaires, where the respondent is interviewed against a pre-set format and where the aggregation of 'open-ended' comments may be difficult to interpret, group discussions enable the skilled inter-viewer to facilitate the interaction between respondents and to explore their responses in far greater depth. This is of vital importance in the identification of appropriate communications dimensions.

An advertising proposition may be rejected for a number of reasons. It may, for example, have the wrong tone of voice; there may be an inconsistency between the visual and verbal dimensions of the message; it may depict the wrong sort of people or environment. Or it may simply be that the given message does not communicate in the way that it was intended. All of these and other facets of the message can be amended with relative ease in order to overcome the objections and enable the proper communication of the message which is desired. By the same token, such feedback can be instrumental in the determination of the most effective commu-nications strategy and of defining the most appropriate positioning for the product or service in the marketplace.

Visuals are commonly used in research, especially in qualitative studies, as they assist in:

- communicating feelings, attitudes and needs that are difficult to articulate;
- identifying intangible dimensions that are difficult to conceive and express;
- stimulating a broader range of thinking on the part of respondents;
- stimulating creativity and interaction in group sessions.

We have already seen that the potential consumers for a product or service can be subdivided in a variety of different ways in order to target a proposition more effec-tively. The socio-economic groupings, together with the important social, environ-mental and attitudinal factors which we have already considered, may be the basis for ensuring the differentiation of a product's positioning from that of its competitors. A great number of the initial directional indicators will derive from quantified stud-ies, since these will enable us to dimensionalise the numbers of consumers who make up certain categories. We can, for example, separate out the number of young vs old, male vs female, high income vs middle income, and similar dimensions.

However, the point has already been made that these are relatively crude meas-ures. It is far more important to consider the attitudinal and other dimensions which are likely to have a far greater bearing on the potential consumer's propensity to buy a particular product or service. It is clear that relatively few products are capable of satisfying all of the consumer's needs simultaneously. If we take a market such as that for instant coffee, we can see that some consumers prefer their beverage strong, oth-ers like to drink it weak. Indeed, given the state of development of this market in most countries, it is immediately apparent that, on this one dimension alone, there are sev-eral distinct groups of consumers whose needs will require a somewhat different product delivery. The process of identifying these differing needs and requirements is of vital importance in the process of product positioning and the determination of the appropriate marketing communications strategy. By using the appropriate mar-ket research techniques we can develop market 'maps' which enable us to see the relative positions of the various brands available in the market.

We can approach this process from two different perspectives. On the one hand, we can identify factors that relate to product differentiation, such as those just described. Here we are concerned to identify the various product attributes that are considered desirable by differing groups of consumers. Alternatively, we can examine the market from the standpoint of the consumers' attitudes and behavioural patterns.

In many markets, product differentiation alone between competing brands is insufficient to achieve the differentiation of competing brands in the eyes of the consumer. The inevitable consequence of converging technology is the fact that competing products rapidly become almost indistinguishable from each other. As Poiesz and Robben (1994) stated:

> Market complexity is increasing and market transparency is decreasing. The constant flow of technological innovation, product adapting and service improvement result in short product life cycles, an increasing knowledge gap between manufacturers and consumers, and a reduction in the physical and psychological differentiation of brands.

That statement becomes even more true today as the pace of change quickens.

Yet, it remains true that consumers adopt very different attitudes towards those same brands based on key dimensions of image. Market research will enable us to identify the image dimensions and to scale them according to the importance that is attached to them by the consumer.

There are two strategic options at this stage. The first is to seek to reinforce consumer perceptions if the brand's position is similar to that desired by consumers. The alternative is to seek to alter brand perceptions if it is found that the brand position differs. A particular technique for identifying the position of a brand in the context of the competitive market is one known as perceptual mapping. This consists of establishing the important dimensions of consumer preference and plotting them on a scale. Then it is possible to discover the extent to which available brands meet the established criteria for choice. An excellent example of perceptual mapping is demonstrated in a paper outlining the contribution of advertising to the Levi Strauss jeans brand in Europe (Baker 1993).

In 1990, the agency – Bogle Bartle Hegarty – and its client undertook a major qualitative research study amongst young European males to identify the attitudes and behaviour with regard to the Levis brand. Some 50 group discussions were held throughout seven separate countries. The primary purpose of the study was to identify the role played by the advertising in the creation of a consistent brand image across the variety of local markets. What emerged presents a fascinating picture both of the particular market and, more importantly, the relevance of the technique.

Marketing communications research

Any product or service is an amalgam of values that are presented to the consumer and reinterpreted by them into some form of whole. Inevitably, therefore, there are many factors beyond those of the product ingredients that influence the consumer to purchase or to refrain from purchasing a particular item.

However, the brand comprises a series of dimensions that are mostly perceptual and intangible. These include the brand name, the reputation of the parent company, quality and value perceptions, and the influences of external forces such as the recommendations of others. Advertising plays a vital role in establishing these dimensions and reinforcing them in the minds of the potential consumer. And, here again, market research can make an important contribution both to the understanding of the important dimensions and in minimising the potential problems resulting from poorly constructed communications messages.

Brand positioning and personality

Segmentation analysis and perceptual mapping techniques enable the creation of a detailed picture in which the brand exists, embracing both consumer typology and product differentiation. By identifying where the brand sits in relation to its competitors, marketing communications can then seek to reinforce the position or to change it. Similarly, we can identify the factors that serve to differentiate the brand from its competitors and provide it with a unique personality in the marketplace.

Brand promise

Advertising needs to provide 'evidence' for the consumer to accept the promise of the brand. This may involve the depiction of a tangible benefit resulting from some emotional value. For example, testimonial advertising showing 'people like me' who are satisfied with the performance of a brand. Alternatively, it may require some depiction of the product in use, demonstrating the outcome of the product's performance.

Effective reach of target consumers

Specific research into patterns of television viewing, newspaper readership and so on, is used to assist in the determination of both media strategy and execution. However, there is an increasingly important dimension of research to identify the appropriateness of the media environment. If we accept Marshall McCluhan's statement that 'the medium is the message', then it follows that the environment in which the advertising is seen will have an important bearing on image dimensions.

Häagen-Dazs determined that, in order to achieve a high-quality positioning in the minds of its consumers – and to differentiate itself from other, 'run-of-the-mill' ice creams, they would only use quality titles in which to place their advertising. The synergy between the medium and the message was apparent. In this instance, the surrounding 'noise' has a 'halo effect' on the advertising, and the same principle applies equally to the placement of an advertising message within specific television programmes.

The contribution to strategic development

Market research has an important role to play in this context. Before we can determine the nature of the communications message itself, we must first identify the appropriate direction for the communications strategy. This, in turn, is dependent on the corporate direction and marketing strategy identified for the company. Several distinct communications strategies can be identified and their appropriateness needs to be considered in the context of any marketing communications campaign.

Pioneer strategy

When a company creates a completely new product and, in the process establishes a new market category, the purpose of the communications message is to ensure that potential consumers are told of the product's existence, its functions, its usage and the location of purchase. When, for example, Sony first introduced the Walkman, the support activity designed for the brand took on these characteristics. Similarly, when Swatch was introduced, it was important that it was not simply seen as just another watch. The marketing communications programme sought to position the product in the vein of a fashion accessory that offered other dimensions than simply telling the time. Inevitably, the thrust of pioneer activity is to develop a market category, rather than simply emphasising the benefits of the brand. Once a category has been established, it is likely that new entrants will begin to compete with the original brand. Accordingly, the owners of that brand must enter a phase of competitive communications. The imperative is to differentiate the brand from its competitors, and to isolate those features and benefits – real or perceived – which will induce potential purchasers to select that brand rather than others.

A third strategy will be that of defensive marketing communications designed to offset the impact of competitive pressures. A good example of this can be seen in the current UK newspaper market, where each move made by one title is immediately matched by a comparable move by one or more of its competitors.

In their book *Integrated Marketing Communications*, Schultz, Tannenbaum and Lauterborn (1992) identify eight key facets of the marketing communications strategy. It needs to:

1 pinpoint customer segments;
2 identify a competitive benefit;
3 understand how the consumer positions the brand;
4 establish a unique, unified brand personality which differentiates the brand from its competitors;
5 establish real and perceived reasons why the consumer should believe the promise of the brand;
6 identify the means by which consumers can be reached effectively;
7 establish the criteria for monitoring success or failure;
8 determine the need for additional research which would further help refine the strategy.

In each of these areas of strategy determination, research techniques are available to assist the process.

Strategy development

Depending on the amount of information that the planner already possesses, it may be necessary to conduct specific research to aid the process of strategic development. This will be specifically concerned with the nature of the message and is designed to identify the strongest possible positioning and consumer proposition that can be made. It is quite likely that the planner will explore a number of different alternatives at this stage, in order to identify the single proposition that is likely to achieve the highest level of impact on the target consumer. Part of this process will involve an exploration of competitor positionings in an attempt to determine whether there is a gap in marketplace that can be adopted by the brand.

Undeniably, market research has a vital role to play in all aspects of marketing and marketing communications. The techniques available are continuously being explored and developed to ensure that we gain a great facility to understand the key consumer processes and the ways in which decisions are made as to which brand (if any) should be purchased. As Alan Hedges (1997) described it: 'Research can heighten the understanding of the market and of the consumer so that we can better understand the job that advertising has to do and the climate in which it has to operate.'

However, research is not a universal panacea. Feldwick (1994), the executive planning director of BMP DDB Needham, outlines the circumstances when the use of market research can be counter-productive.

- When it monopolises resources: Companies are often prepared to spend considerable sums on straightforward research (tracking studies, pre-testing, etc.) to the detriment of more strategic research to gain a real insight into understanding the consumer.
- When it sets simple yardsticks to measure complex objectives: Advertising effectiveness remains a difficult dimension to measure directly, hence intermediate measure are often used. Whilst these have inherent values, they may be dangerous when attempts are made to use them as measures of effectiveness.
- When it paralyses the process of decision making: Since research is often equivocal in its results, management remains responsible for the ultimate decisions. If there is overreliance on research results, in an attempt to gain a definitive answer, the decisions may be delayed or the research used as a reason to avoid decision making.

Advertising pre-testing

Since the production of advertising represents an enormous investment on the part of the company, it is usual to use market research to pre-test the advertising proposition at an early stage in its development. At the outset, this may consist of assessing the impact of several different propositions (as simple concept statements) to determine which of them communicates most effectively. Subsequently, it is likely that the executional approach will also be tested to ensure that it delivers the intended message. There are several methods in which this can be carried out. Sometimes, simple drawings representing frames from the intended commercial will be presented to the target audience. In other instances a slightly more finished version using computer generated images or 'animatics' may be shown. The intention is to avoid huge investment in the final production of a television commercial that fails to deliver the intended message.

Pre-testing is capable of finding out whether an ad has the potential to communicate, but is not predictive of whether people will pay attention in real life. As Gordon (1995) explains: 'While a main message may be played back, this does not necessarily mean that it has been incorporated into the viewer's internal perception of the brand.'

Hedges (1998) argues that much pre-testing of advertising is vastly overrated, both in terms of its predictive accuracy and its ability to shape the in-market effectiveness of any given execution. Instead, it is argued, advertising testing should be devised, run and interpreted with much greater sensitivity and introduced much earlier in the process – ideally, during strategy development.

It is recognised that people consume advertising in a much less conscious and logical way than previously supposed. Moreover, different executions work in different ways, both in terms of their objectives and their creative execution.

Monitoring research

In most instances, the planner does not start from scratch. Since most products and services already exist in the marketplace, it is reasonable to assume that they will have benefited from previous advertising support. It will be important to understand the workings of previous advertising campaigns and to explore the image that advertising will have created in the minds of the consumer. Indeed, such research, often conducted on a regular periodic basis, will not only yield considerable information about the company's own brands, it will also provide a valuable insight into competitor brands.

Tracking studies

A tracking study is a periodic examination of consumer reactions to the brand, its advertising and other activities. Tracking studies can do more than simply provide a basis for the measurement of advertising effectiveness. They can provide the diagnostics that are necessary to make improvements to the campaign. A tracking study can identify, for example, whether a campaign is making the necessary impact on all segments within the overall target market. It can identify if the product message is clearly understood or whether the branding of the advertising is sufficiently strong. If awareness towards the brand is increasing, if attitudes towards the product are being improved; and whether the campaign message is being converted into product trial.

Bond (1993) makes the point that much image data collected about brands tend to be static, in that they reflect a single moment in time. To overcome this problem, many companies conduct image tracking studies, revealing the image of a series of competitive brands over time. Undeniably, this adds to the understanding of the market in that not only is it possible to see the relationship between the brands at a moment in time, but also over time.

The importance of evaluating advertising's effectiveness

Increasingly, there is justifiable pressure to demonstrate the effectiveness of advertising campaigns. Clients need to make the most of their scarce resources and justify the value of their advertising to, sometimes cynical, internal audiences. However, whilst there is a strong need to ensure that the appropriate techniques are utilised for advertising research, there are situations in which such activity can be counter-productive.

The underlying problem of measuring advertising effectiveness is that virtually all of the methods available for measuring and attributing sales variations to advertising are only possible in the short term (McDonald 1992). In the longer term, advertising becomes lost within other influences and its effects become direct and inferential. Against this, Winston Fletcher (1992) argues that:

> no advertiser waits for a year for their advertising to take effect. Advertising must work both immediately and residually. It must generate response both today and tomorrow. Unless short term results are achieved the long term benefits will never materialise. Advertising could not possibly work in the future if it does not work in the present.

However, Schultz (1997) argues that today's technology makes it possible to link marketing expenditures to actual marketplace results. This can be done through financial and customer evaluation models. For example, many service and business-to-business companies can track and monitor their customers' activities, purchases and even defection. They are thus able to construct models of how much they would have to invest to obtain a new customer, how much it would cost to retain that customer and how much that customer would be worth over the 'lifetime value of a customer'. This argument is supported by the views of Schuring and Veerman (1998).

According to Schultz (1998) much of the pressure to measure advertising returns has been driven by the perceived capability of sales promotion, direct marketing and other techniques to demonstrate measurable cost-benefit returns on investment. They assert that, in today's markets, there is virtually no organisation that can separate or isolate advertising from other promotional or communication elements.

In a subsequent paper, Timothy and Schultz (1998) argue that the attempt to evaluate the financial return from investments in advertising have been hampered by the attempts to measure outputs, that is, what we buy, what it does, how it 'works', how we allocate and so on. They suggest that the need is to measure outcomes – what occurs as a result of marketing investments – what do we get back for what we spend?

Franzen (1999) asserts that there are two types of response to brand messages:

- Brand responses occur, partly, as a result of exposure to advertising, although many other factors may affect them, especially including direct experience of the brand itself.
- Mental responses are the effects that the advertising has on the consumer's knowledge of and attitudes towards the brand.

Wilkins (1997) suggests that the diagnostic measures of any TV campaign may include:

Likeability of the campaign
Persuasion
Message communication
Campaign image.

According to Baker (1994), there are four key factors that lead to and facilitate the measurement of an advertising campaign:

- **The strategic impact:** This should compare the brand against pre-existing market psychology, and not only anticipate the needs and responses of the audience, but exceed them.
- **The executional impact:** the message should not only be delivered well, but it should attract the audience's attention and imagination.
- **The media impact:** This is concerned with the effectiveness of the media used and relates to the cost efficiency and innovation of the media deployment.
- **Integration:** This means ensuring that the campaign fits well with the other marketing tools used and achieves cohesive communication to the target audience.

In an article in *Admap*, Terry Prue (1994) suggested key points for the achievement of success through advertising:

- **Persuasion:** The campaign told the target group something that was both interesting and relevant, e.g. the BMW campaign effectively persuades through the communication on various product benefits (the whole being more than the sum of the parts).

- **Involvement:** The building of a closer relationship between the brand and its target audience though the establishment of 'emotional ties' within the advertising. The Boddingtons campaign is involving having been built on 'persuasive truths' about being a smooth-drinking pint. Emotional links are made through the identification of product qualities that are evoked throughout the communication: the creamy head and bright colour.
- **Salience:** The use of creative advertising that is so memorably different that it registers the brand as more significant and worth of purchase consideration (irrespective of the communication content). The Pepperami campaign utilises this approach and has forced the brand into the consciousness of its youth target group.

The largest problem faced by any advertising campaign is that consumers are not actively seeking the information provide by the advertiser. As Applebaum and Halliburton (1993) suggest 'the problem facing advertising is that as much as 98 per cent of the information provided to the consumer is ignored'. Gordon Brown (1994) makes the important point that consumers are not active participants in the advertising process. For the most part, they sit in front of the TV set and passively view both ads and programmes. Sometimes they give their attention to them, on other occasions, not. They are more likely to give their attention to ads which they like. Moreover, Brown argues, they are unlikely to do much processing of the advertising at the time of viewing. They simply store the information contained in the advertising for later use.

There is an increasing need for advertising to work harder to gain people's attention in order to deliver the brand message. And, whilst it may be possible to grab their attention for a short while, it is far more difficult to engage them and build a deeper brand relationship (Brown 2001).

Advertising recall

Recall of advertising is an important measure of its impact on the target audience. According to Juchems (1996) the recall of advertising tends to be structured along a continuum, ranging from simple recall at one end to complex at the other. Categories of recall could include:

- brand name only
- general product benefits (not necessarily linked to the specific brand)
- non-specific details
- long-established familiar slogans
- brand symbols and logos associated with the brand
- current slogans
- elements of an advertising 'story'
- specific arguments used in the campaign
- the whole advertising story or concept
- a story with product arguments integrated.

How to measure advertising's effectiveness

Effectiveness should mean achieving objectives. Communication must be developed with an objective in mind. These might include the need to build a brand image, or to strengthen the brand in people's minds, to defend the position against other brands or to steal brand share. Objectives are of little use if they are not involved in the communications plan. Solid planning is the key to success in advertising. Once the advertiser has obtained a solid understanding of the marketplace and has determined the marketing objectives, they must address three important issues to develop a marketing communications plan:

1 Who do I want to communicate with – who is the target audience, what are their characteristics and where can I find them?
2 What message do I want to communicate to them?
3 How will I communicate with them – what is the most cost-effective medium available?

Effectiveness can be measured according to different factors: the propensity for product purchase, brand awareness, sales figures and the impact of advertising exposures through media (for example, in terms of the recall of the contents of a TV spot).

Advertising builds brand familiarity and keeps the brand salient amongst consumers. Advertising creates interest. Interest is not only generated by what is communicated but also how the message is communicated. Both the message and the execution must be of interest.

Advertising can have its principal effects at three points:

1 it can affect the viewer directly at the time of exposure
2 it can come into play at the point of purchase
3 it can have a role at the time of using the product.

A commercial's effectiveness is likely to be influenced both by the intended message (the message strategy) and by how well that message is conveyed (the execution of the commercial message).

The results of a study by Laskey and Fox (1995) suggest that message strategy and television commercial effectiveness are related but, as might be expected, the relationship is far from simple. The complexity of the relationship suggests that advertisers should use caution when adopting strategies simply because they have been effective for other product categories. The relative effectiveness or ineffectiveness of a message strategy appears to depend on both the product category and on the specific effectiveness measure examined.

The results in fact suggest that, by adopting the same message strategies as many of their competitors, advertisers may, in some cases, be hurting their chances of creating an effective commercial. In several instances, a message strategy that was found to be relatively ineffective for a particular product category was used disproportionately often rather than being avoided. It could be that the relative ineffectiveness of the strategy was due to its overuse rather than its inappropriateness to the product category.

Steiner (2001) states 'Advertising is key to gaining and retaining distribution. In many instances, the retailer is persuaded of the need to stock a particular brand directly as a response to the advertising level supporting that brand.'

Stapel (1998) asserts that it is entirely possible to demonstrate advertising effectiveness. Classified ads elicit a direct response, which is why mail order companies use the medium. Equally, there is considerable evidence of the effectiveness of retailer advertising – indeed, it is often possible to identify the particular part of the ad that had the greatest impact on sales.

A paper from the IPA (Butterfield 1998) provides an analysis of the PIMS database – which now covers more than 3000 companies. It concluded that it is the level of expenditure relative to competitors that is most important. Moreover, advertising works through the mechanism of superior customer value.

The process is illustrated in Figure 8.2.

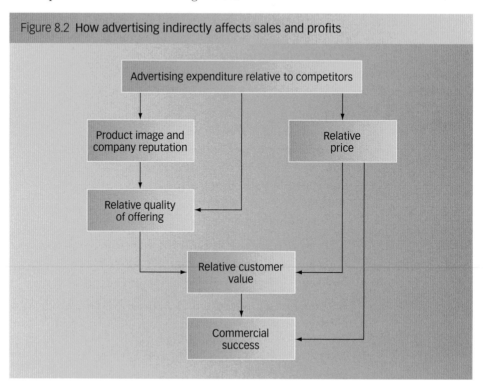

Figure 8.2 How advertising indirectly affects sales and profits

A similar attempt to model the process has been developed by Baker (1999), as shown in Figure 8.3.

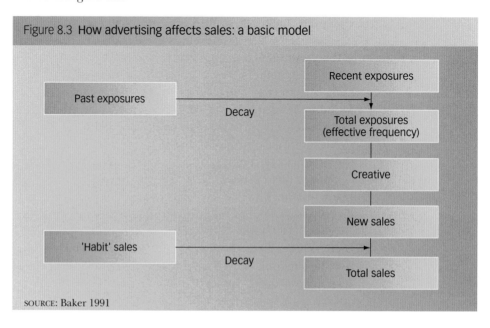

Figure 8.3 How advertising affects sales: a basic model

SOURCE: Baker 1991

Franzen (1994) identifies a series of key facts that have impacted on advertising effectiveness:

- The consumer is overloaded with communication and information. Since 1960, the level of mass marketing has increased eightfold.
- We are becoming increasingly selective about what we attend to.
- Attention and processing are stimulated by relevance. Interest in the product category or brand is the most important factor in influencing attention.
- Attention and processing can be enhanced or adversely affected by the nature of the communications stimulus.
- 30 per cent of commercials are misunderstood. One important cause of this is that the message may not fit with the viewer's preconceptions.

Krugman (1975) indicates that there are a wide range of factors which influence advertising effectiveness. See Figure 8.4.

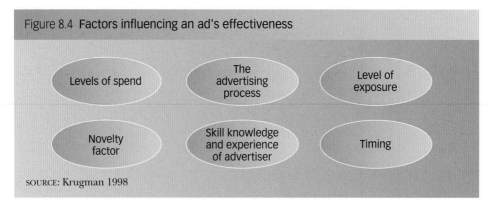

Figure 8.4 **Factors influencing an ad's effectiveness**

Levels of spend

The advertising process

Level of exposure

Novelty factor

Skill knowledge and experience of advertiser

Timing

SOURCE: Krugman 1998

Similarly, Leather et al. (1994) suggest that there are five principal components to underpin viewers' reactions to the commercials shown:

1 whether an advertisement is 'stimulating';
2 its 'relevance';
3 the dynamism inherent or incorporated in its situational vignette, aided and abetted by:
  4 its music quality;
  5 its positive character distinctiveness.

Dyson (1999) reports that – based on the evaluation of advertising at Millward Brown – different advertising executions can have massively different effects for the same budget – a factor of 30 covers the best to worst, but a factor of 2 was quite common.

Similarly, Miller (1998) found that the key difference between highly recalled messages and others is the level of spend. The former are most likely to be supported by well-funded, long-standing advertising campaigns. Indeed, most of the best-recalled slogans have, literally, been on the air for years.

In addition, other factors may play an important part. These will include brand name prominence, brand image, advertising recall, persuasion, the search for information, buying intention and, of course, the purchase decision process.

In his 1999 paper, Farr documents some of the indicators of advertising effect as shown in Table 8.1.

Table 8.1 Indicators of advertising effect

Immediate challenge: driven by news

Measure	Short-term	Long-term
Awareness	Has awareness of claim or product risen?	Is this a step or a blip?
Usership	Did trial or purchase intent increase?	Does this translate into repeat purchases?
Communications	High level of awareness not necessary, but desirable. Is the message new, relevant and credible?	Is the news wearing out?
Core measures	Have perceived performance superiority and relevance increased?	Have these been maintained in the face of 'me-too's'? What evidence is there of emotional bonding?

Immediate challenge: driven by creative impact

Measure	Short-term	Long-term
Awareness	Has saliency risen?	Popularity and familiarity
Affinity	Increases in affinity and status?	Is this a step or a blip? Does it lead to real bonding?
Communications	Are there high levels of branded media awareness? Is it involving, empathetic, emotionally relevant, distinctive among target group?	Signs of freshness, appeal and distinctiveness fading?

Interest and status

Measure	Short-term	Long-term
Awareness	Is awareness of claim or product maintained?	Beware negative trends. Once long-term decline sets in it can be difficult to arrest
Core measures	Movements and measures relating to saliency and popularity?	Are the emotional and status dimensions maintained? Moving?
Communications	Is the advertising topping up the reservoir of associations? Is it involving, empathetic, emotionally relevant, distinctive among target group?	Look for maintenance of freshness, appeal and distinctiveness

Enhancement

Measure	Short-term	Long-term
Core measures	Movements on dimensions relating to communications? Signs of uplift during trial stimulation periods – promotionally driven?	Are users' perceptions reflecting the positioning created via the advertising? Leading to bonding?
Communications	Is the message remembered and linked to the brand? Does it relate to the experience of 'using' the product? Is it creating expectations of what the product would 'feel like' to use? Can these associations positively frame or elevate brand experience?	Is base level of awareness building? Any signs of relevance decline

Similarly, a series of criteria for measuring advertising effectiveness have been developed by Giep Franzen (1994). He proposes that advertising must:

- be perceived with the senses;
- succeed in gaining and retaining our attention;
- be likeable and not irritating;
- contribute to the difference we perceive between the advertised brand and alternatives;
- influence our choice in favour of the advertised brand;
- have a central message that we store in our memory.

Undeniably, advertising enables a greater price premium to be sustained by advertised brands over unadvertised brands in the same market. As Yasin (1995) indicates:

> Apart from issues of brand share, this price premium alone would be a commercially sound rationale for manufacturers spending money on consumer advertising. This aspect of supporting brand strength is confirmed by higher advertising weights being associated with lower own label shares of market.

In many countries, various awards programmes are run by the advertising industry to identify campaigns that demonstrate advertising effectiveness and that can aid the process of gaining a better understanding of how advertising works. The Effie awards are the oldest award programme rewards campaigns for the achievement of advertising effectiveness. They commenced in 1969 within the American Marketing Association. However, some critics argue that the level of proof required is too low. In Canada, the effectiveness scheme, known as the Cassies, are modelled on the UK IPA awards programme, where the levels of proof demanded are much higher.

The Institute of Practitioners in Advertising (IPA) have run the Advertising Effectiveness Awards continuously since 1980. These awards require evidence of advertising effectiveness against a series of rigorous criteria. Indeed, the model has set a trend which has been substantially reflected in the schemes run in other countries. Importantly, as the awards have developed, so too the evaluative criteria have changed, reflecting the changing role of advertising within the marketing communications mix. The awards recognise that the process of advertising evaluation is continuously evolving because of the complexity of the decision chain, and the fact that consumer 'interaction' with the brand prior to purchase is usually much more lengthy and involved (Duckworth 1997). Despite this the debate as to the determinants of effective advertising continues to rage, especially within the advertising trade press.

Several of the case studies used in this text have been taken from the IPA Advertising Effectiveness Awards.

Long-term advertising value

John Philip Jones writing in *Admap* in September 1994 makes a number of observations regarding the short- and long-term impacts of advertising, based on considerable experience and evaluation of brand performance (Jones 1994):

1 A short-term advertising effect is a precondition of a long-term one. To a large degree, a long-term effect is a repetition of a series of short-term effects.

2 The ability of a brand to generate repeated short-term effects depends on the continuity of its advertising schedule.

3 The long-term effectiveness of advertising is also influenced by the brand's internal momentum.

4 50 per cent of advertising campaigns have a noticeable sales effect in both the short and long term.

5 A further 20 per cent of ad campaigns have a noticeable short-term sales effect but no long-term effect, which Jones attributes to the lack of media continuity.

6 30 per cent of campaigns actually result in (or at least coincide with) sales going down. The campaigns are simply too weak to protect the brand from the superior effectiveness of competitive advertising.

Barwise (1999) argues that the effectiveness of advertising can be measured. He states that:

- For most brands, it should be possible to quantify – at least roughly – the impact of advertising expenditure (adspend) on short-term financial performance.

- The demonstrable short-term impact of advertising on sales (or margins) varies widely, but in most cases it is not enough to cover the cost of the advertising.

- In addition to its short-term effects, however, advertising can contribute to long-term shareholder value by increasing 'brand equity', i.e. the brand's ability to support a high market share, a premium price and profitable brand extensions.

- Successful firms do not allow short-term economic conditions to make them abandon their strategy. Instead, they typically maximise long-term value by maintaining or increasing their adspend when the economy slows down and weaker competitors cut back.

- Any reduction in these firms' short-term financial performance is, usually, soon outweighed by increased revenue and profit growth when economic conditions improve.

- Contrary to widespread belief, financial markets do look for long-term shareholder value, not just short-term performance. The markets are also willing to be convinced of the value of brand equity and other intangibles, even if they are sceptical of our ability to quantify this value (never mind the specific long-term contribution of advertising).

- In this context, shareholder reactions depend crucially on the credibility of the firm's strategy, communicated through its actions, financial statements and other corporate communications, and directly by top management.

It has to be remembered that not all advertising is designed to lead directly to sales. For example, some advertising may be aiming for long-term brand image building. Whether it is designed for short-term or long-term purposes, advertising's effectiveness lies in its capability to help stimulate or maintain sales. According to Abraham and Lodish (1990), however, a real and important issue in advertising effectiveness is 'the incremental sales of a product over and above those that would have happened without the advertising or promotion.' If short-term advertising can result in a sustained high level of sales the company is, as they put it, 'getting the most out of advertising'. They suggest that, as a result, much advertising is wasted, largely due to the lack of measures that can show the manager the impact of short-

term advertising on long-term sales. Because of our inability to isolate advertising effects from other effects, and to quantify such effects, many authors have commented that there is no more difficult, complex or controversial problem in marketing than measuring the influence of advertising on sales.

Clearly, it is every company's goal to gain the most from investments in advertising. Contrary to the conventional wisdom that sustained spending in advertising is needed to maintain high levels of sales, the concept of marketing persistence suggests that short-term advertising campaigns can have long-lasting impacts on sales. A study conducted by Zhou et al. (2003) provides a glimpse of the long-term effect of television advertising on sales in China through the use of a marketing-persistence model. Significant marketing persistence was found in sales of consumer durables, whereas there were mixed results in sales of non-durables. Based on the findings, their results show that, as a whole, advertising had long-term effects on sales of consumer durables, but did not have long-term effects on sales of consumer non-durables.

Baxter (1999) argues that the combination of the general data provided by PIMS of aggregated business performance and the cases from the IPA of specific brands and specific advertising campaigns, adds up to a persuasive case for the long-term value of advertising to brands and businesses.

The PIMS study is valuable because it proves that there is a *causal* relationship (not just an associative one) between advertising spend and profitability, and because that relationship is not a simple or direct one, it also articulates the *way* in which advertising impacts on profitability.

The key findings are that:

- Advertising impacts on profitability because it contributes to a key driver of profitability, namely relative customer value.
- The key driver of relative customer value is perceived quality, and there is a direct correlation between advertising and (customer-perceived) quality.
- Successful advertising is therefore that which builds product or service image and company reputation, both of which are key components of perceived quality.
- Successful advertising spends heavily relative to its share of the market: those brands or businesses that invest in advertising to produce a share of voice over and above their share of market outperform their competition.
- It is not just 'any old advertising' that has this effect: spend alone is not enough. The style and content of advertising are also important. Advertising that focuses on product image, company reputation and/or other key attributes that drive customer perceptions of relative quality and hence value will be successful in business terms.

However, Aaker (1991) argues that, as a field, we have been remarkably unsuccessful at measuring/modelling the long-term value of advertising and other brand-building activities. In particular, there are at least four major problems with efforts to estimate long-term value. First, the available independent variable in most historical data sources usually does not tap brand equity dimensions – advertising expenditures might be tracked rather than brand associations or awareness, for example. Second, there is rarely any meaningful change in the independent variable because dramatic changes in strategy are unusual. Third, the period in which changes are monitored is rarely long enough to observe long-term effects, which usually involve years rather than months. Fourth, it is difficult to translate the results that are detected (such as a change in awareness or attitude) to bottom line numbers that relate to shareholder value.

Similarly, Ehrenberg et al. (1998) argue that the main effects of advertising have to be in the medium to long term. This is because for most customers there usually is a long gap (many months or more) between seeing an ad for a particular brand and actually buying that brand. This is so even in the case of 'frequently bought' goods. Competitors then try to combat each other and therefore to negate any positive marketing-mix effects on sales. Hence competition and competitive advertising act mainly to maintain sales.

They continue: 'Such advertising works, we think, if it leaves or strengthens memory traces and associations for the brand in the consumer's mind, so that the brand comes to mind (i.e. is salient) when a purchase occasion for the product arises.'

IMC and research

According to Archer and Hubbard (1996) the vast bulk of market research continues to reflect the structures of disintegrated marketing communications. Much research set out to measure the effectiveness of an element of communication, such as advertising, in isolation of other forms of activity which have been implemented by the organisation. And, the greater the move towards integration, the greater the shortcomings of such research activity become.

Advertising likeability

There is a considerable debate within the industry as to whether advertising needs to be liked in order to be effective. A study by Du Plessis (1994) based on a sample of some 8000 commercials concluded that likeability is not merely entertainment. People will like an ad because it entertains – but also if it gives them relevant news, or if they can empathise with it. They will not like it if it confuses, alienates or bores them.

In a further paper by the same author (1998) he identifies a predictive model based on three important dimensions

1 People like advertising that entertains them. Entertainment is the opposite of being familiar with the ad or the style of advertising.
2 People like ads they can empathise with, which show them how they would like to be.
3 People like ads that give news about products, how they can be useful to them and what they can do with products.

In a similar manner, Jones (1997) concluded that successful campaigns have three general characteristics:

1 they are likeable and offer a reward for watching because they are entertaining and amusing;
2 they are visual rather than verbal;
3 they say something meaningful about the brand being advertised.

In 1990 Biel published his paper entitled 'Love the ad, buy the product' developed a similar point of view to that expressed in papers by Eric Du Plessis (1994, 1998)

that ad liking was the most predictive measure of advertising effectiveness. In it Biel argues that the more liked is the advertising campaign, the greater the exhibited preference for the brand. A sample of consumers were exposed to a series of commercials with the findings as follows:

- Those who were neutral to the advertising showed an improvement in brand preference of 8.2 per cent.
- Those who like the advertising somewhat showed an improvement of 9.5 per cent.
- Those who liked the advertising a lot showed an improvement of 16.2 per cent.

He concludes that it is reasonable to infer that likeable commercials are more persuasive. Based on this study, he has formed five hypotheses:

1 Commercials that are liked get better exposure – if the consumer likes the commercial, they are less likely to avoid it when they have another opportunity to see it.
2 Commercials become brand personality attributes – in those markets where the functional characteristics of the competing brands are perceived to be very similar, advertising itself may be considered as a brand attribute (and differentiator) by consumers.
3 Liking is a surrogate for cognitive processing.
4 Positive affect is transferred from commercial to brand.
5 Liking evokes a gratitude response.

Du Plessis and Foster (2000) suggest that there are five key factors which result in 'ad liking':

1 entertainment value of the advertisement
2 relevant news values
3 empathy with what the ad portrays
4 feelings about the brand being advertised
5 uniqueness of the advertisement.

This point of view is challenged by Rice and Bennett (1998) who state 'Liking does not cause noting, neither does noting cause liking. Usage causes both.'

A further study by Walker and Dubitsky (1994) supports the belief that liking can contribute to effectiveness in more than one way. At the very least, ads that are better liked are more likely to be noticed and remembered. Thus liking should contribute to efficient delivery of the message, leveraging the advertiser's media investment. Further, it is clear that likeability is associated with favourable attitudes toward the brand, and more likeable ads show at least directionally greater persuasive impact.

Case study

APG Creative Planning Awards

Agency AMV. BBDO

Author Kara Miller

Health Education Authority – Anti-smoking campaign

Background

- 1 in every 5 deaths in the UK is caused by cigarette smoking.
- 1 in every 3 16–24 year old girls smoke, and this age group is almost twice as likely to smoke during pregnancy than any other age group. It is for this reason that we chose this group to be our core target.

However, this is a tough target. Young women who smoke experience very few noticeable side effects (nothing serious enough to motivate quitting en masse). Not only do they lack the motivation to quit, they are also extraordinarily adept at creating loopholes to escape anti-smoking messages directed at them.

An analysis of previous research showed that the three main loopholes were:

1 Smoking is just one of the many risks in life. Young smokers make a distinction between immediate, 'personal' reasons for giving up and more remote, 'official' reasons such as long-term health risks (e.g. lung cancer), which seem less relevant.
2 The risks of smoking are too far in the future to worry about now. Young smokers have no meaningful sense of their own mortality and live very much in the here and now.
3 Anti-smoking messages are redundant – 'everybody knows smoking is bad for you'.

To be effective, the anti-smoking message must feel like 'new news'.

Establishing the role for advertising

Our previous campaign used a two-pronged approach: 'Fear' and 'Empowerment'.

Empowerment messages fail because what this group lacks is meaningful, relevant motivation to quit, and many younger smokers do not believe that they are even addicted. While there is a role for advertising that communicates the serious health risks of smoking, a 'fear testimonial' message alone does not block off enough loopholes (very few young people die from a smoking-related illness). An approach was needed that offered immediacy and relevant new news.

The key insight – our target's weak spot. As a result of the above, three key points became clear:

1 There is no scope for even a hint of a prescriptive 'just say no' anti-smoking message. This group, young women, will only respond to messages that offer (or seem to offer) them an informed choice. This is part of their assertion of independence and their rejection of anything that comes from people who patronise them and couldn't possibly understand what it means to be them.
2 Appearance (and from this, positive self-esteem, boys, sex and peer group acceptance) is the key preoccupation. Young women are extremely concerned about their appearance (real and perceived). When it comes to their appearance (skincare, make-up, clothes, hair, etc) they are information hungry and, when reading their magazines, they are willing to plough through acres of pictures, diagrams and juicy detail to discover what's new and true in the world of skincare, hair care and overall image creation. Credible information learned here passes into the grapevine and can very quickly become received wisdom within the peer group.
3 Young women's positive associations with smoking

(aside from peer group acceptance) are mainly to do with appearance:

- When you smoke you look 'sophisticated', 'quietly confident', 'a bit sexy, alluring' and 'more like an adult'.
- The spectre of post-quitting weight gain was, for many young women, seen as more relevant and immediate than cancer.

We decided to research the planner's hypothesis that a credible but scary fact ('smoking makes your skin thinner' – true but probably unusable because everyone in this rather small medical study was over 50 years old) would capture our target's imagination and create a cause for concern where there previously was none.

Many of the girls we spoke to took the skin thinness story and ran with it. These girls internalised the story and gave it their own meanings that were relevant to them now and that tapped into their own individual anxieties about the appearance of their skin.

There was a great deal of familiarity with a wide range of 'scientific' skincare terms (e.g. 'antioxidants', 'amino acids', 'toxins', etc.) which was not particularly surprising given this group's obsession and information hunger with regards to appearance, in general, and skincare specifically. This is the 'language of cosmetics' that cosmetics manufacturers use to sell these girls more and more skin, hair and body products. Each new product requires its own story filled with 'scientific' language to lend it credibility.

The creative brief

Our proposition for the print campaign was every cigarette you smoke is having a detrimental effect on your looks now. Three key points emerged:

1 In order to attract the attention of our rather discriminating target, the visuals used had to be of intrinsic interest to them. Unlike the dark, bewildering visuals we were using which they said bored and repelled them!
2 It is not enough to use long 'scientific' copy to imitate the 'language of cosmetics'. In order to be relevant the copy should be succinct and, to create the same excitement that good cosmetics ads do, it must adopt the aspirational 'Clinique' approach of top skincare scientists at the cutting edge rather than that of an ordinary GP, who they saw as a grey health expert.

3 A tone that was too 'jokey', 'clever-clever', discursive or ironic would undermine the credibility of the message.

Four single-page print ads in the style of a high-quality cosmetics ad campaign but with cigarettes and cigarette ash sullying typical skincare/cosmetic products (facepack, skin cream, translucent powder and a make-up brush).

We worked extremely closely with our media team and when we saw the finished ads – glossy, beautiful, instant fix – we decided that not only were we going to use magazines, for the reasons outlined above, but we were also going to use posters in the London Underground because:

- Although the Underground is not a 'beauty environment' per se, many cosmetics brands advertise there and so there was a natural fit with our 'faux cosmetics' campaign.
- You can't smoke on the tube and so cigarettes are often top-of-mind for many smokers when they travel on the Underground.
- A 'grim reality' strategy of getting to our target when they are feeling lousy, e.g. early in the morning.

Qualitative research commissioned by the HEA showed that by using the language of cosmetics, and also the glamour and simple gloss of the best cosmetics advertisements, the message was found to be believable and extremely relevant.

These ads were found to be an appropriate counter to the 'sophisticated' image the tobacco industry and the movie/fashion world currently give cigarettes.

Quantitative ad tracking showed a 20 per cent increase in the number of 16–24 year olds who claim to have seen advertising with an anti-smoking message (excluding nicotine replacement treatments). Of the smokers who had seen the ads 84 per cent felt that they were aimed specifically at them and almost two-thirds said that the ads had encouraged them to think about giving up. With these ads, we have achieved our goal of inspiring, in our target, the beginnings of meaningful motivation to quit through engendering a sense of identification and instilling a sense of urgency and blocking off escape routes.

SOURCE: This case study is adapted from the paper presented at the APG Creative Planning Awards. The full version is available at www.warc.com and is reproduced by kind permission of the World Advertising Research Center.

Questions

1 What are the stages of the market research process?

2 What are the internal and external sources of information that can be used to gain an understanding of the market?

3 In what ways can market research be used to develop an insight into patterns of consumer behaviour?

4 What are the facets of the development of marketing communications strategy that Schultz, Tannenbaum and Lauterborn identify as being important?

5 What is the role of advertising pre-testing?

6 What methods can be used to evaluate advertising campaigns?

7 What dimensions indicate advertising effectiveness?

9 Defining advertising objectives and strategy

Learning outcomes

In this chapter you will consider:

- the stages of advertising development

- the importance of advertising strategy and the implications for strategy development

- the impact of advertising on the brand at different stages of the product life cycle

- the nature of advertising objectives and how they are determined

- the role of budget planning and the methods used to determine levels of expenditure.

The stages of advertising development

Since the advertising plan is an integral part of the marketing plan, it is imperative that the marketing plan forms the basis of all advertising planning. In many instances both the marketing plan and the advertising plan will be developed together. However, in some cases, the advertising plan will be developed separately.

The development of advertising is a sequential process that must reflect the marketing strategy. Only when the marketing strategy has been determined can the development of advertising strategy begin.

In broad terms, the process of advertising development follows a series of individual steps that are depicted in Figure 9.1.

The background analysis

It is imperative that, as with any other aspect of marketing planning, the starting-point will be a comprehensive analysis of the situation in which the brand exists. Although a great deal may already be known about the brand and its position in the market, it must be remembered that the marketplace is fluid. As such, conditions for the brand are likely to change on a continuous basis. Change might, for example, result from the introduction of a new or improved competitive product that alters consumer expectations of all product offerings. Similarly, it might reflect some underlying change in consumer needs or attitudes. An increased focus on the fat content of foods, as for example has recently occurred both in the UK and in other countries, might enhance the need for the brand to make clear its fat content.

Almost certainly, some form of consumer research would be needed either to confirm existing knowledge or to identify changes that have taken place or are likely to take place in terms of consumer needs and wants.

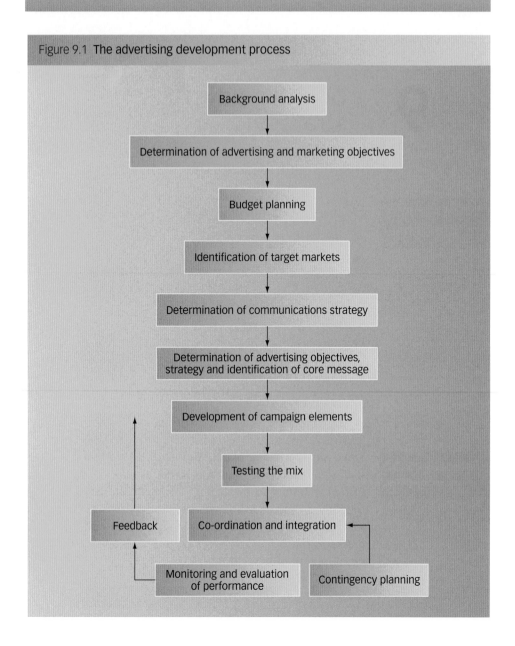

Figure 9.1 **The advertising development process**

Parallel to this would be a detailed analysis of competitive offerings that would be mapped against the identified consumer needs. Not only is it necessary to identify the strengths of competitive products, but also to isolate any potential areas of weakness that might be exploited by advertising.

Finally, in terms of the background analysis, it is important to identify the strengths and weakness of the brand itself. Are there, for example, specific brand associations that need to be reinforced? Conversely, are there particular negative connotations that need to be reversed?

In many instances, it would be appropriate to conduct a thorough SWOT analysis to ensure that all dimensions of the brand situation are identified and understood.

Advertising and marketing objectives

As was noted earlier, there is an intimate relationship between the marketing and the advertising strategies. The former will determine the broader marketing goals to which all of the elements of the marketing mix will contribute. The latter will determine the specific goals that can be fulfilled by advertising. Only when the specific advertising objectives have been decided upon, can the budget be determined.

This is an important part of the development process, since the scale of the advertising budget will substantially impact on the achievement of the defined strategy. This is particularly the case if the budget allocated is too small for the goals determined. A limited budget may constrain the advertising into media which are inappropriate to the task, as we will see later in this chapter when we cover the important dimensions of budget determination.

An important distinction needs to be made between marketing objectives and advertising objectives. The former are concerned specifically with the overarching tasks of marketing. As such, they may be concerned with issues such as pricing policy and profitability, distribution policy and targets, sales volume, etc. The latter deal only with those dimensions which advertising can reasonably be expected to impact upon. These may relate to awareness and perceptions of the brand, brand positioning, brand values and consumer behaviour. We will consider the possible objectives that might be established for an advertising campaign later in this chapter.

As Moriarty (1996) states:

> Setting objectives is the first step in the planning of an advertising campaign. The difficulty is what to base those objectives on. The difficulty is whether to state a behavioural response as a measurement of advertising effectiveness and whether to tie advertising to sales impact.

Clearly, the primary aim of advertising is the achievement of specific communications objectives, any of which may contribute to the creation of a positive purchasing intention. Depending on the position of the brand, advertising may set out to create a basic awareness of the brand, to ensure improved knowledge of the brand and its attributes, create a more favourable image, stimulate positive attitudes, and so on. Ultimately, its function is to sustain the brand as a profitable entity. This is reinforced by the quote from John Bartle (1997), the Managing Director of Bartle Bogle Hegarty: 'Although advertising can be, and is, used in a variety of different ways, its prime contribution is in helping to build and sustain brands for commercial benefit, often leading this process.'

Budget planning

A key aspect of the advertising process is the determination of appropriate levels of expenditure to fulfil the task. The amount of money spent on marketing communications differs widely amongst companies, even within the same industry.

According to Simon Broadbent, author of *The Advertising Budget* (1989), the amount to spend is determined by a process, not a formula. Hence, there is no simple solution. Various methods of budget determination have been suggested and the issue is one of deciding which approach is right for the situation.

The determination of the marketing communications budget cannot be considered in isolation. It is merely a part of the overall budgeting process that affects all aspects of the company's operation. Ultimately, any company must ensure that it remains in profit (at least in the longer term) if its business is to remain viable. As such, there will be a number of demands on the company's income and capital reserves. It may be necessary to improve the quality of production, which will require a significant investment in plant and machinery. Or to augment the sales force in order to achieve better distribution for the products it manufactures; to invest in research and development to ensure that the brand portfolio is maintained and is successful in a competitive environment, and so on.

Advertising, in this context, is part of the overall marketing budget. Inevitably, companies must consider the variety of demands for expenditure from a wide range of different sources, and demands for expenditure on advertising and other forms of marketing communications must compete with all these other areas. Arguably the most important 'competitor' for funds comes from the desire to maintain a competitive price at the point of purchase. Inevitably, if prices are reduced, either to the retailer or the end consumer, there will be a consequence for the overall level of revenue. In many companies, the source from which expenditure is most likely to be withdrawn is that of advertising and other forms of marketing communications.

Identification of target markets

Next we need to define the target market to be exposed to the advertising message. Since it is unusual for any product to appeal to the market as a whole, it is necessary to identify those groups who are likely to be most responsive to the message. It might be:

- existing customers
- potential customers
- consumers who have experienced our brand but who primarily purchase from our competitors
- consumers who are infrequent users of our brand or only use particular sizes or flavours
- people with low awareness of the brand
- people who hold negative attitudes towards the brand.

The decisions made in this area will affect the subsequent development of the media planning strategy.

Advertising strategy

The determination of the appropriate advertising strategy will depend on the market to which the campaign is being applied. Equally, it must consider the consumer decision-making process which is involved in that particular market.

It is clear that there are fundamental differences between the decision to buy a tin of soup and the decision to purchase a television set. Equally, there are differences between buying a CD and buying the equipment to play it on. Advertising will need to work in different ways in each of these situations and reflect the different buying decisions involved.

Effective communication depends on getting the attention of the person you want to communicate with and saying what you want to say in language and with a tone of voice that they can understand. And saying what you want to say to them in terms that have some bearing on their self-interest (Salmon 2001).

Identification of the core message

The core message identifies the precise information that must be conveyed by the advertising campaign. It is important to note that this is not the execution itself, which is determined at the next stage; rather, what message the execution should contain. Communications must be persuasive and differentiate between features and benefits.

Communication often fails because of the belief that what has to be said is inherently boring and the only way to communicate is to be strident and repetitive. Communication may be achieved, albeit often at enormous cost, but it may also build up a resistance to the message.

Moreover, as Franzen (1994) suggests:

> consumers want advertising to take them seriously, and at the same time to be made in such a way that it appeals to them. Advertising should be special in its execution, especially in that it makes proper use of powerful visuals and music. At the same time, it must stick close to the product and the brand, and, in fact, to the everyday lives of ordinary people.

Developing the campaign elements

Once the budget and the core message have been agreed, the team responsible for the campaign can proceed with the campaign development. In outline terms, this will consist of determining the specific components that will feature in the campaign. If the budget is sufficient and the medium is appropriate, it might use television either alone or in combination with some other media.

The team will develop copy and visual content of the appropriate message. In turn, there will need to be an assessment of the media most suitable to the delivery of the message to the defined target audience.

As Spence (1991) states: 'By developing a creative image, the message can be lodged in the consumer's memory and inextricably linked to the brand and its message which can then be recalled at a later date.'

According to Lord Tim Bell (2001) all communication has to be single-minded because it represents a key discipline. People can't remember alternatives – they just become confused.

Testing the mix

In most cases, the agency will explore a number of potential routes to identify the one that will have the most beneficial communications impact. Market research, particularly of a qualitative nature, will be employed to ensure both that the outline executions convey the correct image and, importantly, are clearly understood by the target market. Often, a series of revisions will be required to reflect the findings of this research and to hone the advertising to achieve the most impactful and relevant campaign.

Final production

Once the findings from research have been received, the agency will proceed to the production stage of the advertising. Here again, market research will play an important role in ensuring that there is an appropriate fit between the advertising message and the interpretation placed on it by the desired target audience. There is often a considerable variation between the rough drawings, which will be used in preliminary research to assess consumer response, and the final execution. It will be important to ensure that elements such as the casting of the artists who appear in the advertising, the 'props' used in a photograph or commercial and even the music and voiceover convey the right values.

It is important to note that agencies rarely produce the finished advertising themselves. Rather, they employ the services of specialists in the appropriate area. This might include photographers, television directors (who, in turn, will employ freelance camera and lighting operators, set production and so on). Inevitably, production is an expensive process and considerable sums of money will be invested at this stage. Hence the importance of ensuring that what is to be produced accurately reflects the needs in terms of production values, and comprehension on the part of the reader or viewer. The imperative will be to ensure that risks are reduced as far as is possible.

Implementation

The penultimate stage is the implementation of the advertising campaign. This stage will include, for example, the negotiations for the media time or space to ensure the best placement of the advertising message. After the advertising has been produced, arrangements must be made for the delivery of the advertising to the media and the appearance of the advertising.

Equally, it will be essential to notify the sales force of both the nature of the advertising campaign and its timings. They, in turn, will be able to use the information to persuade retailers to stock the brand and, in some instances, to give the brand special display within their outlets to take advantage of the anticipated consumer demand which will result.

Co-ordination and integration

Most importantly, the agency will ensure that the advertising is not only consistent with the previously agreed objectives but integrates fully with any other marketing communication components which might be used within the overall campaign.

It is important to remember that advertising does not and cannot exist in isolation of the other elements of marketing communications. For any marketing communications plan to work to its maximum demands the total integration of all communications activities. Obviously, not every marketing communications plan embraces all of the elements. However, it is highly likely that the marketing plan will demand the use of, say, sales promotion, sales force incentives and point-of-sale material. Care must be taken to ensure that all of these, and any other elements, are fully integrated to ensure the maximum impact on the target audiences. This is especially important in the context of the nature of the organisations that may contribute to the fulfilment of marketing communications activities. Often, these are independent of the advertising agency and it is important that they are fully briefed as to the specific objectives to ensure that there is consistency in what they produce and the advertising campaign.

As Head (1998) states: 'It is imperative that the strategy identified for advertising aligns and is integrated with other communications strategies.'

Monitoring and evaluation of performance

Once the campaign is under way, it will be important to monitor its performance in the marketplace in order to determine the extent that the defined objectives have been met. As previously, market research techniques will be employed to assist in the evaluative process. Most commonly, advertisers will use devices such as tracking studies to monitor the performance of the advertising over time and to gauge the impact on the desired target audience. Even at this stage, it may be necessary to make additional revisions to ensure that the advertising meets the objectives set for it. Whilst the earlier use of market research may make a valuable contribution to the understanding of the advertising, it is only at the time when the advertising 'goes live' that its true impact on the target market can be properly assessed.

Successful advertising is bounded by two important constraints. Firstly, individuals must be exposed to it and pay some attention. Secondly, they must interpret it in the way that the advertiser intended.

Contingency planning

It is a truism that anything that can go wrong probably will! It is, therefore, both sound practice and prudent to identify a sum of money (usually expressed as a proportion of the overall budget) to be used to remedy deficiencies in the performance of the marketing communications plan. Inevitably, much of the planning process takes place in advance of the implementation of the details of the plan. Whilst steps will be taken to anticipate likely changes which might occur in the marketplace, it is clear that there will be a variety of unforeseen circumstances which may impair the achievement of the desired goals. Competitive product introductions, price changes, alterations in competitive expenditures, may be just a few of the variables that alter once the plan is put into effect.

The need for feedback

The sensible marketer recognises that his plans must operate in a dynamic rather than a static environment. Simply because a plan has been created and approved at senior management level should not imply that it is to be implemented without change. There needs to be constant monitoring and feedback built into the marketing communications plan, to ensure that it reflects the situation which actually obtains rather than the one that was envisaged when the plan was created. Only in this way can the process be amended and adapted to mirror the real market environment.

Having briefly considered the components of the advertising process, it is now possible to deal with the important dimensions in greater depth.

The advertising strategy and strategy development

Michael Head (1998) identifies a series of general principles that, if followed, are capable of producing an effective advertising strategy:

- Did previous campaigns have proper objectives set for them?
- How did those campaigns perform against those objectives?
- What lessons can be learned for future advertising?

It must recognise that much advertising does not deliver in the short term. It works by identifying the appropriate message and repeating it over a sufficient period of time until consumers believe it and act upon it. Accordingly, the strategy must include the length of time required to achieve this impact.

The value of a strategy is that it:

- defines the starting-point
- defines the end point
- describes the process for making the transition
- provides the criteria against which progress can be measured

- provides a platform from which detailed plans can be prepared
- identifies a framework against which research and measurement can take place.

Cowan (1998) argues that an advertising strategy should have three key elements:

1 A target group: This is a group of people defined in terms of the marketing problem. The sort of people who, either from experience or market research, can be influenced by the proposed advertising.
2 A behavioural objective: What do we want the target group to do?
3 A mental objective: What do we want the target group to think, feel, believe or desire once they have seen the advertisement or the campaign?

Leslie Butterfield (1997) has suggested a distinctive format for the determination of advertising strategy (see Figure 9.2). The device adopted is the shape of a diamond in which the vertical dimension indicated the sequence of steps involved in the overall strategy development process. The horizontal dimension represents the variable nature of the breadth of consideration, analysis and research involved at each of those stages.

The important difference between this and other strategy development models occurs in the latter part of the analytical process. In the analysis of the consumer's relationship with the brand, Butterfield suggests that it is important to consider what the product offers the consumer, both as a product and a brand. What they bring to it and the purchase decision process and mechanism. The role for advertising is defined as what advertising can do that will best help to sell the product and how it can go about doing that.

In the determining of creative strategy, the important aspects of brand positioning and target audience identification are considered simultaneously. It is vitally important that segmentation and positioning strategies must fit together seamlessly. Once the strategy has been agreed (usually in the form of the creative brief) management should withdraw from the creative process. As Murphy and Cunningham (1993) note: 'The purpose of developing a statement of creative strategy is to make

Figure 9.2 **The Butterfield diamond framework for strategic analysis**

Definition of the brand's business problem

Interrogation of all aspects of the brand's marketing mix

Analysis of the brand's total marketing situation

Analysis of the consumer's relationship with the brand

Derivation of a realistically defined role for advertising

The advertising objectives and strategy

SOURCE: Butterfield 1997

the advertising more effective by channelling the efforts of the creatives in the most productive direction.'

It is clear that brand awareness is an important facet of brand loyalty. Whilst brand awareness alone cannot ensure brand loyalty, it follows that the reverse must be true. It is for this reason that so much advertising seeks to generate both a positive level of awareness for the brand as well as an inextricable link with the category of product within which it is promoted. It is also clear that once consumers develop an image of a brand, they tend to retain it for a long period of time. In some instances these image dimensions may be linked to specific attributes of the brand. In most cases, however, they represent dimensions of perception which differentiate the product from its competitors. Indeed, in some instances, it is not the product which is the 'best' which occupies the position of leadership in its sector, rather the one that has created the most positive associations for itself in the minds of consumers.

Sometimes, these positive associations derive from a particular association that the brand possesses. Two tea brands have been promoted effectively using specific devices which created a positive identity in the minds of consumers. Tetley tea used the tea folk for many years, whilst its direct competitor, PG, was inextricably linked with the executional device of the chimps, who have featured in their advertising for more than 30 years. Despite the fact that both brands have now moved on, the legacy of these campaigns lives on in the minds of consumers. In other instances, it may be a copy line or style of execution which is associated with the brand and identifies it clearly in the minds of potential consumers.

Next it is necessary to determine what the advertising needs to say. Here again, identifying a clear message strategy will have impact on the media strategy. Advertising messages which need to be long or complex will be different to those which are simple and, for example, need to drive awareness or convey information about price.

How do you want the viewers to feel after seeing the message? The strategy must define in clear terms how the consumer should feel towards the brand. Perhaps we wish them to hold a more favourable image or to ensure that their understanding of the nature of the brand and its functions are more clearly understood.

How do you want them to react after seeing the advertising? The advertising strategy must be specific about what is expected of them as a result of having been exposed to the advertising. It may be that we wish them to purchase the product for the first time, or to use it more frequently. Or perhaps we want to create reasons for the consumer to use the brand on different occasions or for different applications.

Each of these components interact with each other. Necessarily, therefore, strategy development will become an iterative process:

- defining how we want consumers to feel may change the strategy for what we want to tell them
- setting out clearly what we want consumers to do after being exposed to the advertising may require us to rethink which consumer groups we should be targeting.

Before the specific advertising strategy can be determined, several key factors need to be considered in some detail. The important dimensions of branding have been referred to earlier in this book (see Chapter 4). Advertising plays a critical role in the context of the maintenance of the brand image or, in some instances, the creation of a new brand image, if that is the objective.

The role of communications activity, including advertising, over a number of years, is not merely to ensure that a brand has a high level of awareness amongst its target audience, but to bring about brand preference. By creating positive perceptions in the minds of prospective consumers, the brand may be elevated to a position of leadership within its market sector. It will become the norm against which all other competing products are compared. Creative strategy helps advertising do its job in different ways. Perhaps by creating perceptual differentiation, focusing on core competencies, transcending perceived or practical barriers and translating concepts into meaningful images. All of these will contribute to a product or service's position, either formed independently by the consumer or driven by the advertising message.

Implications for strategy development

It is clear that advertising can fulfil fundamentally different strategic roles in the communications process.

- **Routine problem solving**

  For products and services which are bought routinely, the fundamental role of advertising is to reinforce the values associated with the brand, and to ensure a high level of pack recognition at the point of purchase. The consumer will not spend much time evaluating the available alternatives. They will already possess adequate information on which to make the purchase decision, and advertising must ensure that the brand values are sufficiently well known and 'front of mind' to ensure that the brand, at the very least, is included on the shortlist of products to be considered.

- **Limited problem solving**

  For products and services which are purchased on a less regular basis, the primary task of advertising is to provide the necessary levels of reassurance to the consumer that the purchase is an appropriate one. Since the purchase itself is undertaken less frequently, the advertising will need to remind the consumer of the benefits associated with using the brand, and to establish clear advantages relative to the competition. Sometimes, these will be tangible benefits relating to particular attributes of the brand – such as taste, quality, economy and so on. In other instances, these will be emotional benefits such as good motherhood (caring for the needs of the family); or social values (the type of people who use the product or service).

- **Extensive problem solving**

  In the context of products which require more extensive problem solving – that as we have seen previously are normally associated with expensive and very infrequently purchased items – the role of advertising will be both to establish the specific values of the brand, and to provide much of the necessary information upon which the purchase decision will be made.

Sometimes, advertising in such instances will attempt to establish the evaluative criteria that the consumer will use in the making of brand comparisons. It will indicate suggested criteria for choice and, not unreasonably, demonstrate how it performs better than the competition against these given criteria. It is important to make a distinction between the dimensions of purchasing behaviour. Not all products are purchased for rational reasons, although these may be important in the context of justifying the particular purchase to others.

Rational decisions   Some purchasing behaviour is conditioned by the need to take rational decisions as to the nature of purchase. In those instances, it is important to provide the consumer with hard factual evidence that will occasion their purchase. This may take the form of a promotional device, such as a lower price or extra product free. In other instances, it may be some statement of the functional performance of the brand, such as lasting longer than its competitors. In the case of more expensive purchases this may take the form of long copy advertising, factual comparisons, etc.

Image decisions   Many products and services are purchased more because of the image that is associated with them, than the purely functional benefits. In such instances it is important to consider the style and the image which is conveyed by the advertising or the possibility of developing an association with famous names or personalities.

The following are some indications of possible strategies that might be considered:

- **Generic strategy**
  Sometimes, where a brand is in a dominant position in the market, it will simply make a straight claim of product benefit. Heinz Baked Beans or the same manufacturer's Tomato Ketchup both use advertising that has, over a number of years, established them as being synonymous with the category.
- **Competitive strategy**
  In the majority of instances, an advertiser will seek to establish a point of difference between his or her own and competitive products. In some cases, this will be based on a specific dimension of the product (e.g. 'Persil washes whiter' or 'Nescafé – best beans, best blend, best taste'). In others, it will derive from a positioning of the brand that sets it apart, such as 'Avis – we try harder'. In all instances, the objective is to establish some point of advantage that distinguishes the product or service. It is important to remember, however, that such competitive strategies should not be taken to imply that only the particular brand possesses the attribute – rather that they have used the advertising medium to make it their own.
- **Usage expansion strategy**
  Advertising that encourages new or different uses of a brand is referred to as usage expansion advertising (Wansink and Ray 1996). The most typical forms of usage expansion advertising are non-comparison, product comparison and situation comparison ads. A non-comparison ad simply states that the target brand is a reasonable choice for the target situation (e.g., 'Eat Campbell's Soup for breakfast because it is hot and nutritious'). A product comparison ad associates the target brand with the target situation by comparing the target brand with another product already favourably associated with that situation (e.g., 'Eat Campbell's Soup for breakfast because it is hot and nutritious like hot cereal'). A situation comparison ad associates the use of the target brand in the target situation with its use in another situation that is already favourably associated with the brand (e.g., 'Eat Campbell's Soup for breakfast because it is as hot and nutritious as it is with lunch').

Brand image dimensions

Here the advertiser will use other associations to ensure that the product or service is distinguished from its competitors. Häagen-Dazs, for example, does not use basic claims in its advertising to reinforce its quality positioning, rather it associates the brand with desired lifestyle imagery. The long running Levis campaign communicates the values of a 'freedom', 'individuality' and 'originality' rather than asserting that they wear better than rival jeans. Such advertising is a reflection of the desires and aspirations of its consumers, rather than a reflection of specific aspects of the product itself. As such the advertising will seek to convey such dimensions as sensory and pleasurable benefits (as with Häagen-Dazs); intellectual stimulation (as for example, with *The Economist* or the *Sunday Times*) or social approval (as in much of the fashion house Burberry's advertising).

Brand weaknesses can be turned into strengths. The VW was initially seen as an ugly car (in comparison with its competitors). Subsequent advertising proclaimed that it worked better than its competition and the brand was accepted as such by consumers.

Brand planning considerations

Dyson (1999) argues that there are a number of issues that need to be addressed in terms of the development of the advertising strategy:

- Brand strategy: Do we want to grow the brand? If so, sales or profit? Or do we want to milk the brand?
- Brand responsiveness: How well do our different brands respond to advertising? What is the maximum possible return and how quickly do we get there?
- Halo effects and cannibalisation: What happens when we advertise one of our brands? Does it build any of the others in our portfolio or take sales from them?
- Brand profitability: How does this differ by brand and by country? If profit is the focus, there is no point generating sales for unprofitable brands, even if they are responsive to advertising.
- Media costs: Do these vary by brand (maybe because of different target audiences?) Costs will certainly vary by country.
- Market situation: What is the competitive context? What might be the reactions of others to our advertising? Will competitors be more aggressive in some markets than others?
- Operating constraints: Are there any constraints we need to take into account?

Patti and Frazer (1984) developed a planning grid that associated specific strategies with their creative implications (see Table 9.1). Although somewhat dated, the grid still retains much relevance today:

Advertising and the product life cycle

The appropriate advertising strategy will be a function of the stage that the product occupies in terms of the product life cycle. The pre-stage will require a thorough examination of the product in the context of its market and the target consumer audience that need to be informed about its existence. This will entail an analysis of the various alternatives available to the consumer, a detailed consideration of the consumer segments, their needs and wants from the product category and the determination of a match between these and the product or service offering.

Table 9.1 Advertising strategies, their applications and the creative implications

Strategy	Description	Application	Creative implications
Generic	Straight product or benefit with no assertion of superiority	Monopoly or extreme dominance of product category	Serves to make advertiser's brand synonymous with product category; may be offset by higher order strategies
Pre-emptive	Generic claim with assertion of superiority	Most useful in growing or awakening market where competitive advertising is generic or non-existent	May be successful in convincing consumer of superiority of advertiser's product; limited response options for competitors
Unique selling proposition	Superiority claim based on unique physical feature or benefit	Most useful when point of difference cannot be readily matched by competitors	Advertiser obtains strong persuasive advantage; may force competitors to imitate or choose more aggressive strategy
Brand image	Claim based on psychological differentiation usually symbolic association	Best suited to homogeneous goods where physical differences are difficult to develop or which may be quickly matched; requires sufficient understanding of consumers to develop meaningful symbols or associations	Most often involves prestige claims that rarely challenge competitors directly
Positioning	Attempt to build or occupy mental niche in relation to identified competitor	Best strategy for attacking a market leader; requires relatively long-term commitment to aggressive advertising efforts and to understanding consumers	Direct comparison severely limits options for named competitor; counter-attacks seem to offer little chance of success
Resonance	Attempt to evoke stored experiences of prospects to endow product with relevant meaning or significance	Best suited to socially visible goods; requires considerable consumer understanding to design message patterns	Few direct limitations on competitor's options; likely competitive response: imitation
Affective	Attempt to provoke involvement or emotion through ambiguity, humour, or the like, without without strong selling emphasis	Best suited to discretionary items; effective use depends upon conventional approach by competitors to maximise difference; greatest commitment is to aesthetics or intuition rather than research	Competitors may imitate to undermine strategy of difference or pursue other alternatives

SOURCE: Patti and Frazer 1984

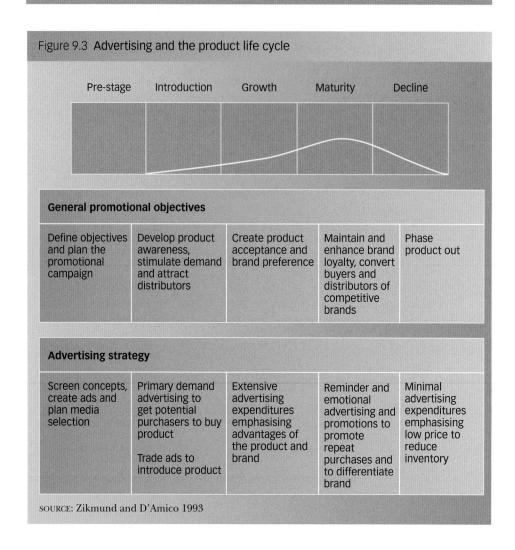

Figure 9.3 Advertising and the product life cycle

Pre-stage	Introduction	Growth	Maturity	Decline

General promotional objectives

Define objectives and plan the promotional campaign	Develop product awareness, stimulate demand and attract distributors	Create product acceptance and brand preference	Maintain and enhance brand loyalty, convert buyers and distributors of competitive brands	Phase product out

Advertising strategy

Screen concepts, create ads and plan media selection	Primary demand advertising to get potential purchasers to buy product Trade ads to introduce product	Extensive advertising expenditures emphasising advantages of the product and brand	Reminder and emotional advertising and promotions to promote repeat purchases and to differentiate brand	Minimal advertising expenditures emphasising low price to reduce inventory

SOURCE: Zikmund and D'Amico 1993

At the introductory stage, the fundamental requirement will be to create product awareness and to stimulate trial of the new product. At the same time, specific trade advertising may be utilised to increase the awareness of the product amongst potential stockists and, thereby, create a wider base of distribution. Subsequently, some of the trialists will go on to become brand loyalists and proceed to repeat purchase of the product; others will simply include it within their personal brand portfolio; and yet others will reject the brand.

Once the product has reached the growth stage it will be important to use advertising to maintain consumer demand and to ensure that the consumer's attention is focused on the advantages of the brand relative to its competition. In the maturity phase, the advertising will be required to maintain customer loyalty. Together with other promotional devices, such as sales promotion, the strategic intent will be to ensure that the existing consumers make repeat purchases on a regular basis whilst encouraging customers of competing brands to switch their custom. Existing consumers will, substantially, be aware of the product's inherent benefits and will not need to be reminded of them. Rather, advertising will take the form of providing some emotional reinforcement of the brand proposition to ensure continued loyalty. Alternative advertising may also be required to stimulate trial amongst those who, for whatever reason, have rejected the brand. Often, this will involve some form of re-presentation of the product proposition, for example, expressing the brand as new or improved.

Finally, during the decline phase, advertising expenditures will be reduced significantly reflecting the decline in brand volumes. The essential requirement will be to ensure that the decline can be slowed, although expenditures may well be directed towards reducing the stocks in the trade. Most often this period will be associated with a series of price-led promotions which will ensure the maintenance of offtake.

Advertising objectives and how they are determined

Defining the advertising objective is the starting-point for campaign development. In simple terms the advertising objective is a specific statement of what the advertising is designed to achieve. This will define, in measurable terms, the role of the advertising, for example, in the context of awareness, brand choice, image change, loyalty or some other aspect of advertising communication. Setting too broad objectives or attempting to achieve too much within a limited budget will undermine the effectiveness of the advertising message. 'Advertising objectives are simply statements describing what is to be accomplished by advertising to capitalise on opportunities and/or overcome problems facing the advertiser during the planning period' (Murphy and Cunningham 1993).

The issue of determining the appropriate objectives is an essential part of advertising campaign planning following the principles established by Russell Colley in his 1961 paper on DAGMAR. It is clear that the objectives establish the essential direction for the campaign. Moreover, as Colley suggests, clear measurable objectives are essential for the subsequent managerial evaluation and control of the advertising effort. One vital aspect of the setting of objectives is that they must be capable of measurement. As he stated in his paper, there is no point having an objective which is not measurable, since it will be impossible to ascertain whether the objective has been met on completion of the campaign. Without such a clear and concise definition of what it is that the advertising is attempting to achieve, it will be impossible to determine whether the campaign has succeeded after its completion.

One issue to be discussed is the link between advertising and sales. Not unreasonably, most companies continue to invest money in advertising in order to stimulate demand for their products. The consequence of this belief is that the additional sales, and the revenue derived from them, will serve to offset the costs of the original investment. The corollary of this belief will be that sales may be considered the arbiter of success.

Unfortunately, there are two important factors which, in most situations, suggest that sales measurement is a less than appropriate evaluation device. Firstly, advertising does not work in isolation of other components of the marketing communications mix, or even the marketing mix. Because all of the elements are inextricably linked, a lack of performance is some other areas may well result in sales targets not being achieved. This does not mean, however, that the advertising campaign has failed to achieve its specific goals. Secondly, in many instances, there is a delay before the impact of advertising is felt. Evidence for this delay is provided in a study of the effects of advertising conducted by Millward Brown (1991).

We have seen earlier that the statement of the advertising objective is important since it will guide the advertising development process. Only by making the objectives clear will it be possible for the creative department to develop a campaign that matches those objectives.

There are many statements of advertising objective and, whilst the following list is not exhaustive, it indicates the type of objectives that might be set for an advertising campaign (Pincott 2001):

- Awareness and saliency:
    - raise the profile of the brand by x per cent;
    - build awareness of brand by x per cent;
    - make consumers aware of brand's promotion;
    - drive saliency;
    - raise awareness of the brand at launch;
    - educate the consumer of the benefits of the brand;
    - reinforce perceptions.
- To maintain brand positioning:
    - revive brand relevance and appeal;
    - reflect the size and status of the brand;
    - remind current and lapsed users that the brand;
    - build on past brand strengths and remedy perceptual weaknesses;
    - enhance the special regard with which the brand is held;
    - change perceptions;
    - reposition the brand;
    - encourage reassessment of the brand.
- To express the brand values in a contemporary manner:
    - change the basis of consumer evaluations of the product category;
    - change behaviour;
    - encourage increased use of the product;
    - gain trial;
    - get kids to ask Mum for the brand;
    - increase penetration of the brand amongst (a defined target group).

Advertising can fulfil a number of roles. As such, the objectives which advertising may be required to meet are somewhat diverse.

Awareness   At various times in the life of a brand, it is important to raise the level of awareness amongst target consumers. Inevitably, this is most often associated with the introduction of a new product. However, either because of competitive or because of other pressures (perhaps the reduction in the levels of advertising support) the levels of awareness of a particular brand may fall, and advertising will seek to improve the levels. In some instances, although the consumer may be aware of the product itself, they will need information as to where to purchase (particularly if it is in limited distribution). Advertising will seek to identify stockists of the product.

Reminder   Reminder advertising can take a number of forms. In some instances, it serves (as with awareness advertising) simply to ensure that the brand is brought towards the front of the mind. In others, it will seek to communicate specific benefits or uses of the brand that may have been forgotten. Kellogg's have used this approach with a previous campaign for Corn Flakes – with the end line 'Too good to be forgotten'. Or, perhaps to suggest new uses which will make it more relevant to the consumer's needs.

Changing attitudes, perceptions and beliefs

From time to time, market research will reveal a dissonance between the stance of the brand and the desired positioning. Perhaps, the image of the brand has become 'old fashioned' or maybe more recently introduced competitor products are seen to have greater relevance to current needs. Although advertising will be designed to counteract these influences, it should be recognised that the task of changing attitudes and perceptions is far more difficult to achieve, but one in which advertising can make a valid contribution. Both Lucozade and Hellmann's Mayonnaise are examples of advertising campaigns that dramatically changed consumer perceptions of the brands.

Reinforcing attitudes

Often the role of advertising is to remind consumers (particularly in the case of routine purchases) of the original reasons why they chose the product. In some instances, such advertising will reassert the original values of the brand either to off-set competitive pressures, or simply to reassure consumers that those brand values have not been changed. Kellogg's, for example, ran a campaign with the broad theme 'If it doesn't say Kellogg's on the box, it isn't Kellogg's in the packet' – to reduce the encroachment of retailer products which might otherwise be confused with the leading brand.

Product line building

In some instances, the volumes for individual product lines, although profitable, will be insufficient to sustain advertising. Here, the manufacturer may seek to communicate values that are common to all product lines which bear the brand name (even though they may well have different functional benefits). Sometimes, although not always, this will take the form of corporate advertising to associate a series of positive values with the parent name in order that it serves to endorse the products with which it is associated.

Relating product to consumer needs

Although a brand may be in common use, the underlying reasons for its purchase may have become confused. Advertising will seek to ensure that the product is seen as being directly relevant to contemporary consumer requirements.

Image

Advertising may seek to convey particular image dimensions in order that the product will be better perceived by the target audience. As we will see in the following chapter, many brands are bought primarily for the image they portray rather than because of their functional benefits. Much perfume advertising is of this nature as, of course, is that for Levis.

This is not to say, however, that image-building advertising is unimportant for low-involvement products. On the contrary, it may be even more important. As Assael (1990) points out, although consumers buy first, they may evaluate a brand after the first few purchases, when brand belief or brand loyalty may be formed.

Even the most well-known brands rely on a combination of periodic brand-image advertising and frequent reminder advertising to stay competitive. In recent years in the cigarette industry, for example, marketers from Philip Morris decided that the grand cowboy image of its flagship brand, Marlboro, had to go hand-in-hand with price promotions. Although the company did not dispense with the cowboy image, it downplayed it. Due to the many choices buyers have in the marketplace, the company let price promotions become a more dominant part of the marketing strategy for its frequently purchased product.

Budget planning

The amount spent on advertising seems to have a considerable impact on the development of strong brand images and identity. Recent research carried out by the IPA demonstrates that there is a correlation between advertising expenditure and brand image development. However, Croft (1998) found that it is not necessarily the total amount spent on advertising, but the ratio between ad expenditure and sales which is important. When influencing consumer perceptions of the quality of the product (and hence its value) it is not just a question of how much a company spends, but of how much more than its competitors relative to their share of the market. Croft emphasises that what matters is advertising that succeeds in building quality perceptions of the product either directly or through the intermediary of product image and company reputation.

Gregory (1997) supports Croft with studies of 220 Fortune 100 companies over a five-year period demonstrating that higher levels of advertising spends were directly related to a greater brand image. Gregory also found that improvements and deterioration in image were directly correlated with levels of financial performance.

A further study by Cobb-Walgren et al. (1995) also showed that brands with greater advertising budgets generate substantially higher levels of brand equity, significantly greater brand preference and purchase intentions.

Research also shows that advertising not only contributes to sales improvement but also to company value (Bell et al. 1999 and Gregory 1997). Studies indicate that advertising has a direct influence of 5 per cent on share price, and that the amount spent on advertising is the main factor in shaping brand image. The research further suggests that brand image has an indirect influence on 70 per cent of all of the other factors which determine the share price such as cash flow, earnings and share price growth.

Biel (1990) indicates that advertising spending plays a dominant role in the brand's marketing mix. Strong brands were more likely to run the same campaign for an extended period of time, changing the executions frequently but not the campaign theme.

A key task is that of determining an effective approach to the setting of a budgetary level. It should be clear that the determination of the correct level of expenditure must depend on proper analysis of the situation, rather than the use of 'norms', rule of thumb, or 'gut-feel'.

Unfortunately, few companies adopt a scientific approach towards budget setting. As described by a senior vice president of one of the largest international grocery products companies:

The most common way that brand managers set budgets is to start the same as last year. At least last year's budget produced last year's results. I've rarely seen zero-based budgeting. The budget and its allocation are typically based on the marketing plan and what needs to be accomplished. Judgement is very much a part of the decision-making process. Models are rarely used.

Low (1999) reports that The Advertising Research Foundation, the American Association of Advertising Agencies and the Marketing Science Institute recently launched a collaborative research project called 'MAX: Managing Advertising Expenditures'. The objective of their efforts is to improve current practice with respect to budgeting and evaluating advertising expenditures. Their project is motivated by the concern that: 'many firms may have been making far from optimal investments in advertising [which] could result in a decline in the value of brands and in lower financial performance.'

On the following pages we set out most of the ways used to determine the budget.

1 Marginal analysis

Several attempts have been made to transfer the learning from the principles of economic theory to that of budget determination. In essence, the principles of marginal analysis suggest that a company should continue to increase its marketing communications expenditure until the point where the increase in expenditure matches, but does not exceed, the increase in income which those expenditures generate.

This can be shown graphically as follows:

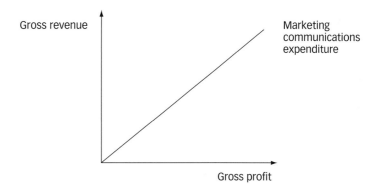

Unfortunately, the application of the theory of marginal analysis does not transfer readily into the real world situation. The first problem to deal with is the fact that the theory assumes that sales are a direct function of marketing communications expenditures. Whilst it is possible to postulate situations in which this might be the case – for example, in the area of direct marketing – even here this may be somewhat wide of the mark. The level of expenditure is only one of the variables that needs to be considered. The theory makes no attempt to consider, for example, the location of the activity in terms, say, of media placement, or of the copy content of the advertisement or sales promotion tool. It simply assumes that every pound spent is likely to achieve the same impact on the market. Clearly, other marketing activities will have an impact on the level of achievement which will render the formula almost incalculable.

Importantly, most marketing communications activities rely on a built in time lag. Even in the area of direct marketing, where a more precise correlation can be established between patterns of expenditure and achievement, it will be necessary to make an allowance for other indirect variables. The nature of the message, its placement, the competitive environment and other factors will all have to be allowed for is the theory is to stand up in practice. Certainly, until the advent of rapid response computer programmes, the amount of detail which would need to be built in to such a calculation proved unwieldy at best.

Several attempts have been made to build econometric models against which to 'test' different levels of expenditure. Suffice it to say that at best they provide some guidance as to the likely impact of the proposals in the real world.

2 Percentage of sales

Probably the most widely used method of budget determination is the calculation of a ratio between past expenditure and sales, sometimes referred to as the advertising:sales ratio. The calculation itself is quite straightforward. The previous year's expenditures are calculated as a percentage of total sales, and the resultant figure is used to calculate the budget for the coming year. Thus, if £12 million worth of sales was achieved against a communications budget of £300 000, the percentage would be 2.5 per cent. Assuming that the sales forecast for the coming year was £15 million this would yield a budget of £375 000. Whilst the process is a quick and easy one, there are flaws in the argument.

In the first place, the data used will be considerably out of date by the time that it is implemented. Since we do not have a full picture of current year sales, we must rely on, at best, the latest 12 months for which we have information on which to base our calculations for next year's activity. Secondly, it creates a situation in which the budget only increases against an expectation of higher sales. If sales are expected to decline, then the future communications budget must be reduced to bring it into line with the defined ratio. The inherent danger is that a brand that is under threat – and losing volume – actually reduces its budgets rather than increasing them. Thirdly, it fails to recognise that marketing communications activity can create sales volume for a brand. The application of the principle, in fact, operates in reverse – with sales being the determinant of expenditure levels.

However, it does demand a close examination of the relationship between the costs of marketing communications, the price charged for the product and the level of profit which is likely to be generated. This is particularly important when considering the specific nature of the ratio to be applied to the calculations. It may be possible, for example, to examine competitive ratios to determine whether the company is operating at, or near the norm for the product sector.

The most important consideration, however, remains the basis on which the ratio itself is established. Many companies set a norm which is rigorously applied. In some cases, it becomes the established company practice, and though it may have been determined after a full consideration of competitive environment, the conditions obtaining at the time of setting the 'norm' will have changed considerably over time. The problem with this approach, therefore, is that there is a tendency to ignore many of the other important variables which may have a direct bearing on the possibility of achieving the desired objectives. Unless the ratio is regularly and consistently reviewed, it may become irrelevant to the contemporary situation which the brand faces.

3 **Percentage of product gross margin**

This approach is, essentially, similar to the previous one except that the gross margin rather than the level of sales is used as the basis of calculating the future level of expenditure. Here, a percentage of either the past or expected gross margin – net sales less the cost of goods – is used.

It has particular relevance to brands with comparatively low production costs set against high unit prices. The manufacturers of such products will be concerned with maintaining the size of the margin, as much as with unit sales volume. The consequence will be to enable such brands to spend more on marketing communications than would necessarily be the case with an A/S ratio in order to maintain their premium price in the marketplace.

As with other ratio methods, it is extremely easy to apply once the specific relationship has been established. But it carries with it many of the same advantages and disadvantages discussed above in the context of the percentage of sales approach.

4 **Residue of previous year's surplus**

This method is entirely based on prior performance whereby the excess of income over costs in the previous year is designated as the budget for the following year. Although simple in principle, it clearly demands that a surplus is achieved in order for monies to be spent in any future period. It fails to recognise the need for investment in growth brands or, for that matter, the impact of competitive activities.

5 **Percentage of anticipated turnover**

This approach is based on the allocation of a fixed percentage of future turnover to the marketing communications budget.

6 **Unit case:sales ratio method**

This method, sometimes referred to as the case rate, requires that brand volumes for the next year are estimated and a fixed sum per unit is allocated towards marketing communications expenditure. It is then a simple process of multiplying the expected sales volume (in units or cases) by the fixed allocation to arrive at a total communications budget. In some instances, comparisons are made between the company's own case rate and those of its competitors to explore the relationships between them

Obviously the approach is a simple one, but it begs the question as to how the case rate itself is calculated. In some instances it may be based on past experience. Usually it is a company or industry norm. Here again, as with other ratio-based approaches, expenditure patterns reflect past achievement or anticipated sales. As such it tends to benefit growth brands and disadvantage those which are declining. It ignores the fact that a brand that is suffering in the marketplace may need to increase its levels of expenditure to arrest the decline, rather than reduce the budget which would be the automatic result of applying the method.

7 Competitive expenditure

Another approach, frequently used, is to base the brand's expenditure levels on an assessment of competitors' expenditures.

Often a calculation is made of the level of category expenditure and a percentage – usually related to a brand's share of market – is chosen as the basis of calculating that brand's expenditure levels. In other instances, an attempt is made to achieve parity with a nominated competitor by setting a similar level of expenditure to theirs. At the very least, this approach has the benefit of ensuring that brand expenditure levels are maintained in line with those of the competition. However, it suffers from the obvious difficulty of being able to determine an accurate assessment of the level of competitive spend.

Whilst it is obviously possible to obtain a reasonable fix on advertising spend from published information – sourced, for example, from Register MEAL – the same is not true of sales promotional spend, and other categories of marketing communications. Figures for the latter are rarely published.

Moreover, it fails to recognise that the expenditure patterns of a competitor may well be dictated by a totally different set of problems and objectives.

Whatever level of expenditure is decided upon, it must also be significant in relation to the spends of competitive brands, and must be deployed with enough continuity that the brand retains high levels of awareness throughout the year (Ewing and Jones 2000).

The annual brand survey published by *Marketing* magazine (2003) in conjunction with Nielsen (the world-wide market research organisation) which is the source of the following figures, provides a comprehensive analysis of many consumer goods markets. For example:

- In the confectionery market, Nestlé Rowntree spent £4.7 million against sales in excess of £141 million for Kit Kat; However, Mars with only slightly smaller sales – between 120 and 125 million – spent only £1.4 million. Cadbury spent £2.2 million defending Roses' sales of some £70 to 75 million, whilst Nestlé Rowntree spent £2.6 million on Quality Street with sales estimated as between £60 and 65 million.

- In the butter and spreads sector Van Den Bergh spent almost £5.2 million on Flora sales in excess of £125 million, whilst Anchor Foods spent slightly more – £5.3 million – against an estimated £115 million sales of Anchor butter. In the same category, Dairy Crest spent £4.1 million against sales of between £50 and 55 million for Clover, whilst St. Ivel spent only £2.3 million on Gold with sales of between £45 and 50 million.

- In the snack foods market, Walkers Crisps – the overall brand leader – spent £6.9 million defending sales of over £388 million. Pringles, the P&G brand, received £2.7 million against sales of £65–70 million. However, Quavers with only slightly smaller sales of £55–60 million received only £1.4 million. Two other roughly comparable brands show the disparity of advertising support. Whilst Golden Wonder spent £1.8 million on sales of £45–50 million, Wotsits received £846 000 against sales of between £40 million and £45 million.

8 **Desired share of voice**

This approach is an extension of the previous one where the management may relate the volume share of the product category to expenditure within the category as a whole, and is primarily related to advertising expenditure. Thus, if a brand has a 15 per cent share of the market in which it competes, and total advertising expenditure for the category is £8 million, in order to retain a proportional share of voice it would need to set a budget of £1.2 million.

By the same token, the company would have a benchmark against which to establish the levels of expenditure required to drive a brand forward. Hence, it might decide to increase its share of voice to say 20 or even 25 per cent in an attempt to gain a greater level of visibility for its brand and a greater share of the overall category.

9 **Media inflation**

This approach makes the simple assumption that a budget – usually the previous year's – should be increased in line with the growth in media costs to ensure a similar delivery of the message to the target audience. At the lowest level, this approach ensures that the real level of advertising expenditure is maintained. However, it fails to acknowledge any of the other variables that will have an impact on the achievement of the marketing objectives. Most importantly, it removes the desire to consider other, more meaningful, media efficiency approaches.

Media, as with most other things, present a competitive environment to the company. When a particular medium increases its price, it should be the cue to re-examine its role within the overall context of the communications programme, rather than simply increasing the budget to reflect the high price being charged.

10 **Objective and task method**

This method is based on a more realistic examination of the specific objectives which the marketing plan needs to meet, and was established as an attempt to apply a more scientific approach to budget determination. The basis of the approach was a paper commissioned by the American Association of National Advertisers and published in 1961 (Colley 1961).

In the paper 'Defining advertising goals for measuring advertising results' (a process henceforth known as DAGMAR) the author, Russell Colley, proposed that advertising should be specifically budgeted to accomplish defined goals or objectives. The DAGMAR approach – also known as the objective and task method – requires that specific objectives for the campaign are defined at the outset.

These may be expressed in terms of, for example, increasing brand awareness, encouraging sampling and trial, promoting repeat purchase and so on. In each case a finite numerical target is given, and the costs of achieving this target are calculated. The resultant budget is, thus, based on a series of goals rather than on past or future results, and is thus the most realistic in marketing terms.

It offers the benefit of being able to monitor the campaign achievement against the targets set, and provides a more accurate guide to budgetary determination for the future. The limitations on the accuracy of the method is the ability to access sufficient information to ensure that all of the relevant variables

can be considered. Although the original paper dealt specifically with the task of establishing advertising budgets, the method is equally applicable to other areas of marketing communications.

11 Experimentation

A guiding principle for budget determination, as with other aspects of marketing, is the need on the one hand to protect the company investment whilst, on the other, ensuring that sufficient new and innovatory approaches are taken to drive the brand forward. It is for this reason that most major marketing companies utilise an experimental approach at various times. Having established the overall marketing communications budget by the normal or most appropriate means, it is possible to create a mini 'test market' for the purposes of experimenting with a variation. By isolating, say, one region of the country, it is possible to experiment with alternative budget constructions. In many cases, and in the absence of definitive data, it is useful to determine the impact of, for example, an increased level of media expenditure or of a particular sales promotion technique.

The benefit of this approach is that the main sources of business are 'protected' in the sense that they receive the 'normal' support levels. Hence, the position of the brand is not unduly prejudiced. By 'hot housing' a different approach, real experience can be gained and the budgetary process enhanced with the additional knowledge. It is an attempt to apply an empirical approach and, thus, a more scientific method to the process of budget determination. However, it is important to restrict the number of 'experiments' in order to ensure that the data are readable against the norm, and that the individual variables can be properly assessed within a real market environment.

12 What we can afford

This approach is based on a management assessment of either the brand itself or the overall company position. In effect, management determines the level of profit desired, or the return on investment, and the marketing communications budget is the amount that remains after calculating that level. Of course, it fails to recognise the contribution of marketing communications itself, and ignores other environmental factors, such as competitive pressure, which might militate against the profit level being achieved. Although this is a somewhat arbitrary approach to the budgetary process, it has to be recognised that the issue of affordability plays an important part within any financial procedures. There will always be competing demands for funds within the company – to support the activities of other brands within the portfolio, to fund areas such as production capability, to finance research and development, and so on. It is a fundamental role of management to determine company priorities and to allocate funds accordingly.

13 New products

One area that demands a separate mention is that of developing a marketing communications budget for a new product. Clearly, past data will be unavailable and, hence, many of the usual budgeting approaches cannot be applied. At the simplest level, the approach to new products is similar that to the objective and task method, described above. Calculations must be made of the amount of money required to achieve the objectives established for the brand.

It must be recognised that, in most instances, new products require investment in advance of sales performance. Indeed, without the appropriate levels of investment in marketing communications, most new products are unlikely to succeed. A realistic timeframe for the achievement of the goals must be established at the outset. It is unrealistic to expect a new product to make a major contribution in the short term.

It is important to restate that there is no hard and fast formula for defining a marketing communications budget. It is important to experiment with a number of the methods described above, and to ensure that the appropriate use is made of previous company experience, industry data, and experimentation. The imperative for all companies is to ensure the building up of a database of information – both within and from competitor knowledge – which can be used to enhance the process.

A considerable argument has raged over the tendency to reduce the levels of advertising spending during periods of economic recession. Some contend that such conditions provide the opportunities to boost market share and take advantage of the increased share of voice whilst other competitors cut back on their spending levels.

Batra and Ray (1986) found that higher levels of advertising exposure led to increasing levels of brand attitudes and purchase intentions.

Raj (1982) found that heavier levels of repetition are effective when the consumer is more familiar with, or loyal to, the brand. The same is true when the message which the advertising seeks to convey is more complex (Arnand and Sternthal 1990).

Similarly when there is a higher level of competitive spending (Burke and Srull 1988) or when there is more advertising clutter (Webb and Ray 1979).

A study by Kamber (2002) specifically investigated the longer-term implications of budget reduction. Amongst other findings, Kamber argues that:

- Companies that maintained or increased spending on advertising during the 1991 recession in the USA had a five-year sales growth rate that was 25 per cent higher than companies that did not.
- There is a positive and statistically significant relationship between adspend during recession and subsequent sales growth.

Berkowitz (2001) states that advertising campaigns typically consist of a variety of activities co-ordinated across several media simultaneously. If medium-specific lag structures do exist (e.g., if television advertising, print advertising, billboard advertising and radio advertising each have their own unique carryover effect), then an advertising budget allocation plan based on multiple lag effects will in all likelihood be very different from one based on a single lag effect. Such medium-specific carryover research becomes even more relevant in the light of recent insights that suggest that budget allocation among media may be more important for advertising spending decisions than total budgeting levels.

Various attempts have been made to develop models to assist in the determination of advertising budgets, particularly in the area of the advertising to sales ratio. However, in general, they provide little guidance to the budget planner (Stewart 1996).

Since the early 1970s there has been a progressive fragmentation of the consultancy sector. Prior to that time, a client could reasonably expect that all of the

elements of a marketing communications campaign would be developed in conjunction with the advertising agency. There followed the emergence of specialist companies within the fields of sales promotion, direct marketing, media planning and others, each of which provided a high level of both input and expertise to the planning of the specific element of the campaign. Inevitably, with this fragmentation of activities, and the more narrow focus adopted by the specialist agencies, the responsibility for determining the most efficient use of resources became a primary responsibility of the brand management team.

Although the ultimate aim of most advertising is to ensure continued sales of the product or service, there is a wide variety of factors that may exert an influence on the outcome. The strength of the sales force and their ability to achieve appropriate levels of distribution will impact upon the advertising's ability to generate consumer sales. However effective and influential the advertising campaign, it cannot achieve the desired objectives if the product is not available at the point of purchase. Similarly, the timing of the campaign relative to the establishment of stocking levels will have an important bearing on the achievement of the desired goals. Advertise too early, and the product will not be available; advertise too late and the product will have been sitting on the shelf for some time with the consequent disillusionment of the retail stockists. Competitive factors will also influence the effectiveness of any advertising campaign.

For the most part, advertising development takes place in isolation of the competitive environment. That is not to say that competitive activity is ignored, rather that its specific nature will not be known in advance. In most cases, competitors will not simply stand by and watch a new campaign diminish their share of market. They may well retaliate with new activity of their own designed to undermine the effectiveness of the campaign.

Eechambadi (1994) attacks the process of advertising budget determination. For the most part, he argues, many companies treat advertising spend as a residual item after all other commitments have been met. The position is further exacerbated by:

- poor targeting by crude demographics;
- little understanding of the links between brand positioning, consumer perceptions and target group behaviour;
- copy testing which bears little relationship to specific advertising strategies;
- wastage in media buying;
- advertising response tracking which is often out of date and not sensitive to current objectives.

Small budgets

Budget limitations affect every marketing decision. Not every brand can afford to increase distribution, employ a larger sales force or make the major capital investments required for growth. If a brand does want to grow, however, it must make the investment to become accessible to more and more consumers. At some point, increased distribution, a larger sales force or additional manufacturing capacity will be essential for growth, and the brand will have to invest in that. The same holds true with marketing communications. As Anschuetz (2002) states:

A brand with a smaller budget will have to focus on reaching fewer consumers until its budget becomes large enough, through growth, to reach even more. There is no question that brands with large marketing budgets have a decided competitive advantage. A smaller brand has to face this reality and make every sum spent work as hard as possible. It still has to grow the total number of category users who buy the brand, including light- and moderate-buying households, not just focus narrowly on a small segment of 'profitable' households.

To all intents and purposes, there are just three main strategic approaches for those wishing to advertise on a small budget:

1 Campaign amplification: This can be achieved either by exploiting to the full the publicity value of the advertising, or by integrating the ads with a more or less spectacular promotion, or both.
2 Selective and focused targeting: This may include area testing and regional roll-outs.
3 Piggy-backing: This means sharing in the activity of a partner with a larger budget.

The vast majority of small budgets are focused. White (1996) points out that campaigns run for a very short period; they are limited to a tight selection of media; they use small spaces; they are only run in a limited geographic area; and they carefully target a very precise group of people using extremely selective media.

If they use mass media, they use TV selectively – by focusing on a particular programme or time, by using a variety of DRTV (direct response TV) deals or by using specific TV channels which are precisely targeted to their selected audience.

A study by Bigne (1995) reveals that the three most commonly used methods remain:

> percentage of sales
> affordable
> task and objective.

The two former remained the most popular and dominated until the early 1980s. The vast majority of budget setting was arbitrary, judgemental and subjective. For the most part, budgets were also determined from the bottom rather than the top of the company, and were merely approved by management.

It was not until some time during the 1980s that closer management scrutiny and a more concerted academic review of budget setting promoted the task and objective method as the most appropriate. Since that time, the use of this method continued to grow to the point when Hung and West (1991) found that it had been adopted by more than 60 per cent of consumer marketers in the USA, Europe and Canada.

Whilst it might be assumed that only smaller less sophisticated companies use other methods to determine budgets, it remains true that many large corporations fail to use any form of modelling to help in budget setting and even amongst those who use task and objective, judgemental methods remain the most commonly employed.

Budgeting for integrated marketing communications

Integrated communication is the key to successful branding. Brand values have to be communicated to the consumer on every available channel in order to ensure that the brand either builds or retains a strong position in the mind of the consumer.

A study by Low and Mohr (1998) highlighted the synergistic effects of the marketing communications allocations on outcomes. Their findings suggest that it is a combination of trade promotion allocations, in conjunction with advertising and consumer promotion allocations, which determines outcome levels. The picture is clearly complex: it suggests that one cannot draw conclusions about the impact of individual marketing communications tools when isolated from other tools in the promotion mix.

It must be recognised that consumers receive marketing communications messages that deal with buyer–seller relationships from a variety of media, including television, magazines and the internet. Each message that the customer receives from any source represents the brand, company or organisation. Unless these messages are co-ordinated, the consumer may become confused and may entirely tune out the message. To prevent this loss of attention, marketers are turning to integrated marketing communications which co-ordinate all promotional activities – to produce a unified, customer-focused promotional message.

Whichever method or methods adopted, however, our task must be to consider the process of budget determination itself. Broadbent (1989) suggests that the process is made up of six separate stages, as follows:

Stage 1   Brand objectives

Here, we must consider the role of the brand within the company and the importance of the brand to the achievement of the overall objectives. The consideration should encompass both the short-term timeframe of the plan, e.g. the year ahead, as well as the longer-term considerations, e.g. over the next three to five years. It is also important to examine the relationship between volume and profit contribution.

At this stage also, the source of the brand's sales should be identified. The larger the audience, the greater the likely budget requirement. By the same token, by adopting a more concentrated approach, the media budget may be lowered.

Stage 2   Review the brand budgets

It is important to consider how the brand has performed in the past, since this will have significant implications on its ability to perform in the future. If a brand has been in decline, then the previous budget will need to be increased if the decline is to be arrested or reversed.

Stage 3   Marketing history and forecasts

As well as a consideration of the brand itself, it is important to consider the market category that will help to place the brand into context. This will reveal a number of important facets which will assist in the brand planning process. Although volume sales may be increasing, it is important to determine whether they are keeping pace with the category as a whole. In fact, the brand may be losing share of market that in the longer term could endanger its position.

It is vitally important to maintain a record of brand performance over time within the market sector in which it operates. That implies maintaining data about competitive brands, advertising and other promotional expenditures, and so on. There are, as has been mentioned, a number of sources which will be important in this context. Nielsen will provide data on retail sales volume and AGB, similarly, will provide a commentary on sales over time, but from the perspective of consumer purchases, whilst media expenditure levels can, within certain limitations, be obtained from MEAL Media Register. By examining this data bank, along with other information streams, it may be possible to identify particular relationships, trends, and the dynamics of the product category.

Stage 4 Assess expenditure effects

Examine the effects of previous advertising and promotional expenditure to determine the level of brand responsiveness to marketing communications activity. Previous experience is a valuable guide to likely future performance. And remember, in this respect it is possible to learn as much from competitor performance as from your own brand.

Stage 5 Set budgets

Consider the application of a number of the standard approaches to budget determination (these are set out in detail above). This is very much a preliminary exercise in budget determination since it will suggest a range of possible amounts to be spent, with affordability and feasibility being checked in the final stage.

Stage 6 Check feasibility

The final stage of this proposed process is ensuring that the budget determined is feasible and practical within the context of the established objectives.

Similarly, Bartle (1999) sets out to summarise the process of planning an advertising campaign. In his paper he establishes a series of stages which need to observed within the planning process:

1 Develop a brand strategy: What is the brand position? What is the competitive context? Who is our target audience? Do we even need to advertise?
2 Decide what this means in terms of targets (for example, percentage change in sales).
3 Convert this into an advertising plan (x per cent extra sales means making y per cent aware of the advertising, and getting z per cent to endorse the specific image)
4 Develop the advertising to meet this strategy.
5 Test the advertising to see how well it delivers against the strategy. Identify at which point we will know how well the advertising works and calculate the size of budget required to achieve the established targets.

Allocating the promotional budget

It is not just the resolution of how the overall budget is calculated, but the allocation of funds within the budget that must be addressed. Again, the emphasis must rest with integrated marketing communications and the identification of the most appropriate and cost-effective communications channels to achieve the specific task. That said, however, it must be recognised that there are no set formulae for allocating budgets between competing communications approaches.

According to research conducted by PIMS Europe, the business of allocating a marketing budget is not only a complex task but, if done incorrectly, can have a devastating impact on a brand's overall profit. The company conducted a study of some 500 US and European FMCG companies. The study was an attempt to determine whether a 'correct' marketing mix exists. The study identifies seven key factors which influence the optimum marketing mix – brand rank; concentration of the trade; pace of innovation; market growth; sister brands; breadth of offering and historic brand image.

It would appear that whatever a brand leader does with its mix, it will always generate better profits than brand number two or three. It suggests that if brand leaders spend less than 50 per cent of their budget on media, they will earn, on average, a 39 per cent return on capital employed over 4 years; whereas a 70 per cent ad spend will cause returns to rise slightly to 43 per cent. However, if a number 2 brand spends between 50 and 70 per cent of its budget on media advertising, it earns its highest possible return at 28 per cent. If it increases this to 70 per cent or more, the profitability is likely to be exactly halved. For also-ran brands, the difference between the optimum and non-optimum mix is the difference between a maximum return of 11 per cent or losses. The penalty for getting the mix wrong is correspondingly greater for brand followers.

However, it is difficult to attach too much importance to the findings. On the one hand, the analysis is somewhat superficial since only two variables – advertising (including direct marketing) and promotion – are considered. One the other, there are confusing correlations between cause and effect. It cannot determine, for example, whether brands are investing heavily in their futures, nor if companies are using their brands as cash cows.

The marketing communications budget should be allocated against an identification of the identity of the target customer and how effectively we can reach him or her. The key decisions should relate to the state of the market (growth or mature), the state of the competitions (few or many competitors) and an understanding of the cost/reward relationship for marketing communications within the industry.

We have already looked at the various methods by which the overall marketing communications budget may be determined. In turn, a series of key strategic decisions must relate to the deployment of that budget against the various elements of the campaign.

Integrated communication is the key to successful branding. Brand values have to be communicated to the consumer on every available channel to make sure that the brand holds a strong position in the heart and the mind of the consumer. In the long run, brands can compete only if they use the full potential of communication options available to them.

Business-to-business advertising

The principles applied to the development of consumer advertising are equally appropriate in the context of business-to-business campaign. However, there are important differences, and these need to be recognised in terms of the strategic understanding of the campaign requirements. In business-to-business campaigns, it must be remembered that the purchaser is not paying directly for the goods or services. He or she has a corporate responsibility to make the correct decision. Moreover, the purchaser may be required to justify his or her decision, both factually and emotionally. The scale of the purchase decision is often large, not just in terms of costs, but in both commitment to the particular supplier over an extended period of time, and in terms of the implications of the purchase decision to the company.

In the business environment, the purchaser is much more likely to develop a personal relationship with the supplier, and the advertising needs to reflect or reaffirm the part that personal contact makes in the decision-making process. Importantly, the purchaser may or may not be a user and, in some circumstances, may well be a consumer of the same companies goods in an individual capacity. Many companies are suppliers both of industrial goods and consumer products (e.g. Lever Bros have an industrial division, whilst Kraft Jacobs Suchard have a catering division which supplies similar products to those sold in conventional retail outlets in a repackaged form).

The notion of integration is just as important in business-to-business communications as it is in consumer marketing. Since there will often be many people involved in the purchasing decision, it is important to recognise that the process of communications is significantly more complex than in the consumer field. Since members of the decision-making unit may be exposed to different components of a single campaign, it is essential that all elements convey, in broad terms, the same message – although there will often be a need to tailor that message specifically to respond to the needs of the individual within the overall target audience.

Advertising accountability	There has been considerable debate in recent years regarding the accountability of advertising. Not unreasonably, client companies want the reassurance that spending money on advertising will deliver results. However, much of that discussion centres on the issue of measurement, according to Kappert (1999). The focus of the debate has been the extent to which the effectiveness of advertising can be measured and translated into a justification of the expenditures entailed.

However, the issue of accountability is somewhat broader than that. Kappert suggests that the debate should embrace a wider agenda:

measurability: it works, but I do not understand how
causality: I understand how it works
controllability: I understand how to make it work.

Various attempts have been made to identify the specific contribution of advertising. For example, in the paper entitled 'Measuring sales response to advertising', Holstius (1990) examines a mathematical correlation between the two forces and demonstrates how they interact with external forces. The results of the study showed that increases in advertising boosted sales and, whenever there was a peak in advertising expenditure, there was a corresponding peak in sales volume.

Case study

IPA Effectiveness Awards 2003

Agency: The Leith Agency

Authors: David Amers and Thea Tetley

Grolsch

Background

In 1615, in a small Dutch town called Grol, Peter Cuyper started brewing Grolsch. In the early 1980s premium strength Grolsch (5 per cent ABV), with its distinctive swing-top bottle, was launched over here. The UK lager market was ripe for foreign premium packaged lager brands. Grolsch quickly gained a high profile. The bottle tops were made famous by the pop group Bros who wore the ceramic tops on their Doc Martens. The 'You can't top a Grolsch' advertising heightened awareness and, by 1989, Grolsch was widely available and selling almost 40 million bottles a year. Unfortunately, Grolsch's good times also came to an abrupt end. From being a leading brand (number five in 1991) it became a marginal brand (16th by 1994). Whilst Grolsch slumped by 41 per cent between 1990 and 1994, premium lager grew from 26 per cent to 35 per cent of the lager market.

A lack of marketing focus in the 1990s had endangered Grolsch. It became marginalised by powerful and aggressive competition from the likes of Stella Artois, Budweiser and Kronenbourg 1664. These brands had clear identities and a sense of heritage and provenance, vital in the premium lager market. By contrast, Grolsch lacked any sense of identity beyond the swing top bottle (and even that was considered gimmicky). It was simply dropping off people's radar.

Brand objectives

For a brand in such poor health, Grolsch was set very ambitious targets:

- double sales to reach half a million barrels by 2002;
- regain top-ten lager brand status by 2002;
- replace Kronenbourg 1664 as the number two premium lager brand by 2010.

The brand needed more than awareness. It required fundamental repositioning.

For Grolsch to succeed it needed to:

- meet contemporary desires for distinction and quality;
- have a personality which today's drinkers could relate to;
- offer the trade a unique point of difference in a crowded market.

The strategy

Grolsch is brewed for a relatively long time and it's this that gives it its distinctive, fuller flavour and a point of difference. This fact has successfully been at the heart of the brand's communication in Holland and the Dutch brand owners were keen that it was used in the UK. However, research showed that UK consumers found the 'brewed longer' story dull and not particularly relevant.

Our brief was clear: communicate successfully the brewed longer message in a way that would make the brand talked about and contemporary. The brand's Dutch provenance was the way forward, for three reasons:

1 Our target audience – mature males who consumed premium brands – bought into the idea that genuine premium lagers originated somewhere other than Britain. Foreign provenance was a reason to believe in product difference and, quite simply, made brands sexier.
2 Our target audience's positive views of Holland were shaped primarily by perceptions of Amsterdam. Amsterdam represented a laid-back, easygoing

approach to life. This character trait would form the basis of an appealing brand personality.

3   Dutchness was also the way of bringing the brewing story to life: the laid-back approach to life applied to the way they brewed their beer.

We developed a new, long-term brand positioning: Grolsch is the laid-back Dutch premium lager, brewed longer for a distinctive taste. From here the creatives forged a straight path to the creative idea: 'A laid-back Dutch hero shows that, as with Grolsch, things are better for not being rushed.'

The new campaign started with an ad featuring some guys trying to rob a bank that was not yet fully built and introduced a new endline: 'We only let you drink it when it's ready'. This provided a strong campaign vehicle and a memorable Dutch hero with his catch phrase – 'Schtop'.

Media

Media was challenged with giving Grolsch a 'big brand' feel. To achieve this, the strategy changed from delivering peaks of awareness to a more year-round buying campaign, focusing on the right quality programmes and a better quantity of centre breaks. As a result, effective share of voice was almost 50 per cent more than actual media expenditure.

How the advertising worked

Consumers responded to the advertising exactly as planned. The new campaign was immediately talked about. With 43 per cent advertising awareness, Grolsch has overtaken Stella Artois (40 per cent) and significantly overshadows Kronenbourg at 22 per cent. Grolsch's advertising is also reported as being the most enjoyable and amusing. Research confirmed the appeal of the Dutch laid-back approach to life to our target audience.

Results

Increased brand predisposition has led to dramatic improvements in Grolsch's fortunes. Grolsch's main target was to sell 500 000 barrels by 2002. It actually exceeded this by 75 000.

Since 1999, Grolsch's on-trade volume sales have more than doubled. Between 2000 and 2001 Grolsch was experiencing on-trade volume growth of +58.4 per cent. Grolsch's second target was to regain share. Grolsch was

working from a small base, but nevertheless, on-trade share of volume and value have both doubled since 1999. Grolsch has achieved its goal of being a top-10 lager again, moving from 14th to 9th in the last two years.

The most concrete measure of increased consumer demand is rate of purchase. Grolsch's rate has more than trebled since campaign launch, going from 26 gallons per month in 2000 to a staggering 80.9 gallons per month in 2002. Consumers are demanding the brand more than ever.

Success has been matched in the off-trade where volume sales have also doubled. Volume and value share have both increased and the brand has risen from a lowly 14th, to 8th in the off-trade lager market. Not only are more households now buying Grolsch, but each purchaser is now spending more money and buying more volume than they did in 2001 (purchasing 3.8 litres more and spending £8.46 more per person in 2003 than in 2001).

Promotional activity

The TV campaign has been supported by a number of promotional initiatives such as Grolsch Dutch beer gardens and Dutch 'sampling trikes' at outdoor events. In the off-trade, 'Grolschware' was introduced allowing consumers to send off for a Dutch 'mayor' glass, a beer skimmer, bottle opener and an aluminium coaster. These cost-effective innovations stand out in the marketplace as a perfect example of how advertising and promotions can reinforce a new brand positioning by working together, allowing Grolsch drinkers not only to see but to experience the laid-back Dutch approach to life.

Return on investment

Grolsch's total retail value in 2002 was £272 million. The brand has smashed its volume targets, trebled on-trade throughput and maintained a price premium.

In just three years, we have transformed Grolsch from a 1980s has-been, lacking in identity and appeal, to a strong, well-rounded brand.

SOURCE: This case study is adapted from the paper presented at the IPA Effectiveness Awards. The full version is available at www.warc.com and is reproduced by kind permission of the Institute of Practitioners in Advertising and the World Advertising Research Center.

Questions

1 Identify the individual stages of the process of advertising development.
2 What is the value of an advertising strategy? What strategies might be adopted for an advertising campaign?
3 What issues need to be addressed in the development of an advertising strategy?
4 Why do advertising campaigns need to be different at the various stages of the product life cycle?
5 What objectives might be set for an advertising campaign? Why is it important to identify campaign objectives at the outset?
6 What implications does the level of budget have for advertising campaign development?
7 Identify the methods by which advertising budgets are determined.
8 What can a company with a small budget do to ensure that its target consumers receive its message?

10 Creative strategy and tactics

Learning outcomes

This chapter will develop your understanding of:

- the role of the creative brief
- creativity in advertising
- the factors to be considered in determining the creative platform
- the nature of advertising appeals and their application
- the variety of formats which can be applied to advertising campaigns
- advertising approaches, including use of celebrities, humour, music, comparative and shock advertising
- the role of non-verbal communications.

In this chapter, we will examine the way in which advertising is developed from a practitioner standpoint. Before proceeding, it will be worth making a distinction between some of the terms that will be used.

The communications objective is a statement of the messages, images or information that the campaign is required to communicate.

The creative platform is the particular device chosen to convey the message.

The advertising execution is the nature of the advertising appeal used to communicate the message to the target audience.

The role of the creative brief

Most advertising agencies use a very precise format for the purpose of briefing creative work. Although the topic headings may differ from agency to agency, the fundamental need is the same in all cases. To provide the creative department with the appropriate guidance to the development of creative materials in a succinct and easily comprehensible form. The creative brief is the basis of all advertising development and should encompass, in summary form, the major findings of research and other inputs upon which the advertising will eventually be based. A contemporary example of a creative brief used by a leading advertising agency is reproduced in Figure 10.1.

Figure 10.1 J. Walter Thompson creative brief

J. Walter Thompson		
Date	Core Team	Timesheet Codes
Media Requirements		Production Budget
Role of Communications		
Target Audience		
Consumer Insight		
The Proposition		
Desired Response		
Reason(s) to Believe		
Brand Personality		
Tone of Voice		
Executional Considerations		

SOURCE: reproduced by kind permission of the J. Walter Thompson agency

The briefing form consists of a single sheet of A4. The former requires the planner to address a series of specific areas as follows:

1 The role of communications

It is here that it is important to provide the context in which the advertising campaign is to be developed. This will include an identification of the current brand situation, the competitive environment. The imperative is to summarise the underlying reasons for doing the advertising and the main tasks that the campaign will be required to perform.

This is designed to isolate the specific task which the creative department is expected to fulfil. This may, for example, take the form of a campaign that builds on the previous advertising heritage of the brand, and which will be used to refresh and update particular aspects of the communication.

It may represent the development of a completely new campaign, sometimes for a new product. It may require the development of a single advertisement for some specific purpose, such as a tie-in with some retailer activity. The major perfume companies often utilise press advertising in this way, with a consumer offer being made available at identified retail outlets. In other instances the company may wish to announce a new store opening.

In some instances, the advertising component will reflect some other form of marketing communications activity that has already been, or is in the process of development. Here the other activity will take the lead, and advertising will provide the means by which the proposition is communicated to a wider audience. Often this will feature a sales promotion offer such as a competition or on-pack lottery which, otherwise would only present its message at the point of purchase and then, predominantly, to existing purchasers of the brand.

2 **The target audience**

The next important stage in the process is the identification of the target audience. Clearly some of the information will be available in the form of specific demographic data – age, sex, class, etc. However, wherever possible, it is important to go beyond these tight (and somewhat restrictive) definitions. If the creatives can be helped to understand the dimensions of the audience (young, old, attitudinal values, lifestyle factors and so on), they will be able to reflect these in terms of the tone and style of the message. Advertising aimed, for example, at a youth market will probably employ different language and tonal values than a campaign designed to support the introduction of a product to an older target audience. By the same token, this information will provide the media department with the key factors by which to isolate the appropriate media to provide the most cost-effective coverage of the defined target audiences.

3 **Consumer insight**

The planner will define the specific aspect that will differentiate the brand from its competitors based on a detailed understanding of the consumers' needs and wants. It may, for example, relate to a particular aspect or benefit that the brand can deliver relative to competition. Alternatively, it might identify some emotional need that other brands are not currently satisfying.

4 **The proposition**

What is the specific message that we wish to convey? What is the single thought that will set our brand apart from its competitors?

Here, the planner has the opportunity to identify the main distinguishing characteristics of the brand, either physical or emotional, and the factors that will ensure that the brand is clearly differentiated from others.

Effective advertising must be based on a careful study of the important consumer dimensions. What can the brand say about itself which will create a clear separation in the minds of consumers between it and its competitors. Although summarised into a very short form (there is only space on the brief for, at most, two short sentences) this a critical aspect of the creative briefing process. It will almost certainly be the culmination of a great deal of research activity and analysis, which has provided the agency with an understanding of the important consumer perceptions of the brand's characteristics.

4 **Desired response**

What is it that we want the consumer to do or feel as a result of seeing the advertising. In some instances, the advertising will be designed to elicit a specific response, such as making a purchase, requesting additional information. In others the campaign will seek to ensure that the consumer adds the brand to his or her portfolio of desirable products.

Alternatively, it might be designed to create some form of emotional bond between the consumer and the brand, perhaps ensuring that they regard it as being contemporarily relevant or 'cool'.

5 **Reasons to believe**

What information will be required to ensure that the consumer believes the proposition? Is there some specific evidence that can be provided to ensure this response?

This will take the form of some – again short – substantiation of the reasons why the consumer should believe the proposition. This may relate to some physical characteristic of the brand. In many instances, it is a direct consequence of the emotional values that the brand represents. If the creative department understand the purpose of the advertising, they can better fulfil the brief.

6 **Brand personality**

How do we want the consumer to perceive the brand? Is the current brand personality (identified from research) still relevant or does it need to be changed or updated?

7 **Tone of voice**

What approach should the advertising take? This is the opportunity to indicate whether the advertising proposition is to be authoritative and serious or amusing and light hearted; fashionable and stylish or down-to-earth and approachable, and so on.

8 **Executional considerations**

Is the brand, for example, associated with a specific advertising style? Should the campaign reflect past advertising or should it take a new direction. Similarly, are there particular elements that need to be included in the advertising? For example, Asda have for many years included a specific mnemonic – someone 'patting' their back pocket. Similarly, Audi advertising has included the endline 'Vorsprung durch Technik'. Perhaps a particular personality spokesperson is used to represent the brand; on other occasions, an underlying theme needs to be reinforced. There may be specific requirements to identify the brand with a logo, and perhaps the identity of the parent company.

The identification of the appropriate media to communicate the message to the target audience is an important dimension of the advertising process. Each of the available media not only has a series of unique characteristics that make it more or less appropriate for the task in hand, they also represent an environment for the message which will serve to enhance or diminish aspects of that message (see Chapter 11).

Elsewhere on the brief, there will be an identification of the production budget that is available. This may have implications for the type of execution that follows since a comparatively small production budget would preclude a lavish execution.

Some agencies, such as Bartle Bogle Hegarty make an important distinction between the actual product and the brand in terms of the creative briefing form (Bartle 1997), as the following examples demonstrate:

Häagen-Dazs ice cream
The product: Super-premium, fresh cream, ice cream.
The brand: The ultimate sensual, intimate pleasure.

Boddingtons ale
The product: Cask-conditioned ale from Manchester.
The brand: The smoothest-drinking bitter – with a Mancunian point of view.

Levis 501s
The product: Five-pocket, western-style heavyweight denim jeans.
The brand: The original and definitive jeans. The embodiment of jeans values (freedom, individuality, rebellion, sex, masculinity, originality and youth).

The creative brief fulfils a vital role in the strategic development of advertising. Although much of the work will have been done separately, it is the framework for the determination of the strategic approach that the advertising will take. As such it fulfils many of the key requirements of the DAGMAR approach described earlier. However, it is also important to recognise that the briefing document fulfils other functions.

From the management perspective, it is the distillation of the major part of the preliminary strategic development that will guide the entirety of the creative process that follows.

For the creative department, it provides an indication of the important directions and the thrust of the communications message, which they will be required to develop. The responsibility of management, in this context, is to establish the broad areas in which the creatives should operate. It should provide a sense of focus and discipline in which they can operate. For the media planners, it will provide the key dimensions of the target audience, which they will seek to reach in the most cost-effective way possible. It will avoid unnecessary waste of time, energy and cost developing creative messages that are inappropriate to the brand or the target audience. And it serves as the benchmark against which the creative work can be assessed.

An alternative description of the briefing process is the paper by Charlie Robertson (1997) in *How to Plan Advertising*.

Henry (1997) offers five key ways in which creatives can develop powerful and distinctive advertising:

1 Find out what everybody else is doing in your marketplace and then do something different.
2 Forget the logical proposition and find the personality of the brand instead.
3 Define the target market so that you like and respect it.
4 Put in creative starters: examples which describe how the strategy might look in its final medium to demonstrate how actionable your brief is.
5 Make it inspiring by making your thinking fresh and unexpected.

The role of creativity in advertising

Considerable debate centres around the role of creativity in advertising. There is little doubt that there is a need for 'The Big Idea' – essential to break through the surrounding clutter and to arouse interest in an otherwise dull product category, as was the case with Tango. However, just because an advertisement is 'creative' does not mean that it will increase sales or turn around a brand that is already in decline. Creativity must be relevant and serve to differentiate the product or service from its competitors in a way that consumers find meaningful. Moreover, the problem is that consumers have become more advertising-literate and consequently it takes increasingly innovative concepts to have an impact on their awareness.

In a paper written in 1984, Mo Drake indicates the extent to which consumers have become advertising-literate:

> Consumers talk about advertising in much the same way as they talk about television programmes. It is a component of their media diet and they are increasingly familiar with the tricks of the industry. In effect, consumers are not only consumers of products, they are also consumers of advertising.

This process is accelerated by the number of programmes that explore the tricks of the advertising trade. Several programmes in the BBC series *How Do They Do That?*, for example, go behind the scenes of a particular advertising execution and explain how the effects were achieved.

The need for creative, highly original advertising is increasingly important in markets where the impact of new ads is limited by the sheer mass of competitive offerings. A memorable idea that clearly focuses on the brand and on relevant communication about the brand can help to break through the clutter. High-impact advertising can go on to build a strong brand over time and generate a long-term response by providing vivid memories to be stored in the mind of the consumer until a time when the brand or product is experienced. These memories prepare expectations of the brand that will be perceived when the brand is experienced, convincing the customer of superior performance.

Creativity is an important aspect of advertising. It is important for design, copywriting, overall campaign strategy and more (Zinkhan 1994). There are, perhaps, many different strategies for being creative, including no visible strategy at all. One creative strategy involves borrowing. That is, a copywriter could borrow an idea from one context and apply it to a completely different context. For instance, melodies (or catchphrases) are borrowed from popular songs and used in commercials to create specific moods or effects. As another example, a copywriter may borrow words or themes from popular literature.

Bovee et al. (1995) describe creativity as 'the ability to produce original ideas or original ways of looking at existing ideas' whilst Schultz and Tannenbaum (1989) argue that:

> What all too often passes for creativity has very little to do with presenting a cogent selling message. Something that is creative is new or different or unique. But advertising that is simply innovative is not necessarily effective in helping motivate customers and prospects to buy . . . it must present the sales message more effectively, not just dramatically or in a more entertaining way.

Creative advertising is a weird form of artistic expression: it aims to satisfy one person (the client) and to persuade another (the consumer). The two sides of the argument are illustrated in a quote from Nissan Europe's vice president of marketing (*Sunday Times* 1995): 'The agency will say that creativity is the most important thing, but obviously to us an increase in sales is most eloquent.'

Creativity encompasses all of the original ideas that are used to develop a campaign. It represents the application of original thinking to establish a particular point. Creative advertising seeks to provide a new and fresh dimension about the brands' proposition. Various attempts have been made to define what elements contribute to an effective advertising campaign (Cummings 1984; Otnes et al. 1995). Creativity is, indisputably, the least scientific aspect of advertising. Yet, according to many, it is the most important.

It can be reasoned that each of the components contained in the above studies represents an element of creativity designed to encourage consumer response. As we can see readily from any of the established models of advertising effectiveness, achieving an impact on the consumer is an integral and vital part of determining the success of any campaign. In order to achieve this impact, advertising must first break through the surrounding noise and achieve some form of sensory reaction. Moreover, in a competitive environment, it is especially important that potential consumers are able to distinguish between competing messages from rival brands. If one brand establishes a particular proposition or benefit, for a second brand to break through it must provide an even greater stimulus and establish a greater empathetic link for it to be recognised. It is this particular need to achieve a bigger impact than competitors that fuels the drive for creativity.

For most large companies, the translation of marketing strategies into persuasive selling language is customarily a task reserved for their advertising agencies' creative departments. That translation is neither trivial nor simple. It is beset by the uncertainties of control and output. As Kover and Goldberg (1995) state:

> Members of the Creative Department: copywriters and art directors who actually make the advertising. Copywriters must produce work that is 'creative'. The production of creative work and creative work by its very nature is largely unpredictable. That unpredictability must be controlled or appear to be controlled by account management before the advertising even reaches clients. In addition, client marketing or advertising managers often feel the need to control the uncertainty surrounding the production of creative advertising.

Understanding why some advertisements are more creative than others is vital, but a fundamental and frustrating limitation is that perceptions of creativity differ depending on whom one asks. It is suggested that creative differences depend on one's role within an agency. Creativity awards judges' perceptions of creativity differ from consumers' perceptions.

Inevitably, therefore, there continues to be considerable debate about the credibility of the various award schemes within the advertising environment, such as those of the Creative Circle and others. In order to assess advertising effectiveness as it related to awards, David Gunn (1995), then Creative Director at Leo Burnett, conducted a survey which invited agencies to evaluate their award winning campaigns against their own predefined objectives. The assessment has been spread over a number of years and provides some interesting findings. 'In 1989, 78 per cent of cases were associated with market success. In 1993, 80 per cent did well in the marketplace and in 1995, 86 per cent of the award winning campaigns increased market share.'

However, there are a number of important points to be made about this study. At best, it is unscientific in so far as the award winners themselves are the arbiters of success. Moreover, the obvious difficulty, even assuming that the associated brands were successful within the timeframe of the advertising campaign, is the fact that the advertising effect cannot easily be distinguished from the other elements of the campaign.

Fletcher (1997) similarly, makes some important points concerning creativity in advertising:

- Many IPA Effectiveness Award winners fail to win creative awards.
- Thousands of campaigns are highly effective but fail to win awards.
- There are many creative award winners that have failed in the marketplace.

According to Koslow et al. (2003) some consensus in developing a definition of creativity has been achieved recently. First, creativity researchers agree that at least one facet must be originality, novelty or newness. Second, creativity researchers agree that originality is not enough and that creativity is therefore multifaceted. However, the question of what constitutes the second factor has been widely debated.

Eccleshare and Lintas (1999) offer one definition:

In advertising, the traditional definition of creativity has been tight. It is about creating something different and involving enough to grab the attention of consumers and communicate with them; creating signals that you understand them and talk their language; and creating a relationship, so that they understand the brand and feel it as their kind of brand.

Indeed, David Ogilvy (1983) suggests three key aspects of the creative process:

1 There is an inherent drama in every product. Our no. 1 job is to dig for it and capitalise on it.
2 When you reach for the stars, you might not quite get one, but you won't come up with a handful of mud either.
3 Steep yourself in your subject, work like hell and love, honour and obey your hunches.

Trevor Beattie, Chairman and Executive Creative Director of TBWA, stresses the importance of ensuring that consumers remember the product: 'No one talks about mediocre ads, products or people. If you can describe the ad without mentioning the brand, it has failed. It is argued that the best practitioners are those who are able to help a client company satisfy its stakeholders' interests for earnings, whilst also creating a strong demand for its products.'

John Bartle (1997) states that:

Real creativity must be measured by the ability to make your expenditure go further, do more than the equivalent spent by your competitors. That is real creativity. The result is advertising which captures both the attention and the imagination and the prize is the brand and the business success.

It must be remembered that different ads for different products have to do different jobs. Creativity is not always vital. In the context of retail advertising, for example, where consumers are, in many instances, simply looking for low prices, the task is to communicate the proposition in a clear and comprehensible manner. However, many ads need to be intrusive because in the main the consumer is not very interested. To achieve this, the ad needs to be new, original and creative. If an advertisement is like all of the others in its category, it will fail to stand out and will remain unnoticed (Fletcher 1997).

Saatchi and Saatchi (1995) have developed a series of criteria for the development of creative advertising. We show these criteria in Table 10.1.

Table 10.1 Saatchi & Saatchi's view of creativity

Fundamentals of creativity	
The role of advertising is to communicate a selling message	Persuasion
The role of creativity is to make the selling message compelling to the consumer	Intrusion/interest
The quality of creativity is dependent on the quality of the brief	Clear thinking/ planning

SOURCE: Saatchi & Saatchi 1995

Kover et al. (1995) argue that the key to understanding advertising is to identify how people respond to it. They assert that advertising works by enabling personal enhancement on the part of the viewer. This demands a need to reinforce the individuals' ideal self and in doing so increase the favourable attitude toward both advertising and the brand or product advertised.

An excellent example of the value of creativity in advertising can be seen from the turnaround of the Tango brand. The introduction of the 'You've been Tangoed' advertisements by Howell Henry Caldecott Lury led to sales over the campaign period rising by an initial 26 per cent, brand awareness increasing from 42 per cent to 72 per cent and agreement that there was no mistaking the orangey taste of Tango by 65 per cent.

Steve Gatfield (1995) then Chief Executive at Leo Burnett suggests that the co-ordination of creativity 'is not a mechanical process, but a fragile art'. Whilst Hooper and White (1994) argue that: 'The idea is the most elusive, intangible and important product of an advertising agency . . . campaigns can succeed or fail on the strength or weakness of the idea.'

Speaking on creativity, John Hegarty (1994), Creative Director of BBH, writing in *Admap* says: 'It's always good to learn about how others have been successful, even if it's only to learn how to do it differently.'

Advertising and the brand personality

Advertising can be used at different stages to establish or reinforce a brand's personality.

1 For new brands, the role of advertising is to create a distinctive new image that will serve to distinguish the brand from its competitors.
2 For mature brands, the advertising can reinforce the existing brand proposition.
3 For ageing brands, advertising can be used to achieve a repositioning in order to reach different target audiences.

As Bartle (1997) states, advertising can best provide the awareness breakthrough, the emotional resonance and the differentiation which will endure and without which even the best product does not leave the factory in any real volume. He goes on to say 'the particular contribution that advertising brings to branding is in helping to build and sustain brands.'

Determining the creative platform

Identifying which creative platform to utilise to convey the appropriate message about a product or service brand is critical to its success in communicating effectively to the target audience. A particular difficulty is ensuring that the advertising stands out from the many others that will be seen by the consumer. According to Winston Fletcher (1994) the average 35-year-old British adult will have seen some 150 000 different commercials, most of them half a dozen times or more. Achieving distinctiveness is, therefore, a paramount consideration and is the driving force behind the creative process. Bland advertising, at best, fails to attract the attention of the consumer. At worst it can undermine the image associated with the brand and result in their shifting to a brand which has more upbeat and positive associations.

Moreover, several recent studies have concluded that as many as half of consumers are 'avoiding' advertisements. The findings of one study conducted (Lowe, Howard-Spink in 1994) suggested that as much as 13 per cent of the money spent on TV advertising (almost £500 million) was wasted due to the phenomenon it called 'advertising avoidance'. One bad ad in a break can put people off the remainder. The analysis was based on BARB data from which three broad segments emerged, all of which were of roughly the same size: non-avoiders who rarely missed commercial breaks; moderate avoiders who saw about 20 per cent fewer ads than non-avoiders. The third group – avoiders – saw only about half as many ads as non-avoiders.

This would appear to correlate with the findings from Target Group Index (TGI). In 1991 it recorded that 33 per cent agreed with the statement 'I enjoy the TV ads as much as the programmes'. That figure is now down to 23 per cent. The research further identified that there is a strong correlation between advertising 'likeability' and awareness. This is reinforced by a variety of previous studies conducted throughout the world by, amongst others Du Plessis (1994) and Millward Brown (1991). A survey conducted by *Adweek* in the United States indicated that more than 40 per cent of Americans actively refuse to buy a product if they do not like the advertising.

The key factors that make people notice advertising are:

1 when the product itself is inherently different;
2 when the advertisement is sufficiently unusual;

3 when the advertisement has some particular, personal relevance;
4 when they seem to keep seeing it, and eventually it penetrates their consciousness (Fletcher 1994).

There are contrasting views on what makes for good advertising. Just as brands exhibit different personalities, so too do the agencies that create the advertising that supports those brands. Most often the choice of which agency to appoint to handle a particular account which be determined as much by the intrinsic approach adopted by the agency as any other factor. Some agencies adopt a 'hard-sell' approach others can be typified as preferring 'soft-sell' advertising.

The former – 'hard-sell' advertising – is an approach in which the advertiser uses specific facets of the product or service to convince the target audience that it is the best available. It often employs comparative techniques to display the particular advantages. This approach is seen commonly in many of the executions used to support the brands of Procter & Gamble. It is often accompanied by a specific injunction to buy now. The advertising within this category utilises a series of logical appeals to the target consumer to communicate the product benefits or attributes. It provides information based on the performance of the product, the particular features it possesses or its ability to provide the means of solving problems with which the consumer has to deal.

'Soft-sell' advertising, by contrast, uses a somewhat more subtle approach to the differentiation of its products. The essential ingredient is the desire to create an image in the minds of the consumers that will, ultimately, lead them to a purchase. Such advertising rarely promotes a specific facet of the brand; seldom do they feature particular product attributes to communicate a reason to buy. Most commonly they deal with images and product associations which will result in the consumer considering the product or service in a more favourable light.

There can be no prescription as to which approach is superior. Indeed, the very simplistic categorisation of advertising into these two groups suggests a more extreme differentiation than actually exists. Most forms of advertising contain elements of both logical and emotional appeals. However, particular clients tend to favour one or other of the approaches in the support of the brands within their portfolio. Both styles of advertising are evidently effective in the creation of brand support. This is an area where the combination of the culture of the client and the role of the account planner are brought together in the creation of an advertising message that will best serve to communicate the role of the brand and contribute to the overall marketing and marketing communications objectives.

The creative challenge: advertising appeals and their application

The primary task facing the creative department is to take all of the inputs and transform this information into a creative idea or advertising execution. Rather than simply stating the attribute or benefits that a product or service possess, they must ensure that the advertising message takes a form which will gain the attention of the potential consumer, arouse their interest and make the advertising memorable. A key consideration will be the extent to which the advertising will be based on a rational or an emotional appeal.

Rational or logical appeals

Many communications messages are based on rational appeals to the consumer. These provide the viewer or reader with specific information relating to the product. Some identify specific features which are found in the product, for example, Club Biscuits have 'more chocolate'; certain attributes which the product or service possesses, e.g. Fairy Liquid washes more dishes than cheaper brands; or benefits which the consumer will derive from using the product, e.g. Neurofen Plus adopts a problem–solution approach in which the commercial associates the problem (back pain) with the ease and comfort delivered by the use of the product.

Rational advertising appeals tend to be used when the manufacturer wishes to convey particular information to the potential consumer. Sometimes, when the product is either superior to its competitors or where the manufacturer wishes to achieve a position of superiority by virtue of being the first or only product in the category to make a particular claim, he or she will use a rational appeal to the consumer. This is commonly seen with the 'first amongst equals' positioning (no-one washes whiter than . . ., for example). These appeals are most commonly used where the product is particularly complex or in those situations where the consumer will require specific information in order to reach a purchasing decision. The computer market is a perfect example of where rational appeals are commonly used. Much business-to-business advertising tends to be of this type, since the buyers involved in the purchasing decision will often possess a high degree of knowledge regarding the products available to them and will require specific information to justify their decision to change the target of their purchasing decision.

In some instances, rational advertising utilises some form of comparison between the company's product and those with which it competes. The Royal Bank of Scotland, for example, directly compares the interest rates charged on its credit card with those of other financial institutions. Similarly, mobile telephone providers often compare their call rates will those of their competitors. In the UK, however, comparative advertising is far less widely used than in the United States, where the format tends to be commonplace. A commonly used format is what might be considered 'generic' comparisons. In these advertisements, the advertiser compares his product with an unidentified competitor – the consumer being left to decide the identity of the 'other' product. This can be seen in such campaigns as, for example, the Daz Challenge.

Such comparative advertising is particularly beneficial to new brands since it enables them to position themselves alongside other well-established products. This device can be effective in attempting to ensure the inclusion of the product within the consumers purchasing portfolio. One.Tel launched a price war against BT with the launch of comparable call packages. The advertising will provide consumers with like-for-like comparisons. Similarly, Asda is running advertising comparing its own brand product with that of the market leader (Andrex). The company was cleared by the ASA to continue to use the claim after submitting evidence that 63 per cent of shoppers do in fact prefer the softness of its toilet roll.

For most brands, however, this comparative route will tend to be rejected, since there is a risk that the rival's product will be promoted by the advertising and will derive additional consumer exposure. A wide variety of rational motives can be used as the basis for advertising appeals. These might include convenience, economy, health, sensory benefits, such as taste, smell, touch and also quality, performance, comfort, reliability, durability, efficiency, efficacy, etc.

Emotional appeals

Increasingly, advertising utilises emotional appeals as the basis of the message to the consumer. We have already seen that the result of convergent technology is the minimising of differences between products within a given category. Clearly, in these situations, any attempt to achieve product differentiation on the basis of a logical appeal to the consumer will fail to achieve sufficient distinction between the manufacturer's brand and its rivals.

Moreover, in a crowded media marketplace, it is clear that consumers like and enjoy advertising that, in turn, enhances their liking of the featured product or service.

David Ogilvy (1963) argues that:

> the greater the similarity between brands, the less part reason plays in brand selection . . . . The manufacturer who dedicates his advertising to building the most sharply defined personality for his brand will get the largest share at the highest profit.

In a similar vein, John Bartle, Managing Director of Bartle Bogle Hegarty, argues that, as the unique selling point (USP) is fast disappearing, then what becomes correspondingly more important is the ESP – the emotional selling point.

A study by de Pelsmacker (1998) demonstrated a range of conclusions about the appeal and understanding of advertising:

- Non-emotional ads lead to the most negative response and the lowest comprehension.
- Humour combined with warmth is better for affective response than warmth alone.
- Warmth rather than humour tends to improve understanding.
- Informative ads create a positive response compared with pure image ads.

Advertising appeals

We can look in more detail at the variety of appeals, both rational and emotional, which are used in contemporary advertising. Indeed, advertising can be classified by the style of appeal used to communicate to the consumer. The advertising appeal refers to the basis or approach used in the advertising to attract the interest and attention of consumers and influence their feelings towards the product.

As Ogilvy and Raphaelson (1982) state:

> Few purchases of any kind are made for entirely rational reasons. Even a purely functional product such as a laundry detergent may offer what is now called an emotional benefit – say the satisfaction of seeing one's children in bright clean clothes. In some product categories, the rational element is small. These include soft drinks, beer, certain personal care products and most old fashioned products.

The most commonly used appeals in advertising are summarised below.

- **Feature appeals:** Ads that use a feature appeal focus on the dominant attributes or characteristics of the product or service. Double Velvet has emphasised the product's softness by depicting scenes from the brand's factory. Employees drop from great heights onto stacks of toilet tissue and use the product as a crash barrier when arriving on their bicycles. The campaign continues the endline 'love your bum' and emphasises the product benefit 'now even softer'. Similarly, Toilet Duck has used its unusually shaped bottle to demonstrate its effectiveness in cleansing toilets.

- **Competitive advantage appeals:** When a competitive advantage appeal is used, the advertiser makes either a direct or indirect comparison to another brand or brands and usually makes a superiority claim on one or more attributes. Historically, the Daz challenge asked housewives to compare their 'usual' product with Daz to see the difference. The Pepsi Challenge, used in a number of markets, demonstrated their product by comparing it with the leading brand. Similarly, AOL made direct cost comparisons with FreeServe in their promotional advertising on television.
- **Price or value appeals:** These are often used to persuade consumer that they are receiving more for their money or making a saving. Price appeals are at their most impactful when combined with some other benefit such as when a company offers high quality at a reduced price. Dixons have recently used the 'price check' principle, underpinned with the promise that they check to ensure that no-one offers same items cheaper than them. Similarly, the Esso Price Watch – 'We never stop watching' – provided the consumer with the same benefit. Asda is currently running advertising with the claim 'voted the lowest priced supermarket for the 7th year running'.
- **Quality appeals:** This is a separate appeal, such as with Sainsbury's 'Fresh food – fresh ideas' campaign. McDonald's has used an airline motif in its advertising for its 'poundsaver' menu. It takes the positive aspects of budget airlines and translates them to a McDonald's restaurant as a metaphor for great value. Hovis has used an animated campaign featuring a cartoon family to maintain the proposition that 'Hovis products are free from artificial preservatives' (see case study at the end of Chapter 4).
- **News appeals:** In these ads some form of new information is provided about the product or service. This approach is commonly used by new products or existing products which have made changes such as improvements or modifications. McVitie's Jaffa Cakes have used a press campaign to emphasise that they've only one gram of fat in them.
- **Product or service popularity appeals:** These appeals focus attention on the wide existing customer base or the market position occupied by the brand, e.g. Hertz no. 1. The RAC states that it is the no. 1 in customer satisfaction.
- **Ego or self-esteem appeals:** Specsavers have been running a campaign which suggests that people 'look better' wearing a pair of spectacles from their range. Toyota advertising features the claim 'A car to be proud of'.
- **Social acceptance appeals:** A recent TV licence campaign depicts non-payers as 'spongers'.
- **Fear or anger appeals:** These are sometimes designed to create an element of shock for the consumer that, in turn, provokes impact and recognition. The possible danger, however, is that as well as shocking the target audience it may also serve to alienate them. Some of the early anti-smoking advertising suffered from this problem. A recent anti-smoking press advertisement depicts two cigarettes arranged in the form of a cross, with the copy 'A quarter of a million people pack

it in every year'. American Express travellers cheques have consistently used the fear factor as the basis of their advertising. The fear of losing travellers cheques highlights the potential consumer risk of a spoilt holiday. A similar approach has been taken by Thomson Holidays with the proposition 'Wouldn't it be nice not to worry about your hotel on the drive from the airport'. Over-the-counter medicines sometimes use a similar fear factor. Diocalm, an anti-diarrhoeal product, uses the fear of contracting a stomach bug whilst on holiday as the platform for its product sale.

- **Star appeals and testimonials:** These appeals enable consumers to identify with their favourite celebrities. The approach attempts to establish empathy amongst the target audience, by presenting the personality in a situation to which the consumer can relate. Seeing a product being endorsed by a famous person can capture attention and convey authenticity for the advertising message. Barclaycard has used the former *Friends* star Jennifer Aniston to front a new campaign, whilst Gary Oldman and Donald Sutherland replaced Samuel L. Jackson in their 'fluent in finance' campaign, stressing the financial expertise of Barclays.

  Characters have been developed as products in their own right. They are marketed laterally across a wide spectrum of product field and media. Characters such as Bart Simpson, the Rugrats and Wallace and Gromit have featured strongly in advertising campaigns (the latter in Jacobs Crackers).

- **Sensory appeals:** These are designed to create a particular image or evoke a response in the mind of the consumer. This approach is commonly taken by drinks manufacturers by evoking a sense of thirst or food manufacturers evoking taste in their advertising.

- **Novelty appeals:** These offer potentially the greatest opportunity for creativity. These ads attempt to catch the attention of the viewer by presenting original perspectives on their proposition. Smirnoff vodka has used this approach with surreal images seen through their bottle. Unilever has used a 'novelty' approach to reinforce the 'blokish' appeal of its Pot Noodle brand. It has had a series of ads using the innuendo positioning of the brand as 'the slag of all snacks'.

Although the above examples serve to illustrate many of the most common appeals used in advertising, it is important to remember that, in many cases, advertising executions contain a combination of both rational and emotional appeals. The imperative is to identify a memorable stance for the brand that will serve to differentiate it from its competitors. If consumers can readily identify with the advertising, more often than not, they will buy the brand.

Appelbaum and Halliburton (1993) provide an alternative listing of appeals that have been used in advertising. They define 'appeal' as any message designed to motivate the consumer to purchase. Although their research was limited to the food and beverage sectors, the list is equally applicable to other categories.

1 loving care
2 relief from stress
3 nostalgia and security
4 personal gratification
5 health appeal
6 friendship and togetherness

7   romance and sex
8   fashionability
9   individuality
10   belongingness to a group
11   separateness from a group
12   social status
13   snob appeal
14   social reward/punishment
15   newness
16   'it's good'
17   natural
18   traditional
19   convenience
20   cost
21   value for money
22   'specials'
23   economy packs
24   country of origin.

An exercise for students would be to try to provide examples from contemporary advertising campaigns to illustrate each of the above advertising appeals.

Styles of advertising/ advertising formats

The different styles of advertising can, similarly, be divided into a relatively small number of groupings. The creative execution style refers to the manner in which a particular appeal is turned into an advertising message, that is, presented to the consumer.

Appelbaum and Halliburton (1993) provide a table illustrating the various formats used within advertising:

1   slice of life
2   story around the product
3   testimonials (by experts)
4   testimonials (by celebrities)
5   testimonials (by ordinary people)
6   talking heads
7   characters associated with the products
8   demonstrations
9   product in action
10   cartoon
11   international versus national.

In the following section we expand on some of these formats and include others which are also popular.

Product as hero

This is advertising which focuses directly on the product and identifies a series of attributes or benefits that can be derived from using the brand. Primarily, it uses a straightforward presentation of information concerning the product or service and is often used with informational and rational appeals where the focus of the mes-

people used in the campaign, they are likely to perceive the featured product or service as being appropriate for themselves. This approach is currently being used in several of the financial services campaigns for companies that help consumers to borrow money to clear their debts.

Mini drama   Both Oxo and Gold Blend have involved the consumer in a developing 'soap' drama which has been extended over many years and has seen considerable changes to reflect the development of consumer lifestyles. The Gold Blend campaign, which was originally launched in 1969, demonstrates the ability of a campaign to evolve whilst retaining the emotional bond with the audience. According to the case study presented in *Advertising Works, 9* (Duckworth 1999), the result has been an increase in brand volume of around 60 per cent at a time when the market was static or declining.

Here, the brand is incorporated into a storyline that dramatises the product benefits. The 'story' may be a short sequence or part of an ongoing story that is developed in subsequent commercials for the brand. The brand seeks to gain added impact from the human interest derived from the ongoing plot for the campaign. The story is not intended to highlight specific product benefits, it uses the story as a means in itself. Often it takes on the language and lifestyle of the intended target group. Such advertising may have strong impact. The current campaign for P&G's Daz uses a similar approach.

Continuing character   This approach uses a central character or personality symbol to deliver the advertising message and with which the product or service can be identified. This approach is often used to transfer the distinctive identities of the characters, and create an associated personality for the brand. John Smith bitter uses the comedian Peter Kay in its 'no nonsense' campaign to present a series of humorous situations surrounding the brand. In some instances the 'continuing character' is an invention of the creative department. In others, advertising features a personality – as is the case of the Renault Clio using Thierry Henri to front its campaign and to reassert its French origins.

Brand heritage and history   This approach can be seen in a variety of advertising campaigns, such as the poster campaign for Jack Daniels whiskey. The advertising stresses some historic dimension of the brand, such as the consistency of its methods of production. The new campaign for Holsten Pils uses the endline 'Still brewed to the 16th century purity law. Just water, barley, malt and hops.' The ads focus on fictional brewers who are still committed to the original standards of quality in the modern Holsten Pils brewery.

Pastiche   Many commercials are derived directly from scenarios established in major films. Indeed, many creatives spend an enormous amount of time watching contemporary movies that provide a guide to contemporary taste and moods. Illustrations of the application of the device are the Mars Delight campaign which spoofs Rambo in one execution and Bruce Lee in another, whilst a campaign for the Mini has used the theme of 'Mini dramas' based on *Mutiny on the Bounty* and *Rio Grande*.

A parody is defined as an artistic work that broadly mimics an author's characteristic style (and holds it up to ridicule). As such, parodies represent a particular kind of borrowing. For a parody to be successful, the audience must readily recognise the

original work which is being mocked. The original work must itself be deeply ingrained in the culture. In some instances, the parody may make the original work even more famous.

In most instances, parodies also have a humorous intent. That is, they strive to make fun of the original work or, at least, try to push the stylistic pretensions of the original to extreme lengths. Modern advertising makes extensive use of parodies. Commercials sometimes parody elements of famous television shows. For example, some ads are presented in the form of an exaggerated soap opera (thus parodying a whole style of shows). Other times, one specific television show may be the object of parody. A more recent departure has been the tendency for some campaigns to spoof other advertising. In the recent execution for John Smith's Bitter, the advertising spoofs the classic Daz doorstep challenge, even to the extent of featuring Danny Baker, who was the presenter in the original commercials. Advertising for O_2 parodies the conventions for car advertising. The ads are shot in such a way that the handset looks like a car. In the voiceover Sean Bean states 'There is a new machine. It is faster, slicker and more technologically advanced than ever before.' An alternative approach is that of the recent campaign for Guinness which spoofs its own previous advertising. In 'surfer' the once brave characters run into the sea, but in contrast to the original execution, retreat quickly because they find that the water is too cold. In another execution, Rutger Hauer, who fronted the long-running 'man with the Guinness' campaign, returns in parody versions of the previous executions.

There are, of course, potential disadvantages associated with the use of parody. Zinkhan (1994) points out that one disadvantage involves the legal ramifications. A second disadvantage is that audience members may not find the parody to be funny. This is a danger associated with any humorous execution. A related disadvantage is that audience members may not readily recognise the original work that is the object of the parody. In this case, the message may remain incomprehensible or (in extreme cases) may result in some audience members being offended.

Spectacular, musical, stage show Commercials using this approach often involve a 'cast of thousands' and inevitably are costly to produce. The Halifax has used this technique in several of their executions.

Non-verbal An increasingly important approach, especially where commercials are intended for use across a variety of different markets, where the use of language to describe the product or its benefits would prove difficult. Two recent campaigns in the car market, one for the Peugeot 397SW, the other for Mercedes SLK-class, both use advertising in which the visual components dominate and where there is no reliance on a voiceover to explain the merits of the car. Nike shoes have been running advertising featuring 'Leo' who outperforms Nike's sporting heroes. The logo (tick) at the end identifies the brand.

Teaser Teaser advertising is commonly used by new products to create an element of intrigue and curiosity and to build excitement and anticipation. Such advertising often uses non-verbal executional cues to communicate. Small ads or advertising placed in unconventional media raises the level of interest. The primary idea is to add intrigue and curiosity to an advertising campaign in the hope that consumers

will 'search' for the main advertising when it eventually appears. A good example is the launch campaign for the Nissan Micra (see Duckworth 1999) and several recent film launches.

Animation Various executions using drawn or computer-generated illustrations have become increasingly popular. Such executions offer important advantages in enabling creation of situations which might be impossible to film in real life. Claymation, the techniques used in the 'Wallace and Gromit' films, was previously used for British Gas, for example, whilst the characters also appear in the advertising for Jacob's Crackers. Both Hovis and Kia Picanto use cartoon treatments.

Fantasy This approach is often used where emotional appeals are relevant. Product or service becomes a central part of storyline. Pirelli, for example, uses images and symbolism to create an association with the brand.

Infomercial This approach adopts a 'news-style' presentation in which the execution is very similar to that of a foreshortened television news programme. The approach has been used widely in the financial services sector.

Shock advertising This is an approach designed to deliberately startle or offend the audience in order to get noticed. Advertisers typically justify shock appeals in advertising for their ability to break through the clutter and get people's attention. Surprise is a significant part of the process because it initialises the processing of advertising information; it attracts attention to the novel stimulus or event. Without doubt, the brand most associated with shock advertising is that of Benetton, which we will examine in more detail later in this chapter.

Advertising approaches or how to get an ad noticed

The following sections describe some of the many approaches that can be taken to make your ad work for the target audience.

Using celebrities

An area of significance in the world of advertising is the use of celebrity personalities to front advertising campaigns. The use of celebrities in marketing communications is not a new phenomenon. Celebrities have been endorsing products since the late nineteenth century. Erdogan (1999) cites Sherman (1985) who states that Queen Victoria endorsed Cadbury's Cocoa. Moreover he argues that as many as one in five marketing communications campaigns in the UK now features a celebrity endorser.

A similar estimate was provided by Till and Shimp (2002) who estimated that around one-quarter of all commercials screened in the United States include celebrity endorsers. They added:

> although celebrity endorsement has a historic presence in Great Britain, the number of celebrity campaigns has increased markedly in recent years. In fact, our findings show that one in five marketing communications campaigns in the United Kingdom feature celebrities.

Advertising has long recognised the value of using spokespersons who are easily identified by the consumer. They recognise the fact that the celebrity has the ability to draw attention to the advertising message. This adds a point of difference to the advertising and assists the process of breaking through in a cluttered media environment. It is hoped that the popularity, respect and admiration that the consumers hold for the celebrity will be transferred to the product or service they are advertising. Celebrity spokespersons have become prevalent in advertisements (Agrawal and Kamakura 1995) and are widely used for gaining attention for brands, but generally the celebrity must be matched to the characteristics of a brand to be effective (Kamins and Gupta 1994).

Celebrities often bring visibility to a brand when acting as spokespersons, particularly in a new brand introduction in which the product is previously unknown to the consumer or when brand switching is desired. In addition, celebrities can produce higher levels of brand and advertisement recall. In general, high-credibility sources, which often include celebrities, are considered to be more persuasive in general communications terms, though in advertising research tends to indicate that highly credible spokespersons are more effective for unfavourably disposed audiences and that only moderately credible endorsers should be used for favourably inclined audiences.

The commercial which featured the greatest number of celebrities was one for the *Sunday Times* to mark the occasion of the paper's relaunch after a long dispute. The Benton & Bowles-produced commercial featured no less than 23 personalities in a 60-second slot and included Sir John Gielgud, Sir Ralph Richardson, Glenda Jackson MP, Sir Richard Attenborough, Joan Collins, Dame Edna Everage, John Thaw and Edward Fox amongst others.

There are several reasons for such extensive use of celebrities. Because of their high profile, celebrities may help advertisements stand out from surrounding clutter, thus improving their communicative ability. Celebrities may also generate extensive PR leverage for brands. As well as promoting established brands, celebrities are used to promulgate new brand images, reposition brands or introduce new ones.

An effective advertising campaign requires the right spokesperson to deliver a persuasive message through appropriate media. Selecting the right spokesperson is a difficult and often complex decision based on critical considerations, such as source credibility and attractiveness, as well as matching the brand or firm's image with spokesperson characteristics. Selecting the right spokesperson to promote a service can be especially challenging because the spokesperson may become the tangible representation of the service in the absence of other defining visual cues.

Although there are no hard and fast rules concerning the use of celebrities in advertising, certain situations suggest their suitability for a consideration of this approach.

1 When inherent differences between competing products are small. Ratneshwar and Chaiken (1991) suggest that celebrity endorsers would be especially effective when consumers' motivation to process message arguments is relatively low.
2 When introducing a new product where the sense of familiarity with the celebrity will be transferred to the product.

3 When a product which has a comparatively small share used a celebrity endorsement to elevate it from anonymity.

4 One of the ad's objectives is to bring about a change of image for a product. The values associated with the celebrity will be transferred to the product (e.g. Lucozade).

Erdogan and Kitchen (1998) indicate that there are many reasons why advertisers align themselves and their brands with celebrities, often at substantial cost:

- Celebrities are believed to possess dynamic qualities that can be transferred to products through marketing communications.
- Because they are famous, celebrities can attract and maintain attention by their presence in advertising, and also achieve high recall results. The use of Gary Lineker has been a constant element of Walkers Crisps advertising and has contributed significantly to the status of the brand.
- Celebrities can easily affect company or product images, and help to reposition an old brand or to introduce a new one. One of the best-known examples is the use of well-known athletes such as Daley Thompson, John Barnes and Linford Christie as the presenters of Lucozade.
- Celebrities with world-wide recognition can assist the task of achieving global marketing communications.

There is an overriding need to ensure that there is a close match between the brand, the target market and the celebrity. Consumer research is important in this context. The source credibility research provides the best understanding of how spokespersons can be more or less effective, depending on their personal characteristics and situational contingencies related to the endorsed product and the targeted audience. Despite a large body of literature on the topic, there continue to be conflicting viewpoints on what constitutes source credibility. In general terms, source credibility can be loosely defined as 'as a communicator's positive characteristics that affect the receiver's acceptance of a message' (Ohanian 1990).

Advertising is more effective when endorsers and firms' products have attributes that match (Kamins 1990; Kamins and Gupta 1994). Although companies may spend ample time and energy finding a celebrity whose image corresponds well with their brands, endorser concerns often do not end there. Problems can arise when the famous person is involved in incidents that change, or even damage, his or her reputation. These circumstances, referred to here as 'negative events', can range widely from accidents that hinder a celebrity's ability to perform to exposure for substance abuse. In a set of laboratory studies, Till and Shimp (1998) find that negative information about a celebrity can damage product evaluations through the associative link between brand and celebrity. Equally, as Kaikati (1987) notes:

> If the advertiser fails to establish a firm connection between the celebrity and the message during the campaign, the celebrity will probably have no special effect beyond generating attention, at best.

Iddiols (2002) identifies five types of endorsement as illustrated in Table 10.2.

Table 10.2 Five types of celebrity endorsement

	Characteristics of types of endorsement	
Testimonial	Celebrity essentially acts as a spokesperson for the brand	Ian Botham – Shredded Wheat
Imported	Celebrity performs a role already well known to the public through TV/film appearances	Neil Morrisey – Homebase Jamie Oliver – Sainsbury's
Invented	Celebrity plays an invented role only seen within the advertising	Prunella Scales – Tesco
Observer	Celebrity takes on the role of observer commenting about the brand, for example, as a customer	Helen Mirren – Virgin
Harnessed	The celebrity's personality is wedded to the storyline	Gary Lineker – Walkers Crisps Jamie Oliver – Sainsbury's

SOURCE: Iddiols 2002

Erdogan and Kitchen (1998) also point out some of the potential dangers inherent in the use of celebrity personalities in advertising campaigns:

- Some companies have been embarrassed when their celebrity has become embroiled in some form of scandal or controversy. Possible the most famous example is that of Michael Jackson, who was the lead personality for Pepsi and who was immediately dropped from the campaign when adverse publicity surrounded his activities. Despite Pepsi's bad experience with Michael Jackson, the brand still managed to pick up two share points through the sponsorship of two of his tours. For an estimated investment of $20 million, the brand generated an extra $1000 million of sales. Similarly, when O.J. Simpson was charged with the murder of his wife, Hertz responded by dropping him from their campaign.
- A celebrity may fade from the limelight during the period of the campaign. A celebrity may become overexposed by acting as the spokesperson for a number of different products. If the celebrity is identified within a number of different commercials or associated with a variety of brands, the consumer may perceive them as lacking in integrity. Tripp, Jensen and Carlson (1994) found that if a celebrity endorses many different products, this will negatively affect consumer perceptions of both the endorser and the advertising. Currently, for example, Andre Agassi appears in a number of commercials for different products. These include T-Mobile and Kia cars amongst others. This can be offset by entering into an exclusivity contract with the personality, although this can be very expensive.
- A celebrity can change his or her public appearance to the detriment of the campaign.

- Celebrities may come to dominate the advertising in a manner that enables recall of them but not the brand which they are advertising.
- There will inevitably be different perceptions of any personality within a given audience. Some people will like the celebrity, others will dislike him or her. The latter may well associate their dislike of the individual with the brand.

The advertiser who chooses to use a celebrity has no control over the celebrity's future behaviour. Any negative news about a celebrity may reduce the celebrity's allure, and therefore the appeal of the brand they endorse. The risk is potentially great for new or unfamiliar brands for which the association set is relatively scant and for which the celebrity is essentially the primary attribute on which consumers form evaluations of the brand. Negative celebrity information may have a much greater effect on such brands than it does on familiar, established brands.

There are a range of issues which will affect the selection of a celebrity appropriate for the brand campaign:

- the need for the personality of the celebrity to fit with the advertising concept;
- the need to match the celebrity to the target audience;
- the cost of acquiring the services of the celebrity (negotiating an appropriate fee can run into hundreds of thousands and, in some cases, millions of pounds), which will be greater if the advertiser seeks to ensure the exclusive use of the celebrity;
- the credibility of the celebrity.

Iddiols (2002) suggests four key measures to assess the dimensions of success for a successful celebrity campaign:

1 the extent to which there is an association between the celebrity and the brand;
2 the extent to which the brand can be said to be imbued with associations derived from the celebrity;
3 the extent to which there is a 'good fit' between the brand and the celebrity;
4 the extent to which the success of the brand (in the short and/or long term) can be said to be linked to the involvement of the celebrity.

The costs of celebrity endorsers

The high cost of celebrity endorsements is evidenced with a number of examples.

- Jamie Oliver has signed a one-year contract to continue to front Sainsbury's advertising for a fee reported to be £1 million.
- David Beckham has a series of contracts for advertising and personal appearances that include Gillette (£7 million); Pepsi (£5 million); Marks & Spencer (£3 million); Adidas (£3 million); Police sunglasses (£1.5 million) and Vodafone (£1 million).
- Michael Owen's deals include Umbro (£5 million); Burton (£1 million); Lucozade (£1 million); Nestlé (£1 million); Asda (£500 000); Persil (£500 000).
- Wayne Rooney, a newcomer to the endorsement scene, has already signed a series of contracts that include Ford (£1 million); Nike (£650 000); Coca-Cola (£500 000); Mastercard (£350 000) and Pringles (£200 000).

However, there can be positive financial benefits derived from the association of a brand with a celebrity name. According to a book by Hamish Pringle (Director General of the IPA), *Celebrity Sells*, Prunella Scale's campaigns for Tesco since 1998 are estimated to have generated an extra £2.2 billion in sales for the supermarket chain. Jamie Oliver is estimated to have generated an additional £1.12 billion over 18 months. This contrasts with the Sainsbury's commercial featuring John Cleese, which was voted the most irritating campaign of the year by *Marketing* magazine.

Other successful celebrity endorsements highlighted by Pringle are:

- Stephen Fry and Hugh Laurie for Alliance and Leicester – £656 million
- Bob Hoskins 'It's good to talk' for BT – £297 million
- Vic Reeves and Bob Mortimer for First Direct – £223 million
- Martin Clunes, Caroline Quentin and Jonah Lomu and others for Pizza Hut – £55 million
- Pauline Quirke for Surf – £21 million
- Chris Eubank and Prince Naseem for The Dairy Council – £21 million

However, the use of a celebrity per se is no guarantee of success. If the match between the celebrity and the product is inappropriate, then the desired impact will not be achieved.

Coca-Cola unveiled a star-studded TV campaign to support its sponsorship of Euro 2004. The ads feature football stars representing teams from across Europe including Wayne Rooney (UK), Luis Figo (Portugal) Ruud Van Nistelrooy (Holland) and Thierry Henri (France). The campaign builds upon Coke's existing on-pack promotion offering free branded footballs. The on-pack promotion was supported by a media campaign including TV ads and break-bumpers on ITV which appeared around live broadcasts of matches during the tournament.

Using animated endorsers

Although human spokespersons and celebrity endorsers have been effective, they are also somewhat risky to use. Moreover, the match between an endorser and a brand is critical to successful advertising, and human endorsers have a way of changing their public persona as they engage in various activities that may denigrate their image in the eyes of the public. Thus, animated characters have come to be thought of as 'safer' because they are created and can be controlled in ways that human endorsers cannot. Little research has been done linking the persuasive effects of animated spokes-characters to the source effects models; given the likelihood that the use of such endorsers represents new opportunities for understanding source effects, it is well worth investigating (Callcott and Lee 1994).

Spokes-characters, animated characters used to endorse brands, do not fall prey to many of the potential problems inherent in human celebrities; certainly, they are not likely to embarrass national sponsors by their off-stage behaviour (Stafford et al. 2002).

Third-party organisation endorsement

A third-party organisation (TPO) endorsement is defined by O'Mahoney and Meeneghan (1997) as product advertising that incorporates the name of a TPO and a positive evaluation of the advertised product that is attributed to the TPO. Observation of current advertising suggests that TPO endorsement may take one of three general forms:

1 the product is ranked against competing products in its class on one or more criterion;

2 the product is awarded a 'seal' of approval by the TPO (though how the seal differentiates among products in the class may be unclear);

3 a subjective, non-comparative statement is made about one or more product attributes.

In their studies, the TPO endorsement groups had means for perceived quality and information value of the ad that were significantly greater than those for the celebrity groups. Expertise appears to be the source effect most responsible for endorsement persuasion in advertising expensive, utilitarian products. Consumers apparently regard the recommendations of expert sources as information that can be internalised to solve problems.

Although TPO endorsements were generally superior to celebrity endorsements for the products advertised in their investigation, O'Mahoney and Meeneghan (1997) state that celebrity endorsements are not without merit. For products high in psychological or social risk and low in financial or performance risk, celebrity endorsements may be more appropriate. In addition, celebrity endorsements are valuable in attracting attention to the ad and the brand

Humour in advertising

Humour is one of the commonly used communication devices in advertising. In the USA Speck (1991) estimated that almost 24 per cent of TV ads used humour. Alden et al. (1993) reported similar levels in international usage of humour:

Whilst it is undeniable that humour can be very effective in communicating a brand message, there are also significant risks associated with the use of humour:

• The impact of humour varies according to age, gender and ethnicity.
• Humour may not travel as a consequence of cultural differences.
• Research has suggested that humour is more appropriate to low-involvement products.
• Humour tends to work best when the audience already holds positive attitudes towards the brand.
• The wearout factor may be somewhat higher with humorous rather than non-humorous ads. The joke simply stops being funny after the viewer has been exposed to the message several times.

Certainly, humour that is well integrated with the brand message and imagery has been shown by various researchers to enhance attention, credibility, recall, evaluation and purchase intention.

Humour is often featured in consumer advertisements, yet its effects and the mechanisms by which they operate have not been fully identified. Previous studies are somewhat contradictory in their findings. Some have shown humour to enhance, others to inhibit, whilst yet others show no effect on consumers' responses to advertisements.

Research by Weinberger et al. (1995) shows that humour may arouse desirable responses by attracting attention, making ads more likeable, and perhaps more memorable. Nevertheless, the same study has also shown that humorous ads do not always elicit more positive brand attitudes and purchase intentions. It can be argued that humour remains one of the least understood elements in advertising. This is particularly important in the context of international advertising since cultural differences establish vastly different 'norms' for humour, resulting in the conclusion that much of what is deemed funny within one society is deemed 'unfunny' elsewhere.

According to Cline et al. (2003) few would dispute the fact that humour can be an effective advertising tool. However, the conditions that determine when it is effective are only now beginning to be understood. Recent work by Alden, Mukherjee, and Hoyer (2000) examined some of the generative mechanisms underlying humour's influence on attitudes. They find that surprise, as a generator of humour, may not be its own virtue. Specifically, humour elicitation is greater when surprise is accompanied by playfulness and warmth. The impact of humour in ads may also depend on the type of humour employed, the type of product being promoted, and the relation of the humour to the product or message. It is important to note that the impact of humour is likely to depend on the interaction of ad characteristics with characteristics of the individual processing the ad.

It has been suggested, by a number of analyses of the contribution of humour to advertising, that humour tends to contribute to recall and liking, but may be slightly less good at persuading or modifying attitudes. Humour can get in the way of an argument, as illustrated by the failed Sainsbury's campaign featuring John Cleese.

A further issue that needs to be considered is the impact of humour of the wear-out factor. What starts out as being a funny commercial on first viewing becomes progressively less so on repeat occasions. Indeed, it may become so irritating that it has the opposite of the intended effect and dissuades people from buying the product.

Music in advertising

Music is often used to set a mood and create favourable associations with brand. A large study regarding the effect of music on advertising was carried out by Stewart and Furse in 1986. They analysed over 1000 commercials and discovered that there was a positive relationship between the musical factors and the level of recall and comprehension. There is considerable evidence that where music has been used before by a brand then the advertising is more easily understood and there is better identification and awareness of the brand being advertised.

Advertisers spend large sums of money on the production of musical ads. Creative fees for an original composition can cost several thousand pounds. The rights to popular songs can cost much more: for example Nike paid £350 000 for the use of The Beatles' song 'Revolution'.

A study by Branthwaite and Ware (1997) identified the common functions of music within advertising:

indicates branding	7%
sings message	7%
borrows a lifestyle	15%
gives pace	34%
background music	38%
creates mood	54%

Music can be used in a number of different ways within advertising:

- to create or enhance the mood and atmosphere of the ad;
- to create or change pace, add drama, imply a lifestyle, create an image, identify a target group;

- to sing a message about the product or brand;
- as a aid to branding;
- as background music, not directly related to the theme of the ad.

Dunbar (1990) claims that music should be considered as a human language, which is just as effective at communication. He identified a series of roles for music in advertising. Music can be used to fill awkward silences in the soundtrack or to provide continuity between disjointed visuals; it can be employed as a comment on the pictures by drawing attention to or enhancing the action on the screen, or used as a brand signature, as in the case of Intel.

Branthwaite and Ware (1997) suggest that music acts as a magnet, attracting the attention of target groups by signifying who the brand is for in terms of lifestyles, age (music era), gender (music and artist appeal) and attitudes (music style). They used the Millward Brown LINK test system to substantiate music effectiveness. Their findings indicated that ads with music were considered more enjoyable to watch and more attention getting compared to those without music. Since enjoyment of advertising is considered a strong determinant of liking, it enhances the viewer's involvement in the ad, promotes absorption of the message and branding, and increases awareness of the advertised brand.

The unique contribution of music in the advertising context lies in its ability to remind the consumer of the brand's existence over long periods of time. By achieving an association with a particular music track, the advertiser benefits when the music is played on radio or television stations, and even without overt mention of the brand name, the music reminds them of the brand. Music has been used to plant a message firmly in the minds of consumers and contributed to word-of-mouth advertising, since the music becomes popular in its own right. Tracks sometimes receive considerable radio exposure, as in the case of Levis.

Indeed, the Levis brand has used musical underpinning extensively in their advertising campaigns, with great success both for the brand and the artists featured. The approach has been continued since the first BBH commercial in 1986 known as 'Laundrette' which featured the Marvin Gaye track – 'I heard it through the grapevine'. Several of the backing tracks used by Levis have reached number 1 in the charts. These include, amongst others, 'Stand by me', Ben E. King in January 1987; 'The joker', Steve Miller in June 1990; and Babylon Zoo in 1995. However, Levis have recently broken with that tradition. The latest campaign featuring its 501 jeans is the first in some 20 years to be aired without a music track.

Research by the Department of Psychology at the University of Leicester, commissioned by Capital Radio, found that music can increase the recall of advertising by 63 per cent if advertisers use the right kind of music. It is claimed that the use of Sting's track 'Desert rose' used in the Jaguar S-Type ads contributed to the increased sales of 35 per cent in the first 10 months of 2000. Similarly, the use of Shaggy's song 'Boombastic' by Levis contributed to a 12 per cent increase in sales.

The variety and diversity of music tracks featured in commercials can be seen from the following examples:

- 'The Israelites', Desmond Dekker, used both by Vitalite (who have recently revived the track after an interval of 12 years) and Sony Tapes;

- 'Fly away', Lenny Kravitz, used by Peugeot;
- 'Music to watch girls by' Andy Williams, used by Fiat Punto;
- 'If everybody looked the same', Groove Armada, used by Mercedes;
- 'Find my baby', Moby, used by Fiat.

Speaking of the use of music, John Hegarty (1995a) of the Levis agency, BBH, stated:

> We are surprised, however, that it took the record industry so long to wake up to what advertising can do. We give a narrative and a stronger sense of image to a song than film of the band could ever do.

There is now a close symbiotic relationship between music and advertising, where the line between promotion and usage has become blurred.

Moby, the last-named artist in the list above, on realising that his music was not getting conventional airplay, determined to use non-traditional methods of getting his music heard. He and his licensing company arranged for every single track on his fourth album – *Play* – to be licensed to ads, television and movies. In June 2000 it was estimated that nearly 600 uses had been gained by music from his album. The list of ads using Moby's music included Galaxy chocolate, the Nissan Almera, Thornton's, Learn Direct, VW Polo, Fiat and Maxwell House.

Some companies extend the use of music tracks once they have become associated with the brand. 'Walking on sunshine' by Katrina and the Waves is used by First Choice not only in their advertising also on their charter flights.

Music can become a memorable and effective branding tool, as was the case when Peugeot used the Lenny Kravitz track 'Fly away' for the 206 model. The same brand used a similar device for their 405 advertising, this time utilising the Roxette track from Topgun. Mercedes Benz have used 'O Lord, won't you buy me a Mercedes Benz' to overcome many of the difficulties associated with non-verbal communications, as did Ford with the Des'ree track 'You gotta be strong'. Recent advertising for Halifax uses music as the focus of the campaign, with employees singing the praises and benefits of the company to the tune of current hits including Ricky Martin's 'Living la vida loca', The Baha Men's 'Who let the dogs out' and Tom Jones's 'Sex bomb'.

In an advertising context, music may contribute to message reception by attracting and holding attention. According to one view (Kellaris and Cox 1993), attention-getting music should attract attention to an ad, thereby enhancing message reception. A paradox arises, however, in that listeners sometimes attend to the music so closely that the message is not processed. In these cases, music is a distraction that inhibits message reception and processing. Similarly, research by Alpert and Alpert (1991) has demonstrated that music in advertising can affect information retrieval amongst viewers, and that purchase intention was higher in those ads with music.

Music can communicate meanings in two distinct ways. First, musical pieces occasionally convey literal meanings by imitating concrete sounds (e.g., bird calls, traffic noises). Second, music has a special ability to convey images, thoughts and feelings more abstractly as well.

Music can be used to evoke a specific mood. According to Cook (1992): 'For a given individual (or for a group) music may evoke a certain mood or associate with specific places, events or images. Such connotations are at once both predictable and also vague and variable.'

Music can also be considered from a global perspective. International advertising must, increasingly, find ways of communicating with a vast array of different audiences. Music often provides the underlying link which enables advertisers to overcome language barriers (Appelbaum and Halliburton 1993).

Milward Brown has tested over 2800 TV ads in the UK and USA, from which Branthwaite and Ware (1997) draw a series of conclusions:

- Enjoyment of ads is enhanced by having music, and:
  prominent music gives more enjoyment than background music;
  well-known music has a greater effect than music which has been adapted or specially written.
- The ad is more engaging when:
  there is prominent music which makes the ad more interesting, involving and distinctive;
  the music used is well known.
- Attention is increased by:
  music in general;
  prominent music as opposed to background music;
  well-known music.
- Brand recognition is improved:
  when the music is familiar and has been used before by the brand;
  if the music has a brand name in it.

Comparative advertising

Comparative advertising is used to compare two or more brands on the basis of one or more product attributes (William and Farris 1975). According to Dwek (1997), the comparative approach accounts for an estimated 35 per cent of all advertising in the USA compared with a meagre 1 per cent in the UK.

Comparative advertising can takes several different forms:

- Knocking copy. This is often used to make comparisons with, for example, the brand leader. Will contain a statement such as 'our product is as good as/better than/cheaper than . . .' One.Tel launched a price war against BT with the launch of comparable call packages. The advertising campaign provides consumers with like-for-like comparisons.
- It may imply a product is better than that of a competitor (brand *x*) but leave it up to the public to make the direct comparison and reach a conclusion on superiority. A campaign for the Peugeot 407 shows competitive cars as toys compared with the real thing.
- Ads may compare specifications such as size, weight or other dimensions of performance.

According to Barry (1993) there are a variety of comparisons that exist in the marketplace today. These include:

- Inferiority comparatives, e.g. 'We're the highest priced computer in the market'.
- Parity comparatives, e.g., 'We fly as many places as other major airlines'.
- Superiority comparatives, e.g., 'We're the finest-tasting soup on earth'.
- Combination comparatives, e.g. 'We may be the highest-priced soup on the market but we're the finest-tasting soup on earth'.
- Direct brand partnership comparatives, e.g. 'The Goodyear Eagle GA. Audi's choice for the flagship of their line.'

Comparisons can be:

- implicit (audience fills in brand) and/or explicit (brand(s) named);
- verbal (words) and/or visual (illustrations);
- brand (specific brand(s) named) and/or category (product class(es) named);
- inferior, parity, superiority, combination claims;
- brand partnerships.

In a study conducted by Donthu (1998) it was found that people are often suspicious about the credibility of the message in comparative advertising. However, this was somewhat dependent on the level of exposure to such advertising that had previously been experienced: 'Attitude towards comparative advertisements was especially negative for respondents in countries where comparative ads were not widely used or are rarely used.'

John Hegarty, Chairman and Creative Director of BBH (Hegarty 1995b), feels that:

> by and large, it [comparative advertising] demeans the brand. Advertising should try to make you beyond comparison. Any comparison implies a similarity. We often talk about brands as personalities, yet usually we do not like people who have a go at other people. We generally prefer those who have confidence in themselves.

Pechmann and Ratneshwar (1991) suggests that when ads compare brands on one or more attributes, consumers may link them together in terms of other attributes and infer similarities. They demonstrated that a low-share sponsor's ad gets the most attention when it is compared to a competitor with many users.

There are many circumstances that can facilitate, necessitate or inhibit the use of comparative advertising. Muehling and Stoltman (1992) suggest that an advertiser may feel forced to respond to a competitive comparison campaign. Recent changes in legal restrictions have changed the climate for conducting comparative advertising. The banks and other financial institutions, for example, have taken advantage of the opportunity to compare interest rates between competing lenders – The Leicester Building Society makes direct comparisons comparing interest rates on current accounts between itself and other lenders.

It is clear from the available research that there are both merits and demerits associated with the use of comparative advertising:
Benefits:

- Comparative advertising can be used to focus attention on particular aspects of the product's relative performance, thus assisting the potential consumer in evaluation and choice.

- May be used to strategically position a brand in the minds of consumers.
- Can influence attitudes towards and perceptions of brand/supplier credibility.
- Enhances message recipients cognition of a brand or supplier.
- Can provide 'free advertising' for lesser-known competitive firms.
- Pinkleton (1977) compiled research that showed that negative comparative advertising creates a greater impression than positive or neutral advertising in the consumers' mind.

Disadvantages:

- There is a possibility of overloading consumers with information.
- May result in misidentification of brand names.
- Competitive brands may counter-argue producing a 'boomerang' effect.
- Credibility of advertising may be tarnished.

A recent survey conducted by OMD for *Marketing* magazine indicates that brands that use comparative advertising risk alienating their target audience. Their research asked whether potential consumers are more or less likely to consider a brand more favourably that compares its prices with those of a rival firm:

31 per cent indicated that they would be more likely
19 per cent said less likely
whilst 50 per cent were not sure.

The same study asked whether consumers believed price comparison ads. The responses were:

Yes   24%
No   76%

One difficulty regarding comparative advertising is that the use of the practice differs between countries. In some, the practice is legal and commonly used. Elsewhere restrictions exist which limit or even ban its application. Moreover, cultural differences may preclude the use of comparative advertising when it is perceived that it offends cultural norms. Table 10.3 indicates the legal status and usage of comparative advertising in a number of selected countries.

Barry (1993) concludes that there is no general evidence for comparative advertising being more effective in terms of awareness generation, communication effectiveness or purchase intentions. Those occasions where it might have more chance of being more effective are where:

1 it has short-term novelty value;
2 it is used to give more credence to a little-known brand;
3 it can be based on objective rather than subjective comparisons;
4 credibility/believability are crucial (e.g. evidence on a serious subject is provided by a recognised independent body).

Table 10.3 Legal status and usage of comparative advertising, by country

Country	Legality?	Usage
Hong Kong	no	–
Korea	no	–
Belgium	no	–
Mexico	yes	very low
Brazil	yes	very low
Japan	yes	very low
France	yes (since 1991)	very low
Italy	yes (since 1993)	very low
India	yes (very recently)	very low
New Zealand	yes (since 1989)	very low
Germany	yes	low
Netherlands	yes	low
Denmark	yes	low
Australia	yes	low
Great Britain	yes	moderate
Canada	yes	high
USA	yes	high

SOURCE: based on Donthu 1998

Fear appeals

As was noted earlier, many advertising campaigns incorporate an element that is designed to elicit 'fear' in the mind of the viewer. According to LaTour and Rotfield (1997), a threat is an appeal to fear, a communication stimulus that attempts to evoke a fear response by showing some type of outcome that the audience (it is hoped) wants to avoid. Fear is an actual emotional response that can impel changes in attitude or behaviour intentions (e.g. toward car safety issues or toward the energy crisis) and consumer actions (e.g. cessation of cigarette smoking or more careful driving habits) and can even influence how readily patients heal after surgery.

The use of fear appeals has become popular because they have been found to increase the interest and persuasiveness of ads. However, fear appeal use in advertising is still not universally accepted. Critics argue that fear appeals are unethical and can 'backfire' or have unintended negative effects on consumers.

Some critics of advertising cite its overly dramatic and increasingly graphic use of fear appeals and such advertising's general lack of social responsibility (La Tour et al. 1996). Additionally, some suggest that improperly used fear appeals damage the credibility of advertisers and create unnecessary fears and worries among audience members.

Despite these criticisms, the use of fear appeals is quite common in many types of advertising campaigns. Indeed, many advertisers have found them to increase interest and persuasiveness of individual ads. Empirical studies (Hyman and Tansey 1990) suggest that subjects remember better those ads that portray fear rather than ads with no emotional content. Moreover, their recall of those ads is better. This is particularly important in the context of the volume of 'media clutter' – satellite and cable TV, remote controls and VCRs – where today's advertising has to work harder for the attention of viewers.

Bennett (1996) conducted a study into the use of fear appeals in advertising and concluded that the stronger the fear arousal, the greater the effect. Moreover, against suggestions elsewhere, there was no evidence of diminishing returns.

Shock advertising

There is little doubt that some advertising purposely breaches social norms with the intent to shock. Probably the most widely publicised cases include the advertising campaigns produced by clothing retailers Benetton and Calvin Klein. Initially, the Benetton campaign used images that were uncontroversial, but the campaign evolved progressively to use images that were both startling and, to some, offensive. Over the years Benetton's advertisements have featured photographs of a slain soldier's bloodied uniform, a white infant nursing at a black woman's breast, a leading American Aids campaigner on his deathbed and the picture of the newborn baby, still covered in blood.

The advertisements have won awards for heightening public awareness of social issues but have also provoked public outrage and consumer complaints. Both the two latter ads elicited large numbers of complaints. The former included many from Aids charities who felt that the image used was gratuitous and demeaning; the latter attracted the greatest number of complaints received by the ASA in its history (BBC 1997).

A shock advertising appeal is generally regarded as one that deliberately, rather than inadvertently, startles and offends its audience. Offence is elicited through the process of violating social norms, encompassing transgressions of law or custom (e.g. indecent sexual references, obscenity), breaches of a moral or social code (e.g. profanity, vulgarity), or things that outrage the moral or physical senses (e.g. gratuitous violence, disgusting images).

However, as Cooper (1997) points out – in an age when consumers are exposed to an estimated 3000 advertisements per day, what does it take to get an advertisement noticed? For many advertisers, the answer is shock. Although opinions vary on whether shock is a legitimate creative technique the trend is so prolific in the United Kingdom that it even has its own name, 'yobbo advertising', which is 'roughly translated as the desire to shock the audience into taking notice by whatever means possible.'

Research by Dahl et al. (2003) suggests that contrary to recent scepticism and concern regarding the negative effects of using shocking advertising content, this type of communications strategy can be effective. The publicity that is often generated, as a consequence of the norm-violating nature of shocking advertisements, need not be considered to be necessarily negative and ineffective. In a public policy context they demonstrate that, although a shock advertisement generates an acknowledgement of norm violation among viewers, it also ensures that subjects remember the message and engage in message-relevant behaviour. In a cluttered advertising environment, shocking advertising content ensures that the message will be heard.

The role of non-verbal communications

The use of non-verbal communications is an increasingly important consideration especially to overcome language difficulties associated with international advertising. However, the approach is equally popular in domestic advertising, designed to differentiate the campaign from other advertising approaches. Several authors indicate that the use of non-verbal communications in advertising has increased during recent years (Phillips 1997). Advertisers have increasingly begun to understand the use and advantages of non-verbal devices (McQuarrie and Mick 1999).

As Biel and Lannon (1993) explain:

> The primary reliance in advertising is virtually always placed on words. Whether the features are unimportant or very important, there is an assumption that there can be no communication, no persuasion except by words. Yet the truth is that almost never are the words the key to persuasion. Non-verbal communications refers to those communicative behaviours which are not part of the formal verbal language system and is based on the transfer of symbols to create shared meaning in the mind of the sender and receiver.

Images have the ability to convey much more information, more accurately and faster than words. They can be absorbed and remembered with much less effort by the viewer. Moreover, images have the potential to provide entertainment that serves the consumer's increasing requirement of advertising. Visual effects draw greater attention to the advertisements and can create an emotional response on the part of the viewer.

Muller (1996) and Chisnall (1995) identify non-verbal communication as facial expressions, eye contact and gaze, body movement (such as hand gestures and posture), touching, space usage, time symbolism, smell, appearance or dress, colour and sign symbolism, tone of voice, sound, and even silence.

Since images can bring us closer to the appearance of reality than words, complex messages can often be portrayed in a much simpler form, with the added benefit that more than one nationality can understand the message. Indeed, messages that might be difficult to express verbally can often be more effectively communicated using images (Morgan 1999). Price is often used as a non-verbal symbol to communicate cheapness, value for money, quality or luxury. Moreover, according to Mead (1990) only 30 per cent of our language is verbal.

Percy and Woodside (1983) claim that visual stimuli are better recognised and recalled that verbal. Similarly, Rosbergen, Pieters and Wedel (1997) argue that non-verbal devices can help to gain attention. Not only do these devices differentiate the ad from those of the competitors, they can get the message to stand out. Pictures in advertisements can grab the particular attention of a targeted audience. For example, women are more likely to notice ads including babies and children.

Non-verbal communication can be used to transfer emotions and attitudes to a brand, educating the consumer about the values of the brand. In the same way, the use of a logo or some other symbol representing the company or the brand can help the consumer to interpret a visual reference. Childers and Heckler (1992) suggest that non-verbal elements included in advertising can have positive effects on memory, especially if relevant to the message. However, they also identified the fact that unexpected elements introduced into the advertising can serve to increase consumer attention to the message.

McCorkell (1990) suggests that because pictures are attention grabbers, they can be used judiciously to give readers several start points at which they can become involved with the advertisement. Others indicate that visual elements in magazine ads are known to attract attention, create associations, or increase the impact of an ad.

Mitchell and Olsen (1981) reached the conclusion, based on a series of laboratory experiments, that presence of illustrations not only contributes towards the development of cognitive associations (beliefs) but also to greater appreciation of the advertisement, a positive attitude towards the ad and maybe the brand.

There are many examples of the use of non-verbal communications being used in contemporary advertising. The recent Levis 'Twisted original' campaign told its story within a 30-second ad using images and sound, without a single word being spoken. As noted earlier, several car manufacturers such as Mercedes and Peugeot are using non-verbal communications advertising.

One of the main factors driving the use of non-verbal communications in advertising is the appearance of multinational and global companies, who are increasingly selling their products to an audience which sometimes encompasses entire regions such as Asia, Western Europe or even the entire globe, confirmed by Messaris (1997).

However, great care needs to be taken in the production of such commercials, especially where they are intended for international use. Although signs and gestures may be used to augment the meaning of language, they may not have the same meaning in other cultures. For example, the traditional hand gesture for OK symbolises a willingness to give money in Japan. Elsewhere the gesture has a more offensive meaning. (HSBC have used this example in an ad to illustrate their 'local knowledge' of a global market.) Symbols can be interpreted in different ways, depending on the cultural reference point. The tiger, a symbol of strength used by Esso throughout much of its advertising, could not be used in Thailand, where the animal has other connotations.

Similarly, hand holding between members of the same sex has a different meaning in some countries, whilst the inappropriate touching between sexes may be considered offensive in some regions. It would be considered an affront in many Arab countries, for example, to see a man and woman embracing in public. Great care needs to be taken in the selection of models. Their ethnic 'look' may affect the acceptability of the advertising message in particular markets. Gillette for example re-shoot their campaign to ensure that the artists reflect the local 'look' for each market area. By the same token, attention must be given to ensuring that the setting is consistent with local requirements. An American-designed kitchen, for example, may evoke a different reaction from a UK kitchen to an English audience. Marieke de Mooij (1994) suggests that all aspects of a commercial must, as far as possible, be neutral. Everything from landscapes and buildings to road signs and car number plates have a national appearance, which will be inconsistent and unconvincing to someone from a different country from the one in which the advertising was shot.

Biel and Lannon (1993) published a paper on the use of visual metaphor – the use of one image to evoke another, and its use in advertising. They seek to demonstrate that visual metaphors are the basis of many powerfully effective advertisements.

Metaphors have been used increasingly as modern advertising has evolved. Advertising employs brand language and symbolism where benefits are conveyed by metaphors and symbols, tapping into universal human myths and archetypes. Indeed, there is evidence that much communication occurs non-verbally. They represent a powerful and often precise way of conveying information, particularly for multinational campaigns.

They describe a number of principles that may govern the use of visual metaphors:

- different rules, e.g. exaggeration enhances acceptability;
- self-explanatory visual metaphors don't require supporting text;
- visual metaphors demand mental processing;
- they are less susceptible to wearing out and can be refreshed;
- they possess many meanings and possess rich overtones;
- they enable the brand to make broad pledges rather than specific promises;
- they are easier to own – they become a property of the brand;
- they are transferable across media;
- they help in defining the brand's territory.

Advertising copy

Slogans and straplines tend to be taken for granted, although research has shown that they are a potentially valuable asset to the advertising and can be useful in terms of assisting response to advertising executions (Crowther 1999). A potent slogan or endline can be part of the way in which advertising is stored. Moreover, at its mention, a host of motivating brand associations can be triggered.

A good endline can transcend a range of campaigns (L'Oréal – 'You're worth it'; Audi – 'Vorsprung durch Technik'; Gillette – 'The best a man can get', etc.). The advertising for Ronseal ('It does what it says on the tin') has passed into common usage.

A paper by Donaghey and Wateridge (1998) indicates some important facets of the endline:

- respondents could consistently attribute famous slogans from the past to brands;
- a jingle helped recall;
- more recent endlines triggered executional recall of ads;
- some endlines work beyond advertising and move into the public dialogue arena.

They indicate that famous slogans from the past were consistently attributed to the correct brand, although few were able to remember many executional details from the advertising that accompanied the slogan. Nevertheless, these slogans still had the power to deliver a message in relation to the brand or to trigger pack or branding device recall (e.g. 'for great lager, follow the bear'). Recall was often assisted when the slogan or ad had been accompanied by a jingle. TSB, Hamlet, Heinz Baked Beans, Martini and Hofmeister fell into this group. Some endlines (mostly more recent), when correctly attributed to the brand, served to trigger sounds and images from the advertising executions themselves, indicating that endlines can operate as a gateway into the creative, with all its associated rational and emotional communications. Kit Kat, Tango and Boddington's endlines are good examples of where this occurs. Finally, some more recent ads, while not bringing the creative to mind in this much detail, were strongly linked to brand logo, symbol, packaging or other branding devices, particularly for the target consumers for the advertising. Moreover, some of these seemed to operate beyond the realms of the advertising idea, in that they appeared to express the brand philosophy, reflecting a brand attitude that mirrored real consumer sentiment. Nike's 'Just do it' and BT's 'It's good to talk' are examples.

Guidelines for evaluating creative output

At its minimum, effective advertising must satisfy the following conditions:

1 it must derive from a sound marketing strategy;
2 it must take the consumer's viewpoint – consumers buy product benefits not attributes;
3 it must be persuasive;
4 it must find a unique way to break through the surrounding clutter;
5 it must prevent the creative idea from overwhelming the strategy.

A series of important questions need to be answered in this context. Is the creative approach consistent with the brand's marketing and advertising objectives? Is the creative approach compatible with the creative strategy and objectives, and does it communicate what it is supposed to? Is the creative approach appropriate to the target audience, for example, does it have street cred as with the Sega and Sony Playstation campaigns? Does the creative approach communicate a clear and convincing message to the consumer? Does the creative execution overwhelm the message? Is the creative approach appropriate for the media environment in which it is likely to be seen? Is the advertising legal decent and honest?

It is essential that advertising creates active involvement. Some aspect of the advertising campaign must secure the attention of the consumer for some longer period of time in order that they can actively process the information contained within it. In this way, the advertising is likely to have a more lasting effect in that it will be committed to memory. Much will depend on the nature and quality of the content of the advertisement. Since research has shown that consumers store very few details of an advertising campaign on first exposure, it is essential that their interest is aroused in order that more details can be absorbed on subsequent viewings. Over time, the consumer builds up a more comprehensive recall of the campaign content and message.

The American Advertising Research Foundation demonstrated that 'likeability' of advertising (du Plessis 1994) is the best predictor of advertising effectiveness. However, others feel that this term is too broad to be used as an accurate measure of advertising effectiveness. Amongst these is Terry Prue (1994) writing in the foreword to *Advertising Works*. He indicates that many ads can be effective without being 'liked'. He proposes the use of an alternative word 'involving'. To demonstrate his thinking he cites road safety and Aids awareness campaigns, both of which can be shown to be effective without necessarily being liked by the target audience. It is reasonable to assume, however, that effective advertising both involves and persuades the consumer.

Case study

APG Creative Planning Awards

Agency: BMP

Author: Jane Cunningham

Terry's Chocolate Orange

Background

Seventy years ago, a chocolate maker at Terry's came up with an idea. He set about trying to create a product that combined the appeal both of fruit *and* of chocolate. And thus the Terry's Chocolate Orange was born. Terry's and BMP had worked together for many years, developing advertising for a whole range of different chocolate products in the Terry's portfolio. Two Chocolate Orange advertising campaigns had been developed together, and the ads – which ran around Christmas – had been reasonably successful in maintaining awareness and creating sales uplifts around the time that they ran. In addition, a number of new Chocolate Orange products had been launched into different sectors of the confectionery market. These attempts at brand extension were a mixed success but the Chocolate Orange bar gained and maintained a small share of its market.

In the mid-1990s, however, Terry's decided to rationalise their portfolio and advertising. Rather than supporting a number of different products, they decided to focus their marketing efforts behind a few key brands that were judged to have the greatest growth potential. Terry's Chocolate Orange was one of these brands. Steep growth targets were set for both the Chocolate Orange and the Chocolate Orange bar and work began on developing the positioning and the advertising in order to meet them.

Understanding the problem

The first problem was that Chocolate Orange was an extremely seasonal product. The Orange itself was mainly given and received as a Christmas gift and, over the years, promotional and advertising support had been focused around that key sales period.

As a result, nearly 90 per cent of sales happened in the three weeks leading up to Christmas. And interestingly – for a variant specifically designed for everyday consumption – the bar was also purchased very infrequently; on average, buyers bought it just 1.7 times a year – a very low figure given that heavy chocolate users eat an average of six bars of chocolate a week. Given that we knew the bar was widely distributed and that very few people claimed they didn't like the taste, we concluded the brand was so heavily associated with Christmas and special occasions that people did not think about buying on an everyday basis.

The second obstacle was the proposed advertising budget. Every year, Nestlé, Mars and Cadbury outspend Terry's ten times over. Moreover, they had supported their brands consistently over time, both in terms of spend and in terms of message. As a result, their brands, benefits and advertising properties were well established and recalled and had a much greater salience and presence than the well-known but rarely thought of Chocolate Orange.

If we were to achieve the growth we needed, we were going to need advertising that did two things. Firstly, we would have to find a way of re-presenting Chocolate Orange so that it had relevance and an application on occasions other than Christmas. And secondly, to compensate for our tiny share of voice, we were going to have to ensure the re-presentation was done in a way that really stood out and was different. Not only did we have to free the brand from its exclusive associations with Christmas, but to do that successfully, we would have to free ourselves from the norms of chocolate advertising in order to be heard.

To do this, we undertook a huge audit of the confectionery market, looking both at competitive positionings and at their presentation. It appeared there were two equally strong conventions determining the shape of the contemporary confectionery market. Almost without exception, chocolate was being presented to consumers in one of two distinct ways: it was depicted either as a serious indulgence or as a piece of light-hearted fun to brighten up the day.

Isolating the opportunity

When we talked to real chocolate eaters, they told us chocolate was neither as serious nor as flip as the advertiser's conventions suggested. Certainly it was a luxury and it gave them a lift, but it was very rarely about the extremes that the advertising depicted. In real life, outside of the overblown dramatisations of advertising land, real people were eating chocolate in a much more down to earth and casual way. In fact, chocolate was – for most people, most of the time – just a little bright spot in their day: something that was certainly seriously indulgent but not something that was particularly serious in itself.

The brand's relationship with Christmas meant that it was associated with happy, cheerful times. The format it came in – segments which you broke off or open to eat – meant that it was considered more playful than standard chocolate. And the chocolate itself – which consumers described as rich, mouth-watering and exotic – meant that Chocolate Orange was well placed to deliver on an indulgence front.

We believed that if we could position Chocolate Orange as the brand of chocolate that offered indulgence with a sense of fun, we could achieve our objective of representing Chocolate Orange in a way that would position it as everyday and give it a relevance and application on a regular basis not just at Christmas.

The creative brief

We defined the opportunity for advertising thus:

> Most chocolate advertising is either about serious indulgence or just loud fun. Terry's Chocolate Orange offers both: really luxurious taste and a sense of humour. The opportunity for advertising is to take a new angle on indulgence and turn it in to something fun.

Our target audience was women who love the taste of chocolate (just the sort of women who had told us in research how real chocolate lovers in real life eat chocolate). The proposition was: 'Terry's Chocolate Orange: Seriously indulgent chocolate that doesn't take itself too seriously.'

The creative idea

The campaign that the creative team came up with featured the perfect embodiment of that attitude: Dawn French – a personality best known for her sense of fun but also well known as a chocoholic. Through her attitude, her personality and the depiction of the lengths she would go to in order to get her hands on a Chocolate Orange, we felt we had the ideal representative of the Chocolate Orange benefit.

SOURCE: This case study is adapted from the paper presented at the APG Creative Planning Awards. The full version is available at www.warc.com and is reproduced by kind permission of the World Advertising Research Center.

Questions

1 For a brand of your own choosing, complete the creative briefing form illustrated at the beginning of this chapter.
2 What is the role of creativity in advertising and why does the issue cause such an intense debate within the industry?
3 What factors need to be considered when attempting to define the creative platform?
4 Consider the various appeals used in advertising. In what circumstances would you consider using a rational rather than an emotional appeal?
5 Why are there so many different advertising formats? What factors might determine the use of a particular format?
6 Identify why celebrities are used in so many advertising executions.
7 What contribution does music make to an advertising campaign?
8 What is the role of non-verbal communications?

11 Media planning, objectives and strategy

Learning outcomes

This chapter will develop your understanding of:

- the role of media planning
- the changing nature of media
- the advantages and disadvantages of the various media channels
- the importance of media strategy
- the issues involved in the development of a media plan
- the issues relating to media scheduling.

If any area of advertising development has changed over recent years, media and media planning must be at the forefront of those that have experienced the greatest changes. On all fronts, any discussion of media has become progressively more complex.

1 The underlying media scene has become dramatically more complicated, with changes in both the number and scope of the available media outlets.
2 The task of the media planner – and, with it, the responsibilities for 'getting it right' – have become more involved.
3 The improvements in technology have provided access to an ever-increasing volume of data. The tasks of media analysis have become more sophisticated.
4 The media role has become, in many instances, a discipline separated from other aspects of advertising planning. Not in the sense that media considerations can be divorced from the overall context of advertising planning but, rather, that the primary responsibility is increasingly moving away from traditional agencies into the hands of media specialists.
5 The need for media planners to adopt an innovative approach in order to break through the surrounding clutter is becoming increasingly important.
6 The requirement for the media function to be accountable is greater than at any other time.

The consequence is that the contribution of media planning has been recognised as being more important to the strategic process. As Bulman (1994) states 'Media is already far more centre stage, media planners can come up with innovative and effective solutions and media planning can break new ground'. Ingram (1998) states that 'Developments, such as relationship marketing, digital TV, the Internet,

E-commerce and the massive increase in data processing gives the opportunity to put media at the heart of the media function'.

Similarly, Martin Sorrell (1997), CEO of the WPP group, indicated that 'Growing awareness of media and audience fragmentation of the prevalence of media clutter and the importance to consumer response have re-focussed attention on the need to relate media and creative closely and the corresponding need to plan media more effectively'.

The primary role of media is to operate within the brand team to construct communications plans that deliver brand messages to potential customers. The strategic role is to identify the means of connecting the brand with potential consumers.

The role of media planning

We have already seen that one aspect of the creation of effective advertising is the determination of the appropriate message to communicate the benefits – real or perceived – of the product or service to a defined target audience. The role of media planning is to identify the most suitable media to carry those messages to that audience.

Branthwaite et al. (2000) have demonstrated that a consumer's impressions of a brand's communications are shaped by the medium through which they are received. A message that is trustworthy and credible in one medium might be viewed with wariness in another – even for the same brand. The extent of the medium's impact varies by country and the status of the medium within that country.

The process of media planning must be seen as overlapping and being concurrent with that of developing the creative message. The interrelationship between the two strands is an inevitable facet of the overall communications process. For obvious reasons, a key influencing factor will be the scale of the overall media budget. The proposed level of expenditure may preclude certain media channels from being utilised. However, it is equally important to consider the nature of the message itself. Identifying what the advertiser needs to say about the product or service will play a major role in the selection of the most appropriate media outlets. King (1997) argues that 'There is a strong case for the media choice to begin to precede the choice of communication strategy solutions and even the creative strategy'.

The determination and fulfilment of media strategy involves a number of separate and distinct tasks, as illustrated in Figure 11.1.

Media planning is the series of decisions an advertising agency has to make regarding the selection and use of media, allowing the marketer to optimally communicate the message to as many of the target market as possible at the minimum cost. Planning today is an executive function because it has become so much more complex than it was years ago.

The media planner is confronted with a wide variety of options – television, radio, print media, posters, ancillary media – several of which may reach the defined audience. The challenge that confronts the media planner is the identification of the most relevant and cost-effective media to fulfil the tasks defined.

Since the marketing communication objectives are only part of the overall marketing objectives, marketers place emphasis on media planners being able to comprehend and hence link their decision making into the overall picture. This would enable media planners to make more rational decisions when the selection process is complicated, as is often the case. Referring to the overall marketing

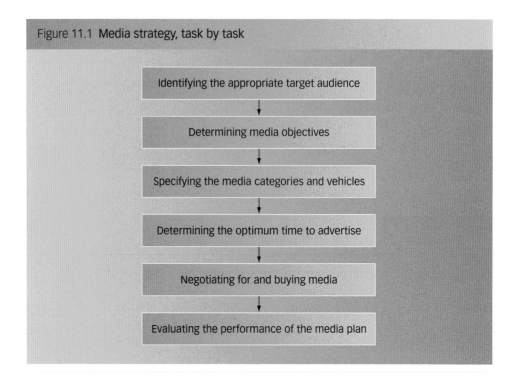

Figure 11.1 Media strategy, task by task

Identifying the appropriate target audience

↓

Determining media objectives

↓

Specifying the media categories and vehicles

↓

Determining the optimum time to advertise

↓

Negotiating for and buying media

↓

Evaluating the performance of the media plan

objectives, in such instances this would allow media planners to align their decisions with the priorities established by their clients.

The scale of media advertising can be seen from Table 11.1 showing the top 20 UK advertisers during 2003.

It is possible to see the comparative levels of UK media expenditure by channel, as shown in Figure 11.2.

Comparable data for other selected countries can be seen in Table 11.2.

The changing nature of media

Recent years have seen a progressive increase in the number and range of the media available to the planner. In the UK alone, we have three terrestrial commercial television stations, ITV, Channel 4 and Channel 5; numerous satellite and cable stations, all of which accept paid-for advertising or programme sponsorship; a wide range of national daily and Sunday newspapers, each vying with the others to provide effective reach of a group of readers; regional and local newspapers, designed to serve the interests of smaller communities; weekly and monthly magazines which respond to the specific interests of particular groups within the population; national and regional commercial radio stations; cinema; poster sites which can be bought on a local, regional or national basis; ancillary media in the form of transport advertising such as that which appears on buses, trains, and even taxi cabs. And an increasing diversity of 'new' media ranging from the internet to till receipts. Finally, as well as 'conventional' advertising, most of these media outlets offer opportunities for sponsorship activity.

This is a continuing process, as can be seen from Figure 11.3, which is taken from the original submission of *The Economist* case study at the end of this chapter.

Table 11.1 Top 20 UK advertisers, 2003

Rank 2003	Rank 2002	Organisation	Spend (£m 2002)	Spend (£m 2002)	Change (%)
1	1	Procter & Gamble	186 976	165 776	12.8
2	2	COI Communications	138 238	120 447	14.8
3	3	BT	96 314	96 721	−0.4
4	5	L'Oréal Golden	90 365	70 830	27.6
5	4	Ford	79 141	94 918	−16.6
6	11	Lever Fabergé Personal Care	69 870	58 646	19.1
7	8	Nestlé	68 727	63 457	8.3
8	13	Orange	62 570	55 717	12.3
9	6	Masterfoods	62 399	67 004	−6.9
10	10	DFS	61 403	59 394	3.4
11	7	Renault	60 651	66 146	−8.3
12	14	Reckitt Benckiser	59 487	53 048	12.1
13	18	Lever Fabergé Home Care	58 979	43 609	35.2
14	9	Vauxhall	58 570	63 382	−7.6
15	–	Hutchison 3G	49 809	37	
16	17	Volkswagen	49 200	45 386	8.4
17	15	Sainsbury's	46 688	48 738	−0.1
18	12	Toyota	48 245	55 966	−13.8
19	24	Kellogg's	43 359	39 413	10.0
20	21	Vodafone	43 340	42 117	2.9

SOURCE: *Marketing Magazine Top 100 Advertisers*, 2003

Figure 11.2 Comparative UK media expenditure by channel, 2001

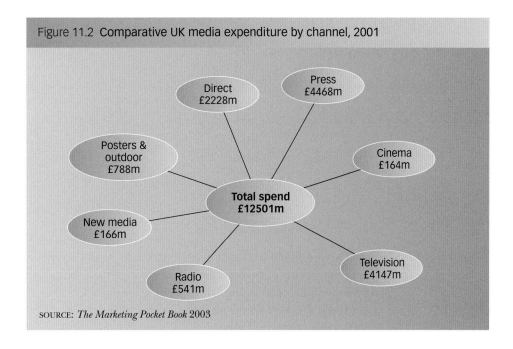

SOURCE: *The Marketing Pocket Book* 2003

Table 11.2 Media expenditure by channel in selected countries

	Television	Radio	Newspapers	Magazines	Cinema	Outdoor	TOTAL
France € millions	2 921	713	2 475	2 233	74	1 085	9 501
Germany € millions	4 396	661	7 495	3 172	178	793	16 695
Italy € millions	3 952	284	1 765	1 302	72	181	7 556
Australia Au $ millions	2 666	702	2 991	563	58	261	7 241
New Zealand NZ$ millions	516	203	628	173	8	37	1 565
USA US$ millions	50 778	17 178	41 830	13 912	n.a.	4 140	127 838
South Africa ZAR millions	3 663	1 416	3 029	1 398	79	428	10 014

SOURCE: *European Marketing Pocket Book* 2003

Figure 11.3 Advertising across media: a continuous process

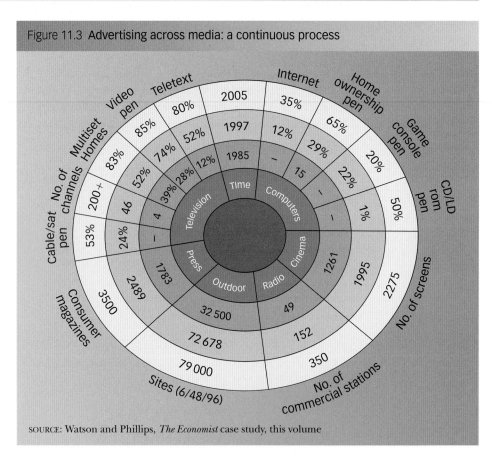

SOURCE: Watson and Phillips, *The Economist* case study, this volume

The inevitable consequence of this explosion in media availability has been the fragmentation of the audiences that each of them covers. When commercial television commenced in the UK in 1955, a single ITV channel provided the only outlet for the advertisers' messages within the medium. Programmes competed for viewership with the output of the BBC, but the consumers' choice was restricted and the advertiser could be reasonably confident of substantial audiences for the programmes in which he or she advertised. The arrival of BBC2 and, more significantly, from the standpoint of paid-for advertising, the commencement of Channel 4 in 1982 provided the consumer with a greater range of programme choices and effectively reduced the numbers viewing any individual programme.

Moreover, it became rapidly apparent that each programme attracted a different sort of audience, dependent upon its nature and content and time of day. Some were more likely to attract a male versus a female audience, some younger rather than older viewers, and so on. The greater the availability of programmes, the more likely that the audience would be spread across them, thus simultaneously reducing the numbers of viewers but, correspondingly, enabling the media planner to use more sophisticated research techniques to identify the precise nature of the viewers and ensure a correspondence with their targeting needs.

This process has continued progressively. The penetration of cable and satellite viewership has continued to rise to a level of around 40 per cent of homes by 2003, with its reach expected to grow in the years ahead, accelerating audience fragmentation. This is particularly important given the natural tendency of terrestrial television to appeal to the relatively older and less prosperous audiences.

A similar process can be seen in other areas of the media. In 1991 there were only 53 regional commercial radio stations compared with 180 in 2003 covering the whole of the UK. Vast numbers of 'dedicated' magazines and periodicals have exploded onto the scene, each of which is targeted to a very specific audience. Here, perhaps more than any other area of the media, titles come and go with great regularity, adding to the complexity of media selection. Even if a particular title achieves an effective coverage of a desirable audience, its success is not guaranteed and its disappearance may require the media planner to seek alternative means of reaching that group of consumers. This phenomenon is not unique to the UK. Similar changes that have taken place over recent years in the context of media availability across Europe.

Despite this audience fragmentation, costs have not moved in the same direction. Despite the fact that the individual media attract smaller audiences, in general, costs have accelerated at a rate faster than inflation. Although this may seem to be a contradiction, in fact it is a simple reflection of the forces of supply and demand.

Although at face value it may seem desirable for advertisers to reach the widest possible audience with their commercial messages, in fact this is rarely the case. The fundamental problem is that all media carry with them a degree of wastage, that is, readers, listeners or viewers who are inappropriate to the advertiser's message. In an ideal world, the advertiser would wish to target his or her message exclusively to those individuals who might be persuaded to purchase his or her product or service. Audience fragmentation may offer the opportunity to limit the exposure of the message to those consumers who most closely correspond to the desired target audience. Media proprietors are aware of the function they fulfil, and charge the advertiser accordingly. Moreover, where competition for the same audience exists – as it does in most cases – the rates which the media can charge are increased by direct competitive demand for the same space or airtime amongst a number of different potential advertisers. The more successful media owners are now better than ever at controlling their inventory.

Rates for a 30-second spot during the final episode of *Friends* on Channel 4 were traded at around £100 000. The rate is about 70 per cent more than a normal episode as advertisers anticipated a record audience of 16–34 viewers. The hour-long episode contained three centre breaks compared to the usual one.

Access to media and their characteristics

Each medium has its own distinctive character that can differ from country to country. This affects consumers' willingness to engage with different media. The feelings instilled by each medium will colour and shape the impressions conveyed, as the media impart a 'spin' to the image and hence the message. The trustworthiness and credibility of the message can be changed by the medium, as can its status and impacts; the aura of some media can lend familiarity and friendliness, while others create suspicion and wariness. This fundamental inequality in media means that responses to global media campaigns are unlikely to be the same everywhere, as consumers approach the media with different feelings and see an ad through different frames of mind, and differing media relationships (*The Marketing Pocket Book* 2003).

The various media channels: their advantages and disadvantages

Each of the available media not only has a series of unique characteristics that make it more or less appropriate for the task in hand, they also represent an environment for the message which will serve to enhance or diminish aspects of that message.

Media can, therefore, be considered in terms of three questions:

1 Does it enable the communication of the advertising message?
2 Does it provide cost-effective coverage of the target audience?
3 Is it the appropriate environment in which to place the message?

Television

Traditionally, television has provided a major means of communicating to a mass market and, as such, is frequently used for the promotion of fast-moving consumer goods. However, as might be expected, the associated costs are extremely high. Not only is airtime expensive, but so too are the costs of producing a commercial for airing. As an indication, a 30-second peaktime commercial (between 7.30 and 10.30 p.m.) on Carlton Television – covering the London area alone – would cost around £55 000. An off-peak spot of the same length in the same region would cost some £7500. The comparable rates for Channel 4 in London – which attracts significantly smaller audiences – would range from £26 000 for a peaktime spot down to £1000 for an off-peak spot. By comparison, a peak spot in the Grampian region – covering Scotland – would cost around £14 000 with an off-peak spot for as little as £250.

The advent of satellite-based television stations has introduced a new dimension to television buying. A peak spot on Eurosport, for example, costs around £12 000. A comparison of the costs for the various TV stations can be seen in Table 11.3.

Production costs are similarly high. It is realistic to expect to spend anything from £250 000 upwards for a 'simple' commercial and something of a slightly more spectacular nature, such as those for British Airways or The Halifax, could cost £1 million or even more. Similarly, using a personality to endorse a brand does not

Table 11.3 Television cost data

	£ cost per 30-second equivalent			
	Adults	Housewives	Adults 16–34	ABC1 adults
National ITV	6.99	10.87	29.57	18.96
National satellite	4.33	6.05	10.68	9.94
London	11.94	19.06	47.81	26.99
Central	7.30	11.45	30.19	19.22
North	4.85	7.34	20.27	15.00
STV	5.13	7.92	21.28	14.63
HTV	5.44	8.72	26.04	14.49

SOURCE: *The Marketing Pocket Book*, 2003

come cheap. A famous name might add a further £100 000–£200 000, and a music track – especially if it is in the charts – could cost the same again!

Programme sponsorship

Programme sponsorship on commercial television has gained in significance representing, as it does, a new way of communicating with the viewers and providing a context for the brand.

Byles and Walford (1991) suggest that the difference between conventional advertising and sponsorship is how they work rather than what they set out to do, and afterwards achieve. Advertising works in a more direct way: creating its own values and context for the product and stimulating the desired consumer response from the way that they perceive the brand. Sponsorship, by contrast, works in an indirect way, by association. It borrows the values of the sponsored event or programme, making them part of the nature of the brand in the minds of the viewer. The creativity in advertising comes in defining the nature of the brand in the minds of the viewer. The creativity in sponsorship comes in determining the nature of the fit between the required brand personality and the donated associations.

Estimates from the media company Carat show total UK sponsorship expenditures rose by 4 per cent to £828 million in 2003, with television accounting from £105 million. A prime reason given for the sponsorship of a TV show is to cut through the clutter of an average commercial break. Ads and the growing number of broadcaster promotions can run to anywhere between 7 and 15 messages a break. A major factor has been the relaxation of the ITC governing sponsorship some three years ago. Sponsoring a TV show is widely seen as an effective way of driving brand awareness and reinforcing (or even changing) consumer perceptions of a brand. It can maximise the impact of existing advertising by increasing brand presence. In some cases, it can be used to drive sales. It can shore up distribution when the broadcast sponsorship is extended at the point of sale. According to Jim Peters, head of sponsorship at Carat, 'television sponsorship fundamentally shifts brand perceptions in a way that conventional TV advertising doesn't.'

The key is to identify a TV programme with the correct fit to the brand and then to develop the association over time. According to Nick Walford, Managing Director of Performance, 'the most effective sponsorships are long-term, such as Ford's 12 year 'Destination Football' association with the Premier League on Sky and the Champions League on ITV.'

Some examples of recent sponsorship deals serve to illustrate the way in which brand owners are seeking to achieve additional exposure for their brands.

- £10m Heinz Tomato Ketchup and Salad Cream sponsorship of ITV's *Emmerdale.*
- £10m Cadbury Trebor Bassett sponsorship of *Coronation Street* for a further two years from 2004.
- The *Daily Telegraph* is spending £4.5 million to sponsor ITV's coverage of the Formula One season. It replaces Toyota which had been the sponsor for the past two seasons. The deal gives the paper credits throughout the 18-race race series. It includes live coverage on ITV1, highlights on ITV2, competitions and sponsorship of the ITV-linked website, which is claimed to attract 82 million visitors each year. The paper is supporting its sponsorship with an F1 fantasy game and F1 supplements. In turn, they have been replaced by LG.
- £4m Talk Talk link-up with the fifth series of Channel 4's *Big Brother.*
- £2m for the Halifax to back ten of Channel 5's property shows, including *Britain's Worst Home* and *Hot Property.*
- £1.5m for Schwartzkopf to sponsor the repeats of all six series of Channel 4's *Sex and the City.*
- £1.5m Cif links to the third series of Channel 4's *How Clean is Your House?* and is backing the deal with £1.5m of marketing activity.
- Britvic soft drink J_2O is investing £1.5 million to sponsor the ITV *Frank Skinner Show.* The tie-in extended the brand's association with other comedy themes such as the Jongleurs comedy club and the London Comedy Festival.
- Nivea signed a £1.7m deal with BskyB to sponsor *24.* The package includes promotions across all Sky's channels, 15-second credits at the start and end of the hour and five six-second break bumpers in the three ad breaks of each programme.
- Ikea is running advertising-funded programming on UKTV. The short programmes *What You Wish For* offer viewers advice on how to transform their home. To adhere to regulations preventing the placement of the advertiser's products in the programming, the interior furnishings will be in the form of animations. The series of 10 two-minute shows will air on UKTV Style and UKTV Bright Ideas.

A key factor for conventional advertising as well as programme sponsorship is not just the size of the audience but its composition. Inevitably, almost any advertiser using television as a medium will have to accept a degree of wastage – that is, viewers who are not interested in his particular message. The task, therefore, is to identify the programmes that are most closely targeted to the desired viewing audience. The consequence is that an advertiser may accept a smaller audience on, say, Channel 4 or for one of the satellite stations, because the viewership is more in line with the profile of the brand. The use of viewing data from such sources as BARB (British Audience Research Bureau) will enable the refinement of the television schedule to ensure that, as far as possible, the viewing audience corresponds with the brand's target group.

The share of total viewing figures (based on BARB for 2002) reveals the following breakdown of all adults (15+) viewing:

BBC1	26.1%
BBC2	11.2%
ITV	24.2%
Channel 4/S4C	10.4%
Channel 5	6.5%
Others	21.7%

The popularity of specific television programmes and their impact on viewing levels was seen with the recent screening of the final episode of *Friends* and the return of *Big Brother*. The former attracted an average audience of 8.6m with an audience share of 36 per cent. Among all 16–34 year adults, the programme had a 62.7 per cent share. *Big Brother* had an average of 6.7m with an audience share of 37.4 per cent.

A study by Bauer and Greyser, reported in LaBarbera et al. (1998) revealed great inconsistencies between the number of commercials watched and the level to which they were seen and interpreted. They suggest that the average adult is exposed to around 46 commercials each day. However, far fewer were actually watched and interpreted – the consequence of selective attention and perceptual defence.

Press

The print media can be subdivided into a number of separate areas for the purposes of media planning. There are a series of national daily and Sunday newspapers which appeal to different social groups, enabling the advertiser to reach significant segments of the population who, at least, can be segmented on socio-economic grounds.

To these can be added a variety of regional titles, which offer coverage on a geographic basis (although their stature is somewhat less). Further there is a wide range of over 3000 media titles which enable the targeting of 'special interest' groups. Whether they are interested in football, fishing, car maintenance or antiques collecting, there will be a number of titles specifically targeted towards the group.

As noted earlier, print media offers the ability to develop a long copy message to the target audience, and similarly sophisticated research tools such as the NRS (National Readership Survey) and TGI (Target Group Index) will enable a profiling exercise to be undertaken.

In 2003 the *Guardian* saw a 9 per cent year-on-year decline in its sales following its decision to launch a compact edition, according to ABC figures. The *Independent* has seen sales increase by 16 per cent over the same period, with its compact edition contributing 140 000 sales. Sales of the compact edition of *The Times* exceeded 200 000 in 2003 (see Table 11.4).

Radio

Since the 1990s British radio has seen a rapid growth in the number of stations available to the consumer. The launch of digital services, satellite, cable and terrestrial platforms increase both the supply and penetration of new radio stations. In 1993 the consumer could access around 10 different stations. In 2003 that number averaged 14 across the UK, whilst those living in London had over 25 stations from which to choose.

Table 11.4 National newspaper circulation trends (selected titles)

Title	2000 (000s)	2001 (000s)	% Change
Sun	3 388	3 284	−3.1
Daily Mirror	2 085	2 018	−3.2
Daily Mail	2 333	2 367	+1.5
All popular dailies	9 912	9 768	−1.5
Daily Telegraph	989	977	−1.2
The Times	676	662	−2.1
Guardian	357	364	+2.0
Independent	201	196	−2.5
Financial Times	180	169	−6.1
All quality dailies	2 403	2 368	−1.5
News of the World	3 776	3 758	−0.5
Sunday People	1 380	1 264	−7.1
Sunday Mirror	1 777	1 708	−3.9
All popular Sundays	10 062	9 843	−2.2
Sunday Times	1 224	1 236	+1.0
Sunday Telegraph	778	769	−1.2
Observer	398	417	+4.8
All quality Sundays	2 611	2 616	+0.2

SOURCE: *National Readership Survey* 2003

The latest audience figures for radio and TV published by Radio Joint Audience Research (RAJAR) and The Broadcast Audio Research Board (BARB), respectively, indicate that, for the first time, radio listening overtook television as the most often used form of media.

The medium enables close targeting of specific audiences. Kiss FM, for example, which targets young adults, features advertising for clubs and new record releases; Classic FM, with a totally different audience profile, has ads for supermarkets, finance and household products. When music releases are advertised on Classic FM they are for a totally different genre. Commercial radio, often regarded as a support medium only, is increasingly gaining credibility in its own right. In, fact, more people listen to a commercial radio station than to the BBC, as Table 11.5 shows.

As we have seen, for the most part, consumers cannot recall the source of the advertising message. Indeed, there is considerable evidence that some radio advertising will be recalled as having been seen on television! Radio may provide the means of achieving comparatively low-cost coverage of an identified target audience since, not only are the rates for using the medium relatively low, but so too are the associated production costs. With four national radio stations and over 180 local radio stations in the UK, the ability to target specific audiences is improving rapidly. The diversity of programming (from jazz through classical; from rock to pop; and a variety of speech-only programmes) listeners can be targeted on a variety of interest dimensions, both nationally and regionally.

Table 11.5 Radio stations ranked by shared of listening

	Share of listening (%) Sept. 2003	Share of listening (%) Sept. 2002	Change %
All commercial	46.2	45.3	0.9
All BBC	40.9	41.4	−0.5
Heart	7.2	6.3	0.9
Capital FM	7.0	8.8	−1.8
Magic	5.0	4.0	1.0
Classic FM	4.5	4.5	0.0
Kiss 100	4.1	4.8	−0.8
Xfm	2.1	2.1	0.0
Jazz FM	2.0	1.9	0.1
talkSPORT	1.5	1.7	−0.2
Virgin	1.2	1.1	0.1

SOURCE: RAJAR

The allocation of frequencies to new radio stations will extend the opportunities for listener segmentation even further, once they are all on air. Historically, audiences for radio are young, downmarket and mostly male. It offers very good regional coverage, although the reach of media is less, and markedly so, compared to TV, newspapers and posters. As with television, radio is purchased on the basis of time-length. A 30-second commercial on Capital Radio (London) would cost around £1800 against a similar spot on Isle of Wight Radio at only £22.

The Radio Advertising Bureau's case study database (available at www.rab.co.uk) provides comprehensive evidence of the effectiveness of radio advertising. There are also examples of radio playing a strategic role, either on its own or in combination with other media channels.

As with television, a new dimension in radio advertising is the sponsorship of programmes. From its outset, the commercial radio stations have recognised an important new revenue opportunity, and one that potentially allows the sponsor to achieve a greater level of affinity with the target audience.

Kellogg's Corn Flakes have extended sponsorship of the Capital FM and Century Networks breakfast shows featuring Johnny Vaughan in a deal reported to be worth £8m. Kellogg's claim that research has shown that listeners have a more positive attitude towards the brand, with 74 per cent agreeing that 'the best way to wake up in the morning is with Kellogg's'. Unilever has agreed a deal to become the exclusive FMCG advertising partner of EMAP music station The Hits. A 12-month tie-up valued at £600 000 covers the promotion of a number of Unilever's youth-oriented brands. It follows a similar agreement between Burger King and the station for exclusivity in the fast food category. The Irish bookmaker Paddy Power is to sponsor the drive time show on talkSPORT. The company is using its sponsorship to build its profile among sports fans.

Whilst these are comparatively long-term relationships between manufacturers and programmes, there is an increasing trend towards short-term sponsorship.

Several of the radio stations offer daily or weekly opportunities for companies to promote their products and services through sponsorship of an 'event', such as a prize giveaway or phone-in competition, and thereby to augment their conventional use of the medium.

Radio listeners are far less promiscuous than TV viewers. In the UK as a whole, according to figures from RAJAR, some 35 per cent listen to a single radio station each week, with a further 29 per cent listening to only two stations. Despite the availability of increased choice, and the proliferation of radio stations, loyalty tends to be significantly higher than in many other media areas. This, of course, has significance for the production of radio commercials. The average radio listener is much more likely to be exposed to a radio campaign than the average TV viewer. More importantly, frequent repetition, a consequence of the relative cheapness of the medium, can eventually 'turn off' even the most avid listener. Today, comparatively few advertisers have got the message that it is important to create a pool of commercials when advertising on radio in order to keep the campaign fresh and interest alive. Given the low costs of radio commercial production this is not expensive to achieve.

Cinema

Over recent years there has been a resurgence in the levels of cinema attendance, a trend which has been experienced worldwide. In the UK current attendances exceed 140 million on an annual basis.

Some regard the medium as an ideal scenario for the communication of brand messages. Commercials projected onto a 40-foot screen in front of a captive audience, with the benefit of stereo sound. Ewing et al. (2001) argue that recent developments have impacted positively on the medium. With television advertising increasingly coming under scrutiny, the cinema provides an ideal complement in many advertising campaigns.

It offers the advertiser a high level of impact with, in general, the absence of the media and environmental clutter associated with alternative media channels. For the most part, there are few distractions for the audience, who are unable to do much else but look at the screen.

Cinema is continuing to attract substantial audiences, with a profile that is significantly younger than for other mainstream media. Since there is an associated decline in television viewing figures amongst the young, cinema has an important role in reaching this audience. The nature of the cinema audience can be seen from Table 11.6.

Table 11.6 Average cinema audience by sex and age

	Average audience	% of UK population
Males	48	49
Females	52	51
15–24	37	15
25–34	24	19
35+	39	66

SOURCE: Cinema Advertising Association/Gallup

Table 11.7 UK cinema admissions, 1984–2000	
Year	**Audience numbers (million)**
1984	54
1990	89
1996	123
1997	130
1998	163
2000	180
SOURCE: Cinema Advertising Association/Gallup	

After the commencement of commercial television, cinema admissions experienced a significant decline, but that situation has now been reversed, as Table 11.7 shows.

Cinema is normally purchased on a screen-by-screen basis. This enables very tightly focused advertising campaigns down to the smallest geographic regions. Additionally, it can be bought by town, TV area, nationally, by film title and by guaranteed audience. An average campaign, providing national coverage, would cost around £30,000 per week. The latest research into the medium reinforces the view that cinema advertising is the most impactful medium amongst those who go.

However, it is important to remember that production costs will make the investment in cinema considerably higher. Not only are the costs involved in producing a cinema commercial as high as those for television, each screen on which the commercial is to be shown requires its own copy.

As in the UK, there has been a worldwide surge in cinema advertising expenditure. Proponents of the medium argue that among cinema's many virtues is its ability to reinforce and complement other media. In 2001, Ewing et al. conducted a study of commercials launched simultaneously on television and in cinema. Their findings confirm that, assuming a set budget constraint, recall scores for commercials shown concurrently in both media are significantly higher than for those launched only on television. Moreover, young adults, a group often considered by advertisers to be evasive and difficult to target via traditional media, can be effectively reached through cinema advertising. Cinema's appeal is not restricted to the youth market, however. It is an underrated and under-utilised medium through which to target older consumers.

It is generally accepted that cinema is a high-impact medium due to the largely captive and attentive audience, compounded by the size of the visual stimulus and the quality of the sound. Add to this, potentially low media and environmental clutter and distractions, as well as the audiences' inability to do anything other than look at the screen (i.e. no 'zipping' or 'zapping').

Posters

Outdoor media are available in a variety of different forms and sizes. Poster sites are available most often in 96-, 48-, 32- and 16-sheet sizes. The medium also encompasses a range of options from taxi cab sides to supermarket trolleys.

Posters and other outdoor media provide the opportunity of reminder advertising. They can be used to reinforce an aspect of the campaign which is developed elsewhere (on television, on radio or in the press) yet enable a tight focus on the brand identity with the featuring of the pack, logo and similar devices. A great advantage of the medium is the fact that sites can be purchased close to the point of purchase, underpinning the brand message close to the moment of purchase. A national campaign of around 1000 48-sheet sites would cost around £300 000 for a month's duration.

The Economist magazine developed its brand message using posters. They delivered visibility on a limited budget, provided a distinctive message for the brand, enabled targeting, provided size and stature and offered a vehicle that enhanced creative clarity and simplicity.

A comparison of media advantages and disadvantages

Table 11.8 summarises the advantages and disadvantages of the different media for advertisers.

Table 11.8 Media advantages and disadvatages

Media	Advantages	Disadvantages
Television	Mass coverage High reach Impact of sight sound and motion High prestige Low cost per exposure Attention getting Favourable impact on image	Low selectivity Short message life High absolute cost High production costs Clutter VCRs Disappearing in commercial break
Radio	Local coverage Low cost High frequency Flexible Low production costs Well-segmented audiences	Audio only Clutter Low attention getting Fleeting messages
Magazines	Segmentation potential Quality reproduction High informational content Longevity Multiple readership	Long lead times Visual only Lack of flexibility
Newspapers	High coverage Low cost per reader Short lead times Ads can be placed in interest sections Timely (currency of advertising) message Reader controls exposure Can be used for coupons	Short life Clutter Low attention getting capabilities Poor reproduction Selective read exposure Limited colour availability
Cinema	Very young audience profile Impact of sound and motion Attractive media environment High attention value Can be tightly focused	High production costs Comparatively long lead times
Outdoor	Location specific High repetition Easily noticed	High cost per contact Poor image Clutter

The new media

The scope of media availability is enormous. The latest area to which attention is being given is that know as 'ambient media'. Croft (1998) defines ambient media as advertising which fits in with the environment. This area encompasses non-traditional areas, such as supermarket trolleys and floor mats, take-away box lids or lamp-post posters. The most common and well-established version of ambient media is taxi cab sides. It is estimated that around 62 per cent of all London taxis now carry an advertising message. Petrol stations offer other opportunities to communicate with the consumer, through petrol pump nozzles.

A new form of ambient media has presented a major opportunity for advertisers. The device uses technology that allows the real-time placement of advertising messages on posters surrounding sporting events. With the increasing complexity of international regulations governing what product categories are allowed to advertise in which countries, the technology may well overcome these difficulties for internationally screened events. Formula 1, for example, is screened worldwide, although certain countries preclude the use of cigarette advertising. The technology will allow for the reinstatement of the brand message only in those countries where such advertising is permitted. It will also enable local advertisers to participate on a national level in events that receive international coverage and where the fees of involvement would otherwise preclude them.

The wide range of ambient media can be seen in Table 11.9.

Table 11.9 The range of ambient media

Ambient media

Retail	shopping centres car parks petrol stations supermarkets post offices fast food outlets	trolley advertising ticket advertising take-away lids postcard racks floor advertising carrier bags
Leisure	cinemas sports stadiums pubs, clubs and restaurants fitness clubs music venues	postcard racks toilet wall advertising beer mats washroom floor advertising
Travel	underground, train and buses/ coaches bus stops petrol and service stations, airports etc.	posters on lorries, coaches and buses petrol pump nozzles, stair riser advertising car park barriers ticket advertising
Other	aerial and mobile media schools, colleges, universities and libraries	sponsored balloons, sky writing posters video screens, payroll advertising bookmarks, litter bins
Community	playgrounds emergency services	sponsorship opportunities
Corporate	company and council buildings	payroll advertising

SOURCE: Shankar and Horton 1999

Once regarded as no more than a 'quirky offshoot' of outdoor advertising, ambient has become a thriving sector in its own right. Research suggests that it is growing faster than any other media sector. According to Concorde, the outdoor media specialist company, ambient media accounted for more than £84 million spend in the year 2000. However, it is difficult to be precise about the real level of expenditure due to the diversity of executions. This increase testifies to the expanding confidence of advertisers in ambient media, as growing numbers recognise its unique ability to target consumers 'when their defences are down'.

Barnes (1999) suggests that the most effective ambient media campaigns are simply placing old ads in new places. In the search for opportunities to avoid the familiar and to create interest, ads have been placed on increasingly obscure surfaces, such as the back of buses, on taxis, airships, petrol pump nozzles and a variety of places in toilets, euphemistically referred to as 'washroom media'.

Ambient media tends to be placed in locations where it can intrude on the individual's consciousness. They provides an innovative way of reaching a defined target audience when consumers are not expecting it, which gives a lot more impact. Some examples provide illustrations of the ways in which ambient media is being used to communicate to specific audiences:

- **DETR** (Department of the Environment, Transport and the Regions) used a series of thermo-dynamic stickers fixed to urinals. In their normal state, the reflect the campaign theme 'Don't Drink and Drive'. However, when urinated on the letters 'r' and 'e' disappear to refine the statement and reinforce the consequences – 'don't drink and die'.

- **Tesco** is installing 40 to 50 screens in each store to capitalise on the opportunities of promoting purchase at the point of sale. The opportunity provided is to target consumers during the last few seconds prior to making a purchase. Initial trials have proved successful with various brands experiencing significant increases in sales volume. Weetabix saw a 10 per cent rise in volume, Guinness 23 per cent and Unilever's 'I can't believe it's not butter' saw a volume uplift of 43 per cent.

- **British Airways** has struck a deal with Nationwide building society to advertising on its cash machines across the UK. When using an ATM users will see a BA video sequence. Advertising will appear during pauses in transactions and will be presented with a reminder featuring BA's logo and web address.

- **Mates**, the second-biggest-selling condom brand in the UK, is targeting women with its latest range and is supporting the launch with a guerrilla campaign which asks women to name their ultimate pleasure. The brand will place postcards in bars across the UK to encourage women to vote by text or by visiting a website. The competition will end with one woman winning her ultimate fantasy. The brand is also to become headline sponsor of 'Formula Woman', a reality TV series about the first ever all-female motor racing championship.

- **Fuller's London Pride** has signed up 200 black-cab drivers as brand ambassadors. They have been briefed to engage passengers in sports chat and to sprinkle the conversation with mentions of the brand and its association with sport. Black cabs will be branded with London Pride ads. The campaign will be supported with press ads in the sports pages of national newspapers as well as the London edition of *Metro* and in the *Evening Standard*. Radio activity will focus on the sports bulletins of Capital Radio, talkSPORT, Virgin, Capital Gold and LBC.

The growth of ambient media is underpinned by the role it can play as part of a fully integrated marketing communications campaign. Certain ambient media offer the opportunity to communicate with potential customers close to and up to the point of purchase, as the above examples illustrate. They also offer the opportunity to enhance the brand image. Since most supermarket purchases are unplanned, ambient media represents the opportunity to supplement existing brand knowledge and influence the purchasing decision.

The importance of media strategy

In many respects, media strategy is as important to the achievement of the overall objectives as the creative approach. However powerful the advertising message, it will be ineffective if it fails to achieve exposure amongst the appropriate target audience. The development of an appropriate media plan commences with a statement of media objectives. But first a definition: media objectives are the translation of marketing and advertising objectives and strategies into goals that can be achieved by media. The media strategy is the translation of those objectives into general guidelines that will control the planner and the use of media. Media strategy is the use of finely tuned approaches that add to brand value, provide presence and get the brand noticed and talked about.

It should be noted that media objectives are different from communications objectives. They define the exact role media has in terms of delivering the brand objectives. The setting of media objectives in a careful and precise way is essential to the success of the media component of the advertising campaign.

These need to cover the following points:

- What target audience should be reached by the media?
- What is the message the advertising wishes to convey?
- To what geographic market(s) should the message be directed?
- How far into the target audience can the advertising reach, given budgetary constraints?
- With what frequency should the message reach the target audience during the campaign period?
- At what times should the message reach the target audience? This needs to address day, time and seasonality issues.
- What type of media provides the best match between the intended market and the actual audience?

Strategic options

Media mix strategies can take a variety of different forms, although they can be broadly identified as two variations. Media mix strategies may be concentrated or assorted.

A concentrated media mix is one in which the budget is concentrated, typically, within a single media type (or at most a very limited number of media vehicles). It offers a variety of benefits. By concentrating the media effort in a limited area, there is a strong chance of dominating that medium compared to competitors. The result is that the advertising expenditure is likely to have greater impact on those consumers exposed to that medium. By limiting the range of media, retailers (especially if directed) will be more aware of the media effort. This will potentially enhance their preparedness to support the campaign. Similarly, by concentrating expenditure into a single or comparatively few media areas, there will often be a negotiating advantage. Remember that media are in competition with each other and will be more likely to offer attractive prices if they feel that they can secure the bulk, or all, of your expenditure in the process. And, by restricting the number of media outlets, there may be considerable savings in terms of production costs.

An assorted mix is one that uses several media types. This is particularly likely if the target audience is subdivided into several discrete groups which can only be reached by the use of separate media channels. Here again, there is a number of advantages to be considered. An assortment of media types enables the delivery of different messages to different target groups. It is an inevitable consequence of the increasing number of media channels. The assortment of media environments may provide a range of opportunities that can be exploited within the media and creative strategies. For example, a medium may be used to create impact, drama, movement, etc. (TV) whilst another may be used to deliver a longer copy message (press). Using an assortment of media channels often provides a means of increasing coverage of the selected target groups (although this is mostly achieved at the cost of frequency).

The proliferation of new media adds complexity to the media landscape. The growing number of media will result in more selective media behaviour, because the attention of the media user is limited by both time and money. In this context, Franz (2000) argues, the strategic planning of the media mix is becoming more crucial for effective communication with the target consumer.

Sissors and Bumba (1993) have identified a series of specific questions to be considered in the setting of media objectives and strategies. See Table 11.10.

Each of the available media will need to be considered in the light of these considerations. The process consists of two separate stages. Initially, the planner must determine which class of media best fulfils the criteria. This involves a comparison and the selection of the broad media classes, for example, television, radio or press, etc., or some combination of these. Table 11.11 shows some of the important variables that will need to be examined.

Only when this category analysis has been completed can the planner move on to select the specific media within classes. This involves a comparison and evaluation of the best media within the chosen category in order to differentiate, using a series of pre-determined criteria, which is the best newspaper, television or radio station and so on.

The media plan

The planning process is, essentially, a cyclical one. It consists of following a series of distinct stages, although in some instances these may overlap and, indeed, the identification of new information will require the return to previous stages to consider whether changes should be made.

Iain Jacob (1997) depicts a model for the generation of a media plan, shown in Figure 11.4.

As can be seen from Figure 11.4, the development of a media plan is a complicated task. It involves several different stages and the use of research data to ensure that the plan is properly constructed, cost-effective and capable of delivering the

Table 11.10 Setting media objectives and strategies: what to ask

Media objectives	Media strategies
What actions should we take as a result of media used by competitors?	Should we use the same media mix as competitors? Should we allocate the same weight as competitors? Should we ignore competitors?
What actions should we take as a result of our brand's creative strategies?	Which media/vehicles are best suited? Any special treatments? Which dayparts?
Who should be our primary and secondary targets?	Which product usage patterns should we consider? Heavy/medium/light users? What distribution of strategic impressions? Which dayparts?
What balance of reach to frequency is required?	What levels of reach and frequency? What levels of effective reach/frequency?
Do we need national and/or local media?	What proportion should go into national media? What proportion into local media?
What patterns of geographic weighting should we use?	Should we weight by spend or ratings points? Where should we place weights? When should we weight (weeks/months)? What weight levels for each market?
What kind of scheduling pattern suits our plans? Continuity/flighting/pulsing?	Should we use one or the other? When should we weight more heavily?
Does media have to support promotions? How?	What proportion of the budget should be use? What media mix?
Is media testing needed? How should it be used?	How many and which markets?
Is budget large enough to accomplish objectives?	Do we need to set priorities? Which must we achieve? Which are optional? Do we need more money than is available?

SOURCE: Sissors and Bumba 1993

desired impact on the chosen target audience. Moreover, it is a task that cannot be carried out in isolation from the other parts of the advertising planning process.

But there are a series of additional factors that the planner will need to take into consideration. Some of these will be objective and based on available data analyses; others will be more subjective, such as a consideration of the media environment. Factors here might include an understanding of the differing patterns of readership or viewership. The point was made earlier that the planner seeks to minimise the wastage involved in the purchase of any media outlet. Inevitably, the broader the appeal of a media channel, the greater the degree of potential wastage, resulting from the fact that members of the audience who will be exposed to the advertising will not be an appropriate target for the message. By conducting an analysis of the viewers of particular television programmes, it is possible to determine the make-up of the audience to ensure that it is aligned as closely as possible with the desired target.

By examining The Target Group Index (TGI) data in Table 11.12, we can see a significant differences between the viewing patterns of *The Bill*, *Friends* and *Channel 4 News*, which affect their suitability for the advertising of particular products and services.

Table 11.11 How media outlets compare: category analysis

Considerations	Terrestrial television	Cable & satellite television	Newspapers
Audience coverage	High with considerable selectivity of audience profile	Moderate, but good profiling opportunities	Very tight focus on socio-economic groupings
Geographic availability	Available on national and regional basis	Stations received across Europe	National, regional and local availability
Attention and interest	Variable	Variable	Moderate
Intrusive nature of media	Potentially high	Potentially high	Moderate/low
Media environment	Good, potential for 'endorsement'	Good, potential for 'endorsement'	Good reference value
Ability to demonstrate product	Very good	Very good	Limited
Availability of colour	Yes	Yes	Sometimes available
Availability of sound	Yes	Yes	No
Creative flexibility	Very high	Very high	Good
Life span of message	Short	Short	Medium
Long copy availability	Limited	Limited	Good
Production costs	High	High	Medium
Production requirements	Lengthy	Lengthy	Short
Planning requirements	Reasonably flexible, minimum two months	Reasonably flexible, minimum two months	Moderate copy dates

The same principle will be applied to other media opportunities since, in turn, this will have an impact on the overall cost and cost-effectiveness of the campaign. But, as with other aspects of media planning, there is a trade off. In many instances, it is possible to reach a dedicated audience who, for example, read a relevant magazine or watch a targeted television programme. Unfortunately, it is also likely that the absolute size of these audiences will be significantly smaller than for more general media activity. Deciding how the message is transmitted is now seen as equally important as the content of the message itself.

Again, it is important to understand the specific nature of the media environment and the extent that the selected medium not only reaches the desired audience, but also serves to act as an endorsement of the message to them.

Table 11.11 How media outlets compare: category analysis (continued)

Magazines	Radio	Outdoor	Cinema
Can isolate interest specific groups	Moderate coverage, but high loyalty	Reasonable coverage but can be tightly focused	Low but selective
Mostly national, but some regional titles	National, regional and local availability	Can be purchased nationally or down to single location	National, regional and local availability
High	Moderate	Low	Highest of all
Moderate/low	Moderate	Low	Highest of all
High level of endorsement	Variable	Low	High
Limited	Poor	Poor	Very good
Mostly	None	Yes	Yes
No	Yes	No	Yes
Good	Good	Moderate	Very high
Long	Short	Short	Long
Good	Limited	No	Limited
Medium	Low	Medium	High
Lengthy	Short	Medium	Lengthy
Long copy dates, minimum three months	Very rapid availability	Moderate copy dates, minimum one month	Moderate, minimum two months

Media information sources

To guide the media planner in the determination of the appropriate media, there are a variety of dedicated information sources. Either in their original form, or when subjected to special analyses, these provide substantial information on viewership, listenership and readership of the various media outlets.

- BRAD – British Rate and Data provides comprehensive details of the rate card costs for all media outlets. Updated monthly, it provides necessary production information and copy dates.
- ACNielsen MEAL – provides a summary of mainstream media expenditures which can be analysed by product category down to brand level. Although based on rate card costs, it provides comparative guidance as to the expenditure patterns of competing products by month and with annual moving totals. There is now a successful rival providing a similar service called MMS.

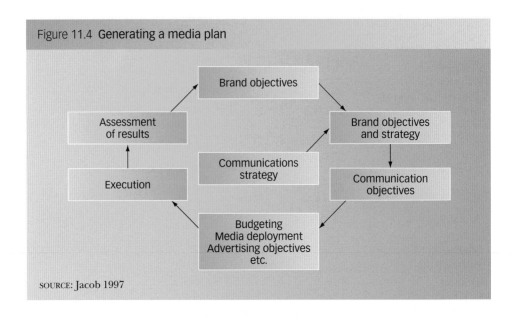

Figure 11.4 Generating a media plan

Brand objectives

Assessment of results

Brand objectives and strategy

Communications strategy

Execution

Communication objectives

Budgeting
Media deployment
Advertising objectives
etc.

SOURCE: Jacob 1997

Table 11.12 Viewing profiles of selected TV programmes, 2003

	The Bill		Friends		Channel 4 News	
	Audience size (000's)	Index	Audience size (000's)	Index	Audience size (000's)	Index
Men	7541	95.0	3032	93.2	2487	122.1
Women	8806	104.7	3664	106.4	1706	79.1
15–24	2325	93.1	2938	287.0	280	43.7
25–34	3044	94.8	2027	154.2	522	63.4
35–44	2390	85.3	848	82.7	620	86.3
45–54	2389	90.8	443	41.1	727	107.7
55–64	2134	107.3	180	22.1	758	148.5
65+	4065	126.4	159	12.1	1285	155.8
ABC1	6937	86.6	3703	112.9	2418	117.7
C1C2	8064	98.1	3583	106.5	1941	92.1
C2DE	9410	112.9	2992	87.6	1774	83.0

SOURCE: TGI

- ABC – The Audit Bureau of Circulation is the source of circulation data regarding newspapers and magazines. It is important to note that readership of publications is usually significantly higher than levels of circulation.
- ABCE – ABCE is the source of data relating to websites.
- NRS – National Readership Survey provides comparative data on readership (AIR). Currently provides information on reading frequency, average issue readership. This latter is important in that it provides an indication of the number of people who claim to have read or looked at a given publication within a specific period of time. This AIR is currently provided from some 244 publications and is subdivided by age, sex, socio-economic group and geographic region. Readerships

are also shown by weight of TV viewing, education, holiday taking, employment and occupational status, shopping expenditure, major expectations, car and home ownership.

- JICREG – The Joint Industry Committee for Regional Press Research provides information relating to regional media with information of average issue readership, cumulative readership and readership duplication.
- CAVIAR – The Cinema and Video Industry Audience Research provides audience data based on age, frequency of cinema going, social grade and sex.
- OSCAR was the comparable data source for the outdoor industry. Now replaced by POSTAR II to provide more relevant and reliable information. Measuring people who actually see a poster (rather than those in an arbitrary catchment area) will provide information on coverage and frequency on a site by site basis.
- AIRC – the Association of Independent Radio Contractors provides regular data and other information on listenership. Important information sourced by RAJAR – Radio Joint Audience Research – provides comparative data for commercial and non-commercial stations, both local and national. A representative sample of the total population is interviewed on a regular basis.
- BARB – The Broadcast Audience Research Board is the provider of research data evaluating television audiences, based on the viewing patterns of almost 4500 households across the UK. BARB provides valuable quantitative information, including the profiles of viewers of specific programmes, TV ratings, coverage build-up and frequency of viewing.
- TGI – The Target Group Index is the source of detailed media analysis enabling an examination of the audience composition by socio-economic and geographic dimensions.

Identifying target audiences

A critical phase of the media planning process will be the identification of the appropriate audience or audiences for the intended message. We have already seen that this is equally important in terms of defining the overall marketing communications objectives. We have already considered the various methods by which target audiences can be identified (Chapter 6) so we will not restate the process here. Suffice it to say that the media planner will use a variety of approaches utilising demographic, geo-demographic, psychographic, lifestyle and product usage information to ensure that the various audiences can be identified properly. Whilst each of these variables, dependent upon the source of the information, may be used individually, it is more likely that they will be used in various combinations, again depending on availability of information within the particular market or sector.

The media planner must identify all media categories that are relevant for integrated approaches. The primary objective is the collection of data measuring affinity to media categories. The data can be used to reconstruct the composition of the individual set of media choices within the specific segment of target consumers. The defined target segment is then checked for its media consumption and its behavioural patterns. This provides the planner with an insight into the primary and secondary channels, which can be effectively used for communication with the target consumers.

Franz (2000) states that the overall objective is to find the perfect mix of communication media. At same time it contributes to the appropriate design of the content and the tonality of the commercial message. The strategic decision is the key to maximum advertising effectiveness.

Media scheduling issues

Media planning essentially revolves around the need to balance two key issues: coverage and frequency. However large the advertising budget, there will never be enough money to maximise both elements, and the planner must determine the balance between the two.

Inevitably, some form of trade-off will have to be made between a campaign which achieves the maximum level of coverage but provides few opportunities for the target audience to see or hear the advertising message and one which narrows the coverage to enable a greater frequency of exposure.

Coverage or reach is the measurement of that percentage of a given target audience who might be exposed to an advertisers' message in a given period through the use of a particular medium. Conventionally, coverage is not concerned with the number of times each individual sees the message, only with the total number of individuals who may see it. As we have seen, specific tools are available to provide the media planner with information in this area.

Frequency is specifically concerned with the number of times that people within the defined target group might be exposed to the message during a given time period. An important consideration here is the word *might*. Effective frequency generally refers to the average number of vehicle exposures (often called opportunities to see or OTS) required to effectively expose the average audience member to an advertising message.

Effective reach and frequency refers to the concept of using these measures in media planning. This is generally done by seeking to maximise effective reach within a particular budget constraint, subject, of course, to other media planning and buying factors. Although reach and frequency measures can provide information on the potential that the medium can provide, they can offer no guarantees that any given individual will notice the advertising.

In order to establish both the budget and advertising goals, planners must estimate the relationship between advertising and advertising response, or what is commonly known as the advertising response curve.

There are a number of reasons why media planners are actively seeking ways of making their advertising more effective. The search proceeds on three levels. Firstly, advertisers are striving to maximise the advertising weight each campaign will deliver for a given expenditure. Secondly, advertising planners are continually trying to improve the calibre of their creative strategies and executions to ensure maximum effectiveness in any given advertising campaign. Thirdly, advertising practitioners are conducting both formal and informal research into the dimensions of advertising message delivery and, in particular, into the two interrelated dimensions of advertising frequency and advertising reach in the hope that these can, in some way, be related to advertising effectiveness.

Media planners can make an important contribution to effective advertising campaigns by ensuring that these campaigns achieve effective reach.

A paper by Murray and Jenkins (1992) sought to define the issues related to effective reach. Their general conclusions are as follows:

1 Three confirmed vehicle exposures to an individual or household in the target audience over a prescribed time period provide a realistic, pragmatic definition of 'effective reach' which can be used as an operational guideline by media practitioners.

2 As a general rule, a 'reach threshold' of 45 per cent of the target audience over an agreed-upon time period is an appropriate minimum level of effective reach. It appears to be closely related to subsequent marketplace success.

3 In television a one-week reach of 45 to 50 per cent, interestingly, is also likely to achieve a four-week effective reach of 45 to 50 per cent.

4 The minimum requirement for effective reach in outdoor media is twelve or more vehicle exposures per month.

5 The minimum requirement for effective reach for radio, television, and newspapers is three or more vehicle exposures per month.

6 The minimum requirement for effective reach in magazines is three or more vehicle exposures per quarter.

According to Leo Bogart (1995), however, it is the quality, the intensity and, above all, the meaning of an experience that counts, rather than its duration or the frequency with which it occurs. The notion of optimum frequency therefore rests on a number of mistaken assumptions. The combination of familiar and unfamiliar elements makes a sequence of exposures to different but related advertisements look more compelling than the same sequence of exposures to the identical ad.

Media context

Media context can be an important situational factor. De Pelsmacker et al. (2002) defined media context as the characteristics of the content of the medium in which an ad is inserted (e.g. articles in a magazine, commercials within a television programme), as they are perceived by the persons who are exposed to them. Media context is important. For example, some types of context may be more appropriate for certain types of advertising than for others. Media context also can make certain needs more salient and stimulate the motivation to pay attention to ads featuring context-congruent products, such as an ad for suitcases inserted into an article on travelling. Many advertisers whose products and services are designed to appeal to international travellers tend to utilise in-flight magazines as a primary medium. Similarly, the manufacturers of sports accessories will achieve more affinity with their target audiences by using a sports-related magazine or radio programme.

When we talk of the media, it is easy to forget that they are brands and, just like any other types of brands, they carry values, expectations and different levels of trust. The media are far more than passive showcases for advertising – brands do not appear in a vacuum. Research by Byfield (2002) shows that advertising effectiveness is conditioned by the context of the media/consumer relationships, and the best media buying and planning understands and exploits those relationships. Effective media placement goes far deeper than simply producing a map of where audiences are available – how we talk to them in the media is just as important, and concentration on this element of media selection will add effectiveness to the communications.

All of the available media channels offer different media contexts:

- TV – the 'broadcast at them' channel;
- Direct mail – the 'personally to you' channel;

- The internet – the 'visit and interact with us' channel;
- Events – the 'go out and interact with them' channel;
- Editorial environment – an ad that is consistent with editorial values will require less frequency.

A paper by Norris and Colman (1994) indicate that the effectiveness of advertising is influenced by the TV programmes in which those ads appear. They suggest that advertisers wishing to optimise attitudes towards their campaigns and to increase purchase intentions should choose programme contexts that are highly involving. However, those whose key objective is to maximise memory for the ad, product or brand should consider low-involvement programmes.

Kasumoto (2002) argues that a similarity in the sense of values between brand users and magazine readers is one of the most important factors in facilitating brand message absorption. The reason being that if the brand users' and the magazine readers' sense of values are similar, the readers will read the brand advertisements with a positive attitude, resulting in high probability brand message absorption. He illustrates his argument as follows: suppose a magazine most of whose readers are strongly interested in environmental issues carries one advertisement for electric cars and another for luxury sedans. In this case, even if both advertisements are placed in advertising spaces with the same advertising readership score, the electric car advertisement is likely to be read more carefully than the luxury sedan advertisement. If, on the other hand, the majority of the readers are luxury oriented, the result will be the opposite.

Dyson (1999) provides a comparison of media properties which illustrates the contribution of the various media channels to advertising effectiveness. See Table 11.13.

Table 11.13 Comparison of media properties

	TV	Outdoor	Print	Internet
Intrusiveness	High	High	Low	Low
Control/selectivity of consumption	Passive	Passive	Active, selective	Active, selective
Episode attention span	Long	Short	Long	Restless, fragmented
Active processing	Low	Low	High	High
Mood	Relaxed, seeking emotional gratification	Bored, understimulated	Relaxed, seeking interest, stimulation	Goal-orientated, needs-related
Modality	Audio/visual	Visual	Visual	Visual (auditory increasing)
Processing	Episodic, superficial	Episodic, semantic	Semantic, deep	Semantic, deep
Context	As individual in interpersonal setting	Solitary (in public space)	Individual, personal	Alone, private

SOURCE: Dyson 1999

Television gives more public status, authority and credibility to a message so it can be more impactful and persuasive, although persuasion tends to wear out with repetition. Radio has low impact and generates less awareness, but it can be targeted to specific audiences. It is also capable of delivering a more specific message (or brand claim) more effectively to people not actively interested in the category through repetition and passive assimilation which are characteristic of the listening format (Branthwaite and Wood 2000).

There are several other issues that the media planner must address, as discussed in the following sections.

The intrusive nature of the message

Some advertising is innately more 'visible' than other campaigns. All advertising has to compete for the attention of the consumer, not merely with other advertising messages, but also with the general 'noise' within the media environment. Most consumers read newspapers or magazines, watch television or listen to radio for the intrinsic benefits that the medium will provide. For an advertising message to communicate effectively, it must break through the surrounding noise in order to impact upon the consumer

If the reader of a newspaper or magazine article is involved with the subject-matter, they may well turn the page without noticing your advertisement. Similarly, the viewer of a television programme may well use the commercial break to leave the room for other purposes. They may well also take the opportunity to 'channel cruise' or, with the increasing penetration of video, to fast-forward the tape to continue watching the programme. In all these cases, the placement of the message will play a significant part in drawing the attention of the individual towards it. This may affect the design and content of the message as well as its position within the media.

The competitive environment

A further consideration will be the comparative level of competitive expenditure. At times when competitors are spending heavily, the weight of their activity may reduce the effective communication of your message. It may be preferable to seek to plan to advertise at times when competitive presence will be lower, in order to gain a greater awareness of your own campaign.

The nature of the message

Advertising which seeks to remind the consumer of knowledge it already possesses, demands a lower frequency of exposure than a campaign which seeks to create awareness in the first instance. Moreover, the more complicated the message which the advertiser wishes to communicate, the greater the number of times it will need to be exposed to the audience for the message to penetrate.

Message length

Some advertisers can build the effective frequency of their message by the utilisation of different time-lengths or space sizes. At the outset of a campaign, longer commercials or larger advertisements may be used to achieve the desired level of penetration through the surrounding clutter and noise. Subsequently, shorter time-lengths or space sizes may serve to assist the consumer in recalling the overall message, or to focus the attention of the consumer on a particular facet of the message.

The number of exposures

There is no consensus as to the 'correct' number of exposures that an advertising campaign should seek to achieve. Although various studies have been conducted in an attempt to ascertain the incremental value of consecutive exposures of an advertisement, the debate continues as to the desired level for any given campaign. Two differing views illustrate the argument.

There is considerable debate as to the level of advertising required to provide effective frequency. A central issue is the lack of a definition of what makes up effective frequency, i.e. the number of exposures to a particular piece of advertising required to elicit the desired response. Moreover, it is reasonable to assume that different responses, such as a change in attitude or a change in behaviour, might require different levels from, say a campaign designed to reinforce current attitudes or behaviour patterns.

One of the major influences on what makes up 'effective frequency' was a paper presented by Krugman (1972). He argued that a consumer requires only three exposures of any ad for the effect to be achieved. This has come to be the media planner's benchmark. His argument is that the first exposure generates a response of 'What is it'?; the second 'What of it?'; whilst the third and subsequent exposures serve as reminders of what has gone before. When Leckenby and Kim (1994) conducted a study amongst the 200 largest advertising agencies as to the basis of media planning, they overwhelmingly responded that they used 'three-plus exposures'.

In contrast, John Philip Jones (1995) argues that sales are generated by a single advertising exposure. His study claims to demonstrate that the extra sales effect of more advertisements becomes progressively smaller as the number of advertisements is increased. He concludes that it is therefore uneconomic to concentrate media into heavy bursts during the period before a consumer buys a brand, because of those diminishing returns. It is more sensible, he submits, to stretch the available funds by buying low frequency over a longer period. This ensures that there are fewer gaps in the brand's advertising schedule, avoiding the danger of the brand becoming vulnerable to competitive encroachment.

Whilst it is true that many papers have been published on the optimum level of advertising frequency, one issue which needs to be considered is the differential level of advertising recall by age. A paper by Dubow (1995) concludes that recall is differentiated by age of viewer. In his study teens (12–17) showed the highest level of recall, followed by young adults (18–34). Over 35s showed a somewhat lower level of brand recall than the other groups.

The impact of successive exposures of an advertisement is shown graphically in Figure 11.5. The authors suggest, as with Krugman, that effective exposure is achieved with the third exposure to the brand and that, thereafter, further advertising serves to reinforce the brand message.

It is important to remember that whilst each medium is capable of achieving significant impact on the target audience – dependent, of course, on the quality of the message – there will remain groups of consumers who will not be exposed to advertising within a single medium. As Wilkins (1997) states 'Some people, for example, who listen to radio or who read newspapers and magazines, may not be exposed to a campaign which is only on television. Inclusion of these media will inevitably increase the reach of the campaign.'

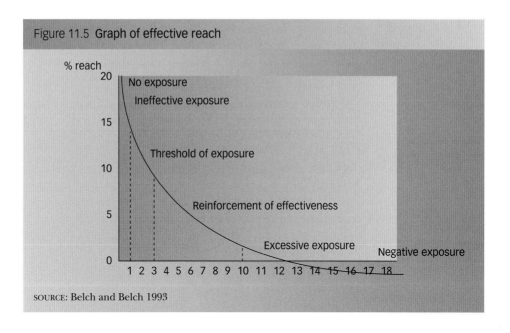

Figure 11.5 Graph of effective reach

SOURCE: Belch and Belch 1993

Wilkins illustrates this premise with a hypothetical campaign, based on three media – television, press and radio. See Figure 11.6.

Indeed, many media plans are developed using different media channels in order to reinforce the advertising message in different ways. For example, television might be selected to achieve initial impact and raise awareness of a brand proposition, whilst print media such as newspapers might be added to the schedule to provide more detailed copy and, therefore, an explanation of what the brand offers. Similarly, outdoor media might be used as a reminder of the brand proposition close to the point of purchase.

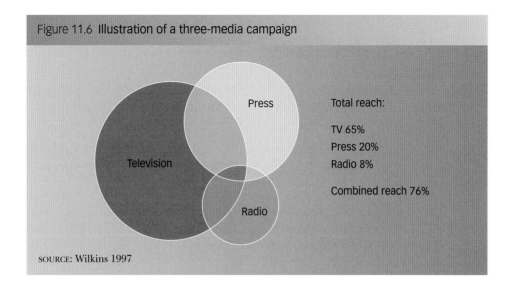

Figure 11.6 Illustration of a three-media campaign

SOURCE: Wilkins 1997

The status of the brand

Brands that have already established themselves within the marketplace will tend to attract more attention than those that are unknown. Accordingly, they can, as a general rule, operate at a lower level of frequency and concentrate more on the reach of their message.

Seasonality factors

In many market categories the volume of sales differs on a monthly basis either because of inherent trends with the sector or because of the brand's propensity to respond to, say, changes in weather conditions. Many products are given as gifts and thus sales peak around Christmas and other gift-giving occasions (Father's Day, Mother's Day, etc.); DIY products tend to experience a seasonal boost in the spring as the weather improves and people turn to home improvement activities; ice cream and soft drinks sales increase dramatically as the temperature rises. In each instance, the media planner will want to capitalise on the market opportunities that these changes represent.

Consumer dimensions

The strategic media planner, as with other areas of planning, need to understand the key aspects of consumer behaviour with the added dimension of media consumption. These will need to be examined in the context of:

- Current users: How many are there and what are they worth to us? What are their motivations to purchase? What do they think of the brand and of competitor brands?
- Competitive brand users: Do they have different motivations and what do they think of our brand?
- Loyalists: What is necessary to retain their loyalty? What might cause them to defect from the brand?
- Non-trialists: What are the reasons for their non-purchase?
- What are the opportunities for growth, within current consumption, from within the category and from current non-usage?

It will be necessary to consider the sources of future business, as illustrated in Table 11.14.

Table 11.14 Potential volume from current users

	Heavy users	**Medium users**	**Light users**
Potential volume	Not saturated but already higher volume	High already Irregular purchasers	High already Tried brand, potential for increased volume
Objective	Maintain 'new' purchasing habit	Prompt purchase on a more regular basis	Secure prime position on repertoire
Communication	Reminder	Encourage greater usage	Encourage usage through motivation
Priority	Medium	High	High

Purchasing patterns

Especially in the area of fast-moving consumer goods, there may be a propensity to purchase products on particular days of the week. Much shopping activity takes places at the weekend and planners may wish to concentrate adverting in the days immediately before to stimulate both awareness of the proposition and the consequent sales.

Advertising wearout

Two papers written in 1998 offer contradictory views on the issue of advertising wearout. On the one hand, Blair and Rabuck (1998) conclude that wearout follows a predictable path influenced by the initial persuasiveness of the advertising and the level of rating points placed behind the campaign. Conversely, Scott and Solomon (1998) conclude that there is no easily identified pattern of wearout. They argue that wearout is a complex phenomenon influenced by a number of interrelated factors and, hence, cannot be predicted.

Adams and Blair (1992) suggest that it is possible to calculate the wearout factor of advertising using an approach that they call 'ARS persuasion'. They argue that whilst both dimensions of persuasive advertising – advertising quality and advertising weight – are both important, it is the latter which is the more important. Moreover, they suggest that the persuasion power of an advertisement is a finite resource that gets used up progressively as the advertising continues to be exposed to the consumer.

Du Plessis (1995) concludes from a study conducted in South Africa that advertising awareness increases with commercial length, with the likeability of the ad and with greater frequency. However, there is no response curve that can be generalised to all commercials. He also states that there is no predictable relationship between impact rates and awareness or retention rates of commercials. Finally he confirms that the repetition of a commercial improves its retention rate in all cases.

Alternative approaches to media scheduling

In the vast majority of instances it is apparent that a single exposure of the advertising message will be insufficient to communicate effectively to the target audience, notwithstanding the comments of Jones (1995) cited above. The more often consumers are exposed to the message, the greater the likelihood that they will understand it. However, this inevitably results in a reduction in the potential for achieving a high level of coverage of the desired audience since the two facets of media planning work inversely. This can be seen graphically in Figure 11.7.

Although a great deal of work has been done to research the balancing of coverage and frequency, as we have seen, there are no definitive answers. Even today, much depends on the skills and experience of the media planner in assembling a media schedule that will achieve the objectives that have been set. However, there is a series of important factors which will affect the overall planning process and raise specific considerations regarding the necessary frequency of the advertising. These will involve a consideration of the marketing background, creative dimensions and the media environment.

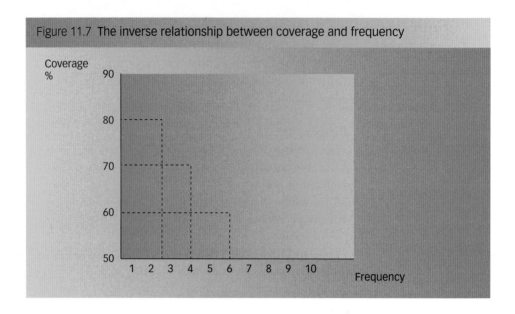

Figure 11.7 The inverse relationship between coverage and frequency

Marketing factors   The key marketing factors are listed below.

- Brand history: Is the brand new or well established? New brands require much higher frequency in order to achieve impact on the consumer, as indeed may a new message from an established brand.
- Brand share: The higher the brand share, the lower the frequency required.
- Brand loyalty: The higher the level of loyalty, the lower the level of frequency required.
- Purchase cycles: The shorter the purchase cycle, the higher the required frequency to maintain front of mind awareness.
- Usage cycle: Products used on a very regular basis will be used up and need to be replaced comparatively frequently. A high level of advertising frequency is desirable in order to maintain 'front-of-mind' awareness as in the case of, for example, soap powders.
- Competitive share of voice: Higher frequency is required when a high level of competitive noise exists and when the goal is to match or beat competitors. This may vary by season, e.g. the car market increases at those times of the year when new licence plates are issued.
- Target group: The nature of the target group in terms of their ability to learn and absorb messages has an effect on frequency levels.

Creative factors   The key creative factors are as follows:

- Message complexity: The simpler the message, the less frequency required.
- Message uniqueness: The more unique the message the less frequency required.
- New vs continuous campaigns: New campaigns require greater frequency to register the message.
- Image vs product sell: Creating image demands greater frequency.
- Message variation: Single messages require less frequency than multiple messages.

However, the trade off is that multiple messages may reinforce values of brand and maintain level of interest in overall proposition.

- Wearout: High frequency may lead to message wearout, as when the target consumer becomes bored with the advertising message and further insertions not merely cease to have an impact but can actually result in a diminution of interest in the brand. Tracking studies can be useful in identifying campaign wearout. The point was made earlier that, based on experience with radio, the audience tends to be more dedicated. Given the comparatively low costs of using the medium – both airtime and production – it is possible to achieve a comparatively higher level of frequency of exposure, even on a limited budget, and there is, therefore, a greater propensity for wearout.

Media factors The key media factors are as follows. The more complex ones are discussed separately below.

- Clutter.
- 'Zipping and zapping'.
- Attention.
- Scheduling: Continuous scheduling requires less frequency than flighting or pulsing.
- Number of media used: The lower the number of media used the lower the level of frequency required.
- Repeat exposures.
- Media environment.

Clutter: It is increasingly true that advertising must compete, within its media environment, for the attention of the viewer, reader or listener. Media outlets that carry a high volume of advertising may well diminish the likelihood of the consumer remembering a particular advertisement for a brand. In the context of television, there are additional considerations.

'Zipping and zapping': There is widespread recognition that one of the problems facing advertisers is the extent to which viewers switch channels or 'zap' commercials without actually viewing them. Modern technology enables television viewers to record programmes for subsequent viewing and enhance the likelihood that the commercials contained within will not be observed. There is little doubt that these practices often result in the viewer receiving only partial exposure to television commercials. Indeed, such is the concern that ITV announced in February 2004 that it is to shorten commercial breaks. Following a study commissioned by ITV it was found that the more commercials viewers see, the fewer they remember. This is in line with findings of a study conducted by Biu and Lee (2001) in the USA which found, not surprisingly, that 'non-zappers' can recall more of the brands advertised than zappers. However, those brands which are recalled by zappers are those which are placed at the end of commercial breaks, implying that they 'return to the channel' or slow down the video in order not to miss the re-commencement of the programme they are viewing.

Consumers' avoidance of television commercials has been described as 'zipping', 'zapping', 'flipping', 'flicking', and 'grazing'. Regardless of the different names used to describe the reactions of consumers to irritating ads, each of the many studies has examined the impact of viewer control over ad exposure when watching television and concluded that, when consumers are given a means to avoid ads, many do just that. Abernethy (1991) found that viewers are likely to either leave the room or change the channel to avoid ads. Other television viewers simply participate in another activity or ignore the ads altogether and focus on something else.

A specific study conducted in 1993 (Gilmore and Secunda) investigated the extent to which zipped commercials impact on viewer comprehension. A number of groups were exposed to TV programmes containing commercials and were shown a variety of combinations of normal speed commercials and zipped ads. They were invited back to a second session, following which they were questioned on recall, recognition and product attributes for the commercials seen.

The study found that:

1   Previous exposure significantly reduced the recall difference between commercials presented at zipped and normal speed. Similar results were obtained for brand name recognition and attribute recall.
2   The greater the number of times an ad was seen at normal speed, the greater the recall and recognition of the zipped commercial.
3   If there was no normal speed exposure to the commercial prior to seeing the zipped commercial, then there was a large difference between normal and zipped speed recall and recognition.

Attention: The greater the attention getting values of the ad, the less frequency required. Conversely, low attention getting ads require greater frequency. This is an important factor to consider in the context of international and global campaigns, since the attention catching nature of a particular campaign may well be culturally bound and, hence, have less impact in some countries than others. Moreover, as we will see in Chapter 13, the level of understanding of the 'language' of advertising in different markets may impose different requirements.

Repeat exposures: Media that allow for repeat exposures require less frequency, for example, monthly magazines. However, Kirmani (1997) found that at extremely high levels of repetition of an ad that was already attention getting, perceptions about the manufacturer as well as about brand quality deteriorated. Consumers appeared to be inferring that 'if it's advertised too much, there must be something wrong'.

Although the ad may wear out, the benefits of repetition for perceptions of the manufacturer and perceived brand quality may make the increased repetition worthwhile. The notion that the amount of repetition may be perceived as a signal of quality is reaffirmed.

Media environment: As we have already seen, a further consideration is that of the impact of the message within a given medium. The media environment will be a critical factor in terms of the way that the message is received and interpreted by the target audience. In some instances, as noted earlier, the nature of the advertising campaign will, itself, determine the broader issues of media selection: Television versus press or radio, and so on. However, it is in the area of the specific selection of the

timing of the appearance of the commercial, the press titles or radio stations selected, that will have the greatest level of influence on the advertising message.

These considerations will often be reflected in the way in which the media campaign is laid down. In some instances, in order to achieve the maximum level of impact, media expenditure will be concentrated into a relatively short period. There are three alternative approaches that the media planner can adopt – burst, drip or pulse.

1 Burst advertising: Often associated with awareness objectives, the burst campaign (sometimes referred to as 'flighting') compacts media activity into a series of relatively short timeframes, with relatively long periods of absence from media activity in between, as illustrated in Figure 11.8.

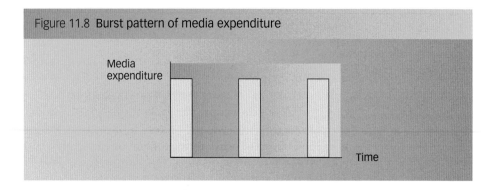

Figure 11.8 Burst pattern of media expenditure

2 Drip advertising: An alternative approach, mostly associated with reminder campaigns, is to extend the time scale of the advertising message over a long period, as shown in Figure 11.9.

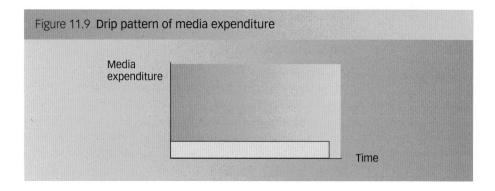

Figure 11.9 Drip pattern of media expenditure

The drip campaign provides continuity of the message, although at the cost of impact.

3 Pulse advertising: A compromise between the two is the development of a pulsing campaign. Here a comparatively low level of media activity is maintained over a long period of time, with periodic increases in the expenditure pattern, often associated with seasonal or other influences on buyer activity. See Figure 11.10.

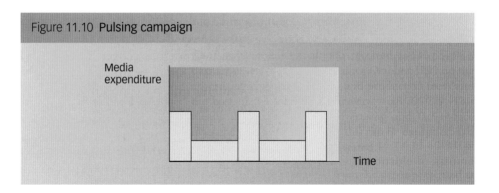

Figure 11.10 Pulsing campaign

Media expenditure

Time

Implementing the media plan

No media schedule is ever perfect. The aim must be to maximise the effectiveness of the campaign elements by the careful determination of the format in which the schedule is planned and the specific content of the media in which the advertising will appear.

Here again a number of factors will be important, especially the nature of the media buying process.

All media outlets have what is known as a rate card cost. This is the amount of money that the media proprietor seeks to earn from the sale of a particular time slot or space in a newspaper. Every month, BRAD (British Rate and Data) publishes a comprehensive listing of all media opportunities and their respective costs. From this it is possible to determine the rate card cost of, say, a page in the *Sunday Times*, or a 30-second TV spot on Carlton Television at different times of day. In practice, few media buyers will pay the asking price, but will negotiate down to a lower level.

This will be dependent on the value of that audience to different potential buyers. Since all media have a finite amount to sell, they can only achieve the greatest price when the demand for what they have to sell exceeds the supply. If the demand is at a lower level, the media proprietor will offer a discount to attract buyers who would otherwise not be interested at the full price. In some instances, such discounts will be available in return for making a commitment to the media outlet, for example, agreeing to place a series of consecutive advertisements in the same magazine or on the same radio station, or in return for an agreed share of the overall brand expenditure.

The negotiating skills of the media buyer are of extreme importance to the delivery of a cost-effective schedule. By understanding the media environment it may be possible to negotiate savings of as much as 15 or 20 per cent of the rate card cost which, in turn, will have a major impact on the overall delivery of the complete schedule.

Other media considerations

The placement of the advertising must reflect the advertising objective. We have already seen that the media environment is one of the important considerations in this context. However, there may well be other considerations.

There is as much creativity in media planning as there is in advertising content. Identifying a suitable but unusual media vehicle may well provide the element that differentiates a manufacturer's advertising from that of its competitors. Several

examples, taken from recent campaigns, illustrate the application of creativity in the media context.

Recently, Pretty Polly adopted an unusual stance to its poster buying by negotiating a format that had not previously been used. They took a conventional landscape format and turned it on its side. Despite the fact that the company had to negotiate the building of special poster sites to house the advertising message, the campaign achieved both distinctiveness and noticeablity, both essential components of any advertising campaign, together with major PR exposure. The same format was, adopted by Peugeot for its 406 campaign, and for the launch of the film title *Van Helsing*.

When Häagen-Dazs entered the UK market in 1991, they adopted an unconventional approach to media planning. Unlike other manufacturers in the sector, they identified the need to use the selected media to assist in the positioning of the brand. By examining the interests of their target consumers, they matched these with titles that reflected them. Accordingly, their initial schedule consisted of national newspapers – albeit with a regional bias to reflect their pattern of retail distribution – together with a selection of upmarket women's magazines (such as *Vogue*, *Tatler* and *Cosmopolitan*). The impact of seeing unconventional advertising in an unconventional media environment played a significant role in establishing the unique identity that became the property of the brand. (The case study on which this example is based is available in a more detailed form in Baker 1993.)

A further innovative media approach is that known as 'road blocking'. This is a device whereby a commercial is aired simultaneously on all available or relevant channels to ensure coverage of the whole audience, including channel switchers. Recently used by Peugeot, a single commercial could be seen on all available television channels. The same approach is commonly used by advertisers introducing new products, to ensure the maximum level of awareness amongst television viewers.

Contingency planning

In all instances, it is important to have a contingency budget to respond to circumstances that represent change from the planning phase. Since the planning process takes place before implementation, significant changes may occur within the relevant variables that affect the effectiveness of implementation.

Such changes may include:

- Changes in economic conditions: The sales of many products respond specifically to changes in economic circumstances. These may be broadly based, for example, a downturn or improvement in the general economic environment, or may be more specific, such as a budget that increases or decreases the tax on a specific product category.
- Changes in sales: The brand may achieve greater or lower levels of sales than those anticipated. These may require a redeployment of support, especially if there are strong regional variations in performance.
- Changes in the competitive environment: It is important to remember that media planning takes place in the absence of specific knowledge of competitor plans. They may take the decision to, say, upweight their media expenditure at specific times of the year, or to introduce a new product. Necessarily, the brand will need to respond to these changes.

The need to retain flexibility is important in media planning. Sometimes the opportunity to take advantage of market opportunities is only possible if part of the budget remains unspent and uncommitted. Periodically, media outlets will be left with unsold space or time and will offer it to existing or desired advertisers at 'bargain' rates.

Evaluation of the media plan

To ensure that the media campaign continues to deliver against its targets, a proper evaluative process must be implemented. Whether this takes the form of periodic ad hoc research activity to investigate specific dimensions of the advertising effectiveness or continuous market research in the form of a tracking study is somewhat less important than the fact that appropriate objective measurements are taken.

A factor which affects viewers watching of commercials is what Kaufman and Lane (1994) refer to as 'Polychronic Time Use': 'people tend to combine several different activities within the same amount of clock time'.

Media planners have identified deficiencies in BARB's assessment of television viewing. Whilst presence in front of a TV set accounts for nearly 25 hours per week, the time spent actually watching TV accounts for less than 17. Research studies into viewing habits have revealed that much TV 'viewing' is more likely to be characterised by a semi-attentive glance rather than the enraptured gaze. Many people are actually engaged in some other activity whilst 'watching' TV, e.g. reading a newspaper, book or magazine, pursuing some form of hobby, chatting, preparing food, etc. This may also be associated with the problems of zipping and zapping referred to earlier.

Research undertaken by Roberts (1996) reviewed the results of detailed analyses of the short-term effects of some 21 FMCG brands enabling the following conclusions:

- Whilst the magnitude of short-term effects is highly variable, those effects are greatest when the brand has something new to say – most usually when the brand itself is new or has been re-formulated, or when the brand has been without advertising for a considerable period.
- For established brands, consumer response to repeated exposures usually shows a saturation effect after four to five exposures in four weeks.
- For new brands or relaunches, the saturation level is much higher.
- Advertising tends to stimulate purchasing from new or occasional buyers rather than to encourage repeat purchasing from regular buyers.
- Advertising response is significantly greater when it coincides with sales promotions.

A further study by the same author (1998) provided additional evidence:

- Despite most of the brands included in the study being well established and in mature markets, TV advertising contributed incremental sales in the short term. This means that the benefit is not confined to the purely defensive role of sustaining the brand for the longer term.
- Advertising has a memorable effect on purchasing for up to 14 days after it was seen.
- Concentrated exposure immediately prior to purchase (i.e. within three days) produces significantly greater results.

- In the short term those who are least loyal to the brand respond most to the advertising.

The changing face of media implementation

It has been argued by Jacobs (1995) that no other agency function has undergone such dramatic changes as that of media management. In the mid-1970s several members of the agency media fraternity left to start dedicated media agencies of their own. The process of media planning and buying shifting to the media independents had begun. And, what had previously been considered as an agency business function emerged as a business in its own right. At the same time, there was recognition that creative media solutions could have a dramatic effect on the impact of the advertising.

Today, in most cases, the media specialists have been acquired by the major agency groupings. Since the media function is highly profitable in its own right, the major players have consistently demonstrated their desire to ensure that this profitability is retained by them.

However, it presents somewhat of a dichotomy to agency owners. On the one hand, they want their media companies to grow and to attract third party client business. On the other, they have the need to sell the benefits of a 'one-stop shop' providing a totally integrated communications solution to its clients.

As mentioned earlier, the development of the media independent and media dependents has been one of the most important factors within the overall advertising environment. Initially, perhaps to gain more recognition and status for their areas of responsibility, small groups of media specialists broke away from their parent agencies and established independent media consultancies whose sole contribution to the advertising process was the development and evaluation of media campaigns. However, as the pace quickened, clients saw the advantages of having the media function separated from the others. In the first place, they could receive independent advice divorced from the creative process. The media specialist could be remunerated on a different basis – that of achievement – and, indeed, many media companies were rewarded for their efforts on the basis of the percentage improvements over agreed targets that they could achieve. In some cases, these specialists were used to assist in the evaluation of the performance of one or more conventional agencies, assessing the achievements of each of them in order that the client could determine which was performing best. And, of course, there was the possibility of achieving significant cost savings. Not only could the basic level of remuneration for the media specialist be reduced but by placing all of the media planning and buying into one specialist agency the company could achieve bulk buying discounts. Instead of having separate agencies buying on behalf of different brands within the company's portfolio, one agency could be appointed to handle all of the buying. And, the aggregation of the budgets made the negotiating position ever stronger.

In some respects, the process has now come full circle. Traditional agencies, not wishing to lose out on the media revenue have, progressively, taken stakes in or bought out the independent media operators. Today, many of them are wholly owned subsidiaries of the major advertising agency groups. Table 11.15 shows the top ten media specialists, all of which are now part of larger agency groups.

Moreover, the nature of media planning and buying is now wholly different from that of, say, the 1980s and 1990s. Today's media specialist has the advantage of highly

Table 11.15 Top 10 UK media agencies, 2004

Rank 2003	Rank 2002	Agency	Ownership	Billings y/end Dec. 2003 (£m)	Billings y/end Dec. 2002 (£m)	Year-on-year % change
1	3	MediaCom	Grey Global	610.93	550.06	11.06
2	1	ZenithOptimedia	Publicis	605.90	697.42	−13.12
3	4	Mindshare	WPP	556.75	480.77	15.80
4	2	Carat	Aegis	519.17	573.46	−7.86
5	5	OMD UK	Omnicom	427.31	400.46	6.70
6	7	Initiative Media	Interpublic	415.04	365.79	13.46
7	6	Starcom Motive	Publicis	388.62	372.36	4.36
8	8	Universal McCann	Interpublic	325.10	287.31	13.15
9	9	PHD	Omnicom	262.98	276.08	−4.74
10	10	Starcom MediaVest	Publicis	260.11	272.25	−4.46

SOURCE: *Campaign* (2004)

sophisticated IT-based facilities that enable the interrogation of media data on a level never previously imagined. What, at best was a long and laborious exercise several years ago, can now be completed rapidly and provide the planner with information to guide the media planning process.

Media neutral planning

A new consideration in the context of media planning is what is now termed 'media neutral planning'. In some respects, it parallels the growth in the consideration of integrated marketing communications in the sense that it is concerned with the best approach towards reaching the target audience effectively without a bias towards particular media channels.

Mitchell (2003) identifies the key drive behind MNP as 'the client's desire for accountability' and regards 'all the means of contact, interaction and influence in the lives of consumers' as being a broader definition of media.

The MNP Best Practice Group (2004) asserts that 'open planning' is a more appropriate term to define the process and define it as 'a rigorous process for the selection of communication options which combines facts with imagination to drive the continual improvement to overall ROI'.

In 2002 *Campaign* magazine published a series of essays by media specialists offering their views on media neutral planning. The editorial director, Dominic Mills, in his introduction states: 'it's about an unbiased selection of media depending on the consumer's relationship with the brand and in the context of the message that needs to be deployed.' He adds 'Before you allocate spend across different media channels, all the options must be considered without bias.'

Case study

IPA Effectiveness Awards 2002 SILVER AWARD

Agency: Abbot Mead Vickers BBDO

Authors: Annabelle Watson and Clare Phillips

The Economist

Introduction

A revolution has taken place in the media. Since 1985 there have been over 1500 magazine launches, over 300 new TV channels, more than 200 new radio stations and the number of websites has increased from zero to millions. This dramatic fragmentation has left media owners needing to fight even harder for consumers' time and money. This paper shows how a media brand established in 1843 can compete successfully in today' increasingly competitive media market.

The advertising problem

In 1988, the need was recognised for a new advertising campaign. People's choice of media was expanding. However, people's time to consume this expanding media remained unchanged. As a result, *The Economist*, with its traditional positioning as a weekly newspaper, was competing for share in a highly aggressive marketplace. A publication with a worthy and rather intellectual image could easily be driven out of readers' repertoires, as was the case for the weekly *Business Magazine*, forced to close in the recessionary early 1990s.

The advertising objective and strategy

The objective was to encourage more people to read *The Economist* by positioning it as an essential weekly read and a brand with which they wanted to be associated. The campaign's target audience was ambitious, busy business people. The campaign needed to both consolidate the customer base and acquire new readers. Qualitative research provided the key that unlocked the new strategy. When people spoke about the publication, even if they found it hard-going, they almost all revered it. They did so because of what it said about them. We found that there was a link between *The Economist* and success – an emotional link that would prove to be extraordinarily powerful.

Rather than advertising content as most of our competitors did, we decided to dramatise the emotional benefit of reading *The Economist*. The creative strategy was to play on the cachet of reading *The Economist* – if you were a reader, you were part of an exclusive club of successful people. The price of admission was the price of the magazine. The creative guidelines insisted that the tone of the advertising reflect the personality of the successful club – clever, urbane – with an undercurrent of wit to move the brand away from its somewhat stuffy image.

The media strategy

The use of posters supported the creative insight of suggesting that readers are an exclusive 'club' of successful people. If exclusivity is defined as much by those who are not members of the club as by those who are, then using a broadcast medium was vital to bringing the creative strategy to life. This loyalty to posters also created a point of difference in its competitive set – no other newspaper or magazine has made significant use of the medium, allowing *The Economist* to 'own' the news category in outdoor.

A further benefit of using posters was the creative opportunity built on the characteristics of poster exposure:

- Major sites bought on a two-week basis alongside commuter routes into city centres meant that each poster would be seen repeatedly by consumers on their daily journey to work. It gave them time to decipher the double meanings and wordplay that became an integral part of the campaign.
- Posters also allow for several executions within each campaign which create a more rounded expression of the brand.

Finally, the medium formed a vital part of the message and the two mutually reinforced the brand communication.

Not only have the media and advertising strategies remained consistent over time, but the campaign creative has been consistent through the line. Everything from direct mail and point-of-sale material, to corporate gifts such as eye masks and matchboxes, have a consistent look and tone. The brand proposition has evolved over the past 14 years to reflect the changing business, social and economic climates.

Effectiveness of the advertising

The consistency and continuity of *The Economist* brand campaign has paid dividends:

- **Increased circulation:** During the campaign, *The Economist* increased its circulation by 64 per cent (from 86 000 in 1988 to 141 000 in 2001). This is against a backdrop of decline in newspapers and magazines of 20 per cent over the past 15 years. Most of *The Economist*'s 'competitors' – the quality dailies and news magazines – have suffered declines in circulation over the period.
- **Increased loyalty:** In the case of *The Economist*, increasing customer loyalty means increasing the subscriber base. Over the 14-year campaign, the number of subscribers in the UK has increased, from 37 000 in 1988 to 72 000 in 2001 – an increase of 95 per cent. As a proportion of total circulation, this is an increase from below 50 per cent in 1988 to 64 per cent in 2001.

- **Strengthened readership profile:** *The Economist*'s ad revenues are dependent not only on circulation but also on the profile of its readership. So it was not enough just to increase readership. *The Economist* had to attract more of the right kind of readers. Since 1988 the magazine has increased the proportion of ABs by almost 10 per cent.
- **Increased advertising revenues:** Between 1988 and 2001 *The Economist* increased the cost of a single-page advertisement at a faster rate than the competition.

Econometric modelling shows a direct effect of advertising on circulation. The models reveal that every £1000 spent on advertising generates 60 news-stand sales and 6.4 subscriptions. Each year we spend approximately £1 million on the brand campaign, so that figure generates 60 000 news-stand sales and 6400 subscriptions. This equates to 2.4 per cent of news-stand sales and 5.7 per cent of subscriptions.

The advertising doesn't just generate new customers, it generates loyal customers. It encourages people to form a relationship with *The Economist*, literally 'buying into' the brand by going straight to subscription. Advertising awareness built rapidly in the early years of the campaign and has continued at high levels ever since, despite a decreasing share of voice. *The Economist*'s ad awareness still outstrips the competition who have spent on average three-and-a-half times more on advertising. Relative to the competition, *The Economist* has extremely high spontaneous brand awareness.

The advertising has also increased quality perceptions. Tracking shows that 'intelligence', 'cleverness', 'well informed' and 'witty' are the key communication take-outs from the advertising. These advertising messages have remained consistent during the campaign and over time have translated into brand image.

SOURCE: This case study is adapted from the paper presented at the IPA Effectiveness Awards. The full version is available at www.warc.com and is reproduced by kind permission of the Institute of Practitioners in Advertising and the World Advertising Research Center.

Questions

1 Describe the tasks involved in the fulfilment of the media strategy.

2 Why has the explosion in media channels made the task more difficult, on the one hand, and made close targeting more easily achieved?

3 Identify the key characteristics of the available media channels.

4 How does programme sponsorship differ from conventional advertising and what are the benefits it can provide?

5 Why is the identification of target audiences a key consideration in media selection?

6 Describe the different approaches that the media planner can adopt – drip, burst or pulse – and when each would represent the optimum method of deploying the media budget.

12 Other areas of advertising

Learning outcomes

By the end of this chapter you should be familiar with:

- the increasing use of advertising in the corporate and business-to-business sectors

- the issues of services advertising

- advertising in the non-profit sector (charity and cause-related activities)

- the growth of interactive advertising and direct-response mechanisms

- the implications of the growth of the internet and its use as an advertising medium.

The corporate and business-to-business sectors

Corporate brand management

Recent years have seen the emergence of a new area of activity within the field of marketing communications and advertising. There has been a marked progression from supporting the consumer brand to that of supporting the corporate brand.

There is a growing recognition of the corporate brand as a valuable asset (Bickerton 2000). Moreover, research conducted by Fombrun and Rindova (1998) underpins the role of marketing communications in this context. They concluded: 'In sum, these analyses indicate that communication benefits may result not only from the amount and frequency of communications but from the variety of issues about itself that a firm reveals through its communications.'

Companies, even small ones, conduct their business in the glare of the public spotlight. Every day, newspapers from *The Times* to the *Sun* – the latter read by nearly a quarter of UK adults – reveal the affairs of large and small companies alike. They identify the companies behind the brands, reveal the decisions taken by management and the resultant business outcomes.

This media coverage extends far beyond the financial performance of the company. The organisation's record as an employer, its latest senior management hirings and firings, its plans for the future, and its record on environmental matters are just some of the issues which are being brought into public focus through the pages of the newspapers.

Multinational corporations are increasingly exposed to communications challenges both domestically and internationally. The result of mergers and acquisitions has meant even greater emphasis on ensuring that corporations project a consistent global corporate identity. A multinational company's personality is rapidly becoming a major factor in consumer choice between its products and those of a competitor. According to Melewar and Saunders (1998) some companies opt for a unified global brand. The degree of adaptation of the identity depends on whether competitive advantage is derived from co-ordinating activities centrally or devolving them to operational markets.

According to Alan Cooper (1999) two themes emerge from these factors:

- consumers are becoming more exposed to companies as businesses and brand owners, and want to know more about them;
- companies need actively to manage their reputations, rather than to react to issues and crises as they arise. Public trust is the reward for the former, public suspicion for the latter.

The more well known a company becomes, through direct experience of its brands or proactive communication about its activities and policies, the more positive its reputation is likely to be. This applies to all audiences, not just consumers.

Various studies have indicated that product purchase decisions are, in part, influenced by the consumer's view of the parent company. The extent to which the consumer holds the company in high regard and hold positive views about the company's 'good citizenship' will positively influence them to purchase products or services from that company. Fombrun (1996) argues that corporate credibility influences purchase intent because consumer perceptions of the trustworthiness and expertise of a company are part of the information they use to judge the quality of the company's products and therefore whether they want to buy them or not. Lafferty and Goldsmith (1999) and Lafferty et al. (2000) similarly found that corporate credibility had a positive effect on purchase intentions.

As Biehal and Sheinin (1998) state 'Corporate advertising has, in consequence, become a significant business activity. That fact is important for brand managers because consumers' knowledge formed from corporate advertising may influence the way they think about brands the company markets.'

Because it is more cost effective to sell to current customers than new ones, Duncan and Moriarty (1998) argue that corporate focus should place more emphasis on relationships than transactions. Corporate focus should also be on stakeholders rather than just customers, as this helps companies to avoid sending conflicting messages to overlapping stakeholder/customers.

There are important organisational implications. Because relationship marketing is more communication-intensive, cross-functional management is needed to plan and monitor messages for strategic consistency and inconsistency. In fact, few large companies have a management system in place to ensure that communications messages are consistent across the variety of sources from which they emanate. In many instances they maintain 'independent' departments responsible for advertising, public relations, corporate publications such as the annual report, and so on. The consequence is all too often the issuing of contradictory messages.

In a book by Willmott (2003) the argument is put forward that a detailed analysis of several studies into the impact of various 'citizenship' initiatives demonstrates the clear impact of these programmes on both profits and share price. He argues that people are increasingly judging commercial organisations on their values and wider roles and behaviour in society.

The use of corporate societal marketing (CSM) appears to be on the rise in line with the increasing recognition of the vast potential of CSM programmes as a direct response to the focus on major organisations. Corporate societal marketing's aim is defined as being to 'encompass marketing initiatives that have at least one non-economic objective related to social welfare and use the resources of the company and/or one of its partners' (Wilmott 2003). One factor driving this growth in CSM is the realisation that consumers' perceptions of a company as a whole and its role in society can significantly affect a brand's strength and equity.

Hoeffler and Keller (2002) state that there is little doubt that corporate societal marketing programmes are poised to play a more important role in brand marketing. They can add important values to the organisation such as:

- building brand awareness,
- enhancing brand image,
- establishing brand credibility,
- evoking brand feelings,
- creating a sense of brand community,
- eliciting brand engagement.

A recent leading article (*Market Leader* 2002) provided hard evidence of the importance of corporate social responsibility. It indicated that 90 per cent of French consumers said they would pay more for 'sustainable and ethically produced goods and services if they have guarantees about the production process'. Another study affirmed that some 70 per cent of European consumers reflect on a company's commitment to social responsibility when they are about to buy something. Figures such as these more than suggest that the consumer brands that respond accordingly will enjoy massively improved sales.

Esso, a company that has been the source of much international controversy, have developed a corporate campaign stressing their environmental credentials: 'We're all for reducing emissions'. Here the company highlights the strides it has made in the energy efficiency of its refineries. Another ad informs of the company's sponsorship of Stanford University's Global Climate and Energy Project. Similarly, MG Rover has mounted a corporate campaign indicating how the company is supportive to the economy in a number of areas.

A further drive towards the development of corporate communications has been the recognition that most large companies maintain substantial portfolios of products and brands. Whilst the largest of these are of significant size and can afford advertising budgets, there are also many smaller brands whose profitability cannot support such expenditure. By establishing the corporate identity in the minds of consumers it acts as an 'umbrella' to ensure that smaller brands bearing the company's name are positively received by consumers.

Business-to-business advertising

Ivey (1995) argues that in the business-to-business (B2B) context, the convention is to establish the corporate brand rather than a branded product. There are several reasons for this approach:

1 Where technology is changing rapidly, it is crucial that the relationship is established with the supplier's company, not the individual product, to ensure that the original supplier handles the upgrading.

2 Business services, such as accounting, do not have products. It remains true, therefore, that it is the quality of the people and the values to which they adhere that are being sought, and these must reflect the performance at the company level.

3 Many supplies require back-up services in terms of after-sales care or flexibility or speed of delivery. These values must, similarly, relate to the corporate brand rather than the specific services themselves.

It is important to recognise that targeting and segmentation of the B2B market is more complicated than in the case of conventional brands. There is often a variety of decision makers and others who exert an influence on the decision taken – managers, finance and end users, each of whom fulfils a different role and may well have significantly different motivations related to the purchase.

The business buyer differs from other customers in a variety of ways. Often he or she may not be an individual at all, but part of a decision making unit (DMU). And the outcome of their buying decision can carry enough weight to make or break those involved. Business buyers, in consequence, are obliged to make more considered decisions.

Business-to-business dealings tend to be characterised by a more rational buying process: longer-term relationships, greater product complexity, larger amounts of money being exchanged, greater use of group decisions and the creation of specific product/service mixes to meet the particular needs of an organisation. Moreover, it must be recognised that B2B buyers are not spending their own money and are therefore accountable for their purchase decisions and their outcomes. Various authors have indicated that it is far more common to see rational appeals being used for B2B advertising, with quality and price being particularly strong influencers (Garber and Dotson 2002).

Business-to-business is different because buyer motivation and its context are more structured and complex than in a consumer environment. Alanko (2000) argues that integration of B2B marketing is strategic for the whole enterprise. He suggests that the primary need is that of gaining an understanding of the processes of business, motivators and structures. The key differentiator is that the focus of analysis is not on product, although it may appear to be so, but on how two organisations can come together and add value to each other's businesses.

Business communications are about supporting the selling company throughout the buying process. This involves:

• making sure that the company gets onto the buyer's list of potential suppliers;
• helping the company when the buyer is going through an initial evaluation;
• working to get on the shortlist;
• making sure that the company comes across as powerfully as possible when the buyer is examining the shortlist;
• providing buyer reassurance in the final decision.

Brand communication aims to position the company competitively, create long-term opportunities, predispose buyers towards the company's offering and pave the way for the selling efforts.

One important issue is the need to communicate the selling company's values to all of those individuals involved in the decision-making process. Whilst most industry sectors have dedicated media channels, such as trade magazines, which are read by many people in the company, these may not reach all of the people who can influence the purchasing decision. Sometimes, therefore, it is appropriate to recognise the broader influence of 'conventional' media in this respect.

When the author was involved in the development of advertising for Compass, one of the world's largest catering and service providers, research indicated that the trade publications, whilst reaching many of those in the target group, failed to affect decision influencers, particularly those at board level. Accordingly, an advertising campaign was produced using mainstream media that communicated the values of the company to those individuals, to significant effect.

Services advertising

The past 30 years has seen vast growth in the service economy. However, comparatively little attention has been given to the advertising of services. Grove et al. (1997) suggest that advertising may play an important role for a number of reasons:

- The higher level of perceived risk associated with the purchasing of services suggests that marketers may need to create specific messages to help remove apprehensions on the part of consumers.
- Advertising may help consumers to visualise the service that helps overcome the intangibility of the service provision.
- Advertising may present an indication of service quality and help overcome the perceived inability of service consistency.

What makes service brands different is the level of contact between the business and the consumer. In most instances, it involves the customer in direct contact with the company, its personnel or both.

Successful service brands succeed by focusing effort as much on how the product is delivered to customers as on its precise nature. Delivery is recognised as critical to the offer. For this reason, service brands are, for the most part, more complex than FMCG brands. They are crucially dependent on the recruitment, training and motivation of people, especially those in direct contact with the customer.

White (1996) argues that the successful service brand requires five basic elements:

1 desirable, marketable products;
2 clear, strong, motivating positioning;
3 an appropriate culture to sell the product to its target market;
4 an operational approach that allows for continuous development;
5 an integrated communications programme to achieve fruitful contacts with actual and potential customers.

Because services are less tangible, Cutler and Javalgi (1993) argue that services advertising should attempt to provide more tangibility. They recommend a number of approaches:

- use 'vivid' language in the advertising;
- provide cues for the service, e.g. the Direct Line telephone, Churchill's dog, etc.;
- use emotion to make the service seem more real, concrete and vivid.

Stockdale (1995) provides an overview of best practice in financial services advertising based on a series of IPA Effectiveness Award winning campaigns. He identifies the problem that only a small number of individuals are actively seeking financial services at any given time, leaving advertisers with the choice between targeting a small number of active consumers or seeking to pre-influence the behaviour of a larger number of currently inactive consumers.

Using these case studies, he illustrates a number of advertising strategies employed in the financial services market:

- understanding the influences of advertising in a sales process consisting of a dialogue between independent financial advisors and consumers (Scottish Amicable);
- using TV-led branding to sustain perceived differences (Direct Line);
- capitalising on an organisation's ethical heritage to reposition itself to compete with other financial institutions (Co-operative Bank);
- creating an advertising theme to accommodate different products (Alliance & Leicester).

The non-profit sector

Charity advertising

A further area that has seen considerable expansion in recent years has been charity advertising. For many years, the Charities Act precluded organisations from using advertising to promote their causes. However, recent changes in the law have enabled charities to advertise. None the less, despite the removal of this barrier, a specific difficulty remains. Very few charitable bodies have sufficient money to afford to mount major campaigns in mainstream media.

According to *Admap* (2003) nominal adspend by charities rose 16 per cent to £54.4m (nominal because much charity advertising is heavily discounted or undertaken on a pro bono basis). Charity ads are spread across the main media as follows: TV (36 per cent), national newspapers (24 per cent) and radio (10 per cent).

The top 10 charity advertisers are shown in Table 12.1.

Table 12.1 Top 10 UK charity advertisers

Charity	March–February 2002 (£000)	March–February 2003 (£000)
Cancer Research UK	4 717	6 833
NSPCC	1 996	5 165
RSPCA	3 036	2 379
World Vision	1 818	2 174
Christian Aid	1 650	1 570
British Heart Foundation	2 392	1 465
Plan International UK	716	1 450
British Red Cross	1 521	1 444
National Canine Defence League	1 822	1 218
Oxfam	1 866	1 218
Total charity advertising	46 975	54 502

SOURCE: *Admap* 2003

By comparison with many FMCG products, these sums are comparatively small. Moreover, the table does not show the vast number of smaller charities whose income levels are even smaller than those indicated above.

Two factors, however, have served to enable these bodies to use conventional advertising. The first is the fact that as new media channels have emerged, with the consequent fragmentation of audiences, so some media costs have been reduced to the level of affordability. Many charities use satellite and cable channels rather than terrestrial stations, where the cost of advertising is significantly lower. And, as mentioned above, some TV stations are prepared to discount their charges or provide free airtime since the presence of charity advertising may be perceived by them as enhancing their overall stature.

The second factor has been the increased interest in cause-related marketing. It was noted above that a number of large organisations have recognised the values inherent in 'adopting' a cause to enhance their image of social responsibility. Many charitable bodies have developed relationships with major corporations who provide the necessary funding to enable the charities to develop advertising campaigns.

Cause-related marketing

Cause-related marketing can be defined as a commercial activity by which business and charities or causes form a partnership with each other to market an image, product or service for mutual benefit. As Goodyear (2000) states: 'What characterises cause-related marketing is that it is long-term and very much part of the promotional strategy of both the corporation and the charity.'

A recent example of such a relationship can be seen in Vodafone's three-year commitment to the National Autistic Society (NAS). The activity is one of many examples of a brand attempting to bolster its reputation through a cause-related campaign. As well as pledging to raise £6 million for the NAS over three years, the company will also work on three specific projects. It is setting up a 24-hour helpline which will offer help and advice on autism by phone or online. It is developing a support programme that will offer a network of assistance to families. It will also use advertising – both to its existing customer base and to the wider public – to raise awareness of autism.

The same company is also funding a TV campaign on Channel 4 for the British Special Olympics whereby 30-second spots on the channel ask viewers to donate skills, time and money. Additionally, free airtime has been secured for the campaign on Eurosport and CNBC, with the ad also being shown in football stadia.

Similarly, the British Red Cross is running a national drive to add 10 000 donors to its current base of 185 000. Advertising, featuring the endline 'I owe my life' will feature beneficiaries of the charity's services. The campaign uses 170 48-sheet posters across the country together with 40 6-sheet posters in the car parks of Asda, a corporate partner of the charity.

Interactive and direct response advertising

Infomercials

An infomercial can basically be described as a programme-length paid advertisement that promotes an organisation's product or image through information and persuasion (Balasubramanian and Kumar 1997). Typically, they last anything from 15 minutes to two hours. They provide the opportunity for the advertiser to present a detailed product story, to make an emotional connection with the consumer and to drive sales through retail and direct marketing channels. They appear in a number of different formats, focusing on product demonstrations, expert or celebrity testimonials, a talk-show format or a dramatisation using a 'slice of life' format. As Singh et al. (2000) state, infomercials offer the opportunity to provide long messages and offer a detailed discussion of the attributes of the promoted product. They feature product demonstrations that help viewers to learn more about the product.

Usually a direct response element is associated with infomercials (e.g. a free telephone number) so that interested viewers can call to order the item being advertised or to seek additional information (Chapman and Beltramini 2000).

Today, infomercials represent a form of advertising that is of very considerable commercial significance. In one US estimate, advertisers were reported to have spent some $800 million on infomercial time. In the UK, this figure is significantly lower, although it is growing very rapidly. Not only are infomercials increasingly popular, they are also attracting a number of well-known brands to advertise in this format.

Infomercials are not a new form of advertising. In the UK, the device took on a somewhat different form in which a programme was designed to enable the featuring of manufacturer's products. The presenter and others would discuss the merits of the product, which had paid for its presence in the segment. This form of 'product placement' was outlawed and it was not until the arrival of satellite television that the infomercial returned. Essentially, the format is the same, although in most instances, the infomercial is sponsored by and features a single company's products.

There is an increasing number of these direct-response television devices which can be split into three broad categories:

- short-form commercials, usually of 2–3 minutes' duration;
- infomercials;
- home shopping channels devoted entirely to selling products on television, usually 24 hours a day.

Martin et al. (2002) argue that infomercials are more likely to be seen as effective by consumers who value expert comments, demonstrations, product comparisons and bonus offers. It is the ability to create persuasive arguments based on product demonstrations, testimonials from satisfied users and experts that is the key to infomercial success.

The study by Agee and Brett (2001) demonstrates that often, and against expectations, responses to infomercials are somewhat planned. Their survey determined that only a small segment (13 per cent) responded to an infomercial with an impulse purchase. Most purchases resulted from the viewer having seen it several times.

According to Alba and Lynch (1997) the convergence of technological, economic and cultural forces has made possible a new and revolutionary distribution channel known generically as interactive home shopping (IHS). Although only in its infancy, IHS has the potential to change fundamentally the manner in which people shop as well as the structure of the consumer goods and retail industries.

Interactive advertising

For most of advertising's existence, it has largely been a passive device. Advertising, using a variety of media channels, sent messages to consumers. It did not have the facility to enable any form of immediate response or interactivity. As Stern (1994) explains:

> the [traditional] commercial was old-fashioned passive viewing. The biggest single challenge the advertising community has in modern television is how do you keep your viewer engaged to your message? The facility to order a brochure or catalogue, get a product demonstration, access interactive services such as home shopping and banking, and link to a Website and Teletext page from the comfort of our homes is now available to viewers in many parts of the world.

As Johnson (1999) states: 'Television has the potential to change from a generally passive medium to one in which the viewer increases the level of control they have over the messages they wish to receive.'

Interactivity is the key. The advent of new technologies at the end of the last century has changed the fundamental nature of advertising. The introduction of cable, mobile phones, WAP, the web and digital interactive television, together with CD-ROM, interactive kiosks, TiVo and Bluetooth amongst other technologies, has enabled instant response to an advertising message. In whatever way the advertising message is received, an increasing number of consumers have the opportunity to interact with it.

Interactivity has been defined in many ways, for example, as the facility for persons and organisations to communicate directly with one another regardless of distance or time. Deighton (1997) considers interactivity to have two primary features: the ability to address a person and to gather and remember the response of that person. Steuer (1992) suggests that interactivity is 'the extent to which users can participate in modifying the format and content of a mediated environment in real time'.

Stern (1994) defines interactive advertising as: 'a dialogue between human and machine [interactive], based on integrated digital streams of video, audio text, and graphics [multimedia]'. It is a product of the alliance between telephones, computers, and television that gives consumers control over advertising by enabling them to manipulate 'what they see on the screen in real time'.

According to Deighton et al. (1996) interactivity has already made major inroads into marketing budgets since the mid-1990s in the form of direct mail, catalogue retailing, telemarketing and the incorporation of response devices into broadcast advertising. Developments in data storage and transmission, however, hold out the promise of new and better interactive tools to manage relations with customers and to link the networked corporation to its channels and its collaborators.

Although the world wide web may be the ultimate interactive medium, there is still much that can be done with the less exotic interactive technologies. For example, when a broadcast advertisement elicits a response such as a freephone call –

which is then stored in a computer database and which triggers a personalised direct mailing – that sequence represents a form of low-tech interactivity. A sales representative calling on customers is also engaging in low-tech interactivity. The web, however, promises high-tech interactivity. When a consumer visits a website, many cycles of messages can be exchanged in a short time. When the consumer visits some time later, the dialogue can resume just where it left off. The web medium is potentially as subtle, as flexible, as pertinent and as persuasive as one-on-one dialogue. It boasts a better memory than the most diligent salesperson and has none of the salesperson's distaste for repetitive tasks. Although other media may be more gripping, the web is uniquely responsive.

Many arguments have been put forward in favour of the new media outlets. These include:

- Digital media can combine sound, image and text in unlimited ways – and add interactivity – and the more creative media have always supplanted pre-existing ones.
- New media let advertisers individually tailor the information sent to consumers.

Interactive television (iTV) represents a new medium that combines conventional brand advertising with direct-response mechanisms. Since its inception, TV advertising has taken a number of different formats across the world. As creative agencies, technology providers, broadcasters and platforms grapple with executing iTV ad campaigns, and with the increasing proliferation of iTV ad technologies worldwide, we are seeing a number of different creative deliveries, vastly different results and different levels of functionality.

Interactive TV banner advertising and sponsorship have been introduced across a number of platforms and countries throughout the world. Similar to that of the internet, banners and sponsorship are either served or broadcast into content partner areas, navigation or electronic programme guides, linking the viewer to a designated advertiser's site.

Moreover, as Johnson (2002) states, interactive TV events are becoming increasingly popular, and broadcasters and advertisers are devising new ways for advertisers to benefit and become involved. iTV advertising elements are being incorporated into large events: indeed some argue that they are the lynchpin that many advertisers base their campaign around. Either using enhanced TV or in a stand-alone environment (pop-ups or integration into the site), there are a number of new ways advertisers are incorporating themselves into major iTV events. It is also evident that this type of interactivity is moving closely towards programme sponsorship.

Response advertising

Response advertising seeks to establish direct interaction with consumers, to influence immediate purchase decisions using techniques designed to elicit response, conversion and to establish lifetime value. Interactive television creates a connection between traditional television advertising and direct response mechanisms by linking the consumer into a real-time dialogue.

Fox and Burrows (2001) make three important points:

- TV viewers are passively exposed to advertising which must emotionally engage them in order to foster attention to the brand message;

- direct mail respondents receive information that personally engages them in the product with materials specifically designed to elicit a response;
- internet surfers actively engage in making decisions that affect their choice of interaction.

Although their work was limited to the internet, the findings of Ditto and Pille (1998) are equally applicable to other forms of direct-response media. They identified three categories of consumer impact which these media provide:

- Informational: The most basic level where the website is fundamentally a means to provide the same information available through traditional marketing. The information provided enables the customer to learn about the enterprise but it is not interactive. It is, therefore, a one-way process similar to conventional marketing.
- Transactional level: A transactional website provides more than static information by enabling communication with the customer. Customers can have a 'virtual tour' and can find out more about their particular needs. The information and tools provided enable customers to contact the enterprise by e-mail, telephone or by other means.
- Relational level: The internet provides interactivity with customers. The enables the development of a continuous relationship from the original transaction. It is possible to involve customer groups with similar needs and a 'virtual' community can be established involving customers with the enterprise. The internet can act as a medium to develop a relationship between enterprises and customers.

The internet as an advertising medium

Without doubt, the medium that has the potential to make the greatest changes to conventional advertising is that of the internet. In well under a decade the internet has evolved into an important medium for advertisers and marketers for both branding and direct-selling purposes. As a central part of the fast-expanding digital economy, the internet has attracted an enormous amount of advertising revenues. According to an industry report, internet advertising revenue reached $4.62 billion in 1999 (Internet Advertising Bureau 1999). Although this is a small portion of overall advertising spending (estimated to be over $200 billion in 1999), total spending on the internet has now exceeded that of outdoor advertising. Driving this rapid growth is the fact that the internet has been drawing sizeable audiences from other media. The number of Americans using the internet has grown exponentially in the past few years, from fewer than 5 million in 1993 to as many as 110 million in 1999 (U.S. Department of Commerce 1999).

It is important to place the internet into some context. According to a paper by Foster (2000) the top 165 internet sites delivered 952 million impressions. During the same period, commercial television channels delivered 55 000 million impressions. Thus, the internet delivered a number of impressions equivalent to 1.73 per cent of those delivered by commercial television, which places it alongside one of the UK's smaller satellite or cable channels.

Fast, broadband internet connections are now available and web page designers are working on ways to bring exclusivity and entertainment value to their sites. The growth in internet users has been phenomenal, the rate of adoption outstripping any previous new communications technology. An NOP user survey conducted in

2001 indicated that there were over 12 million users in the UK alone. Other studies have indicated that the figure may be even greater.

Technological innovations also have made the internet an attractive medium for advertisers. Today, server-based technologies enable advertisers to display banner ads according to user profiles and interests and in ways that were not possible before. As an advertising medium, the internet offers all the elements of other media and much more. Banner ads can include not only graphics and texts but also streaming audio and video. Java and Shockwave technologies can be used to deliver highly dynamic and interactive banner ads. Such interactive and personalisable technologies have made the internet an effective and accountable medium with unlimited creativity.

The essence of the web is still its unique ability to bond communities on a global, regional, national and local scale. The web has grown dramatically because the world is made up of communities and we interact with many, knowingly or unknowingly, on a daily basis. If someone raves about a certain pop star, they are a member of a fan community. If you are a birdwatcher you belong to the ornithological community. If you buy any product bought by more than one person, you become a member of the community that buys that product. Successful community websites identify and serve a community that will find group interaction useful. The recent petrol prices exposé has been given significant extra weight because the internet has allowed everyone with the same feelings to go to boycott-the-pumps.com and sign a petition that will be passed to Downing Street.

As a marketing communication medium there are a number of ways in which the web is different from other communications media. In particular, approaches for grabbing the attention in traditional media need to be reinterpreted in an environment in which the viewer only sees what is on a small screen. The potential for the internet is to assist the consumers in gathering information pertinent to a purchasing decision. In the digital age, consumers can mine a variety of websites for the information they require when they require it. Importantly, it is available when the consumer wants it, rather than when the advertiser decides that second-tier media should be used (or when they can afford it). Customers approach the web in a number of different ways, and exercise a variety of search strategies. The spectrum ranges from attempting to locate a specific item (sometimes referred to as directed or purposeful searching) through aimless or general 'browsing'.

One of the most important facets of the web as a communications medium is that, unlike others, its audience has a greater degree of control over exposure to material. They can actively choose which website they wish to visit, when they want to visit it and how they wish to interact with it. Unlike other media, the internet's links and e-mail provides the consumer with the opportunity to interact both with the site itself and the company it is promoting. The internet is more than just an advertising medium; it is a transactional medium. Consumer awareness and the desire to purchase, prompted by information gained from the web can immediately be translated into actionable leads and, ideally, concrete sales. Many users of the internet do so to gain information on product details, best prices and alternatives.

As Gallagher et al. (2001) indicate, a characteristic that distinguishes the web from other media, including print, is that it changes users from passive 'targets' of communications to active manipulators of content. Users decide what to see and in what order. Experienced web users like having this control and expect web documents to have appropriate links to related material. Readers do not have the same expectations of print documents.

Internet advertising differs from traditional media advertising in many ways. Among the most salient characteristics, according to Rowley (2001), are:

1 unlimited delivery of information beyond time and space;
2 unlimited amounts and sources of information;
3 the ability to target specific groups or individuals;
4 the potential audience is global and unidentified, but once contact has been made, individuals can be identified and targeted;
5 the internet is available at any time and in any location.

The capacity for interactivity is greater on the web than with any other mass media. What this interactivity implies for the media audience is that it confers them with the ability to 'choose and respond' to a particular advertisement of their liking. This is especially important in light of the current shift in advertising strategy that favours the effectiveness of deriving maximum response from selected target groups over the efficiency of providing maximum exposure to many unknown audience groups with a minimum cost.

However, many users feel disappointed with sites that fail to offer this facility and, in general, are unlikely to return to them. Few companies use their websites to their full potential. For many, the promotional usages are little different from existing forms of communication. They contain product news, catalogues of products and services, and similar items that are merely web translations of other printed sources of the same material.

A recent study conducted by Bruner and Kumar (2000) suggests that, with the tremendous growth of e-commerce, firms are increasing the amount of money spent on web-based marketing communications, sometimes at the expense of traditional media. However, it remains true that most firms may still have to depend on traditional media to influence their target market's attitudes towards their ads and their brands. This is particularly true when the target market includes segments of the population whose experience with the web is limited.

Various researchers have investigated the effectiveness of web presence in contributing towards the fulfilment of promotional objectives. They suggest that it is effective for:

• creating brand, product and corporate awareness and image;
• providing product and other information;
• generating qualified leads;
• handling customer complaints, queries and suggestions.

Web retailing

Web-based retailing is taking its place as a new retailing environment. It removes the traditional constraints on retailers and provides for a new form of transactional value enhancement. The web can operate like an electronic interactive catalogue. It allows people to browse, collect information and buy. There are some interesting examples of e-commerce sites, such as Amazon, Bol, CDnow, Lastminute, Google, Ebay and Thinknatural.

However, the great 'dot-com' boom of the late 1990s was followed by the early demise of many of the players. It had been widely assumed that the internet was a new medium that enabled those with a new proposition to 'play by new rules'. An analysis of the collapse of those companies by Burkitt (2000) demonstrated that the same rules that apply to the 'old economy' apply equally to dot-coms. He describes the reasons for their early failure under seven headings:

1 no clear proposition
2 poor branding
3 lack of memorability
4 questionable targeting strategies
5 lack of charm in execution
6 product delivery problems
7 no profit margin.

The web provides retailers with a variety of new opportunities (Griffith and Kampf 1998):

- To use the web as a virtual store where products are offered directly to customers.
- To use their web presence as a form of communication in which they can advertise their products or increase their corporate presence. It represents a new medium by which additional information can be provided to customers.
- To offer increased perceived value to the customer through additional customer services. The web enables traditional retailers, for example, the opportunity to provide customers with 24/7 access to their offerings.
- To provide a new strategic tool for their businesses.

Cleaver (2000) argues that the internet is developing a fresh business culture that is altering the relationships that customers will have with their suppliers or brand owners. It is possible that, over time, retailers will use their physical presence to showcase what they sell, to create interest and experience for customers, and use the web in parallel as the purchasing and fulfilment medium.

Slack et al. (2001) have also noted that:

the advantage of internet selling is the increased reach (the number of customers that can be reached and the number of items they can be presented with) and richness (the amount of detail which could be provided concerning both the items on sale and the customers' behaviour in buying them.

If traditional selling involved a trade-off between reach and richness, the internet effectively overcomes this trade-off.

The true potential of the net as a distribution channel is not yet fully understood. There are, clearly, specific threshold price levels at which online commerce can work. There is a number of examples of the direct selling of high-cost products from cars to holidays that are profitable for an e-commerce site. Similarly, high-volume sales of low-margin products such as books and CDs can also work. However, the one-off sale of individual low-price items such as FMCG products cannot be profitable. There is evidence that consumers who frequently access the internet engage in online purchasing more often for books, computer products, education, electronic goods, entertainment, internet-related products and travel than consumers who access the internet less frequently (Kwak et al. 2002).

The economics of distribution places limits on the degree to which FMCG companies can adopt one to one online trading as a distribution channel. The only way these products can be sold online at a profit is through e-baskets. Tesco Direct enables consumers to put together e-baskets of products from its virtual shelves.

The advantage of these sites is to provide relaxed home shopping and cheaper selling prices, through the removal of retailer profits. Some sites like Letsbuyit.com cleverly merge the community and commerce elements of consumers' use of the internet. Letsbuyit encourages the creation of communities of buyers for the same product and uses their collective buying power to purchase on better terms.

Foster (2000) provides the example of Carprices.com in the US, which allows active car buyers to get dealers bidding for their purchase. Car manufacturers are now bidding to deal with the consumer and obtain their business. Traditionally, US car buyers pay an 8 per cent margin to the dealer. Carprices.com claims its buyers only pay a 2 per cent margin.

Three factors are critical to the profits of online sellers:

1 driving traffic to the site,
2 getting initial sales,
3 securing repeat business.

Driving customers to sites has proven to be expensive and highly competitive (Peterson et al. 1999). Some 'dot-com' sellers are reported to have spent 25 to 50 per cent of their total budget on advertising and marketing. In an extreme case, one online seller apparently paid millions of dollars for banner ads on a leading portal that brought in only $100,000 of sales. Increased demand for advertisements in major and support media has created substantially higher prices and a glut of dot-com advertisements has made it harder for sellers' messages to get attention and to be remembered. The consequent failure of dot-com companies to achieve profitability has been widely reported.

Once a site has traffic, it must convert the shoppers and surfers into purchasers, and then into repeat purchasers. As in conventional retailing, repurchase rates and amounts are a critical driver of future profits. However, research indicates that repeat rates are often disappointingly low. As one industry figure noted, internet marketers might spend $45 'to acquire a customer who generally spends $35 and never comes back'. Loyal customers tend to spend greater amounts and may refer others to the site. For example, Amazon.com's book-selling operation is now profitable, and repeat purchases comprise over 70 per cent of its sales.

Given the absence of physical exposure and contact, trust may be particularly important in the online buying experience. Consumers may have heard of unscrupulous or unreliable online sellers, and they may be concerned about customer service levels should performance not match a site's claims or offers. Exchanges that involve credit card information or other potentially sensitive data (e.g. records of books bought as gifts) may be based on electronic communication alone. Moreover, even buyers who are loyal over time may not know the physical location of an e-business. Trust levels may therefore affect shoppers' willingness to buy, and their willingness to return to the site.

There remain a number of specific barriers to e-shopping, as Flood (2000) points out:

- fraud concerns
- hassle and stress factors
- contentment with real-world shopping
- concern with giving away too many personal details.

Many consumers feel manipulated by website owners. Roberts (2001) indicates that there is a general belief that companies will try to ensnare unwary visitors to their site into divulging personal information (for subsequent bombardments with sales messages). Novice consumers feel that the internet has taken on the marketing tactics of the bazaar – and needs to be treated with as much caution.

The internet and brands

Sutherland (2000) argues that brands are an essential component of the internet. He suggests that consumers need the familiarity of existing brands that are well established in their minds and already hold connotations for them. The tendency of major companies to create new brands for internet users denies them the opportunity of exploiting the existing heritage of established brands (Prudential became Egg; Yellow Pages became Yell, and so on).

The internet can be used to fulfil three major branding objectives (Swiffen-Green 2002):

- awareness, generated through the frequent exposure of simple messages;
- understanding through more complex messages in banners, pop-ups and microsites;
- relevance through appropriate placement, and targeted or customised content.

Brands today are not just bought, they are experienced by their consumers. In the age of the internet, the consumer is more empowered than ever before. A good or bad experience of a brand can be expressed on the internet is such a way that other consumers decisions can be impacted. On sites such as Amazon, the comments of other readers/purchasers can drive or inhibit subsequent purchases. Moreover, sites such as Kelkoo enable brand comparisons to be made in seconds, without the need to embark on a major information search.

Boutie (1996) argues that in the context of the new media, every brand fan can become an evangelist. They can spread the brand message and influence other consumers. Evidence of this occurring is widely and readily available. Many websites invite consumer feedback on the quality and efficacy of products.

Internet approaches

The demand for greater knowledge about how to create a successful brand presence on the internet continues to increase. At a recent meeting that included both internet and consumer goods companies, much of the discussion revolved around how the formal features of websites might be better utilised to create strong brands. A recent study suggests that larger, more complex internet ads may be more memorable, communicate more information and be more likely to engage consumers. Many marketers are beginning to demand that web content providers accommodate advertisements that use techniques known as 'rich media', that can enable both banners and bigger ads to include animation, sound and even full video. Despite this, most large consumer goods companies have been slow to adopt the use of advanced web design tools like animation and sound.

One of the most important dimensions that differentiates the new media from traditional media is the level of realism provided. New media can incorporate levels of vividness and interactivity that traditional media cannot. Not only is interactivity a fundamental difference between traditional media and online media, but the various online tools also differ in their degree of interactivity. In their 2002 paper, Yui and Schrum compared the seven most popular forms of online marketing tools on their degree of interactivity: They identified the most popular tools as:

- internet presence sites (company websites),
- web communities (websites that serve as a channel for information exchange between people with similar interests or beliefs),
- online stores,
- banner ads,
- pop-up ads,
- e-mail newsletters
- unsolicited e-mails (spam).

A further device is the use of cookies to track web users' site visiting habits. By tracking the sites visited, it is possible to build up a pattern of behaviour so that banner advertising can be located on those sites most likely to be visited (Derricott and Firouzabadian 2000).

There is a variety of internet advertising vehicles:

- text links which appear to be part of the editorial and are effective at driving traffic;
- banners and buttons which can be integrated into the editorial;
- rich media banners (including video and interactive) which, generally, have more impact than static banners;
- pop-ups, which are highly intrusive devices that can offer substantial branding information and calls to action;
- interstitials, which intrude on viewers as they move from one page to another;
- sponsorships, which link advertiser brand values with the established values of the media owner;
- webvertorials, which are a web-based version of the advertorial in which the advertiser's brand values are overtly displayed using the media owner's design and editorial to add credibility;
- e-mail can be used to attach complex branding information;
- desktop customising tools which change cursors, standard buttons and desktop design to reflect an advertiser's symbols.

Foster (2000) makes the point that internet surfers seek content, which is vital to the success of any medium. The top UK websites are content-rich. He states that one example of this is bbc.co.uk. It possesses three things that many websites do not – high-speed, accurate, sought after information; powerful database search facilities and the authority of the BBC brand. It delivers over 100 million impressions per month. The new online technologies provide the potential to improve depth and accuracy of search, speed of delivery or content refinement in a way better than previously possible. It is this that will attract new users.

Other key sites include sports information sites such as Cricinfo, Soccernet and Football365. The UK top site list also includes a number of financial investor sites such as Motley Fool. These sites serve a specific need for information which is valued by users. The newer and more accurate the information, the more value it has.

However, websites containing bland, outdated or irrelevant content fail to attract visitors. Those with poor content or low utility struggle to gain an audience. Many FMCG brands have websites. These include sites about chocolate, detergents, beauty products, alcoholic and soft drinks, food products, and so on. They do not offer any consumer usefulness and yet their corporate owners often wonder why they do not deliver traffic.

The competition to make use of use of broadband connections and create attractive sites is tempting designers to use more graphic images, more blinking text, more animation, more sound, more full-motion video, and so on. The surge in online advertising sees many major brands choosing to promote their products and services through banner advertisements on frequently visited pages such as Yahoo or Hotmail, the most popular sites for advertisers being large portals and search engines.

Lynch (2001) evidences that great expenditures are made to improve the quality of retail websites (e.g. ease of use, provision of helpful graphics, usefulness of search engines, completeness of information). In addition to the product, online vendors who provide quality functional and technical components on their websites increase the utility and value provided to the customer. The effort and investment placed on improving websites suggests that online sellers expect site quality to influence shoppers' likelihood of buying during this visit and making return visits.

New technologies allow for the provision of 'rich media'. Instead of static images, these allow for full movement and colour. Moreover, by co-operation with the internet service provider, it is possible to deliver these rich media directly to their customers.

According to the Internet Advertising Bureau in 2000, banner ads are the most popular advertising format on the web, accounting for 55 per cent of online ads. Ideally, banner ads induce consumer clicking, which links the consumer to the brand's target communication (usually the company website) and ultimately to a purchase. However, with an average of only a 1 per cent clickthrough rate, evidence suggests that the use of clickthrough or direct-response measures is likely to undervalue the web as an advertising medium. (A clickthrough rate is the percentage of the consumers seeing the ad who click on it.)

As the number of internet users increases daily, internet advertising grows in importance as one of the elements of the communications mix. Because of the controversy surrounding the effectiveness of banner advertising, many companies are seeking alternative formats for capturing online consumers. Research by Becker-Olsen (2003) provides an empirical investigation of the effects of banner advertising and sponsored content on website communities and their advertisers. Her studies demonstrate that web communities and advertisers both benefit from sponsored content. Specifically, sponsored content can be an effective advertising tool to engender positive response toward an advertiser and increase feelings of customer responsiveness, product quality, category leadership and even purchase intention. In addition, there is evidence that these types of messages are processed differently, indicating to communications managers that program objectives should drive the decision as to whether sponsored content, banner advertising or some combination of the two will be most effective.

The research also supports other findings that banner advertising can have positive company effects. It reinforces the lesson that banner ads need to be highly relevant to the site and the audience, as well as provide some added value, such as entertainment or, in this case, promotional inducement.

Against this, Derricott and Firouzabadian (2000) argue that banner advertising has inherent limitations. They liken it to some television advertising, where the main objective is to get as many people as possible to see the banner ad, with no real consideration of the need for effective targeting.

The physical size restrictions of the banner mean that the content is usually static images or basic animations. The result has been clickthrough rates as low as 0.5 per cent. Some marketers are using vertical portals, that is, banners placed on websites which are devoted to specific topics, such as cars, sports, entertainment, etc. These enable somewhat more precise targeting.

Emotional experiences during site use may also influence outcomes. Marketers know there is a better chance of winning customers if they 'feel good'. Positive affect speeds consumer decision making and enhances product recall with positive associations. Boutie (1996) argues that this dimension could be particularly important in those product categories where peer group assessment is an important dimension of the purchasing decision process. Indeed, he suggests that many companies will invest in 'brand ambassadors' to spread the positive message of the brand.

The traffic to a particular website can be maximised through:

- Paid advertising: This will include ads in traditional media as well as banner ads placed on web pages, such as those of search engines.
- Publicity and word-of-mouth: The web provides many opportunities for users to communicate with each other. Importantly, communication can be either positive or negative. The web provides an opportunity for disaffected customers to get their voice heard and represents a potential threat to business in the longer-term as e-business becomes more established.
- Portals and search engines: these can be useful intermediaries for producers in a specific market sector.
- Site and search design: An easy-to-use interface is an essential ingredient of a good website.

Measuring internet effectiveness

The web provides increased opportunities for measuring effectiveness. The facility to measure sources of traffic, and whether transactions take place enables the gathering of more detailed information about customer behaviour. According to Rowley (2001) there is a variety of measures that can be used:

- traffic
- visit duration
- conversion rate (visit to purchase)
- sales value

- number of transactions
- number of users.

A paper by Briggs and Stipp (1999) summarises the results of a large number of research projects conducted over recent years to explore the effectiveness of different types of advertising on the web. They concluded that:

- advertising on the internet can be very effective;
- for most forms of advertising, the web should not be regarded as a substitute for advertising in traditional media;
- internet advertising works best if it is part of a co-ordinated campaign that includes traditional advertising;
- clickthrough is not necessary for effects;
- reaching the right audience is key since online browsers are actively looking for information and, therefore, if the ad is not perceived as relevant they will pay little attention;
- creative execution plays a major role and can impact on the effectiveness of the use of the internet significantly.

Despite the internet's phenomenal growth, measurement and pricing practices on the web are far from being standardised. Most advertisers recognise that, for the internet to become a fully viable advertising medium, there must be uniform measures so that they can make direct comparisons with other media in campaign planning and evaluations. Because the internet enables advertisers to track responses to online ads, some argue that advertisers should pay for their internet ads on the basis of responses or performances. Others argue that such pricing and measurement methods would dismiss banner advertising's brand-building value and force web publishers to assume accountability for the creativity and effectiveness of messages.

A study by Millward Brown (1999) suggests that rich media significantly enhance brand perception, brand loyalty, purchase intent and click rates.

Research conducted by Fuyuan (2002) found that:

- An overwhelming number of the agencies surveyed frequently use cost per 000 (CPM) to price banner advertisements. Approximately one-third of the agencies use clickthroughs. Cost per outcome/action is the least-used pricing method. This shows that, despite the technical ability of the internet to track more precise user responses and actions, CPM remains a favourite pricing method.
- When using measures to gauge advertising effectiveness, most agencies indicate using clickthroughs and outcomes/actions rather than exposures or impressions. This indicates that, when it is feasible, interaction and performance-based benchmarks are favoured as measures of advertising effectiveness.
- Despite industry efforts to provide voluntary measurement metrics and guidelines, many agencies still consider the lack of standardisation and auditing as major problems facing internet banner advertising.
- Generally speaking, pre-testing banner ads is not common practice among interactive agencies. For those using pre-tests, the measures commonly used are clickthroughs and outcomes. Traditional measures such as awareness, attitude, and memory are less popular.

E-mail advertising

A further use of the internet is the ability to use e-mails as the basis of marketing campaigns. The internet enables virtual and real-time one-to-one communication. E-mail is the most popular manifestation of this. It enables the exchange of information and ideas in an efficient way. According to recent studies, e-mail is second only to the telephone as a form of technology used for communications. However, it offers significant advantages over the former in that it provides the vehicle for the delivery of a multimedia experience, incorporating graphics, audio and video files.

There is a variety of applications. Internet communication can take place in chat and news groups which is real-time, text-based communication between groups of users with a shared interest. News groups, similarly, allow virtual bulletin board-based communication between individual users and groups with a shared interest.

Increasingly it is the recipient rather than the sender who define whether e-mail and internet marketing works. The consequence has been to develop a new application known as permission-based marketing (Godin 1999). This is the automated use of e-mail to deliver content-rich messages to people who have voluntarily provided their contact details to a specific company or organisation. It overcomes the difficulties associated with the fact that people are becoming increasing discerning about which e-mails they choose to consider.

It offers the opportunity to forge a real two-way link between the sales and marketing department and it customers, whose previous visits to websites provided no real information.

In permission marketing, each e-mail from the customer generates a response from the company (and is noted in the customer database). A further action generates a further response and so on. Increasingly, the relationship becomes more personalised (Farris 2001).

Consumers provide interested marketers with the information about the types of advertising messages they would like to receive. The marketers then use this information to target advertisements and promotions to the consumer. This is seen as reducing clutter and lowering search costs for the consumer while increasing the targeting precision of marketers. Marketers obtain the trust of the consumer and build two-way relationships with consumers.

Permission marketing builds on relationship and one-to-one marketing by adding a new twist – customer-initiated targeting. When consumers target marketers and control the terms of the relationship, it is possible that it will lead to increased involvement and participation.

Cassady (2002) indicates that there are three key motivations for these companies and those planning to use permission marketing:

- **Better-targeted marketing communications:** Focusing on consumers who will be interested in what you have to offer is common sense. It ensures consumers get the mail they want and advertisers achieve the responses they need. It is basically creating a dialogue and a transparent exchange of information between consumers and advertisers, ensuring that the mail consumers receive is anticipated and welcomed. This has to be better than the non-permission route of buying huge lists of consumers, mailing or e-mailing them and, not surprisingly, annoying the majority of them merely to get adequate response rates.

- **Profitability:** It has not been unknown for response rates to increase by up to 400 per cent when compared with using traditional sources of data. Indeed, 60.5 per cent of those using permission data agreed that using opt-in files attracted more profitable customers.
- **Making good use of a customer database:** Permission marketing is about building relationships with customers and maximising the value of these relationships. The mechanics of permission marketing are key to this – listening to customers and providing them with what they want.

| **Experiential marketing** | Several authors suggest that the new media offers manufacturers a higher degree of involvement with the consumers. A new dimension is emerging under the heading of experiential marketing. O'Keefe (2000) suggests that experiential marketing represents a major new opportunity by providing consumers with an experience that matches the brand attributes. Consumers can participate with the brand in an interactive mode – examples are Ford, Citroen, Guinness, Nike and Levis. In some instances (Guinness) consumers are invited to download a screensaver which acts as a constant reminder of the brand promise. |

Case study

IPA Effectiveness Awards 2002 Grand Prix

Agency: Bartle Bogle Hegarty

Authors: Dan Goldstein and Mary Daniels

Barnados

Background

Barnados is one of Britain's oldest children's charities. For much of its history, however, it was known for running a number of orphanages. This case study shows how a campaign of integrated communications enabled Barnados to divorce itself from its orphanage past and embrace the future. In 1966 Barnardos began closing its orphanages. Over the next 35 years the charity was relatively quiet and there was little communication to the public about its new areas of work. This lack of dialogue had had a profound effect on how the charity was seen, particularly amongst younger age groups. For these people, 88 per cent spontaneously associated Barnardos with homes, orphanages and institutions. It was these people that Barnardos was looking to recruit and yet the charity's function appeared irrelevant to them in today's society.

The brand problem: the importance of donations

An increase in state funding experienced over the 1990s meant that Barnardos was becoming far too reliant on the public sector. This had compromised the charity's ability to lobby and campaign amongst MPs, a major area of the charity's work. Money from donations gives Barnardos the opportunity to work in areas too politically sensitive to be funded by the state, e.g. the charity's work with young asylum seekers. Donations are the only source of income that enables the charity to grow and invest in new projects.

The reason Barnardos' donations income was under threat lay in the profile of the charity's donor base. The people donating to Barnardos were old; over half were over 65. The vast majority of Barnardos' donor base was recruited via the charity's direct mail programme. It was clear that Barnardos needed not only new donors but a new profile of donor – younger, committed in their method of payment, longer term and higher value.

The brand challenge

The brand challenge was a considerable one – to replace Barnardos' orphanage past with a new vision. BBH identified a common and powerful theme. It was based on the unique way in which Barnardos approached childcare, one that differed from other children's charities, notably the NSPCC.

Where other charities intervene in the immediate circumstances, affecting the well-being of the child, Barnardos works to ensure the child's long-term 'emotional health'. Through this process Barnardos changes the future for children. The power of this thought lies in its 'truth' as an observation on how we develop as human beings and how our experiences shape all of our lives.

The next task was to communicate Barnardos' new purpose to all 12 500 people who work for the charity. A series of 'brand roadshows' travelled the country and visited each of the 16 regional offices. Within each office the new vision was presented to the heads of each department who in turn ran their own workshops for their own staff. By autumn 1999 all the people working for Barnardos understood that their efforts, their passion and commitment was in the pursuit of a single definable cause: children's futures.

The communications plan

The communications activity had a single objective: to recruit younger people into the brand to ensure future donations income. To this end, a broad target of 35–55-year-olds was selected. This age group not only gave more money in donations but they had more reason to care about children's futures being likely to have young children of their own. The task was to turn this lost generation of brand rejecters into active brand supporters.

Advertising was to reposition the brand as modern and deserving to the 35–55-year-olds. As well as this central objective, it needed to impact opinion formers. Face-to-face recruitment: a new channel to bring in new donors. Direct mail would see some of its budget cut in order to fund the face-to-face activity.

The advertising dramatised the 'future thought' in all its power. Children were shown acting out their future lives as a result of their disadvantaged childhood: a 4-year-old robs a bank; a 6-year-old solicits as a prostitute; an infant injects heroin. The copy described the troubled circumstances of their childhood, explaining how their lives took such a destructive path. A second campaign showed images of dead adults.

The advertising was in many ways designed to shock because it had to. We needed to present a cutting-edge, modern organisation at the forefront of childcare and shake people from an entrenched view that Barnardos ran orphanages and was therefore redundant today. During the process of developing the advertising the creatives were provided with case histories and visited some of the projects themselves. All the individuals in the advertising were based on real individuals and the ones used were not the most 'shocking'.

Media

The media choice for the advertising was the broadsheet press, the role of which fulfilled several strategic functions. A good coverage of the 35–55-year-old target audience; a readership who were more likely to be responsive to the advertising's 'challenging' content; and a medium read by 'social influencers' not just potential donors.

The advertising itself was of a serious subject matter, one that was felt to be in line with a broadsheet's editorial tone. The size of the layout presented an ideal format to provide the advertising even greater levels of power and impact. The immediacy of a newspaper environment helped position Barnardos as relevant in today's world.

How the re-launch impacted on the business

Since 21 October 1999 Barnardos' total income has increased by £46.6m on the 29-month-period before the relaunch. The fastest-growing source of income was from the 'direct marketing' programme. As a whole, direct marketing increased its contribution by 86 per cent over the same time period prior to relaunch.

Recruitment activity began in London during October 1999, tying in with the advertising launch. To date (February 2002) Barnardos has both recruited and retained 107 205 people via this method and the programme continues with no sign of exhaustion. As the base of recruits grows so too does the income from this source, totalling over £4m.

The combined communications strategy in recruiting the lost generation of younger donors had been highly effective. The majority (58 per cent) of the new recruits were the previously brand-rejecting 35–55-year-old age group. The addition of over 100 000 face-to-face recruits shifted the entire age profile of Barnardos' donor base. It has also increased the quality of donors. In September 1999 (the month prior to relaunch) only 3 per cent of Barnardos' donor base were using committed methods of payment. By February 2002 29 per cent of donors were committed.

It was advertising's role to drive the change in the way people defined Barnardos. Of all communications it was the advertising that had attracted the most awareness. For face-to-face to successfully recruit people in such high volumes the advertising needed to start changing their opinions from the outset. The power of the advertising's content ensured that it did.

Barnardos was now seen to be more modern, in line with other children's charities. People's spontaneous association of Barnardos with orphanages began to decline, a trend that continued through the life of the campaign. The net result of these perception shifts meant that people now saw Barnardos as more deserving.

Total communications effect

As well as repositioning Barnardos in the minds of potential donors, the relaunch also needed to create a change in how the opinion leader audiences perceived the charity. The advertising was the major communications channel to influence journalists, amongst whom the campaign had high awareness, second only to the big-spending NSPCC. Not only were they aware of the advertising but they were impressed by the charity's relaunch.

The campaign's provocative and shocking content made Barnardos a subject of a national debate, which took place in newspapers, magazines and on TV. The Committee of Advertising Practice (CAP) urged media owners not to run the controversial 'Heroin baby' execution. This was contrary to public opinion: there were only ever 28 complaints made to the Advertising

John Donaldson | AGE 23

Standards Authority (ASA): 57 per cent of people agreed that the advertising was 'shocking but effective'. Even Barnardos' head office received over 300 phone calls of support.

The value of the PR surrounding the 'Heroin baby' execution is alone worth £630 000. The nature of this coverage is far from simply a mention in editorial and in many cases is equivalent to free advertising space.

Face-to-face donors have already contributed over £4m to Barnardos since October 1999. The 'lifetime' value of these people over four years, including the income Barnardos has already received, is £15 681 961. Barnardos' total expenditure since October 1999 on the advertising (including agency and production fees) and the cost of the face-to-face activity = £8 766 779. This means the return on the advertising and face-to-face investment is £10 212 756. Or this can be expressed as a return of £2.16 on every £1 invested.

SOURCE: This case is adapted from the paper presented at the IPA Effectiveness Awards. The full version is available at www.warc.com and is reproduced by kind permission of the Institute of Practitioners in Advertising and the World Advertising Research Center.

Questions:

1 Why are an increasing number of companies opting for corporate campaigns over the development of individual branded messages?
2 How can small charities overcome the budget deficiencies to mount effective advertising campaigns targeted at their potential supporters and donors?
3 What benefits does the sponsor gain from links with charitable bodies?
4 Consider the role of infomercials compared to conventional advertising. What are the advantages and disadvantages of each?
5 How does interactive media enhance the prospect of establishing a 'dialogue' with consumers?
6 Identify the deficiencies of the internet as an advertising medium.
7 Why have so many internet companies failed to achieve their growth potential? What are the factors which inhibit many consumers from using the internet as a 'shopping' facility.

13 The development of international advertising

Learning outcomes

This final chapter aims to give you a grounding in:

- the growth of international marketing

- the reasons for the development of global brands

- the management of global brands and the implications for global branding

- the nature of the international consumer and the factors affecting international advertising

- the move towards global marketing communications.

The growth of international marketing

The years since the Second World War have seen an increasing tendency towards the internationalisation of brands. Indeed, the term used to describe the process – 'globalisation' – is itself comparatively recent. Increasingly, companies are recognising that their competitiveness, even in domestic markets, is a reflection of their ability to develop their brands on a global basis. Their focus, progressively, must be to develop products and services that satisfy a wider range of consumer needs. With this growth comes increased expertise, successive product improvements and economies of scale. As domestic markets have reached positions of virtual saturation, manufacturers have turned to new and often distant markets to ensure a continuation of their growth potential.

As Boyfield (2000) states, the dramatic explosion in global marketing can be attributed to a variety of factors:

- the liberalisation and privatisation of former state monopolies,
- the emergence of the internet as a new source of consumer information,
- a relaxation of outmoded retail regulations,
- the entry of new players challenging domestic incumbents,
- stricter competition rules adopted by national governments,
- a wave of merger and acquisition activity.

Mary Goodyear (2000) argues that the evolution of marketing is both consistent and predictable, and is based on the effects of time and economic growth, rather than culture. She contends that the process of 'consumerisation' is a response to increased choice and competition in the marketplace together with increased power and discrimination on the part of the consumer.

She suggests that the stages are progressive, and are as follows:

1 commodity selling
2 primitive marketing
3 classic branding
4 customer-driven marketing
5 post-modern marketing
6 cause-related marketing (a stage which is likely to dominate in marketing-sophisticated environments).

Multinational vs global marketing

We can make an important distinction between these two approaches to foreign markets – which have significant implications for the determination of marketing communications strategies.

The multinational company readily perceives the fundamental differences between the various markets it serves. In general, it believes that its success is dependent on the development of individual marketing and marketing communications programmes for each of its territories. As a result, it tends to operate through a number of subsidiaries which, for the most part, act independently of each other. Products are adapted, or developed independently, to meet the needs of the individual markets and the consumers within. By the same token, the other elements of the marketing mix are, similarly, developed on a local basis. Although there may be some cross-fertilisation of ideas through some form of central function, the primary aim is to satisfy the needs of individual country markets, rather than the specific identification of common elements that might allow for the standardisation of activities.

As Kanso (1992) states: 'Multinationals using a standardised approach believe that consumers anywhere in the world have the same basic needs and desires and therefore can be persuaded by universal appeals.'

The global organisation strives towards the provision of commonality, both in terms of its products and services, and the propositions which support them. As far as possible, it attempts to standardise its activities on a world-wide basis although, even within this concept, there is some recognition of the need for local adaptation to respond to local pressures. The fundamental objective is the identification of groups of buyers within the global market with similar needs, and the development of marketing and marketing communications plans that are standardised as far as possible within cultural and operational constraints.

As Grein and Ducoffe (1998) state:

Client companies are increasingly managing their businesses on broad regional or global basis. They wish to use more standardised campaigns around the world that they consider easier to administer. The desire to identify a unified brand image and position around the world has increased the impetus towards the globalisation of advertising agencies.

The impetus for a more detailed examination of the implications of international marketing was provided by a seminal article by Theodore Levitt (1983) in the

Harvard Business Review. The thrust of his argument in 'The Globalisation of Markets' is that a variety of common forces, the most important of which is shared technology, is driving the world towards a 'converging commonality'. The result, he argues, is 'the emergence of global markets for standardised consumer products on a previously unimagined scale'. Levitt suggested that 'companies must learn to operate as if the world were one large market, ignoring superficial regional and national differences'. However, this is far from being an accepted view. Philip Kotler (1994), among others, considers globalisation as a step backwards to the so-called 'production era' of business, when organisations were more concerned about producing as many standardised products as possible, rather than worrying about satisfying individual consumer needs and wants.

From a personal standpoint, I would argue that it is the convergence of communications that has, and will continue to have, a far greater impact and will assist those companies that are seeking to develop both standard products and standard marketing communications approaches. We have already seen that consumer motivations toward the purchasing of products and services are the result of the influence of a wide range of factors. One central factor that impacts upon many, if not all, of them is the mass media. As the peoples of the world are exposed to the same messages via television, film and other media, it is inevitable that their attitudes towards the products and services depicted will move towards a common central point. Slogans or icons on T-shirts seem familiar even in another language. Coca-Cola and Nike are everywhere. Search engines work in the same way; Napster allows everyone to listen to popular bands, a cacophony of different ethnic restaurants open next door to one another, internet cafés abound and consumption cultures – of coffee, for example – unite people across borders and across continents.

Irrespective of our location, it is likely that most of us will listen to the same music. The bands that top the charts in one country enjoy similar levels of success in others. The same films – which country has not yet been exposed to the *Harry Potter* movies, *Shrek 1* and *2* or *Troy* to name but a few – the same television programmes, the same computer programmes, and even the same articles in the media.

Whilst it is undeniable that cultural differences will continue to prevail, at least into the foreseeable future, so too we are witnessing the coming together of many attitudes and beliefs, which enhance the potential for products and services which respond to those common and shared values.

Simon Anholt (2002) suggests that several entirely new kinds of international business are now commonplace in a wide range of industries. These include

- global start-ups
- small global businesses
- global businesses with one office
- global businesses based in 'developing' countries.

In the past corporations only became global through the slow evolution from simple export marketing, via third-party licensee or distributor marketing, to global brand building directly from the country of origin. The process often took many decades. Indeed many of today's multinationals began their international growth at the beginning of the last century.

Many of the new international businesses have little fixed presence outside their market of origin. They de-duplicate as many corporate functions as possible, centralising such areas as NPD, finance, administration and, often, production. They use digital media to inform, distribute and sell. With internet, WAP and database technologies, they can sell things almost anywhere. These companies are seldom inspired to build global brands merely because the notion appeals. They are compelled to, because in the new economy a global brand may be their only real asset. The window of opportunity for new products was always brief, but increased competitiveness means that the temporary monopoly enjoyed by a new product might only last a few weeks before it is outperformed and underpriced by a crowd of imitators. Consequently, the only way in which these companies can achieve payback on their research and development efforts is by launching simultaneously in as many countries as possible.

The development of global brands

It is inevitable that the progressive standardisation of products results in significant economies of manufacture which, potentially, leads to lower prices and a more competitive positioning for the brand. The high investment in product development will be rapidly amortised if the market for the resulting product is global and enormous rather than domestic and limited. Such developments, however, will not obviate the need in many instances to adapt the product to meet 'special' local needs, however these are occasioned.

Some manufacturers perceive the world of the future to be one in which global brands dominate. The perceived benefits of a single world-wide brand identification outweigh those of country-specific products with separate brand identities. However, it is important to remember that, even here, it is not essential that the product delivered in each market is identical – only that the branding and the imagery associated with it are the same.

The arguments put forward in favour of global brands are widely known and compelling:

- They provide high economies of scale due to the standardisation of product platforms.
- Technology which is now present in most products is itself an inescapable homogenising force.
- The world has become a global village thanks to global media, CNN and the internet.
- At the segmentation level there is much more resemblance between executive working women living in New York and Paris than between themselves and other groups within their own country. As a result, nations and countries are no longer considered relevant criteria for market segmentation. Moreover with an increasing number of open markets being created, such as the EC, aiming at the disappearance of all trade, legal and fiscal barriers in the Euro zone.
- At the consumer level, both common observation and recent empirical studies have shown that brands perceived as global induced better quality ratings, which in turn increased desire to buy.

- Lastly, as distributors themselves go global, they expect their suppliers to do the same.

According to Anholt (2002), international branding is no longer a choice, it has become a necessity. The new global communications channels, the mobility of the consumer, the globalisation of the economy, the internet and the 'vigilante consumer' have ensured that no brand building can ever take place in geographic isolation. It is no longer tenable for a brand to adopt different positionings in different territories; and a brand that fails to express its core values consistently from country to country will leak equity until it learns to be true to itself.

Few companies can afford fragmentation and inefficiency. The process of briefing, managing, co-ordinating and monitoring the work of many separate agencies is a major task, even for mature companies, with marketing offices in each country. For the emerging international marketers who sell direct to the consumer worldwide, or who rely on agents or distributors abroad, adequate management of brand communications becomes almost impossible.

International marketing in the twenty-first century is not about ignoring or over-riding cultural differences, but about understanding, accommodating and harnessing them in the service of global brand building.

Even where it is necessary to subjugate the current brand identity in favour of a single consistent world-wide brand mark, major manufacturers have determined that the long-term benefits are likely to outweigh the short-term losses. Despite enjoying considerable consumer acceptance in the UK with their Marathon brand, Mars opted for a standardisation of the brand under the name of Snickers across all markets. The same policy has now been applied to Opal Fruits, renamed as Starburst. In a similar manner, Unilever have standardised the name of their household cleanser as Cif, replacing the brand names used in various countries such as Jif, Vif, etc.

However, the arguments in favour of the global approach are not accepted by all. In March 2000, Coca-Cola's then CEO Douglas Daft announced the company's new 'think local, act local' marketing strategy. As Quelch (2003) pointed out, having embraced Levitt's vision for decades, executives in America's global companies began to appreciate that they had taken their global brand strategies too far. With their centralised decision making and standardised marketing programmes, they had lost touch with the new global marketplace.

As sales slumped, global brand owners started to listen more closely to their local business partners about how to adapt product attributes and advertising messages to local tastes. They began delegating more authority over product development and marketing to local managers. And they started developing and promoting local executives to take over from expatriates.

Meanwhile, some US multinationals like Philip Morris and Coca-Cola ramped up their acquisition of local brands – for the same reasons that investors diversify a stock portfolio. Today, two-thirds of Coca-Cola's sales in Japan are from local beverage brands, and the company now owns more than 100 local beverage brands world-wide. In some cases, the global brand owners are financing totally separate companies. Unilever India, for example, has set up the free-standing Wheel organisation as a low-cost enterprise that markets quality, low-priced local brands to the mass market.

Byfield and Caller (1996) argue that brands hold the same value in whichever markets they occupy. However, the reasons for purchase may differ. Klaus Wustrack (1999) provides the example of Alcatel to illustrate this point. He found that customers for mobile phones had different reasons for purchase depending on their country of residence. Women in the UK purchased mobile phones as a means of security; middle-class consumers from China bought mobile phones as a status symbol; whilst those in South Africa found that due to the lack of fixed wire infrastructure, it was actually easier to buy a mobile.

Even the usage of the word 'brand' has to be re-interpreted in the international context. According to Mary Goodyear (1996) Western marketers tend to focus on the product as brand; in Japan and Korea 'brand' tends to refer to the corporate entity. The consequence is that it tends to be evaluated over a much longer time scale. Individual 'brands' can come and go, but the total corporate share become the centre of long-term planning. Mitsubishi and Daewoo are good examples of this, with both companies maintaining diverse interests in a wide variety of, sometimes, unrelated markets.

It is important to recognise that, in developing countries, brands play a significantly smaller role in terms of the regular shopping process. Many products that have become brands in Western society (bread, biscuits, milk, sugar) remain as commodities which continue to be purchased loose (without packaging) in other parts of the world.

Trust is a key dimension of a brand. A recent survey conducted by Reader's Digest identified the World's most trusted brands. The results are summarised in Table 13.1.

Table 13.1 The world's most trusted brands

Category	Number of winning brands	Brands winning in more than 3 countries	Number of countries
Mobile phone	1	Nokia	14
Credit card	2	Visa	13
Skin care	3	Nivea	12
Camera	4	Canon	10
PC	6	IBM (4); Dell (3)	
Hair care	6	Pantene (5) L'Oréal (4)	
Soap powder	6	Ariel (6) Persil (3)	
Car	7	Mercedes (4) VW (4)	
Toothpaste	7	Colgate	6
Cosmetics	8	Avon (4) Nivea (3)	
Pain relief	10	Aspirin	7
Kitchen appliance	11	Miele	4
Petrol retailer	11	Shell	3
Soft drink	12	Coca-Cola	3

SOURCE: Reader's Digest 2004

As globalisation is increasing, the scope and rationale for local differentiation is being reduced. In practice, the number of truly standardised global brands is limited – Burger King, BMW, Mazda, Coke and Pepsi. Many brands – like Kit Kat and Colgate – are global in name but have shown significant differences in positioning, branding and packaging from country to country. The reality of globalisation is that usually some decisions are standardised, whilst others are tailored to local needs. For example, ClubMed attempts to standardise its villages, quality and advertising themes, but not its promotional activities and budgets. Very often global brands coexist with local brands. As Pawle (1999) indicates:

> The attributes of brands are often common globally. It is remarkable how stable brand images often are in different cultures, despite somewhat different packaging in some cases and despite the lack of a global advertising campaign. There are, however, significant differences in the ways that people in different cultures respond to brand images, including how products are used.

According to Aaker and Joachimsthaler (1999) global brands are 'brands whose positioning, advertising strategy, personality, look and feel are in most respect the same from one country to another'.

Byfield and Caller (1996) describe three distinct categories of global brand:

1 long-term international brands (mostly American), which are exploiting a universal heritage;
2 new products, which have been developed with a global consumer in mind;
3 brands which have begun life in one or more markets and then have been exported to others.

They argue that the crucial issue is that brands hold the same values in whichever markets they are available. It is evident that brands can become irrelevant if their image is not kept in step with changes in society.

The world's leading brands are familiar to people in virtually every country in the world. The Interbrand survey assesses some 350 brands against a series of criteria as follows:

- brand weight: the extent of the dominance of a brand over its market;
- brand length: the extent of brand extension outside of its original category;
- brand breadth: the strength of the brand across age, gender, nationality and religion;
- brand depth: a measurement of consumer commitment to the brand.

Based on these dimensions, the top 20 global brands in 2003 were as shown in Table 13.2.

The scale of expenditures of the world's global marketers can be seen in Table 13.3.

For many years, Procter & Gamble has promoted its global brands, progressively eliminating small local competitive brands before axing its own stronger local versions. Although many of these were category leaders in a particular country market, they were none the less removed from the portfolio in favour of brands that the company could market on an international basis. In 2000, Unilever announced a similar policy, with plans to axe three-quarters of their 1400 brands within a timescale of 3–5 years.

Table 13.2 Top 20 global brands, 2003

	2003 ($ billions)	2002 ($ billions)	Percentage change
Coca-Cola	70.45	69.64	+1
Microsoft	65.17	64.09	+2
IBM	51.77	51.19	+1
GE	42.34	41.31	+2
Intel	31.11	30.86	+1
Nokia	29.44	29.97	−2
Disney	28.04	29.26	−4
McDonald's	24.70	26.38	−6
Marlboro	22.18	24.15	−8
Mercedes	21.37	21.01	+2
Toyota	20.78	19.45	+7
Hewlett-Packard	19.86	16.78	+18
Citibank	18.57	18.07	+3
Ford	17.07	20.40	−16
American Express	16.83	16.29	+3
Gillette	15.98	14.96	+7
Cisco	15.79	16.22	−3
Honda	15.63	15.06	+4
BMW	15.11	14.43	+5
Sony	13.15	13.90	−5

SOURCE: Interbrand 2003

Table 13.3 Top 10 multinational advertisers, 2002

	Company	US $ million
1	Procter & Gamble	4497
2	Unilever	3315
3	General Motors	3218
4	Toyota	2405
5	Ford	2387
6	Time Warner	2349
7	Daimler Chrysler	1800
8	L'Oréal	1683
9	Nestlé	1547
10	Sony Corp.	1513

SOURCE: *Advertising Age* 2002

The proponents of globalisation can demonstrate the enormous economies that are made when several local brands are replaced by one single world-wide offering. The opportunities to feature these brands in international media events such as the World Cup, the Olympics, Formula 1, etc. are undeniable.

Quelch (1999) suggests that the degree of standardisation of global brands will be dependent on the product category. In culture-bound categories like food, there will be larger cultural and national food differences, but with a product like a PC the criteria are basically the same everywhere. He asserts that the impact of the Euro Zone will encourage further movement towards pan-European branding. The introduction of a single currency has made differential pricing across borders more transparent, with the consequence that brands will become subject to diversion, i.e. where parallel imports are made between high- and low-price countries. He suggests that the biggest consumers of global brands are the youth market – today, one teenager is much like any other, regardless of borders.

Duffy and Medina (1998) suggest that as long as domestic environments remain fundamentally different to foreign environments, then there will be the need for adaptability.

Attracted by such high-profile examples of success, many companies are tempted to try to globalise their own brands. The problem is, that goal is often unrealistic. Consolidating all advertising into one agency and developing a global advertising theme – often the cornerstone of the effort – can cause problems that outweigh any advantages. And edicts from on high – 'Henceforth, use only brand building programmes that can be applied across countries' – can prove ineffective or even destructive. Managers who move toward creating a global brand without considering whether such a move fits well with their company or their markets risk major damage to the brand. Kapferer (2000) cites several reasons for that.

First, economies of scale may prove elusive. It is sometimes cheaper and more effective for companies to create ads locally than to import ads and then adapt them for each market. Moreover, cultural differences may make it hard to pull off a global campaign: even the best agency may have trouble executing it well in all countries. Finally, the potential cost savings from 'media spill-over'- in which, for example, people in France view German television ads – have been exaggerated. Language barriers and cultural differences have made realising such benefits difficult for most companies.

Second, forming a successful global brand team can prove difficult. Developing a superior brand strategy for one country is challenging enough; creating one that can be applied world-wide can be daunting (assuming one even exists). Teams face several stumbling blocks: they need to gather and understand a great deal of information, they must be extremely creative, and they need to anticipate a host of challenges in execution. Relatively few teams will be able to meet all those challenges.

Third, global brands can't just be imposed on all markets. For example, a brand's image may not be the same throughout the world. Honda means quality and reliability in the United States, but in Japan, where quality is a given for most cars, Honda represents speed, youth and energy. And consider market position. Cadbury in the United Kingdom and Milka in Germany have pre-empted the associations that connect milk with chocolate; thus neither company could implement a global positioning strategy.

However, there remain significant opportunities for local brands, even those from international companies. Kapferer (2000) reports on the recent successful introduction of a new cigarette brand from BAT to Russia. Yava Gold was the product chosen to challenge the position of Marlboro, a local brand. Similarly, in the Czech Republic, Danone focused their attention on Opavia, a local brand, rather than launching one of their internationally known branded products.

In another paper, the same author (Kapferer 2002) indicates that following the analysis of the many cases where local brands hold strong if not dominating market shares and qualify as real assets for their companies, a number of explanatory variables emerge. They can be grouped under six factors:

1 structural factors, such as frequency of purchase;
2 brand equity factors, such as being perceived as an institution;
3 competitive factors;
4 corporate general strategy;
5 organisational factors linked to the corporate culture and orientation;
6 environmental factors such as the nationalistic feelings of the country.

The management of global brands

Companies adopt varied approaches to the management of global brands. Research conducted by Focus (Aitchison 1995) indicated that, amongst the companies surveyed in their study representing a cross-section of major international brands, there was a general consensus that there should be conformity of product or service delivery. The varied attitudes and approaches to international branding issues can be seen from the following company statements:

> 'In our business, globally-consistent product performance and packaging, coupled with visual consistency, is a pre-requisite.' (Shell)

> 'We are committed to standard product performance with a consistent presentation across all markets.' (Kellogg's)

However, a key factor was the ability to recognise and respond to consumer needs:

> 'A global brand has an appeal than can transcend political, ethnic, social or cultural boundaries.' (IBM)

> 'We create and satisfy the same need, using the same values in each country.' (Coca-Cola)

The research suggests that successful global brands satisfy at least one of three categories of consumer needs – physiological, personal utility or self-worth. In each instance, however, the satisfaction of those needs also requires the endorsement of brand values and positionings that themselves have universal relevance. Without such endorsement, the brand remains open to competition from locally produced brands, either 'me-too' or those of an innovative nature.

As Anholt (1998) states: 'Understanding the personality of a brand is crucial as it conditions every marketing activity, if well understood and communicated will provide the coherence that brands need in order to survive intact around the world.'

Planners and marketing teams spend a great deal of time and effort trying to define a single meaningful identity for their brands that can be implemented across international markets. If it is possible to identify a single, succinct motivating identity, it is possible that it can generate a single advertising strategy and, ultimately, a single campaign.

Marketing managers in consumer goods companies often customise brand image across international markets. The study findings show that the extent to which managers customise versus standardise brand image is related to variations in national environmental market conditions. When markets differ in cultural uncertainty avoidance, individualism, and national socio-economics, managers tend to respond by using an image customisation strategy. When markets do not differ cross-nationally in those conditions, managers are much more likely to use an image standardisation strategy (Roth 1995).

A major benefit of globalisation is efficiency and economies of scale:

'A global brand gives us significant economies of scale right across the board – in media and production costs, sponsorship, manufacturing and management costs.' (International food and drinks manufacturer)

'Global branding gives us major cost efficiencies in marketing and production as well as a powerful tool to control our brand through joint ventures and third party distributors' (Global brewer)

'We ended up with too many centres of manufacturing across Europe, with too many products and with too many brand names; we have been rationalising on all fronts.' (Pedigree petfoods)

'Our consistent brand image and wide availability is very important to our customers – they themselves are very international in outlook.' (Bacardi)

Differing attitudes and approaches are evidenced towards the development of international marketing communications campaigns:

'We impose strong control from HQ, with clearly defined brand and advertising strategy being passed down to the local offices. All advertising is approved at HQ and local freedom is largely limited to local promotion and distribution activity.' (Bacardi)

'The development of the British Airways brand and its sub brands (such as Club World) is managed from Head Office. A partnership process between head office and the regions, jointly agrees a 3 year plan.' (British Airways)

'The HQ marketing function underpins our national marketing decisions. We put forward our plans and budgets with an overall brand framework.' (Moulinex)

It is possible to describe a strategic matrix of international brand options. Figure 13.1 is taken from Hankinson and Cowking (1996).

Brand standardisation is an international marketing strategy which consists of producing one product and selling it in the same way everywhere in the world, with the same specification and characteristics. Research carried out by Rieisenbeck and Freeling (1991) indicates that successful global marketers are those that ensure

Figure 13.1 Strategic matrix of international brand options

		Product formulation	
		Standardised	Adapted
Brand proposition	Standardised	Fully global e.g McDonalds	Product adaptive e.g Shell
	Adapted	Proposition adaptive e.g Gordon's Gin	Fully adaptive e.g Nescafé

SOURCE: Hankinson and Cowking 1996

that they standardise the core elements of their brands. Their findings indicate that the companies that did not change or compromise the core elements of their brand – those which they consider to be at the heart of their business – proved most successful. Adaptation was implemented in other dimensions of the marketing mix to ensure global branding success.

Aaker and Joachimsthaler (1999) suggest five guidelines to be effective in global brand management:

1   It should include an analysis of the customers and brand associations that resonate with the, its competitors so it can differentiate itself from its competitors via its communication plan. Lastly, it should carry out an audit of the brand with its heritage, image, strengths and vision.

2   Fixation on product attributes should be avoided. The majority of strong brands go beyond functional attributes and deliver emotional benefits, through brand personality, user imagery, intangibles associated with the company, innovativeness, or reputation for quality, and symbols associated with the brand.

3   Communication should be made effective internally throughout the company. Everyone should have a clear understanding about the company's objectives for brand building to be a success.

4   Brand equity, measurement and goals are very important; without these brand building will be all talk and no real action. Brand equity should be measured in terms of customer awareness, customer loyalty, brand personality and associations that resonate with the public.

5   The process needs to tie in global brand strategies with country brand strategies, which can be done via a top-down approach beginning with a global brand strategy then country brand strategies following from it. The bottom up approach would be global brand strategies build around country brand strategies. Country strategies are grouped by similarity, which can be based on market maturity, or by

its competitive context. Although there will be differences in brand strategies for these groupings, the global brand strategy should be able to find the common elements and, over time, should be able to capture synergies.

International branding considerations

In the development of companies, many find themselves forced to seek further opportunities to continue the process of brand expansion. In many cases, these opportunities exist by expanding into new countries. The benefits which can be derived from the economies of production, and the apparent similarity of the markets in other countries, has attracted some brands to expand beyond their original marketplaces. The process of developing international brands is very similar to that adopted for national brands although, inevitably, it is both more complex and more time consuming – especially if the underlying desire is to achieve parity of brand image in all of the markets in which the product is sold.

A series of fundamental questions must first be asked about how products in the category are expected to perform in different markets. The functional areas of a product may be different from country to country. Despite the fact that many consumers in different countries all drink instant coffee, for example, should not suggest that their expectations of product performance are the same. People in almost all of the Latin countries, for example, tend to drink their coffee much stronger than, say, in the UK. Offering the same blend to all markets might lead to acceptance in some, but would find rejection in most. The evaluation of the performance of washing powders might be the same in most markets – 'How white do they get my clothes?' – but factors such as the way in which the product is used may have an important bearing. Is the penetration of automatic washing machines similar or do many consumers in some markets still wash by hand?

Understanding the brand personality is, arguably, even more important in the international context. We have seen that the dimensions of brand personality are, largely, perceptual. They relate to the images that have been created over time by the various aspects of marketing communications. Equally important, however, they relate to elements of consumer behaviour in the different markets. In some markets, the use or possession of a particular product may have no meaning beyond its functional purposes. In others, it may be regarded as a symbol of success or affluence. Setting, what for some is an aspirational product in a mundane environment – but a wholly appropriate setting for others – for advertising purposes is likely to undermine the values associated with the brand. It is important to ensure that there is an adequate 'fit' between the positioning of the brand and the perceptions of the consumers in all of the markets in which it is to be sold.

Ultimately, of course, it may be possible to alter the underlying perceptions and reach a point at which all markets share a common view of the brand. Until that time is reached, however, it is important that the brand continues to deliver against the expectations of the consumers who purchase it.

There are important international dimensions to aspects of branding:

1 **Certain products have strong associations with particular countries.** Pasta with Italy; perfume with France. This has an impact on the brand name decision, even

if the product does not originate from the particular country. Japan has been long associated with high-quality products in the fields of high technology. Many electrical products have adopted Japanese-sounding brand names even though they are manufactured elsewhere. Both Germany and Japan enjoy strong reputations for the production of high-quality cars. Recently, Cadbury's were ordered to withdraw a chocolate bar sold under the name of 'Swiss Chalet' because it implied that the product was Swiss.

This notion of 'country of origin' has been suggested by a number of writers to have a 'halo effect' on the purchasing decision, particularly in those circumstances where the consumer is unfamiliar with the particular brand (Johansson et al. 1995; Min Han 1990).

Country-of-origin image refers to 'buyers' opinions regarding the relative qualities of goods and services produced in various countries. Parameswaram and Pisharodi (1994) argue that few multinational marketers and advertisers make full use of their product's favourable country of origin image (or successfully overcome the liability associated with an unfavourable one).

2 **The image of imported products as opposed to products produced in the home country.** This ethnocentricity has an important bearing, which may be either positive or negative. France has long had a reputation for biasing consumption to domestically produced products. Its car market enjoys a significantly higher penetration of domestically produced cars than most other countries.

The opposite impact of the country of origin can be seen from an example provided in a paper by Bilkey and Nes (1982) in which they cite a Puerto Rican shoe manufacturer which exported its entire production to New York and then re-imported them in order that they could advertise the shoes as being from New York. The manufacturer felt that the shoes would be better received as being made in New York than in their own country.

3 **The national image of the manufacturing company,** e.g. Waterford Glass is seen as being an Irish product, although part of its production is sourced from Poland.

David Head (1998), writing in the *International Journal of Advertising*, suggests that there are three distinct categories of 'made in' appeals:

1 Appeals to national pride and the patriotism of consumers.
2 Appeals that highlight stereotypical attributes of a country and associate those attributes with a specific brand.
3 Appeals that suggest a particular expertise which is associated with a country. Switzerland is associated with manufacturing expertise in the field of watches, for example.

The majority of international brands were originally conceived on a national level and developed to achieve recognition within their original markets. Brand names were more often selected because of the impact in their own national context. This can lead to particular problems when the product is exported to other markets.

A major brand of lemonade in France is sold under the name of Pschitt; whilst

Zit is a soft drink in Greece; one of the leading brands of toilet tissues in Scandinavia is retailed under the name of Krapp; Fanny is a canned tuna product; Skum a Swedish confectionery; Colon is a Spanish brand of washing detergent. Each of these products might encounter difficulties in other markets!

International brands share a number of consistent characteristics:

1 The products all share a long-term orientation. The majority of recognised international brands have established long-term consumer awareness and recognition which, in turn, achieves brand goodwill. Coca-Cola was first introduced in 1886. Ivory Soap is over 100 years old; Kellogg's first produced corn flakes in the 1880s. Avon was adopted as the name for the company previously trading as the California Perfume Company. Today it has an estimated 1.6 million representatives in over 100 countries. Cadbury started manufacturing drinking chocolate in 1831 and eating chocolate in the early 1870s (the use of the name Bourneville was a reflection of the then prestige of French chocolate). Production of the safety razor by King Camp Gillette commenced in 1903. George Eastman produced the first Kodak camera in June 1888 and has been associated with photographic products since that time. Lego, synonymous with children's toys, is a derivative of the Swedish words 'leg godt' (play well). The company first introduced its product in the 1930s and today produces 97 per cent of its products for export – to over 106 countries.

2 International brands are mostly those products that have established a consumer reputation based on considerable and cumulative advertising expenditure. The advertising budget for Kellogg's was as high as $1 million in 1911. Heinz adopted the slogan '57 varieties' in the late 1880s, even though the company manufactured more than 60 even then. The copy line has remained unchanged since that time.

3 According to Shalofsky (1987) many of these international brands have a basic credibility which relates to their national image. Marlboro cigarettes and Coca-Cola share an American heritage. Buitoni (now owned by Nestlé) is synonymous with Italy, the home of good pasta.

The international consumer and international advertising

Understanding the international consumer

If marketing communications demands a thorough understanding of consumers and the environmental factors that surround them, this is even more true of marketing communications in an international context. Where we can reasonably expect to understand important facets of consumer behaviour in a domestic context, this is far less likely to be the case in different and separate markets where culture, tradition and other factors may result in vastly different meanings being attached to the communications message.

Market research will play an important part in identifying those areas of similarity in order to allow for the development of a single consistent message, if that is the objective. It should be clear that, in order to develop an effective multinational or global communications strategy, a number of 'new' dimensions will have to be considered, beyond those which would be appropriate for a single-market communications strategy.

The model of communications, discussed earlier in Chapter 2, needs some re-examination in the international context. See Figure 13.2.

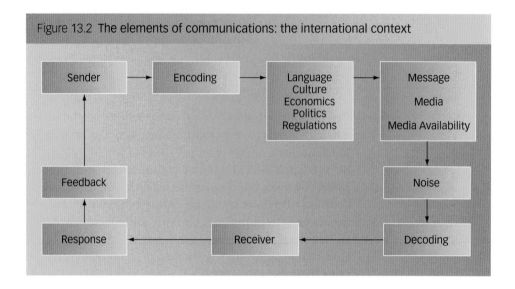

Figure 13.2 The elements of communications: the international context

Language

Language is an obvious discriminating factor in the international context. It has been suggested that there are over 3000 different languages in current use. Some are indigenous to a single country or region, others are commonly spoken in several different countries. Many countries are multilingual. Canadian law requires that all product packaging be produced in both English and French; in Belgium, potential consumers may speak French or Flemish; India has over 200 distinct languages or dialects.

Although English is increasingly the lingua franca of many major international businesses (many companies are American owned and insist that business is conducted in their own tongue), it was Winston Churchill who suggested that the USA and Britain were two nations separated by a common language. This can be illustrated by a series of examples demonstrating different meanings attached to the same words. Recently, an American advertiser described his product, in a domestic campaign, as 'a little bugger'. The word has a somewhat different meaning in the UK. Brand names may suggest different connotations in different markets. The brand name Durex is the leading brand of contraceptives in the UK whilst in Australia it is a major brand of adhesive tape!

Increasingly, international advertising campaigns feature words in English, although their appearance is scheduled for countries where English is not the mother tongue. Whilst on the surface, this might not appear to pose a problem, it may have negative consequences if the words used can be incorrectly translated. The Vauxhall Nova, for example, was introduced to Spain where the word literally means 'doesn't go'. A previous Pepsi campaign slogan – 'Come alive, you're in the Pepsi generation' was translated into German. Unfortunately, the German slogan meant 'come alive out of the grave'!

Multinational communications campaigns often fail because the message is simply translated rather than reinterpreted. This is not simply merely a semantic difference. Not only is it true that specific words often will not have a correspondence in another language, sometimes the true translation will have a negative impact on the target audience. Colgate Palmolive launched its Cue toothpaste in France without first establishing the meaning of its brand name. To its surprise, it subsequently discovered that the word is a pornographic expression. Schweppes discovered that its leading tonic water product translated in Italy to bathroom water.

As Garcia (1998) states:

> The problem is not the language itself, but is reflected in the language. One language represents only one cultural framework. Speakers of different languages not only say things differently, they experience things differently and the fact that there are rarely direct translations (especially for abstract words) is a reflection of this.

Anholt (1993) states that: 'advertising works when consumers believe they are being spoken to by somebody who understands them, who knows their needs and talks and feels just as they do – not a foreigner speaking to them through an interpreter.' Unfortunately, several campaigns fail to recognise this important fact and come across as 'foreign' commercials intended for another market.

Culture and tradition

A critical dimension of international marketing communications is the divergent nature of the cultures in which the activity will be seen. Culture, as discussed earlier, is that complex whole which includes knowledge, beliefs, art morals, customs and the various other capabilities and habits which are acquired as a member of a particular society.

Arguably, this is one of the most difficult areas of multinational communications. Perceptions that are based on tradition and culture are extremely difficult to overcome. Fundamental areas, such as pack colours or symbols, may have totally different meanings resulting from cultural interpretation.

Culture is learned behaviour, passed on from one generation to another. Often it is a difficult barrier for the outsider to cross, substantially because we tend to observe other people in the context of our own cultural values. In many cases, the differences between societies are quite subtle and may not be immediately apparent. They may influence, for example, the ways in which people relate to each other, the roles of men and women within society, eating habits, relationships with authority and dress habits, both within the working environment and in informal situations. Any of these elements may be a component of a marketing communications campaign which, in order to communicate effectively, must be considered within the context of the cultural values of the society in which the campaign is to be run.

When Disney introduced its theme park to Paris, it adopted the same style of operation as had been successful elsewhere. As in the USA and Japan, alcoholic drinks were banned. Subsequently, however, they were forced to change their policy when they recognised the French tradition of drinking wine with meals.

At a superficial level, cultural values can be modified over time, resulting in the creation of a form of 'global culture'. Sometimes, this is the result of people working within multinational companies, which may seek to impose constant values in all of the countries in which they operate. Equally, some of the imagery created by brands may become accepted within many, otherwise, diverse cultures.

Work conducted by the Henley Centre for Forecasting has suggested that there are important factors of consumer convergence throughout Europe and elsewhere.

The increasing domination of Anglo-American culture in terms of music, films and so on carry with them a variety of cultural and brand values. Films, particularly those of American origin, gain almost immediate world-wide distribution. This is less true in reverse. Music and film material developed elsewhere gains, at best, limited distribution and often only in exclusive 'arts' theatres.

Most significantly, the cultural values, sometimes derived from religious views, result in markedly different attitudes towards products and services. Several examples will illustrate. It would be an anathema to show pork or shellfish ingredients in a product intended for a predominantly Jewish market; the same would apply to beef in Hindu communities or alcohol for Muslims. Several years ago, McDonald's suffered from a failure to understand the cultural dimensions of one of its markets. Orthodox Jews in Israel campaigned for the removal of McDonald's advertising from television. The advertising standards committee at Israel's Channel 2 network put their weight behind the proposed ban, since it recognised that the campaign offended religious observers.

Similarly, Nike was forced to withdraw a line of training shows because the logo, intended to look like flames, resembled the word 'Allah' in Arabic and offended Muslims. The company was also forced to remove a poster that showed a basketball player with the headline 'They called him Allah'.

Whilst the specific advertising message might avoid such obvious errors, it is important to remember that the surroundings in which the message is set (a home, a retail outlet, etc.) may, similarly, contradict existing cultural beliefs in some markets. In some markets, for example, it would be inappropriate to depict a woman wearing Western clothes; in others, a commonly used motif of a man stroking a woman's skin to connote smoothness would be regarded as taboo.

Even large brands sometimes fail to appreciate the significance of local cultural factors. Retail audits suggest that Pepsi controls up to 80 per cent of the Saudi Arabian market. Several years after entering the market Coca-Cola has been unable to gain a significant share. Much of Coke's advertising has featured images of everyday people – predominantly Western – to whom the Saudi people found it difficult to relate. Pepsi has tended to take an impersonal approach, featuring just the brand logo itself, without the use of people. If people are used, they will be Middle Eastern. By these means, Pepsi has identified itself as part of the Saudi Arabian society.

Equally, the nature of the individual purchase decision may vary as a result of cultural influences. The role of the family may, in certain circumstances, be more important in the final determination of which products and services to purchase. This is particularly true in parts of Asia. For example, the discretion over the use of income is heavily influenced by the expected contribution to the family. The tradition of deference to parental wishes affects patterns of buying in clothing, leisure expenditure, etc. (Redding 1982).

The differences between Western and Asian cultures are summarised in Table 13.4.

Byfield and Caller (1996) indicate that different peoples, from different backgrounds and cultures, receive and decode messages differently. Responses to advertising around the world differ, but they are not static. Further, they demonstrate that may respondents, particularly those in central Europe, want advertising to be information-led. Advertising showing Western-style images often produced discon-

Table 13.4 Differences between Western and Asian cultures

Western individualism		Asian collectivism
Beliefs in competition, challenge, self-expression	Values	Beliefs in harmony, co-operation, avoiding confrontation
Personal responsibility, independence		Shared responsibility, interdependence
Doing one's 'own thing'		Public self and 'face'
Question authority		Respect for authority, age and seniority
Nuclear family, self and immediate family	Sources	Extended family, blood/kinship and work groups
'I' and 'me'		'Us' and 'we'
Guilt and conscience	Control	Shame and 'face'

SOURCE: Cooper 1997

tentment, either because there were insufficient funds to buy the offerings, or because the advertisements were perceived as inappropriate. Moreover, as Anholt (1993) indicates:

> Advertising is so intimately linked with the popular culture, the social fabric, the laws, the advertising conventions, the buying habits, the aspirations, the style, the humour, and the mentality of people that messages just cannot be communicated in precisely the same way in different countries.

In developed countries, consumers have well-developed relationships with brands. In the developing world, millions of people who are new to the concept of branding are receiving broadcast messages about them. These messages reach people with varying degrees of education and experience and who have, at best, only a limited knowledge about the brand and what the advertisement is saying. They can only decode commercial communications within their own context and experience.

The influence of cultural values on brands – some cultural drivers are different, particularly in the East, where collectivism and reluctance to create social conflict – means that there are differences in the way that consumers respond to brands.

Understanding cultural differences is often considered a prerequisite for successful international advertising. The reasoning is that consumers grow up in a particular culture and become accustomed to that culture's value systems, beliefs and perception processes. Consequently, they respond to advertising messages that are consistent with their culture, rewarding advertisers who understand that culture and tailor ads to reflect its values. Matching advertising appeals to culture is advisable for advertisers, especially in the case of sharply contrasting cultures. A study by Zhang and Gelb (1996) suggests that an advertiser who takes such a market seriously will seek to align message with culture.

As with many other elements of popular culture, advertising has developed its own particular systems of meaning. These are by no means universal across borders according to the target market, but rather are often culturally defined and frequently vary from country to country.

Becatelli and Swindells (1998) illustrate this with several examples. German advertising tends to reflect the nation's cultural psyche with frequent references to ecology, individuality and the 'man against the elements' motif which has been ingrained in German culture since the naturalist movement of the eighteenth and nineteenth centuries, while also reflecting a marked interest in hedonistic consumption and technology. Historically, French advertising has been notable for its thematic representations of personal style, idiosyncrasy and patriotism which occasionally verges on the jingoistic.

Further cultural factors which relate to global advertising are discussed below.

- **Perception:** The perception of shapes, colours and symbols varies across cultures. White is the colour of birth and, in the West, it is usually associated with weddings; in China, Japan and India the colour symbolises mourning. Green, a colour normally associated with freshness and good health in the West, is sometimes associated with disease elsewhere. The colour is favoured in Arab countries but forbidden in Indonesia. Black is often seen as the universal colour of mourning, however, in many Asian countries mourning is white, in Brazil it is purple, yellow in Mexico and dark red in parts of Africa. Red suggests good fortune in China, but death in Turkey. In India, the owl is a symbol of bad luck, the equivalent of the black cat. The stork, which in the West is associated with birth, symbolises maternal death in Singapore (Copeland and Griggs 1986).

   International marketers must gain a cultural understanding of the meaning of both colours and symbols in order to ensure that their packaging and product design and even advertising messages communicate the appropriate and desired values. As Jacobs et al. (1991) comment: 'marketers in a particular nation often take colour for granted, having experienced certain colour associations all their lives, and do not even question whether other associations may exist in different societies'.

   Signs (physical symbols that stand for something other than themselves) and rules and conventions (either implicit or explicit) that determine how they can be combined to form more complex messages. The successful combination of messages requires a common sharing of those same rules and conventions; the more we share the same codes, the closer our two meanings are to each other.

- **Motivation:** As Usenier (1996) points out, it is important to consider the motivations to own, to buy, to spend, to consume against the background of the intended market. He suggests that Maslow's hierarchy of needs should be re-addressed in the international context. Importantly, Maslow's argument that needs must be satisfied at each level before the higher-order needs appears to be contradicted within specific societies. In certain developing countries, for example, the population may have more basic survival needs, yet some of those same cultures encourage self-actualisation in a manner that does not imply material consumption and therefore appear to go against Maslow's thesis.

- **Learning and memory:** The level of literacy is shaped by the education system. Prior experiences of product categories will have an important bearing upon the acceptance (or otherwise) of a new product launched into a foreign market.

- **Meaning:** Edward Hall (1976) has provided a concept to explain the cultural framework of meaning. He distinguishes between low and high context where the former place an emphasis on words and the latter are more reliant on contextual cues. In low-context societies, such as Germany and much of Scandinavia, advertising tends to be more logical, scientific and provides evidence to substantiate the product claims being made. In high-context countries, such as Japan and China, advertising tends to be more intuitive and appeals to the consumers' emotions. Advertising formats which are extensively used in many European campaigns – which provide a focus on the merits of a particular product, often making comparative claims, for example – fail to have an real impact in high context marketplaces

- **Age:** Consider the respective valuation of younger and older people within society. Also, how is purchasing power distributed across generations.
- **Self-concept:** How do people consider their roles and, importantly, how do particular products and services relate to these roles? Ownership of a car may have purely functional values in some markets; elsewhere the car is an extreme symbol of status within society. Following the breakdown of the barriers between Eastern and Western Europe, many car marques sold in the former Eastern bloc because of the status values associated with their names.
- **Group influence:** To what extent are individuals influenced in their attitudes and buying behaviour by their group? How does consumer behaviour reflect the need to self actualise individual identity or to manifest group belonging?
- **Social class:** Are social classes important locally? Is social class demonstrated through consumption? What types of products or services do social status minded consumers buy? Are there exclusive shops?
- **Sex roles:** Who makes the decisions? In Japan, the housewife makes the majority of major purchases. More significantly, she receives her husband's pay cheque and allocates a sum of money for him to spend on personal requirements, including his lunch. In this context, targeting the housewife is a major priority for major Japanese advertisers. Who shops – he, she or both?
- **Decision making:** Family models (nuclear vs extended family) differ markedly between countries. In some, particularly where the extended family is paramount, the family 'elder' may exert a disproportionate influence on the nature of the products and service purchased; elsewhere it is important to consider the influence of children on the decision-making process.
- **Purchase:** The patterns of purchasing frequency differ markedly between countries, sometimes resulting from differences in income levels, on other occasions the results of patterns of usage. In some parts of the East, for example, fresh produce is bought on a daily basis whereas elsewhere shopping, even for fresh ingredients, may be carried out weekly and the resultant purchases stored in the fridge or freezer.
- **Motivational factors and aspirations:** These are, similarly, different from one country to another, leading to difficulties in communicating aspirational 'norms' where such values either do not exist or have different parameters.
- **The loyalty/purchasing environment:** In most Western countries, consumers expect their 'favourite' brands to be available on a regular basis in the outlets they frequent. Elsewhere, factors of distribution may have an important influence on availability. In some instances, consumers become accustomed to purchasing from the product category rather than expecting to be able to purchase any given brand. Similarly, the influence of salespersons may have greater or lesser importance in different markets.

- **Post-purchase:** Here again a distinction can be drawn between Western and developed markets with those of the underdeveloped nations. Expectations of product quality will inevitably differ between them. Similarly, there may be different 'cultures' which relate to the nature of consumer complaints.
- **Standards of living:** Products that are consumed on a daily basis may be considered as luxuries in others – particularly if the relative cost is high. Cigarettes, for many purchased in packets of 20, are sold singly in some African markets, with the resultant difficulties of the lack of packaging to communicate brand values. Elsewhere, the incidence of fridges may preclude the sale of some packaged convenience foods, and so on. However, it is evident that some developing markets often 'leapfrog' earlier stages of evolution which have been witnessed in the West. The mobile telephone market is evidence of this fact.

Advertising literacy

Goodyear (1991) identified a series of differences in marketing literacy across different parts of the world:

- At the immature level there is an emphasis on the manufacturer's description of the product with repetitious, factual messages.
- At the next stage, the emphasis remains on the products' attributes, but there is an awareness of the consumer's freedom of choice in a competitive market.
- Subsequently, the emphasis shifts from the product to the brand and from attributes to consumer benefits.
- At this level, the advertiser has 'given' the brand to the consumer and there is little acknowledgement of the selling functions of advertising. Brand values are sufficiently well known at this stage for them to be expressed, either in shorthand form (by a brief glimpse of the pack, or some symbol associated with the brand) or by suffusion throughout the execution. The advertiser asks the consumer to identify with what he or she is shown, and the persuasive device is reinforcement.
- At the most sophisticated level, the focus is no longer on either the brand or the consumer, but the advertising itself. Where the brand does appear, it is usually in a highly symbolic form. It is the ad that provides the stimulation and the entertainment, sometimes with little or no direct reference to the brand. Where the brand does appear, it is usually in a highly symbolic form.

O'Donohoe (1994) argues that advertising literacy is not only the skill to be able to understand and transfer the meanings from an advertisement, but also the ability to use those meanings within the social context. Advertising literacy becomes a significant factor employed by many consumers to locate their social groups and their identities within those groups, because advertising literacy is used by social group members to evaluate each other.

The rate of development seems to be dependent on a number of factors:

1 The amount of exposure to television and film. People have to learn how to see, and consumers have to learn to see through the camera's eye. The conventions of fast cutting, dissolves, flashbacks etc. are not innately understood.
2 The amount of exposure to advertising. The more advertising people are exposed to, the more they appreciate that it is a form of communication that is largely separate from the other content of the media, and that it is a communi-

cation that has its own conventions. Before that separate identity is recognised, there is a lot of confusion between programme and commercial, and a lack of understanding about the advertising message.

3 Level of industrialisation consumerisation. Advertising conventions, especially those that focus on the added values and imagery of brands, only have meaning for those societies where branded goods are common. Societies where people think about goods in terms of brand values and associated imagery are likely to have high advertising literacy. In societies where product differentiation is the level at which most discrimination is made, then it is likely that the advertising will be at a different and lower level.

4 Certain national cultural factors. Some countries, because of their national or traditional culture, are better able than others to develop advertising sophistication.

The West is certainly populated with consumers at the most sophisticated level of advertising literacy. They know what is going on. They have access to vast amounts of information about the world in which they live, the products, brands and services that they use. However, they also harbour deep cynicism about the motives and tactics of suppliers of goods and services.

Legal and regulatory requirements

There are few common standards for marketing communications across all markets – although there are progressive moves towards harmonisation is some areas, such as the EC. Yet tobacco advertising, for example, is still commonplace in many parts of Europe, whilst limited or totally prohibited in others. Most countries now see condom advertising as part of the global campaign to control Aids. However, in certain countries, with strong religious beliefs, such advertising would be unthinkable.

There are increasingly complex differences when marketing across borders. Either morally or from the standpoint of regulations, the situation differs from market to market. In the UK, for example, there has been no problem with advertising confectionery (although this may change). In Finland, however, there are not only restrictions on the advertising of confectionery products, but also sugar taxes designed to directly cut consumption. In Sweden there is a complete ban on advertising directed at children under the age of 12. In Germany comparative and price advertising are heavily restricted. Rules on prizes and promotional draws are also constrained. In Germany it is against the law to cold call or mail shot a prospect even if you have the person's card (Haigh 1996).

The controls imposed on such activities as advertising and sales promotion will vary significantly between countries. What is considered perfectly acceptable in one country may be regarded as offensive in another.

- **Restrictions on product types:** Many countries impose bans or other forms of limitation on the specific types of products and services that may be advertised freely. Many countries, for example, have complete prohibitions on the advertising of cigarettes, others control the promotion of alcohol. Tougher restrictions on advertising to children currently exist in Greece, Sweden, Norway and parts of Belgium, where bans on toy advertising are in place. In France the use of children in food ads is banned and in Canada and Sweden, advertising to children during children's programmes is banned.

- **Comparative advertising:** Comparative advertising is almost common place in the USA. Elsewhere, as in Germany, comparative claims can only be made following fairly rigorous tests of the statements. In the UK, comparisons have tended to be less direct – e.g. Brand *x*. However, a change in the law has enabled manufacturers to make overt comparisons with named brands. In Japan, such comparisons tend not to be made more for cultural than for legislative reasons.
- **Taxation on advertising:** Some countries impose comparatively high levels of taxation on advertising expenditure. This adds significantly to the raw media costs and, for some smaller companies, may preclude access to mainstream media based activity.
- **Locally produced advertising:** Several countries restrict the use of advertising that is produced outside of that country. For example, Australia requires that commercials must be produced with local crews in attendance.

Media availability and usage

A primary consideration, especially in the context of global campaigns, is the need to access constant media outlets. After all, if a major aim of standardisation is to eliminate costly production, then the same media must be available in all markets. However, not only are certain media not available to the marketer in some areas – certain countries, for example, have only limited television penetration, whilst others do not allow advertising – the patterns of usage may also differ. In some countries, spot advertising throughout the day is commonplace. In others, all advertising is grouped together and broadcast at set times of the day.

Other aspects of media are equally important. In different markets, different media have a different status, such that advertising placed in them has greater or lesser credibility. This is particularly the case in those markets where media have a distinct religious or political orientation.

Since the arrival of universally available mass media, people in advanced cultures have access to far more information about their world. Satellite television has transformed broadcasting. The skies are now cluttered with sophisticated technologies capable of beaming messages around and across the globe. The key element for global marketing communications is that whatever is broadcast is indiscriminate by nature. Wherever the signal can be received, so can the message irrespective of nationality, culture etc. Star TV, for example, covers some 43 countries and an estimated 3000 million people.

Similarly, the emergence of the internet has also had a dramatic impact on the spread of information and the impact on consumers' lives. Distance is irrelevant and the transfer of information instantaneous. When Justin Timberlake 'accidentally' ripped off Janet Jackson's costume during the 2004 SuperBowl event the largest ever number of hits were made on the site showing the incident.

Cultural and content experiences affect the media value to consumers in different countries. Elms (2001) suggests that far more Britons and Germans have exposure to loose inserts in the press. However, in the main, they pay less attention to them, perhaps because they are so widespread. Many French and Spanish consumers pay more attention to inserts – possibly because they confront them less frequently.

Not only are the same movies and television programmes available simultaneously in many countries, but more and more people are able to receive international media brands. This increasing globalisation of media (CNN, MTV, *Vogue*, *Cosmopolitan*, *Reader's Digest*, etc.) means that brand owners can, at least in theory, target an international audience with a single communication. However, this approach will only work if different cultural values do not interfere with the way in which either the media or the advertising is received (Ford and Phillips 1998).

The web is more than just a global medium: it is an excellent means to deliver 'local' marketing communications. While there may be some conflict between websites in different countries where brands have a different positioning, the real strength of the web and other new media tools is to deliver personalised marketing messages. These could be web pages that are delivered to the browser based on previous purchase or visit activity.

The competitive environment

Just as consumers differ between markets, so do the brands available to them. Identifying the aspirational values for a brand, in order to define a unique positioning, becomes more difficult as the number of markets is increasing and the competitors differ in their stances. Often, a desired positioning is already occupied by another brand in a particular market. And, as we have seen, the relative position of a brand – leader or follower – will have important implications for communications strategy determination. It is extremely unlikely that all but a very few brands occupy the same position in all of the markets in which they are available.

It is clear from the above, that the task of developing a singular marketing communications strategy, whilst not insuperable, is an extremely difficult one. Many companies have accepted that, in order to achieve their communications objectives, they must adopt a somewhat different stance. Indeed, such consensus as exists suggests that the policy towards multinational marketing communications campaigns should be based on the statement – 'Think globally, act locally'. Inherent in this statement is the acceptance of the fact that common communications strategies can be developed across all markets, but that their implementation must be effected on a local basis, in order to reflect the multitude of differences which – despite convergency – continue to exist.

The move to global marketing communications

In the same way that we have seen the progressive move towards the standardisation of brands, so too, there has been the movement towards the development of standardised marketing communications programmes. The rapidly accelerating costs of producing separate campaigns for individual markets and the difficulties of co-ordinating separate campaigns in physically close markets, together with the desire for the establishment of a single world-wide identity for its brands, have induced many companies to explore the potential of single campaign development across many if not all markets. Inevitably, there are polarised views on the merits of such moves. At one extreme, as a response to the pressures indicated above, some companies have developed central campaigns which provide the core of all of their marketing communications activity in all markets.

The logic behind global brands suggests that brand communications should also be globalised, and that should include advertising. Global advertising is claimed to provide benefits of economy, of control, and of consistency, and to enable the brand owner to leverage (rare) creative brilliance across the world. As brands have moved up the corporate agenda, their control within large multinational corporations has tended to become more centralised, and this has heightened management's leanings toward centralised advertising. This depends, however, as much on corporate culture as on the cultures of the target markets.

At the same time, the agency networks have made it easier for their clients to globalise campaigns, through the extension of their networks, through changes in their structures to create international brand groups, and through the development of global media agencies. The development of global media and global media owners has encouraged the process. The evolution of the full service multinational agency is seen by many to be the obvious response to two of the must fundamental issues of the 1990s – the integration of marketing communications and the globalisation of brands.

Central or local control of marketing communications?

In the past, companies have adopted a range of strategies for marketing on a global or multi-country basis. These may be summarised as:

- highly centralised, with one product and one set of communications (one sight, one sound, one sell);
- central control, with limited local adaptation of products and communications;
- central control, with products and communications developed locally to fit the global template;
- totally local, offering different products and communications in different countries.

- **Centralisation:** This approach emphasises a high level of central control over all forms of marketing communications. All aspects of the marketing communications planning process are determined centrally. It obviously provides a high degree of control over promotional activity and affords the opportunity for complete integration. It eliminates many of the problems associated with diffuse campaigns in separate markets and eases the tasks of co-ordination. For the most part, the same campaign is used in all markets in which the company operates.

  There is a number of problems associated with the centralised approach. The company may lack the ability to deal speedily with changes as they occur in individual markets; may not be able to deal with competitive challenges; and may inhibit managerial and entrepreneurial initiative in individual markets.

- **Decentralisation:** All, or at least most, of the important decisions relating to advertising and other forms of marketing communications are taken at a local level. This enables campaigns to be planned within the context of the particular local requirements and to reflect the needs of local consumers. Much more focus can be achieved, particularly in the context of dealing with such issues as culture, tradition, political and legal factors. As might be expected, local managers tend to be more supportive of this approach as it provides them with a greater level of flexibility to develop their own communications campaigns. Importantly, local efficiency can often be improved and the company can respond more speedily to competitive and other pressures.

- **Combination:** Here, the decision-making process in relation to marketing communications is shared between the head office and local managers. For example, the broad strategy may be determined centrally with individual implementation left to local managers. There are many variations on this theme. In some cases, policy decisions may be centralised but the specific details of implementation may be planned at a local level. Often this results in a significant duplication of effort, with each country developing individual and separate response to the communications requirements. Photo shoots and the preparation of campaign materials will often be replicated with significant cost implications. To overcome this disadvantage, some companies go somewhat further in the planning process. Here, not only is the strategy determined centrally, but the main thrust of advertising may be developed there also. The preparation of materials will be planned and co-ordinated to avoid duplication but local managers will be provided with a range of materials in order that they can 'personalise' or tailor the execution to meet their individual requirements. For many years, the Outboard Marine Corporation adopted this approach to its European activities. After consultation with area managers (responsible for one or more European countries) a consistent look was adopted for the brand advertising, with separate campaigns being developed for Evinrude and Johnson power boat engines. Photographic shoots were planned to ensure that all regional requirements were catered for (to take account of such factors as boating styles, environmental and legal factors, and so on). Individual managers were then able to call off their specific advertising requirements within this central framework.

An adaptation of this approach, which is gaining support, is the grouping of markets which share common factors. These can then be handled out of a central location or a regional hub. Whilst Smirnoff developed a common global campaign 'pure thrill' for its vodka brand, depicting distorted images which became clear when seen through the bottle, the specific images chosen varied from country to country. For example in Brazil, the image chosen was that of the famous statue of Christ above the city of Rio de Janeiro, although in this instance depicted with a football; in the USA, the Hollywood sign above the hills of Los Angeles was illustrated with the 'W' being composed of the legs of two people.

By now, a growing number of companies, and their managers, have experience of advertising across country borders and cultural divides, and companies have evolved a range of strategies for dealing with the problems this raises. There is a continuum of campaigns, from the tightly controlled and co-ordinated at one end ('global'), through various degrees of adaptation of a common campaign idea ('glocal') to almost total national autonomy ('local'). Recently, there has been a marked swing away from the global end of the spectrum, as advertisers have increasingly come to accept that opportunities for truly global advertising are rare.

For a number of years Coca-Cola have run essentially similar campaigns in many markets, with all or most of the elements being constantly applied in all of the territories in which they operate. Their sponsorship of the 1994 World Cup, for example, was featured prominently on cans sold as far apart as Thailand and Malaysia and the UK. In the past, identical advertising, save only for the language of the voiceover, has been run by the brand across all territories.

At the other end of the spectrum is a wide range of international brands which continue to develop 'local' advertising propositions which, in their view, enable them to more readily reflect the needs and desires of the individual markets in which they operate.

Between these two positions are those brands which adopt a common communications strategy but allow for the local development of specific executions. In these instances, there is cohesion in the underlying message of the brand in all of its markets, but room for the development of tightly focused and tailored propositions which reflect the subtleties and nuances of the local market place.

Some manufacturers have developed this approach to the position where they develop 'pattern book' communications campaigns. An overall stance for the brand will be taken centrally, with semi-finished examples of advertising and sales promotional approaches laid down by the centre. These, however, provide the 'shell' of activity and the local operations have the flexibility to adjust the specific content to meet their local requirements. We need to understand that 'just because something applies in one market does not mean it applies elsewhere' (Elms 2001). Companies that localise their advertising strategy have acknowledged this issue and use different ads for different markets, thus adapting to local market conditions. Standardisation might mean cost savings but localisation may result in higher economic returns.

It is this latter area which has witnessed the greatest growth over recent years. Indeed, even the ubiquitous Coca-Cola have recognised the need to develop specific messages for individual markets to respond to pressures on the brand's position. The company has always prepared a pool of commercials for international use. In April 1997 it unveiled 16 new commercials in the 'Always Coca-Cola' campaign. However, the regional companies are no longer forced to use them. The head office continues to generate brand strategy but, subject to their approval, the local markets can develop creative work more in tune with the local environment. The company claims that 'our marketing structure translates global into local'.

Standardised versus local communications

Academicians and practitioners alike are still divided on the advisability of using standardised (universal) or localised advertising approaches in international campaigns. Advertisers who use the standardised approach argue that consumers anywhere in the world have the same basic needs and desires and can therefore be persuaded by universal appeals. On the other hand, advertisers who follow the localised approach assert that consumers differ from country to country and must accordingly be reached by advertising tailored to their respective countries.

Research conducted by Kanso (1992) reveals that the majority of the studied firms are guided by the localised approach. Such a finding, compared with findings of previous studies, suggests that the standardisation of advertising is on the decline.

Overall, the findings suggest that human wants and needs are more or less universal, but the way to address these wants and needs is not. Communication is largely determined by cultural conditions. To minimise advertising blunders, American firms should consider each foreign business opportunity as a unique challenge. What is needed for successful international advertising is a global commitment to local vision.

We have already seen that the proponents of standardised communications campaigns cite the cost savings to be accrued from the development of a single campaign, together with the comparative ease of co-ordination, as partial justifications for the move towards common global marketing communications activities. It cannot be denied that the cost savings may be enormous. With the average cost of production of a television commercial being of the order of £200 000 to £300 000 and, very often, very much more than that, brands such as Nike often spend millions of their commercials, not least because of the number of international personalities featured in the advertising. Moreover, if several creative teams are working in different parts of the globe to resolve the communications needs, the time involved and the associated costs will be considerable. And if, as we have seen, there is an underlying commonality of requirements, much of that time will be spent covering the same ground as others in the search for the communications message.

Not only does a standardised process eliminate the problems of conflict arising from dissimilar messages being communicated in adjacent territories, it also saves a considerable amount of management time involved in resolving such difficulties. Similarly, management would otherwise be need to be involved – within each market – in the briefing and approval of creative work, the development of separate sales promotion campaigns, PR activity and, even, packaging changes. Equally, agencies can develop an ever-increasing pool of knowledge which they can bring to bear on their clients requirements. According to Tom Sutton of J. Walter Thompson: 'The interaction of different types of talent in different countries started to contribute everywhere. The cross-fertilisation of ideas, the exchange of people, the exposure to new situations, all helped to bring a stronger whole.'

As well as saving time by dealing with one agency, the multinational client can derive savings in several important areas. Importantly, one consistent creative strategy can be developed to cover the entirety of the territories in which the company operates. The 'through the bottle' campaign for Smirnoff developed by Lowe Howard-Spink ran almost unchanged in some 43 countries with some sections being cut to ensure local relevance and application. For example, several different end shots were developed to cater for the different vodka mixers that were used in different markets. IBM's 'subtitles' campaign was made for only a reported £150 000 and ran in 26 separate countries. Similarly, BBH's campaigns for Levis run virtually unchanged all over the world.

Ultimately, the key benefit results in the creation of a single consistent image for the brand across all markets. The management and monitoring of the campaign can be more consistent, and the implementation process simplified.

Against these, however, it can be argued that there are a number of significant disadvantages. Inevitably, if the brand is at a different stage in its development it may be less responsive to a marketing communications campaign developed for all markets, than to one specifically designed to deal with its own particular needs. We have already seen that different objectives, such as creating awareness, stimulating repeat purchase, and so on, will require different motivations and, hence, different messages. Similarly, in order to ensure universal appeal and comprehension, the resultant execution may be bland and boring and satisfy none of the individual requirements satisfactorily. This may, in turn, inhibit the opportunity to generate sales volume and result in management frustration.

Indeed, the problem is often one of motivation for staff both within the company and the agencies it uses. Since they may be uninvolved with the development of the marketing communications programme, they may perceive it as being irrelevant to their needs. And they will often feel no commitment to its successful implementation. Often, since multinational campaigns take a long time to create and produce, this reduces the ability, on a local level, to respond rapidly to local pressures.

Sometimes, the attempt to globalise the image results in costly blunders. When Elida Gibbs paid $3 million to entice Steffi Graf to appear in their Sure commercials, it discovered belatedly that she was only well known in her home country – Germany – and the UK and USA. Elsewhere, her endorsement of the product held little significance.

International campaigns are often criticised as appealing to the 'lowest common denominator'. If the campaign is to work at its most effective level, there must be a concentration on identifying the highest denominator, both strategically and executionally. It is important to concentrate on issues such as common life stage, common youth culture, common aspirations of common cultural associations, and similar common values.

We can identify several forces driving this move towards global integration:

- economies of scale
- learning benefits
- globally integrated competitors
- homogenisation of consumer preferences
- multinational customers
- high investment intensity
- high technological intensity
- pressures for cost reduction.

Against these we can identify several alternate forces calling for local responsiveness:

- diverse consumer preferences
- differences in marketing infrastructure (media availability, distribution channels, etc.)
- legal framework
- physical environment
- transportation methods and costs
- availability of substitutes
- market structure differences (competition, prices, etc.)
- government policies
- administrative costs of integration
- flexible manufacturing.

Harvey (1993) attempts to define the important variables which impact on the desire to adopt standardised advertising in international markets:

- Product variables: The constancy of the product offering across different markets.
- Competitive variables: The structure of the competitive environment and the mix between domestic and foreign competitors.
- Organisational experience and control variables: The level of international experience within the organisation.
- Infrastructure variables: The ability to standardise elements within the advertising process – media, advertising agencies, and production facilities.
- Governmental variables: The restrictions placed on communications.
- Cultural and societal variables.

Spurred by Levitt's (1983) article on the globalisation of markets, the focus of much international advertising research of the 1980s and 1990s and beyond has been on whether advertising can be standardised across markets. De Mooij (1998) states that some have argued that almost complete standardisation of advertising programmes is possible, while others have countered that adaptations must be made due to cultural, legal or other factors.

The debate concerning the applicability of standardised international advertising has gone on for almost four decades amongst international marketers, advertising agencies, and academicians. A paper by Onkvisit and Shaw (1999) examines recent evidence that deals with this strategy in an indirect manner. It discusses why the research approaches that have been utilised so far have made it difficult to test the validity of the concept of standardisation.

Solberg (2000) similarly indicates that the standardisation/adaptation issue in international marketing has generated much debate and interest among both academics and practitioners. Even though many researchers have addressed the issue, it still remains an underresearched field of international marketing. The contradictory findings of different researchers in this area may reflect the fact that some aspects have been overlooked or are ill defined. For example, the more mechanical measurement of the degree of standardisation of different marketing mix elements may conceal more fundamental organisational dimensions, such as market knowledge, the nature of the decision-making process (e.g. planning or distribution of decision power), degree of internationalisation, and so forth.

More advertisers are standardising strategy even if they are adapting executions. It is usually possible for brand positioning to be global even when it may not be feasible to standardise executions.

Discussions of segmentation in global markets have generally focused on segmenting countries into homogenous groups using a base of segmentation such as religion, economic status, geography, culture, or political system. This traditional method ignores the possibility of segments that cut across national boundaries (Taylor 2002).

The controversy over the standardisation of advertising campaigns has focused on the appropriateness of variation within advertising content from country to country. Three schools of thought have emerged: standardisation, localisation and compromise.

- **Standardisation:** Proponents of this view argue that because of faster communication there is a convergence of art, media activity, living conditions and cultures and, consequently, and that advertising can and should follow suit. Levitt (1983) attributed the success of McDonald's, Pepsi cola and Coca-Cola to the fact that they are globally standardised, sold everywhere and welcomed by everyone. Standardised strategies and campaigns appear most appropriate and effective when the product is utilitarian and the message is informational. In these cases, reasons for buying or using the product (service) are rational – and less likely to vary in different cultures. Glue, batteries, gasoline are such products.
- **Localisation:** The opposite view is localisation. According to this school of thought, advertisers have to consider insurmountable barriers among countries. Such barriers include: differences in culture, taste, media infrastructure and economic development, and consumers' resentment of international corporations' attempts to homogenise their differing tastes and cultures. Given these considerations, it becomes necessary to design specific advertising programmes to achieve impact in local markets

- **Compromise:** A main problem relating to the analysis of international advertising practices is that standardisation is not one option; rather, the multinationals are faced with a complex choice in terms of the form and extent of standardisation.

  Here though the campaign is developed to provide uniformity in direction but not necessarily in detail. In other words, pattern standardisation calls from the outset for the development of a single promotional theme along with flexibility in campaign execution to adapt to the various local markets (Kanso and Nelson 2002).

For most products, it is generally considered more appropriate and effective to gear strategies and campaigns to local customs and cultures: 'think global, act local.'

- Often, product usage varies according to the culture. This applies to most foods, and beverages such as coffee and tea.
- For many products, the benefits are more psychological than tangible, requiring and understanding of the psychologies of different cultures. Sweets, snacks and clothing are examples of products with intangible benefits.
- When the method of selling is an emotional appeal, advertisers must recognise the vast differences in emotional expression that exist throughout the world. Some societies are highly demonstrative and open, while others are diffident, aloof or private.
- Perhaps the riskiest method of selling is humour. There are vast differences in humour even within a culture – not to mention differences among different cultures.

In addition, advertisers must consider a multicultural, adaptable and flexible strategy or campaign if the brand is in different stages of development or of varying stature across different markets.

- A commercial designed for a mature market will not necessarily work well in a developing market.
- A commercial designed to support a brand's leadership position in a market where it is number 1 does not necessarily have the characteristics required to succeed in a market where the brand is number 5.
- A commercial in a market where the product/brand is unique or one of a few has quite a different task than a commercial in a market where competition among brands is rife.

Sriram and Gopalakrishna (1991) conducted an analysis of 40 separate countries in order to identify common elements that might enable the adoption of standardised advertising. They concluded that 'advertisers should view standardisation not as the transferability of an entire campaign across countries, but as a strategy that makes unified themes, images and brand names possible'.

When Hite and Fraser (1998) surveyed international advertisers, they found that:

- only 9 per cent were using totally standardised advertising in all markets;
- 37 per cent used completely localised advertising;
- the majority, 54 per cent, had local agencies tailor an umbrella strategy theme to the customs, values and lifestyles of their native markets.

Payne (2002) points out that the global marketer's job (and budget) can be made a little easier if a strategy or campaign is aimed at a targeted market segment that may have many common characteristics regardless of nationality. For example, senior business people share a certain universal level of sophistication and cosmopolitanism. This segment often has a great deal in common that can be addressed by one campaign, strategy or execution for luxury products.

Finally, what truly is meant by the global market? We are far from one world. There may be certain similarities among sectors of the world market. For example, several European nations, or Europe and the United States, can possibly be addressed together by a global strategy, although this is by no means a foregone conclusion. Equally, a 'Latin strategy' could reach out to the Mediterranean and Adriatic, and to South and Central America and Puerto Rico as well. Yet, advertisers probably should not expect a campaign to work equally well in the United States and Japan, or in the United States/Europe and the Middle East. Certain parts of the world are just too far apart to be advertised to in the same voice.

The development of multinational communications agencies

Globalisation (or at least internationalisation) has been the driving forced behind many of the changes in the advertising scene. The multinational agencies followed their clients into the marketing into which they were expanding. Tharp and Jeong (2001) indicate that since the 1980s there have been radical change in the advertising agency business. The increasing dominance of global markets for brands in a wide variety of product categories, enterprises and industries has favoured the growth of global network communications agencies.

The top 10 global agencies now control more than 80 per cent of global media billings. These agencies are substantially the same companies in Europe, Latin America, Africa and the USA. Asia is the major exception, where local Japanese agencies dominate the region. The large agency networks have benefited from the overall growth in world-wide trade as well as the expansion of their multinational clients and brands.

A major consequence of these mergers and acquisitions is that debate surrounding international advertising has substantially been overtaken by agency practices. In the majority of cases, the preferred solution is 'glocalisation' – a hybrid strategy that involves the establishment of global objectives, whilst implementation tends to be decentralised.

They argue that the management of a global agency requires four areas of expertise:

1 Agency planning and strategic thinking must be increasingly brand focused. What the brand stands for must be acceptable to consumers in various cultural environments, but the link from consumer to brand must be based on compatible values. A direct result of this is that global agencies have adopted strategic planning models that operate across their networks.
2 Consumer values, research and knowledge are important to the successful development of agency/client strategic planning.
3 There is an increasing need for cross-cultural experience for communications decision makers.
4 Experience with particular clients and brands needs to be shared across the network.

In some cases agencies expand into international markets because they see them as being strategically significant, for example, in the emerging economies of Eastern Europe. More often agencies become multinational by being pulled along by their multinational clients and then picking up local business later. Other agencies have had to become international to avoid the risk of losing business.

The last three decades have seen as rapid and dramatic consolidations of agencies into mega networks. By acquiring agencies specialising in complementary services such as sales promotion, media buying and research in various countries, agencies can get closer to offering their clients a consistent 'one-shop' facility on a global basis. WPP now owns J. Walter Thompson, Ogilvy & Mather, Bates Rainey, Kelly Campbell Roalfe/Y&R, all of which are leading advertising agencies, together with a number of smaller agencies. Similarly, it owns Hill & Knowlton, specialising in public relations, and Millward Brown, a market research agency, together with several other specialist communications companies. In the field of media, WPP now owns MediaEdge:CIA, MindShare, amongst others to be the fourth-largest media group in the world.

There has been the progressive 'internationalisation' of the service companies to the point where few do not have representation in all of the key markets. As a result of mergers, acquisitions and alignments, the major practitioners in the fields of marketing communications have subsidiaries or associates in all the major countries of the world. Increasingly, global clients are appointing global agencies to hand and co-ordinate their marketing communications business, across all of their territories.

Recently, for example, Johnnie Walker, the Diageo-owned drink brand, appointed Arc to handle its advertising world-wide (*Campaign* 2004b), whilst TBWA was appointed to handle Pedigree Petfoods similarly on a global basis (*Campaign* 2004a).

Indeed, the key requirement to inclusion on the shortlist for many such accounts is the extent to which the companies have the ability to service the business on a multinational basis. Often, companies will maintain a roster of agencies to handle their business, particularly where they have multiple brands. In most case, the same agency will be used across the brand in all markets. Examples of this practice may be seen with Procter & Gamble, Mars and others. Other clients which have followed the same philosophy are Colgate Palmolive, Bayer and Reckitt & Colman. A significant factor is the easier process of exporting successful advertising campaigns into different markets often saving considerable costs.

Multinational agencies

As noted above, the trend has been for the large agencies either to acquire or establish branches in all those markets in which they might reasonably expect to generate international client opportunities. Indeed, some of this process has been client-inspired, in the sense that the agency is encouraged to establish an office in a country in which the client is intending to operate.

Over the past two decades, led originally by agencies of American origin, but more recently by British and Japanese agencies, groupings have been assembled to respond to client needs.

Such has been the growth of this process that the lists of the top 10 agencies in most countries are broadly similar in content – although not in order – to each other.

Table 13.5 World's top 10 advertising groups, 2002

		Billings US ($m)
1	Omnicom	7536
2	Interpublic	6204
3	WPP	5782
4	Publicis	2712
5	Dentsu	2061
6	Havas	1842
7	Grey	1200
8	Hakuhodo	861
9	Cordiant	788
10	Asatsu	340

SOURCE: *Advertising Age* 2002

Table 13.6 Top 10 multinational advertising agencies, 2001

		Billings US ($m)
1	Dentsu	2078
2	McCann Erickson	1858
3	BBDO Worldwide	1612
4	J. Walter Thompson	1536
5	Euro RSCG	1441
6	Grey	1321
7	DDB Needham	1215
8	Ogilvy & Mather	1135
9	Leo Burnett	1072
10	Publicis Worldwide	1066

SOURCE: *Advertising Age* 2002

Today, most of the world's advertising business is in the hands of advertising agencies that maintain global networks of offices that operate in most countries throughout the world. The top 10 agencies have control of approximately one-third of the world's advertising billings. Advertising agencies have consistently expanded internationally to satisfy a number of needs including:

- servicing current clients
- exploiting new markets
- countering the efforts of competing agencies
- satisfying the need for potential investment opportunities.

Many high-profile companies, including Citibank and IBM, have replaced the multi-agency rosters handling their campaigns and consolidated them in single agency networks. As the number of multinational brand roll-outs continues and the number of brands conceived as pan-regional or multinational continues to grow, the impetus for globalisation in the advertising industry is likely to increase.

Independent networks

To offset the competitive threat posed by the multinationals, networks and confederations have been formed to provide the global coverage demanded by some client companies. CDP Europe, Alliance International and ELAN (European Local Advertising Network) are three examples of such groups.

From the agency perspective, these associations meet the clients' needs to operate on a global basis, while preserving their own independence. Usually, these groupings are based on like-minded philosophies, with agencies of similar views of the marketing communications process coming together – creative style, media prowess, the role of planning, and so on.

Local independents

In many countries, newly emergent agencies guard their independence jealously and, at least in the short term, are prepared to forego some international accounts. Indeed, many such agencies remain independent in the longer term as a means of offering their own unique positioning in a crowded market.

The selection of an agency for international business

The principles underlying the selection of an agency to handle business across a number of markets are, essentially, the same as those involved in the appointment to handle an account within a single market, as detailed in Chapter 5. Obviously, the decision as to agency selection will, to a large degree, be governed by the strategic direction of the company. As such, there are a number of separate options to be considered:

1 the appointment of a single, multinational agency;
2 the appointment of an international agency network;
3 the appointment of a series of local agencies.

Before deciding on its agency, any client must consider a set of important criteria in the international context.

- **To what extent is it planned to implement a single communications strategy in all markets?** For those companies wishing to pursue a global communications strategy, it is sensible to consider only the first and second options. The benefits of already established links will ensure the speedy transfer of knowledge and understanding which, in turn, should facilitate the process of implementation in the variety of countries in which the campaign will run.
- **To what extent will the intended agency be precluded from operating in other market areas?** Some companies adopt a strict policy whereby the incumbent agency is precluded not only from handling directly competitive business but also from those other areas in which the client company has an interest. This, it has to be said, is becoming an increasingly untenable situation. As multinational companies expand their businesses, both horizontally and vertically, they embrace ever more diverse market segments.

Acquisitions of companies and brands result in their taking an interest in markets far beyond their original businesses. P&G have interests in diverse fields including hair care preparations, sanitary protection, cough and cold remedies, soap powders and toothpaste, to name just a few. Apart from their coffee interests, Nestlé operate in the following markets: confectionery, bottled waters, cereals, tinned soups, and yoghurts and mousses. Here again, the list is only a partial one.

Clearly, to function profitably, the multinational agencies have to think carefully about client conflicts, current and for the future, before taking on a new account. Though the short-term increase in billings might be attractive, their tenure of a particular client might inhibit their growth potential in the future. In turn, therefore, some agencies with otherwise desirable credentials may be precluded from consideration.

- **Do the multinational or network agencies possess all the appropriate skills in all markets?** Often, a multinational agency may have relatively weak representation in one or more of the markets considered important to the company. The same is equally true of agency networks, where not all of the participants may have the same reputation and skills.

- **Are there specific local skills that need to be accessed?** In some instances, a local independent agency may have a far greater in depth knowledge or understanding of the market, the consumers or the general environment, which it may be important to access. Indeed, the independent local agency may have greater prowess, for example, in media planning or creativity. It should not be assumed that simply because an agency is part of a wider international grouping it will possess all of the skills required.

  Where co-ordination is not a requirement, some companies have taken the decision to locate the creative development with one agency – usually referred to as the 'lead' agency – and to appoint several local agencies to handle the implementation. In other instances, they have chosen to appoint the 'best' agency in each market, to ensure access to the necessary skills in all areas.

- **How will the company cope with co-ordinating the campaign globally?** Deploying company personnel to the co-ordinating task may be one solution. An alternative, particularly where a multinational agency is appointed, is to devolve that responsibility to the agency. Usually, a senior member of the agency structure is appointed to the specific role of ensuring consistency, both of creative work and implementation, throughout all markets. It will be his or her role to ensure cohesion between all aspects of the campaign in all markets although, ultimately, it will be the client's responsibility to determine whether the role has been fulfilled adequately.

  This internal agency role is, often, of considerable importance to other aspects of the smooth running of the campaign. The task involves overcoming the 'not invented here' syndrome, whereby the local brand management team responsible for the implementation of the activity may feel detached from it, since it was created elsewhere. Similarly, the international co-ordinator may have the responsibility for allocating funds between branches to ensure that such tasks as market research are carried out adequately. In many cases, although the work is an important aspect of the understanding of the communications task in the market, the branch office may not generate sufficient income to afford their contribution.

Agency structures tend to mirror those of their clients. Accordingly, many agencies have appointed 'world-wide' account directors, planning directors and others to ensure co-ordination and consistency across a diversity of offices spread throughout the world. Often, although not always, these 'world-wide' directors will be located in close proximity to the client's headquarters, although there has been an increasing tendency amongst clients to develop a 'hub' approach, in which a regional office is identified as the centre or location for the management of a particular areas of business activity.

As Grein and Ducoffe (1998) point out, the nature of the co-ordination required between countries differs markedly. Some client companies are highly sophisticated and know precisely what they require from their agencies; others require more guidance in the development of advertising strategies. Some companies have one campaign that runs around the world in an unmodified form; others employ less standardised campaigns.

International marketing and marketing communications strategy

The development of the international marketing plan covers the same dimensions as those of the domestic planning process, with any or all of the following areas being subject to review for potential changes:

- **Brand name and logo:** Some companies seek to impose a consistency of brand identity across all markets in which they operate – as we have seen, Mars have committed substantial expenditure to re-identifying the Marathon brand as Snickers. Wanadoo recently mounted a campaign to identify the change in their name from Freeserve, the name used elsewhere in Europe.
- **Product specification:** Nestlé adopts the same identification for a number of its products across all markets, but allows for variances in the nature of the product itself.
- **Packaging:** will the same packaging be appropriate for all markets? Increasingly, manufacturers are overcoming some of the difficulties by printing important information in several languages.
- **Product positioning and strategy:** will the same positioning be viable across all territories in which the product is present. Often, the brand position in one country may be identical to that of a competitor product in a different market.
- **Pricing:** How much to charge for a brand may well be dependent on local conditions.
- **Advertising strategy and execution:** Depending on the company attitudes it will need to determine whether it wishes to pursue a standardised, localised or compromise strategy. Similarly, it will need to determine through market research whether the executional device will travel across markets. The media strategy will be affected by the availability and relevance of media channels in different countries.

Table 13.7 Pros and cons of the global approach

Pros	Cons
Cost savings/economies of scale in production, packaging and communications	Local needs sacrificed to lowest common denominator
Pooled budgets means potential better marketing mix	Temptation to be cost driven versus consumer driven
Smaller countries get access to higher-quality thinking and production	Temptation to 'force fit' solutions
The brand is consistent in overlapping media areas, and to international travellers	Local gaffes more common
Ability to 'deal' on regional/global media opportunities	Potentially less responsive to rapidly changing market needs

SOURCE: Clifton 1997

International advertising

Rita Clifton (1997) has defined international advertising as an approach 'seeking a common perspective across markets . . . but not in as ambitious a way as global advertising which seeks to standardise as much as possible'.

The effectiveness of advertising is substantially dependent on the cultural and linguistic attitudes of the target population. Advertising often uses colloquial language which may have limited understanding across national boundaries and is seldom capable of being translated effectively.

In the context of international advertising, it is important that the same appeal will motivate consumers in different countries to buy the product. This is not as easy as it sounds, since as we have seen, different countries attach different meanings to the same values. In a society such as China, for example, the use of the 'individuality' appeal would be less than appropriate, since the cultural norm is one in which group membership and conformity is a highly cherished cultural value.

Marieke de Mooij (1991) argues that: 'Advertising, to be effective, must derive from and be part of a culture sharing the language and values of the target audiences.' However, global brands such as Coke and Pepsi have worked their way around this problem by developing 'universal' themes based on common imagery, lifestyle concepts and heroes.

On the international scene, a commercial that is dominated by visuals is often superior to one which is copy-heavy. Nowhere is it truer that 'a picture is worth a thousand words'. McCollum Spielmam (1992) argue that international advertisers should fully utilise television's visual dimension to demonstrate features or illustrate the benefits. Psychological benefits are also amenable to visual demonstration. The TV medium is ideally suited for non-verbal communication. Music is often an enhancement, serving as a lingua franca. Brand symbols, trade marks or emblems can be potent visual devices in markets where the brand has stature and the symbol is meaningful. An approach that is dramatic, unique and distinctive should be tested to see if it has met the basic rules and preconditions of its targeted culture.

Consumers in developing markets will need to be told about the functional nature of the product, whilst sophisticated, advertising-literate consumers will expect more. They will want advertising that entertains, makes them laugh and gives them a sense of being in touch with what's going on.

We need to be aware that the comprehension of an advertising message is substantially dependent on the level of advertising literacy. In most Western developed nations, consumers grow up surrounded by advertising. In effect, they grow up speaking two 'languages' – their mother tongue and the 'language' of advertising. The consequence is that they rapidly become aware of the nature of the advertising process and comprehend a variety of shorthand devices and metaphors to 'explain' the relevance of brands. Elsewhere, advertising is a comparatively new phenomenon. Potential consumers need to be reminded of the functional benefits of the brand since the emotional context (so familiar in Western advertising) will have little or no relevance to them.

The advertising proposition must be approached from a multi-lingual perspective from the outset. Good international advertising seeks to avoid subtleties of language, nuances, puns and idiomatic expressions. These are rarely capable of translation into different languages. Some languages require more physical space in which to express the same meaning. When an ad is translated directly from English to German, for example, it will require approximately 25 per cent more space. It is equally important to understand that humour doesn't travel easily. Avoid using translators who have been away from their home country for a long period of time. Language changes over time and someone who is separated from the current version of the language may not be aware of subtle changes. Equally, check out each language version in the country in which the material is to appear. The Spanish used in Spain is significantly different from that used in say, Mexico. Equally, Canadian French is different to the language used in France.

Mary Goodyear (1996) differentiates the components of advertising literacy in the following table:

Table 13.8 **The components of advertising literacy**

Low consumerisation	High consumerisation
Product attributes	Product benefits
Focus on product	Focus on usage
Rational	Emotional
Realistic	Symbolic
Fact	Metaphor
Maker's language	Brand language
Salesperson	Consumer
Pack shot	Consumption
Left brain	Right brain
Selling	Buying

SOURCE: Goodyear 1996

The importance of developing an understanding of advertising literacy is, according to Goodyear, is the need to anticipate the audience for the company's products and services, and to produce creative work which is familiar enough to be recognised, and new enough to have saliency.

While different cultures may differ in their response to advertising, how different nationalities process advertising is the same. That is, a good creative idea features something interesting or involving which holds the viewer's attention. These creative magnifiers need to be related to both the strategic communication, or it may not be conveyed, and the brand or it may not be recalled. 'The export of advertising messages, signs and symbols with a particular meaning in one part of the world will not necessarily decode identically in others' (Cramphorn 1996).

There are obstacles to global success, as we have seen, and the factors that are pertinent in determining success include:

- **Brand position:** The advertising needs will vary depending upon whether this is a new product, a relatively unknown brand or an established healthy brand. A brand's position can vary from market to market.
- **Market context:** Competition differs from market to market, so determining whether the sector is growing or stable, and the strength and positioning of competitive brands is important to campaign success. Without this understanding, a strategy or style which was intended to be leveraged uniquely for the brand may prove a failure, since competitors may have already laid claim to it in certain countries.
- **The advertising history of the brand:** We must be careful not to force the continuation of an existing campaign for new country launches: what worked well previously for the campaign may not work outside its country of origin, since the established ad style and branding devices are unfamiliar (Green and Aubury 1997).

Clifton (1997) develops a scale to illustrate those concepts which are more or less less to travel across the globe. This is shown in Figure 13.3.

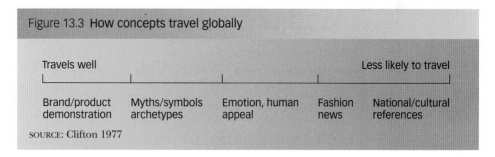

Figure 13.3 **How concepts travel globally**

Travels well				Less likely to travel
Brand/product demonstration	Myths/symbols archetypes	Emotion, human appeal	Fashion news	National/cultural references

SOURCE: Clifton 1977

The tone of voice must be clearly established and verified in the context of local requirements. In some countries what appears as an authoritative statement elsewhere may be misconstrued as a directive – and possibly rejected. Translated words may have different meanings. One way to overcome this is by using a method known as back translation. The original piece is translated into the language in which it is intended to appear. A second translator converts the translation back into the original language and the two versions are compared for inconsistencies.

It is important to consider the dimensions of media availability and relevance, since these may play an important part in determining whether a consistent campaign can be implemented across all markets. On a wider basis, and looking at only one media outlet – television – it can be seen that access to the medium differs markedly in different parts of the world. See Table 13.9.

Table 13.9 People per TV in selected countries	
Country	**No. per set**
USA	1.2
UK	2.3
Germany	2.6
Hong Kong	3.6
Turkey	5.7
Indonesia	16.7
India	31.3
Kenya	111.1
Laos	143.0
Nepal	500.0

Even where the medium is widely available, its role in the overall communications mix differs markedly.

Similar principles apply to the consideration of other media opportunities. Newspaper coverage, for example, is a function of the levels of literacy in different markets. To illustrate the point, over 50 per cent of the inhabitants of India and 27 per cent of those of China are functionally illiterate. This would impose severe limitations on a press-based campaign mounted in either of those two countries.

Even if a particular medium is available, the quality may be significantly different from what is normally associated with that channel. Newsprint quality in some countries is so poor that quality reproduction may be unobtainable. Similarly, whilst television may be available, colour may not be. This will affect the interpretation of advertising which uses colour as a major component of the message. Further, where there is a limited availability of media, or where shortages of time or space are common, the rates charged for advertising will tend to be considerably higher.

International market research

A critical area of international marketing communications is the role of market research.

Given the complexities involved in developing creative work for implementation in separate markets – especially given the cultural and environmental factors mentioned earlier – market research must be used at all stages to ensure that the intended message communicates effectively. It can never be assumed that, simply because a campaign works effectively in one or more markets, it will work equally well elsewhere. Specific research testing of the concepts and executions will be required in all markets in which it is intended to run.

Bannister et al. (1997) illustrate the areas in which research can make a contribution in the international context:

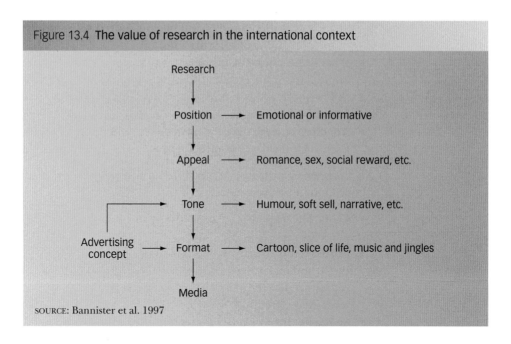

Figure 13.4 **The value of research in the international context**

SOURCE: Bannister et al. 1997

In the same way, advertising evaluation must reflect an understanding of how individuals responds to ads, rather than determining how advertising works on average. The problem with averages is that they can be achieved in many different ways and may not accurately reflect response levels in different countries.

Typically, people respond to advertising in two different ways:

1 They react to the creative material itself. Can it gain and sustain their attention?
2 They react to the communication of the brand ideas. Are these ideas relevant to them? And do they strengthen their bonds with the brands?

Individual responses to advertisements vary enormously. These responses are influenced by their culture, their lifetime learning and their continually developing experiences. When people respond positively to the ad itself, they are much more inclined to respond positively to the brand's ideas that it contains.

However, the task of conducting market research on an international basis is subject to a series of important considerations. The most important of these is **comparability of international data**. Whilst it is often true that, certainly in developed nations, there is access to considerable amounts of secondary data, what is less certain is the compatibility of the information. Even if the data exist, the problem of definition may make the information of low comparative value.

Several factors need to be examined:

- **How were the data collected?** The way in which the data were obtained will have an obvious impact on the potential for comparison. In some instances, data will be collected by government bodies, in others they will be obtained by commercial companies. Some information will be available as 'hard' facts whilst other information will be based on estimates.
- **When were the data collected?** In most countries, data are collected on a periodic basis. However, the intervals between collection may vary considerably. The

result is that the marketer will be confronted with significant time gaps in terms of the availability of information.

- **What is the source of the data?** As noted above, data will be collected by different bodies, some governmental, others commercial. Inevitably, some information will be more reliable than others and it is important to verify the source before assuming that data are comparable.
- **Are there enough data?** In the less developed nations, reliable data may not exist. Even such things as population statistics may be, at best, rough estimates.

If problems exist with secondary data, there are even greater problems with the collection of primary data.

- **Cost:** The expense of collecting information in different countries will vary markedly.
- **Attitudinal differences:** Much primary research will be designed to determine the attitudinal values of the intended target audience. But it is important to recognise that the values on which such attitudes are based may, themselves, be somewhat different.
- **Semantic differences:** The meaning of words will have a bearing on the interpretation of the research findings.
- **Availability of research skills:** In some countries, even basic research skills may not exist. Accordingly, it may be necessary to bring in specialists from elsewhere to carry out the work.
- **Infrastructure:** In order to conduct some forms of research, reliable information and infrastructure must be available. For example, the researcher may wish to conduct a series of interviews by telephone. Not a problem where the penetration of telephones is widespread, but in many countries the penetration of telephones may be at a very low level. Transport may not be available in order to access people living in rural communities. Sampling may be made difficult by the lack of adequate street maps or house numbers.
- **Literacy:** This will have an impact on the potential for collecting data from self-completion questionnaires.
- **Preparedness to participate:** In some countries, it may be impossible to collect data because of the lack of willingness to participate in research programmes. Certain topics may be taboo. Individuals may be reluctant to provide information to a stranger.

There are five basic problems that have hindered the development of international advertising research:

1 There are too many descriptive studies of advertising content and not enough research on why various executional techniques are effective in specific markets.
2 There has been a preoccupation with questions of whether campaigns should be standardised, to the detriment of seeking answers for pragmatic execution across markets.
3 There is a lack of rigour in establishing equivalence in studies comparing data from multiple countries, both in terms of study design and data analysis.
4 There is a lack of knowledge about whether, and when, targeting segments that cut across national boundaries (i.e. inter-market segmentation) can be effective.

5 Not enough focus has been give to the control of international advertising campaigns, both in terms of who makes the decisions and the extent to which they are effectively implemented.

Global integrated marketing communications (GIMC)

Grein and Gould (1996) proposed the concept of globally integrated marketing communications to add an international dimension to that of the promotional disciplines. They argued that co-ordinated global management of both countries and the promotional tools was increasingly essential to achieve effective communications outcomes.

They contend that no matter whether the company adopts standardised or adapted marketing communications, both approaches benefit from global managerial co-ordination. They define GIMC as 'a system of active promotional management which strategically co-ordinates global communications in all of its component parts both horizontally in terms of countries and organisations and vertically in terms of promotional disciplines.'

Case study

IPA Effectiveness Awards 2003

Agency: The Union

Author: Mark Reid

VELUX roof windows

Background

VELUX has been manufacturing the world's leading brand of roof windows for over 60 years. The company has a presence in over 40 countries around the world. These markets have the climate and architectural styles that are perfect for roof windows. The company's vision is to improve the living environment within the home, through the concept of 'the living attic'. VELUX believe that 'the living attic' creates 'the best room in the house'.

The issue

Like many international organisations, VELUX constantly grapples with the issue of what level of centralisation/consistency they apply to their marketing/advertising across different markets. For VELUX the issue has been complicated by the fact that the brand is at different stages of development in different markets. This is due to a combination of differing circumstances – competition, maturity, distribution, etc.

In order to acknowledge these differing market dynamics, whilst implementing a degree of consistency across various markets, VELUX has segmented markets as being 'high awareness' or 'low awareness'. This split is demonstrated by the fact that brand awareness ranges in Europe from 25 per cent (UK) to over 80 per cent in some other European countries. Over time VELUX has identified a strong correlation between levels of brand awareness and business performance in individual markets – essentially the better the brand awareness, the better the business performance.

The task

The agency was asked to create advertising to run in the 'low-awareness' markets. These are classified as having less than 30 per cent total brand awareness. Markets such as Poland and the UK, together with half a dozen others, all fell into this category.

The task as defined by the client brief was to create a powerful, well-branded advertising idea. VELUX's experience in the other markets indicated that the higher overall brand awareness was, the greater the likelihood that VELUX would be the specified brand when the customer was deciding which brand of roof windows to purchase. The international dimension was the most challenging aspect of producing a new campaign for VELUX.

The creative challenge

International campaigns demand that the communication works against a number of audiences (with slightly different mindsets). But all too often this leads to lowest common denominator advertising – advertising that can run in all markets, but doesn't really work in any. However, given that the VELUX campaign for 'low-awareness' markets would be covering a footprint from the northernmost tip of Norway to the southernmost tip of Spain and from the west of Ireland to the east of Croatia, it was clear that finding a creative idea to successfully straddle the geography was going to be a big challenge.

A single international campaign made a lot of sense in terms of cost effectiveness. With the relative expense of TV production costs the potential savings to VELUX over a large number of markets were enormous. In order to find this creative idea it was important to understand what 'hot buttons' we could press that would be relevant in the various markets.

One cannot over-emphasise the climatic, socio-economic, political and cultural differences these widely different markets. However, as far as the marketing of VELUX was concerned, research highlighted that there was consistency regarding the various female mindsets being united in a shared aspiration of wanting more room in their houses. Therefore the idea of utilising the attic to create additional space under their sloping roof was one that has a great deal of appeal across all the markets within which VELUX operates.

Research also helped highlight that a loft conversion is a very real solution for these people who are keen to improve their living environment, but are less keen to incur the hassle and expense involved in moving house.

The role for advertising was to trigger the thought process that leads the audience to consider 'transforming' their roof space. Once this was achieved, sales for VELUX were highly likely given its role as dominant market player.

The creative brief

The guiding strategic principle for the development of the creative brief was that we were not selling roof windows per se, we were selling the transformation of the attic into the 'best room in the house'. If we could successfully sell this concept to consumers, logic said we would sell more VELUX roof windows.

> A LOFT CONVERSION WITH VELUX WINDOWS
> CAN HELP TRANSFORM YOUR LIVING
> ENVIRONMENT

However, whilst this sentiment would ensure that there would be consistency in terms of communication, it was imperative that the 'look' of any advertising was capable of working across a number of different markets. Specifically this meant that any advertising had to work equally well in countries such as Britain and Norway, where the loft space is converted into a vibrant living space, as well as countries like Poland and Croatia, where the loft conversions are much more basic affairs.

The creative solution

The television execution at the heart of the campaign was based around a group of toys that sadly had been rejected and left in a dark and dingy attic. Clearly the toys were not happy about this! They therefore came to

life and initiated a chain of events that would set them free (be a rediscovered toy) whilst giving the home owner the benefit of an airy living space with plenty of daylight they would enjoy. The 'Toys' and VELUX would help create 'the best room in the house'. A wide range of collateral material including press ads, point of sale and direct mail was also produced in order to leverage as much value as possible out of the core creative vehicle and ensure the campaign could run across the specified markets.

Campaign effectiveness

The objective for the campaign was very simple – to improve VELUX brand awareness in 'low-awareness' markets. In order to measure this key brand metric in the UK, a series of surveys has been conducted using the BMRB omnibus. A total of eight waves were conducted between April 2001 and May 2002. Given the task was very much one of driving awareness, TV was very quickly identified as the key medium. However, a key requirement from a client perspective was to ensure optimal appropriation of the media budget. To this end the media schedule contained a blend of national activity, regional activity and upweights. This would enable a more scientific analysis of the build (and crucially the decay) of brand awareness dependent on different media weights.

The first burst of television activity was in April/May of 2001 and consisted of a national burst of 540 TVRs. The effect of this burst was to increase brand awareness by 9 per cent. That the increase was a function of the impact and strong branding of the 'Toys' advertising is demonstrated by the fact that there was an 80 per cent increase in advertising awareness for VELUX. This figure rose from 10 per cent to 18 per cent over the course of the first burst of advertising.

The performance of the advertising is even more powerful when we look at the pre- and post-figures against the core target audience for VELUX – adults aged between 35 and 54. Amongst this group total brand awareness after this first burst of advertising increased by 18 per cent. Again that this was primarily due to advertising is demonstrated by the fact that advertising awareness amongst this 35–54 age group improved 61 per cent, increasing from 18 per cent to 29 per cent.

A regional burst was factored into the 2001 media campaign. The objective of this upweight was to gauge the effect of sustained support of the creative vehicle over time. It would also help us better understand the dynamics of 'wearout/wear in' of the 'Toys' commercial. Therefore a burst of 550 TVRs ran in the Granada TV region in October 2001. Prior to this burst total brand awareness in the Granada TV region was 29 per cent, after the burst of advertising, this had increased significantly to 45 per cent. Over the same period in Granada, advertising awareness for VELUX doubled from 14 per cent to 30 per cent.

This improvement in awareness was not solely focused on the UK, however. In Poland, VELUX saw its brand awareness increase by 42 per cent after the advertising campaign. It was a similar picture in the Netherlands and Hungary, which both saw brand awareness improved by one third.

Crucially, however, there seems to be strong evidence that these improvements in awareness also translated into improvements in terms of the number of people wanting to find out more about VELUX and also the number of people choosing to fit VELUX roof windows. Specifically, in the UK in the first month of the campaign the VELUX call centre received 40 per cent more phone calls than they normally received. Likewise the number of hits into the website spiked massively by 225 per cent compared to the previous period. (The URL was included at the end of the commercial.)

This increase in interest in the VELUX brand has reassuringly had a positive impact on the VELUX business. This is demonstrated by the improvement in sales over a three-year period. ('Toys' ran in 2002 as well as 2001.)

BRINGING LIGHT TO LIFE

VELUX
ROOF WINDOWS

UK sales	(index)
2000	100
2001	112
2002	130

The 'Toys' have also give VELUX a sustainable advertising property that has the potential to support the brand's advertising in years to come. The campaignability of 'Toys' is demonstrated by the fact that the commercial has already been utilised in a number of non-'low awareness' markets. The second 'Toys' adventure is also in the pipeline and about to launch in the UK and other European markets.

SOURCE: This case study is adapted from the paper presented at the IPA Effectiveness Awards. The full version is available at www.warc.com and is reproduced by kind permission of the Institute of Practitioners in Advertising and the World Advertising Research Center.

Questions:

1 Identify the factors that are encouraging the growth of international and global marketing
2 What alternative approaches can be applied to the management of global brands?
3 What factors need to be considered in the context of international branding?
4 What factors differentiate the international consumer from the domestic consumer? Why is it vital to understand these dimensions before embarking on the development of an international advertising campaign?
5 Should advertising be controlled centrally or locally? What are the advantages and disadvantages of each method?
6 How have advertising agencies responded to the move towards global communications?
7 What criteria need to be considered when appointing an advertising agency to handle an international account?

Appendix: useful websites

Organisation	Web address
Account Planning Group (UK)	
Produces a range of papers on advertising planning issues and oversees the annual account planning awards for advertising effectiveness.	www.arsite.org
Ad Brands (USA)	
Provides a variety of profiles of both brands and advertising agencies.	www.adbrands.net
Ad Forum (USA)	
USA advertising news source with editions for Germany, France, Spain and the UK. It also offers a variety of other resources.	www.adforum.com
Ad Resources (USA)	
US sources for internet advertising.	www.clickz/resources/adres
Ad Slogans (UK)	
Site relating to advertising slogans which includes a special student section.	www.adslogans.co.uk
The Advertising Association (UK)	
The Advertising Association is the representative body of the advertising and promotions industry and maintains an information centre that can be accessed by students by appointment. The ASA also produces the official UK and European advertising expenditure figures.	www.adassoc.org.uk
Advertising Educational Foundation (USA)	
Provides resource to access advertising related content on the web.	www.aef.com
Advertising Information Group (UK)	
Develops position papers on a variety of advertising-related topics.	www.aig.org
Advertising Research Foundation (USA)	
Information source that provides articles on current research within the advertising industry together with guidelines and papers on advertising standards.	www.amic.com/arf

Organisation	Web address
Advertising Standards Authority (UK) The ASA is the independent self-regulatory body in the UK. The site provides access to the codes of practice and information on adjudications, together with other material.	`www.asa.org`
Advertising Standards Authority for Ireland Codes of practice developed to regulate the Irish advertising industry.	`www.asai.ie`
The Advertising Standards Authority of New Zealand The New Zealand regulatory body which provides access to the codes of practice and other information.	`www.assa.co.nz`
American Advertising Museum Wide variety of information with access to many past advertising campaigns.	`www.admuseum.org`
The American Association of Advertising Agencies The national trade association representing the advertising business in the USA.	`www.aaaa.org`
Associacion de Autocontrol de la Publicidad (Spain) The Spanish advertising regulatory body.	`www.autocontrol.es`
L'association des agences conseils et communication (France) The French association of advertising and marketing communications agencies. The site provides a variety of useful information and has an English version.	`www.aaac.fr`
Association of Accredited Advertising Agencies (Hong Kong) Provides information about the advertising industry and access to a variety of information resources.	`www.aaaa.com.hk`
Association of National Advertisers (USA) Marketing resource centre.	`www.ana.net`
Australasian Promotion Marketing Association Publishes a range of news articles and statistics relating to the advertising and promotional industry.	`www.apma.com`
Australian Association of National Advertisers Source for papers on advertising effectiveness, self-regulation and other issues affecting the advertising industry.	`www.aana.com.au`
Australian Direct Marketing Association The main body for the provision of material relating to information based marketing.	`www.adma.com.au`
Brand Channel Interbrand's information site. It provides a great number of current articles on branding issues, together with much additional information.	`www.brandchannel.com`

Organisation	Web address
Brand Republic UK news and information source.	www.brandrepublic.com
Bureau de Verification de la Publicité (France) The French advertising regulatory body.	www.bvp.org
Canadian Advertising Research Foundation Provides access to a variety of resources relating to advertising research.	www.carf.ca
Committee of Advertising Practice (UK) UK advertising industry body that creates and enforces the various codes of practice.	www.cap.org.uk
Direct Marketing Association (UK) The website of the UK direct marketing association provides news, articles papers and an online library.	www.the-dma.org
History of Advertising Trust (UK) Maintains a substantial archive of historic advertising material and campaigns.	www.hatads.org
Incorporate Society of British Advertisers Articles on advertising and related subjects together with best practice guides.	www.isba.org.uk
Infotrac You will have received a password to access this extremely useful site. It will provide you with access to a wide range of academic journals and other material that is of great value to those studying the subject of advertising.	
Institute of Advertising Practitioners in Ireland News, publications and other information including articles on advertising effectiveness.	www.iapi.ie
Institute of Communications and Advertising (Canada) Contains a great deal of information on advertising agencies, publications and other material. The site also contains links to other relevant websites.	www.ica-ad.com
Institute of Practitioners in Advertising (UK) UK advertising trade body providing a resource centre with special section for students.	www.ipa.co.uk
Instituto dell'Autodisciplina Publicitana (Italy) Provides access to the Italian codes of advertising practice and also has an English version.	www.iap.it
Interbrand Interbrand's international site contains much valuable information including the results of the global brand survey.	www.interbrand.com

Organisation	Web address
International Advertising Association (UK) The UK chapter of the IAA with information relating to the industry.	www.iaaukchp.co.uk
International Advertising Association (USA) Source of a range of surveys and reports relating to the advertising industry.	www.iaaglobal.org
Internet Advertising Bureau (UK) The IAB provides news, articles and case studies relating to internet advertising.	www.iab.uk.net
Internet Advertising Bureau (USA) The American IAB provides a similar resource to that of the UK site plus a range of internet statistics.	www.iab.net
Journal of Interactive Advertising Full access to articles from this academic journal.	www.jiad.com
Market Research Society (UK) Site for the UK market research society which provides access to a wide range of data and other material.	www.mrs.org.uk
Radio Advertising Bureau (UK) Many articles on radio advertising and radio effectiveness together with access to radio ads.	www.rab.co.uk
UK Sponsorship Database of sponsorship news and information.	www.uksponsorship.com
The World Advertising Research Centre (UK) Publishers of a range of pocketbooks on advertising and related statistical information. An excellent online resource for information on the advertising industry. WARC also publishes a variety of books and monographs on advertising related topics, together with the influential industry journal *Admap*.	www.warc.com
Zenith Optimedia Marketer's Portal A superb site providing links to many of the above websites and a wide range of other sources of information.	www.marketersportal.com

References

Chapter 1

Abernethy, A.M. (2001), 'Self-regulation and television advertising: a replication and extension', *Journal of Advertising Research*, vol. 41, iss. 3.

Abernethy, A.M. and Franke, G.R. (1996), 'The information content of advertising: a meta-analysis', *Journal of Advertising*, vol. 25, iss. 2.

Advertising Association (2003), *Advertising Statistics Yearbook*.

Arnold, W. (2001) 'Responding to the future of interactive advertising', *Admap*, May.

Baggozzi, R.P. and Moore, D.J. (1994), 'Public service advertisements: emotion and empathy guide prosocial behaviour', *Journal of Marketing*, Jan.

Bandyopadhyay, S., Kindra, S. and Sharp, L. (2001), 'Is television advertising good for children? Areas of concern and policy implications', *International Journal of Advertising*, vol. 20, iss. 1.

Banerjee, S. and Gulas, C.S. (1995), 'Shades of green: a multi-dimensional analysis of environmental advertising', *Journal of Advertising*, vol. 24, iss. 2.

Berger, R. (1999), 'The effects of commercial advertising on children', *International Journal of Advertising*, vol. 18, iss. 4.

Boddewyn, J.J. (1991), 'Controlling sex and decency in advertising around the world', *Journal of Advertising*, vol. 20, iss. 4.

Boddewyn, J.J. (1998), 'Advertising and self-regulation: true purpose and limits', *Journal of Advertising*, vol. 19, iss, 2.

Boutlis, P. (2000), 'A theory of postmodern advertising', *International Journal of Advertising*, vol. 19, iss. 1.

Brenkert, G.E. (2002), 'Ethical challenges of social marketing', *Journal of Public Policy & Marketing*, vol. 21, iss. 1.

Bullimore (1995), 'A brand's eye view of response segmentation in consumer brand choice behaviour', *Journal of Marketing*, vol. 32, iss. 1.

Bush, A.J. and Bush, V.D. (1994), 'The narrative paradigm as a perspective for improving ethical evaluations of advertisements', *Journal of Advertising*, vol. 23, iss. 3.

Cane, A. (1999), 'Are you ethical? Please tick yes or no on researching ethics in business organisations', *Journal of Business Ethics*, vol. 20, iss. 3.

Carrigan, M. and Attalla, A. (2001), 'The myth of the ethical consumer – do ethics matter in purchase behaviour?' *Journal of Consumer Marketing*, vol. 18, iss. 8.

Debating Society (2003), minutes available online at www.debatingsociety.org.uk.

De Chernatony, L. and McDonald, M. (1992), *Creating Powerful Brands*, Butterworth Heinemann.

Ehrenberg, A. and Barnard, N. (1977), 'Advertising and product demand', *Admap*, May.

Feldwick, P. (1997), 'Above the line advertising. Is it still a key tool for building brands?', ESOMAR conference paper.

Fletcher, W. (1993), *A Glittering Haze*, NTC Publications.

Fletcher, W. (1999), *Advertising, Advertising: Advertising's Public Benefits*, Profile Books.

Ford-Hutchinson, S. and Rothwell, A. (2002), 'The public's perception of advertising in today's society', *Advertising Standards Authority*, Feb.

Goodyear, M. (2000), 'Marketing evolves from selling to citizenship', *Market Leader*, 12.

Gordon and Langmaid (1999), MRS conference paper.

Gordon, W. and Ryan, C. (1982), 'How do consumers feel advertising works?', *Journal of the Market Research Society*, 39.

Hardesty, D.M., Carlson, J.P., and Bearden, W.O. (2002), 'Brand familiarity and invoice price effects on consumer evaluations: the moderating role of scepticism toward advertising', *Journal of Advertising*, vol. 31, iss. 2.

Harker, D. and Harker, M. (2000), 'The role of codes of conduct in the advertising self-regulatory framework', *Journal of Macromarketing*, vol. 20, iss. 2.

Hyman, M.R. and Tansey, R. (1990), 'The ethics of psychoactive ads', *Journal of Business Ethics*, 9.

Interbrand (2004), 'Global brand survey', available online at www.interbrand.com.

Jones, J.P. (1995), 'Advertising's impact on sales and profitability', Advertising effectiveness conference, 16 Mar.

Kerr, G. and Moran, C. (2002), 'Any complaints? A review of the framework of regulation in the Australian advertising industry', *Journal of Marketing Communications*, 8.

Kiely (1993) cited in Eagle et al. (1999), 'Perceptions of integrated marketing communications', *International Journal of Advertising*, vol. 18, iss. 1.

Klein, N. (2000), *No Logo*, Flamingo Books.

Kotler, P. (1972), 'What consumerism means for marketers', *Harvard Business Review*, 50, May/June.

Kotler, P. and Levy, S.J. (1969), 'Broadening the concept of marketing', *Journal of Marketing*, 33.

Kroeber-Riel cited in Appelbaum, U. and Halliburton, C. (1993), 'How to develop international advertising campaigns that work: examples of the European food and drink industry', *International Journal of Advertising*, 12.

Leiss, W., Kline, S. and Jhally, S. (1986), *Social Communication in Advertising*, Methuen Publications.

Levitt, T. (1960), 'Marketing myopia', *Harvard Business Review*, July/Aug.

Li, H., Edwards, S.M. and Joo-Hyun, L. (2002), 'Measuring the intrusiveness of advertisements: scale development and validation', *International Journal of Advertising Research*, vol. 31, iss. 2.

Mittal, B. (1994), 'Public assessment of TV advertising: faint praise and harsh criticism', *Journal of Advertising Research*, vol. 34, iss. 1.

Mole, C. (1999), 'Winning in a converging world', *Market Leader*, 4.

Murphy, C. (2000), 'Ugly business, advertising unpopular products', *Marketing*, 7 Sept.

Ogilvy, D. (1983), *Ogilvy on Advertising*, Pan Books.

Pollay, R. (1986), 'The distorted mirror: reflections on the unintended consequences of advertising', *Journal of Marketing*, 50.

Pollay, R.W. and Gallagher, K. (1990), 'Advertising and cultural values: reflections in the distorted mirror', *International Journal of Advertising*, vol. 9, iss. 4.

Reeves, R. (1961), *Reality in Advertising*, MacGibbon & Kee.

Reidenbach, R.E. and Robin, D. (1988), 'Some initial steps toward improving the measurement of ethical evaluations of marketing activities', *Journal of Business Ethics*, 7.

Richards, J. and Curran, C.M. (2002) 'Oracles on advertising: searching for a definition', *Journal of Advertising*, vol. 31, iss. 22.

Robin, D.P. and Reidenbach, R.E. (1998), 'Social responsibility, ethics and marketing strategy: closing the gap between concept and application', *Journal of Marketing*, 51.

Rogers, M. and Smith, K.H. (1993), 'Public perceptions of subliminal advertising: why practitioners shouldn't ignore this issue', *Journal of Advertising Research*, Mar./Apr.

Rust, R.T. and Oliver, R.W. (1994), 'The death of advertising', *Journal of Advertising*, vol. 23, iss. 4.

Schultz, D.E. and Barnes, S.E. (1995), *Strategic Advertising Campaigns*, NTC Business Books.

Scipione, P.A. (1997), 'Too much or too little? Public perceptions of advertising expenditures', *International Journal of Advertising Research*, vol. 37, iss. 3.

Shimp, T.A. (1997), *Advertising and Promotion: supplemental aspects of integrated marketing communications*, Dryden Press.

Treise, D. and Weigold, M.F. (1994), 'Ethics in advertising: idealogical correlates of consumer perceptions', *Journal of Advertising*, vol. 23, iss. 3.

World Advertising Research Centre (2004).

Zinkhan, G.M. (1994), 'Advertising ethics: emerging methods and trends', *Journal of Advertising*, vol. 23, iss. 3.

Zinkhan, G.M., Bisesi, and Saxton, M.J. (1989), 'MBA's changing attitudes toward marketing dilemmas: 1981–1987', *Journal of Business Ethics*, 8.

Chapter 2

Ambler, T. (1998), 'Myths about the mind', *International Journal of Advertising*, vol. 17, iss. 4.

Ambler, T. (2000), 'Persuasion, pride and prejudice: how ads work', *International Journal of Advertising*, vol. 19, iss. 3.

Barnard, N. and Ehrenberg, A.C.S. (1998), 'Advertising and brand attitudes', *Admap*, Mar.

Barry, T.E and Howard, D.J. (1990), 'A review and critique of the hierarchy of effects', *International Journal of Advertising*, vol. 9, iss. 2.

Belch, G.E. and Belch, M.A. (1993), *Introduction to Advertising and Promotion: An Integrated Marketing Communications Perspective*, Irwin, 2nd edition.

Blackston, M. (2000), 'Pay attention! This advertising is effective', *Admap*, Mar.

Boulding, W., Lee, E. and Staelin, R. (1994), 'Mastering the mix: do advertising, promotion and sales force activities lead to differentiation?' *Journal of Marketing Research*, vol. 31, iss. 2.

Brierley, S.B. (1995), *The Advertising Handbook*, Routledge.

Buck, S. (2001), *Advertising and the Long-term Success of Premium Brands*, WARC.

Campbell, M. and Dove, B. (1998), 'Evaluating the impact of advertising on sales', *Admap*, Feb.

Colley, R. (1961), 'Defining advertising goals for measured advertising results', Association of National Advertisers.

Duckworth, G. (1995), 'How advertising works – the universe and everything', *Admap*, Jan.

Ehrenberg, A.S.C. (1974), 'Competitive advertising and the consumer', *Journal of Advertising Research*, vol. 14, iss. 2.

Ehrenberg, A. (1997), 'How do consumers come to buy a new brand?' *Admap*, Mar.

Ehrenberg, A. (2000), 'Repetitive advertising and the consumer', *Journal of Advertising Research*, vol. 6, iss. 40.

Ehrenberg, A., Barnard, N. and Sharp, B. (2001), 'Decision models or descriptive models: a brief critique', *Marketing Research*, vol. 13, iss. 3.

Ehrenberg, A., Barnard, N., Kennedy, R. and Bloom, H. (2002), 'Brand advertising as creative publicity', *Journal of Advertising Research*, vol. 42, iss. 4.

Foote, Cone and Belding (1979), 'How advertising works: an FCB strategy planning model'.

Foxall, G.R. and Goldsmith, R.E. (1994), *Consumer Psychology for Marketing*, Routledge.

Franzen, G. (1999), 'Brands and advertising: how advertising effectiveness influences brand equity', *Admap*.

Hall, M. (1998), 'How advertising works: new steps on the advertising timeline', APG conference paper.

Heath, R. (2002), 'Understanding advertising: how the best ads work', *Admap*, Apr.

Jones, J.P. (1995), 'Single source research begins to fulfil its promise', *Journal of Advertising Research*, vol. 35, iss. 3.

Jones, J.P. (1998), 'The essential role of communications', *Admap*, Jan.

Juchems, A. (1996), 'The role of awareness in the advertising process', *Admap*, July/Aug.

Krugman, H.E. (2000), 'Memory without recall, exposure without perception', *Journal of Advertising Research*, vol. 40, iss. 6.

Lavidge, R.J. and Steiner, G.A. (1961), 'A model for predictive effects of advertising effectiveness', *Journal of Marketing*, October.

Little, J. (1994), cited in Ehrenberg, A., Barnard, N. and Sharp, B. (2001), 'Decision models or descriptive models: A brief critique', *Marketing Research*, vol. 13, iss. 3.

Lowe, Howard-Spink (1995), study reported in *Campaign*, 8 Dec.

McDonald, C. (1992), *How Advertising Works: A Review of Current Thinking*, The Advertising Association/ NTC Publications.

Meyers-Levy, J. and Prashant, M. (1999), 'Consumers' processing of persuasive advertisements: an integrative framework of persuasion theories', *Journal of Marketing*, vol. 63, iss. 4.

Prue, T. (1998), 'An all-embracing theory of how advertising works', *Admap*, Feb.

Romaniuk and Sharp (2002).

Rossiter, J.R., Percy, L. and Donovan, J.R. (1991), 'A better advertising grid', *Journal of Advertising Research*, vol. 31, iss. 5.

St. Elmo Lewis cited in Strong, E.K. (1925), *The Psychology of Selling*, McGraw-Hill.

Stern, B.B. (1994), 'A revised communication model for advertising: multiple dimensions of the source, the message and the recipient', *Journal of Advertising*, vol. 23, iss. 2.

Strong, E.K. (1925), *The Psychology of Selling*, McGraw-Hill.

Swindells, A. (2000), 'The myth of consumer choice', MRS conference paper.

Vakratsas, D. and Ambler, T. (1999), 'How advertising works: what do we really know?' *Journal of Marketing*, vol. 63, iss. 1.

Walford, N. (1992), 'How it works: sponsorship effects and advertising campaigns', *Admap*, July.

Weilbacher, W.M. (2001), 'Does advertising cause a "hierarchy of effects"?' *Journal of Advertising Research*, vol. 41, iss. 6.

Weilbacher, W.M. (2003), 'How advertising affects consumers', *Journal of Advertising Research*, vol. 43, iss. 2.

White, R. (1998), 'The blind alleys of recall', *Admap*, Jan.

White, R. (1999), 'What can advertising really do for brands?' *International Journal of Advertising*, vol. 18, iss. 1.

Yeshin, T. (ed.) (1993), *Inside Advertising*, Institute of Practitioners in Advertising.

Chapter 3

Alanko, J. (2000), 'The case for integration in B2B marketing', *Admap*, Sept.

American Association of Advertising Agencies (1993), *Marketing News*, 18 Jan.

Archer, J. and Hubbard, T. (1996), 'Integrated tracking for integrated communications', *Admap*, Feb.

Brannan, T. (1995), *A Practical Guide to Integrated Marketing Communications*, Kogan Page.

Caywood, C., Schultz, D. and Wang, P. (1991), 'Integrated marketing communications: a survey of national consumer goods advertisers', Northwestern University Report, June.

Cleland, K. (1995), 'A lot of talk, little action on IMC', *Business Marketing*, Mar.

Cook, W. (1994), 'The end of the line', *Marketing*, 24 Feb.

Cornellisen, J.P., Lock, A.R. and Gardner, H. (2000), 'Theoretical concept or management fashion: examining the significance of IMC, *Journal of Advertising Research*, vol. 40, iss. 5.

Cornellisen, J.P., Lock, A.R. and Gardner, H. (2001), 'The organisation of external communications disciplines: an integrative framework of dimensions and determinants', *International Journal of Advertising*, vol. 20, iss. 1.

Duncan, T. and Everett, S. (1993), 'Client perceptions of integrated marketing communications', *Journal of Advertising Research*, vol. 33, iss. 3.

Duncan, T. and Moriarty, S.E. (1998), 'A communication-based marketing model for managing relationships', *Journal of Marketing*, vol. 62, iss. 2.

Fletcher, W. (1998), 'Marketing skills can make sweet music together', *Marketing*, 12 Feb.

Franz, G. (2000), 'Better media planning for integrated communications', *Admap*, Jan.

Grein, A. and Ducoffe, R. (1998), 'Strategic responses to market globalisation amongst advertising agencies', *International Journal of Advertising*, vol. 17, iss. 3.

Grein, A.F. and Gould, S.J. (1996), 'Globally integrated marketing communications', *Journal of Marketing Communications*, vol. 2, iss. 3.

Griffin, T. and McArthur, D.N. (1997), 'A marketing management view of integrated marketing communications', *Journal of Advertising Research*, Sept./Oct.

Grondstedt, T.A. (1996), 'How agencies can support integrated communications', *Journal of Business Research*, vol. 37, iss. 3.

Grondstedt, T.A. and Thorson, E. (1996), 'Five approaches to organise an integrated marketing communications agency', *Journal of Advertising Research*, vol. 36, iss. 2.

Iddiols, D. (2000), 'Marketing Superglue: client perceptions of IMC', *Admap*, May.

Jeans, R., 'Integrating marketing communications', *Admap*, Dec. 1998.

Kitchen, P.J. and Schultz, D.E. (1999), 'A multi-country comparison of the drive for IMC', *Journal of Advertising Research*, Jan./Feb.

Kitchen, P. and Schultz, D.E. (2000), 'The status of IMC: a 21st century perspective', *Admap*, Sept.

Lannon, J. (1994), 'What brands need now', *Admap*, Sept.

Lannon, J. (1996), 'Integrated marketing communications from the consumer end', *Admap*, Feb.

Linton, I. and Morley, K. (1995), *Integrated Marketing Communications*, Butterworth Heinemann.

Low, G.S. (2000), 'Correlates of integrated marketing communications', *Journal of Advertising Research*, May.

McArthur, D.N. and Griffin, T. (1997), 'A marketing management view of integrated marketing communications', *Journal of Advertising Research*, vol. 37, iss. 5.

Mitchell, H. (1995), 'Client perceptions of integrated marketing communications', Cranfield.

Nilson, T.S. (1992), *Value Added Marketing*, McGraw Hill.

Novak, G.J. and Phelps, J. (1994), 'Conceptualizing the integrated marketing communications phenomenon: an examination of its impact on advertising practices and its implications for advertising research', *Journal of Current Issues and Research in Advertising*, vol. 16, iss. 1.

O'Donoghue, D. (1997), chapter 8 in Cooper, A. (1997), *How to Plan Advertising*, 2nd edition, Cassell.

Ogilvy, D. (1993), *Ogilvy on Advertising*, Prion.

Picton, D., and Hartley, B. (1998), 'Measuring integration: an assessment of the quality of integrated marketing communications, *Journal of Advertising*, vol. 7, iss. 4.

Proctor, T. and Kitchen, P. (2002), 'Communication in post-modern integrated marketing', *Corporate Communications*, vol. 7, iss. 3.

Reid, M. (2003), 'IMC – performance relationship: further insight and evidence from the Australian marketplace', *International Journal of Advertising*, vol. 22, iss. 2.

Schultz, D.E. (1999), chapter 8 in Jones, J.P. (ed.) (1999), *The Advertising Business*, Sage.

Schultz, D.E and Kitchen, P.J. (1997), 'Integrated marketing communications in US advertising agencies: an exploratory study', *Journal of Advertising Research*, vol. 37, iss. 5.

Schultz, D.E., Tannenbaum, S.I. and Lauterborn, R.F. (1992), *Integrated Marketing Communications: Putting It Together and Making It Work*, NTC Business Books.

Schultz, D.E., Tannenbaum, S.I. and Lauterborn, R.F. (1995), *The Marketing Paradigm – Integrated Marketing Communications*, NTC Business Books.

Shimp, T.A. (1996), *Advertising Promotion: Supplemental Aspects of Integrated Marketing Communications*, Harcourt.

Smith, P. (1996), 'Benefits and barriers to integrated marketing communications', *Admap*, Feb.

Solomon, M.R. and Englis, B.G. (1994), 'The big picture: product complementarity and integrated communications', *Journal of Advertising Research*, Jan./Feb.

Van Raaij, W.F. (1998), 'Integration of communication: starting from the sender or receiver?' in *Effectiveness in Communication Management*.

Yeshin, T. (1996), 'The development and implications of integrated marketing communications', DMB&B study.

Chapter 4

Aaker, D.A. (1996a), *Building Strong Brands*, The Free Press.

Aaker, D.A. (1996b), 'Measuring brand equity across products and markets', *California Management Review*, vol. 38, iss. 3.

Aaker, D.A. and Keller, K.L. (1990), 'Consumer evaluations of brand extensions', *Journal of Marketing*, vol. 54, iss. 3.

Aaker, J. (1997), 'Dimensions of measuring brand personality', *Journal of Marketing Research*, vol. 24, iss. 3.

Agres, S.J. and Dubitsky, T.M. (1996), 'Changing needs for brands', *Journal of Advertising Research*, vol. 36, iss. 1.

Ambler, T. (1997), 'Do brands benefit consumers?' *International Journal of Advertising*, vol. 19, iss. 3.

Barnard, N., Ehrenberg, A.C.S. and Scriven, J. (1998), 'Branding and values', *Admap*, vol. 33, iss. 6.

Barnard, P. (1993), 'Brandscapes', *Admap*, Mar.

Bartle, J. (1997), chapter 2, in L. Butterfield (ed.), *Excellence in Advertising*, Butterworth Heinemann.

Bateson, J.E.G. (1995), *Managing Services Marketing*, The Dryden Press.

Belen del Rio, A., Vazquez, R. and Iglesias, V. (2001), 'The effects of brand associations on consumer response', *Journal of Consumer Marketing*, vol. 18, iss. 5.

Bennett, P.D. (ed.) (1998), *Dictionary of Marketing Terms*, American Marketing Association.

Biel, A.L. (1990), 'Strong brand, high spend', *Admap*, Nov.

Biel, A.L. (1991), 'The brandscape: converting brand image into equity', *Admap*, vol. 26, iss. 10.

Biel, A.L. (1997), 'Discovering brand magic: the hardness of the softer side of branding', *International Journal of Advertising*, vol. 16, iss. 3.

Birkin, M. (1995a), 'The future of the brand: why brands are valued', *Admap*, Mar.

Birkin, M. (1995b), 'Why brands are valued', *Admap*, Mar.

Blackett, T. (1996), 'The valuation of brands', *Admap*, July/Aug.

Blackston, M. (1993), 'The levers of brand power', *Admap*, Mar.

Blackston, M. (1995), 'The qualitative dimension of brand equity', *Journal of Advertising Research*, July/Aug.

Brandt, M. and Johnson, G. (1997), 'Power brand building: technology brands for competitive advantage', *International Data Group*.

Broniarczyk, S.M. and Alba, J.W. (1994), 'The importance of the brand in brand extensions', *Journal of Marketing Research*, 31, May.

Buck, S. (2000), 'The triumph of the premium brand', *Market Leader*, Winter.

Buck, S. and Passingham, J. (1997), 'Brands vs. private label', *TN AGB*.

Burt, M. (1994), in *Campaign*, 5 Aug.

Buzzell, R.D. and Gale, B.T. (1987), *The PIMS Principles: Linking Strategy to Performance*, Collier Macmillan.

Campbell, M. and Dove, B. (1998), 'Evaluating the impact of advertising on sales', *Admap*, Feb.

Cleaver, C. (2000), 'Brands, the web and brand strategy', *Admap*, June.

Clifton, R. and Maughan E. (2000), *The Future of Brands*, Macmillan.

Clemmow, S. (1997), 'The role for advertising', in A. Cooper (ed.), *How to Plan Advertising*, Cassell.

Cooper, A. and Simmons, P. (1997), 'Brand equity lifestage: an entrepreneurial revolution', *TBWA Simmons Palmer*, Sept.

Cooper, R.G. (1998), 'The new product process: a decision guide for management', *Journal of Marketing Management*, vol. 3, iss. 3.

Cowley, D. (1999), *Understanding Brands by 10 People who Do*, Kogan Page.

Davis, S. (1994), 'Securing the future of your brand', *Journal of Product and Brand Management*, vol. 3, iss. 2.

Davis, S. (2002), 'Brand asset management: how business can profit from the power of the brand', *Journal of Consumer Marketing*, vol. 19, iss. 14.

De Chernatony, L. and Dall'Olmo Riley, F. (1997), 'Expert views about defining services brands and the principles of services branding', Open University working paper series.

De Chernatony, L. and Dall'Olmo Riley, F. (1998), 'Defining a brand: beyond the literature with expert's interpretations', *Journal of Marketing Management*, 14.

De Chernatony, L. and McDonald, M. (1992), *Creating Powerful Brands*, Butterworth Heinemann.

De Chernatony, L. and McDonald, M. (1998), *Creating Powerful Brands*, 2nd edition, Butterworth Heinemann.

Dibb, S. and Simkin, L. (1993), 'The strength of branding and positioning in services', *International Journal of Service Industries Management*.

Doyle, P. (1989), 'Building successful brands: the strategic options', *Journal of Marketing Management*, 5.

Doyle, P. (1997), 'Building successful brands', in L. Butterfield (ed.), *Excellence in Advertising*, Butterworth Heinemann.

Doyle, P. (1998), 'Brand equity and the marketing professional', *Market Leader*, 1.

Duckworth, G. (1996), *Advertising Works, 9*, IPA/NTC.

Farquhar, P.H., Han, J.Y., Herr, P.M. and Ijiri, Y. (1992), 'Strategies for leveraging master brands', *Marketing Research*, 4, Sept.

Farr, A. (1996), 'Advertising and brand equity', *Admap*, Apr.

Feldwick, P. (1997), 'Do we really need "brand equity"', *Journal of Brand Management*, vol. 4, iss. 1.

Feldwick, P. (1998), 'What is brand equity anyway, and how do you measure it?' *Journal of Product and Brand Management*, vol. 7, iss. 2.

Financial Times (1997), 23 June.

Ford-Hutchinson, S. (1996), 'Understanding brand leadership', Market Research Society conference paper.

Ford-Hutchinson, S. (1998), 'Brand stretch – much discussed but seldom demonstrated', Market Research Society conference paper.

Fournier, S. (1995), 'Understanding consumer-brand relationships', Harvard Business School working paper.

Griffiths, C. (1992), 'Brand as verb', *Admap*, July/Aug.

Haigh, D. (1996), 'Brands', *Marketing Business*, Mar.

Hankinson, G. and Cowking, P. (1995), 'What do you really mean by a brand?', *Journal of Brand Management*, vol. 3, iss. 1.

Hart, S. and Murphy, J. (1998), *Brands: The New Wealth Creators*, Macmillan Business.

Heath, R. (1998), 'What can advertising realistically achieve?' *Admap*, June.

Hegarty, J. (2001), private interview.

High, D. (1994), 'Taking brands offshore', *Admap*, Nov.

Howard, D. (1997), 'Stretching a point', *Admap*, Mar.

Jeavons, C. and Gabbott, M. (2000), 'Trust, brand equity and brand reality in Internet business relationships: an interdisciplinary approach', *Journal of Marketing Management*, 16.

Kapferer, J.N. (1992), *Strategic Brand Management*, 2nd edition, Kogan Page.

Keller, K.L. (2000), 'The brand report card', *Harvard Business Review*, vol. 78, iss. 1.

Kim, P. (1990), 'A perspective on brands', *Journal of Consumer Marketing*, vol. 7, iss. 3.

King, S. (1991), 'Brand building in the 1990s', *Journal of Marketing Management*, 7.

Kotler, P. and Armstrong, G. (1996), *The Principles of Marketing*, 7th edition, Prentice Hall.

Kotler, P., Armstrong, G., Saunders, J. and Wong, V. (2001), *Principles of Marketing*, 3rd European edition, Prentice Hall.

Louro, M.J. and Cunha, P.V. (2001), 'Brand management paradigms', *Journal of Marketing Management*, 17.

Lury, A. (1998), *Brandwatching*, Black Hall Publishing.

McEnally, M. and de Chernatony, L. (1999), 'The evolving nature of branding: consumer and managerial considerations', *Academy of Marketing Science Review*, 2.

McWilliam, G. (1993), 'The effect of brand typology on brand extension fit: commercial and academic research findings', *European Advances in Consumer Research*, 1.

Macrae, C. (1991), *World Class Brands*, Addison Wesley.

Macrae, C. (1995), 'Branding – a core business process', *Journal of Brand Management*, Apr.

Marketing (1997), 'Sleeping with the enemy', 5 June.

Marketing (2003), 'Biggest brands, 2003', 28 August (based on A.C. Nielsen figures).

Meenaghan, T. (1995), 'The role of advertising in brand image development', *Journal of Product and Brand Management*, vol. 4, iss. 4.

Mihailovic, P. (1995), 'Time to scrap the rules', *Journal of Brand Management*, Aug.

Morrin, M. (1999), 'The impact of brand extensions on parent brand memory structures and retrieval processes', *Journal of Marketing Research*, vol. 36, iss. 4.

Oakenfull, G. and Gelb, B. (1996), 'Research-based advertising to preserve brand equity but avoid "genericide"', *Journal of Advertising Research*, vol. 36, iss. 5.

Ogilvy, D. (1983), *Ogilvy on Advertising*, Pan Books.

Onkvisit. S., and Shaw, J.J. (1989), 'The international dimension of branding', *International Marketing Review*, 6.

O'Reilly, T. (1996), interviewed on 'Branded', transmitted on BBC2, 22 Feb.

O'Shaughnessy, J. (1995), *Competitive Marketing: A Strategic Approach*, 3rd edition, Routledge.

Park, C.W. and MacInnis, J.D. (1986), 'Strategic brand concept-image management', Journal of Marketing, vol. 50, Oct.

Park, C.W., Milberg, S. and Lawson, R. (1991), 'Evaluation of brand extensions: the role of product feature similarity and brand concept consistency', *Journal of Consumer Research*, 18, Sept.

Patterson, M. (1999), 'Re-appraising the concept of brand image', *Journal of Brand Management*, vol. 6, iss. 6.

Plummer, J.T. (1985), 'How personality makes a difference', *Journal of Advertising Research*, vol. 24, iss. 6.

Rangaswamy, A., Burke, R.R. and Oliva, T.A. (1993). 'Brand equity and the extendability of brand names', *International Journal of Research in Marketing*, vol. 10, iss. 3.

Reader's Digest (2004), 'Most trusted brands'.

Reddy, S.K., Holak, S.L. and Bhat, S. (1994), 'To extend or not to extend: success determinants of line extensions', *Journal of Marketing Research*, vol. 31, iss. 2.

Reynolds, T., Gutman, J. and Schultz, D. (1984), 'Advertising is image management', *Journal of Advertising Research*, vol. 24, Feb.

Roedder, J.D., Loden, B. and Joiner, C. (1998), 'The negative impact of extensions: can flagship brands be diluted?', *Journal of Marketing*, 62.

Roth, M.S. (1992), 'Depth versus breadth strategies for global brand image management', *Journal of Advertising*, vol. 21, iss. 2.

Sampson, P. (1993), 'A better way to measure brand image', *Admap*, July/Aug.

Schuring, J. and Veerman, D. (1998), 'High brand equity: a mixed blessing', *Admap*, Nov.

Selame, E. (1997), 'What's in a name', *Bank Marketing*, vol. 29, iss. 2.

Siracuse, L. (1998), 'Looks aren't everything: creating competitive advantage with brand personality', *Journal of Integrated Communications*.

Southgate, P. (1994), *Total Branding by Design*, Kogan Page.

Sunde, L. and Brodie, R.J. (1993), 'Consumer evaluations of brand extensions: further empirical results', *International Journal of Research in Marketing*, vol. 10, iss. 1.

Tauber, E. (1988), 'Brand leverage: strategy for growth in a cost control world', *Journal of Advertising Research*, 28.

The Economist (1996), 14 November.

Trout, J. with Rivkin, S. (1996), *The New Positioning*, McGraw Hill.

Uncles, M. (1995), 'Branding – the marketing advantage', *Journal of Brand Management*, Aug.

Upshaw, L. (1995), *Building Brand Identity: A Strategy for Success in a Hostile Marketplace*, John Wiley & Sons.

Walker, D. and Dubitsky, T. (1994), 'Why liking matters', *Journal of Advertising Research*, vol. 34, iss. 3.

Walter Thompson, J. (n.d.), *Directory of Market Research Terminology*.

Weilbacher, W.M. (2001), 'Does advertising cause a "hierarchy of effects"?', *Journal of Advertising Research*, vol. 41, iss. 6.

White, R. (2000), 'Chameleon brands: tailoring brand messages to consumers', *Admap*, July.

Chapter 5

Bartle, J. (1985), 'Account planning, has it a future?' *Admap*, Dec.

Beard, F.K. (2002), 'Exploring the use of advertising agency review consultants', *Journal of Advertising Research*, vol. 42, iss. 1.

Beard, F.K. and Kim, K. (2001), 'Linking the use of advertising agency review consultants to agency search outcomes', *Journal of Advertising Research*, vol. 41, iss. 2.

Beltramini, R.F. and Pitta, D.A. (1991), 'Underlying dimensions and communication strategies of the advertising agency–client relationship', *International Journal of Advertising*, vol. 10, iss. 2.

Butterfield, L. (1985), 'Account planning and the client relationship', *Admap*, Nov.

Campaign (2004a), 'Top 300 Agencies', *Campaign* 27 Feb.

Campaign (2004b), 'Why accounts move', 27 Feb.

Carter, S. and Rainey, M.T. (1998), 'Should the agency decide the advertising?', *Market Leader*, Winter.

Collins, J.V.C. and Porras, J.I. (1997), *Built to Last*, Harper Business.

Duncan, G. and Lace, J. (1998), 'Agency remuneration: time for a new paradigm?', *Admap*, Oct.

Eagle, L., Kitchen, P., Hyde, K., Fourie, W. and Pasisetti, M. (1999), 'Perceptions of integrated marketing communications among marketers and ad agency executives in New Zealand', *International Journal of Advertising*, vol. 18, iss. 1.

Fortini-Campbell, L. (1992), *Hitting the Sweet Spot: How Consumer Insights Can Inspire Better Marketing and Advertising*, The Copy Workshop.

Hackley, C.E. (2003), 'Account planning: current agency perspectives on an advertising enigma', *Journal of Advertising Research*, vol. 43, iss. 2.

Hall, E. (1997), 'Does planning have a future?, *Campaign*.

ISBA (2000), 'How advertisers pay their agencies', ISBA, July.

Jones, J.P. (1998), *The Advertising Business*, Sage Publishing.

Jones, M. (2001), 'What are today's clients looking for?', *Admap*, May.

King, S. (1989), 'The anatomy of account planning', *Admap*, Nov.

Kover, A.J. and Goldberg, S.M. (1995), 'The games copywriters play', *Journal of Advertising Research*, Aug.

Kugelman, S. (1998), quoted in the *AAA Agency Magazine*, Summer.

Kulkarni, M.S., Vora, P.P. and Brown, T.A. (2003), 'Firing advertising agencies', *Journal of Advertising*, vol. 32, iss. 3.

Lace, J.M. (2000), 'Payment by results: is there a pot of gold at the end of the rainbow?', *International Journal of Advertising*, vol. 19, iss. 2.

Lannon, J. (1986), 'New techniques for understanding consumer reactions to advertising', *Journal of Advertising Research*, vol. 26, iss. 4.

Mitchell, P.C. and Sanders, N.H. (1995), 'Loyalty in agency–client relations: the impact of the organisational context', *Journal of Advertising Research*, Mar./Apr.

Newman, J. (1994), 'What is the client relationship to account planning?' *American Association of Advertising Agencies Agency Magazine*, Oct.

Ogilvy, D. (1983), *Ogilvy on Advertising*, Prion.

Pollitt, S. (2000), *Pollitt on Planning*, Admap Publications.

Patti, C.H. and Frazer, C.F. (1984), *Advertising: A Decision Making Approach*, Dryden Press.

Reeves, R. (1961), *Reality in Advertising*, MacGibbon & Kee.

Surguy, J. (2001), 'Incentivising agency performance', *Admap*, May.

West, D. and Ford, J. (2001), 'Advertising agency philosophies and employee risk taking', *Journal of Advertising*, vol. 30, iss. 1.

Aaker, D. (1982), *Advertising Management*, Prentice Hall International.

Alreck, P.L. and Settle, R.B. (1999), 'Strategies for building consumer brand preference', *Journal of Product and Brand Management*, vol. 8, iss. 2.

Anschuetz, N. (2002), 'Why a brand's most valuable customer is the next one it adds', *Journal of Advertising Research*, vol. 42, iss. 1.

Baldinger, A.L. and Rubinson, J. (1996), 'Brand loyalty: the link between attitude and behaviour',

Chapter 6

Journal of Advertising Research, vol. 36, iss. 6.

Barnard, N. and Ehrenberg, A.S.C. (1997), 'Advertising: strongly persuasive or nudging?', *Journal of Advertising Research*, vol. 37, iss. 1.

Belk, R.W. (1988), 'Possessions and the extended self', *Journal of Consumer Research*, 15.

Buck, S. (2001), *Advertising and the Long-term Success of the Premium Brand*, WARC.

Burdick G. (1997), 'The power of the visual message', *Admap*, Nov.

Debating Society (2004), minutes available online at www.debatingsociety.org.uk.

De Chernatony, L. and McDonald, M. (1998), *Creating Powerful Brands*, 2nd edition, Butterworth Heinemann.

Dube, L. (1996), Chattopadhay, A. and Letarte, A., 'Should advertising appeals match the basis of consumer's attitudes?', *Journal of Advertising Research*, Nov./Dec.

Ehrenberg, A.C.S. (1972), *Repeat Buying: Theory and Applications*, North Holland Publishing Company.

Engel, J.F., Kollat, D.T. and Blackwell, R.D. (1968), *Consumer Behaviour*, Holt, Rinehart & Winston.

Elliott, R. (1997), 'Existential consumption and irrational desire', *European Journal of Marketing*, vol. 31, iss. 3/4.

Elliott, R. and Wattasuwan, K. (1998), 'Brands as symbolic resources for the construction of identity', *International Journal of Advertising*, vol. 17, iss. 2.

Flatters, P. (2003), 'Re-thinking the consumer', *Admap/WARC*, May.

Gordon, W. and Ryan, C. (1982), 'How do consumers feel advertising works?', Market Research Society conference paper.

Gordon, W. and Valentine, V. (2000), 'The 21st century consumer: an endlessly moving target', *Market Leader*, Winter.

Graeff, T.R. (1996), 'Using promotional messages to manage the effects of brand and self-image on brand evaluations', *Journal of Consumer Marketing*, vol. 13, iss. 3.

Heath, R. (2000), 'Low-involvement processing', *Admap*, Apr.

Heath, R. (2001), 'Low involvement processing – a new model of brand communication', *Journal of Marketing Communications*, 7.

Hirschman, E.C. and Thompson, C.J. (1997), 'Why media matters: towards a richer understanding of consumers' relationships with advertising and mass media', *Journal of Advertising*, vol. 26, iss. 1.

Howard, J.A. and Sheth, J.N. (1969), *The Theory of Buyer Behaviour*, Wiley.

Ilsley, C. and Baldinger, A. (1998), 'Managing brand health through the marriage of attitudes and behaviour', ESOMAR conference paper.

Jamal, A. and Goode, M.M.H. (2001), 'Consumers and brands: a study of the impact of self-image congruence on brand preference and satisfaction', *Marketing Intelligence and Planning*, vol. 19, iss. 7.

Juchems, A. (1996), 'The role of awareness in the advertising process', *Admap*, July/Aug.

Katona, G. (1963), in S. Koch (ed.), *Psychology: A Study of a Science*, McGraw-Hill.

Lannon, J. (1991), 'Developing brand strategies across borders', *Marketing & Research Today*, Aug.

Lannon, J. (1996), 'Integrated communications from the consumer end – part II', *Admap*, Mar.

Lannon, J. and Cooper, P. (1983), 'Humanistic advertising – a holistic cultural approach', *International Journal of Advertising*, vol. 2.

Leith, A. and Riley, N. (1998), 'Understanding need states and their role in developing successful marketing strategies', *JMRS*, vol. 40, iss. 1.

Long, M.M. and Schiffman, L.G. (2000), 'Consumption values and relationships: segmenting the market for frequency programs', *Journal of Consumer Marketing*, vol. 17, iss. 3.

Lury, G. (1998), *Brandwatching*, Blackhall.

Marketing Week (1997), 17 Apr.

Maslow, A.H. (1954), *Motivation and Personality*, Harper & Row.

McNeal, J. (1999), *Kids as Consumers*, Sage.

Nicosia, F. (1966), *Consumer Decision Processes: Marketing and Advertising Implications*, Prentice Hall.

Olney, T.J., Holbrook, M.B. and Batra, R. (1991), 'Consumer responses to advertising: the effects of ad content, emotions and attitude toward the ad on viewing time', *Journal of Consumer Research*, vol. 17, iss. 1.

Perry, Sir M. (1998), cited in Lury, G., *Brandwatching*, Blackhall.

Shapiro, S. and Shanker, K.H. (2001), 'Memory-based measures for assessing advertising effects: a comparison of explicit and implicit memory effects', *Journal of Advertising*, vol. 30, iss. 3.

Sirgy, J. (1982), 'Self concept in consumer behaviour: a critical review', *Journal of Consumer Research*, vol. 9, Dec.

Solomon, M.R., *Consumer Behaviour*, 3rd edition, Prentice Hall International, 1996.

Swindells, A. (2000), 'The myth of consumer choice', Market Research Society conference paper.

Tyrell, B. (1994), Henley Centre for Forecasting.

Valentine, V. and Gordon, W. (2000), 'The 21st century consumer: an endlessly moving target', *Market Leader*, 11.

Vigneron, F. and Johnson, L.W. (1999), 'A review and a conceptual framework of prestige seeking consumer behaviour', *Academy of Marketing Science Review*, vol. 99, iss. 1.

Webster, F. and Wind, Y. (1973), 'A general model for understanding organisational buying behaviour', *Journal of Marketing*, 2.

Yeshin, T. (ed.) (1993), *Inside Advertising*, Institute of Practitioners in Advertising.

Chapter 7

Adams, A.J. and Van Auken, S. (1995), 'Observations: a new approach to measuring product category membership', *Journal of Advertising Research*, Sept./Oct.

Ambler, T., Broadbent, S. and Feldwick, P. (1998), 'Does advertising affect market size? Some evidence from the United Kingdom', *International Journal of Advertising*, Aug.

Anschuetz, N. (1997), 'Building brand popularity: the myth of segmenting to brand success', *Journal of Advertising Research*, vol. 37, iss. 1.

Baker, C. (ed.) (1995), 'Boddingtons case study', *Advertising Works, 8*, IPA/NTC.

Barnathan, J., Kuntz, M. and Khermouch, G. (2001), 'The best global brands', *Business Week*, 6 Aug.

Bhat, S. and Reddy, K. (1998), 'Symbolic and functional positioning of brands', *Journal of Consumer Marketing*, vol. 15, iss. 1.

Bond, J.R.P. and Morris, L. (2002), 'People are different if you know how to look', Market Research Society conference paper.

Cobb-Walgren, C.J. and Ruble, C.A. (1995), 'Brand equity, brand preference and purchase intent', *Journal of Advertising*, vol. 24, iss. 3.

De Chernatony, L. and McDonald, M. (1998), *Creating Powerful Brands*, 2nd edition, Butterworth Heinemann.

Donthu, N. and Gilliland, D.I. (2002), 'The single consumer', *Journal of Advertising Research*, vol. 42, iss. 6.

Ehrenberg, A.C.S and Barnard, N. (1997), 'Advertising and product demand', *Admap*, vol. 32, iss. 5.

Englis, B.G. and Solomon, M.R. (1995), 'To be or not to be: lifestyle imagery, reference groups and the clustering of America', *Journal of Advertising*, vol. 24, iss. 1.

Hibbert, S.A. (1995), 'The market positioning of British medical charities', *European Journal of Marketing*, vol. 29, iss. 10.

Hofmeyr, J. and Rice, B. (1999), 'The impact of consumers commitment to existing brands on new product launch strategies', ESOMAR conference paper.

Holbrook and Hirchman (1991), 'The consumers' ability to process brand information from ads', *Journal of Marketing*, Oct.

Holt, D.B. (2002), 'Why do brands cause trouble? A dialectical theory of consumer culture and branding', *Journal of Consumer Research*, vol. 29, iss. 1.

Kates, S.M. and Goh, C. (2003), 'Brand morphing: implications for advertising theory and practice, *Journal of Advertising*, vol. 32, iss. 1.

Keller, K.L., Sternthal, B. and Tybout, A. (2002), 'Three questions you need to ask about your brand', *Harvard Business Review*, vol. 80, iss. 9.

MacMillan, I.C. and McGrath, R.G. (1997), 'Discovering new points of differentiation', *Harvard Business Review*, vol. 75, iss. 4.

Marsden, P. (2002), 'Brand positioning: meme's the word', *Marketing Intelligence and Planning*, vol. 20, iss. 5.

Meeneghan, T. (1995), 'The role of advertising in brand image development', *Journal of Product and Brand Management*, vol. 4, iss. 4.

Mitchell, A. (1983), *Nine American Lifestyles: Who We Are and Where We Are Going*, Macmillan.

Muniz and O'Guinn (2001) cited in Kates, S.M. and Goh, C. (2003), 'Brand morphing: implications for advertising theory and practice, *Journal of Advertising*, vol. 32, iss. 1.

Myerson, J. (2003), in 'Creative business', *Sunday Times*, 18 Feb.

Park, C.W., Jaworski, B.J. and MacInnis, D.J. (1986), 'Functional and expressive attributes as determinants of brand-attitude', *Research in Marketing*, 10.

Plummer, J. (1974), 'The concept and application of lifestyle segmentation', *Journal of Marketing*, Jan.

Preston, C. (2000), 'The problem with micro-marketing', *Journal of Advertising Research*, vol. 7, iss. 1.

Roberts, J.P. (1999), 'Psychographics comes of age', *Admap*, June.

The Times (1997), 27 Sept.

Trout, J. and Ries, A. (1986), *Positioning: The Battle for Your Mind*, McGraw Hill.

Upshaw, L.B. (1995), *Building Brand Identity: A Strategy for Success in a Hostile Marketplace*, John Wiley & Sons.

Woods, R. (1993), 'Why has advertising gone blank?' *Brandweek*, 22 Feb. 22.

Woodward, P. (1999), 'Are your favourite brands about to become roadkill?'. *Admap*, Apr.

Chapter 8

Aaker, D. (1991), 'Are brand equity investments really worthwhile?', *Admap*, Sept.

Abraham M.M. and Lodish L.M. (1990), 'Getting the most out of advertising and promotion', *Harvard Business Review*, vol. 90, iss. 3.

Applebaum, U. and Halliburton, C. (1993), 'How to develop international advertising campaigns that work: example of the European food and beverage sector', *International Journal of Advertising*, vol. 12,

Archer, J. and Hubbard, T. (1996), 'Integrated tracking for integrated communications', *Admap*, Feb.

Baker, C. (ed.) (1993), 'Jeans sans frontieres', in *Advertising Works*, 7, IPA/WARC.

Baker, C. (1994), *Advertising Works*, 8, IPA/NTC.

Baker, P. (1999), 'Surely there are lasting effects of advertising', *Admap*, July/Aug.

Barwise, P. (1999), 'Advertising for long-term shareholder value', *Admap*, Oct.

Baxter, M. (1999), 'Advertising and profitability: the long-term returns', *Admap*, July.

Biel, A.L. (1990), 'Love the ad. buy the product', *Admap* Sept.

Bond, J. (1993), 'How brand image affects your share', *Admap*, Mar.

Brown, G. (1994), 'The awareness problem: attention and memory effects from TV and magazine advertising', *Admap*, Jan.

Brown, M. (2001), 'The total brand experience as mainstream communication', *Admap*, Feb.

Brown, S.P. and Stayman, D.M. (1992), 'Attitudes and consequences of attitude toward the ad', *Journal of Consumer Research*, vol. 19, iss. 1.

Butterfield, L. (1998), 'How advertising impacts on profitability', IPA.

Crimp, M. and Wright, L.T. (1995), *The Marketing Research Process*, 4th edition, Prentice Hall.

Crouch, S. and Housden, M. (1996), *Marketing Research for Managers*, 2nd edition, Butterworth Heinemann.

Duckworth, G. (1997), *Advertising Works 9*, IPA/WARC.

Du Plessis, E. (1994), 'Likeable ads work best, but what is likeability?', *Admap*, May.

Du Plessis, E. (1998), 'Advertising likeability', *Admap*, Oct.

Du Plessis, E. and Foster, C. (2000), 'Like the ad. Like the brand? Chicken or egg?' *Admap*, Dec.

Dyson, P. (1999), 'How to manage the budget across brand portfolio', *Admap*, Dec.

Ehrenberg, A., Barnard, N. and Scriven, N. (1998), 'Justifying our advertising budgets', *Admap*, Mar.

Farr, A. (1999), 'Measuring the health of your brand', *Admap*, July/Aug.

Feldwick, P. (1994), 'When "accountability" becomes a problem', *Admap*, Sept.

Fletcher, W. (1992), *A Glittering Haze: Strategic Advertising in the 1990s*, NTC Publications.

Franzen G. (1994), *Advertising Effectiveness*, NTC Publications.

Franzen, G. (1999), 'The brand response matrix', *Admap*, Sept.

Goodyear, M. (1994), 'Keeping up with the Jones's', *Admap*, Sept.

Gordon, W. (1995), 'Advertising pre-testing works – or does it?', *Admap*, Mar.

Hedges, A. (1997), *Testing to Destruction*, 2nd edition, revised by S. Ford-Hutchinson and M., Hunter-Stewart, IPA.

Jones, J.P. (1994), 'Advertising's woes and advertising accountability', *Admap*, Sept.

Jones, J.P. (1997), 'Is advertising still salesmanship?' *Journal of Advertising Research*, vol. 37, iss. 3.

Juchems, A. (1996), 'The role of awareness in the advertising process', *Admap*, July/Aug.

Krugman, H. (1975), 'Advertising: better planning, better results', *Harvard Business Review*, Mar./Apr.

Laskey, Henry A. and Fox, Richard J. (1995), 'The relationship between advertising message strategy and television commercial effectiveness', *Journal of Advertising Research*, vol. 35, iss. 2.

Leather, P., McKechnie, S. and Amirkhanian, M. (1994), 'The importance of likeability as a measure of advertising effectiveness', *International Journal of Advertising*, vol. 13, iss. 3.

McDonald, C. (1992), *How Advertising Works*, Advertising Association and NTC Publications.

Miller, S. (1998), 'Brand salience versus brand image: two theories of advertising effectiveness', *Journal of Advertising Research*, vol. 38, iss. 5.

Poiesz, B.C. and Robben H.S.J. (1994), 'Individual reactions to advertising', *International Journal of Advertising*, vol. 13, iss. 1.

Prue, T. (1994), 'How advertising works: the 1994 IPA Advertising Effectiveness Awards', *Admap*, Nov.

Rice, B. and Bennett, R. (1998), 'The relationship between brand usage and advertising tracking measurements', *Journal of Advertising Research*, vol. 38, iss. 3.

Schultz, D. (1997), 'Making marcom an investment', *Marketing Management*, Fall.

Schultz, D.E. (1998), 'Determining how brand communications works in the short and long terms', *International Journal of Advertising*, vol. 17, iss. 4.

Schultz, D.E., Tannenbaum, S.I. and Lauterborn, R.F. (1992), *Integrated Marketing Communications: Putting it Together and Making it Work*, NTC Business Books.

Schuring, R.J. and Veerman, D. (1998), 'High brand equity: a mixed blessing', *Admap*, Nov.

Stapel, J. (1998), 'Advertising and sales: an historical perspective', *Admap*, Feb.

Steiner, R.L. (2001), 'Manufacturers' brand advertising and how it influences manufacturers' and retailers' margins', *Journal of Marketing Communications*, 7.

Timothy, A. and Schultz, D.E. (1998), 'Rethinking brand communications measurement', *Admap*, Dec.

Walker, D. and Dubitsky, T.M. (1994), 'Why liking matters', *Journal of Advertising Research*, vol. 34, iss. 3, May/Jun.

Wilkins, J. (1997), 'TV or not TV?', Market Research Society conference paper, Mar.

Yasin, J. (1995), 'The effects of advertising on fast-moving consumer goods', *International Journal of Advertising*, vol. 14, iss. 2.

Zhou, N., Zhou, D. and Ouyang, M. (2003), 'Long-term effects of television advertising on sales of consumer durables and non-durables', *Journal of Advertising*, vol. 32, iss. 2.

Chapter 9

Anand, P. and Sternthal, B. (1990), 'Ease of message processing as a moderator of repetition effects in advertising', *Journal of Marketing Research*, vol. 27, iss. 3.

Anschuetz, N. (2002), 'Why a brand's most valuable customer is the next one it adds', *Journal of Advertising Research*, vol. 42, iss. 1.

Assael, H. (1990), *Marketing Principles and Strategy*, 2nd edition, Dryden Press.

Bartle, J. (1997), 'The advertising contribution', in L. Butterfield (ed.), *Advertising Excellence*, Butterworth Heinemann.

Batra, R. and Ray, M. (1986), 'Situational effects of advertising repetition', *Journal of Consumer Research*, vol. 12, iss. 4.

Bell, Lord Tim (2001), private interview.

Bell, R.D. and Bucklin, E.R. (1999), 'The role of internal reference point in the category purchase decision', *Journal of Consumer Research*, 26.

Berkowitz, D. (2001), 'The impact of differential lag effects on the allocation of advertising budgets across media', *Journal of Advertising Research*, vol. 41, iss. 2.

Biel, A.L. (1990), 'Strong brand, high spend', *Admap*, Nov.

Bigne, J.E. (1995), 'Advertising budget practices: a review', *Journal of Current Issues and Research in Advertising*, vol. 17, Fall.

Broadbent, S. (1989), *The Advertising Budget*, IPA/NTC Business Books.

Burke, R.R. and Srull, T.K. (1988), 'Competitive interference and consumer memory for advertising', *Journal of Consumer Research*, vol. 15, iss. 1.

Butterfield, L. (1997), 'Strategy development', in L. Butterfield (ed.) *Excellence in Advertising*, Butterworth Heinemann.

Cobb-Walgren, C.J., Ruble, C.A. and Donthu, N. (1995), 'Brand equity, brand preference and purchase intent', *Journal of Advertising*, vol. 24, iss. 3.

Colley, R.M. (1961), 'Defining advertising goals for measured advertising results', Association of National Advertisers.

Cowan, D. (1998), 'Strategy, strategy, strategy', *Admap*, Feb.

Croft, M. (1998), 'Joking aside', *Marketing Week*, 11 June.

Dyson, P. (1999), 'How to manage the budget across brand portfolio', *Admap*, Dec.

Eechambadi, N.V. (1994), 'Does advertising work?' *McKinsey Quarterly*, 3.

Ewing, M.T. and Jones, J.P. (2000), 'Agency beliefs in the power of advertising', *International Journal of Advertising*, vol. 19, iss. 3.

Franzen, G. (1994), *Advertising Effectiveness: Findings from Empirical Research*, NTC.

Gregory, J.R. (1997), 'Ranges of advertising efficiency', *Journal of Brand Management*, vol. 4, iss. 6.

Head, M. (1998), 'Define the strategy', *Admap*, May.

Holstius, K. (1990), 'Measuring sales response to advertising', *International Journal of Advertising*, 1.

IMBI (2001), 'How advertising affects the sales of packaged goods brands', Millward Brown International.

Kamber, T. (2002), 'The brand manager's dilemma: understanding how advertising expenditures affect sales growth during a recession', *Brand Management*, vol. 10, iss. 2.

Kappert, C. (1999), 'Marketing campaign evolution', *Admap*, Sept.

Low, George S. (1999), 'Setting advertising and promotional budgets in multi-brand companies', *Journal of Advertising Research*, vol. 39, iss. 1.

Low, G.S. and Mohr, J.J. (1998), 'Brand manager's perceptions of marketing communications budget allocations: synergistic and differential effects on outcomes', *American Marketing Association Conference Proceedings*.

Marketing (2003), 'Annual brand survey', 3 July.

Moriarty, S.E. (1996), 'Effectiveness, objectives and the EFFIE awards', *Journal of Advertising Research*, Jul./Aug.

Murphy, J.H. and Cunningham, I. (1993), *Advertising and Marketing Communications Management*, Dryden Press.

Patti, C.H. and Frazer, C.F. (1984), *Advertising: A Decision Making Approach*, Dryden Press.

Pincott, G. (2001), 'How to tell if your advertising is working', *Admap*, Jan.

Raj, S.P. (1982), 'The effects of advertising spending on high and low consumer segments', *Journal of Consumer Research*, vol. 9, iss. 1.

Salmon, J. (2001), private interview.

Spence, S. (1991), 'Creativity and its implications for advertising development and research techniques', *Marketing and Research Today*, Aug.

Stewart, D. (1996), 'Allocating the promotional budget: revisiting the advertising and promotion-to-sales ratio', *Marketing Intelligence and Planning*, 14 Apr.

Wansink, B. and Ray, M.L. (1996), 'Advertising strategies to increase usage frequency', *Journal of Marketing*, vol. 60, iss. 1.

Webb, P. and Ray, M.L. (1979), 'Effects of TV clutter', *Journal of Advertising Research*, vol. 19, iss. 3.

White, R. (1996), 'Taking on the big boys: how to make the most of a small budget', *Admap*, Oct.

Zikmund, W.G. and D'Amico, M. (1993), *Marketing*, 4th edition, West Publishing Company.

Chapter 10

Agrawal, A. and Kamakura, W.A. (1995), 'The economic worth of celebrity endorsers: an event study analysis', *Journal of Marketing*, vol. 59, iss. 3.

Alden, D.L., Hoyer, W.D and Lee, C. (1993), 'Identifying global and culture specific dimensions of humour in advertising', *Journal of Marketing*, vol. 57.

Alden, D.L., Mukherjee, A. and Hoyer, W.D. (2000), 'The effects of incongruity, surprise and positive moderators on perceived humour in television advertising', *Journal of Advertising*, vol. 29, iss. 2.

Alpert, J.I. and Alpert, M.I. (1991), 'Contributions from a musical perspective on advertising and consumer behaviour', *Advances in Consumer Research*, vol. 18.

Applebaum, U. and Halliburton, C. (1993), 'How to develop international advertising campaigns that work: example of the European food and beverage sector', *International Journal of Advertising*, vol. 12.

Barry, T.E. (1993), 'Comparative advertising: what have we learned in two decades?' *Journal of Advertising Research*, vol. 33, iss. 2.

Bartle, J. (1997) 'The advertising contribution', in L. Butterfield (ed.), *Excellence in Advertising*, Butterworth Heinemann.

BBC (1997), *My Greatest Mistake*, BBC Television, Mar.

Bennett, R. (1996), 'Effects of horrific fear appeals on public attitudes towards aids', *International Journal of Advertising*, vol. 15, iss. 3.

Biel, A.L. and Lannon, J. (1993), 'Steel bullet in a velvet glove? Harnessing visual metaphor in brand building', *Admap*, Apr.

Bovee, C.L., Thill, J.V., Dovel, G.P. and Wood, M.B. (1995), *Advertising Excellence*, McGraw Hill.

Branthwaite, A. and Ware, R. (1997), 'The role of music in advertising', *Admap*, July/Aug.

Branthwaite, A. and Ware, R. (1997), 'Music in advertising', ESOMAR conference paper.

Callcott, M.F. and Lee, W. (1995), 'A content analysis of animation and animated spokes-characters in television commercials', *Journal of Marketing*, vol. 59, iss. 4.

Childers, T.L. and Heckler, S.E. (1992), 'The role of expectancy and relevancy in memory for verbal and visual information: what is incongruency?' *Journal of Consumer Research*, vol. 18, iss. 4.

Chisnall, P.M. (1995), *Consumer Behaviour*, 3rd edition, McGraw Hill.

Cline, T.W., Altsech, M.B. and Kellaris, J.J. (2003), 'When does humour enhance or inhibit ad responses?' *Journal of Advertising*, vol. 32, iss. 3.

Cook, G. (1992), *The Discourse of Advertising*, Routledge.

Cooper, A. (ed.) (1997), *How to Plan Advertising*, 2nd edition, Cassell.

Crowther, J. (1999), 'What a little endline can do', *Admap*, Jan.

Cummings (1984), cited in Ried, L.N., King, K.W. and Delorme, D.E. (1998), 'Top level creatives look at advertising then and now', *Journal of Advertising*, vol. 27, iss. 2.

Dahl, D.W., Frankenberger, K.D. and Manchanda, R.V. (2003), 'Does it pay to shock? Reactions to shocking and non-shocking advertising content among university students', *Journal of Advertising Research*, vol. 43, iss. 3.

De Mooij, M. (1994), *Advertising Worldwide*, 2nd edition, Prentice Hall.

De Pelsmacker, P. (1998), 'Advertising characteristics and the attitude towards the ad', *Marketing and Research Today*, Nov.

Delorme, D.E. (1998), 'Top level creatives look at advertising then and now', *Journal of Advertising*, vol. 27, iss. 2.

Donaghey, B. and Wateridge, S. (1998), 'The endline: important tool or hackneyed device?' *Admap*, Nov.

Donthu, N. (1998), 'A cross-country investigation of recall and attitudes towards comparative advertising', *Journal of Advertising*, vol. 27, iss. 2.

Drake M. (1994), 'The basics of creative development research, *International Journal of Advertising*.

Du Plessis, E. (1994), 'Likeable ads work best, but what is likeability?' *Admap*, May.

Du Plessis, E. (1995), 'Understanding and using likeability', *Journal of Advertising Research*, vol. 34, iss. 5.

Duckworth, G. (1999), 'Case study', *Advertising Works*, 9, IPA/NTC.

Dunbar, D.S. (1990), 'Music and advertising', *International Journal of Advertising*, vol. 9, iss. 3.

Dwek, R. (1997), 'Compare and contrast', *Management Today*, Mar.

Eccleshare, W. and Lintas, A. (1999), 'Optimising creative potential', *Admap*, June.

Erdogan, B.Z. (1999), 'Celebrity endorsement: a literature review', *Journal of Marketing Management*, 15.

Erdogan, Z. and Kitchen, P. (1998), 'Getting the best out of celebrity endorsers', *Admap*, Apr.

Fletcher, W. (1994), 'The advertising high ground', *Admap*, Nov.

Fletcher, W. (1997), 'Cutting through the haze', *Admap*, Apr.

Gatfield, S. (1995), 'Brand building and the agency', *Admap*, Jan.

Gunn, D. (1995), 'Do creative commercials sell?' *Campaign*, 22 Sept.

Hegarty, J. (1994), 'Factors behind success: the 1994 IPA Award winners', *Admap*, Dec.

Hegarty, J. (1995a), 'The bottom line', *Sunday Times, Culture*, 26 Nov.

Hegarty, J. (1995b), *Campaign*.

Henry, H. (1997), 'How to write a great brief', *Admap*, Nov.

Hooper and White (1994), *How to Produce Effective TV Commercials*, 3rd edition, NTC Business Books.

Hyman M.R. and Tansey, R. (1990), 'The ethics of psychoactive ads', *Journal of Business Ethics*, vol. 9, iss. 2.

Iddiols, D. (2002), 'The fame game: using celebrities effectively', *Admap*, Dec.

Kaikati, J.G. (1987), 'Celebrity advertising', *International Journal of Advertising*, 6.

Kamins, M.A. (1990), 'An investigation into the "match up" theory hypothesis in celebrity advertising: when beauty may only be skin deep', *Journal of Advertising*, vol. 19, iss. 1.

Kamins, M.A. and Gupta, K. (1994), 'Congruence between spokesperson and product type: a match up hypothesis perspective', *Psychology and Marketing*, vol. 11, iss. 6.

Kellaris, J.J. and Cox, A.D. (1993), 'The effect of background music on ad processing: a contingency explanation', *Journal of Marketing*, vol. 57, iss. 4.

Koslow, S., Sasser, S.L. and Riordan, E.A. (2003), 'What is creative to whom and why? Perceptions in advertising agencies', *Journal of Advertising Research*, vol. 43, iss. 1.

Kover, A.J., Goldberg, M. and James, W.L. (1995), 'Creativity vs. effectiveness? An integrating classification for advertising', *Journal of Advertising Research*, vol. 35, iss. 6.

Kover, A.J. and Goldberg, S.M. (1995), 'The games copywriters play: conflict, quasi-control, a new proposal, *Journal of Advertising Research*, vol. 35, iss. 4.

La Tour, M.S. and Rotfeld, H.J. (1997), 'There are threats and (maybe) fear-caused arousal: theory and confusions of appeals to fear and fear arousal itself', *Journal of Advertising*, vol. 26, iss. 3.

La Tour M., Snipes, R.L. and Bliss, S.J. (1996), 'Don't be afraid to use fear appeals: an experimental study', *International Journal of Advertising*, Mar./Apr.

McCorkell, G. (1990), *Advertising that Pulls Response*, McGraw-Hill.

McQuarrie, E.F. and Mick, D.G. (1999), 'Visual rhetoric in advertising: text interpretive, experimental and reader response analyses', *Journal of Consumer Research*, vol. 26, June.

Mead, R. (1990), *Cross Cultural Management Communications*, John Wiley & Sons.

Messaris, P. (1997), *Visual Persuasion: The Role of Images in Advertising*, Sage Publications.

Millward Brown (1991), 'How advertising affects the sales of packaged goods', Millward Brown International.

Mitchell, A.A. and Olsen, J.C. (1981), 'Are product attributes beliefs the only mediator of advertising effects on brand attitude?' *Journal of Marketing Research*, Aug.

Morgan, R. (1999), 'A visual way to explore brand imagery', *Admap*, vol. 34, iss. 9.

Muehling, D.D. and Stoltman, J.J. (1992), 'An investigation of factors underlying practitioners' attitudes toward comparative advertising', *International Journal of Advertising*, vol. 11, iss. 2.

Muller, B. (1996), *International Advertising: Communicating Across Cultures*, Wadsworth Publishing.

Ogilvy, D. (1963), *Confessions of an Advertising Man*, Pan Books.

Ogilvy, D. (1983), *Ogilvy on Advertising*, Prion.

Ogilvy, D. and Raphaelson, J. (1982), 'Research on advertising techniques that work and don't work', *Harvard Business Review*, vol. 18, July–Aug.

Ohanian, R. (1991), 'The impact of celebrity spokespersons perceived image on consumers' intention to purchase', *Journal of Advertising Research*, Feb./Mar.

O'Mahoney and Meenaghan 1997/98.

Otnes, Oviatt and Tviese (1995), cited Ried, L.N., King, K.W. and Delorme, D.E. (1998), 'Top level creatives look at advertising then and now', *Journal of Advertising*, vol. 27, iss. 2.

Pechmann, C. and Ratneshwar (1991), 'The use of comparative advertising for brand positioning: association versus differentiation', *Journal of Consumer Research*, Sept.

Percy, L. and Woodside, A.G. (1983), *Advertising and Consumer Psychology*, Lexington Books.

Phillips, B.J. (1997), 'Thinking into it: consumer interpretation of complex advertising', *Journal of Advertising*, vol. 26, iss. 2.

Pinkleton, B. (1977), 'The effects of negative comparative advertising on the candidate evaluations and advertising evaluations', *Journal of Advertising*, vol. 26.

Pringle, H. (2004), 'Celebrity sells', Wiley.

Prue, T. (1994), *Advertising Works*, 6, IPA/NTC.

Ratneshwar, S. and Chaiken, S. (1991), 'Comprehensions' role in persuasion: the case of its moderating effect on the impact of source cues', *Journal of Consumer Research*, vol. 18.

Robertson, C. (1997), chapter 4 in Cooper, A. (ed.). *How to Plan Advertising*, 2nd edition, Cassell.

Rosbergen, E., Pieters, R. and Wedel, M. (1997), 'Visual attention to advertising – a segment level analysis', *Journal of Consumer Research*, vol. 24, iss. 3.

Saatchi & Saatchi (1995), *Developing Effective Creativity*.

Schultz, D.E. and Tannebaum, S.I. (1989), *Essentials of Advertising Strategy*, 2nd edition, NTC Business Books.

Speck, P.S. (1991), 'The humorous message taxonomy: a framework for the study of humorous ads', *Current Issues and Research in Advertising*, vol. 13.

Stafford, M.R., Stafford, T.F. and Day, E.A. (2002), 'Contingency approach: the effects of spokesperson type and service type on service advertising perceptions', *Journal of Advertising*, vol. 31, iss. 2.

Stewart, D.W. and Furse, D.H. (2000), 'Analysis of the impact of executional factors on advertising performance', *Journal of Advertising Research*, vol. 40, iss. 6.

Sunday Times (1995), Culture, 16 July.

Till, B.D. and Shimp, T.A. (1998), 'Endorsers in advertising: the case of negative celebrity information', *Journal of Advertising*, vol. 27, iss. 1.

Tripp, C., Jensen, T.D. and Carlson, L. (1994), 'The effects of multiple product endorsements by celebrities on consumer's attitudes and intentions', *Journal of Consumer Research*, vol. 20, iss. 4.

Weinberger, M.G., Spotts, H.E., Campbell, L. and Parsons, A.L. (1995), 'The use and effect of humour in different advertising media', *Journal of Advertising Research*, vol. 35, iss. 3.

William, L. and Farris, P. (1975), 'Comparative advertising: problems and potential', *Journal of Marketing*, 39, October.

Zinkhan, G.M. (1994), 'The use of parody in advertising', *Journal of Advertising*, vol. 23, iss. 3.

Chapter 11

Abernethy (1991), cited in Li, H., Edwards, S.M. and Lee, J-H. (2002), 'Measuring the intrusiveness of advertisements: scale development and validation', *Journal of Advertising*, vol. 31, iss. 2.

Adams, A.J. and Blair, M.H. (1992), 'Persuasive advertising and sales accountability: past experience and forward validation', *Journal of Advertising Research*, vol. 32, iss. 2.

Baker, C. (ed.) (1993), *Advertising Works*, 7, IPA/WARC.

Barnes, J. (1999), 'Creating a difference with ambient media', *Admap*, Feb.

Belch, G.E. and Belch M.A. (1993), *Introduction to Advertising and Promotion*, Irwin.

Biu, A.C. and Lee, R. (2001), 'Zapping behaviour during commercial breaks', *Journal of Advertising Research*, vol. 41, iss. 3.

Blair, M.H. and Rabuck, M.J. (1998), 'Advertising wearin and wearout: ten years later – more empirical evidence and successful practice', *Journal of Advertising Research*, vol. 38, iss. 5.

Bogart, L. (1995), 'Is there an optimum frequency in advertising?' *Admap*, Feb.

Branthwaite A. and Wood, K.. (2000), 'The medium is part of the message: the role of media for shaping the image of the brand', ESOMAR conference paper, Nov.

Branthwaite, A., Wood, K. and Schilling, M.C.M. (2000), 'The medium is part of the message', ESOMAR paper, Nov.

Bulman, J. (MD of B&J Media Services) (1994), interviewed in *Campaign* 16 Sept.

Byfield, S. (2002), 'Media creativity: three dimensions for better communications planning', *Admap*, May.

Byles, D. and Walford, N. (1991), 'Advertising's brother: why TV sponsorship is an agency's business', *Admap*, May.

Campaign (2004), 'Campaign's top 300 agencies', 27 Feb.

Croft, M. (1998), 'Joking aside', *Marketing Week*, 11 June.

De Pelsmacker, P., Guens, A. and Anckaert, P. (2002), 'Media context and advertising effectiveness: the role of context appreciation and context/ad similarity', *Journal of Advertising*, vol. 3, iss. 2.

Dubow, J.S. (1995), 'Advertising recognition and recall by age – including teens', *Journal of Advertising Research*, Sept./Oct.

Du Plessis, E. (1995), 'Ad advertising burst is just a lot of drips', *Admap*, July/Aug.

Dyson, P. (1999), 'How to manage the budget across brand portfolios', *Admap*, Dec.

Ewing, M.T., du Plessis, E. and Foster C. (2001), 'Cinema advertising re-considered', *Journal of Advertising Research*, vol. 41, iss. 1.

European Marketing Pocket Book (2003), WARC.

Franz, G. (2000), 'Better media planning for integrated communication', *Admap*, Jan.

Gilmore, R.F and Secunda, E. (1993), 'Zipped TV commercials boost prior learning', *Journal of Advertising Research*, Nov./Dec.

Ingram, C. (1998), interviewed in *Campaign* 16 Sept.

Jacob, I. (1997), 'Making the most of media', in Butterfield, L., *Excellence in Advertising*, Butterworth Heinemann.

Jacobs, B. (1995), 'Advertising agencies and the management of media', *Admap*, Apr.

Jones, J.P. (1995), 'Advertising's impact on sales and profitability', IPA conference paper, Mar.

Kaufman, C. and Lane, P. (1994), 'In pursuit of the nomadic viewer', *Journal of Consumer Marketing*.

King, S. (1997), *Admap* Feb.

Kirmani, A. (1997), 'Advertising repetition as a signal of quality: if it's advertised so much, something must be wrong', *Journal of Advertising*, vol. 26, iss. 3.

Krugman, H.E. (1972), 'How potent is TV advertising?' American National Advertisers workshop paper.

Kusumoto, K. (2002), 'Affinity-based media selection: magazine selection for brand message absorption', *Journal of Advertising Research*, vol. 42, iss. 4.

LaBarbera, P.A., Weingard, P. and Yorkston, E.A. (1998), 'Matching the message to the mind: advertising imagery and consumer processing styles', *Journal of Advertising Research*, 38, Sept./Oct.

Leckenby, J.D. and Kim, H. (1994), 'How media directors view reach/frequency', *Journal of Advertising Research*, Sept./Oct.

Marketing (2003), *Marketing Magazine Top 100 Advertisers*.

Marketing Pocket Book (2003), The Advertising Association/WARC.

Mills, D. (2002), 'Introduction', *Campaign*, 5 Nov.

Mitchell, P. (2003), 'Demystifying media neutrality', *Journal of Database Marketing*, vol. 10, iss. 4.

Murray, G.B. and Jenkins, J.R.G. (1992), 'The concept of "effective reach" in advertising', *Journal of Advertising Research*, vol. 32, iss. 3.

National Readership Survey (2003), NRS Ltd.

Norris, C. and Colman, A. (1994), 'Putting ads in context: how television programmes affect viewer reaction to ads', *Admap*, Jan.

Roberts, A. (1996), 'What do we know about advertising's short-term effects?' *Admap*, Feb.

Roberts, A. (1998), 'Measuring the short-term effects of TV advertising', *Admap*, Apr.

Scott, D.R. and Solomon, D. (1998), 'What is wearout anyway?' *Journal of Advertising Research*, vol. 38, iss. 5.

Shankar, A. and Horton, B. (1999), 'Ambient media: advertising's new media opportunity?' *International Journal of Advertising*, vol. 18, iss. 3.

Sissors, J.L. and Bumba, L. (1993), *Advertising Media Planning*, 4th edition, NTC Business Books.

Sorrell, M. (1997), 'Beyond the millennium: the future of the ad agency', *Admap*, Jan.

The MNP Best Practice Group (2004), 'The communications challenge, A practical guide to media-neutral planning', Account Planning Group.

Wilkins, J. (1997), 'TV or not TV?' Market Research Society conference paper, Mar.

Chapter 12

Admap (2003), 'Charity adstats', *Admap*, May.

Agee, Y. and Brett A.S. (2001), 'Planned or impulse purchases? How to create effective infomercials', *Journal of Advertising Research*, vol. 41, iss. 6.

Alanko, J. (2000), 'The case for integration in B2B marketing', *Admap*, Sept.

Alba, J. and Lynch, J. (1997), 'Interactive home shopping: consumer, retailer and manufacturer incentives to participate in electronic marketplaces', *Journal of Marketing*, vol. 61, iss. 3.

Balasubramanian, S.K. and Kumar, V. (1997), 'Explaining variations in the advertising and promotion costs/sales ratio: a reanalysis', *Journal of Marketing*, vol. 61, iss. 1.

Becker-Olsen, K.L. (2003), 'And now, a word from our sponsor', *Journal of Advertising*, vol. 32, iss. 2.

Bergen, M. and John, G. (1997), 'Understanding co-operative advertising participation rates in conventional channels', *Journal of Marketing Research*, vol. 34, iss. 3.

Bickerton, D. (2000), 'Corporate reputation versus corporate branding: the realist debate', *Corporate Communications: An International Journal*, vol. 5, iss. 1.

Biehal, G.J. and Sheinin, D.A. (1998), 'Managing the brand in a corporate advertising environment: a decision-making framework for brand managers', *Journal of Advertising*, vol. 27, iss. 2.

Boutie, P. (1996), 'Will this kill that?' *Journal of Consumer Marketing*, vol. 13, iss. 4.

Briggs, R. and Stipp, H. (1999), 'How internet advertising works', *Marketing and Research Today*, May.

Bruner, G.C. and Kumar, A. (2000), 'Web commercials and advertising hierarchy of effects', *Journal of Advertising Research*, Jan./Feb.

Burkitt, H. (2000), 'East dotcom, east dotgo', *Market Leader*, Winter.

Cassady, B. (2002), 'Is permission marketing the future?' *Admap*, Mar.

Chapman, P.S. and Beltramini, R.F. (2000), 'Infomercials revisited: perspectives of advertising professionals', *Journal of Advertising Research*, vol. 40, iss. 5.

Cleaver, C. (2000), 'Brands, the web and brand strategy', *Admap*, June.

Cooper, A. (1999), 'What's in a name?', *Admap*, June

Cutler, B.D. and Javalgi, R.G. (1993), 'Analysis of print ad features: services versus products', *Journal of Advertising Research*, Mar./Apr.

Deighton, J. (1997), 'Commentary on exploring the implications of the internet for consumer marketing', *Journal of the Academy of Marketing Science*, vol. 25.

Deighton, J., Sorrell, M., Salama, E., Levin, M., Webster, F.E., Carter, D., Barwise, P., Haeckel, S.H., Hundt, R., Hoffman, D.L., Novak, T.P. and Day, G.S. (1996), 'The future of interactive marketing', *Harvard Business Review*, vol. 74, iss. 6.

Derricott, C. and Firouzabadian, M. (2000), 'Internet advertising: exciting new opportunities ahead', *Admap*, May.

Ditto, S. and Pille, B. (1998), 'Marketing on the internet', *Healthcare Executive*, vol. 13, iss. 5.

Duncan, T. and Moriarty, S.E. (1998), 'A communication-based marketing model for managing relationships', *Journal of Marketing*, vol. 62, iss. 2.

Farris, J. (2001), 'Permission-based email marketing: the new frontier', *Admap*, Mar.

Flood, V. (2000), 'Brand building in the age of e-commerce: have the "rules" changed?', Market Research Society conference paper.

Fombrun, C.J. (1996), *Reputation*, Harvard Business School Press.

Fombrun, C.J. and Rindova, V.P. (1998), 'Reputation management in global 1000 firms: a benchmarking study', *Corporate Reputation Review*, vol. 1, iss. 3.

Foster, S. (2000), 'The evolution of the new media species', *Admap*, Sept.

Fox, N. and Burrows, D. (2001), 'Direct marketing will knock spots off TV advertising', *Admap*, Mar..

Fuyuan, S. (2002), 'Banner advertisement pricing, measurement, and pre-testing practices: perspectives from interactive agencies', *Journal of Advertising*, vol. 31, iss. 3.

Gallagher, K., Foster, D. and Parsons, J. (2001), 'The medium is not the message: advertising effectiveness and content evaluation in print and on the web', *Journal of Advertising Research*, vol. 41, iss. 1.

Garber, L. and Dotson, M.J. (2002), 'A method for the selection of appropriate business-to-business integrated marketing communications mixes', *Journal of Marketing Communications*, vol. 8.

Godin, S. (1999), *Permission Marketing: Turning Strangers into Friends, and Friends into Customers*, Simon & Schuster.

Goldsmith, R.E., Lafferty B.A. and Newell, S.J. (2000), 'The impact of corporate credibility on consumer reaction to advertisements and brands', *Journal of Advertising Research*, vol. 29, iss. 3.

Goodyear, M. (2000), 'Marketing evolves from selling to citizenship', *Market Leader*, vol. 12.

Griffith, D.A., and Krampf, R.F. (1998), 'An examination of the web-based strategies of the top 100 US retailers', *Journal of Marketing Theory and Practice*, vol. 6, iss. 3.

Grove, S.J., Pickett, G.M and Stafford, M.R. (1997), 'Addressing the advertising of services: a call to action', *Journal of Advertising*, vol. 26, iss. 4.

Hoeffler, S. and Keller, K.L. (2002), 'Building brand equity through corporate societal marketing', *Journal of Public Policy & Marketing*, vol. 21, iss. 1.

Ivey, E. (1995), 'Building business brands', *Admap*, June.

Johnson, I. (1999), 'What's the value of interactive advertising?' *Admap*, Feb.

Johnson, I. (2000), 'Interactive TV advertising: a worldwide perspective', *Admap*, June.

Kwak, H., Fox, R.J. and Zinkhan, G.M. (2002), 'What products can be successful promoted and sold via the Internet?' *Journal of Advertising Research*, vol. 42, iss. 1.

Lafferty, B. and Goldsmith, R.E. (1999), 'Corporate credibility's role in consumers' attitudes and purchase intentions when a high versus a low credibility endorser is used in the ad', *Journal of Business Research*, vol. 44, Feb.

Lynch, P.D. (2001), 'The global internet shopper: evidence from shopping in twelve countries, *Journal of Advertising Research*, vol. 41, iss. 3.

Market Leader (2002), 'Corporate social responsibility and the bottom line; how strong is the connection?' *Market Leader*, 18, Autumn.

Martin, B.A., Bhimy, A.C. and Agee, T. (2002), 'Infomercials and advertising effectiveness: an empirical study', *Journal of Consumer Marketing*. vol. 19, iss. 6.

Melewar, T.C. and Saunders, J. (1998), 'Global corporate identity: standardisation, control and benefits', *International Marketing Review*, vol. 15, iss. 4.

Millward Brown (1999), 'The wired digital rich media study', Millward Brown Interactive, Jan.

O'Keefe, T. (2000), 'Fresh marketing strategies that attract savvy consumers', *American City Business Journal*, Jan.

Peterson, R.A., Balasnramanian, S. and Bronnenberg, B.J. (1997), 'Exploring the implications of the internet for consumer marketing', *Journal of the Academy of Marketing Science*, vol. 25, iss. 4.

Roberts, L. (2001), 'Return to first principles', *Admap*, Jan.

Rowley, J. (2001), 'Remodelling marketing communications in an internet environment', *Internet Research: Electronic Networking Applications and Policy*, vol. 11, iss. 3.

Singh, M., Balasubramanian, S.K. and Chkraborty, G. (2000), 'A comparative analysis of three communications formats: advertising, infomercial and direct experience', *Journal of Advertising*, vol. 29, iss. 4.

Slack, N., Chambers, S. and Johnson, R. (2001), *Operations Management*, 3rd edition, Prentice Hall.

Stern, B. (1994), 'A revised communication model for advertising: multiple dimensions of the source, the message and the recipient', *Journal of Advertising*, vol. 23, iss. 2.

Steuer (1992), cited in Stern, B.B. (1994), 'A revised communication model for advertising: multiple dimensions of the source, the message and the recipient', *Journal of Advertising*, vol. 23, iss. 2.

Stockdale, M. (1995), 'Best practice in financial services advertising', *Admap*, May.

Sutherland, R. (2000/2001), 'Dispatches from a weary cyberspace wanderer', *Market Leader*, Winter.

Swiffen-Green, J. (2002), 'Can internet advertising be used for branding?' *Admap*, Jan..

Willmott, M. (2003), *Citizen Brands: Putting Society at the Heart of your Business*, Wiley & Sons.

White, R. (1996), 'Developing the service brand', *Admap*, Nov.

Yui, L. and Shrum, L.J. (2002), 'What is interactivity and is it always such a good thing? Implications of definition, person, and situation for the influence of interactivity on advertising effectiveness', *Journal of Advertising*, vol. 31, iss. 4.

Chapter 13

Aaker, D.A. and Joachimsthaler, E. (1999), 'The lure of global branding', *Harvard Business Review*, vol. 77, iss. 6.

Advertising Age (2002), *Top 50 Global Marketers outside the USA*, special issue November.

Aitchison, G. (1995), 'Global branding', Market Research Society conference paper, Mar.

Anholt, S. (1993), 'Adapting advertising copy across national frontiers', *Admap*, Oct.

Anholt, S. (1998), 'Developing international advertising campaigns', *Commercial Communications*, May.

Anholt, S. (2000), 'Updating the international advertising model', *Admap*, June.

Bannister, L., Riley-Smith, P. and Maclay, D. (1997), 'Global brands, local contexts', *Admap*, Oct.

Becatelli, I. and Swindells, A. (1998), 'Developing better pan-European campaigns', *Admap*, Mar.

Bilkey, W.J. and Nes, E. (1982), 'Country of origin effects on product evaluation', *Journal of International Business*, Spring/Summer.

Boyfield, K. (2000), 'Why survival will rely on branding skills', *Market Leader*, Winter.

Byfield, S. and Caller, L. (1996), 'Building brands across borders', *Admap*, June.

Campaign (2004a), special supplement, 30 Jan.

Campaign (2004b), special supplement, 1 July.

Clifton, R. (1997), 'Planning to go global', *Admap*, Oct.

Cooper, P. (1997), 'Western at the weekends', *Admap*, Oct.

Copeland, L. and Griggs, L. (1986), *Going International*, Plume Books.

Cramphorn, M. (1996), 'Where does your ad work?' *Admap*, June.

De Mooij, M. (1991), *Advertising Worldwide*, 2nd edition, Prentice Hall.

De Mooij, M. (1998), 'Global marketing and advertising: understanding cultural paradoxes', *International Marketing Review*, vol. 15, iss. 3.

Duffy, M. and Medina, J. (1998), 'Standardisation versus globalisation: a new perspective of brand strategies', *Journal of Product and Brand Management*, vol. 7, iss. 3.

Elms, S. (2001), 'Multi-country communication planning', *Admap*, Jan.

Ford, R. and Phillips, A. (1998), 'Targeting European teenagers', *Admap*, June.

Garcia, S. (1998), 'When is a cat not a cat?' *Admap*, Oct.

Goodyear, M. (1991), 'The 5 stages of advertising literacy', *Admap*, Mar.

Goodyear, M. (1996), 'Divided by a common language', Market Research Society conference paper.

Goodyear, M. (2000), 'Marketing evolves from selling to citizenship', *Market Leader*, 12.

Green, A. and Aubury, C. (1997), 'Global copy testing: lessons from experience', *Admap*, Oct.

Grein, A.F. and Gould, S.J. (1996), 'Globally integrated marketing communications', *Journal of Marketing Communications*, vol. 2, iss. 3.

Grein, A. and Ducoffe, R. (1998), 'Strategic responses to market globalisation among advertising agencies', *International Journal of Advertising*, vol. 17, iss. 3.

Haigh, D. (1996), 'Accountability', *Marketing Business*, Oct.

Hall, E. (1976), *Beyond Culture*, Anchor Books.

Hankinson, G. and Cowking, P. (1996), *The Reality of Global Brands*, McGraw Hill.

Harvey, M.G. (1993), 'A model to determine standardisation of the advertising process in international markets', *Journal of Advertising Research*, vol. 33, iss. 4.

Head, D. (1998), 'Ad slogans and the made in concept', *International Journal of Advertising*, vol. 7.

Hite, R.E. and Fraser, C. (1988), 'International advertising strategies of multinational corporations', *Journal of Advertising Research*, Aug./Sept.

Interbrand (2003), 'Top 20 global brands', available online at www.interbrand.com.

Jacobs, L., Keown, C. and Ghymn, K. (1991), 'Cross cultural colour comparisons: global marketers beware', *International Marketing Review*.

Johansson, J., Douglas, S.P. and Nonanka, I. (1985), 'Assessing the impact of country of origin on product evaluations,' *Journal of Marketing Research*.

Kapferer, J-N. (2000), 'In defence of local brands', *Market Leader*, 9.

Kapferer, J-N. (2002), 'Is there really no hope for local brands?' *Journal of Brand Management*, vol. 9, iss. 3.

Kanso, A. (1992), 'International advertising strategies: global commitment to local vision', *Journal of Advertising Research*, Jan./Feb.

Kanso, A. and Nelson, R.A. (2002), 'Advertising localisation overshadows standardisation', *Journal of Advertising Research*, vol. 42, iss. 1.

Kotler, P. (1994), *Marketing Management: Analysis, Planning, Implementation and Control*, 7th edition, Prentice Hall.

Levitt, T. (1983), 'The globalisation of markets', *Harvard Business Review*, vol. 61, iss. 3.

McCollum Spielman (1992), 'Global advertising: standardised or multi-cultural', *Journal of Advertising Research*, vol. 32, iss. 4.

Min Han, C. (1990), 'Country image: halo or summary construct', *Journal of Marketing Research*.

O'Donohoe, S. (1994), 'Advertising uses and gratifications', *European Journal of Marketing*, 28.

Onkvisit, S. and Shaw, J.J. (1999), 'Standardized international advertising: some research issues and implications,' *Journal of Advertising Research*, vol. 36, iss. 6.

Parameswaram, R. and Pisharodi, R.M. (1994), 'Facets of country of origin image: an empirical assessment', *Journal of Advertising*, vol. 23, iss. 1.

Pawle, J. (1999), 'Mining the international consumer', *Journal of the Market Research Society*, vol. 41, iss. 1.

Payne, M. (2002), 'Going local: creating effective multi-country strategies', *Admap*, Feb.

Quelch, J. (2003), 'The return of the global brand', *Harvard Business Review*, vol. 81, iss. 8.

Reader's Digest (2004), *Number of different winning brands across Europe*.

Redding, S.G. (1982), 'Cultural effects on the marketing process in Southeast Asia', *Journal of the Market Research Society*.

Riesenbeck, H. and Freeling, A. (1991), 'How global are global brands?' *McKinsey Quarterly*, vol. 4.

Roth, Martin S. (1995), 'Effects of global market conditions on brand image customisation and brand performance', *Journal of Advertising*, vol. 24, iss. 4.

Shalofsky, I. (1987), 'Research for global brands', *European Research*, May.

Solberg, C.A. (2000), 'Educator insights: standardisation or adaptation of the international marketing mix: the role of the subsidiary/representative', *Journal of International Marketing*.

Sriram, V. and Gopalakrishna, P. (1991), 'Can advertising be standardised among similar countries?' *International Journal of Advertising*, vol. 10, 2.

Taylor, C.R. (2002), 'What is wrong with international advertising research?' *Journal of Advertising Research*, vol. 42, iss. 6.

Tharp, M. and Jeong, J. (2001), 'Executive insights: the global network communications agency', *Journal of International Marketing*, vol. 9, iss. 4.

Usenier, J-C. (1996), *Marketing Across Cultures*, 2nd edition, Prentice Hall.

Wustrack, K. (1999), 'One-touch sweeps the budget', *Admap*, Feb.

Zhang, Y. and Gelb, B.D. (1996), 'Matching advertising appeals to culture: the influence of products' use conditions', *Journal of Advertising*, vol. 25, iss. 3.

Index